SO-BAW-474

Table of Contents

American Casino Guide

2008 Edition

Written and Edited By
Steve Bourie

Contributing Writers
Bill Burton
Anthony Curtis
Bob Dancer
John Grochowski
H. Scot Krause
Max Rubin
Jean Scott
Henry Tamburin

This book is dedicated to the memory of Scott Barr.
A truly great guy who will forever be missed by his friends and family.

American Casino Guide - 2008 edition

Copyright ©2008, Casino Vacations Press, Inc.

Published By:
Casino Vacations Press, Inc.
P.O. Box 703
Dania, Florida 33004
(954) 989-2766

e-mail: info@americancasinoguide.com
website: americancasinoguide.com

3 9082 10533 3358

ISBN-13: 978-1-883768-17-1
ISSN: 1086-9018

About Your Guide

This guide has been written to help you plan your visit to casino gambling areas and also to help you save money once you are there. The first edition of this guide began 17 years ago as an eight-page newsletter and it has continued to grow each year as casino gambling has spread throughout the country. We have listed information on all of the states that offer any type of traditional casino table games or slot machines (including video lottery terminals). We have also included stories to help you understand how casinos operate; how video poker and slot machines work; how to make the best plays in blackjack, craps, roulette and baccarat; and how to take advantage of casino promotional programs. Additionally, we have included a casino coupon section that should save you many times the cost of this book.

Virtually every casino has a "comp" program whereby you can get free rooms, food, shows or gifts based upon your level of play at their table games. If you plan on gambling during your trip to the casino, you should call ahead and ask their marketing department for details on their programs. There are also stories in this book to help you understand how "comp" programs work and how to best take advantage of them.

One more suggestion to save you money when visiting a casino is to join their slot club. It doesn't cost anything and you would be surprised at how quickly those points can add up to earn you gifts, cash, food or other complimentaries. Also, as a slot club member you will usually receive periodic mailings from the casino with money-saving offers that are generally not available to the public.

When using this guide please remember that all of the listed room rates reflect the lowest and highest prices charged during the year. During holidays and peak periods, however, higher rates may apply. Also, since the gambling games offered at casinos vary from state to state, a listing of available games is found at the start of each state heading. We hope you enjoy your guide and we wish you good luck on your casino vacation!

Your Best Casino Bets - Part I

by Henry Tamburin

The majority of casino players leave too much to chance when playing in a casino. To put it bluntly, they don't have a clue as to how to play. They are literally throwing their money away with little chance of winning. Luck most certainly has a lot to do with your success in a casino but what really separates the winners from the losers is the skill of the players. Granted, there is no guarantee that you will win, but on the other hand, there is no guarantee that you must lose. My objective in this article is to educate you on the casino games so that at the very least, you'll be able to enjoy yourself in the casino with maximum play time and minimum risk to your bankroll.

Let's begin our understanding of casino gambling by learning how casinos win as much as they do. They don't charge admission, and they certainly don't depend on the luck of their dealers to generate the income they need to pay their overhead. In fact, they guarantee themselves a steady income by having a built in advantage, or house edge, on every bet. Think of it as a very efficient hidden tax that generates them a guaranteed daily profit.

Here's an example of how this works. Suppose we take a coin and play heads or tails. Every time you lose a flip of the coin you pay me $1. Every time you win a flip, I pay you 90¢. Would you play? I hope you said no. Here's why. In this simple game I would have an advantage over you and I created that advantage by not paying you at the true odds of one-to-one (or $1).

Casinos do this very same thing to create their advantage. They simply pay off winning bets at less than the true odds. For example, the true odds of winning a bet on number 7 on roulette are 37-to-1 (the latter means you have 37 chances to lose vs. one chance to win). If you get lucky and the roulette ball lands in the number seven slot, you'd expect the casino to pay you 37 chips as winnings for the one chip you bet on number 7 (37- to-1 payoff). If they did that, the casino's advantage would be zero. However, as I mentioned above, the casinos create their advantage by paying off winning bets at less than true odds. In the case of our bet on number 7, the winning payoff is 35 chips (instead of 37 chips). The two chips the casino quietly kept is what pays their bills. Mathematically, the casino advantage is 5.26% on this bet which simply means day in and day out, the casino expects to win (or keep) 5.26% of all money wagered in roulette.

The casino games with the lowest casino advantage (less than 1.25%), and your best bets, are blackjack, craps, baccarat, and video poker. Now don't sell the ranch and run over to your nearest casino just yet. These games, plus table poker, are your best bets but you must learn how to play these games properly to enhance your chances of winning. Here are some tips to get you started:

BLACKJACK - This is your best casino game, but you must learn how to play your hands (when to hit, stand, double-down, split, etc.). This is known as the basic strategy. Learn it and you can reduce the casino's advantage to virtually zero. And if you learn how to keep track of the cards as they are played (i.e. card counting) you can actually turn the tables on the casino and have the edge over them! Do not try to play blackjack if you haven't learned the correct basic strategy. If you do, your chances of winning are slim. Also, it's wise not to make any side bets that may be offered on your table and please stay away from any game which only pays 6-to-5 for an untied blackjack. Blackjack tournaments are also popular and here players compete against other players with the player with the most chips at the end of the round advancing. Tournament prizes can be substantial. Playing and betting strategy for blackjack tournaments, however, is different than playing blackjack in a casino so bone up on your tournament skills before considering playing in a tournament.

CRAPS - The game of craps intimidates most casino players because of the complicated playing layout and the multitude of bets. In fact craps is an easy game to play. And it also has some of the best bets in the casino (and also some of the worst). Your best bet is the pass line with odds and come with odds. Next best is a place bet on six or eight. Stay away from all other bets on the layout because the casino's advantage is too high. If you really enjoy the game of craps you might consider learning dice control – it's not an easy skill to learn and it requires a lot of practice but if you get good at it, you can have the edge over the casino.

ROULETTE - Every bet on the American roulette layout (with 0 and 00 on the wheel) has a high casino advantage. That goes for bets straight up on numbers that pay 35-to-1, as well as even money wagers on red or black. Atlantic City players get a break. If you bet on an even money payoff bet and 0 or 00 hits, you lose only half your wager. This cuts the casino's advantage in half. Also, some casinos offer a European layout with only one zero. This is a better bet than wheels with 0 and 00.

BACCARAT - Many casinos offer a low stakes version called mini-baccarat. Not a bad game to play. If you bet on the bank hand, the casino's edge is only 1.17%. And when you play baccarat, there are no playing decisions to make which makes the game very easy to play. However, this game is fast with many decisions per hour. It's best to play slowly. One way is to only bet on the bank hand after it wins (meaning you won't be betting on every hand which will slow down your play).

BIG SIX WHEEL - Stay away from spending a lot of time (and money) at this game. The casino's advantage is astronomical (11% to 26%). Its drawing card for the novice player is the low minimum bet ($1). Save your money for the better games.

CARIBBEAN STUD POKER - This popular cruise ship game has found its way to land and dockside casinos. Unlike regular table poker where players compete against each other, in this game the players play against the house. But the rules favor the casino and their advantage is about 5%. The part of this game that appeals to players is the progressive jackpot side bet. You should not make this side bet, however, unless the jackpot exceeds $280,000 for the $1 ante and the $1 jackpot bet.

PAI GOW POKER - Strange name for a casino game. The game is a cross between Pai Gow, a Chinese game of dominoes, and the American game of seven-card poker. Players are dealt seven cards and they must arrange (or set) their cards into a five-card poker hand and a two-card poker hand. Skill is involved in setting the two hands which can help reduce the casino's advantage.

SLOT MACHINES - Casinos earn more money from slot machines than all the table games combined. The casino's advantage varies from one machine to another. Typically the higher denomination machines ($1 and up) pay back more than the nickel, quarter and fifty-cent machines. Slots are not your best bet in the casino, but here are a few tips: It's wise to play one coin only in machines where all the payouts increase proportionally to the number of coins played (i.e, there is no jackpot for playing maximum coins). However, if the machine has a substantial jackpot when you play maximum coins, then you should play always play the maximum number of coins the machine will accept or you won't be eligible for a bonus payoff for the jackpot. Don't waste hours looking for a machine that's "ready to hit." Join the slot clubs, always use your slot club card when you play, and try to schedule your play time when the casino offers multiple points. Joining is free and you'll be rewarded with discounts and other freebies. Machines that have lower jackpots pay smaller amounts more frequently which means you normally get more playing time for your money. Playing machines that have bonus rounds and fancy graphics may be fun, but the house edge on these machines is usually higher than traditional reel spinning machines. Likewise, the house edge is higher for linked machines that have those life-changing mega jackpots. Some casinos now certify their machines to return 98% or more and these machines are your best bets. Also, consider playing in slot tournaments where you are competing against other players, rather than the house, and the prizes can be substantial.

VIDEO POKER - Your best bet if you enjoy playing slot machines. Skill is involved as well as learning to spot the better payoff machines. For example, on the classic jacks-or-better game, always check the full houseand flush payoff schedule. The machines on jacks or better pay nine coins for a full house and six coins for a flush for each coin played. These machines are known as 9/6 machines. They are readily available; seek them out. The same analogy holds for bonus poker, double bonus, deuces wild, joker wild, etc., video poker games. There are good pay schedules and bad ones, and it's up to you to know the difference and play only the higher paying schedules with the correct playing strategy (readily available on the Internet, in books, and on strategy cards).

KENO - This casino game has a very high casino advantage (usually 20% and up). Stay away if you are serious about winning.

RED DOG - This is the casino version of the old acey-deucey. The stakes are low, but the casino edge is a wee-bit steep (3.5%). If you play, only make the raise wager when the spread between the two cards is seven or more.

SIC BO - This is an oriental game in which players bet on the outcome of the roll of three dice. There are lots of bets on the layout, some that pay odds of 150-to-1. However, most have a very high casino advantage. Your best bet is a bet on the big or small wager.

LET IT RIDE - This casino table game is based on the all-American game of poker. Like Caribbean Stud Poker, players compete against the house rather than against each other. What makes this game so unique is that the players can remove up to two of their initial mandatory three bets if they don't think they can win. The objective is to end up with a five-card poker hand of at least 10's or higher. The higher the rank, the greater the payoff; up to 1,000-to-1 for the royal flush. The casino edge is about 3% and about 70% of the hands will be losing hands. If you are lucky enough to catch a high payoff hand, be smart, push your chair back, and take the money and run!

THREE CARD POKER - One of the more successful table games in recent years, You can wager on either the Ante/Play or Pair Plus. You win your Ante/Play bet if your three card poker hand beats the dealer's hand. If you wager Pair Plus, you win money if your three card hand contains at least a pair or higher (the higher the ranking hand, the greater the payout). There are different paytables – the best pays 4-1 for a flush rather than 3-1. The optimum playing strategy is to raise on Q-6-4 or higher and avoid playing the Pair Plus if the flush pays only 3-1.

Henry Tamburin has more than 30 years of experience as a casino player, author, columnist and instructor. More than 7,500 of his articles on casino gambling for have been published in numerous national gaming publications including Casino Player magazine. He is also the author of numerous books and instructional videos, edits the popular Blackjack Insider newsletter (www.bjinsider.com), and is the Lead Instructor for the Golden Touch Blackjack course (www.goldentouchblackjack.com). You can visit his web site at http://www.smartgaming.com

Your Best Casino Bets - Part II

by Steve Bourie

In the previous story Henry gave you his choices for your best casino bets based on which ones offer you the best mathematical odds. Now, Henry is a great mathematician who is truly an expert at crunching numbers to figure out what the theoretical odds are, but what about real life? By this I mean - at the end of the week, or the month, or the year, how much does a casino really make from blackjack, or craps, or roulette? Sure, you can do the math to calculate the casino advantage on a bank hand in mini-baccarat as 1.17%, but at the end of the day what percent of those bets on mini-baccarat actually wind up in the hands of the casino? Is it precisely 1.17%? Or is it less? Or is it more? And, if you knew how much the casino truly averaged on all of the games it offered, which one would turn out to be your best bet based on that information?

To find the answer to this question I began my search by looking at the annual gaming revenue report issued by Nevada's State Gaming Control Board. It lists the win percentages, based on the drop (an explanation of this term later), for all of the games offered by the casinos and you might be surprised at which game had the lowest win percentage. Go ahead and take a guess...nice try, but you're wrong! The answer is bingo, where casinos only won .70% of the money they handled! The first column below lists the actual win percentages based on the "drop" (an explanation of "drop" follows shortly) for Nevada's various games for the fiscal year from July 1, 2006 through June 30, 2007:

GAME	WIN %	ADJUSTED WIN %
Keno	27.41	27.41
Race Book	15.13	15.13
Slot Machines	6.02	6.02
Sports Pool	7.09	7.09
Caribbean Stud Poker	29.29	5.85
3-Card Poker	26.36	5.27
Pai Gow Poker	21.81	4.36
Let It Ride	21.79	4.36
Roulette	19.94	3.99
Pai Gow	19.38	3.87
Craps	13.22	2.64
Twenty-One	12.59	2.52
Mini-Baccarat	11.77	2.35
Baccarat	11.65	2.33
Bingo	.70	.70

Usually bingo would rank as one of the games with the worst odds, but not in Nevada where it's sometimes used as a "loss leader." Just like your local Kmart runs especially low prices on a couple of items to bring you into the store where they believe you'll buy some other items, Nevada casinos use bingo to bring people into their casinos, believing that while they're there they'll play other games and also develop a loyalty to that casino. Actually, some years the casinos offering bingo actually lose money on the game rather than make money. So, if you're a bingo player Nevada casinos are the best places you'll ever find to play your game.

Before we start analyzing the other numbers, you'll first need a brief explanation of how the win percentages are calculated and we'll start off with a basic lesson in how casinos do their accounting.

Casinos measure their take in table games by the *drop* and the *win*. The *drop* is the count of all of the receipts (including cash and credit markers) that go into the drop box located at the table. Later, an accounting is made to see how much more (or less) they have at that table than they started with. This amount is known as the *win*.

What the first column in the table shows you is how much the casinos won as a percentage of the drop. For example, on the roulette table for every $100 that went into the drop box the casino won $19.94 or 19.94%. What it doesn't tell you, however, is how much the casinos won as a percentage of all the bets that were made. In other words, the drop tells you how many chips were bought at that table, but it doesn't tell you how many bets were made with those chips. For example, if you buy $100 worth of chips at a blackjack table and play $10 a hand you don't bet for exactly 10 hands and then leave the table, do you? Of course not. You win some hands and you lose some hands and if you counted all of the times you made a $10 bet before you left the table you would see that your original $100 in chips generated many times that amount in bets. In other words, there is a multiplier effect for the money that goes into the drop box. We know that for every dollar that goes into the drop box there is a corresponding number of bets made. To find out exactly what that number is I asked Henry for some help. He replied that there is no exact answer, but during a 1982 study of the roulette tables in Atlantic City it was discovered that the total amount bet was approximately five times the amount of the buy-in. This means that for every $100 worth of chips bought at the table it resulted in roughly $500 worth of bets being made.

The multiplier effect for the money that goes into the drop box is also dependent on the skill of the player. A blackjack player that loses his money quickly because he doesn't know good playing strategy will have a much lower multiplier than a player who uses a correct playing strategy. For purposes of this story, however, we'll assume that they balance each other out and we'll also assume that all games have the same multiplier of five. We can now return to our win percentage tables and divide by five the percentages for those games that have a multiplier effect. These new adjusted numbers let us know approximately how much the casinos actually won as a percentage of the amount bet on each of those games. Keep in mind, however, that there are four game categories that do not need to be adjusted: keno, bingo, race book and sports pool; plus slot machnes. All of these need no adjustment because there is no multiplier factor involved. The casinos know the exact total of the bets they take in and the exact total of the bets they pay out.

After calculating our adjusted win numbers we can now go back and take another look at which games are your best casino bets. The worst game, by far, is keno with its 27.41% edge. Next comes the race book with 15.13%, followed by slot machines at 5.92%; and then sports betting which has a casino win rate of 7.09%. However, that number actually deserves a closer look because there are really five different types of bets that make up that 7.09% figure: football - 7.63%; basketball - 5.18%; baseball - 5.53%; sports parlay cards - 27.94%; pari-mutuel sports betting - 18.46%; and other sports (golf, car racing, etc.) - 7.12%. As you can see, all sports bets carry a relatively low house edge, except for sports parlay cards and pari-mutuel sports betting.

Next on our list is Caribbean stud poker at 5.85%; three-card poker at 5.27%; pai gow poker at 4.36%; let it ride at 4.36%; roulette at 3.99%; and pai gow at 3.87%.

Finally, we come to the four best casino bets that all have roughly the same edge of less than three percent: craps at 2.64%; twenty-one (blackjack) at 2.52%; mini-baccarat at 2.35%; and baccarat at 2.33%

So there you have it. Baccarat is your best casino bet! Henry said it was a good game to play and he was right. But didn't he also say that blackjack was your *best* casino bet? Was he wrong about that? Not really, because he prefaced it by saying "you must learn how to play your hands."

You have to remember that of all the table games offered in a casino (other than poker) only blackjack is a game of skill. This means that the better you are at playing your cards, the better you will be able to beat the house average. The 2.52% figure shown is just an average and if you learn proper basic strategy you can cut it down even more, which would then make it your best bet. Good luck!

More Fun at the Casino

by Jack Short

Each year, millions of new players arrive on the casino scene. Most are unaware their casino experience can be enhanced by knowing more about the games of chance they are about to play.

Casino players today have a huge advantage over the Las Vegas visitor of years ago. Today, hundreds of books exist that give insight into the games you wish to play. Valid literature is available from your local library or bookstore. Some titles are considered "core" or "must read" by librarians. The *American Casino Guide*, which you are reading, is an example of a text you should read annually.

Examples of other basic literature are Jean Scott's *The Frugal Gambler* and Stanford Wong's *Basic Blackjack*. These books will inform you on money management, wagering strategies and the best games to play. Experienced players can find books that go into depth on any casino game. The more you know the nuances of a game, the higher your level of enjoyment and the possibility of a winning day.

It's a bit like going to a ballgame with your dad. The first time, you simply saw a lot of guys playing ball. As the years went by, you gained new insights and the enjoyment level went up. The same with casino games – the more you know, the higher the satisfaction of being at the casino.

Jack Short is Executive Director of the National Gambling Literacy Organization (NGLO), a low-profile non-profit (501C3) group that primarily keeps the public libraries in America informed as to what gambling literature is valid and should be in their collections for this genre.

NGLO feels the casino scene can be a positive life experience for the majority of players if approached with common sense and a thorough grasp of the games they want to play.

NGLO encourages players to stay alert to the dangers of gambling addiction. Jack Short can be contacted at NGLO@webtv.net; or PO Box E, Avon, CT 06001.

Casino Comps

by Steve Bourie

In the world of casino gambling a "comp" is short for complimentary and it refers to anything that the casino will give you for free in return for your play in their casino.

Naturally, the more you bet, the more the casino will be willing to give you back. For the truly "high roller" (those willing to bet thousands, tens of thousands or even hundreds of thousands on the turn of a card) there is no expense spared to cater to their every whim, including: private jet transportation, chauffeur-driven limousines, gourmet chef-prepared foods, the finest wines and champagnes, plus pampered butler and maid service in a $10 million penthouse suite. But what about the lower-limit bettor?

Well, it turns out that pretty much any gambler can qualify for comps no matter what their level of play and if you know you're going to be gambling anyway, you might as well ask to get rated to see what you can get on a comp basis.

When you sit down to play be sure to tell the dealer that you want to be rated and they'll call over the appropriate floorperson who will take down your name and put it on a card along with information on how long you play and how much you bet. The floorperson won't stand there and constantly watch you, instead they'll just glance over every once in awhile to see how much you're betting and note it on the card. If you change tables be sure to tell the floorperson so that they can continue to track your play at the new table.

Usually a casino will want you to play for at least three hours and virtually all casinos use the same formula to calculate your comp value. They simply take the size of your average bet and multiply it by: the casino's advantage on the game you're playing; the decisions per hour in your game; and the length of your play in hours. The end result is what the casino expects to win from you during your play and most casinos will return anywhere from 10% to 40% of that amount to you in the form of comps.

So, let's say you're a roulette player that averages $20 a spin and you play for four hours. What's that worth in comps? Well, just multiply your average bet ($20), by the casino's advantage in roulette (5.3%) to get $1.06, which is the average amount the casino expects to make on you on each spin of the wheel. You then multiply that by the number of decisions (or spins) per hour (40) to get $42.40, which is the average amount the casino expects to make on you after one hour. Then, multiply that by the total hours of play (4) to get $169.60, which is the average amount the casino expects to make on you during your four hours of play. Since the casinos will return 10% to 40% of that amount in comps, you should qualify for a minimum of $16.96 to a maximum of $67.84 in casino comps.

One thing to keep in mind about comps is that you don't have to lose in order to qualify. The casino only asks that you put in the time to play. So, in our example if, after four hours of gambling, our roulette player ended up winning $100, they would still be eligible for the same amount of comps.

The last thing to mention about comps is that some casino games require skill (blackjack and pai gow poker), or offer various bets that have different casino advantages (craps) so those factors are sometimes adjusted in the equation when determining the casino advantage in those games. Just take a look at the chart below to see how the average casino will adjust for skill in blackjack and pai gow poker as well as for the types of bets that are made in craps.

Game	Game Advantage	Decisions Per Hour
Blackjack	.0025 (Card Counter) .01 (Good Basic Strategy) .015 (Soft Player)	70
Roulette	.053	40
Craps	.005 (Pass Line/Full Odds) .01 (Knowledgeable) .04 (Soft)	144
Baccarat	.012	70
Mini-Baccarat	.012	110
Pai Gow Poker	.01 (Knowledgeable) .02 (Average)	25

Comp City U.S.A.

by Max Rubin

Casino Comps have always been synonymous with Las Vegas, high rolling, and living large. Certainly everyone who plays the high and fast game—and there aren't that many of them—has come to expect to be treated like a potentate at the casino's expense. But most gamblers still don't realize that the overwhelming majority of the billions of comp dollars dished out by casinos every year are spent on the average guy, and you don't have to risk a spare $10,000 to beat the system.

Fact is, the comp system is designed to reward gamblers at every level. Even if you play nickel slots or blackjack at $5 a hand, your action makes you eligible for something in the grand comp plan. The trick to getting your share is to understand what you're entitled to and then get more.

What Gets What - The first step is to size up your threshold for risk and to determine how much money you've got to play the game with. Casinos have one simple goal: take your money. That means that how much you wager—or how much they think you wager—is the prime determinant in how much in comps they're willing to give you. But you've gotta be careful. The strategy isn't to increase the amount that you gamble to get comps. On the contrary, it's to stay at your normal level, get the comps you qualify for, and use them to enhance your result (by either mitigating losses or augmenting wins). The following provides a good overview of what you can expect to get.

At the lowest levels, you'll have to be content with little comps, things like comped parking and funbook freebies. You get those just for showing up.

The next rung on the comp ladder is free drinks, which even the lowly single-nickel slot player (or someone who pretends to be) can get by flagging down a cocktail waitress. You only have to step up your play a little—quarter slots and $5-$10 table games—to graduate to the next level, which is where it starts getting good. These comps include free snack bar food, breakfasts in the coffee shops, and rounds of drinks at the bar. Double that action and you'll start getting the best buffets, dinner in the coffee shops, invitations to low-level events, and the little-known but highly valuable "casino rate" on a room (a discount that can knock up to 50% off the retail price). The two-fold secret to getting these comps is simple: If you play table games, ask for them. If you play machines, join the slot club.

It's no mystery that casinos give better comps to bigger players, and if you regularly bet $25-$100 a hand, or plug dollars into machines, you can look forward to gourmet meals and free seats in the showrooms in all but the most elegant Vegas megastores. Once you graduate to the $100-$350 bet level, it's essential to get "rated" if you're playing table games, which means the pit bosses have to log all of your action. If you're playing multi-coin dollar machines and use your VIP card, they're already tracking every coin you shove down the gullet of the no-armed bandits, so all you have to do is put in your hours to be put in a suite.

Beyond the $350-a-hand table game and $5-a-pull machine level, the sky's the limit for comps: private multi-room penthouse suites, limo rides, $500 rounds of golf, trips to the Super Bowl, shopping sprees at Neiman's, the works. Many of the high rollers who get this treatment have casino lines of credit in excess of $1 million, and at these levels, a strange symbiotic bond is forged between the casino and the gambler. The casino is happy because its winnings far exceed the expense of hosting the gambler. The gambler is happy because he considers the attention and status he receives a fair trade for the risk he's willing to take (and the losses he's willing to fade).

The biggest change in the evolution of the comp system over the past five years is that you can now get the comps you want where you want. There are now very few major cities in America that are more than 100 miles from a bona fide big-bet store, and earning comps has become easier—geographically at least—than ever before.

Some of the newer venues—especially in California, where they're still getting their feet wet and don't have sophisticated management or comp-tracking systems, and places like Illinois and Mississippi, which have brutal tax structures that don't leave much for the masses—make it fairly tricky to earn comps on the Vegas level. But that's not to say you can't get a comp-bang for your gambling buck outside Nevada. You can, and in some places with inadequately trained staffs and/or outdated comp systems, it actually gets easier. You just have to be more diligent in doing the research necessary to know which casinos are ripe for the taking.

Comp Wizardry - Now that you know that the prizes are out there—and everywhere—you might be wondering how well you can play the comp game. The bottom line is, anyone with a lick of sense can play it well. You can master perfect basic strategy blackjack, which is the skill-level you need to achieve, for about $2 (use one of the cards they sell in virtually every casino gift shop), and you can learn how to exploit the loopholes in every casino's comp system by reading my book, *Comp City, A Guide to Free Casino Vacations*. The book details the step-by-step techniques used by "comp wizards" to beat casinos at their own game by getting a dollar's worth of comps for every dime they lose. Short of taking this crash course in comp strategy, just asking for meals and tickets and line passes, and using your rating card every time you play is 90% of what you need to know in 95% of America's casinos, especially at the lower levels. They're giving away millions every day. Don't miss out on your share.

Max Rubin is a former casino idustry executive, author
of the book "Comp City - A Guide to Free Casino Vacations"
and co-host of CBS TV's Ultimate Blackjack Tour

Taking Advantage of Slot Clubs

by H. Scot Krause

Slot Clubs originated in Atlantic City over 25 years ago as a way to begin recognizing and rewarding the casino's good players. Today, slot clubs are the casino's most powerful marketing tool and the player's best benefit the casino has to offer. It's the best of both worlds for both the player and the casino.

To begin, perhaps the word "club" is a little misleading, since there are no dues to pay, meetings to attend or any of the usual aspects associated with joining a club. You do get a slot club membership card (also called a player's card) which is your key to unlocking the benefits and rewards of the casino you're playing in.

Typically, your slot club membership card is a plastic card, with your identifying number on it, that you will use while playing at any of the casino's slot or video poker machines or while playing table games. It resembles a credit card, but only in its appearance, and is in no way an actual credit card. I mention that because there are some people who actually, mistakenly believe they will be inserting a credit card into their slot machine and play on credit, and therefore they refuse to get their player's card and are basically denied any and all benefits they are entitled to!

So let's start at the beginning and walk through the slot card program, when and why to do it and discuss some benefits, rewards and perks.

When you enter any casino for the first time, ask someone immediately where you can find the slot club or players club booth before you put any money at play. At the booth, or club, you should find a rather friendly group of employees who will get you started, signed up and get your card for you pronto.

You'll probably need to fill out a short application form or at least give your identification card to the clerk. It's simply a way to register the card in your name. You usually don't need to give your social security number if you don't want to, but always give your birthday and anniversary dates when asked. They help identify you with the casino in case others have your same name and many times the birthday benefits are nothing short of fantastic.

Always ask the slot club personnel about how to use the card and any other current promotions or benefits in addition to using your card. There will usually be a brochure or literature available that you can take explaining all the club benefits. There may also be a sign-up bonus such as a free gift or free points when you register. Be sure to ask. Sometimes an easily obtainable coupon may be required, and the clerks can tell you where or how to get one. Finally, I like to request two cards when I join, and you might like to do the same. You'll find that you may lose one, or want to play two machines at one time. That's it! You're on your way.

When you're out on the casino floor, you'll notice a slot on the machines that your card fits into. When you decide which machine you want to play, put your card in the slot and leave it in the entire time you play that machine. (Note: Take a moment to look for the card reader slot and not the bill acceptor. If you accidentally put your card in the bill acceptor you'll probably strip the magnetic reader off your card and it won't work).

Most machines will have some type of reader that will display your name, points earned or at least let you know your card has been accepted. It's not a swipe card, and you must leave it in the machine while you play. It's simply counting the coins, or credits, that go through the machine while you're playing and giving you credit in the form of points for the amount of money that cycles through the machine. (Some casinos consider time on the machine as well as money being cycled, but that is a little more rare than in years past). Now, while you're playing, you'll be earning valuable points that become redeemable for anything from cashback to restaurant complimentaries (refered to as "comps") show tickets, gifts, reduced room rates or free rooms, to almost any amenity you may want or require.

Be sure to keep your card in the machine until you have completed your play and cashed all coins out of the machine. Some clubs base their points on a coin-out system, rather than coin-in. Of course, these rewards are based on total play and your rewards may vary according to point formulas created exclusively for the casino at which you're playing. I do caution you not to continue to play beyond your comfortable gambling range and budget just to earn a point level or comp. Let the comps fall in place as you play or when you return again in the future. Which brings me to another interesting thought. I've heard players refuse to get a card because they believe they won't return to the casino again. First of all, you never know what your future plans may hold. Second, you may earn enough points while you're on this trip to at least earn a small comp or some cash back before you leave. You'll at least get on the casino's mailing list for future specials and events. You may win a jackpot that will allow you to return sooner that you originally thought was possible. And finally, with as many consolidations and buy-outs as there are in the casino business today, the casino you're playing at today may be owned by someone else tomorrow, who may in turn, be closer to your home, and you'll be able to use your points with them. There's just no good excuse not to get a player's card at any casino you visit.

Here are a couple other tips when you plan to visit a casino and need to get a slot club card. Sometimes you can apply or sign-up in advance by mail registration or visiting the casino's website on the Internet. They will often mail you the card in advance or have it already prepared for you when you get to the casino. Call and ask ahead of time for this service and you'll save time and won't have to stand in long lines when you hit the casino floor. Sometimes, when you receive your card by mail or Internet sign-up, you'll get additional offers, coupons, gifts and funbook offers along with it.

Many casinos now employ slot club ambassadors, cash hosts, or enrollment representatives who will sign you up on the casino floor, making it even easier for you to enroll in the club. They often have additional incentives or perks they can give you when you sign up with them. You might also check to see if a card you have from another casino might work where you're playing now. Many casino corporations are beginning to combine their clubs to offer you benefits at any of their respective properties. We're sure to see more of this as consolidations and mergers continue to take place.

Now, let's take a little closer look at the benefits and reasons why you want to belong to these slot clubs. Obviously, the casinos want your business and will go to great lengths to have you return. In addition to the points you're earning while playing, which will entitle you to various comps as mentioned previously, your most valuable asset from joining the slot club will be your mailing list advantage. Offers to slot club members are mailed often and repeatedly for room specials, many times even free room offers, meal discounts (two for ones), and often other free offers. We've been mailed match play offers, double and triple point coupons, show and movie theater tickets, spa specials, gifts and gift certificates, drawing tickets, and a myriad of other offers.

The casino offers are based on levels of play, and better offers including lavish parties, Superbowl and New Year's Eve invitations, free participation to invited guest slot tournaments, limousine services, and even free round-trip airfare, are offerd to the casino's best players. Don't rule yourself out just because you don't think you'll reach those levels of play to be awarded those opportunities. Everyone is rewarded in some way for even the most nominal play. Just wait until your birthday rolls around and I can almost guarantee you'll get some fabulous offers from the casinos to spend your celebration with them!

Finally, we'll now take a look at some of the myths regarding slot clubs and player's cards and dispose of them accordingly. Here are some of the arguments I've heard against slot club cards, or excuses as to why players don't use them...

"I never win when I play with my card." The truth is your results would be the same regardless if you had a card in or not. There is no relation between the card counting coins through the machine and what comes up on the screen when you push the button. The card just records how much money is wagered. It has no memory of whether you have won or lost and it doesn't care.

"I don't want to be tracked," or "I don't want the casino to know how much I'm playing," or "I don't want the IRS to have my records." In fact, you do want the casino to track you so you can be rewarded for your play. They have no way of knowing you, or how they can help and reward you unless they know who you are, what you're playing and how much you're spending. The IRS does not have access to your gambling activities, but you, in fact, do. The slot club can provide you with a year end win-loss record of your play that may help you offset wins with losses for tax purposes.

"I don't need a card, I'm a local," or "I'm a tourist." Basically, you're one or the other, but either way you still should have a card. The casino's computers usually separate locals from tourists and tailor their offers accordingly. If you're going to play anyway, get a card!

"I always lose those cards." You can always have another card made. Get extras made. Why play without it? It's like losing your wallet. The card has so much value for you, yet you leave it in the machine. You don't forget your airline frequent flier card at the airport, or your grocery savings card when you go shopping, do you?

"I don't need a card, I'm leaving in an hour." It doesn't matter how long you will be staying or how soon you will be leaving. Remember that all-important mailing list, and that you just might return some time in the future or play at a sister property somewhere else. (Don't worry. Most casinos do not sell their mailing list names. They want you for themselves and are very selfish!)

All-in-all, I've never heard of one good reason not to join a slot club. In fact, I hope I've given you enough good reasons to always join every slot club at every casino you ever visit. Good luck and happy slot clubbing!

H. Scot Krause is a freelance writer and researcher, originally from Cleveland, Ohio. He is an 11-year resident of Las Vegas who reports, researches, and writes about casino games, events and promotions for The American Casino Guide as well as other publications and marketing/consulting firms.

Slot Clubs And Comps

by Steve Bourie

Before you start playing any kind of electronic gaming machine in a casino, whether it be a slot, video poker, video blackjack, or video keno machine, you should first join the casino's slot club to reap the rewards that your play will entitle you to. What is a slot club you ask? Well, it's very similar to a frequent flyer club, except that in these clubs you will earn cash or comps (free food, rooms, shows, etc.) based on how much money you put through the machines.

Virtually every major casino in the U.S. today has a slot club and joining is quite simple. Just go to the club's registration desk, present an ID, and you'll be issued a plastic card which is very similar to a credit card. When you walk up to a machine you'll see a small slot (usually at the top, or on the side) where you should insert your card before you start to play. The card will then record how much money you've played in that particular machine and then, based on the amount you put through, you will be eligible to receive cash (sometimes) and comps (always) back from the casino. Naturally, the more you gamble, the more they will give back to you.

Some casinos will give you a free gift, or some other kind of bonus (extra slot club points, free buffet, etc.) just for joining and since there's no cost involved, it certainly makes sense to join even if you don't plan on playing that much. As a club member you'll also be on the casino's mailing list and you'll probably be receiving some good money-saving offers in the mail. Additionally, some casinos offer discounts to their club members on hotel rooms, meals and gift shop purchases.

While almost no casino will give you cashback for playing their table games, virtually all casinos will give you cashback for playing their machines. The amount returned is calculated as a percentage of the money you put through the machines and it basically varies from as low as .05% to as high as 1%. This means that for every $100 you put into a machine you will earn a cash rebate of anywhere from five cents to $1. This may not seem like a great deal of money but it can add up very quickly. Additionally, some casinos (usually the casinos with the lower rates) will periodically offer double, triple or quadruple point days when your points will accumulate much more rapidly.

One other point to make about cashback is that the vast majority of casinos (about 90%) offer a lower cash rebate on their video poker machines than they do on their slot machines. Generally, the rate is about one-half of what the casino normally pays on its slot machines. As an example, on the Las Vegas Strip all of the following casinos offer their slot players a rebate of .67% but reduce that rate to .33% for video poker play: Treasure Island, Mirage, New York New York, Bellagio and Luxor. The reason for the reduced rate is that video poker is a game of skill and knowledgeable players can achieve a greater return on video poker games than they could on slots. Since the casino will make less money on video poker games they simply reduce their cash rebates accordingly. This is very important to keep in mind, especially if you're a bad video poker player, because you'll probably only be earning half the cash rebate you could be getting by just playing the slots.

Of course, the best situation is to be a smart video poker player and to find a casino that offers the same cash rebate to all of its player regardless of what kind of machine they play. This way you could be playing a good video poker game, combined with a good cash rebate, and this will allow you to be playing at a near 100% level! Quite a few of the "locals" casinos in Las Vegas that have low cash rebates (.05% to .15%) offer the same rate of return regardless of the type of machine.

One final point to make about cash rebates is that not all clubs will allow you to get your cashback immediately. In Atlantic City, for example, most of the casinos will send a voucher to your home address which you must bring back to the casino (usually within 90 days) to receive your cash. You should always make it a point to ask if your cashback from the slot club is available immediately. If not, you may find yourself being mailed a voucher that is worthless to you.

While not every casino's slot club will give you back cash it is standard for every slot club to allow you to earn "comps" for your machine play. "Comps" is short for complimentaries and it means various things that you can get for free from the casino: rooms, meals, shows, gifts, etc.

Once again, the comp you will earn is based on the amount of money you put through the machines but it is usually at a higher level than you would earn for cashback. After all, the real cost to a casino for a $15 meal is much less than giving you back $15 in cash so the casinos can afford to be more generous.

When it comes to casino slot club comp policies they basically fall into one of three categories. Some casinos have clubs that allow you to redeem your points for either cash at one rate, or comps at a reduced rate that will cost you fewer points. In these clubs, for example, you might have a choice of redeeming your 1,000 points for either $10 in cash or $20 in comps.

Another option (one that is commonly used by many "locals" casinos in Las Vegas) is for the casino to set a redemption schedule for each particular restaurant, or meal. For example: breakfast is 800 points, lunch is 1,200 points and dinner is 1,600 points. These are popular programs because players know exactly what is required to earn their comp.

At the other extreme is the practice of many casinos to base their comps on your total machine play but not to tell you exactly what's required to achieve it. At the Mirage, Caesars Palace and Treasure Island in Las Vegas, for example, you will earn cashback at a set schedule but you'll never quite know what you need to earn a food comp. You just have to go to the slot club booth, present your card, and ask if you can get a buffet or restaurant comp. The staff will then either give it to you or say you need some more play on your card before they can issue you a food comp.

And which casinos have the best slot clubs? Well, that would really be dependant on what's most important to you. If you're visiting from out of town you would probably want a slot club that's more generous with room comps so you could save money on your accomodations. However, if you're going to be playing at a casino near your home you would be more interested in which casino offers the best cashback rate and food comps. Whatever the situation, be sure to give most of your play to the casino that offers the best benefits for you and you'll soon be reaping the rewards of slot club membership!

Using Casino Coupons

by Jean Scott

An overwhelming majority of gamblers in a casino are playing negative-expectation games, meaning the house has the mathematical edge, and they will usually lose money in short order. Remember, you can only win in the long run if you're not giving the casino that little "admission fee," its edge, on every bet. That's not to say it's not possible to win on a negative-expectation game one day, or one trip, or even for several trips in a row. But in the long run, if you play negative-expectation games, the house edge will see to it that you're a long-term loser.

Couponing affords you the opportunity to turn things around and have the edge in your favor. For example, if you're lucky enough to have a blackjack coupon that makes your first card an automatic ace, you're playing with a whopping 52% edge. No, you won't win on every coupon, no matter how big the edge, but you will get to the winning long-term much faster.

Therefore, because couponing takes the edge away from the casino and gives it to you, it is possible to gamble with a much smaller bankroll. Because you always have the edge, and sometimes quite a large one, you'll likely become an overall winner more quickly than playing a regular game without a coupon. Of course, you must make coupon bets that are compatible with your bankroll. If you have only a couple of hundred dollars, you better stick with $5-$10 and/or one-bet coupons. It takes a larger bankroll to play some large-bet or extended-time-play coupons, i.e. $25 matchplays or getting paid double for blackjack for the first hour of play. But if you make an effort to track down a lot of those smaller coupon plays, you'll be surprised how soon you can build up your bankroll for the bigger plays that yield even greater profits.

Couponing is an extremely important tool even for casino visitors who are playing positive-expectation games. For the skillful video poker player at the quarter level or the blackjack card counter who makes only low-level

bets, couponing may be the first line of defense against the casino edge. My husband Brad and I played quarter video poker for many years, and all during that time our per-hour profit rate in couponing far exceeded what we had made in video poker and became an important contributor to building our gambling bankroll so we could progress to higher denomination play.

Coupons for free or reduced-price food, drinks, hotel rooms, or shows are "found" money if you're not getting these amenities comped. I've known couples that paid full-price for a show when there was a 2-for-1 coupon in the unopened freebie magazine right in their hotel room. People are given a coupon book when they check into a casino hotel-and the maid finds it on the dresser after they check out, a coupon for $5 in free coin, with no playing requirement, still intact. (And guess who the maid sometimes knows that loves "leftover" coupons!)

Casinos used to be famous for their bargain-priced meals, rooms, and show tickets, but this is changing quickly; Las Vegas especially is going upscale. So if you're are on a limited budget, you'll find that the time and effort you spend looking for the non-gambling coupons will allow you to afford some of the higher-price splurges. Even though we play enough to get all the free drinks we usually want in a casino, I always carry a few drink coupons in my purse in case we want to meet friends in the lounge and not face a big bar bill. Now let's take a look at the different kinds of coupons offered to gamblers.

Matchplay - Whether it says "$5 matchplay" or "Bet $5 and We Will Pay You $10 If You Win," it means the same: The casino is giving you money. However, you can't take this money and stick it in your pocket. The "free" money must be used for a bet and comes with a condition: You must risk some of your own money at the same time.

Here's how it works: We'll use as an example the most common matchplay-a $5 coupon for blackjack. You go to a blackjack table and sit down at an empty space, placing your coupon on the betting circle for your seat, with a $5 bill on top of the coupon. Some casinos let that bill play; some exchange it for a $5 chip. In either case, you now have a $10 bet riding on this hand-your own $5 investment plus an extra bet of $5 that the casino has given you by "matching" your bet. If you win, the casino pays off at $10. If you lose, the casino merely takes away the coupon and the $5 of your own money that you put up.

This is how it works in general for all table games and all denominations of matchplay coupons. If you have a $25 matchplay, then the casino matches that amount and you have a $50 bet. You're paid off at $50 if you win, while giving up only your own $25 (and the coupon) if you lose. You will win about half the time on matchplay bets, depending on the game and the type of bets you make. A rule of thumb to figure out the value of a matchplay coupon is to cut the amount in half and subtract the house edge, which averages around 3%, depending on the game, the bet, and/or your skill level. I usually just subtract 10 cents on a $5 matchplay as a round figure. This renders a $5 matchplay worth about $2.40-plus. A $25 matchplay is worth about $12-plus ($25 divided by 2 minus 50 cents).

Non-Even-Money Matchplay Coupons - Almost all matchplays can be used only on even-money bets. However, if you get one that allows non-even money bets, the optimal use is to bet it on the longest longshot available-like straight-up on a number at roulette.

Example: If you're betting a $100 matchplay (use it once and lose it whether you win or lose) at single-zero roulette, taking a shot at straight-up on a number yields an expected value (EV) of $94.59 ($3,500 payoff/37 possible outcomes). If you bet on the banker at baccarat, your EV is about $49.47.

The problem is that you pay for your extra EV on this bet in roulette with *extreme* variance, but if you expect to get many more of these matchplays, it can make sense to maximize your EV in this way.

Lucky Bucks - This kind of coupon generally adds a dollar or two extra on an even-money bet. For example, with a 7-for-5 coupon, you put down the coupon with a $5 chip or bill and if you win, you're paid an extra $2. Like matchplays, you win on average about half the time, so the coupon is worth just a few cents less than half the bonus, about 97 cents.

There are also occasional 3-for-2 and 2-for-1 lucky bucks, but you often can't find a table with minimums that allow you to bet that small, and you're usually not permitted to use them with a larger bet even if you explain that you still only expect the same dollar bonus. I've given up trying to educate dealers (and even pit bosses) that this is actually to their advantage, since I'm putting more money at risk for the same measly bonus. (I guess I'm getting too old to argue over small change. Brad says it's about time!)

First Card Is An Ace - Put this coupon in the betting spot on a blackjack table with the bet listed on the coupon (usually $5) and it becomes your first card, a valuable ace. The dealer skips you on the first-card deal around, then gives you a second card. You play out the hand the same as if you were dealt a first-card ace, getting paid immediately if you're lucky to score a blackjack. Otherwise you hit, stand, split, or double as usual.

This coupon gives you an enormous 52% edge, although a bit more long term than other coupons, since you often have to split or double, which involves putting more money at risk. But it still doesn't take too many of these coupons to become an overall winner and to make this your favorite coupon, as it is mine.

Free Play - This is usually a coupon you get as a bonus reward for past play at a casino and an incentive to come back, sometimes referred to as bounce-back cash. If the coupon is for slot play, you usually have to go to the slot club to have credits activated on a slot or video poker machine and you have to play them through once before you can cash out your winnings.

If the coupon is for chips, you usually get special non-negotiable chips at the cage. These chips cannot be exchanged for cash, like regular chips, but must be played. These chips are usually *not* matchplay, but can be bet alone, with no money of your own at risk. When you win a bet with this kind of chip, you're paid in regular chips that you *can* cash in. You can usually continue to bet with these special non-negotiable chips until you lose them; therefore their worth is the face value of the chip.

Read the rules for all free-play coupons carefully and note any special instructions or restrictions. They're often date specific. The table-game chips might be "for one play only," and the ones for slot credits might specify or exclude certain machines

Jean Scott is one of the country's most renowned and successful gamblers and has appeared on many TV shows, including *48 Hours*, where Dan Rather gave her the nickname of Queen of Comps. Her first book, *The Frugal Gambler*, has been a best-seller for nine years. She also wrote a sequel, *More Frugal Gambling,* and a tax guide for gamblers. She provides a complete resource package for video poker players, from beginners to the experienced: the *Frugal VP* software program which goes with her new book, *Frugal Video Poker*, and the must-have *Frugal Video Poker Scouting Guide*. Her Web site is queenofcomps.com.

Video Poker From A to Z

Frugal Video Poker is the most comprehensive and detailed book ever written on preparing and practicing for, then playing, video poker. It takes you step-by-step as far as you want to go, from basic to highly skilled.

Beginners are walked through the basics of play, learning to first distinguish between good and bad paytables, then playing them properly. Experienced players can fill in the inevitable gaps in their study to grasp the complete picture. For experts, *Frugal Video Poker* covers special opportunities, such as tournaments, promotions, progressives, and the cutting-edge games; an extensive resource section paves the way to advanced study.

And everyone can benefit from the detailed lessons in using readily available video poker computer tutorials, specifically the *Frugal VP* software.

Frugal Video Poker
Jean Scott, Viktor Nacht
316 pages • Order #1483 • $14.95

To order visit ShopLVA.com
or call 1-800-244-2224

Breaking The Bank at Monte-Carlo

by Steve Bourie

Yes, I know. This is supposed to be a book about American casinos. However, there are three important reasons why this story was included in this year's book.

First, you will know how U.S. casinos vary from their counterparts in another country. Second, you will learn the history of one of the world's most famous casinos. Third, and most important of all, I can write-off the entire cost of my trip to Europe as a business expense. Now, sit back, relax and enjoy the story!

Because of my extensive knowledge of casino gambling and travel, I am sometimes contacted by other publications to write stories for them.

In early 2005 I was hired to write an article about "The World's 10 Coolest Casinos" for a major magazine and in that story, I mentioned only four U.S. casinos: Bellagio, Wynn Las Vegas, Foxwoods and Borgata. The other six casinos were in foreign countries and although they weren't in any ranked order, one casino on the list stood out as the most important to me: Monte-Carlo.

As a kid, growing up in New York, I remember the casino at Monte-Carlo as being the most famous in the world. There were songs and stories written about it; movies were made about it and, of course, there was the famous wedding of American actress Grace Kelly to Monaco's Prince Rainier which brought even more notoriety to the area.

With such a fabled history, I had always wanted to visit Monte-Carlo and in April, 2007 my wife and I made our first trip there. It's truly a beautiful area and here are some travel tips for when you're ready to plan your own trip there, plus details on my attempt to "break the bank" at the casino.

Monaco is an independent principality located along the Mediterranean Sea in Southern Europe. Only three miles long by a half-mile wide, it is sandwiched between the French Riviera to the west and the Italian Riviera to the east. It is the world's second smallest independent state after The Holy See (Vatican) and the population is 30,000, but only 7,000 people, known as Monégasques, are natural born natives.

Many people mistakenly believe that Monaco and Monte-Carlo are the same, but the principality is divided into five distinct districts and Monte-Carlo is but one of them. The other four are: Monaco-Ville, Fontvieille, Moneghetti and the Condamine.

The usual route to Monaco involves flying to Paris and that's where we started our adventure. While in the "city of lights" you should definitely plan on staying a few days to take in the usual sights: Eiffel Tower, Louvre, Notre Dame, a walk down the Champs Elysées and a sight-seeing boat trip along the Seine.

The Paris subway, known locally as the Metro, is excellent and provides service to most any area of the city. On our arrival at the Charles de Gaulle Airport we took a bus directly into Paris, but after realizing how fast and easy it was to use the Metro, we took it back to the airport when we were ready to leave. Not only was it faster, it was also about half the cost of the bus.

You can save money on Metro fares by buying a pass at the ticket booth at any station. The "Paris Visite" pass entitles you to unlimited travel on the metro, buses and some other local train lines for your choice of one, two, three or five consecutive days. Along with the pass, you are also given a coupon book for discounts on various attractions.

There are three options for getting to Monte-Carlo from Paris: driving, flying or taking a train. Since we didn't have a lot of time, the 600-mile drive was out of the question. Nice is the airport closest to Monte-Carlo and an Internet search revealed that Air France offered seven flights each day with an hour-and-a-half flying time and a round-trip fare of $144. The TGV (Train à grande vitesse), which is a high-speed train that travels at speeds up to 186 m.p.h., was the most intriguing option, but the travel time was still more than five hours and the cost was double that of flying.

Upon arrival at the Nice airport you can take a 45-minute bus ride to Monte-Carlo for $22, or an eight-minute helicopter ride for about $80. In researching our trip on the official Monaco website at www.visitmonaco.com I learned that you can buy a one-year membership in *Le Club Diamant Rouge de Monaco* for $55 and it offers some great values.

Le Club is operated by the Monaco Government Tourist Office and its membership card provides free admission to all of Monaco's museums, the aquarium and the casino, plus discounts or perks at several hotels, spas and other travel service providers. The free admissions alone amount to about $90 in savings, but best of all, card members receive a free helicopter flight from the Nice airport to Monaco and a 20% discount on the purchase of a flight back. There is a requirement that you stay at least one night at one of 10 participating hotels in order to buy the card, but chances are you will be staying at one of those hotels anyway. For more details go to www.clubdiamantrouge.com (or call 800-371-CLUB) and while visiting the web site, be sure to check out the auctions link which allows you to bid on various hotel packages, some of which include dining options, spa visits and other extras. You can also visit the auction site separately by going to www.monacoauction.com

My wife doesn't like to fly and we have a close friend who was injured in a helicopter crash, so in planning our trip it was understandable that she was hesitant to opt for the helicopter ride. A friend of hers, however, pointed out that she should look at it as a once-in-a-lifetime opportunity to see a beautiful city from a fantastic point of view and, after giving it much thought, she finally agreed - provided we took the bus back to the airport. I agreed to her request and it's rather ironic that in looking back on our trip we were in agreement that the helicopter flight was a major highlight and the return bus ride via the mountainous roads was scarier than the helicopter ride!

The visitmonaco.com web site has a wealth of information for visitors and I also found it useful for planning our hotel reservations. The site breaks down hotels by category, with four star deluxe being the highest and two star being the lowest. I started at the top and visited all five of the four star deluxe hotel web sites first. The rates started at about $525 per night, but I noticed that one property, Hotel Metropole, offered a special rate of about $320 per night. The rate was nonrefundable and required a 30-day minimum advance reservation, but the savings were substantial, so I booked it. Everything turned out great as both the hotel and room were beautiful, plus the service from all of the staff was excellent.

We arrived on Sunday afternoon and were leaving Tuesday morning, so we really didn't have a lot of free time. Naturally, the casino was the top priority and I had made an appointment through the public relations department to meet a representative from the casino for a tour shortly after our arrival at the hotel.

There are actually five casinos in Monaco (you can access information about all of them at www.casinomontecarlo.com.) and the original Casino de Monte-Carlo is the largest. Just across the street is the Café de Paris, which functions as both a sidewalk cafe and restaurant, plus the rear of the facility houses the Casino Café de Paris with the area's largest number of slot/video poker machines: 436.

Three blocks away, in the Fairmont Hotel, is the Sun Casino and about a mile further east, inside the Monte-Carlo Bay Resort, is the Bay Casino which has no table games, just slots and video poker. The fifth casino, open only during the summer months, is appropriately named Casino d'Été (Summer Casino) and can be found in Le Sporting Monte-Carlo, an entertainment complex housing restaurants, a disco and a live events center with a retractable roof.

All casinos are owned by the Société des Baines de Mer (SBM) which has been in existence since 1863 and is a publicly traded company with 69% of its shares owned by the Principality of Monaco. Employing more than 3,000 people, SBM also owns and operates five hotels, 30 restaurants, and several other sports club and entertainment venues in Monaco.

After a brief rest in our hotel room we walked three blocks to the main casino and went to the reception desk in the main lobby to ask about meeting our representative. All casino guests are required to stop at the desk to show their passport. Part of the reason for the ID check is to make sure you are not a native Monégasque, as they are not allowed into the casino. Guests must also be at least 18 years of age and pay an admission fee of 10 Euros (about $14). This is the only casino in Monaco that charges an entrance fee and it seems that many visitors are gawkers rather than gamblers and don't mind paying the fee.

As a member of *Le Club* all we had to do was show our membership card and we were given free admission. Guests staying at many of the better hotels in Monaco, as well as previously rated players, are also given free admission.

If you haven't been to Monte-Carlo, it's possible that you may have already seen it in a James Bond movie. The casino, as well as Monaco's main harbor area are shown in the James Bond movie, *Goldeneye*, starring Pierce Brosnan. The film includes an exterior shot of the casino when Bond arrives in his Aston Martin and he is then shown inside the casino playing Chemin de Fer (Baccarat) pitted against the evil female agent Xenia Onatopp. The main harbor area, Port Hercule, is shown in the next day's action scene when Onatopp steals a helicopter from a battleship docked in the port.

The casino was also featured in *Never Say Never Again*, starring Sean Connery as James Bond. In one scene the action follows Domino Petachi, played by Kim Basinger, as she plays at a roulette table. Shortly, thereafter, Bond plays a high-stakes video game against the main villain, Maximilian Largo. Of course, Bond wins, and rather than collecting the $267,000 from Largo, he says "I'll settle for one dance with Domino." Connery and Basinger then perform their dance in what seems to be a ballroom, but in reality it is the atrium that houses the reception desk and the entrance into the casino's gaming floors.

A call from the reception desk to the casino's marketing department brought the guide for our tour down to the lobby in a few minutes. Her name was Nathalie and her primary job was that of a casino host. Similar to that position in a U.S. casino, her job was to greet players and accommodate their needs. As we walked through various areas of the casino it seemed that she was very good at her job because she seemed to know many of the players. To communicate with the casino's international clientele, Nathalie was fluent in four languages and she had no problem switching from one to another when greeting her clients during our tour. I had assumed that most of the casino's customers were from France, but she dispelled that myth when she told us that "the majority of our customers are from Italy."

An aerial view of the Place du Casino. At the top of the circular driveway is the Casino de Monte-Carlo. To the left of the driveway is the Café de Paris with its outdoor dining area. To the right is the Hotel de Paris.

Casino de Monte-Carlo was originally built in 1863 on the site of an olive grove. It was the first casino to be built in Europe and was designed by Charles Garnier, who also designed the Paris Opera House. Nathalie explained that the first room we entered, Salle de l'Europe (European Room), was the original casino when the facility first opened and the other rooms were added on to the building throughout its 144-year history. The games in this room were all roulette, except for one called Trente et Quarante (30 and 40).

I had read about dress rules being enforced in the casino, with men required to wear jackets and ties, but the crowd in this room was dressed rather casually, including sneakers. I asked Nathalie about the dress code and she explained that it only applied for entrance to the casino's back rooms, called Salons Privés (Private Salons), after 10 p.m. The American Room was the next area we visited and it housed all 11 of the casino's blackjack tables, as well as one craps table.

As we entered the next gaming area, the White Room, it was quickly evident that this room housed all of the casino's slots and video poker games (about 120 in total). As we checked out the assortment of games, Nathalie pointed out that, "unlike most American casinos, we have large windows to let in sunlight, plus clocks on the walls." She also let us know that there was one other area of the casino with about 60 slots/video poker machines. It was situated directly by the main entrance just before reaching the reception desk so visitors didn't have to pay a fee to play the games. An interesting fact is that in the U.S. the average casino makes about 70 percent of its profit from electronic machines, but in Monaco most players prefer table games and only about 40 percent of the profits are generated by machines.

The last area of the casino we visited was the Salons Privés. There is another entrance fee of 10 Euros required to enter this area but, once again, our membership in *Le Club* allowed us to visit this area at no extra charge. It was about 5:30 on a Sunday afternoon so it was pretty empty, but it was interesting to see these two additional gaming areas which are both named after architects who worked on the casino: Salle Touzet and Salle Medecin.

An interesting part of the Salle Medecin was that it featured Les Privés, a restaurant specializing in French food. Located at the rear of the room, it's built on a terrace and has large picture windows showcasing panoramic views of the Mediterranean Sea just a few blocks away.

In one of the gaming rooms there was an antique elevator which served as a private entrance to the Cabaret de Monte-Carlo, a showroom located one floor below the casino. We didn't get to see the Cabaret as it's only open seasonally, but Nathalie did let us take a look into an even more private area of the casino.

"We have four 'Super Private Rooms' available for our higher limit players" she said as she proceeded to lead us into one that was discreetly located in the confines of the regular Private Salons. After leaving that room, she walked us out some doors and down a flight of stairs that led to a private entrance on the side of the casino. From that spot, we then proceeded to another of the special rooms. Evidently, this was the route for the exclusive "high rollers" who didn't have to bother going through the main reception area. Surprisingly, these rooms were plainly decorated, but it was a wonderful treat to get access to an area that most visitors to the casino never get to see.

I asked Nathalie about comping programs for players and her reply was that it was similar to U.S. casinos, with different levels of players eligible for varying comps. She said that players were rated and given a designated players club card based on their "action." Crystal was the entry level card which afforded free admission to the casino, followed by Silver, Gold and Diamond. She suggested that anyone wanting more information could send an email to their marketing department at marketingcasinos@sbm.com.

To get a better idea of what betting levels were required for a complimentary room I later looked on the www.montecarlocasino.com web site and saw that a free two-night stay required depositing a minimum of 8,000 Euros ($11,200) with the casino, plus gambling for a minimum of four hours per day with an average bet of at least 100 Euros ($140).

After touring the casino I must say that it was very different from what we have in the U.S. While many American casinos are imploded to make way for a more hip, modern gambling palace, the emphasis here was most definitely on the past. The rooms were all very ornate, with lots of marble, chandeliers, candelabras, mahogany woodwork, stained glass, frescoes, sculptures and many turn-of-the-century paintings adorning the walls. It was like stepping into a time warp and being transported back 100 years.

Old European elegance was in abundance: from the lavish decor, to the tuxedo-clad croupiers, to the strange and eery quietness. American casinos are usually bristling with loud noises emanating from both players and machines, but this casino was different. Most players were huddled around roulette tables, quietly placing their bets and hardly a peep could be heard from the blackjack tables. Even the lone craps table was deadly silent.

Yes, it was very different, but I liked it and I was ready to try my luck at the tables. Unfortunately, we were exhausted from our trip and I had to put off my play until the next day.

The following morning we slept late and went for a walk to explore the city. We took our map and headed for the city's main harbor, Port Hercule. From there we headed to the Oceanographic Museum and Aquarium, which was a pleasant way to spend a few hours. There were several other places of interest we wanted to visit, but time was short and we needed to have a late lunch and then visit the three other casinos.

We chose the Café de Paris for our lunch destination and it is a must stop for anyone visiting Monaco. Situated diagonally across from the main casino, you can enjoy a cocktail, coffee or light snack at this outside cafe while watching the comings and goings at the world's most famous gaming venue. A major highlight for us was seeing the large collection of exotic cars parked outside the casino. There was the usual assortment of Ferraris, Porsches and Lamborghinis, but we also witnessed the arrival of a Mercedes-Benz SLR McLaren. The SLR McLaren is the world's fastest automatic transmission automobile and has a retail selling price of slightly more than $450,000. Upon seeing that fascinating car, I believe I said "that's a car you don't see every day," but I was wrong because we did see another one the next day in the window of the local Mercedes dealer. Yes, this was an interesting way to enjoy a leisurely lunch, but of course it came at a somewhat hefty price as we enjoyed a club sandwich priced at $16 (and it only came with three sections instead of four - what did they do with that other section?), plus an $11 bottle of Heineken beer.

After lunch we visited the other three casinos and it turned out that they all looked very much like their American counterparts. One surprise was that the two casinos with table games offered only American-style roulette with double-zero wheels, rather than the single-zero European game found in the big casino.

Later that night we headed back to the Monte-Carlo casino to try our luck Once again, the tables weren't very crowded and our first stop was to check out the video poker.

The Jacks or Better game at the two Euro level ($2.80) was very good and, it turned out, the best VP game in the casino. It had a standard 9/6 paytable, except it paid 300 coins for a royal flush, rather than 250. Also, in order to get a higher payoff of 18,000 coins for the royal, rather than the standard 6,000, you had to make a maximum bet of 20 coins. If you bet one coin at a time, the return was 98.47%, but if you bet the maximum 20 coins, it brought the return up to 99.79% (because of the added bonus on the royal).

At the one Euro level ($1.40) the paytables dropped to a standard 8/5 (97.28% return) with 250 for the royal and 4,000 when you bet the maximum five coins, for .50 Euros it was lowered to 7/5 (96.15%) and for .20 Euros, the paytable dropped to 6/5 (95.00%).

We played one coin at a time on the two Euro game, but stopped about 20 minutes later after losing 40 Euros. It should be pointed out that you need to exchange dollars for Euros at the main cashier cage before gambling. However, the conversion rate is very good because you don't have to pay the usual transaction fee which most currency exchanges charge.

I didn't have a lot of cash with me, but I definitely wanted to play some roulette and I figured I'd take a shot with the last 60 Euros ($84) left in my gambling bankroll. Normally, I wouldn't play roulette in a casino, but here they had a much better game than found in most U.S. casinos.

All of the tables had single-zero wheels which cut the house edge down to 2.70%, rather than the 5.26% casino advantage you would face on a double-zero wheel. Even better, if you played any even money bet: odd/even; high/low; or red/black; and the ball landed in zero, you only lost half of your bet. This brought the casino's edge on these bets down to 1.35%, making it the best roulette game you can find.

As it turned out there were two types of roulette games offered: English and European. The only difference between the two was in the kind of chips that were used on the table. In the European version all of the chips at the table must represent their actual value. In other words, the chips were all 5 Euros, 10 Euros, 25 Euros, etc. The English version, however, was similar to the game found in U.S. casinos where the chips can represent any value and each person has their own uniquely colored chips. Other than that one difference, the games were identical.

Again, I don't play roulette very often, but I sometimes get matchplay vouchers that need to be played only on roulette and my usual method is to bet on red or black. Also, rather than trying to guess which color to play, I simply bet the

A roulette table at the Casino de Monte-Carlo. Players sit along the sides of the table and the croupiers sit at the ends. The sticks, or "rakes," in the center of the table are used to push the chips around the table.

same color that came in on the previous spin. Roulette is purely a game of luck and this method is no better or worse than any other method for choosing what to bet, but it does save me the dread of deciding what to do on each spin. Another thing I like about this method is that if I lose, I can blame it on the system, rather than myself, for picking the wrong color. My wife didn't want to play or watch, so I told her what I was planning to do, left her at a nearby seat and then headed over to the European game.

Of course, 60 Euros isn't a big bankroll, but I was sure that with a little bit of luck I too could become as famous as Joseph Jaggers, otherwise known as "The Man Who Broke The Bank at Monte-Carlo." In 1873, Jaggers, an English engineer, hired people to secretly record the outcome of every spin at each roulette table and then analyzed the results. Believing he found a "biased" wheel in which certain numbers won more often than others, Jaggers parlayed his hunch into an impressive fortune over the course of three days. The casino finally figured out what he was doing and took countermeasures such as switching wheels and replacing frets (the dividers between the numbers). Denied his advantage, Jaggers lost back some of his winnings, but he still left the casino with more than $3 million (in today's dollars) and never returned.

In reality, "breaking the bank at Monte-Carlo" doesn't mean that someone wins *all* of the casino's money - that has never happened. The phrase simply means that all of the chips at a particular roulette table have been won by a player and the chips must be replenished from the casino's reserves. The table is closed while a new supply of chips is brought over and then the game continues.

Okay, maybe I would need more than a *little* bit of luck, but evidently, I didn't have to win all of the casino's money, just all of the chips on the table, and this made my job much simpler. A look at the placard by the table showed that the minimum bet was only five Euros - well within my bankroll's range - so I was ready to begin my quest! I bought in for 60 Euros right at the table and I was given 12 chips, valued at five Euros each.

The first thing I noticed was that the table was much wider than an American table and the players were seated on two sides of the table, rather than on one side as in U.S. casinos. Also, the croupiers were placed at both ends of the table. In the U.S. the roulette staff would be working only on the long side of the table that is located inside the pit area.

I looked at the table's electronic display board to see what color had just won and I was eager to bet on it to repeat. I soon discovered that the betting square I wanted was on the opposite side of the table and I couldn't reach it. Rather than asking the croupier for help, I gently tossed my chip across the felt and it landed exactly in the right spot, but I knew this was going to be a problem for my future bets.

When that bet lost, the next color I had to bet was on my side and that made things easy. However, when that lost, I needed to make my bet back on the other side and I decided to ask the croupier for help in placing the bet. In response, he handed me one of the little sticks they use to move the chips around the table and jokingly said "we make you work at this table!" I then used the stick, also known as a "rake," whenever I had to place a bet on the other side of the table and I was having fun shoving my chips around the table. Regrettably, that was the only fun I had because the winning colors alternated between red and black for nine of the first 10 spins and I busted out within 15 minutes. Oh well, there went my dreams of "breaking the bank" and buying my very own SLR McLaren.

A few minutes later, I walked over to break the news to my wife and I could see that she wasn't the least bit fazed, by my stroke of bad luck. "That was a bad idea to bet that way," she said. "But it wasn't my fault, it was the system's fault," I replied. "It could just as easily have gone the other way with a lot of repeat colors winning. I just had some bad timing."

"Bad timing? Sure, whatever you say, let's go," she answered. As we left the casino, hand-in-hand, I turned around to take one last look at the table where I had played and I couldn't help but notice on the display board that red had just come in five times in a row. "See," I said, "it wasn't such a bad system after all." Watch out Monte-Carlo, I'll be back!

Slot Machines

by Steve Bourie

Virtually anyone who visits a casino, even for the first time, is familiar with a slot machine and how it operates: just put in your money, pull the handle and wait a few seconds to see if you win. It isn't intimidating like table games where you really need some knowledge of the rules before you play and it's this basic simplicity that accounts for much of the success of slot machines in the modern American casino.

As a matter of fact, the biggest money-maker for casinos is the slot machine with approximately 65 percent of the average casino's profits being generated by slot machine play. As an example, in Nevada's fiscal year ending June 30, 2007 the total win by all of the state's casinos was a little more than $12.7 billion. Of that amount, $8.3 billion, or slightly more than 65 percent, was from electronic machine winnings.

With this in mind, you must ask yourself, "can I really win money by playing slot machines?" The answer is a resounding yes...and no. First the "no" part: in simplest terms a slot machine makes money for the casino by paying out less money than it takes in. In some states, such as Nevada and New Jersey, the minimum amount to be returned is regulated. In Nevada the minimum is 75 percent and in New Jersey it's 83 percent. However, if you look at the slot payback percentages for those particular states in this book you will see that the actual average payback percentages are much higher. In New Jersey it's close to 92 percent and in Nevada it's slightly more than 94 percent. Even though the actual paybacks are higher than the law requires, you can still see that on average for every $1 you play in an Atlantic City slot machine you will lose 8¢ and in a Las Vegas slot machine you will lose 5¢. Therefore, it doesn't take a rocket scientist to see that if you stand in front of a slot machine and continue to pump in your money, eventually, you will lose it all. On average, it will take you longer to lose it in Las Vegas rather than Atlantic City, but the result is still the same: you will go broke.

Gee, sounds kind of depressing, doesn't it? Well, cheer up because now we go on to the "yes" part. But, before we talk about that, let's first try to understand how slot machines work. All modern slot machines contain a random number generator (RNG) which is used to control the payback percentage for each machine. When a casino orders a slot machine the manufacturer will have a list of percentage paybacks for each machine and the casino must choose one from that list. For example, a manufacturer may have 10 chips available for one machine that range from a high of 98% to as low as 85%. All of these chips have been inspected and approved by a gaming commission and the casino is free to choose whichever chip it wants for that particular brand of machine.

In almost all instances, the casino will place a higher denomination chip in a higher denomination machine. In other words, the nickel machines will get the chips programmed to pay back around 87% and the $25 machines will get the chips programmed to pay back around 98%. A casino can always change the payback percentage, but in order to do that it must go back to the manufacturer to get a new RNG that is programmed with the new percentage. For this reason, most casinos rarely change their payback percentages unless there is a major revision in their marketing philosophy. And what exactly is a random number generator? Well, it's a little computer chip that is constantly working (as its name implies) to generate number combinations on a random basis. It does this extremely fast and is capable of producing hundreds of combinations each second. When you pull the handle, or push the spin button, the RNG stops and the combination it stops at is used to determine where the reels will stop in the pay window. Unlike video poker machines, you have no way of knowing what a slot machine is programmed to pay back just by looking at it. The only way to tell is by knowing what is programmed into the RNG.

As an example of the differences in RNG payout percentages I have listed below some statistics concerning various slot manufacturers' payback percentages in their slot machines. Normally, this information isn't available to the public, but it is sometimes printed in various gaming industry publications and that is where I found it. The list shows the entire range of percentages that can be programmed into each machine:

A.C. Coin and Slot
   Bingo Nights Slotto   87.90% - 97.00%
   Super Slotto Celebration   85.60% - 95.65%

Anchor Gaming
   Fishin' Buddies   86.99% - 96.99%
   Wheel of Gold Money Multiplier 92.78%

Aristocrat
   Boot Scootin' (20-line)   87.20% - 97.15%
   Moon Festival   87.57% - 95.42%
   Mr. Woo   90.63% - 92.17%
   Tiki Talk   87.95% - 94.86%
   Wild Panda   88.00% - 95.00%

Atronic
   Bamboo Forest   86.00% - 96.00%
   Crimson Fire   86.00% - 96.00%
   Deal or No Deal The Show   86.00% - 96.00%
   IC Money   85.20% - 97.02%
   King Kong Cash   86.00% - 90.00%
   Sphinx (2-reel, 5-line)   90.99%

Bally Gaming
    Black & White 5 Times Pay   84.49% - 96.72%
    Black & White Sevens   87.00% - 95.00%
    Blazing 7's Double (reel)   88.00% - 95.98%
    Hee Haw   88.00% - 96.00%
    Hot Shot Progressive   86.06% - 96.03%
    Movie Star Betty Boop   88.02% - 90.14%
    Mystic Lamp   86.00% - 96.00%
    Playboy Get Lucky Wheel   88.00% - 90.00%
    S&H Green Stamps   86.00% - 96.00%

IGT
    Addams Family   88.00% - 93.50%
    Austin Powers   88.00% - 98.00%
    Beverly Hillbillies Cash For Crude   85.00% or 88.00%
    Dick Clark's Censored Bloopers   85.01% - 98.01%
    The Joker's Wild   87.00% - 90.00%
    Elephant King   85.03% - 98.04%
    Enchanted Unicorn   85.00% - 98.00%
    Fortune Cookie   85.03% - 98.01%
    I Dream of Jeannie   86.01% - 96.97%
    Jeopardy   90.00%
    My Rich Uncle   92.50%
    Neon Nights   87.53% - 98.03%
    Neptune's Exploration Inc.   85.00% - 94.00%
    Pink Panther   88.00% - 95.00%
    Price Check   85.00% - 98.00%
    Red White and Blue   85.03% - 97.45%
    Soul Train Mystery Progressive   87.59% - 94.27%
    Texas Tea   87.00% - 97.00%
    Viva Las Vegas   87.50% - 87.80%
    Wheel of Fortune Super Spin/Wild   87.50% - 89.40%
    White Orchid   90.00% - 98.00%

WMS Gaming
    Brazilian Beauty   87.00% - 96.00%
    Cash Crop   86.36% - 94.92%
    Money To Burn   86.41% - 94.77%
    Monopoly Chairman of the Board   86.36% - 94.87%
    Monopoly Party Train   87.82% or 88.25%
    MonopolySuper Grand Hotel   87.10% - 92.09%
    Life of Luxury   90.10%
    Pac-Man   88.00% - 94.00%
    Village People Party   87.04% - 93.97%
    Who Dunnit?   86.01% - 94.89%

Once again, keep in mind that casinos generally set their slot paybacks based on each machine's denomination. Therefore, nickel machines will probably be set towards the lower number and $5-$25 machines will be set towards the higher number.

Okay, now let's get back to the "yes" part. Yes, you can win money on slot machines by using a little knowledge, practicing some money management and, mostly, having lots of luck. First, the knowledge part. You need to know what kind of player you are and how much risk you are willing to take. Do you want to go for the giant progressive jackpot that could make you a millionaire in an instant or would you be content walking away just a few dollars ahead?

An example of a wide-area progressive machine is Nevada's Megabucks where the jackpot starts at $7 million. These $1 machines are located at more than 125 Nevada casinos around the state and are linked together by a computer. It's fine if that's the kind of machine you want to play, but keep in mind that the odds are fairly astronomical of you hitting that big jackpot. Also, the payback percentage is lower on these machines than the average $1 machine. During Nevada's fiscal year ending June 30, 2007 Megabucks averaged around 88% payback while the typical $1 machine averaged a little less than 95%. So, be aware that if you play these machines you'll win fewer small payouts and it will be very difficult to leave as a winner. Unless, of course, you hit that big one! If you really like to play the wide-area progressive machines your best bet is probably to set aside a small percentage of your bankroll (maybe 10 to 15 percent) for chasing that big jackpot and saving the rest for the regular machines.

One other thing you should know about playing these wide-area progressives is that on most of them, including Megabucks, you will receive your jackpot in equal payments over a period of years (usually 25). You can avoid this, however, by playing at one of the casinos that link slot machines at their own properties and will pay you in one lump sum. The Circus Bucks slots at Circus Circus casinos in Nevada offer this as well as the Million Dollar Babies at Caesars Palace.

Knowledge also comes into play when deciding how many coins to bet. You should always look at the payback schedule posted on the machine to see if a bonus is payed for playing the maximum number of coins that the machine will accept. For example, if it's a two-coin machine and the jackpot payout is 500 coins when you bet one coin, but it pays you 1,200 coins when you bet two coins, then that machine is paying you a 200-coin bonus for playing the maximum number of coins and you should always bet the maximum two coins to take advantage of that bonus. However, if it's a two-coin machine that will pay you 500 coins for a one-coin bet and 1,000 coins for a two-coin bet, then there is no advantage to making the maximum bet on that machine and you should only bet the minimum amount.

Knowledge of which casinos offer the best payback percentages is also helpful. When available, we print that information in this book to help you decide where to go for the best return on your slot machine dollar. You may want to go to the Las Vegas Strip to see the free pirate show at Treasure Island, but take a look at the slot machine payback percentages for the Strip-area casinos in the Las Vegas section and you'll see that you can get better returns for your slot machine dollar by playing at the off-Strip area casinos.

The final bit of knowledge you need concerns slot clubs. Every major casino has a slot club and you should make it a point to join the slot club before you insert your first coin. It doesn't cost anything to join and as a member you will be able to earn complimentaries from the casinos in the form of cash, food, shows, drinks, rooms or other "freebies." When you first join the club you'll be issued a card (similar to a credit card) that you insert into the machine before you start to play and it will track how much you bet, as well as how long you play. Naturally, the more money you gamble, the more "freebies" you'll earn. Just make sure you don't get carried away and bet more than you're comfortable with just to earn some extra "comps." Ideally, you want to get "comps" for gambling that you were going to do anyway and not be pressured into betting more than you had planned.

Now let's talk about money management. The first thing you have to remember when playing slot machines is that there is no skill involved. Unlike blackjack or video poker, there are no decisions you can make that will affect whether you win or lose. It is strictly luck, or the lack of it, that will determine whether or not you win. However, when you are lucky enough to get ahead (even if it's just a little) that's where the money management factor comes in. As stated earlier, the longer you stand in front of a machine and put in your money, the more likely you are to go broke. Therefore, there is only one way you can walk away a winner and that's to make sure that when you do win, you don't put it all back in. You really need to set a "win goal" for yourself and to stop when you reach it. A realistic example would be a "win goal" of roughly 25 percent of your bankroll. If you started with $400, then you should stop if you win about $100. The "win goal" you decide on is up to you, but keep in mind that the higher your goal, the harder it will be to reach it, so be practical.

And what if you should happen to reach your goal? Take a break! Go have a meal, see a show, visit the lounge for a drink or even just take a walk around the casino. You may have the urge to keep playing, but if you can just take a break from the machines, even it's just for a short time, you'll have the satisfaction of leaving as a winner. If, later on, you get really bored and find that you just *have* to go back to the machines you can avoid a total loss by not risking more than half of your winnings and by playing on smaller denomination machines. If you made your winnings on $1 machines, move down to quarters. If you won on quarters, move down to nickels. The idea now is basically to kill some time and have a little fun knowing that no matter what happens you'll still leave as a winner.

And now, let's move on to luck. As stated previously, the ultimate decider in whether or not you win is how lucky you are. But, is there anything you can do to help you choose a "winning" machine? Not really, because there is no such thing. Remember, in the long run, no machine will pay out more than it takes in. There are, however, some things you could try to help you find the more generous machines and avoid the stingy ones. Keep in mind that all slot machine payback percentages shown in this book are averages. Some machines are programmed to pay back more and some machines are programmed to pay less. Also, like everything else in life, machines have good cycles where they pay out more than average and bad cycles where they pay out less than average. Ultimately, what you want to find is a high-paying machine in a good cycle. Of course if I knew how to find that machine I wouldn't be writing this story, instead I'd be standing in front of it with a $100 bill in my hand and looking for the change attendant. So, I guess you'll have to settle for my two recommendations as to how you *might* be able to find the better paying machines.

First, is the "accounting" method. With this method you start with a pre-determined number of coins and after playing them you take an accounting of your results. If you have more than you started with you stay at that machine and start another cycle. Just keep doing this until the machine returns less than you started with. As an example, let's say you start with 20 coins. After playing those 20 coins you count how many you got back. If it's more than 20 you start over again with another 20 coins and then do another accounting. If, after any accounting, you get back less than the 20 you started with, stop playing and move on to a different machine. This is an especially good method because you have to slow down your play to take periodic accountings and you will always have an accurate idea of how well you are doing.

The other method is even simpler and requires no math. It's called the "baseball" method and is based on the principle of three strikes and you're out. Just play a machine until it loses three times in a row, then move on to another machine. Both of these methods will prevent you from losing a lot in a machine that is either set for a low payback or is going through a bad cycle; yet both can still allow you to take advantage of a high payback machine or one that is going through a good cycle. Good luck!

Slot Tournaments

by Steve Bourie

Slot tournaments are special contests arranged by casinos where participants who get the highest scores on slot machines within an allotted amount of time, or credits, are awarded cash or prizes. Some slot tournaments are offered free of charge but most require an entry fee.

Virtually every casino today offers slot tournaments and they're used by each casino's marketing department as a promotional tool to generate more business for the casino. An interesting thing about slot tournaments is that they aren't necessarily designed as money-making events for the casino.

Some casinos will give back all of the entry fees in the form of prizes and some won't. Those casinos that give back all of the money are happy to have the tournament's contestants in their hotel rooms and playing in their casino. The thinking at these casinos is that the tournament is generating extra business and they don't have to make money off the tournament itself. These are the best kinds of tournaments to play in but they aren't always easy to find. In other instances the casinos look at tournaments strictly as a money-making venture and they'll keep part of the entry fees for themselves. In either case, tournaments can sometimes provide extra value to you and they are occasionally worth looking into.

Each month *Las Vegas Advisor* gives information on upcoming tournaments in that city and many gaming magazines do the same for all of the major casinos throughout the country. These publications don't list much more than the required entry fee so you'll have to call each casino for more information on the specifics. You can probably get that information over the phone but it's best to ask for a brochure to be mailed to you. This way, you'll have an official written record of the tournament rules and regulations.

When looking at the prize structure of the tournament be sure to add up the total cash value of all the prizes and compare it to the total amount of money the casino will be getting in entry fees. For instance, if the entry fee is $200 and they're limiting the tournament to 200 entrants then the casino is generating $40,000 in entry fees. Are they offering that much in cash prizes? If so, then it's a good tournament. If they're only offering $25,000 in cash, then the casino is keeping $15,000 and you may want to shop around for a different tournament that offers you more "equity." By equity we mean the value you'll be receiving in relation to the cost to enter. Positive equity means the casino is giving back more in cash and benefits than it's charging to enter the tournament. Negative equity means just the opposite: the casino is charging more than it's giving back in cash and benefits. You should always try to find a positive equity tournament.

Another thing you'll need to add into the equation when considering your equity are the extra "freebies," or discounts, that the casino will add to the package. Most casinos will host a welcoming party for the contestants, plus a free lunch or dinner and an awards banquet at the end when the winners are announced. Generally, all casinos will also offer a discounted room rate to tournament participants and some will even throw in a surprise gift for everyone. If you don't need a room then that benefit won't add anything to the value you'll be receiving but for some players a discounted room rate could mean the difference between a positive and negative equity situation. Each tournament is different and you should be sure to add up the total of all the benefits you'll receive when deciding which tournament you want to enter.

One more thing to keep in mind when looking at a tournament's structure is how the prizes are distributed. If too much is given to the top finishers that leaves less to be distributed among the other contestants. The chances are pretty good that you're not going to win one of the top prizes so it will help if the lower-tier prizes are worthwhile.

One last thing to remember about tournaments is that in many of them it pays to enter early. Most tournaments offer an "early-bird" discount if you enter by a certain date and the entry fee rises after that date. The discount can be as high as 25 percent and, once again, the reduced rate could make the difference between a positive and a negative equity situation.

Once you've found the tournament that offers you the most equity you'll need a strategy for winning. What's the best strategy? Get lucky! Slot tournaments are pure luck and there really isn't anything you can do to help you win. So, just keep pushing that spin button and hope for a good score!

Personally, I only like to play games of skill (like blackjack and video poker) so I usually don't play in slot tournaments. There was, however, one instance where I played in a tournament because of the value it offered.

Keep in mind that the following story took place many years ago, but the information is still valid for comparing the value offered by a slot tournament. My friend Marvin and I were planning a trip to Las Vegas to attend the World Gaming Congress and Expo at the city's main convention center. This event is held each year and it's the world's largest trade show for the casino industry. The event took place during the middle of the week but we also wanted to stay over for the weekend. Unfortunately, the room rates are much higher on weekends and the hotels usually don't discount their rates very much on those days. After calling around to check rates we decided to look in the *Las Vegas Advisor* to find out about slot tournaments.

Boulder Station was having its *All Treats, No Tricks* slot tournament that same weekend. The entry fee was $199 but by entering before a certain date, the fee was reduced to $149 and there was a total of $40,000 in prize money up for grabs. The rules required 268 entrants, or else the total prize money could be reduced, but based on that required number the casino would be receiving $39,932 in prize money (assuming all early entrants) and awarding $40,000 in prize money which made this a slightly positive equity situation. Additionally, everyone received a t-shirt, a welcoming cocktail party, lunch at the *Pasta Palace,* an awards celebration and a reduced room rate of $25 for Friday and Saturday evening.

We had stayed at Boulder Station before and we both liked the property very much. We called the hotel's reservation department and they told us it would be $99 per night on Friday and Saturday. That was $198 for the two nights, plus 9% tax, for a total of $215.82 By entering the slot tournament our cost would be $149, plus $50 for the room for two nights, plus 9% tax (only on the room), for a total of $203.50 Hey, you want to talk about positive equity? This thing was great! Not only were they giving back all of the prize money, but in this case it was actually cheaper to enter the slot tournament than to get the room by itself!

The rules allowed us to enter as a team for the $149 fee and that also got us into the activities together. At the welcoming party we had an unlimited choice of alcoholic beverages or sodas, plus a large selection of finger sandwiches and other snacks. The *Pasta Palace* is a good restaurant and we had a great lunch there.

We weren't very lucky in the tournament and didn't finish high in the standings. Actually, we received the lowest cash prize which was $40. That brought our actual cost for the room and the tournament down to $163.50 which was still $52 cheaper than just getting the room by itself. Plus, we got the t-shirt, welcoming party and lunch as an added bonus.

As you can see, we saved some money by entering the slot tournament and we also had a lot of fun. You can do the same thing by checking out some of the tournaments that are available the next time you're planning a trip to a casino. Just use the toll-free numbers in this book to call the casino marketing departments, or pick up the latest issue of *Las Vegas Advisor,* or a general gaming magazine, for information on current tournaments.

Video Poker

by Steve Bourie

Okay, who knows the main difference between video poker and slot machines? C'mon now, raise your hands if you think you know it. If you said "a slot machine is a game of luck and video poker is a game of skill" then you are correct! When you play a slot machine there is no decision you can make which will affect the outcome of the game. You put in your money; pull the handle; and hope for the best. In video poker, however, it is your skill in playing the cards which definitely affects the outcome of the game.

Okay, who knows the other major difference between video poker and slot machines? Well, you're right again if you said "you never know what percentage a slot machine is set to pay back, but you can tell a video poker machine's payback percentage just by looking at it." Of course if you knew that answer then you also knew that video poker machines almost always offer you better returns than slot machines (provided you make the right playing decisions).

Now for those of you who didn't know the answers to those two questions, please read on. You others can skip the rest of this story as I am sure you're eager to get back to your favorite video poker machine.

First, let's cover the basics. Video poker has virtually the same rules as a game of five card draw poker. The only difference is that you have no opponent to beat and you can't lose more than your initial bet. First, you deposit from one to five coins in the machine to make your bet. You are then shown five cards on the video screen and your goal is to try to make the best poker hand possible from those cards. Since it is a draw game, you are given one opportunity to improve your hand. This is done by allowing you to discard from one, up to all five cards from your original hand. Of course, you don't have to discard any if you don't want to. After choosing which cards you want to keep (by pushing the button below each card), you then push the deal button and the machine will replace all of the other cards with new cards. Based on the resulting final hand the machine will then pay you according to the pay schedule posted on the machine. Naturally, the better your hand, the higher the amount the machine will pay you back.

That's pretty much how a video poker machine works from the outside, but what about the inside? Well, I had a few questions about that so I visited International Game Technology, which is the world's largest manufacturer of video poker machines (as well as slot machines), in January 2001 and spoke to their chief software engineer, James Vasquez. Here's what Jim had to say in answer to some questions about how his company's machines work:

Let's talk about the difference between video poker and slot machines. It's my understanding that with video poker you can't control the number of winning and losing combinations programmed into the computer chip, instead its based on a 52-card deck with a fixed number of combinations. Is that correct?

Vasquez: Yes, assuming there are no wild cards.

When the cards are dealt is it done on a serial basis where it's similar to cards coming off the top of a deck? Or, parallel where there are five cards dealt face up and one card is unseen underneath each of the initial five cards?

Vasquez: It's serial and the five later cards aren't determined until there is more player interaction at the time of the draw.

They aren't determined at the time of the deal?

Vasquez: No. They're determined at the time of the draw. That varies with the jurisdictional regulation actually. Some lottery jurisdictions tell you that you have to draw all 10 at once. Different jurisdictions write into their rules how they want it done, specifically on poker, because it's a simpler game and they understand it. They say they either want all 10 done at once, or however they want.

How is it done in Nevada? All ten at once, or five and five?

IGT: In Nevada it's five and five.

The talk with Jim Vasquez confirmed that in most regulated jurisdictions video poker machines use a Random Number Generator to shuffle a 52-card deck and then choose five cards to display to the player. (By the way, when played without wild cards, there are exactly 2,598,960 unique five-card poker hands possible.) Then, when the deal button is pushed, the next group of cards is chosen and dealt to the player.

One point must be made here regarding random outcomes in video poker machines. Please note that *gaming regulations* always require video poker machines to have random outcomes. You should be aware that there are casinos operating in places that *do not* have gaming regulations. Examples are cruise ships which operate in international waters, some Indian reservations that are not subject to state regulations, and virtually all Internet casinos. You should also be aware that the technology exists for machines to be set so they do not act randomly. These machines can be actually programmed to avoid giving the players better hands and they wind up giving the house a much bigger advantage. These machines are illegal in Nevada, New Jersey, Colorado and all other states that pattern their gaming regulations after those states. You may, however, come across them in unregulated casinos.

One final point you should keep in mind - IGT is not the only manufacturer of video poker machines. There are quite a few others and they may engineer their machines to work in a different manner. Their RNG may not stop in the same way and their draw cards may be dealt differently. IGT, however, is by far the largest and it is the type of machine you will most often encounter in a casino.

Now that you understand how a video poker machine works let's learn how to pick out the best paying ones. In the beginning of this story it was mentioned that "you can tell a video poker machine's payback percentage just by looking at it." That's true, but it takes a little bit of knowledge to know the difference among all the different types of machines. An example of some of the different machines available are: Jacks or Better, Bonus, Double Bonus, Double Double Bonus, Joker Poker and Deuces Wild. To make it even more confusing, not only are there different machines, but each of those machines can have a different pay schedule for the same hand.

Fortunately, every video poker machine's payback percentage can be mathematically calculated. Not only does this let you know which machines offer you the best return, but it also tells you the best playing decisions to make on that particular machine based on the odds of that combination occurring. The bad news, however, is that it's fairly impossible to do on your own so you'll have to either buy a book that lists all of the percentages and strategies or buy a computer program that does the work for you. Take a look at the tables on the next few pages and you'll see some different types of video poker games and their payback percentages (when played with maximum coin and perfect strategy). For those of you with a computer there are several software programs on the market that can determine the exact payback percentage for any video poker machine. They retail for prices from $29.95 to $59.95 and besides calculating percentages they will also allow you to play video poker on different types of machines and analyze hands to show you the expected return for each play. You can set these games to automatically show you the best decision each time or you can set them to just warn you if you make a wrong decision on your own.

If you have no desire to get quite that serious about learning video poker then I'll try to provide some general tips to help you out. First, you'll need to find the machines that offer you the highest returns. One of the best is the 9/6 Jacks or Better machine. Of course, you're probably wondering "what is a 9/6 Jacks or Better machine?" Well, the Jacks or Better part refers to the fact that you won't win anything from the machine unless you have at least a pair of Jacks. The 9/6 part refers to the payback schedule on this kind of machine.

As stated earlier, each machine can have a different payback schedule and there are at least 20 different kinds of payback schedules available on Jacks or Better machines. In Las Vegas the two most common Jacks or Better machines you will find are 8/5 and 9/6. Here's a comparison of their pay schedules (per coin, for five-coin play):

Hand	9/6	8/5
Royal Flush	800	800
Straight Flush	50	50
4-of-a-Kind	25	25
Full House	**9**	**8**
Flush	**6**	**5**
Straight	4	4
3-of-a-Kind	3	3
Two Pairs	2	2
One Pair J's	1	1

As you can see, the schedules are identical except for the better payoffs on the 9/6 machines for Flushes and Full Houses. The payback on a 9/6 machine is 99.5% with perfect play, while the 8/5 machines return 97.3% with perfect play. Of course, it doesn't make any sense to play an 8/5 machine if a 9/6 machine is available. Yet, you'll often see lots of people playing an 8/5 when a 9/6 can often be found in the same casino. The reason they do that is because they don't know any better; you do. Always look for the 9/6 machines. They can be usually found in most downtown Las Vegas casinos at the quarter level and in many Strip casinos at denominations of $1 and higher. In other states they won't be found as easily, and sometimes, not at all.

One other common machine you will come across is an 8/5 Jacks or Better progressive. These feature the same 8/5 pay table as above except for the royal flush which pays a jackpot amount that is displayed on a meter above the machine. The jackpot will continue to build until someone hits a royal flush; then it will reset and start to build again. When the progressive jackpot (for five coins) on a 25¢ machine first starts out at $1,000 the payback is only 97.30%, but when it reaches $2,166.50, the payback is 100%.

Another good tip is to restrict your play to the same kind of machine all the time. Each video poker machine has its own particular strategy and what works best on a Jacks or Better machine is definitely much different from what works best on a Deuces Wild machine. I usually only play 9/6 Jacks or Better machines because that is what I practice on and I automatically know the best decision to make all the time. Keep in mind that when you calculate the payback percentage for a video poker machine the number you arrive at is based on perfect play. As an example, a 9/6 Jacks or Better video poker machine has a 99.5 percent payback with perfect play. This means that, theoretically, it will return $99.50 for every $100 played in the machine, but only if the player makes the correct decision every time. If you make mistakes, and most players do, the return to the casino will be higher. If you play several different kinds of

Jacks or Better Pay Table Variations
(Per coin with maximum coin played and perfect strategy)

9/6 with 4,000 coin jackpot		9/6 with 4,700 coin jackpot	
Royal Flush	800	Royal Flush	940
Straight Flush	50	Straight Flush	50
4-of-a-kind	25	4-of-a-kind	25
Full House	*9*	*Full House*	*9*
Flush	*6*	*Flush*	*6*
Straight	4	Straight	4
3-of-a-kind	3	3-of-a-kind	3
2 Pair	2	2 Pair	2
Jacks or Better	1	Jacks or Better	1
Payback	**99.54%**	**Payback**	**99.90%**

8/5		7/5	
Royal Flush	800	Royal Flush	800
Straight Flush	50	Straight Flush	50
4-of-a-kind	25	4-of-a-kind	25
Full House	*8*	*Full House*	*7*
Flush	*5*	*Flush*	*5*
Straight	4	Straight	4
3-of-a-kind	3	3-of-a-kind	3
2 Pair	2	2 Pair	2
Jacks or Better	1	Jacks or Better	1
Payback	**97.28%**	**Payback**	**96.15%**

6/5	
Royal Flush	800
Straight Flush	50
4-of-a-kind	25
Full House	*6*
Flush	*5*
Straight	4
3-of-a-kind	3
2 Pair	2
Jacks or Better	1
Payback	**95.00%**

Bonus Poker Pay Table Variations

(Per coin with maximum coin played and perfect strategy)

7/5 Bonus		8/5 Bonus	
Royal Flush	800	Royal Flush	800
Straight Flush	50	Straight Flush	50
Four Aces	80	Four Aces	80
Four 2s 3s 4s	40	Four 2s 3s 4s	40
Four 5s-Ks	25	Four 5s-Ks	25
Full House	*7*	*Full House*	*8*
Flush	*5*	*Flush*	*5*
Straight	4	Straight	4
3-of-a-kind	3	3-of-a-kind	3
2 Pair	2	2 Pair	2
Jacks or Better	1	Jacks or Better	1
Payback	**98.02%**	**Payback**	**99.17%**

9/6 Double Bonus		9/7 Double Bonus	
Royal Flush	800	Royal Flush	800
Straight Flush	50	Straight Flush	50
Four Aces	160	Four Aces	160
Four 2s 3s 4s	80	Four 2s 3s 4s	80
Four 5s-Ks	50	Four 5s-Ks	50
Full House	*9*	*Full House*	*9*
Flush	*6*	*Flush*	*7*
Straight	5	Straight	5
3-of-a-kind	3	3-of-a-kind	3
2 Pair	1	2 Pair	1
Jacks or Better	1	Jacks or Better	1
Payback	**97.81%**	**Payback**	**99.11%**

10/7 Double Bonus		10/7 Triple Bonus	
Royal Flush	800	Royal Flush	800
Straight Flush	50	Straight Flush	50
Four Aces	160	Four Aces	240
Four 2s 3s 4s	80	Four 5s-Ks	120
Four 5s-Ks	50	Four 2s 3s 4s	75
Full House	*10*	*Full House*	*10*
Flush	*7*	*Flush*	*7*
Straight	5	Straight	4
3-of-a-kind	3	3-of-a-kind	3
2 Pair	1	2 Pair	1
Jacks or Better	1	*Kings or Better*	*1*
Payback	**100.17%**	**Payback**	**98.52%**

Deuces Wild Pay Table Variations

(Per coin with maximum coin played and perfect strategy)

Short Pay		Full Pay	
Natural Royal Flush	800	Natural Royal Flush	800
Four Deuces	200	Four Deuces	200
Wild Royal Flush	25	Wild Royal Flush	25
5-of-a-kind	15	5-of-a-kind	15
Straight Flush	9	Straight Flush	9
4-of-a-kind	*4*	*4-of-a-kind*	*5*
Full House	3	Full House	3
Flush	2	Flush	2
Straight	2	Straight	2
3-of-a-kind	1	3-of-a-kind	1
Payback	**94.34%**	**Payback**	**100.76%**

Not So Ugly (NSU) Deuces		Deuces Deluxe	
Natural Royal Flush	800	Natural Royal Flush	800
Four Deuces	200	Four Deuces	200
Wild Royal Flush	25	Natural Straight Flush	50
5-of-a-kind	*16*	Wild Royal Flush	25
Straight Flush	*10*	5-of-a-kind	15
4-of-a-kind	*4*	Natural 4-of-a-kind	10
Full House	*4*	Wild Straight Flush	9
Flush	*3*	Wild 4-of-a-kind 4	
Straight	2	Full House	4
3-of-a-kind	1	Flush	3
Payback	**99.73%**	Straight	2
		3-of-a-kind	1
		Payback	**100.34%**

machines it becomes increasingly harder to remember the correct play and you will make mistakes. Therefore, it only makes sense to memorize the correct decisions for one kind of machine and to always play on that same kind of machine (of course, in order to learn those proper strategies, you may want to buy that book or software).

Now that you've decided which machines to play, you'll need some help with strategy. On the next two pages are charts that will give you an excellent simple strategy for both 9/6 and 8/5 video poker machines. These charts were derived from calculations using a video poker software computer program and give you a near-perfect strategy. They aren't 100% perfect but they are close to it and will only be fractionally incorrect in some situations. The only difference between the two tables is shown in the poker hands that have been *italicized* in the 8/5 strategy tables.

Simple Strategy Table For 9/6 Jacks or Better

1. Royal Flush
2. Straight Flush
3. 4 of a kind
4. 4 card Royal Flush
5. Full House
6. Flush
7. 3 of a kind
8. Straight
9. 4 card Straight Flush
10. Two Pairs
11. 4 card inside Straight Flush
12. Pair of Jacks or higher
13. 3 card Royal Flush
14. 4 card Flush
15. 4 card straight with 3 high cards
16. Low Pair
17. 4 card Straight with 2 high cards
18. 4 card Straight with 1 high card
19. 3 card Inside Straight Flush with 2 high cards
20. 3 card Straight Flush with 1 high card
21. 4 card Straight with no high cards
22. 3 card Double Inside Straight Flush with 2 high cards
23. 3 card Inside Straight Flush with 1 high card
24. 3 card Straight Flush with no high cards
25. 4 card Inside Straight with 4 high cards
26. 2 card Royal Flush with no Ace or 10
27. 2 card Royal Flush with Ace and no 10
28. 3 card Double Inside Straight Flush with 1 high card
29. 3 card Inside Straight Flush with no high card
30. 4 card Inside Straight with 3 high cards
31. 3 high cards with no Ace
32. 2 high cards
33. 2 card Royal Flush with 10 and no Ace
34. 1 high card
35. 3 card Double Inside Straight Flush with no high card
36. All New Cards

Simple Strategy Table For 8/5 Jacks or Better

1. Royal Flush
2. Straight Flush
3. 4 of a kind
4. 4 card Royal Flush
5. Full House
6. Flush
7. 3 of a kind
8. Straight
9. 4 card Straight Flush
10. Two Pairs
11. 4 card inside Straight Flush
12. Pair of Jacks or higher
13. 3 card Royal Flush
14. 4 card Flush
15. 4 card straight with 3 high cards
16. Low Pair
17. 4 card Straight with 2 high cards
18. 4 card Straight with 1 high card
19. 3 card Inside Straight Flush with 2 high cards
20. 3 card Straight Flush with 1 high card
21. 4 card Straight with no high cards
22. 3 card Double Inside Straight Flush with 2 high cards
23. 3 card Inside Straight Flush with 1 high card
24. 3 card Straight Flush with no high cards
25. 4 card Inside Straight with 4 high cards
26. 2 card Royal Flush with no Ace or 10
27. 2 card Royal Flush with Ace and no 10
28. *3 high cards with no Ace*
29. *4 card Inside Straight with 3 high cards*
30. *3 card Double Inside Straight Flush with 1 high card*
31. *2 high cards*
32. *3 card Inside Straight Flush with no high card*
33. 2 card Royal Flush with 10 and no Ace
34. 1 high card
35. 3 card Double Inside Straight Flush with no high card
36. All New Cards

To use any chart just look up your hand and play it in the manner that is closest to the top of the chart. For example: you are dealt (6♣,6♦,7♥,8♠,9♣). You keep (6♣,6♦) rather than (6♦,7♥,8♠,9♣) because a low pair (#16) is higher on the chart than a four-card straight with no high cards (#21). Remember to always look for the highest possible choice on the chart when there are multiple ways to play your hand. As another example: you are dealt (8♣,8♦, J♥,Q♥,K♥). You keep (J♥,Q♥,K♥) rather than (8♣,8♦) because a three-card royal flush (#13) is higher on the chart than a low pair (#16). As a final, but radical, example of how to play your hand by the chart what would you do if you're dealt (6♥,10♥,J♥,Q♥,K♥)? Yes, you have to break up your flush by discarding the 6♥ and go for the royal flush because the four-card royal flush (#4) is higher on the chart than the pat flush (#6). When looking at the 9/6 chart there are a few things that should seem rather obvious:

1) A low pair is relatively good. Of the 36 possible hands, a low pair is #16 which means there are 20 hands worse than a low pair. If you look at the 15 hands that are better than a low pair eight of them are pat hands that require no draw. Of the other seven hands, six of them are four card hands and the remaining hand is a three-card royal flush.

2) Don't hold three cards trying to get a straight or flush. Nowhere on the chart do you see that you should hold three cards to try for a straight or flush. In some instances you should hold three cards to try for a straight flush, but *never* a straight or flush.

3) Rarely draw to an inside straight. Inside straights (6,7,_,9,10) appear only twice on the chart and only in rather bad positions: #30 (with three high cards) and #25 (with four high cards). It is much easier to draw to an outside straight (_7,8,9,10_) where you can complete your straight by getting the card you need on either end. Open end straights appear four times on the chart and in much higher positions than inside straights: #21 (with no high cards), #18 (with one high card), #17 (with two high cards) and #15 (with three high cards).

4) Don't hold a kicker. A kicker is an unpaired card held with a pair. For example (8,8,K) or (K,K,9) are examples of hands where an extra card (the kicker) is held. *Never* hold a kicker because they add no value to your hand!

If you would like to make your own video poker strategy charts there are some special software programs that will allow you to do this. Some of these specialized programs are included in the regular video poker game playing software and some can be purchased separately. Either way, they will allow you to generate your own video poker strategy charts on your home computer. You can then print out the strategy charts and bring them with you into the casino.

For your information there are exactly 2,598,960 unique poker hands possible on a video poker machine (when played without a joker). On a 9/6 Jacks or Better machine a royal flush will occur about once every 40,000 hands; a straight flush about every 9,000 hands; four-of-a-kind about every 425 hands;

Other Video Poker Game Pay Tables

(Per coin with maximum coin played and perfect strategy)

Pick'Em Poker (five coin payout)

Royal Flush	6,000
Straight Flush	1,199
4-of-a-kind	600
Full House	90
Flush	75
Straight	55
3-of-a-kind	25
Two Pair	15
Pair 9's or Better	10
Payback	**99.95%**

All American Poker

Royal Flush	800
Straight Flush	200
4-of-a-kind	40
Full House	8
Flush	8
Straight	8
3-of-a-kind	3
Two Pair	1
Pair Jacks or Better	1
Payback	**100.72%**

Double Joker Full-Pay

Natural Royal Flush	800
Wild Royal Flush	100
5-of-a-kind	50
Straight Flush	25
4-of-a-kind	*9*
Full House	5
Flush	4
Straight	3
3-of-a-kind	2
2 Pair	1
Payback	**99.97%**

Double Joker Short-Pay

Natural Royal Flush	800
Wild Royal Flush	100
5-of-a-kind	50
Straight Flush	25
4-of-a-kind	*8*
Full House	5
Flush	4
Straight	3
3-of-a-kind	2
2 Pair	1
Payback	**98.10%**

a full house about every 87 hands; a flush about every 91 hands; a straight about every 89 hands; three-of-a-kind about every 14 hands; two pairs about every 8 hands; and a pair of Jacks or better about every 5 hands. The interesting thing to note here is that both a flush and a straight are harder to get than a full house, yet a full house always has a higher payback. The majority of the time, about 55% to be exact, you will wind up with a losing hand on a 9/6 machine.

The next bit of advice concerns how many coins you should bet. You should always bet the maximum amount (on machines returning 100% or more) because it will allow you to earn bonus coins when you hit the royal flush. Example: For a royal flush on a 9/6 machine with one coin played you receive 250 coins; for two coins you get 500; for three coins you get 750; for four coins you get 1,000 and for five (maximum) coins you get 4,000 coins! This translates into a bonus of 2,750 coins! A royal flush can be expected once every 40,400 hands on a 9/6 machine; once every 40,200 hands on an 8/5 machine; and once every 32,700 hands on an 8/5 progressive. The odds are high, but the added bonus makes it worthwhile. If you can't afford to play the maximum coins on a positive machine then move down to a lower denomination machine. And, if you absolutely insist on playing less than the maximum, be sure to play only one at a time. It doesn't make any sense to play two, three or four coins, because you still won't be eligible for the bonus.

One important thing to keep in mind when you look at the total payback on these video poker machines is that those numbers always include a royal flush and the royal flush plays a *very* big factor in the total return. As a matter of fact, the royal flush is such a big factor on video poker machines that you are actually expected to lose until you get that royal flush. Yes, even by restricting your play to video poker machines with a more than 100% payback you are *still* expected to lose money until you hit a royal flush. Once you hit that royal flush it will bring your cash back up to that 100% level but until it happens you should be fully aware that you are statistically expected to lose money.

According to video poker expert Bob Dancer, "on a 25¢ Jacks or Better 9/6 machine you will lose at a rate of 2.5% while you are waiting for the royal to happen. Another way to look at this is quarter players who play 600 hands per hour can expect to lose about $18.75 per hour, on average, on any hour they do not hit a royal." You really have to keep in mind that there are no guarantees when you play video poker. Yes, you are expected to get a royal flush about once every 40,000 hands but there are no guarantees that it will happen and if you don't get that royal flush it could cost you dearly.

A final tip about playing video poker concerns slot clubs. Every major casino has a slot club and you should make it a point to join the slot club before you insert your first coin. It doesn't cost anything to join and as a member you will have the opportunity to earn complimentaries from the casinos in the form of cash, food, shows, drinks, rooms or other "freebies." When you join the club you'll be issued a card (similar to a credit card) that you insert in the machine before you start to play and it will track how much you bet, as well as how long you play. Naturally, the more money you gamble, the more freebies you'll earn. Just make sure you don't get carried away and bet more than you're comfortable with just to earn some extra comps. Ideally, you want to get comps for gambling that you were going to do anyway and not be pressured into betting more than you had planned. Many clubs will also give you cash back for your play and that amount should be added into the payback percentage on the kind of machine you'll be playing. For example: at Treasure Island in Las Vegas, the slot club rebates .33% in cash for your video poker play (.67% for slots). By only playing 9/6 Jacks or Better machines with a return of 99.54% you can add the .33% rebate to get an adjusted figure of 99.87%. This means that you are, theoretically, playing an almost even game, *plus* you're still eligible for other room and food discounts on top of your cash rebate.

Choosing Your Core Video Poker Play

by Jean Scott

Jean Scott has been financially successful as a video poker player for 18 years, slowly moving from low-roller quarter play to much higher denominations. She shows you the detailed steps how to do this in her new book, *Frugal Video Poker,* which includes lessons that help you use the *Frugal VP* software for faster progress. The new *Frugal Video Poker Scouting Guide* completes this complete VP tool kit. Her Web site is queenofcomps.com.

You choose good casino plays by looking for good video poker games and adding good slot club benefits. Your first step is to select your core game. In this article, I discuss the factors you can consider in making your decision.

Personal Makeup - The first factors to think about are the personal ones. What are your goals when you go to a casino? What is your personality type? Do you want to choose a lower-EV (expected value) game that's the most fun for you, even though you know your bankroll won't last as long? Or would you rather choose one that isn't quite as exciting, but you know in the long run you'll lose less? Would you rather play a lower-EV game that has a simpler strategy or take the time to learn a more difficult one so you can play at a higher EV? Only you can make these kinds of choices—and no one else has the right to judge your decision.

Casino Location - Another factor you might want to consider is location. Some people choose one high-EV core game and never play video poker unless they can play that game, even if it means avoiding their local casinos and as often as possible visiting far-away ones that have their chosen game. Others choose a lower-EV game because they want to play often and it's the best play in their area.

There can be very good reasons to choose a lower-EV game in a casino near you. Many casinos send generous weekly cash or free-play coupons to locals. Some hold numerous drawings and offer promotions that players who can visit the casino frequently will be able to take advantage of. I discuss this in detail in my book, *Frugal Video Poker*, and show you how you can figure out the value of these kinds of benefits. Many times they will compensate for lower pay schedules.

However, you have to face reality here. Many casinos offer only very low-paying VP paytables. No amount of extra benefits would put the games into a position where the long-term losses are acceptable to players who want to play heavily and often. These games are an option only for the very light recreational player who's willing—once in a while—to take a shot at a gamble with odds no better than a slot machine.

Cash vs. Comps - Some casinos give cash for points, while others only offer comps. In either case, if your points are worth a stated dollar amount, you can figure out the percentage that this adds to your game by using the "Slot Club Calculator" in the *Frugal VP* software program.

If the points in the casino where you're considering playing can be redeemed for cashback, there's no decision — a dollar is a dollar is a dollar. However, if the points can only be used for comps, you must decide if you really want and will actually use them; in other words, are they worth the same amount to you as if they were given in cash? Evaluating comps is a personal decision. One man's pleasure is another one's yawn.

Real-Life Examples - Here are some examples of people I've known — although I haven't used their real names — and how they made their decision about what game to play and where to play it. Hopefully, their experiences will be helpful in making your own decision.

• Riverboat Sam is a 65-year-old retired railroader who lives in the Midwest with a riverboat casino just five miles from his house and two more about an hour's drive away. Before his wife died, she converted him from craps to video poker and taught him about using accurate strategy. They usually visited the two casinos that were farther away, because both had 9/6 JoB (Jacks or Better) and they had that strategy down pat. They occasionally visited the casino close by and had learned the strategy changes for its best game, 9/5 JoB. Now he only plays at the nearby casino, even thought he knows that the EV of 9/5 JoB is 1.09% lower than the 9/6 version. He sticks with the nickel machines, but realizes this still costs him about $1.36 more per hour than 9/6 ($.25 per bet, based on 500 hands per hour). It's worth it to him not to have to drive so far, especially at night, since his eyes aren't as good as they used to be. Besides, all his railroad cronies go to this nearby casino and he enjoys the company of old friends. They all flirt with the young change girls who know them by name and they eat long lunches together in the casino buffet most weekdays.

He strictly budgets what he takes to the casino. If his daily-session VP bankroll doesn't last as long as he'd like to stay in the casino, he sits in the race book and watches horse races and chats with his friends. He always plays more on the two-a-week senior double-point days than on days when he gets single points. He keeps track of his wins and losses, as well as the slot club benefits and comps, and says that this entertainment has cost him about $100 a month since his wife passed away three years ago. He says that's a small price for the fun that has helped alleviate his loneliness—and it has saved him from the high price of gasoline and his own cooking.

• Curt and Cindy are highly paid executives with stressful high-tech jobs in California's Silicon Valley. They fly to Reno or Vegas for a weekend every month or so to relax at high-denomination VP machines. They play at such a high level that the casino floods them with luxurious comps and extra benefits. They're smart and understand the concept of game EV, but they choose to play Double Double Bonus, although higher EV games are available. They tell me that they work at monotonous tasks 60 hours a week—they get away to a casino for excitement and love the thrill of a kicker game. They have a large gambling bankroll, so they don't worry about the dry stretches and just play on, anticipating those jackpots. They've practiced DDB on the computer, so they know the strategy quite well. I've talked to them about the financial advantage of switching to JoB, which is available in the casinos where they play, and they tried to switch. But they got bored too quickly and went back to their beloved DDB.

Still, they may have made a better choice than it seems on the surface. Casinos can become suspicious of players who play only the best VP games—and in some cases, may take countermeasures, such as cutting off their goodie mailings or becoming stingy with comps. Curt and Cindy will never have to worry about this happening to them—they'll always be welcome at the casinos with outstretched hands full of freebies.

• Jim and Joyce, a young couple with two school-age children, live in the Midwest, close to the Canadian border, where there are only a few scattered small Indian casinos. Because they have no nearby competition, they all offer very poor VP. The best schedule pays back only 96.15%. Jim and Joyce used to drive a half-hour to one of these casinos two or three times a month, dropping the kids off at volunteer grandparent babysitters along the way. They studied VP and fell in love with Deuces Wild, but the best Deuce schedule they could find had an EV of only 94.34%. So they played slowly on the machine with the best paytable available, 7/5 JoB with the big casino edge of 3.85%.

Jim and Joyce both had good jobs and this was their major entertainment choice, so they could afford the average loss, which was about $19 per hour for each quarter machine. (A slow-rate 400 hands an hour is $500 coin-in for each machine. Multiply that by the casino's 3.85% edge, and you get a $38-an-hour loss for the two of them.) Playing two hours in one evening, their expected average loss was $76, perhaps reduced by a comped meal once in a while. Of course, they were thrilled with an occasional big jackpot—but most of the time they lost, and sometimes they lost big time.

After a few months, they sat down and added up the monthly cost of this pastime, realizing that even if they had average luck, they were putting out $150-$200 a month. So they decided to stay home and rent a movie, or eat out, or find some other low-cost entertainment for those nights they used to spend in the casino. They started socking away most of the money they used to spend there and surfed the Internet regularly, looking for cheap airfares to Las Vegas, where they can now fly every few months or so and play all day long on their game of choice, quarter full-pay Deuces Wild. They say that they don't feel deprived, but enjoy immensely these frequent vacations for no more than they used to spend at their home casino. In fact, they report, they're doing so well on this high-EV game and getting so many free room offers in the mail from their play in Vegas casinos that they're well on their way to having all these vacations cost just a fraction of their saved bankroll.

• The next example is a composite of scores of retired couples we've met— and given suggestions to—who've moved to Las Vegas because VP is their favorite entertainment choice. Most don't aspire to make money gambling, since they have adequate pensions and investments for a secure financial future, but they enjoy the comp side benefits, especially free meals and shows, that VP play brings. Most soon realize that these comps "cost" too much if they're losing more on the games than the comps are worth. So, if they haven't studied how to choose a good VP game and use accurate strategy, they soon decide to either cut out the gambling and pay for their own meals and shows or start learning how to reduce their losses. Many of these retirees, because they have the time and motivation, read, practice, and learn the ropes of the slot club/comp systems until they become extremely skilled VP players, "accidentally" making it a financially profitable hobby as Brad and I have done.

Video Poker From A to Z

Frugal Video Poker is the most comprehensive and detailed book ever written on preparing and practicing for, then playing, video poker. It takes you step-by-step as far as you want to go, from basic to highly skilled.

Beginners are walked through the basics of play, learning to first distinguish between good and bad paytables, then playing them properly. Experienced players can fill in the inevitable gaps in their study to grasp the complete picture. For experts, *Frugal Video Poker* covers special opportunities, such as tournaments, promotions, progressives, and the cutting-edge games; an extensive resource section paves the way to advanced study.

And everyone can benefit from the detailed lessons in using readily available video poker computer tutorials, specifically the *Frugal VP* software.

Frugal Video Poker
Jean Scott, Viktor Nacht
316 pages • Order #1483 • $14.95

To order visit ShopLVA.com
or call 1-800-244-2224

Choosing Video Poker Games

by John Grochowski

Way back in the early 1990s when the nationwide expansion of gambling was at its beginning and riverboat casinos were new, I asked a riverboat slot director why there was so little video poker on his floor.

``Our guests aren't ready for it,'' he told me. ``When we opened, we didn't know what everybody was going to play. We assumed it would be about normal for the Las Vegas Strip. We opened with about 17 percent video poker, and they sat there empty. All anyone wanted to play was the slots. So we dropped to 9 or 10 percent video poker.''

Things have changed. Slot directors move to other jobs at other casinos, and player tastes change. The current slot director at that same riverboat told me in 2000 that he now has 18 percent video poker, and players can't get enough of it. If he was starting from scratch, he'd turn 20, maybe even 25 percent of his floor over to video poker. What happened?

Video poker, it seems, is an acquired taste. You can see that clearly in casino gambling's capital city. Las Vegas visitors who stick to the Strip will see video poker taking up roughly 15 percent of the slot floors -- a little more in some casinos, a little less than others. But get off the Strip and check out the places that cater to the locals, places such as the Fiesta and Santa Fe in northwest Las Vegas, or Sunset Station and The Reserve to the southeast in Henderson. There you'll see row after row after row of video poker, 50 percent or more of the slot floor.

The difference is in the experience of the players. What the Las Vegas locals know, and what regular players in newer gaming markets are learning, is that they get a better run for their money on video poker than on the slots. Whereas slots on the Las Vegas Strip return an average of a little more than 95 percent of coins played to dollar players and a little less than 93 percent to quarter players. Even the bad video poker games, the ones that experts warn to stay away from, return 95 percent with expert play. The good machines return 99 percent, even 100 percent or more in the long run -- although even on those machines there will be more losing sessions than winners, balanced out in the long run by the odd royal flush.

Video poker does it with a high hit frequency, too. On most Jacks or Better-based games, about 45 percent of all hands bring some return. That's a percentage slots were unable to approach until the advent of multiline, multicoin video slots, and on those games many "winners" bring returns of less than the wagers.

Not every player has access to those 100-percent machines. In new gaming markets, where demand for a place to play frequently outstrips available space, slot directors are able to use games that will maximize their profit margins. They know they can use a Jacks or Better game that pays 7-for-1 on full houses and 5-for-1 on flushes instead of a full-pay game that returns 9-for-1 and 6-for-1, and they'll still get plenty of play. There are good machines out there, too, but it's up to the player to learn to tell the difference.

JACKS OR BETTER: In video poker, when the casino wants to change the long-term payback percentage of a game, it changes the pay table. Given the same strategy, players get winning hands no more or less frequently, but some hands pay a little more or a little less.

In Jacks or Better, the base game around which many video poker variations are built, the payoffs that usually are changed are full houses and flushes. We look for games that pay 9-for-1 on full houses and 6-for-1 on flushes, with the full pay table being 250-for-1 on royal flushes (jumping to 4,000 coins with a five-coin wager), 50-for-1 on straight flushes, 25-for-1 on four of a kind, 9-for-1 on full houses, 6-for-1 on flushes 4-for-1 on straights, 3-for-1 on three of a kind, 2-for-1 on two pair and 1-for-1 on pairs of Jacks or better.

For each unit that the payoff on full houses or flushes drops, we lose about 1.1 percent of our long-term payback. On an 8-5 Jacks or Better game, with one-unit drops in both spots on the pay table, our average return drops to 97.3 percent. Drop the full house payback again to 7-for-1, and a 7-5 machine drops to 96.2 percent.

Given better options, a video poker player in the know would walk away from that 7-5 game. In Las Vegas, he might even leave the casino and look for a better deal next door or across the street. That's tough to do on a riverboat, or in a Native American casino that's miles away from the next option. So a player who finds the best video poker in a casino is 7-5 Jacks or Better has a decision to make. Does he take up table games? Does he just go home and skip his night's entertainment? Or does he sigh, decide that at least a 96-percent game is better than he'd get on the slots, and play anyway? Most take the third option.

BONUS POKER: The "bonuses" in Bonus Poker are on certain fours of a kind. Four 2s, 3s or 4s will bring you 40-for-1 and four Aces will bring 80-for-1 instead of the 25-for-1 that is standard on Jacks or Better and on the remaining quads in Bonus Poker.

Other than that, the pay table is the same as in Jacks or Better, with reduced paybacks on full houses and flushes. We look for games that pay 8-for-1 on full houses and 5-for-1 on flushes. That's a 99.2 percent game with expert play. Bonus Poker games often have 7-5 and 6-5 versions, with overall returns dropping about 1.1 percent for each unit the flush payoff drops.

There are no major strategy differences between Bonus Poker and the versions of Jacks or Better that pay 5-for-1 on the flush. Learn to play 8-5 Jacks, and you're ready for Bonus Poker.

DOUBLE BONUS POKER: If everyone could play this game perfectly and played only the best available version, the casinos would be supporting us instead of the other way around. Double Bonus Poker, which in its full-pay version pays 10-for-1 on full houses, 7-for-1 on flushes and 5-for-1 on straights, returns 100.17 percent in the long run with expert play.

The full pay table is as follows: 250-for-1 on royal flushes (jumping to 4,000 coins with a five-coin wager), 50-for-1 on straight flushes, 160-for-1 on four Aces, 80-for-1 on four 2s, 3s and 4s, 50-for-1 on four of a kind, 10-for-1 on full houses, 7-for-1 on flushes, 5-for-1 on straights, 3-for-1 on three of a kind, 1-for-1 on two pair and 1-for-1 on pairs of Jacks or better.

A few important things to note: Two pair pays only 1-for-1 instead of the 2-for-1 Jacks or Better players get. More of the overall payback is tied up in the higher end of the pay table. With five coins wagered, four Aces bring an 800-coin jackpot. I've had more than one former slot player tell me that Double Bonus is the game that pried them away from the reels, with a realistic secondary jackpot worth walking away with making the difference.

Few play at expert level, and the casinos are in no danger of losing money. There are some tricky little moves in this game that average players miss. For example, if we're dealt a full house that includes three Aces, our best play is to break up the full house and go for the fourth Ace. We'd never do that in Jacks or Better or Bonus Poker. Also, the 7-for-1 payback on flushes dictates that we hold three parts of a flush. Given 10 of diamonds, 8 of clubs, 6 of diamonds, 4 of hearts, 2 of diamonds, in 10-7 Double Bonus we'd hold the three diamonds, whereas in Jacks or Better we'd discard all five.

To change the payback percentage, the casino changes payoffs on full houses, flushes and sometimes straights. It's common to see Double Bonus games with 9-7 (99.1 percent) and 9-6 (97.8 percent pay tables), and I sometimes see pay tables as low as 8-5-4, paying 8-for-1 on full houses, 5-for-1 on flushes and 4-for-1 on straights. The 8-5-4 game pays only 94.2 percent with expert play, making it problematic as to whether a video poker player is really any better off on that game than on the reel slots.

DOUBLE DOUBLE BONUS POKER: The big change as compared to Double Bonus is that there are extra bonuses available on some fours of a kind provided the fifth card is a certain denomination. If four Aces are accompanied by a 2, 3 or 4, the usual 160-for-1 jackpot jumps to 400-for-1 -- a 2,000-coin bonanza with five wagered. If four 2, 3s or 4s are accompanied by an Ace, 2, 3 or 4, the 80-for-1 payoff jumps to 160-for-1.

Straights drop back to 4-for-1 on all versions of this game. The full-pay Double Double Bonus game pays 9-for-1 on full houses and 6-for-1 on flushes, and returns 98.9 percent with expert play.

It's not unusual to see Double Double Bonus in an 8-5 format, leaving a 96.8 percent game, and I've even seen 7-5, a 95.7 percent pay table in the long run with expert play.

One quick strategy tip: Do not hold fifth-card kickers without already having the four of a kind. If you're dealt three Aces, a 2 and a 9, discard both the 2 and the 9. Give yourself two chances to draw the fourth Ace instead of just one.

DEUCES WILD: Someday, I'm going to write a book with nothing but Deuces Wild pay tables and strategy variations. There are countless versions of Deuces Wild. Most video poker books focus on strategy for full-pay Deuces Wild, which is available only in Nevada. The 100.8 percent payback with expert play is too strong for regulators' tastes in most gaming markets and the only place you can find the game is in Nevada. It's a great game if you can find it. Most players can't find it anywhere.

Let's compare it to another game that video poker fans sometimes call "Illinois Deuces." It doesn't say "Illinois" on the machine -- it just says Deuces Wild. Manufacturers and casino operators leave it to the player to tell the difference among pay tables, if they can.

The game isn't limited to Illinois. It's available nationwide. It just has that nickname because it rose to popularity in the early '90s at the Par-A-Dice casino in East Peoria, Illinois. Look at the following pay tables, and guess which one is the full-pay game, returning 100.8 percent, and which is Illinois Deuces, returning 98.9 percent.

Variation No. 1: Natural royal flush 250-for-1 (jumps to 4,000 coins for a five-coin bet); four 2s 200-for-1; royal flush with wild cards 25-for-1; five of a kind 15-for-1; straight flush 9-for-1; four of a kind 5-for-1; full house 3-for-1; flush 2-for-1; straight 2-for-1; three of a kind 1-for-1.

Variation No. 2: Natural royal flush 250-for-1 (jumps to 4,000 coins for a five-coin bet); four 2s 200-for-1; royal flush with wild cards 25-for-1; five of a kind 15-for-1; straight flush 9-for-1; four of a kind 4-for-1; full house 4-for-1; flush 3-for-1; straight 2-for-1; three of a kind 1-for-1.

The differences look minor, right? No. 1 pays 5-for-1 on four of a kind, while No. 2 pays only 4-for-1. But No. 2 pays 4-for-1 on full houses and 3-for-1 on flushes, but up a notch from the payouts on No. 1. So which is better? It's No. 1.

Some players fall into the trap of thinking that in poker, full houses and flushes are more common than four of a kind, so No. 2 must be the better game. That's exactly what the operators want you to think. In Deuces Wild, we get four of a kind more often than full houses and flushes combined. If you have two pair and one of the pair consists of 2s, you have four of a kind. If you have three 9s, an 8 and a 2, the wild deuces doesn't become an 8 to complete a full house, it takes the place of a 9 to give you four of a kind.

One major strategy difference comes when we're dealt two pairs. If we have two 9s and two 8s, strategy tables that focus on full-pay Deuces will tell you to keep only one pair. But in Illinois Deuces, where we get less for four of a kind and more for a full house, our best play is to keep both pairs and make a one-card draw for a full house. Let's try one more variation:

Variation No. 3: Natural royal flush 250-for-1 (jumps to 4,000 coins for a five-coin bet); four 2s 200-for-1; royal flush with wild cards 25-for-1; five of a kind 16-for-1; straight flush 13-for-1; four of a kind 4-for-1; full house 3-for-1; flush 2-for-1; straight 2-for-1; three of a kind 1-for-1.

Again, we have a Deuces variation that differs from full-pay in three places on the pay table. As in Illinois Deuces, four of a kind is reduced to 4-for-1, and we know that's important. Five of a kind goes up to 16-for-1 from the usual 15-for-1, and there's a big jump on straight flushes, to 13-for-1 from 9-for-1.

Those jumps aren't nearly enough to make up the difference. This game, nicknamed ``Colorado Deuces'' but available nationwide, returns only 96.8 percent with expert play.

There's no easy road map to all the variations of Deuces Wild. The key thing to remember is that changes on the low end of the pay table in Deuces Wild or any other video poker game have a greater effect than those higher on the pay table. With few exceptions such as four-of-a-kind in Deuces Wild, hands lower on the pay table occur more frequently than those higher up. An increase on full houses to 4-for-1 helps the player much more often than a bigger increase on straight flushes, and so makes a bigger difference in the long-term return.

So it goes with any video poker game. In Double Bonus, the four-of-a-kind bonuses, the enhanced payoffs on full houses, flushes and straights all are offset by one decrease low on the pay table -- the drop from 2-for-1 to 1-for-1 on two pair. When you next find an unfamiliar pay table, be aware. Any boost high on the pay table might look attractive, but check out what you're giving up to get it.

John Grochowski writes a weekly syndicated newspaper column on gambling, hosts a casinos radio show on WCKG-FM (105.9) in Chicago and is author of the "Casino Answer Book" series from Bonus Books.

The Video Poker Answer Book

By *Chicago Sun-Times* Gaming Columnist John Grochowski

This book should be required reading for any video poker player. In *The Video Poker Answer Book*, author John Grochowski gives his easy-to-understand insights into how the machines work and the best strategies for attacking up-to-date variations on this casino standard.

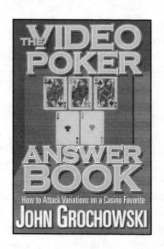

How does the player recognize a high-paying machine? How do bonuses on certain rare hands affect strategy? Does the best method of play change on new machines that have the customer play three, four five, 10 or even 50 hands at once?

John Grochowski is one of the nation's leading gaming writers. His columns on casino gambling have appeared in the *Chicago Sun-Times*, he hosts a casinos radio show on WCKG-FM (105.9) in Chicago and he's also a regular contributor to *Midwest Gaming and Travel*, plus numerous other gaming magazines.

With answers to more than 300 questions, *The Video Poker Answer Book* is a natural companion to his other best-selling gambling books - *The Casino Answer Book* and *The Slot Machine Answer Book* - which both drew rave reviews. The 277-page *Video Poker Answer Book* sells for **$14.95** in bookstores everywhere, or order it online at: www.casinoanswerman.com/books.html

The Proof Is In the Tasting . . . NOT!

by Bob Dancer

Let's say you go to an Italian restaurant you've never visited and see minestrone soup on the menu. The description boasts, "Fresh vegetables, pasta, and beans in a light tomato broth — a vegetarian classic." There are zillion different recipes for minestrone, and you now know that this one isn't made with beef or chicken broth, as many are. Other than that, you don't know much. Maybe the beans are red and maybe white. Maybe this version contains spinach and/or zucchini, and maybe it doesn't. It probably has at least some garlic, but how much?

In this case, the only way to know for sure how this particular chef makes this popular dish is to order it and try a spoonful. If you're knowledgeable about minestrone, you can now estimate how much basil, oregano, garlic and other spices are in there.

I'm not an expert in this. If you put two bowls of minestrone side by side, I can usually spot several differences — color of broth, vegetables used, smell, etc. But ask me a month later to describe the differences and I can't. The information just doesn't stick with me. The exact taste of food isn't one of my priorities.

In video poker, things are very much the opposite than the situation described above. You can learn everything you need to know about a game by looking at the pay schedule, denomination, slot club, and current promotions — assuming you know how to read the code. There is no additional information available by tasting — for me anyway. Your score over five minutes or five hours tells you absolutely nothing relevant about whether or not you should keep playing.

Many people have a tough time accepting this concept. After all, in most things in life, you learn as you go. But not here.

I think the big reason that people want to learn as they go is because they DON'T ALREADY KNOW. When I go into a casino, I can tell at a glance the return on this particular Jacks or Better game, or that particular Deuces Wild game. The reason I understand these things is that I've studied pay schedules enough so it's second-nature to me.

But many people haven't studied that hard or that long. When they get to the casino, they don't know if this particular game is a good one or bad one. What should people like this do?

My first advice (rarely taken) is that they shouldn't play this trip. They should go through the casino writing down pay schedules. When they return home, they should enter those pay schedules into a computer program like Video Poker for Winners to determine how much the game is worth. If the game returns under 98%, I recommend it never be played. (Personally, I only play games that return in excess of 100% when you include the slot club and promotions, but I know that many players have lower standards).

If the game return is high enough, go ahead and practice the game and play during your next trip. Whether you won on your last trip or lost on your last trip is irrelevant. Even tight machines pay off sometimes and loose machines sometimes overhold. Over million of hands, things will average out, but over a few hundred or few thousand hands, anything can happen.

But if you don't know which games are best, and you insist on ignoring my advice and playing anyway on this trip, how should you decide which game to play? We are now delving into a position of making decisions when we don't have enough information. We FREQUENTLY don't have enough information about a number of things. But we have to cope as best we can.

Every person has their own technique for dealing with this kind of situation. My technique, alluded to earlier, is not to play unless I KNOW what the game is worth and how to play it, and further, I also know it returns in excess of 100%. If that is not your rule, fine. You have to live with whatever rule you make. But playing for a half hour is NOT the way to gain useful information. Whether you win $1,000 in that half-hour or lose $1,000 in that half-hour, it tells you absolutely nothing about whether it's an intelligent gamble for you to undertake next time.

Bob Dancer is America's best-known video poker writer and teacher. He has a variety of "how to play better video poker" products, including Winner's Guides, strategy cards, videos, and the award-winning computer software, Bob Dancer Presents WinPoker, his autobiography Million Dollar Video Poker, and his recent novel, Sex, Lies, and Video Poker. Dancer's products may be ordered at www.bobdancer.com.

Where's The Best Place to Play?

by Bob Dancer

Every month I get at least three emails with some variation of the following: "I'll be in Las Vegas next month and I want to know the best place to play video poker."

It's very understandable why this information is desired. After all, if you only have ten playing hours in a trip, you don't want to spend eight of them scouting for a good game to play. But I can't help with the problem unless I know a LOT more information that was included in the email. Information such as:

A - What denomination you do you play? If you only play for quarters, and I tell you the best game for ten dollar machines, it doesn't help you at all.

B - What game(s) do you know how to play? Many players only know 9/6 Jacks or Better, for example. This is not a profitable choice for Las Vegas, by in large, but knowing ANY game well is better than not knowing a game well. Still, if I tell you where a good Deuces Wild game is, it doesn't do you any good.

C - Do you already have a room reservation? If you're staying in the northwest part of the Vegas valley, good games in the southeast aren't particularly attractive. If you don't have a room, are you planning to stay where you play? Some casinos have much better hotels associated with them than others. Is this a priority for you?

D - Are meal comps important to you, and if so, how much of a lesser game are you willing to tolerate to get better meals?

E - Is security an issue? Some casinos are in a rough part of town. This is less of a concern to young, healthy males than to senior couples.

F - Is breathing mandatory? Some casinos with otherwise acceptable games are extremely smoky. Does this eliminate them from consideration for you?

G - Do you have another agenda for the weekend other than good video poker? Do you care how old and/or wealthy the other patrons in the casino are? Do you care if the pool has optional topless sunbathing? Do you care whether the cocktail waitresses serve your particular brand of beer? Is Country Western music playing in the background a plus or a minus?

H - Where have you obtained preferred status? Although names vary, many casinos have a regular card, a gold card, and a diamond card. These sometimes come with extras that can affect which game is best. Similarly, if you need to play $50,000 at one casino on this trip to maintain your preferred status, that strongly limits where you can play.

I - How frequently do you come to Las Vegas? This can affect what kind of slot club is useful. Some casinos in Vegas offer same day cash back and others send you checks in the mail, for which you must come back to collect them. If you are an irregular visitor to Vegas, this affects the choice.

J - Are you planning on having a car for the trip? If not, do you have an aversion to riding the city bus or monorail, or paying higher prices for a cab or limo?

K - Do you have travel companions that affect your choice? Some casinos don't welcome children, for example, and others have movie theaters, child-watching facilities, and video arcades. Sometimes being near a shopping center or being in a casino with a great sports book is mandatory for someone in your party.

Even if you give me all of this information, the choice of where to play might not be unique. There are "chocolate or vanilla" decisions where different people will come up with different conclusions. How can I possibly know all your preferences?

I spend time each month scouting casinos, but when I do, I'm generally looking at $5 and higher machines, which are the ones I'm personally interested in playing. I am reasonably familiar with the best quarter and dollar games in most casinos, but it's not a priority to me to stay up to date on this. And since I live in the southeast section of the valley, it's often four or five months between scouting trips to the northeast.

For the casinos I frequent, I know what kind of mail they send to Las Vegas locals — or at least the high roller locals. But they often send very different offers to out-of-towners, or the low rollers or the mid rollers. And the casinos I don't frequent, I often have no idea at all. And this can affect where to play.

I have no idea what the casino promotions will be next month. I am fairly fluent on current promotions (I co-write with Jeffrey Compton a weekly column about these at www.casinogaming.com), but if you are asking me a month in advance, I often have no way of knowing what these will be because the casinos themselves haven't decided, let alone announced, what they will be. If you wait until the last minute to make your plans, airfare is considerably higher and some hotels are sold out.

Sharing information about video poker is part of what my professional career is all about. But sometimes I'm asked to share more than I can possibly deliver.

Bob Dancer is America's best-known video poker writer and teacher. He has a variety of "how to play better video poker" products, including Winner's Guides, strategy cards, videos, and the award-winning computer software, Bob Dancer Presents WinPoker, his autobiography Million Dollar Video Poker, and his recent novel, Sex, Lies, and Video Poker. Dancer's products may be ordered at www.bobdancer.com.

Blackjack

by Steve Bourie

Blackjack is the most popular casino game in America and one of the biggest reasons for that is its relatively simple rules that are familiar to most casino visitors. Blackjack also has a reputation as being "beatable" and although that is true in some cases, the vast majority of players will always be playing the game with the house having a slight edge over them.

At most blackjack tables there are seven boxes, or betting areas, on the table. This means that up to seven people can play at that table and each player has their own box in front of them in which they'll place their bet. Now, before you take a seat at any blackjack table the first thing you should do is to take a look at the sign that's sitting on each table because it will tell you the minimum amount that you must bet on each hand. If you're a $5 player you certainly wouldn't want to sit at a table that has a $25 minimum so, once again, be sure to look before you sit down.

Once you're at the table you'll need chips to play with and you get them by giving your cash to the dealer who will exchange it for an equal amount of chips. Be careful, however, that you don't put your cash down into one of the betting boxes because the dealer might think you're playing it all on the next hand!

After everyone has placed their bets in their respective boxes the dealer will deal out two cards to each player. He will also deal two cards to himself; one of those cards will be face up and the other face down. Now, if you've ever read any brochures in a casino they'll tell you that the object of the game of blackjack is to get a total of cards as close to 21 as possible, without going over 21. However, that really isn't the object of the game. The true object is to beat the dealer and you do that by getting a total closer to 21 than the dealer, or by having the dealer bust by drawing cards that total more than 21.

The one thing that's strange about blackjack is that the rules can be slightly different at each casino and this is the only game where this happens. If you play baccarat, roulette or craps you'll find that the rules are virtually the same at every casino in the U.S. but that isn't the case with blackjack. For example, in Atlantic City all of the casinos use six or eight decks that are always dealt from a little rectangular box called a *shoe* and the cards are always dealt face up. In Las Vegas, some casinos will offer that same kind of game while others will offer games that use only one or two decks that are dealt directly from the dealer's hand and all of the cards will be dealt face down. To make it even stranger, some casinos in Las Vegas will offer both kinds of games in their

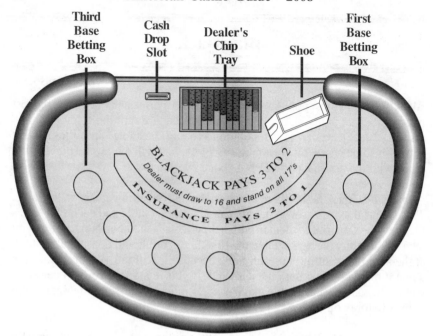

Typical Blackjack Table Layout

casinos and the rules will probably change when you move from one table to another. There can also be other rule variations concerning doubling down and splitting of pairs but we'll talk about those later. For now, just be aware that different casinos can have different blackjack rules and some of those rules will be good for you while others will be bad for you. Hopefully, after reading this story you'll know the good rules from the bad ones and which tables are the best ones to play at.

For our purposes, we'll assume we're playing in a casino that uses six decks of cards that are dealt out of a shoe and all of the player's cards are dealt face up. By the way, whenever you play blackjack in a casino where the cards are dealt face up don't touch the cards. In that kind of game the dealer is the only who is allowed to touch the cards and if you do happen to touch them they'll give you a warning not to do it again - so, don't touch the cards!

After the cards are dealt the players must determine the total of their hand by adding the value of their two cards together. All of the cards are counted at their face value except for the picture cards - jack, queen and king which all have a value of 10 - and the aces which can be counted as either 1 or 11. If you have an ace and any 10-value card you have a blackjack which is also called a natural and your hand is an automatic winner, unless the dealer also has a blackjack in which case the hands are tied. A tie is also called a ***push*** and when that happens it's a standoff and you neither win nor lose. All winning blackjacks are paid at 3-to-2, or one-and-a-half times your bet, so if you bet $5 and got a blackjack you would be paid $7.50

If the dealer has an ace as his up card the first thing he'll do is ask if anyone wants to buy ***insurance***. When you buy insurance you're betting that the dealer has a blackjack by having a 10 as his face down card. To make an insurance bet you would place your bet in the area just above your betting box that says "insurance pays 2-to-1" and you're only allowed to make an in-surance bet of up to one-half the amount of your original bet. So, if you originally bet $10 you could only bet a maximum of $5 as your insurance bet. After all the insurance bets are made the dealer will check his face down card and if it's a 10 he'll turn it over and all of the insurance bets will be paid off at 2-to-1. If he doesn't have a 10 underneath, the dealer will then take away all of the losing insurance bets and the game will continue. By the way, according to basic strategy, insurance is a bad bet and you should never make an insurance bet.

If the dealer has a 10 as his up card the first thing he'll do is check to see if he has an ace underneath which would give him a blackjack. If he does have an ace he'll turn it face up and start collecting the losing bets that are out on the table. If he doesn't have an ace underneath the game will continue. In some casinos, however, the dealer won't check his hole card until after all of the hands are played out.

If the dealer doesn't have an ace or a 10 as his up card the game continues and the dealer will start with the player to his immediate left to see if they want another card. If a player wants another card they indicate that with a hand signal by tapping or scratching the table with their finger to show they want another card. Taking a card is also known as ***hitting*** or taking a hit. If a player doesn't want another card they would just wave their hand palm down over their cards. Not taking another card is known as ***standing***. The reason hand signals are used is because it eliminates any confusion on the part of the dealer as to exactly what the player wants and it also allows the security people to follow the game on the closed-circuit cameras that are hung from the ceiling throughout the casino.

Keep in mind that the hand signals will be slightly different if you're playing in a casino where the cards are dealt face down and you're allowed to pick them up. In that situation a player would signal that they wanted another card by scratching the table with the edges of the two cards they're holding. If they didn't want another card, they would simply place their two cards under the bet in their box.

In either case, if a player draws another card the value of that card is added to the total of the other cards and the player can continue to draw cards unless he gets a total of more than 21 in which case he busts and loses his bet.

When a player doesn't want any more cards, or stands, the dealer then moves on to the next player and after all of the players are finished then it's the dealer's turn to play. While each player can decide whether or not they want another card the dealer doesn't have that option and he must play by a fixed set of rules that require him to draw a card whenever his total is 16 or less and to stop when his total is 17 or more. If the dealer goes over 21 then he has busted and all of the players remaining in the game will be paid 1-to-1, or even money, on their bet.

If the dealer doesn't bust then each player's hand is compared to the dealer's. If the player's total is higher than the dealer's then they win and are paid even money. If the player's hand has a total that is lower than the dealer's hand then the player loses his bet. If the player and the dealer have the same total then it's a tie, or a push and neither hand wins. After all of the bets have been paid off, or taken by the dealer, a new round begins and new hands are dealt to all of the players.

When deciding how to play your hand there are also three other options available to you besides standing or hitting. The first is called *doubling down* and most casinos will allow a player to double their bet on their first two cards and draw only one more card. To do this you would place an amount equal to your original bet right next to it and then the dealer would give you one more card, sideways, to indicate that your bet was a double down. To double down in a game where the cards are dealt face down you would turn up your original two cards and tell the dealer you wanted to double down. Then, after you double your bet, the dealer would give you one more card face down. Some casinos may have restrictions on this bet and may only allow you to double down if the total of your two cards is 10 or 11, but it's always to your advantage if they allow you to double down on any two cards.

Another thing you can do is *split* your cards if you have a pair and then play each card as a separate hand. For example, if you had a pair of 8's you would place a bet equal to your original bet right next to it and tell the dealer you wanted to split your pair. The dealer would then separate your two 8's and give you one card on your first 8. Unlike doubling down, however, you are not limited to only getting one card and you can play your hand out normally. When you were finished with your first hand the dealer would then give you a card on your other 8 and you would play that hand out. Although you aren't usually limited to just one card on your splits, there is one instance where that will happen and that happens when you split aces. Almost all casinos will give you just one card on each ace when you split them. Also, if you get a 10-value card with your ace it will only count as 21 and not as a blackjack so you'll only get even money on that bet if you win. Besides splitting pairs you can also split all 10-value cards such as jack-king or 10-queen but it would be a very bad idea to do that because you would be breaking up a 20 which is a very strong hand and you should never split 10's. By the way, if you wanted to split a pair in a casino where the cards are dealt face down you would simply turn your original two cards face-up and tell the dealer that you wanted to split them.

The last option you have is not available in most casinos but you may come across it in a few Las Vegas Strip casinos and it's called *surrender*. With the surrender option you're allowed to lose half of your bet if you decide you don't want to play out your hand after looking at your first two cards. Let's say you're dealt a 10-6 for a total of 16 and the dealer has a 10 as his face-up card. A 16 is not a very strong hand, especially against a dealer's 10, so in this case it would be a good idea to surrender your hand and when the dealer came to your cards you would say "surrender." The dealer would then take half of your bet and remove your cards. Surrender is good for the player because in the long run you will lose less on the bad hands you're dealt and you should always try to play in a casino that offers the surrender option.

All right, we've covered the basics of how to play the game of blackjack and all of the possible options a player has, so the next question is how do you win? Well, the best way to win is to become a card counter, but for the average person that isn't always possible so let's start off by taking a look at basic blackjack strategy.

Computer studies have been done on the game of blackjack and millions of hands have been analyzed to come up with a basic formula for how to play your hand in any given situation. The main principle that these decisions are based on is the dealer's up card because, remember that the dealer has no say in whether or not he takes a card - he must play by the rules that require him to draw a card until he has a total of 17 or more. Now, according to these computer calculations the dealer will bust more often when his up card is a 2,3,4,5 or 6 and he will complete more hands when his up card is a 7,8,9,10-value card or an ace. Take a look at the following chart that shows how each up-card affects the dealer's chance of busting:

Chance The Dealer's Up Card Will Bust

2	35%
3	38%
4	40%
5	43%
6	42%
7	26%
8	24%
9	23%
10	21%
Ace	11%

As you can see, the dealer will bust most often when he has a 5 or 6 as his upcard and he will bust the least amount, approximately 11% of the time, when his upcard is an ace. This means it's to your advantage to stand more often when the dealer's upcard is a 2 through 6 and hope that the dealer will draw cards that make him bust. It also means that when the dealer's upcard is a 7 through ace he will complete more of his hands and in that situation you should draw cards until you have a total of 17 or more.

Now let's show you how to play your hands by using the basic strategy and we'll start off with the *hard hand* strategy and hard hand means a two-card total without an ace. A hand with an ace is known as a **soft hand** because the ace can be counted as either a 1 or an 11. So, if you had an ace-6 you would have a soft 17 hand and if you had a 10-6 you would have a hard 16 hand. Later on we'll take a look at how to play soft hands, but for now we'll concentrate on the hard hand totals. Oh yes, one more thing, the following basic strategy applies to casinos where they deal more than one deck at a time and the dealer stands on soft 17, which is the situation you'll find in the majority of casinos today. So, keep in mind that the strategy would be slightly different if you were playing against a single deck and it would also be slightly different if the dealer hit a soft 17.

Whenever your first two cards total 17 through 21, you should stand, no matter what the dealer's up card is.

If your cards total 16, you should stand if the dealer has a 2 through 6 as his upcard otherwise, draw a card. By the way, 16 is the worst hand you can have because you will bust more often with 16 than with any other hand. So, if that's the case then why would you want to ever hit a 16? Well, once again, those computer studies have shown that you should hit a 16 when the dealer has 7 through ace as his upcard because in the long run you will lose less often. This means that yes, 16 is a terrible hand, but you should hit it because if you don't you will lose even more often than when you do take a card.

If your cards total 15, you should also stand if the dealer has a 2 through 6 as his upcard otherwise, draw cards until your total is 17 or more.

The same rules from 15 and 16 also apply if your cards total 14. Stand if the dealer has a 2 through 6, otherwise draw cards until your total is 17 or more. The same rules also apply if your cards total 13. Stand if the dealer has a 2 through 6, otherwise draw cards until your total is 17 or more.

When your cards total 12 you should only stand when the dealer has a 4, 5 or 6 as his upcard, remember - those are his three weakest cards and he will bust more often with those cards, so you don't want to take a chance on busting yourself. If the dealer's upcard is a 2 or a 3, then you should take just one card and stop on your total of 13 or more. Finally, if the dealer has a 7 through ace as his upcard then you should draw cards until your total is 17 or more.

When your cards total 11 you would always want to hit it because you can't bust, but before you ask for a card you should consider making a double down bet. If the casino allows you to double down then you should do that if the dealer has anything but an ace as his upcard. After you double down the dealer would give you just one additional card on that hand. If the dealer's upcard is an ace then you shouldn't double down. Instead, you should hit the hand and continue to draw until your total is 17 or more. If the casino doesn't allow you to double down then you should just hit your hand and then, depending on your total, play it by the rules you were given for the hands that totaled 12 through 21. Meaning, if you had an 11 and the dealer had a 5 as his upcard, you should take a card. Then let's say you draw an ace which gives you a total of 12. Well, as noted before, if you have a 12 against a dealer's 5 you should stand and that's how you should play that hand.

If your total is 10 you would, once again, want to double down unless the dealer showed an ace or a 10. If the dealer had an ace or a 10 as his upcard you should hit your hand and then use the standard rules for a hand valued at 12 through 21. Therefore, if you had a 10 and the dealer had an 8 as his up card you would want to double down and take one more card. If you weren't allowed to double, then you would take a hit and let's say you got a 4 for a total of 14. You should then continue to hit your hand until your total is 17 or more.

If your total is 9 you would want to double down whenever the dealer was showing a 3,4,5 or 6 as his upcard. If the dealer had a 2 as his upcard, or if he had a 7 through ace as his upcard, you should hit your hand and then use the standard playing rules as discussed before. So, let's say you had a 9 and the dealer had a 4 as his upcard you would want to double down and take one more card. If you weren't allowed to double then you should take a hit and let's say you got a 2 for a total of 11, you would then take another hit and let's say you got an ace. That would give you a total of 12 and, as mentioned previously, you should stand on 12 against a dealer's 4.

Finally, if your total is 8 or less you should always take a card and then use the standard playing rules that were already discussed.

Now, let's take a look at splitting pairs, but keep in mind that the rules for splitting will change slightly depending on whether or not the casino will allow you to double down after you split your cards. Most multiple-deck games allow you to double down after splitting so that's the situation we'll cover first and then we'll talk about the changes you need to make if you're not allowed to double down after splitting.

Basic Strategy - Single Deck

Dealer stands on soft 17 · Double on any 2 cards · Double allowed after split

Your Hand	Dealer's Upcard									
	2	3	4	5	6	7	8	9	10	A
17	ALWAYS STAND ON HARD 17 (OR MORE)									
16	-	-	-	-	-	H	H	H	H*	H
15	-	-	-	-	-	H	H	H	H*	H
14	-	-	-	-	-	H	H	H	H	H
13	-	-	-	-	-	H	H	H	H	H
12	H	H	-	-	-	H	H	H	H	H
11	ALWAYS DOUBLE									
10	D	D	D	D	D	D	D	D	H	H
9	D	D	D	D	D	H	H	H	H	H
8	H	H	H	D	D	H	H	H	H	H
A,8	-	-	-	-	D	-	-	-	-	-
A,7	-	D	D	D	D	-	-	H	H	-
A,6	D	D	D	D	D	H	H	H	H	H
A,5	H	H	D	D	D	H	H	H	H	H
A,4	H	H	D	D	D	H	H	H	H	H
A,3	H	H	D	D	D	H	H	H	H	H
A,2	H	H	D	D	D	H	H	H	H	H
A,A	ALWAYS SPLIT									
10,10	ALWAYS STAND (NEVER SPLIT)									
9,9	Sp	Sp	Sp	Sp	Sp	-	Sp	Sp	-	-
8,8	ALWAYS SPLIT									
7,7	Sp	Sp	Sp	Sp	Sp	Sp	Sp	H	-*	H
6,6	Sp	Sp	Sp	Sp	Sp	Sp	H	H	H	H
5,5	NEVER SPLIT (PLAY AS 10 HAND)									
4,4	H	H	Sp	Sp	Sp	H	H	H	H	H
3,3	Sp	Sp	Sp	Sp	Sp	Sp	Sp	H	H	H
2,2	Sp	H	Sp	Sp	Sp	Sp	H	H	H	H

- =Stand   H=Hit   D=Double   Sp=Split   *= Surrender if allowed

shaded boxes show strategy changes from chart on next page

Basic Strategy - Single Deck

Dealer stands on soft 17 · Double on any 2 cards · Double <u>NOT</u> allowed after split

Your Hand	Dealer's Upcard									
	2	**3**	**4**	**5**	**6**	**7**	**8**	**9**	**10**	**A**
17	ALWAYS STAND ON HARD 17 (OR MORE)									
16	-	-	-	-	-	H	H	H	H*	H*
15	-	-	-	-	-	H	H	H	H*	H
14	-	-	-	-	-	H	H	H	H	H
13	-	-	-	-	-	H	H	H	H	H
12	H	H	-	-	-	H	H	H	H	H
11	ALWAYS DOUBLE									
10	D	D	D	D	D	D	D	D	H	H
9	D	D	D	D	D	H	H	H	H	H
8	H	H	H	D	D	H	H	H	H	H
A,8	-	-	-	-	D	-	-	-	-	-
A,7	-	D	D	D	D	-	-	H	H	-
A,6	D	D	D	D	D	H	H	H	H	H
A,5	H	H	D	D	D	H	H	H	H	H
A,4	H	H	D	D	D	H	H	H	H	H
A,3	H	H	D	D	D	H	H	H	H	H
A,2	H	H	D	D	D	H	H	H	H	H
A,A	ALWAYS SPLIT									
10,10	NEVER SPLIT (ALWAYS STAND)									
9,9	Sp	Sp	Sp	Sp	Sp	-	Sp	Sp	-	-
8,8	ALWAYS SPLIT									
7,7	Sp	Sp	Sp	Sp	Sp	Sp	H	H	-*	H
6,6	Sp	Sp	Sp	Sp	Sp	H	H	H	H	H
5,5	NEVER SPLIT (PLAY AS 10 HAND)									
4,4	NEVER SPLIT (PLAY AS 8 HAND)									
3,3	H	H	Sp	Sp	Sp	Sp	H	H	H	H
2,2	H	Sp	Sp	Sp	Sp	Sp	H	H	H	H

- =Stand   H=Hit   D=Double   Sp=Split   *= Surrender if allowed

Basic Strategy - Multiple Decks

Dealer stands on soft 17 · Double on any 2 cards · Double allowed after split

Your Hand	Dealer's Upcard									
	2	3	4	5	6	7	8	9	10	A
17	ALWAYS STAND ON 17 (OR MORE)									
16	-	-	-	-	-	H	H	H*	H*	H*
15	-	-	-	-	-	H	H	H	H*	H
14	-	-	-	-	-	H	H	H	H	H
13	-	-	-	-	-	H	H	H	H	H
12	H	H	-	-	-	H	H	H	H	H
11	D	D	D	D	D	D	D	D	D	H
10	D	D	D	D	D	D	D	D	H	H
9	H	D	D	D	D	H	H	H	H	H
8	ALWAYS HIT 8 (OR LESS)									
A,8	ALWAYS STAND ON SOFT 19 (OR MORE)									
A,7	-	D	D	D	D	-	-	H	H	H
A,6	H	D	D	D	D	H	H	H	H	H
A,5	H	H	D	D	D	H	H	H	H	H
A,4	H	H	D	D	D	H	H	H	H	H
A,3	H	H	H	D	D	H	H	H	H	H
A,2	H	H	H	D	D	H	H	H	H	H
A,A	ALWAYS SPLIT									
10,10	ALWAYS STAND (NEVER SPLIT)									
9,9	Sp	Sp	Sp	Sp	Sp	-	Sp	Sp	-	-
8,8	ALWAYS SPLIT									
7,7	Sp	Sp	Sp	Sp	Sp	Sp	H	H	H	H
6,6	Sp	Sp	Sp	Sp	Sp	H	H	H	H	H
5,5	D	D	D	D	D	D	D	D	H	H
4,4	H	H	H	Sp	Sp	H	H	H	H	H
3,3	Sp	Sp	Sp	Sp	Sp	Sp	H	H	H	H
2,2	Sp	Sp	Sp	Sp	Sp	Sp	H	H	H	H

- =Stand   H=Hit   D=Double   Sp=Split   *= Surrender if allowed

Basic Strategy - Multiple Decks

Dealer stands on soft 17 · Double on any 2 cards · Double <u>NOT</u> allowed after split

Your Hand	Dealer's Upcard									
	2	3	4	5	6	7	8	9	10	A
17	ALWAYS STAND ON HARD 17 (OR MORE)									
16	-	-	-	-	-	H	H	H*	H*	H*
15	-	-	-	-	-	H	H	H	H*	H
14	-	-	-	-	-	H	H	H	H	H
13	-	-	-	-	-	H	H	H	H	H
12	H	H	-	-	-	H	H	H	H	H
11	D	D	D	D	D	D	D	D	D	H
10	D	D	D	D	D	D	D	D	H	H
9	H	D	D	D	D	H	H	H	H	H
8	ALWAYS HIT 8 (OR LESS)									
A,8	ALWAYS STAND ON SOFT 19 (OR MORE)									
A,7	-	D	D	D	D	-	-	H	H	H
A,6	H	D	D	D	D	H	H	H	H	H
A,5	H	H	D	D	D	H	H	H	H	H
A,4	H	H	D	D	D	H	H	H	H	H
A,3	H	H	H	D	D	H	H	H	H	H
A,2	H	H	H	D	D	H	H	H	H	H
A,A	ALWAYS SPLIT									
10,10	ALWAYS STAND (NEVER SPLIT)									
9,9	Sp	Sp	Sp	Sp	Sp	-	Sp	Sp	-	-
8,8	ALWAYS SPLIT									
7,7	Sp	Sp	Sp	Sp	Sp	Sp	H	H	H	H
6,6	H	Sp	Sp	Sp	Sp	H	H	H	H	H
5,5	NEVER SPLIT (PLAY AS 10 HAND)									
4,4	H	H	H	H	H	H	H	H	H	H
3,3	H	H	Sp	Sp	Sp	Sp	H	H	H	H
2,2	H	H	Sp	Sp	Sp	Sp	H	H	H	H

- =Stand   H=Hit   D=Double   Sp=Split   *= Surrender if allowed
shaded boxes show strategy changes from chart on previous page

As noted earlier, when your first two cards are the same most casinos will allow you to split them and play them as two separate hands so let's go over the basic strategy rules on when you should do this.

The first thing you should remember is that you always split aces and 8's. The reason you split aces is obvious because if you get a 10 on either hand you'll have a perfect 21, but remember that you won't get paid for a blackjack at 3-to-2, instead it'll be counted as a regular 21 and you'll be paid at even money. If you have a pair of 8's you have 16 which is a terrible hand and you can always improve it by splitting your 8's and playing them as separate hands.

The next thing to remember about splitting pairs is that you never split 5's or 10's. Once again, the reasons should be rather obvious, you don't want to split 10's because 20 is a great hand and you don't want to split 5's because 10 is a great hand to draw to. Instead, you would want to double down on that 10 unless the dealer was showing a 10 or an ace as his upcard.

2's, 3's and 7's should only be split when the dealer is showing a 2 through 7 as his upcard. Split 4's only when the dealer has a 5 or 6 as his upcard (remember 5 and 6 are his weakest cards!), 6's should be split whenever the dealer is showing a 2 through 6 and finally, you should always split 9's unless the dealer is showing a 7, 10 or ace. The reason you don't want to split 9's against a 10 or an ace should be rather obvious, but the reason you don't want to split them against a 7 is in case the dealer has a 10 as his hole card because in that case your 18 would beat out his 17.

If the casino will not allow you to double down after splitting then you should make the following three changes: For 2's and 3's only split them against a 4,5,6 or 7; never split 4's; and for a pair of 6's only split them against a 3,4,5 or 6. Everything else should be played the same.

Now, let's take a look at how to play *soft hands* and, remember, a soft hand is any hand that contains an ace that can be counted as 1 or 11. For a soft hand of 19 or more you should always stand.

For soft 18 against a 2,7 or 8 you should always stand. If the dealer shows a 9, 10 or an ace you should always take a hit and for a soft 18 against a 3,4,5 or 6 you should double down, but if the casino won't allow you to double then you should just stand.

For soft 17 you should always take a hit, but if the casino allows you to double down, then you should double against a dealer's 3,4,5 or 6.

For soft 16 or a soft 15 you should always take a hit, but if the casino allows you to double down then you should double against a dealer's 4,5 or 6.

For soft 14 you should always take a hit, but if the casino allows you to double down then you should double against a dealer's 5 or 6.

Finally, for a soft 13 you should always take a hit, but if the casino allows you to double down then you should double against a dealer's 5 or 6.

The last thing we need to cover is surrender which, as noted before, isn't offered in many casinos but it is an option that does work in your favor and if available, you should play in a casino that offers it. The surrender rules are very simple to remember and only apply to hard totals of 15 or 16. If you have a hard 16 you should surrender it whenever the dealer has a 9, 10 or ace as his upcard and if you have a hard 15 you should surrender it whenever the dealer has a 10 as his upcard. That's all there is to surrender.

Now that you know how to play the game and you have an understanding of the basic strategy let's take a quick look at how the rule variations can affect the game of blackjack. As noted before, various computer studies have been made on blackjack and these studies have shown that each rule change can either hurt or help the player by a certain amount. For example, a single-deck game where you can double on any first 2 cards (but not after splitting pairs), the dealer stands on soft 17 and no surrender is allowed has no advantage for the casino when using the basic strategy. That's right, in a game with those rules in effect the game is dead even and neither the casino nor the player has an edge!

Take a look at the following chart and you'll see how some rules changes can hurt you or help you as a player. Minus signs in front mean that the casino gains the edge by that particular amount while plus signs mean that you gain the edge by that amount.

RULES THAT HURT YOU		RULES THAT HELP YOU	
Two decks	-0.32%	Double after split	+0.13%
Four decks	-0.49%	Late surrender	+0.06%
Six decks	-0.54%	Resplit Aces	+0.14%
Eight decks	-0.57%	Double anytime	+0.20%
Dealer hits soft 17	-0.20%		
No soft doubling	-0.14%		
BJ pays 6-to-5	-1.40%		
BJ pays 1-to-1	-2.30%		

As you can see, it's always to your advantage to play against as few decks as possible. The house edge goes up substantially as you go from 1 deck to 2, but the change is less dramatic when you go from 2 to 4, or from 4 to 6, and it's barely noticeable when you go from 6 to 8. You can also see that you would prefer not to play in a casino where the dealer hits a soft 17 because that gives the dealer a slight edge. You would also want to play in a casino where you're allowed to double down on your soft hands or else you would be giving another added edge to the casino.

You can also see from these charts that you would want to play in a casino where you were allowed to double down after splitting cards and you would also want to play in a casino that offered surrender. The other two rules variations that help the player are somewhat rare but they were put in to show you how these rules changes can affect your odds in the game. Some casinos will allow you to resplit aces again if you draw an ace to one of your original aces and this works to your advantage. Also, some casinos will allow you to double down on any number of cards rather than just the first two. In other words, if you got a 2- 4-3-2 as your first four cards you would then be allowed to double down on your total of 11 before receiving your 5th card. If they allow you to do this then, once again, you have a rule that works in your favor.

The point of showing you these charts is to help you understand that when you have a choice of places to play you should always choose the casino that offers the best rules. So, if you find a single-deck game with good rules you could be playing an even game by using the basic strategy, or at worst be giving the casino an edge of less than one-half of 1%.

Now, there is one way that you can actually have the edge working in your favor when you play blackjack and that's by becoming a card counter. As mentioned before, card counting is not for the average person but it really is important that you understand the concept of card counting and if you think you'd like to learn more about counting cards then it's something you can follow up on later.

Many people think that to be a card counter you have to have a photographic memory and remember every single card that's been played. Fortunately, it's not quite that difficult. Actually, the main concept behind card counting is the assumption that the dealer will bust more often when there are a lot of 10's in the deck and that he will complete more hands when there are a lot of smaller cards in the deck. Now, if you stop to think about it, it makes sense doesn't it? After all, the dealer has to play by set rules that make him take a card until he has a total of 17 or more. If there are a lot of 2's, 3's and 4's in the deck the dealer won't bust very often when he draws cards, but if there are a lot of 10's in the deck then chances are he will bust more often when he is forced to draw cards.

The card counter tries to take advantage of this fact by keeping a running total of the cards that have been played to give him an idea of what kind of cards remain in the deck. If there are a lot of 10 cards remaining in the deck then the counter will bet more money because the odds are slightly in his favor. Of course, if there are a lot of small cards remaining then the counter would only make a small bet because the odds would be slightly in favor of the dealer. Another thing that the card counter can do is to change his basic strategy to take advantage of the differences in the deck.

There are at least a dozen different card counting systems but let's take a quick look at a relatively simple one (it's also the most popular) and it's called the *high-low* count. With this system you assign a value of +1 to all 2's, 3's, 4's, 5's and 6's, while all 10's, Jacks, Queens, Kings and Aces are assigned a value of -1. The remaining cards: 7, 8 and 9 have no value and are not counted.

$$+1 \ = \ 2, 3, 4, 5, 6$$
$$-1 \ = \ 10, J, Q, K, A$$

When you look at these numbers you'll see that there are an equal number of cards in each group: there are five cards valued at +1 and five cards valued at -1. This means that they balance each other out and if you go through the deck and add them all together the end result will always be a total of exactly zero.

What a card counter does is to keep a running total of all the cards as they're played out and whenever the total has a plus value he knows that a lot of small cards have appeared and the remaining deck is rich in 10's which is good for the player. But, if the total is a minus value then the counter knows that a lot of 10-value cards have appeared and the remaining deck must be rich in low cards which is bad for the player. To give you an example of how to count let's say the following cards have been dealt on the first hand from a single deck:

$$2, 3, 3, 4, 5, 5, 5, 6, \ = \ +8$$
$$J, K, Q, A, \ = \ -4$$
$$Total \ = \ +4$$

As you can see, there were eight plus-value cards and four minus-value cards which resulted in a total count of +4. This means that there are now four more 10-value cards than low cards remaining in the deck and the advantage is with the player. Naturally, the higher the plus count, the more advantageous it is for the player and counters would be proportionally increasing their bets as the count got higher. The card counter would also be using the same basic strategy we spoke about previously, except for certain instances where a slight change would be called for.

On the other hand, if the count is negative, a card counter will always bet the minimum amount. Of course, they would prefer not to bet at all, but the casinos don't like you to sit at their tables and not bet so the counter has to bet something and the minimum is the least they can get by with.

There is one more important thing to explain about card counting and it's called the *true count*. The true count is a measure of the count per deck rather than a *running count* of all the cards that have been played and to get the true count you simply divide the running count by the number of decks remaining to be played. As an illustration, let's say you're playing in a six-deck game and the count is +9. You look at the shoe and estimate three decks remain to be played.

You then divide the count of +9 by three to get +3 which is the true count. As another example, let's say you're in an eight-deck game with a count of +12 and there are six decks left to be played. You divide +12 by six to get +2 which is the true count. To put it another way, a +2 count in a double-deck game with one deck left to be played is the same as a +4 count in a four-deck game with two decks left to be played, which is the same as a +6 count is a six-deck game with three decks left to be played, which is the same as a +12 count in an eight-deck game with six decks left to be played.

For the card counter, it is crucial to always take the running count and then divide it by the number of decks remaining in order to get the true count because all betting and playing decisions are based on the true count rather than the running count.

Of course, if you're playing in a single-deck game the running count and the true count are initially the same. The more you get into the deck, however, the more weight is given to the running count because there is less than one deck remaining. So, if the running count was +3 and only a 1/2-deck remained you would calculate the true count by dividing +3 by 1/2 (which is the same as multiplying by 2/1, or 2) to get a true count of +6. As another example, if the running count was +2 and about 2/3 of the deck remained you would divide +2 by 2/3 (the same as multi-plying by 3/2 or, 1 and 1/2) to get +3.

As you can see, the count becomes much more meaningful as you get closer to the last cards in the deck and that's why casinos never deal down to the end. Instead, the dealer will insert a plastic card about 2/3 or 3/4 of the way in the deck and when that card is reached the dealer will finish that particular round and then shuffle the cards. How far into the deck(s) that plastic card is inserted is known as the *penetration point* and card counters always look for a dealer that offers good penetration. The card counter knows that the further into the deck(s) the plastic card is placed the more meaningful the true count will be and the more advantageous it will be for the card counter.

So, now that you know how those card counters keep track of the cards, what kind of advantage do you think they have over the casino? Well, not too much. Depending on the number of decks used, the rules in force, and the skill of the counter, it could be as much as 2% but that would be at the high end. Probably 1% would be closer to the actual truth. This means that for every $1,000 in bets that are made the card counter will win $10. Not exactly a huge amount but there are people out there who do make a living playing the game.

Bad Blackjack Games

By Henry Tamburin

Over the past several years changes have been made to the game of blackjack which have not been good for the player. Most of these changes began in Las Vegas, but they have spread to other gaming areas.

Many casinos have installed continuous shuffling machines (CSM's) on their blackjack tables. These devices allowed the dealers to reshuffle after every hand, which makes card counting futile. But CSM's not only hurt card counters; they have a negative effect on the average player. The reason is because the casinos get 20% more hands played on average per hour with these devices because there is no downtime for manual shuffles. Unless a player slows down when he plays, he will be playing more hands per hour and his potential hourly loss will increase (remember the casinos have the edge over the average player). My advice is to stay away from any CSM dealt game.

Many casinos also offer a single-deck blackjack game where players get paid only 6-5 on an untied blackjack hand instead of the traditional 3-2 payout. This one rule change boosts the casino's edge by 1.4%. Likewise, some casinos pay only even money on blackjack which increases the house edge by 2.3%. Stay away from any game that doesn't pay 3-2 on a blackjack.

Some casinos also offer a single-deck game called Super Fun 21. The game uses a single deck of cards (which most players know has better odds) and a whole bunch of player favorable rules (like doubling on any number of cards and being able to surrender even after doubling). But player blackjacks (except in diamonds) only pay even money. The latter negates all the player favorable rules resulting in a game with an 85% increase in casino's edge (up to 0.95%).

Many casinos are also converting their rules to "dealer hit soft 17" from dealer stand on soft 17. That tiny rule change increases the house edge over players by 0.2%. And that assumes the player knows the changes to the basic playing strategy, which many do not.

Henry Tamburin is the author of six best-selling books including Blackjack: Take The Money & Run. For a free copy of his Blackjack Insider newsletter visit his website at www.smartgaming.com.

Craps

by Steve Bourie

At first glance the game of craps looks a little intimidating because of all the various bets you can make but actually the game itself is very simple, so first let me explain the game without any reference to the betting.

Everyone at the craps table gets a turn to roll the dice, but you don't have to roll if you don't want to. The dice are passed around the table clockwise and if it's your turn to roll you simply take two dice and roll them to the opposite end of the table. This is your first roll of the dice which is also called the "come-out" roll. If you roll a 7 or 11 that's called a "natural" and you win, plus you get to roll again. If you roll a 2,3 or 12 those are all called "craps" and you lose, but you still get to roll again. The only other possible numbers you can roll are 4,5,6,8,9 or 10 and if one of those numbers shows up, then that number becomes your "point" and the object of the game is to roll that number again before you roll a 7.

If a 7 shows up before your "point" number does then you lose and the dice move on to the next shooter. If your "point" number shows up before a 7 does, then you have made a "pass." You then win your bet and you get to roll again. That's all there is to the game of craps.

Now that you know how to play the game, let's find out about the different kinds of bets you can make. Two of the best bets you'll find on the craps table are in the areas marked "pass" and "don't pass". When you bet on the "pass" line you're betting that the shooter will win. To make a pass line bet you put your bet right in front of you on the pass line. Pass line bets are paid even-money and the house edge on a pass line bet is 1.41% You can also bet on the "don't pass" line in which case you're betting that the shooter will lose. To make a don't pass bet you put your bet in front of you in the don't pass area. Don't pass bets are also paid even-money and the house edge on them is 1.40%

In reality, the odds are always 1.41% against the shooter and in favor of the "don't pass" bettor by that same amount. Of course, if you're a "don't pass" bettor the casinos don't want to give you a bet where you have an edge so they have a rule in effect on "don't pass" bets where on the come out roll if the shooter throws a 12, you don't win. You don't lose either, the bet is just considered a "push," or tie, and nothing happens. In some casinos they may make 2 instead of 12 the number that's a push. Just look on the don't pass line and you'll you see the word "bar" and then the number that the casino considers a push. In our illustration it says bar 12, so in this casino your bet on the don't pass line will be a push if the come-out roll is a 12. This rule is what gives the casino its advantage on don't pass bets and it doesn't matter whether the casino bars the 2 or 12 the result is the same 1.40% advantage for the house.

All right, let's say you put $10 on the pass line and you roll the dice. If you roll 7 or 11 you win $10 and if you roll 2,3 or 12 you lose $10. So, what happens if you roll any of the other numbers? Well, as I said before, that number becomes your point and you have to roll that number again before you roll a 7 in order to win your pass line bet.

Once your point is established the dealer at each end of the table will move a marker into the box that corresponds to your point number to let everyone at the table know what your point is. The marker that's used has two different sides. One side is black with the word "off" and the other side is white with the word "on." Before any point is established the marker is kept in the Don't Come box with the black side facing up until you roll a point number and then the dealer turns it over to the white side and moves it inside the box that contains your point number.

For example let's say your come-out roll is a 4. The dealer simply turns the marker over to the white side that says "on" and places it in the 4 box. This let's everyone know that 4 is your point and that you will continue to roll the dice, no matter how long it takes, until you roll a 4, which will make you a winner, or a 7, which will make you a loser.

Now, keep in mind that once your point is established you can't remove your pass line bet until you either win, by throwing your point, or lose, by rolling a 7. The reason for this is that on the come out roll the pass line bettor has the advantage because there are 8 ways to win (by rolling a 7 or 11) and only 4 ways to lose (by rolling a 2, 3 or 12). If a point number is rolled, no matter what number it is, there are then more ways to lose than to win and that's why the bet can't be removed. If you were allowed to remove your bet everyone would just wait for the come-out roll and if they didn't win they would take their bet back which would give them a big advantage over the house and, as you know, casinos don't like that, so that's why you can't remove your bet.

As previously noted, the pass line is one of the best bets you'll find, but there is a way to make it even better because once your point number is established the casino will allow you to make another bet that will be paid off at the true odds. This is a very good bet to make because the casino has no advantage on this bet.

In this instance, since your point was 4, the true odds are 2-to-1 and that's what your bet will be paid off at: $2 for every $1 you bet. This is called an "odds bet," "taking the free odds" or "betting behind the line" and to make this bet you simply put your chips directly behind your pass line bet. There is a limit to how much you're allowed to bet and for many years most casinos allowed a maximum of 2 times the amount of your pass line bet. Nowadays, however, many casinos offer 5 times odds and some casinos are even allowing up to 100 times odds. In Las Vegas, Casino Royale is one casino that offers 100 times odds.

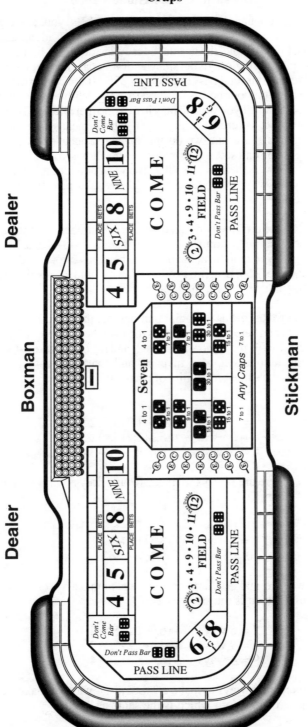

Typical craps table layout

Because the casino has no advantage on these bets you are effectively lowering the house edge on your total pass line bet by taking advantage of these free odds bets. For example, the normal house edge on a pass line bet is 1.41% but if you also make a single odds bet along with your pass line bet you will lower the house edge on your total pass line bets to .85%. If the casino offers double odds then the edge on your bets is lowered to .61%. With triple odds the edge is lowered to .47% and if you were to play in a casino that allowed 10 times odds the edge would be lowered to only .18% which means that, statistically speaking, over time, that casino would only make 18¢ out of every $100 you bet on that table. As you can see, the more the casino allows you to bet behind the line, the more it lowers their edge, so it's always a good idea to take advantage of this bet. By the way, free odds bets, unlike regular pass line bets, can be removed or reduced, at any time.

All right, let's make our free odds bet on our point number of 4 by putting $20 behind the line. Then we continue to roll until we either roll a 4 or a 7. If a 4 came up we would get even money on the pass line bet, plus 2-to-1 on the free odds bet, for a total win of $50. But, if we rolled a 7, we would lose both the pass line bet and the free odds bet for a total loss of $30.

In this example we used 4 as our point number, but there are 5 other numbers that could appear and here are the true odds for all of the possible point numbers: the 4 and 10 are 2-to-1; the 5 and 9 are 3-to-2; and the 6 and 8 are 6-to-5. You'll notice that the numbers appear in pairs and that's because each paired combination has the same probability of occurring.

$$7 = 6 \text{ ways} \qquad 1+6,6+1,2+5,5+2,3+4,4+3$$
$$6 = 5 \text{ ways} \qquad 1+5,5+1,2+4,4+2,3+3$$
$$8 = 5 \text{ ways} \qquad 2+6,6+2,3+5,5+3,4+4$$

As you can see there are 6 ways to make a 7 and only 5 ways to make a 6 or 8. Therefore, the true odds are 6-to-5.

$$7 = 6 \text{ ways} \qquad 1+6,6+1,2+5,5+2,3+4,4+3$$
$$4 = 3 \text{ ways} \qquad 1+3,3+1,2+2$$
$$10 = 3 \text{ ways} \qquad 4+6,6+4,5+5$$

There are 6 ways to make a 7 and only 3 ways to make a 4 or 10, so the true odds are 6-to-3, which is the same as 2-to-1;

$$7 = 6 \text{ ways} \qquad 1+6,6+1,2+5,5+2,3+4,4+3$$
$$5 = 4 \text{ ways} \qquad 1+4,4+1,2+3,3+2$$
$$9 = 4 \text{ ways} \qquad 3+6,6+3,4+5,5+4$$

and finally, there are 6 ways to make a 7, but just 4 ways to make a 5 or 9, so the true odds here are 6-to-4 which is the same as 3-to-2.

It's important that you remember these numbers, because 1.- you want to make sure that you're paid the right amount when you do win and 2.- you want to make sure that when you make your odds bets you make them in amounts that are paid off evenly.

As an example, if your point is 5 and you have $5 on the pass line, you wouldn't want to bet $5 behind the line because at 3-to-2 odds the casino would have to pay you $7.50 and they don't deal in change. When making the odds bet on the 5 or 9 you should always bet in even amounts and in the situation just mentioned most casinos would allow you to add an extra $1 so you would have $6 out and they could pay you $9, if you won. The only other situation where this occurs is on the 6 and 8 where the payoff is 6-to-5. So, in that instance you want to make your bets in multiples of $5. Also, if your pass line bet is $15, most casinos will allow you to bet $25 behind the line because, if you win, it's quicker for them to pay you $30, rather than dealing in $1 chips to give you $18 for $15. When situations like this exist, it's good to take advantage of them and bet the full amount you're allowed because that helps to lower the casino edge even more.

We've spent all this time talking about pass line betting, so what about don't pass betting? Well, everything applied to pass line betting works pretty much just the opposite for don't pass betting. If you put $10 on don't pass you would win on the come out roll if the shooter rolled a 2 or 3, you would tie if the shooter rolled a 12, and you would lose if the shooter rolled a 7 or 11. If any other number comes up then that becomes the shooter's point number and if he rolls a 7 before he rolls that same point number, you will win. If he rolls his point number before he rolls a 7, you will lose.

Don't pass bettors are also allowed to make free odds bets to back up their original bets, however, because the odds are in their favor they must lay odds rather than take odds. This means that if the point is 4 or 10, the don't pass bettor must lay 2-to-1, or bet $10 to win $5; on 5 or 9 he must lay 3-to-2, or bet $6 to win $4; and on 6 or 8 he must lay 6-to-5, or bet $6 to win $5. By taking advantage of these free odds bets the casino advantage is slightly lowered on the total don't pass bets to .68% with single odds; .46% with double odds; .34% with triple odds and .12% with 10 times odds. If you want to you can remove, or reduce the amount of your free odds, bet at any time. To make a free odds bet on don't pass you should place your odds bet right next to your original bet and then put a chip on top to connect the two bets. Keep in mind that when you make a free odds bet on don't pass the casino will allow you to make your bet based on the payoff, rather than the original amount of your don't pass bet. In other words, if the casino offered double odds, the point was 4 and you had $10 on don't pass, you would be allowed to bet $40 because you would only win $20 which was double the amount of your original $10 bet. Since you have to put out more money than you'll be getting back, laying odds is not very popular at the craps table and you'll find that the vast majority of craps players would rather bet with the shooter and take the odds. Statistically speaking, it makes no difference whether you are laying or taking the odds because they both have a zero advantage for the house.

One last point about don't pass betting is that once the point is established, the casino will allow you to remove your don't pass bet if you want to - but don't do it! As noted before, on the come out roll the pass line bettor has the advantage because there are 8 rolls that can win and only 4 that can lose, but once the point is established, there are more ways the shooter can lose than win, so at that point the don't pass bettor has the advantage and it would be foolish to remove your bet.

Now, let's take a look at the area marked come and don't come. Since you already know how to bet pass and don't pass, you should easily understand come and don't come because they're the exact same bets as pass and don't pass, except for the fact that you bet them after the point has already been established.

Let's say that the shooter's point is 6 and you make a come bet by putting a $5 chip anywhere in the come box. Well, that's just like making a pass line bet, except that the shooter's next roll becomes the come-out roll for your bet. If the shooter rolls a 7 or 11, you win. If a 2, 3, or 12 is rolled you lose, and if anything else comes up then that becomes your point and the shooter must roll that number again before rolling a 7 in order for you to win. In this example if the shooter rolled a 4 the dealer would move your $5 come bet up into the center of the 4 box and it would stay there until either a 4 was rolled, which would make you a winner, or a 7 was rolled which would make you a loser. The house edge on a come bet is the same 1.41% as on a pass line bet. You are allowed free odds on your come bet and you make that bet by giving your chips to the dealer and telling him you want to take the odds. The dealer will then place those chips slightly off center on top of your come bet to show that it's a free odds bet. By the way, if you win, the dealer will put your winnings back in the come bet area so be sure to pick them up off the table or else it will be considered a new come bet.

One other point to note here is that when you make a come bet your bet is always working on every roll, even a come-out roll. However, when you take the odds on your come bets they are never working on the come-out roll. That may sound a little confusing, but here's what it means. In our example the shooter's initial point was 6 and then we made a $5 come bet. The shooter then rolled a 4 which became the point for our come bet. The dealer then moved our $5 come bet to the middle of the 4 box at the top of the table. We then gave $10 to the dealer and said we wanted to take the odds on the 4. On the next roll the shooter rolls a 6 which means he made a pass by rolling his original point number. The next roll will then become the shooter's come-out roll and the odds bet on our 4 will not be working. If the shooter rolls a 7 the pass line bettors will win and we will lose our $5 come bet because he rolled a 7 before rolling a 4. The dealer will then return our $10 odds bet because it wasn't working on the come-out roll. Now, if you want to, you can request that your odds bet be working on the come-out roll by telling the dealer. Then he'll put a marker on top of your bet to show that your odds bet is in effect on the come-out roll.

Naturally, don't come betting is the same as don't pass betting, except again for the fact that the bet isn't made until after the point is established. In this case let's say the point is 5 and you make a don't come bet by placing a $5 chip in the don't come box. Well, once again, that's just like making a don't pass bet except that the shooter's next roll becomes the come-out roll for your bet. If the shooter rolls a 2 or 3, you win. If a 7 or 11 is rolled, you lose. If a 12 is rolled it's a standoff and if anything else comes up then that becomes your point and the shooter must seven-out, or roll a 7, before rolling that point number again in order for you to win. In this example if the shooter rolled a 10 the dealer would move your $5 don't come bet into the upper part of the 10 box and it would stay there until either a 7 was rolled, which would make you a winner, or a 10 was rolled which would make you a loser. The house edge on a don't come bet is the same 1.40% as on a don't pass bet and you can make a free odds bet on your don't come bet by giving your chips to the dealer and telling him you want to lay the odds. The dealer will then place those chips next to and on top of your don't come bet to show that it's a free odds bet. The final point to note here is that don't come bets, as well as the free odds bets on them, are always working - even on the come-out roll.

Now let's talk about place betting and that refers to the 6 numbers you see in the area at the top of the table: 4,5,6,8,9 and 10. Anytime during a roll you can make a bet that one of those numbers will appear before a 7 and if it does you will receive a payoff that is slightly less than the true odds. For example: the true odds are 2-to-1 that a 4 or 10 will appear before a 7. However, if you make a place bet on the 4 or 10 you will only be paid off at 9-to-5 and that works out to a casino advantage of 6.67%

The true odds of a 5 or 9 appearing before a 7 are 3-to-2, but on a place bet you would only receive a payoff of 7-to-5 which works out to a casino edge of 4.0%. Finally, on the 6 and 8 the true odds are 6-to-5 that one of those numbers will appear before a 7, but on a place bet you would only be paid off at 7-to-6 which means the casino would have an edge of 1.52% on this bet.

As you can see, making a place bet on the 6 or 8 gives the casino its lowest edge and this means that a place bet on the 6 or 8 is one of the best bets you will find on the craps table.

When you want to make a place bet you aren't allowed to put the bet down yourself, you have to let the dealer do it for you. To do this you would just drop your chips down onto the table and tell the dealer what bet you wanted to make. For example you could put three $5 chips down and say "Place the 4,5 and 9." The dealer would then put $5 on the edge of the 4 box, $5 on the edge of the 5 box and $5 on the edge of the 9 box. You'll notice that when the dealer puts your bets on the edge of the boxes they will always be placed in an area that corresponds to where you're standing at the table and this helps the dealer to remember who placed that bet.

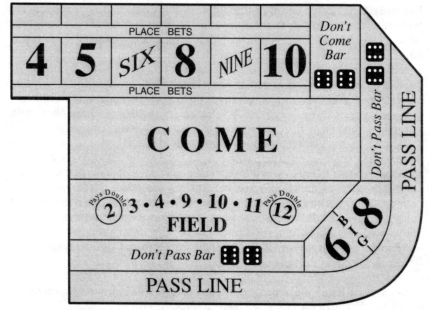

Enlargement of right side of craps layout

When making a place bet you don't have to bet more than one number and you don't have to bet the same amount on each number. You should, however, make sure that you always bet in multiples of $5 whenever you bet on the 4,5,9 or 10 and in multiples of $6 whenever you bet the 6 and 8. This will allow you to always get the full payoff on your bet. If, for example, you bet $3 on the 6 and you won you would only get back even-money, or $3, rather than the $3.50 which your bet should have paid and this results in an even bigger advantage for the casino. Another thing about place bets is that, unlike pass line bets, you can remove your place bets at any time and you do that by telling the dealer you want your bet down and he will take your chips off the table and return them to you. You could also tell the dealer that you didn't want your bet to be working on any particular roll or rolls and you do this by saying for example "off on the 5." The dealer would then put a little button on top of your bet that said "off" and he would remove it when you told him you wanted that number working again.

When we spoke about come bets before I mentioned that come bets are always working on every roll, but that's not the case with place bets because place bets are never working on the come-out roll. If you wanted to, however, you could ask for your place bet to be working on the come out roll by telling the dealer you wanted it working and he would place a button on top of your bet that said "on" to show that your bet was working on the come-out roll.

One last point about place bets is that when you win the dealer will want to know what you want to do for your next bet and you have three choices: if you want to make the same bet just say "same bet" and the dealer will give you your winning chips and leave your original place bet on the table. If you don't want to bet again, just say "take it down" and the dealer will return your place bet along with your winnings. And if you want to double your bet just say "press it" and the dealer will add your winning chips to your other place bet and return any extra chips to you. For example, if you won a $10 place bet on the 5 the dealer would have to give you back $14 in winning chips. If you said "press it" the dealer would add $10 to your place bet and return the remaining $4 in chips to you.

Besides, place betting there is also another way to bet that one of the point numbers will show up before a 7 does and that's called buying a number. A buy bet is basically the same as a place bet except you have to pay a commission of 5% of the amount of your bet and then if you win, the casino will pay you at the true odds. When making a buy bet you should always remember to bet at least $20 because 5% of $20 is $1 and that's the minimum amount the casino will charge you. The reason for the $1 minimum is because that's the smallest denomination chip they have at the craps table and they won't make change for anything under $1. The casino edge on any buy bet for $20 works out to 4.76% so let's take a look at a chart that shows the difference between buying and placing the point numbers.

Point Number	Casino Edge Buy Bet	Casino Edge Place Bet
4 or 10	4.76%	6.67%
5 or 9	4.76%	4.00%
6 or 8	4.76%	1.52%

As you can see the only numbers that you would want to buy rather than place are the 4 and 10 because the 4.76% edge on a buy bet is lower than the 6.67% edge on a place bet. For 5 and 9 the 4.76% edge on a buy bet is slightly worse than the 4.00% edge on a place bet and for the 6 and 8 the 4.76% is a hefty three times higher than the 1.52% edge on the place bet.

To buy the 4 or 10 you would just put your chips down on the layout and tell the dealer what bet you wanted to make. For example, if you put down $21 and said "buy the 10." The dealer will then keep the $1 chip for the house and put your $20 in the same area as the place bets but he'll put a button on top that says "buy" to let him know that you bought the number rather than placed it. Buy bets, just like place bets, can be removed at any time and are always off on the come-out roll. Also, if you do remove your buy bet you will get your 5% commission back.

Besides buy bets where you're betting with the shooter and hoping that a point number will appear before a 7 does, there are also lay bets where you're doing just the opposite - you're betting against the shooter and hoping that a 7 will appear before a point number does.

Lay bets are also paid at the true odds and you have to pay a 5% a commission of the amount you will win rather than the amount you're betting. Once again, when making a lay bet you should always remember to make them based on a minimum payoff of $20 because 5% of $20 is $1 and that's the minimum amount the casino will charge you.

Lay Number	Payoff	Casino Edge
4 or 10	$40 for $20	2.44%
5 or 9	$30 for $20	3.23%
6 or 8	$24 for $20	4.00%

For 4 and 10 you'll have to lay $40 to win $20 and the casino edge is 2.44%; for the 5 and 9 you'll have to lay $30 to win $20 and the casino edge is 3.23%; and for the 6 and 8 you'll have to lay $24 to win $20. The casino edge on that bet is 4.00%.

To make a lay bet you would just put your chips down on the layout and tell the dealer what you wanted to bet. For example, if you put down $41 and said "lay the 10." The dealer would then keep the $1 chip for the house and put your $40 in the same area as the don't come bets but he'll put a button on top that says "buy" to let him know that it's a lay bet. Lay bets, unlike buy bets, are always working on come-out rolls. Lay bets are, however, similar to buy bets in that they can be removed at any time and if you do remove your lay bet you will also receive your 5% commission back.

There are only a few other bets left located on the ends of the table to discuss and two of them are the big 6 and the big 8 which are both very bad bets. To bet the big 6 you place a chip in the big 6 box and then if the shooter rolls a 6 before rolling a 7 you win even money, or $1 for every $1 you bet. To bet the big 8 the same rules would apply: you put your bet in the box and then hope that the shooter rolls an 8 before rolling a 7 so you could win even money on your bet. The big 6 and big 8 can both be bet at any time and both are always working, even on the come-out roll. The casino edge on both the big 6 and the big 8 is 9.1%, which is the biggest edge we've seen so far. But, if you think back about some of the other bets we discussed doesn't this bet sound familiar? It should. This bet is the exact same as a place bet on the 6 or 8, but instead of getting paid off at 7-to-6 we're only getting paid off at even-money! Why would you want to bet the big 6 or big 8 at a house edge of more than 9% instead of making a place bet on the 6 or 8 at a house edge of only 1.5%? The answer is you wouldn't - so don't ever make this bet because it's a sucker bet that's only for people who don't know what they're doing.

The last bet we have to discuss on the player's side of the table is the field bet which is a one-roll bet that will pay even money if a 3,4,9,10 or 11 is rolled and 2-to-1 if a 2 or 12 is rolled. To make a field bet you would just place your chip anywhere in the field box and at first glance it doesn't seem like a bad bet. After all, there are 7 numbers you can win on and only 4 numbers you can lose on! The only problem is that there are 20 ways to roll the 4 losing numbers and only 16 ways to roll the 7 winning numbers and even after factoring in the double payoff for the 2 and 12 the casino winds up with a hefty 5.6% advantage. In some casinos they pay 3-to-1 on the 2 (or the 12) which cuts the casino edge in half to a more manageable 2.8%, but as you've seen there are still much better bets you can make. By the way, if you win on a field bet the dealer will put your winning chips right next to your bet so it's your responsibility to pick them up, or else they'll be considered a new bet!

Now, let's take a look at some of the long-shots, or proposition bets in the center of the table. When you look at these bets one of the first things you'll notice is that, unlike the bets on the other side of the table, the winning payoffs are clearly labeled. The reason they do that is so you can see those big payoffs and want to bet them, but as you'll see, although the payoffs are high, so are the casino advantages.

All of the proposition bets are controlled by the stickman and he is the person who must make those bets for you. So, if you wanted to make a $1 bet on "any craps" you would throw a $1 chip to the center of the table and say "$1 any craps" and the stickmen would place that bet in the proper area for you. Then if you won, the stickman would tell the dealer at your end of the table to pay you. You should also be aware that they will only pay you your winnings and keep your original bet in place. If you don't want to make the same bet again, you should tell the stickman that you want your bet down and it will be returned to you.

There are only four proposition bets that are not one-roll bets and they are known as the "hardways." They are the hard 4, hard 6, hard 8 and hard 10. To roll a number the hardway means that the number must be rolled as doubles. For example 3 and 3 is a hard 6, but a roll of 4-2, or 5-1 are both called an easy 6, because they are easier to roll than double 3's.

To win a bet on hard 10 the shooter has to roll two 5's before rolling a 7 or an easy 10 such as 6-4 or 4-6. To win a bet on hard 4 the shooter has to roll two 2's before rolling a 7 or an easy 4 such as 3-1 or 1-3. The true odds of rolling a hard 4 or hard 10 are 8-to-1, but the casino will only pay you 7-to-1 which works out to a casino advantage of 11.1% on both of these bets.

To win a bet on hard 6 the shooter must roll two 3's before rolling a 7 or an easy 6 such as 5-1, 1-5; or 4-2, 2-4. To win a bet on hard 8 the shooter must roll two 4's before rolling a 7 or an easy 8 such as 6-2, 2-6 or 5-3, 3-5. The true odds of rolling a hard 6 or hard 8 are 10-to-1, but the casino will only pay you 9-to-1 which works out to a casino advantage of 9.1% on both of these bets.

As noted before, all of the other proposition bets are one-roll bets which means that the next roll of the dice will decide whether you win or lose. As you'll see, the house edge on all of these bets is very high and they should all be avoided.

Two different types of proposition bets layouts

For the any craps bet you will win if a 2,3,or 12 is thrown on the next roll and lose if any other number comes up. The true odds are 8-to-1 but the casino will only pay you at 7-to-1 which gives them an edge of 11.1% on this bet and you'll notice that the stickman can put your bet either in the any craps box or, more likely, he'll put it on the circled marked "C" which stands for craps. The reason your bet will be placed in the "C" circle is that it's put in the circle that corresponds to where you're standing at the table and it makes it easier for the stickman to know who that bet belongs to.

For a craps 2 bet you win if the next roll is a 2 and lose if any other number shows up. The true odds are 35-to-1 but the casino will only pay you 30-to-1 which means that the edge on this bet is 13.9% In some casinos the odds for this bet will be shown as 30-for-1 which is actually the same as 29-to-1 and this results in an even bigger edge of 16.7% for the casino

A craps 12 bet works the same as a craps 2 bet, except that now you will only win if a 12 is thrown. Again, the true odds are 35-to-1 but you will only be paid at 30-to-1 which means the casino edge on this bet is the same 13.9% as in the last craps 2 bet. Also if the bet is shown on the layout as 30-for-1 the casino edge is raised to 16.7%

For a craps 3 bet you will only win if the next throw is a 3. The true odds are 17-to-1, but the casino will only pay you 15-to-1 which results in a casino advantage of 11.1% Once again, in some casinos the payoff will be shown as 15-for-1 which is the same as 14-to-1 and the house edge in that casino is an even higher 16.7%

The 11 bet is similar to the craps 3 bet, except that now the only number you can win on is 11. The true odds of rolling an 11 are 17-to-1, but the casino will only pay you 15-to-1 which gives them an 11.1% advantage. Additionally, if the payoff is shown on the layout as 15-for-1 rather than 15-to-1 the casino edge will be even higher at 16.7% By the way, because 11 sounds so much like 7 you will always hear 11 referred to at the table as "yo" or "yo-leven" to eliminate any confusion as to what number you are referring to. So, if you wanted to bet $5 on 11 you would throw a $5 chip to the stickman and say "$5 yo" and then he will either place it in the 11 box or place it on top of the "E" circle that corresponds to where you're standing at the table.

With a horn bet you are betting on the 2,3,11 and 12 all at once. A horn bet has to be made in multiples of $4 because you're making 4 bets at one time and you'll win if any one of those 4 numbers shows up on the next roll. You'll be paid off at the odds for the number that came in and you'll lose the rest of your chips. For example, if you make an $8 horn bet, this is the same as betting $2 on the 2, $2 on the 3, $2 on the 11 and $2 on the 12. If the number 2 came in you would get paid off at 30-to-1 so you would get back $60 in winnings and the casino would keep the $6 that you lost for the three $2 bets on the 3,11 and 12. The only advantage of a horn bet is that it allows you to make 4 bad bets at once rather than one at a time.

The last proposition bet we have to look at is also the worst bet on the craps table and it's the any 7 bet. With this bet you win if a 7 is rolled and lose if any other number comes up. The true odds are 5-to-1, but the casino will only pay you at 4-to-1 which gives them an edge of 16.7%

So there you have it! We've gone over all the possible bets you can make and now it's time to tell you how to win at the game of craps. Unfortunately, as you've seen, craps is a negative expectation game which means that every bet you make has a built-in advantage for the house. Actually, there is one bet that the casino has no advantage on and do you remember the name of that one? That's right it's the free odds bet and it's great that the casino has no advantage on that bet but the only way you're allowed to make that bet is to first make a negative expectation bet on pass/don't pass or come/don't come, so in essence, there are no bets you can make where you have an advantage over the house and in the long run the game of craps is unbeatable.

So, if that's the case then how do you win? Well, in reality there is only one way to win in craps and that way is to get lucky! Of course, this is easier said than done, but you will find it much easier to come out a winner if you only stick to the bets that offer the casino its lowest edge and those are the only bets you should ever make.

If you want to bet with the shooter I suggest you make a pass line bet, back it up with the free odds and then make a maximum of two come bets that are also both backed up with free odds. For example if double odds are allowed, you could start with a $5 pass line bet and say a 4 is rolled. You would then put $10 behind the line on your 4 and make a $5 come bet. If the shooter then rolled an 8 you would take $10 in odds on your come bet on the 8 and make another $5 come bet. If the shooter then rolled a 5 you would take $10 in odds on your come bet on the 5 and then stop betting. The idea here is that you always want to have a maximum of three numbers working and once you do, you shouldn't make anymore bets until one of your come numbers hits, in which case you would make another come bet, or if your pass line bet wins and then you would follow that up with another pass line bet. The important thing to remember is not to make more than two come bets because you don't want to have too much out on the table if the shooter rolls a 7. By using this betting system you'll only be giving the casino an edge of around .60% on all of your bets and with just a little bit of luck you can easily walk away a winner.

If you wanted to be a little more aggressive with this betting system there are some modifications you could make such as making a maximum of three come bets rather than two, or you could add place bets on the 6 and 8. Remember that a place bet on either the 6 or 8 only gives the casino a 1.52% advantage and that makes them both the next best bets after pass/don't pass and come/don't come. To add the place bets you would start off the same as before, but after you've made your second come bet you would look at the 6 and 8 and if they weren't covered you would then make a $6 place bet on whichever one was open or on both. By adding the place bets on the 6 and 8 you would always have at least three numbers in action and you could have as many as five covered at one time.

One final option with this system is to gradually increase the amount of your pass line and come bets by 50%, or by doubling them, and then backing them up with full odds, but I would only suggest you do this if you've been winning for a while because it could get very expensive if the table was cold and no one was rolling many numbers. Of course, if the table got real cold you could always change your strategy by betting against the shooter and the strategy for that is basically just the opposite of the one I just told you about.

To bet against the shooter you would start with a $5 don't pass bet which you would back up with single free odds and then bet a maximum of two don't come bets that are both backed up with single odds. The reason you don't want to back up your bets with double odds is because when you're betting against the shooter you have to lay the odds which means you're putting up more money than you'll be getting back and, once again, it could get very expensive if a shooter got on a hot roll and made quite a few passes.

For an example of this system let's say you start with a $5 don't pass bet and a 4 is rolled. You would then lay the odds by putting $10 next to your $5 don't pass bet and then make a $5 don't come bet. If the shooter then rolled an 8 you would lay $6 in odds on your don't come bet on the 8 and make another $5 don't come bet. If the shooter then rolled a 5 you would lay $9 in odds on your come bet on the 5 and then stop betting. The idea here is that you always want to have a maximum of three numbers working and once you do that, you shouldn't make anymore bets until, hopefully, the shooter sevens out and all of your bets win. If that does happen, then you would start all over again with a new don't pass bet. Once again, the important thing to remember is not to make more than two don't come bets because you don't want to have too much out on the table if the shooter gets hot and starts to roll a lot of numbers. With this system you'll always have a maximum of three numbers in action and you'll only be giving the casino an edge of about .80% on all of your bets. Some options to bet more aggressively with this system are to increase your free odds bets to double odds rather than single odds and also to make three don't come bets, rather than stopping at two. The choice is up to you but remember that because you must lay the odds and put out more money than you'll be getting back you could lose a substantial amount rather quickly if the roller got hot and made a lot of point numbers.

Now, one last point I want to make about betting craps is that the bankroll you'll need is going to be much bigger than the bankroll you'll need for playing any other casino game. If you're betting with the shooter you'll have one $5 pass line bet with double odds and two come bets with double odds which means that you could have as much as $45 on the table that could be wiped out with the roll of a 7. If you're betting against the shooter you'll have $5 on don't pass with single odds and two don't come bets with single odds which means you could have as much as $44 on the table that could be wiped out if the shooter got on a "hot" roll and made a lot of numbers. As I said before, you need to have an adequate bankroll to be able to ride out the losing streaks that will eventually occur and you need to be able to hold on until things turn around and you start to win.

So how much of a bankroll is enough? Well, I would say about 7 times the maximum amount of money you'll have out on the table is adequate and 10 times would be even better. In both of our examples then you should have a bankroll of at least $300. If you don't have that much money to put out on the table then you might want to consider having less money out on the table by making only one come or don't come bet rather than two or maybe even just limiting your bets to pass and don't pass along with the free odds.

Just remember that it doesn't matter whether you want to bet with the shooter or against the shooter - both of these systems will give you the best chance of winning because they allow the casino only the slightest edge and with a little bit of luck you can easily come out a winner. Good luck!

Roulette

by Steve Bourie

Virtually all American casinos use a double-zero roulette wheel which has pockets numbered from 1 to 36, plus 0 and 00 for a total of 38 pockets. This is in contrast to Europe where a single-zero wheel is used and the game has always been the most popular in the casino.

There are usually six seats at the roulette table and to help the dealer differentiate what each player is betting every player is assigned a different color chip which they purchase right at the table. Each table has its own minimum chip values and that information is usually posted on a sign at the table. As an example let's say a table has a $1 minimum chip value. This means that when you give the dealer your money the colored chips he gives you in return must have a minimum value of $1 each. So, if you gave the dealer $50 he would ask what value you wanted on the chips and if you said $1 he would give you 50 colored chips.

If you prefer, you could say you wanted the chips valued at $2 each and he would just give you 25 chips rather than 50. You can make the value of your colored chips anything you want and you'll notice that when the dealer gives you your chips he'll put one of your chips on the railing near the wheel with a marker on top to let him know the value of your chips. Later on when you're done playing at that table you must exchange your colored chips for regular chips before leaving. The colored chips have no value anywhere else in the casino so don't leave the table with them.

Besides the minimum chip value, there is also a minimum amount that must be bet on each spin of the wheel. Once again, the minimums are probably posted on a sign at the table. If it says $2 minimum inside/$5 minimum outside this means that when betting on any of the 38 numbers that pay 35-to-1 the total of all your bets must be $2. You could make two different $1 bets or one $2 bet, it doesn't matter except that the total of all your bets on the numbers must be at least $2. The $5 minimum outside means that any of the outside bets that pay 2-to-1, or even money, require that you bet $5 each time. On the outside bets you can't make a $3 bet and a $2 bet to meet the minimums - you have to bet at least $5 every time. After you've exchanged your cash for colored chips you're ready to place your first bet so, let's see what your options are:

You can make a *straight* bet where you only bet on one number and if it comes in you'll be paid 35-to-1. The casino advantage on this bet is 5.26% and by the time you're done with this roulette section I'm sure you'll be very familiar with that number.

Another choice you have is to do a *split*. This is where you put a chip on the line that separates two numbers. If either number comes up you'll be paid at 17-to-1. The casino advantage on this bet is 5.26%.

If you put a chip in an area that splits 4 numbers this is called a ***corner*** bet and if any one of those 4 numbers comes in you will be paid off at 8-to-1. The casino advantage on this bet is 5.26%.

If you put a chip at the beginning of a row of 3 numbers, this is called a ***street*** bet and if any one of those 3 numbers shows up you will be paid off at 11-to-1. The casino advantage on this bet is 5.26%.

You can also put a chip on the line between two streets so that you have a ***double street*** covered and if any one of those 6 numbers come in you'll be paid off at 5-to-1. The casino advantage on this bet is?... you guessed it...5.26%.

The only other bet you can make on the inside numbers is the ***5- number*** bet where you place one chip in the upper left corner of the number 1 box. If any one of those 5 numbers comes in you'll be paid off at 6-to-1 and what do you think the casino advantage is on this bet? Nope, I gotcha... it's 7.89%. Actually, this is the worst possible bet on the roulette table and the only bet you'll come across that doesn't have a 5.26% house edge on the double-zero roulette wheel. You should never make this bet.

One quick word here about "to" and "for" when discussing odds. Whenever the odds are stated as "to" this means that in addition to the stated payoff you also receive your original bet back. In other words, if you won your single number bet in roulette you would receive 35-to-1, which is a 35-chip payoff, plus you'd still keep your original one-chip bet, so you end up with 36 chips. Now if the odds are stated as "for" that means you do not receive back your original bet. If the odds in your single number bet were 35-*for*-1 you would still receive a 35-chip payoff but the casino would keep your original one-chip bet so you would only end up with 35 chips. The only place in a casino where the odds are always stated as "for" is in video poker. You might also come across it on a couple of craps bets where the odds are stated as "for-one" rather than "to-one" in order to give the casino a slightly better edge.

Now, getting back to our roulette examples, let's look at all of the outside bets that you can make and keep in mind that the house edge on all of these outside bets is...do you remember the number?...that's right...5.26%.

There are three bets you can make that will pay you even money, or 1-to-1, which means that if you win, you will get back one dollar for every dollar you bet:

Red or black - If you put a chip on red then a red number must come up in order for you to win. If the ball lands on a black number, 0 or 00 - you lose. The same thing goes for black - you lose if it comes in red, 0 or 00 and you win if the ball lands on a black number.

Odd or even - If you put a chip on odd then the ball must land on an odd number in order for you to win. If it lands on 0, 00, or an even number - you lose. If you bet on even, you win if an even number shows up and lose if the ball lands on 0, 00 or an odd number.

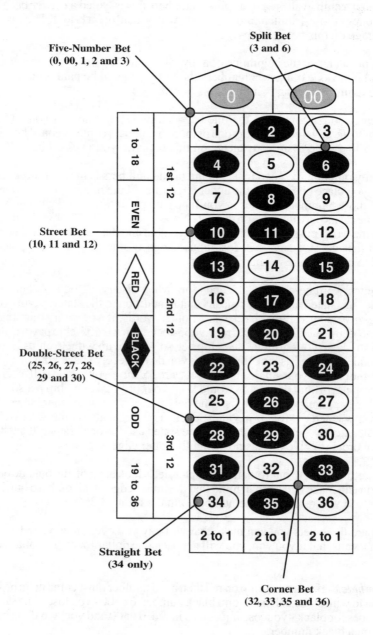

Typical felt layout for placing bets on American double-zero roulette wheel

1 through 18 and 19 through 36 - If you bet on 1 through 18, then you win if a number from 1 through 18 comes in and you lose if the ball lands on 0, 00 or a number higher than 18. Similarly, if you bet on 19 through 36, you win if one of those numbers comes in and you lose on 0, 00 or any number lower than 19.

The only other bets left are the *dozens* and columns bets. If you look at the roulette betting layout you can see three areas that each correspond to 12-number sections on the table. The one marked 1st 12 covers the numbers from 1 to 12, the one marked 2nd 12 covers the numbers from 13 to 24 and the other one that's marked 3rd 12 covers the last section of numbers from 25 to 36. If you bet on the 1st 12 you would win if a number from 1 to 12 came in and you would lose if anything else came in, including 0 or 00. The same principle holds true for each of the other dozen bets where you would win if a number in that section came in and you would lose if anything else showed up. All dozens bets pay 2-to-1.

The last bet to look at is the *column* bet and that is also a bet that pays 2-to-1. There are three possible column bets you can make and you'll notice that each area corresponds to the numbers in the column directly above it. So, if you put a chip under the first column you will win if any of the numbers in that column come in and you will lose if any other number, including 0 or 00 shows up. Once again, the same rule is in effect for each of the other columns where you would win if the number appears in the column above your bet and you would lose if it doesn't.

All right, now you know all the possible bets and you know how to make them at the table. So, the next question is "How do you win?" and the answer to that is very simple - You have to get lucky! And that's the ONLY way you can win at roulette. As you found out earlier, every bet, except for the 5-number bet, which I'm sure you'll never make, has a house edge of?...that's right...5.26%. So, feel free to put your chips all over the table and then just hope that you're lucky enough to have one of your numbers come up. You see, it just doesn't matter what you do because you'll always have that same house edge of 5.26% working against you on every bet you make.

Now, you may have heard of a system for roulette where you should place your bets only on the numbers that are evenly spaced out around the wheel. For example, if you wanted to play only four numbers, you could bet on 1, 2, 31 and 32 because when you looked at a roulette wheel, you would notice that if you divided it into four equal parts, you would have a number that appears in each of the four sections. So, is this a good system? Well, actually it's no better and no worse than any other roulette system. The fact is that it's purely a matter of chance where the ball happens to land and it makes no difference whether the numbers you choose are right next to each other or evenly spaced out on the wheel. Each number has an equal chance to occur on every spin of the wheel and the house edge always remains at 5.26%.

You can probably tell that I wouldn't recommend roulette as a good game to play because there are other games that offer much better odds, but if you really insist on playing the game I have three good suggestions for you. #1 - Go to Atlantic City! In Atlantic City if you make an even-money outside bet, like red or black, odd or even, 1 through 18 or 19 through 36 and if 0 or 00 come up, the state gaming regulations allow the casino to take only half of your bet. Because you only lose half of your bet this also lowers the casino edge on these outside bets in half to 2.63%. This rule is only in effect for even-money bets so keep in mind that on all other bets the house edge still remains at that very high 5.26%.

The second suggestion I have for you also involves some travel and here it is: Go to Europe! The game of roulette began in Europe and many casinos over there use a single-zero wheel which makes it a much better game because the house edge on a single-zero roulette wheel is only 2.70%. To make it even better, they have a rule called "en prison" which is similar to the Atlantic City casino rule. If you make an even-money outside bet and the ball lands on 0 you don't lose right away. Instead, your bet is "imprisoned" and you have to let it ride on the next spin. Then, if your bet wins, you can remove it from the table. Because of this rule, the casino edge on this bet is cut in half to 1.35% which makes it one of the best bets in the casino and almost four times better than the same bet when it's made on a standard double-zero roulette wheel in the United States.

Now, if you're not into traveling and you don't think you can make it to Atlantic City or Europe, then you'll just have to settle for suggestion #3 which is: Win quickly! Naturally, this is easier said than done, but in reality, if you want to win at roulette the best suggestion I can give you is that you try to win quickly and then walk away from the table because the longer you continue to bet the longer that big 5.26% house edge will keep eating away at your bankroll. One major principle of gambling is that in order to win you must only play the games that have the lowest casino edge and, unfortunately, roulette is not one of them.

Before closing out this look at roulette, let's take a minute to examine one of the most famous betting systems of all time and the one that many people frequently like to use on roulette. It's called the Martingale system and it is basically a simple system of doubling your bet whenever you lose. The theory behind it is that sooner or later you'll have to win and thus, you will always come out ahead. As an example, let's say you're playing roulette and you bet $1 on red, if you lose you double your next bet to $2 and if you lose that then you double your next bet to $4 and if you lose that you double your next bet to $8 and so forth until you eventually win. Now, when you finally do win you will end up with a profit equal to your original bet, which in this case is $1. If you started the same system with a $5 bet, you would have to bet $10 after your first loss, $20 after your second loss and so forth, but whenever you won you would end up with a $5 profit.

In theory, this sounds like a good idea but in reality it's a terrible system because eventually you will be forced to risk a great amount of money for a very small profit. Let's face it, even if you only wanted to make a $1 profit on each spin of the wheel, sooner or later you will hit a major losing streak where you will have to bet an awful lot of money just to make that $1 profit. For example, if you go eight spins without a winner, you would have to bet $256 on the next spin and if that lost then you'd have to bet $512. Would you really want to risk that kind of money just to make $1? I don't think so. You may think that the odds are highly unlikely that you would lose that many bets in a row, but eventually it will happen and when it does you will suffer some astronomical losses. One other problem with this system is that eventually you won't be able to double your bet because you will have reached the casino maximum, which in most casinos is $500 on roulette. Just keep in mind that the Martingale system works best when it's played for fun on paper and not for real money in a casino. If it was truly a winning system it would have bankrupted the world's casinos years ago.

Baccarat

by Steve Bourie

When you think of Baccarat you probably think of a game that's played by the casino's wealthiest players who sit at a private table and can afford to bet tens of thousands of dollars on the flip of a card and you know what? You're right! The game of Baccarat has always had a reputation as being for the richest gamblers and that usually scared off the average player, but nowadays more and more people are discovering that Baccarat is really a good game for the small stakes player because 1.-it has a relatively small advantage for the casino and 2.-it's very simple to play.

The mini-Baccarat table is the kind of Baccarat table you're most likely to find in the standard American casino and the game is played pretty much the same as regular Baccarat except that in the mini version all of the hands are dealt out by the dealer and the players never touch the cards. Other than that, the rules are virtually the same. Oh yes, one other difference you'll find is that the betting minimums will always be lower on mini-Baccarat and it's usually pretty easy to find a table with a $5 minimum.

Now, as noted before, the game of Baccarat is very simple to play and that's because the only decision you have to make is what bet you want to make from the three that are available: player, banker or tie. After the players make their bets the game begins and two 2-card hands are dealt from a shoe that contains 8 decks of cards. One hand is dealt for the banker and another hand is dealt for the player. The values of the two cards in each hand are added together and the object of the game is to have a total as close to 9 as possible. After the values of the first two cards in each hand are totaled, a third card can be drawn by either the player, the banker or both. But, the decision as to whether or not a third card should be drawn is not decided by the dealer or the players - it is only decided by the rules of the game.

Actually the name Baccarat comes from the Italian word for zero and as you'll see there are lots of zeros in this game because when you add the cards together all of the 10's and all of the face cards are counted as zeros, while all of the other cards from ace though 9 are counted at their face value. So, a hand of Jack, 6 has a total of 6; 10,4 has a total of 4; king, 7 has a total of 7; and ace, queen which would be a great hand in blackjack, only has a total of 1. The other thing about adding the cards together is that no total can be higher than 9. So, if a total is 10 or higher you have to subtract 10 to determine its value. For example, 8,8 totals 16 but you subtract 10 and your total is 6; 9,5 has a total of 4; 8,3 has a total of 1; and 5,5 has a total of 0.

Once again, the object of the game of Baccarat is to have a total as close to 9 as possible, so after the first two cards are dealt if either the player or banker hand has a total of 9 then that's called a "natural" and that hand is the winner. If neither hand has a total of 9 then the next best possible hand is a total of 8 (which is also called a "natural") and that hand would be the winner. If both the player and the banker end up with the same total then it's a tie and neither hand wins.

Now, if neither hand has an 8 or a 9 then the rules of the game have to be consulted to decide whether or not a third card is drawn. Once that's done, the values of the cards are added together again and whichever hand is closest to a total of 9 is the winner. If both hands end up with the same total then it's a tie and neither hand wins.

If you want to bet on the player hand just put your money in the area marked "player" and if you win you'll be paid off at even-money, or $1 for every $1 you bet. The casino advantage on the player bet is 1.36%. If you want to bet on the banker hand you would place your bet in the area marked "banker" and if you win, you'll also be paid off at even-money, but you'll have to pay a 5% commission on the amount you win. So, if you won $10 on your bet, you would owe a 50¢ commission to the house. The 5% commission is only required if you win and not if you lose. The dealer will keep track of the amount you owe by putting an equal amount in a small area on the table that corresponds to your seat number at the table. So, if you're sitting at seat #3 and won $10 on the bank hand the dealer would pay you $10 and then put 50¢ in the #3 box. This lets him know how much you owe the casino in commissions and when you get up to leave the table you'll have to pay the dealer whatever amount is in that box. After adjusting for that 5% commission the casino advantage on the banker bet is 1.17%

Finally, if you want to bet on a tie you would place your bet in the area marked "tie" and if you win you'll be paid off at 8-to-1, or $8 for every $1 you bet. The big payoff sounds nice but actually this is a terrible bet because the casino advantage is a very high 14.1% and this bet should never be made.

As you've seen, the casino advantage in Baccarat is very low (except for the tie bet) and the rules are set in advance so no decisions are made by either the players or the dealer about how to play the cards. This means that, unlike blackjack where you have to decide whether or not you want another card, you have no decisions to make and no skill is involved. This also means that Baccarat is purely a guessing game, so even if you've never played the game before you can sit at a table and play just as well as anyone who's played the game for 20 years! This is the only game in the casino where this can happen and that's why I tell people that Baccarat is an especially good game for the beginning player because you need no special knowledge to take advantage of those low casino edge bets.

The only part of Baccarat that gets a little confusing is trying to understand the rules concerning the draw of a third card, but remember, the rules are always the same at every table and they'll usually have a printed copy of the rules at

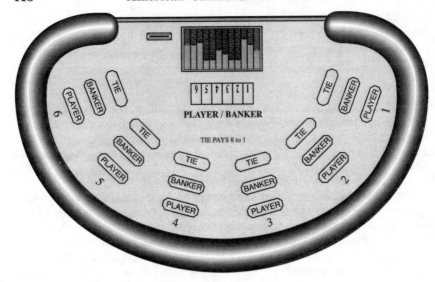

A Sample Mini-Baccarat Table Layout

the table and will give you a copy if you ask for it. After playing the game for awhile you'll start to remember the rules on your own, but until then here's a rundown on how it works:

As noted before, if the first two cards in either hand total 8 or 9, then the game is over and the highest total wins. If the totals are both 8 or both 9 then it's a tie and neither hand wins. For any other total the rules have to be consulted and it's always the player hand that goes first. If the player hand has a total of 6 or 7, it must stand. The only other totals it can possibly have are 0,1,2,3,4 or 5 and for all of those totals it must draw a card.

PLAYER HAND RULES

8,9	STANDS (Natural)
6,7	STANDS
0,1,2,3,4,5	DRAWS

There, that wasn't too hard to understand was it? If the player hand has a total of 6 or 7 it stands and for anything else it has to draw a card. Well, that was the easy part because now it gets a little complicated.

After the player hand is finished the banker hand must take its turn and if its first 2 cards total 0,1 or 2 it must draw a card. If its two cards total 7 it must stand and if the total is 6 it will stand, but only if the player hand did not take a card.

BANK HAND RULES

8,9	STANDS (Natural)
0,1,2	DRAWS
6	STANDS (If player took no card)
7	STANDS

The only other possible totals the bank can have are 3,4,5 or 6 and the decision as to whether or not a 3rd card is drawn depends on the 3rd card that was drawn by the player hand.

When the banker hand has a total of 3 it must stand if the player's 3rd card was an 8 and it must draw if the player's 3rd card was any other card.

IF BANK HAS 3 and
Player's third card is 8 - BANK STANDS
Player's third card is 1,2,3,4,5,6,7,9,10 - BANK DRAWS

When the banker hand has a total of 4 it must stand if the player's 3rd card was a 1,8,9, or 10 and it must draw if the player's 3rd card was any other card.

IF BANK HAS 4 and
Player's third card is 1,8,9,10 - BANK STANDS
Player's third card is 2,3,4,5,6,7 - BANK DRAWS

When the banker hand has a total of 5 it must draw if the player's 3rd card was a 4,5,6 or 7 and it must stand if the player's 3rd card was any other card.

IF BANK HAS 5 and
Player's third card is 1,2,3,8,9,10 - BANK STANDS
Player's third card is 4,5,6,7 - BANK DRAWS

When the banker hand has a total of 6 it must draw if the player's 3rd card was a 6 or 7 and it must stand if the player's 3rd card was any other card.

IF BANK HAS 6 and
Player's third card is 1,2,3,4,5,8,9,10 - BANK STANDS
Player's third card is 6 or 7 - BANK DRAWS

There you have it - those are the rules of Baccarat concerning the draw of a third card. As you saw they were a little complicated, but remember that you don't have to memorize the rules yourself because the dealer will know them and play each hand by those rules, but you can always ask for a copy of the rules at the table to follow along.

Now let's try some sample hands: The player hand has queen,9 for a total of 9 and the banker hand has 4,4 for a total of 8. Which hand wins? Both hands are naturals, but the player hand total of 9 is higher than the banker hand total of 8, so the player hand is the winner.

If the player hand has 4,2 for a total of 6 and the banker hand has ace, jack which totals 1, what happens? The player hand must stand on its 6 and the banker hand must always draw when it has a total of 0,1 or 2. Let's say the bank draws a 7 and wins 7 to 6.

What happens when the player hand has king, 5 and the bank hand has 2,4? The player hand must draw and let's say it gets a 7 for a total of 2. The banker hand has a total of 6 and if it could stand on that total it would win because its 6 is higher than the 2 held by the player. Of course, if you were betting on banker that's exactly what you would want to happen but, unfortunately for you, the rules require the bank hand to draw another card whenever its first two cards total 6 and the third card drawn by the player is a 7. So now, instead of having a winning hand you have to hope that the card you draw isn't a 5, which would give you a total of 1 making you a loser. You also wouldn't want to draw a 6 because that would give you a total of 2 which would give you a tie. In this case let's say that the bank hand goes on to draw an 8 which gives it a total of 3 and it wins 3 to 2.

Baccarat Rules Summary

Player Hand
When the first
two cards total

0-1-2-3-4-5	**Draws**
6-7	**Stands**
8-9	**Natural (Banker cannot draw)**

Banker Hand

When the first player's two cards total	DRAWS when player's third card is	STANDS when third card is
0-1-2	**Always Draws**	
3	1-2-3-4-5-6-7-9-0	8
4	2-3-4-5-6-7	1-8-9-0
5	4-5-6-7	1-2-3-8-9-0
6	6-7	1-2-3-4-5-8-9-0
7		**Stands**
8-9		**Stands (Natural)**

If the Player's hand does not draw a third card,
then the Banker's hand stands on a total of 6 or more.

A 12-Seat Baccarat Table Layout

If the player hand has 3,ace for a total of 4 and the banker hand has 8,7 for a total of 5, what happens? The player hand must draw and say it gets a 9 for a total of 3. Once again, the banker hand would like to stand on its total because it would win, but the rules have to be consulted first and in this case when the banker's first 2 cards total 5 and the player's third card drawn is a 9 the banker hand must stand, so the banker hand wins 5 to 3.

Finally, let's say the player hand has 4,3 for a total of 7 and the banker hand has 6,10 for a total of 6. The player hand must always stand on totals of 6 or 7 and the banker hand must also stand on its total of 6 because the player hand didn't take a third card. The player hand wins this one 7 to 6.

All right, now that you know how to play Baccarat we come to the important question which is - how do you win? Well, as I said before, if you bet on player you'll only be giving the casino a 1.36% edge and if you bet on banker you'll be giving the casino an even more modest edge of just 1.17%. While both of these are pretty low edges to give the casino you're still stuck with the fact that the casino will always have an edge over you and in the long run the game of Baccarat is unbeatable. So, if that's the case then how do you win? Well, the answer to that is very simple - You have to get lucky! And that's the ONLY way you can win at Baccarat. Of course, this is easier said than done, but fortunately, in the game of Baccarat, you have the option of making two bets that require no skill and both offer the casino a very low edge especially when you compare them to roulette where the house has a 5.26% advantage on a double-zero wheel and slot machines where the edge is about 8% to 10% I always stress the point that when you gamble in a casino you have to play the games that have the lowest casino edge in order to have the best chance of winning and with that in mind you can see that Baccarat is not that bad a game to play for the recreational gambler.

Now let's take a quick look at one of the most common systems for betting on Baccarat. One thing that many Baccarat players seem to have in common is a belief in streaks and the casinos accommodate these players by providing scorecards at the table that can be used to track the results of each hand. Many players like to bet on whatever won the last hand in the belief that it will continue to come in and they hope for a long streak.

The thinking for these players is that since Baccarat is purely a guessing game it's just like guessing the outcome of a coin toss and chances are that a coin won't alternately come up heads, tails, heads, tails, heads, tails but rather that there will be streaks where the same result will come in for awhile. So, is this a good system? Well, actually, it's no better and no worse than any other system because no matter what you do you'll still have the same casino edge going against you on every bet you make: 1.36% on the player and 1.17% on the banker. The one good thing about a system like this though is that you don't have to sit there and guess what you want to play each time. Instead, you go into the game knowing how you're going to play and you don't have to blame yourself if your guess is wrong, instead you get to blame it on your system!

Starting Hands in Limit Hold'em Poker

by Bill Burton

No Limit Texas Hold'em is the most popular form of the game for big poker tournaments. However in a casino card room you will find more people playing limit poker which has structured betting rounds. In low limit games you will usually need to show down the best hand.

This means the most important decision you will make when playing Texas Hold'em is choosing your starting hands. Most players lose because they play too many hands. There are 169 possible two-card starting hands. Of these 169 hands there are only about 75 that are profitable to play. Not all of these hands can be played from every position and some of them require more players entering the pot to be profitable.

Suited cards are a little more powerful than unsuited cards because of their flush potential however many novice players put too much value on suited cards. When you start with two suited cards you will only make a flush five percent of the time. Many novice players make the mistake of playing any two suited cards. The combination of starting hands will fall into four categories.

Pocket Pairs - Big pairs are powerful starting hands. A pair of Aces is the best starting hand but a pair of deuces is a weak hand that can only be played in late position in an un-raised pot. Some medium pairs can win, but with the smaller pairs you will be looking to make a set (trips) or possibly a straight draw. The odds of being dealt a pair are 16-to-1 or about one in every 17 hands. The odds of being dealt a specific pair such as aces are 220-to-1.

Connectors - Cards that are next to each other are called connectors. They can be suited or unsuited. These are hands like K-Q, J-T or 9-8. Connectors are used in making straights. Suited connectors can make straight flushes, straights or flushes.

Gapped Cards - Gappers have one or more gaps between them. These are cards like Q-T, J-9 or A-8. The smaller the gap the easier it is to make a straight. With a hand that has a gap you are looking to fill an inside straight if you play these or possibly a flush if they are suited. As with the connectors the suited cards have more potential.

Big Cards - Cards of a higher value than 10 are considered big cards. Suited cards are more valuable than unsuited cards. These hands still fall into the categories of connectors or gapped hands, but because of the higher value they can sometimes stand on their own if you pair them on the flop. Big cards play better against fewer players.

A pair of aces is the strongest starting hand before the flop. With only two cards there is nothing higher. Aces do not always stand up as the winning hand after the flop especially if there are a lot of players involved in the hand. In a heads up situation a pair of aces will win about 80 percent of the time, however against 10 players they will only win about 35 percent of the time.

The weakest starting hand is an unsuited seven and deuce. There are five gaps between the two cards making a straight impossible. Because they are not suited you cannot make a flush either.

Position - There is an adage that says "The Key to success in Business is Location, Location, Location". Well to paraphrase that saying "The key to success in Texas Hold'em is "Position, Position, Position." Yet the majority of the newer players and some of the older ones either have no idea about the importance of position or they simply choose to ignore it. Before we even start to discuss starting hands you need to understand the importance of position. A starting hand that you would throw away in early position may very well be a hand you would raise with in late position or if you are on the button.

Your position is determined by where you sit in relationship to the dealer's button. Unlike seven card stud, where the betting order changes with each betting round, the order is fixed in Texas Hold'em. Before the flop the person to the left of the big blind bets first. After the flop the first active player to the left of the dealer button acts first. If you are in early position you will remain there for all betting rounds. (Even though the blinds make their decision last before the flop, the have actually acted first by posting the blind bets.)

There are seven positions in a 10 handed Hold'em game.
Small Blind – Player posting small blind
Big Blind – Player posting big blind
Under the Gun (UTG)- Player who acts first after the big blind
Early – The two players after UTG
Middle – The two players after early.
Late – The two players after middle
Button- The player with the dealer button.

When you are in early position you have a distinct disadvantage because you have no idea what the players acting after you will do. It is possible that the pot could be raised and re-raised after you enter the hand. For this reason you need to have a much stronger hand if you want to play from earl position. Before you call the blind with a hand from early position you should ask yourself if you would play that hand if you knew the pot would be raised. If you would not call a raise with that hand then you should not play.

In poker, knowledge is power. The more information you have, the better chance you have of accessing your opponent's hands. The later you act in the round the more information you have. When you are in late position you have already seen what the players before you have done. If there has been a raise and or re-raise you know that some players potentially have strong hands and you can fold. If there have been no callers, and you are last to act you can sometimes steal the blind merely by raising with a marginal hand because of your position. You will hear players refer to this play as a positional raise.

In late position after the flop you have more information to help you decide how to play. If you have a strong hand, you can raise if your opponents bet or you can bet if everyone has checked. You may decide to check to gain a free card if you have a drawing hand. If there have been bets or raises before you, and your hand was not helped by the flop, you can fold without it costing you an additional bet.

In early position you do not have this luxury after the flop. If you bet there is a chance that you will be raised. If you have nothing and check in hopes of seeing the turn for free a player in later position will surely bet and you will have to fold. If you have a strong hand and check in the hopes of check raising there is a chance that everyone else will check and you will lose some bets that would have gone into the pot.

Texas Hold'em is a game of many variables. Your hand, your opponents, your position and the action that preceded you are all factors that have to be taken into account during a hand. Players who think that they can play the same hand from any position are not going to be winners in the long run. Learning to play the right hand from the right position will go a long way in improving your game.

Basic Starting Hand Recommendations - Here are some guidelines for starting hands that I recommend you play when you are starting out. Even if you are an experienced player who might not be winning at the tables you might want to try playing just these hands. They are fairly tight but will give you a good foundation to work with until you learn a little more about the game or get back on the winning track.

In Early Position - Raise with A-A, K-K and A-Ks from any position. (s denotes suited cards) Call with A-K, A-Qs, K-Qs and Q-Q J-J, T-T and fold everything else.

In Middle Position - Call with, 9-9, 8-8, A-Js, A-Ts, Q-Js, A-Q, K-Q

In Late Position - Call with A-Xs, K-Ts, Q-Ts, J-Ts, A-J, A-T and small pairs. (note "X" denotes any card) It takes a stronger hand to call a raise than it does to make one. If there is a raise before it is your turn to act you should fold. Why put in two bets with marginal hands?

The Blinds - Once you post your blind the money no longer belongs to you. Many players feel they must defend their blinds by calling all raises even with marginal hands. Don't waste money on marginal hands and don't automatically call with the small blind if you have nothing. Saving a half bet will pay for your next small blind.

Starting Hand Chart - I developed a chart of the complete starting hands which is published in my book. You can view it in color online and even order a copy for $1 at: http://casinogambling.about.com/od/poker/a/arrow.htm. The hands are broken down by position.

Keep Learning - This quick lesson in starting hands should give you enough information to get you started in a limit Hold'em game. However if you want to be a consistent winning player you need to study the game and learn as much as possible. Even the professional players will tell you they are students of the game and are always learning.

Until Next time remember: Luck comes and goes...Knowledge Stays Forever.

Bill Burton is the Casino Gambling Guide and columnist for the Internet portal About.com located at: www.casinogambling.about.com He is the author of "1000 Best Casino Gambling Secrets" and "Get the Edge at Low Limit Texas Hold'em" available online at www.billburton.com. He is also an instructor for Golden Touch Craps: www.thecrapsclub.com

A Few Last Words

by Steve Bourie

When I sit down to put this book together each year I try to make sure that everything in here will help to make you a better and more knowledgeable gambler when you go to a casino.

I try to include stories that will help you understand how casinos operate, how to choose the best casino games and also how to play those games in the best way possible.

My philosophy with this book is that gambling in a casino is a fun activity and, according to research studies, for about 98% of the people who visit casinos this statement is true. The vast majority of people who gamble in casinos are recreational players who enjoy the fun and excitement of gambling. They know that they won't always win and they also realize that over the long term they will most likely have more losing sessions than winning ones. They also understand that any losses they incur will be the price they pay for their fun and they only gamble with money they can afford to lose. In other words, they realize that casino gambling is a form of entertainment, just like going to a movie or an amusement park, and they are willing to pay a price for that entertainment. Unfortunately, there are also some people who go to casinos and become problem gamblers.

According to Gamblers Anonymous you may be a problem gambler if you answer yes to at least seven of the following 20 questions:

1. Do you lose time from work due to gambling?
2. Does gambling make your home life unhappy?
3. Does gambling affect your reputation?
4. Do you ever feel remorse after gambling?
5. Do you ever gamble to get money with which to pay debts or to otherwise solve financial difficulties?
6. Does gambling cause a decrease in your ambition or efficiency?
7. After losing, do you feel you must return as soon as possible and win back your losses?
8. After a win, do you have a strong urge to return and win more?
9. Do you often gamble until your last dollar is gone?
10. Do you ever borrow to finance your gambling?
11. Do you ever sell anything to finance your gambling?

12. Are you reluctant to use your "gambling money" for other expenses?
13. Does gambling make you careless about the welfare of your family?
14. Do you ever gamble longer than you planned?
15. Do you ever gamble to escape worry or trouble?
16. Do you ever commit, or consider committing, an illegal act to finance yourgambling?
17. Does gambling cause you to have difficulty sleeping?
18. Do arguments, disappointments, or frustrations create within you an urge to gamble?
19. Do you have an urge to celebrate good fortune by a few hours of gambling?
20. Do you ever consider self-destruction as a result of your gambling?

If you believe you might have a gambling problem you should be aware that help is available from The National Council on Problem Gambling, Inc. It is the foremost advocacy organization in the country for problem gamblers and is headquartered in Washington, D.C. It was formed in 1972 as a non-profit agency to promote public education and awareness about gambling problems and operates a 24-hour nationwide help line at 1-800-522-4700, plus a website at www.ncpgambling.org Anyone contacting that organization will be provided with the appropriate referral resources for help with their gambling problem.

Another good source for anyone seeking help with a gambling problem is Gambler's Anonymous. They have chapters in many cities throughout the U.S. as well as in most major cities throughout the world. You can see a list of all those cities on their website at www.gamblersanonymous.org or contact them by telephone at (213) 386-8789.

A third program, Gam-Anon, specializes in helping the spouse, family and close friends of compulsive gamblers rather than the gamblers themselves.If you are adversely affected by a loved one who is a compulsive gambler, then Gam-Anon is an organization that may benefit you. They have a website at www.gam-anon.org that lists the cities which host meetings. They can also be contacted by telephone at (718) 352-1671.

I sincerely hope that none of you reading this book will ever have a need to contact any of these worthwhile organizations, but it was an issue that I felt should be addressed.

ARIZONA

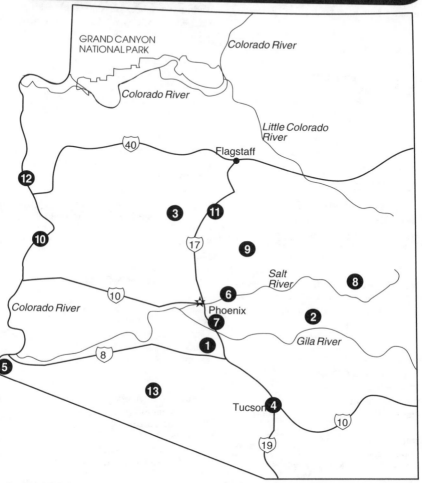

In mid-1993 Arizona's Governor Symington signed a compact with the state's tribes that allowed them to offer slot machines on their reservations.

The compact originally didn't allow for any table games but in early 2003 blackjack was added as a permissible table game. The casinos are also permitted to offer video versions of craps and roulette.

Arizona tribes aren't required to release information on their slot machine percentage paybacks, however, according to the Arizona Department of Gaming, the terms of the compact require each tribes' machines to return the following minimum and maximum paybacks: video poker and video blackjack - 83% to 100%, slot machines - 80% to 100%, keno - 75% to 100%. Each tribe is free to set its machines to pay back anywhere within those limits.

All Arizona casinos have slots, video poker and video keno. Optional games include: blackjack (BJ), Spanish 21 (S21), let it ride (LIR), poker (P), live keno (K), bingo (BG) and off-track betting (OTB).

The minimum gambling age is 21 and all casinos are open 24 hours. For more information on Arizona call the state's Office of Tourism at (602) 364-3700 or visit their website at: www.azot.com

Apache Gold Casino Resort

P.O. Box 1210
San Carlos, Arizona 85550
(928) 475-7800
Map: **#2** (90 miles E. of Phoenix)
Website: www.apachegoldcasinoresort.com

Toll-Free Number: (800) APACHE-8
Rooms: 147 Price Range: $54-$89
Suites: 10   Price Range: $89-$150
Restaurants: 2   Liquor: Yes
Buffets: L-$9.95/$8.95 (Sun)
          D-$12.95/$16.95 (Fri/Sat)
Casino Size: 10,000 Square Feet
Other Games: BJ, P, K, BG
Overnight RV Parking: Must use RV park
Senior Discount: Food discount if 55+
Special Features: Hotel is off-property and is Best Western. 18-hole golf course. Convenience store. 60-space RV Park ($12 per night) w/full hookups and dump station.

Blue Water Casino

11300 Resort Drive
Parker, Arizona 85344
(928) 669-7777
Website: www.bluewaterfun.com
Map: **#10** (160 miles W. of Phoenix)

Toll-Free Number: (888) 243-3360
Rooms: 200 Price Range: $39-$125
Suites: 25 Price Range: $99-$299
Restaurants: 4   Liquor: Yes
Buffet: B- $6.95 L-$7.95 D-$9.95
Other Games: BJ, P, K, BG
Overnight RV Parking: Free/RV Dump: No
Senior Discount: Various buffet discounts

Bucky's Casino & Resort

530 E. Merritt
Prescott, Arizona 86301
(928) 776-1666
Website: www.buckyscasino.com
Map: **#3** (91 miles S.W. of Flagstaff, Junction of Hwy. 69 & Hwy. 89)

Toll-Free Number: (800) SLOTS-44
Room Reservations: (800) 967-4637
Rooms: 81   Price Range: $104-$149
Suites: 80 Price Range: $129-$199
Restaurants: 3 Liquor: Yes
Other Games: BJ, P
Overnight RV Parking: No
Special Features: Located in Prescott Resort Hotel. Free on-site shuttle service. Gas station with RV dump and mini-mart.

Casino Arizona 101 & Indian Bend

9700 E. Indian Bend
Scottsdale, Arizona 85256
(480) 850-7777
Website: www.casinoaz.com
Map: **#6** (15 miles N.E. of Phoenix)

Toll-Free Number: (877) 7-24-HOUR
Restaurants: 1 Liquor: Yes
Casino Size: 40,000 Square Feet
Other Games: BJ, P, K, OTB
Overnight RV Parking: Free/RV Dump: No

Casino Arizona 101 & McKellips

524 N. 92nd Street
Scottsdale, Arizona 85256
(480) 850-7777
Website: www.casinoaz.com
Map: **#6** (15 miles N.E. of Phoenix)

Toll-Free Number: (877) 7-24-HOUR
Restaurants: 5 Liquor: Yes
Buffets: B-$9.95(Sat)/ $17.50 (Sun) L-$9.95
          D-$14.50/$19.50 (Fri/Sat)
Other Games: P, BJ, K, OTB
Overnight RV Parking: Free/RV Dump: No
Special Features: 500-seat showroom.

Casino Del Sol
5655 W. Valencia
Tucson, Arizona 85757
(520) 883-1700
Website: www.casinodelsol.com
Map: **#4**

Toll-Free Number: (800) 344-9435
Restaurants: 2 Liquor: Yes
Casino Size: 22,500 Square Feet
Other Games: BJ, P, BG
Overnight RV Parking: Free/RV Dump: No
Special Features: 4,400-seat amphitheater.

Casino of the Sun
7406 S. Camino De Oeste
Tucson, Arizona 85757
(520) 883-1700
Website: www.casinosun.com
Map: **#4**

Toll-Free Number: (800) 344-9435
Restaurants: 2 Liquor: No
Buffets: B- $10.25 (Sun) L-$7.25/ $10.95 (Sat)
D-$8.30/ $10.95 (Sat)
Other Games: BJ
Overnight RV Parking: Free/RV Dump: No
Special Features: Smoke shop. Gift shop. 50%
food discount on Tuesdays and Thursdays.

Cliff Castle Casino & Hotel Lodge
555 Middle Verde Road
Camp Verde, Arizona 86322
(928) 567-7999
Website: www.cliffcastle.net
Map: **#11** (50 miles S. of Flagstaff)

Toll-Free Number: (800) 381-SLOT
Room Reservation Number: (800) 524-6343
Rooms: 82 Price Range: $79-$100
Suites: 2 Price Range: $110-$120
Restaurants: 5 Liquor: Yes
Buffets: D-$7.95 (Fri Only)
Casino Size: 14,000 Square Feet
Other Games: BJ, P
Overnight RV Parking: Free/RV Dump: No
Special Features: Casino is in Cliff Castle
Lodge. Bowling alley. Kid's Quest childcare
facility.

Cocopah Casino & Bingo
15136 S. Avenue B
Somerton, Arizona 85350
(928) 726-8066
Map: **#5** (13 miles S.W. of Yuma)
Website: www.cocopahresort.com

Toll-Free Number: (800) 23-SLOTS
RV Reservations: (800) 537-7901
Restaurants: 2 Liquor: Yes
Buffets: B- $11.99 (Sun) L-$7.75 D-$17.95
(Fri)/ $11.95 (Sat-Sun)
Other Games: BJ, BG
Overnight RV Parking: Must use RV park
Special Features: 135-space RV park ($28
summer/$32 winter). 18-hole golf course. $3
off lunch buffet for slot club members.

Desert Diamond Casino - I-19
1100 West Pima Mine Road
Sahuarita, Arizona 85629
(520) 294-7777
Website: www.desertdiamondcasino.com
Map: **#4**

Toll-Free Number: (866) 332-9467
Restaurants: 2 Liquor: Yes
Buffets: L-$6.85/$12.85 (Sun) D-$8.85
Casino Size: 15,000 Square Feet
Hours: 9am-4am/24 Hours (Fri/Sat)
Other Games: BG, BJ, K
Overnight RV Parking: Free/RV Dump: No
Special Features: 2,500-seat event center.

Desert Diamond Casino - Nogales
7350 S. Nogales Highway
Tucson, Arizona 85706
(520) 294-7777
Website: www.desertdiamondcasino.com
Map: **#4**

Toll-Free Number: (866) 332-9467
Restaurants: 2 Liquor: Yes
Casino Size: 15,000 Square Feet
Other Games: BJ, P, K, BG
Overnight RV Parking: Free/RV Dump: No

Fort McDowell Casino
P.O. Box 18359
Fountain Hills, Arizona 85269
(602) 837-1424
Website: www.fortmcdowellcasino.com
Map: **#6** (25 miles N.E. of Phoenix)

Toll-Free Number: (800) THE-FORT
Restaurants: 5 Liquor: Yes
Buffets: L/D-$12.95/$20.95 (Fri/Sat)
            L/D-$15.95 (Sun)
Other Games: P, K, BG
Overnight RV Parking: No
Special Features: Free local shuttle. Gift shop.

Gila River Casino - Lone Butte
1200 S. 56th Street
Chandler, Arizona 85226
(520) 796-7777
Website: www.wingilariver.com
Map: **#7** (10 miles S.W. of Phoenix)

Toll-Free Number: (800) WIN-GILA
Restaurants: 3 Liquor: Yes
Buffet: L- $8.95 D-$12.95
Casino Size: 10,000 Square Feet
Other Games: BJ
Overnight RV Parking: Free/RV Dump: No

Gila River Casino - Vee Quiva
6443 N. Komatke Lane
Laveen, Arizona 85339
(520) 796-7777
Website: www.wingilariver.com
Map: **#7** (10 miles S.W. of Phoenix)

Toll-Free Number: (800) WIN-GILA
Restaurants: 2 Liquor: Yes
Casino Size: 15,000 Square Feet
Other Games: BJ, P, BG
Overnight RV Parking: Free/RV Dump: No

Gila River Casino - Wild Horse
5512 W. Wild Horse Pass
Chandler, Arizona 85226
(520) 796-7727
Website: www.wingilariver.com
Map: **#7** (25 miles S.E. of Phoenix)

Toll-Free Number: (800) WIN-GILA
Restaurants: 1 Liquor: Yes
Buffets: L-$8.95 D-$12.95
Casino Size: 20,000 Square Feet
Other Games: BJ, P, K, BG
Overnight RV Parking: Free/RV Dump: No

Golden Hasan Casino
PO Box 10
Ajo, Arizona 85321
(520) 362-2746
Website: www.desertdiamondcasino.com
Map: **#13** (125 miles S.W. of Phoenix)

Restaurants: 1 Snack Bar
Hours: 10am-12am Daily
Overnight RV Parking: No

Harrah's Ak Chin Casino Resort
15406 Maricopa Road
Maricopa, Arizona 85239
(480) 802-5000
Website: www.harrahs.com
Map: **#1** (25 miles S. of Phoenix)

Toll-Free Number: (800) HARRAHS
Rooms: 142 Price Range: $99-$245
Suites: 4 Price Range: Casino Use Only
Restaurants: 4 Liquor: Yes
Buffets: L-$8.99/$13.99 (Sun)
            D-$11.99/$17.99 (Fri/Sat)
Casino Size: 43,000 Square Feet
Other Games: BJ, P, K, BG
Overnight RV Parking: Free/RV Dump: No
Senior Discount: Various Mon/Thu if 50+
Special Features: Free local shuttle.

Hon-Dah Resort Casino
777 Highway 260
Pinetop, Arizona 85935
(928) 369-0299
Website: www.hon-dah.com
Map: **#8** (190 miles N.E. of Phoenix)

Toll-Free Number: (800) 929-8744
Rooms: 126 Price Range: $89-$109
Suites: 2 Price Range: $150-$180
Restaurants: 1 Liquor: Yes
Buffets: B- $6.95 L-$7.95
        D-$10.95/$15.95 (Fri-Sat)
Casino Size: 20,000 Square Feet
Overnight RV Parking: Must use RV park
Other Games: BJ, P
Special Features: 258-space RV park ($23 per night). Convenience store. Gas station.

Mazatzal Casino
P.O. Box 1820
Hwy. 87, Milemarker 251
Payson, Arizona 85547
(928) 474-6044
Website: www.777play.com
Map: **#9** (90 miles N.E. of Phoenix)

Toll-Free Number: (800) 777-7529
Restaurants: 2 Liquor: Yes
Casino Size: 35,000 Square Feet
Other Games: BJ, P, K, BG (Mon-Thu)
Overnight RV Parking: Free/RV Dump: No
Senior Discount: 10% off food if 55 or older
Special Features: Offers Stay & Play packages (Sun-Thu) with local motels. Free shuttle.

Mojave Crossing Casino
101 Aztec Road
Fort Mojave, Arizona 86426
(928) 330-2555
Map: **#12** (10 miles S. of Bullhead City)

Restaurants: 1 Liquor: Yes
Casino Size: 35,000 Square Feet
Othe Games: Only Machines
Overnight RV Parking: No
Special Features: 3,000-seat event center.

Paradise Casino Arizona
450 Quechan Drive
Yuma, Arizona 85364
(760) 572-7777
Website: www.paradise-casinos.com
Map: **#5** (244 miles W. of Tucson)

Toll-Free Number: (888) 777-4946
Restaurants: 1 Liquor: Yes
Other Games: BJ, BG
Overnight RV Parking: Free/RV Dump: No
Special Features: Part of casino is located across the state border in California. Poker offered in CA casino. 10% food discount with slot club card.

Spirit Mountain Casino
8555 South Highway 95
Mohave Valley, Arizona 86440
(928) 346-2000
Map: **#12** (15 miles S. of Bullhead City)

Toll-Free Number: (888) 837-4030
RV Reservations: (928) 346-1225
Restaurants: 1 Snack Bar Liquor: Yes
Casino Size: 12,000 Square Feet
Other Games: Only Machines
Overnight RV Parking: Must use RV park
Special Features: Adjacent to 82-space Spirit Mountain RV park ($17 per night). Convenience store. Gas station.

Yavapai Casino
1501 E. Highway 69
Prescott, Arizona 86301
(928) 445-5767
Website: www.buckyscasino.com
Map: **#3** (91 miles S.W. of Flagstaff)

Toll-Free Number: (800) SLOTS-44
Restaurants: 1 Snack Bar Liquor: Yes
Other Games: BJ, P
Overnight RV Parking: Free/RV Dump: No
Special Features: Located across the street from Bucky's Casino. Free local-area shuttle bus.

ARKANSAS

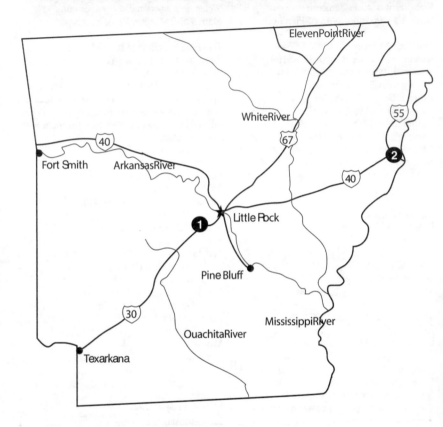

Arkansas has two pari-mutuel facilities featuring "electronic games of skill," which are defined as "games played through any electronic device or machine that affords an opportunity for the exercise of skill or judgment where the outcome is not completely controlled by chance alone."

The games offered are video poker, video blackjack, and "skill" slots where you have two opportunities to spin the reels. The "skill" factor comes into play because after seeing the results of your first spin you then have to decide whether to keep none, one, two, or all three of the symbols on each reel before you spin them again.

Gaming regulations require that all of the electronic games of skill must return a minimum of 83%.

For the six month period from November 2006 through April 2007, the average gaming machine's return at Oaklawn was 90.65% and at Southland it was 90.92%

The minimum gambling age is 21 for slots and 18 for pari-mutuel wagering. For more information on visiting Arkansas call the state's tourism office at (800) 628-8725 or visit their web site at: www.arkansas.com.

Oaklawn Jockey Club
2705 Central Avenue
Hot Springs, Arkansas 71902
(302) 674-4600
Website: www.oaklawn.com
Map: **#1** (55 miles S.W.. of Little Rock)

Toll-Free Number: (800) 625-5296
Restaurants: 3
Hours: 11am-12am/2am (Fri/Sat)/11pm (Sun)
Admission: Free Parking: Free
Overnight RV Parking: No
Special Features: Live throroughbred racing
Mid-January through Mid-April. Daily
simulcasting of horse racing.

Southland Park Gaming & Racing
1550 North Ingram Boulevard
West Memphis, Arkansas 72301
(870) 735-3670
Website: www.southlandgreyhound.com
Map: **#2** (130 miles E. of Little Rock)

Toll-Free Number: (800) 467-6182
Restaurants: 4
Hours: 10am-2am (Mon-Sat)
          Noon-2am (Sunday)
Admission: Free Parking: Free
Preferred Parking: $3/Valet Parking: $5
Buffets: L-$6.95
          D-$11.95/$13.95 (Fri)/$14.95 (Sat)
Overnight RV Parking: No
Special Features: Live greyhound racing Mon/
Wed-Sat. Daily simulcasting of greyhound and
horse racing.

CALIFORNIA

California's Indian casinos are legally allowed to offer electronic gaming machines, blackjack, and other house-banked card games. The games of craps and roulette are not permitted. However, some casinos do offer modified versions of craps and roulette that are played with cards rather than dice or roulette wheels.

Most California card rooms also offer some form of player-banked blackjack, but because they are prohibited by law from playing blackjack, the game is usually played to 22 rather than 21. Additionally, players must pay a commission to the house on every hand they play. The amount will vary depending on the rules of the house but, generally, it's about two to five percent of the total amount bet. There are about 90 card rooms in California and you can see a listing of them on the Internet at: *http://ag.ca.gov/gambling/game/cardroomlist.php*

California's tribes aren't required to release information on their slot machine percentage paybacks and the state of California does not require any minimum returns.

Unless otherwise noted, all California casinos are open 24 hours and offer: slots, video poker, and video keno. Optional games offered include: baccarat (B), blackjack (BJ), Spanish 21 (S21), mini-baccarat (MB), poker (P), pai gow poker (PGP), Caribbean stud poker (CSP), let it ride (LIR), three card poker (TCP), four card poker (FCP) bingo (BG), casino war (CW) and off track betting (OTB).

The minimum gambling age is not uniform at all casinos; it is 21 at some casinos and 18 at others. Unless noted otherwise, all casino are open 24 hours.

Although most of the casinos have toll-free numbers be aware that many of those numbers will only work for calls made within California. Also, many of the casinos are in out-of-the-way locations, so it is advisable to call ahead for directions, especially if you will be driving at night.

For more information on visiting California contact the state's department of tourism at (800) 862-2543 or www.visitcalifornia.com.

Agua Caliente Casino
32-250 Bob Hope Drive
Rancho Mirage, California 92270
(760) 321-2000
Website: www.hotwatercasino.com
Map: **#3** (115 miles E. of L. A.)

Toll-Free Number: (866) 858-3600
Restaurants: 4 Liquor: Yes
Buffets: B-$7.99 L-$11.99/$23.99 (Sun)
   D-$17.99/$23.99 (Fri-Sat)/$12.99 (Mon)
Other Games: BJ, MB, CSP, TCP,
         P, PGP, BG (Sat-Thu)
Overnight RV Parking: Only offered at
            adjacent Flying J truck stop
Special Features: Associated with Spa Casino.
Offers card version of craps.

Augustine Casino
84001 Avenue 54
Coachella, California 92236
(760) 391-9500
Website: www.augustinecasino.com
Map: **#8** (125 miles E. of L. A.)

Toll-Free Number: (888) 752-9294
Restaurants: 1 Liquor: Yes
Buffets: L-$9.95
      D-$11.95
Other Games: BJ, TCP, S21
Overnight RV Parking: No

Barona Valley Ranch Resort and Casino
1932 Wildcat Canyon Road
Lakeside, California 92040
(619) 443-2300
Website: www.barona.com
Map: **#1** (15 miles N.E. of San Diego)

Toll-Free Number: (888) 7-BARONA
Room Reservations: (877) 287-2624
Rooms: 397 Price Range: $129-$299
Suites: 9 Price Range: Private Use Only
Restaurants: 8 Liquor: Yes

Buffets: B/L-$13.99/$16.99 (Sat-Sun)
D-$17.99/$20.99(Fri-Sat)/$21.99 (Mon/Thu)
Other Games: BJ, BG, B, MB, P, CSP, PGP,
TCP, LIR, CW, OTB
Overnight RV Parking: Free/RV Dump: No
Special Features: Offers card versions of
roulette and craps. Food court. Wedding
chapel. 18-hole golf course. Buffet discounts
for slot club members.

Bear River Casino
11 Bear Paws Way
Loleta, California 95551
(707) 733-9644
Website: www.bearrivercasino.com
Map: **#38** (10 miles S. of Eureka)

Toll-Free Number: (800) 761-2327
Hours: 9am-5am Daily
Restaurants: 2 Liquor: Yes
Buffet: D- $15.95 (Wed)
Casino Size: 31,000 Square Feet
Other Games: BJ, S21, P, PGP, TCP
Overnight RV Parking: No

Black Bart Casino
100 Kawi Place
Willits, California 95490
(707) 459-7330
Map: **#11** (130 miles N. of San Francisco)

Restaurants: 1 Deli Liquor: No
Hours: 8am-2am/24 hours (Fri-Sat)
Casino Size: 6,000 Square Feet
Other Games: Slots Only
Overnight RV Parking: Free/RV Dump: No

Black Oak Casino
19400 Tuolumne Road North
Tuolumne, California 95379
(209) 928-9300
Website: www.blackoakcasino.com
Map: **#5** (100 miles S.E. of Sacramento)

Toll-Free Number: (877) 747-8777
Restaurants: 3 Liquor: Yes
Buffet: Brunch-$12.95 (Sat-Sun)
        D-$8.99 (Mon-Wed)/$19.99 (Thu)/
$17.95 (Fri-Sun)
Casino Size: 22,000 Square Feet
Other Games: BJ, TCP, LIR, CW
Overnight RV Parking: Free/RV Dump: No

Blue Lake Casino
777 Casino Way
Blue Lake, California 95525
(707) 668-9770
Website: www.bluelakecasino.com
Map: **#34** (10 miles N. of Eureka)

Toll-Free Number: (877) BLC-2WIN
Restaurants: 2 Liquor: Yes
Buffet: B/L- $7.95/$12.95(Sun)
        D-$14.95/$16.95(Wed)/$19.95 (Fri)
Other Games: BJ, S21, P, TCP, FCP,
        BG (Sun-Wed)
Overnight RV Parking: Free/RV Dump: No

Cache Creek Indian Bingo & Casino
14455 Highway 16
Brooks, California 95606
(530) 796-3118
Website: www.cachecreek.com
Map: **#2** (35 miles N.W. of Sacramento)

Toll-Free Number: (800) 452-8181
Room Reservations: (888) 772-2243
Rooms: 173 Prices: $139-$189

Suites: 27 Prices: $159-$319
Restaurants: 9 Liquor: Yes
Buffets: B- $19.95 (Sat-Sun)
        L-$14.00
        D-$18.00/$25.00 (Fri-Sat)
Casino Size: 18,000 Square Feet
Other Games: BJ, P, CSP, LIR, PGP, TCP, B,
        MB, CW, BG (Mon-Thu)
Overnight RV Parking: Free/RV Dump: No
Senior Discount: $2 off buffet if 55 or older
Special Features: Offers card versions of craps
and roulette. Full-service spa.

Cahuilla Creek Casino
52702 Highway 371
Anza, California 92539
(951) 763-1200
Website: www.thefriendliestcasino.com
Map: **#19** (30 miles S. of Palm Springs)

Restaurants: 1 Liquor: Yes
Buffets: Brunch-$9.99 (Sun)
Other Games: BJ
Overnight RV Parking: Free/RV Dump: No

Casino Pauma
777 Pauma Reservation Road
Pauma Valley, California 92061
(760) 742-2177
Website: www.casinopauma.com
Map: **#20** (35 miles N.E. of San Diego)

Toll-Free Number: (877) 687-2862
Restaurants: 1 Liquor: Yes
Buffets: B-$4.95 L-$5.95
        D-$8.95/$14.95 (Fri-Sun)
Casino Size: 35,000 Square Feet
Other Games: BJ, P, PGP, TCP, LIR
Overnight RV Parking: Free/RV Dump: No
Senior Discount: 50% off lunch buffet if 55+
Special Features: Offers card versions of craps
and roulette.

Cherae Heights Casino
P.O. Box 635
Trinidad, California 95570
(707) 677-3611
Website: www.cheraeheightscasino.com
Map: **#4** (25 miles N. of Eureka)

Toll-Free Number: (800) 684-BINGO
Restaurants: 3 Liquor: Yes
Other Games: BJ, S21, P, PGP, TCP,
        BG (Wed-Sun)
Overnight RV Parking: Free/RV Dump: No

Chicken Ranch Bingo
16929 Chicken Ranch Road
Jamestown, California 95327
(209) 984-3000
Map: **#5** (100 miles S.E. of Sacramento)

Toll-Free Number: (800) 752-4646
Restaurants: 1 Snack Bar Liquor: No
Hours: 9am-1am Daily
Casino Size: 10,000 Square Feet
Other Games: Slots only, BG (Thu-Sun)
Overnight RV Parking: Call ahead for permission
RV Dump: No

Chukchansi Gold Resort & Casino
711 Lucky Lane
Coarsegold, California 93614
(559) 692-5200
Website: www.chukchansigold.com
Map: **#25** (35 miles N. of Fresno)

Toll-Free Number: (866) 794-6946
Rooms: 190 Prices: $99-$199
Suites: 6 Prices: Casino Use Only
Restaurants: 7 Liquor: Yes
Buffets: B- $14.99 (Sun) L-$8.99
        D-$13.99/$16.99 (Fri/Sat)
Other Games: BJ, S21, MB, TCP, PGP, LIR
Overnight RV Parking: Free/RV Dump: No
Senior Discount: $5.99 lunch buffet if 55+
Special Features: Offers card version of craps.

Chumash Casino Resort
3400 East Highway 246
Santa Ynez, California 93460
(805) 686-0855
Website: www.chumashcasino.com
Map: **#13** (40 miles N.W. of Santa Barbara)

Toll-Free Number: (800) 728-9997
Room Reservations: (800) 248-6274
Rooms: 89 Prices: $195-$250
Suites: 17 Prices: $280-$550
Restaurants: 3 Liquor: No
Buffets: B- $12.95 (Sat-Sun) L-$7.99 D-
$9.99/$15.99 (Fri-Sat)/
            $19.95 (Wed)
Casino Size: 94,000 Square Feet
Other Games: BJ, P, PGP, BG (Sun-Wed),
        TCP, LIR
Overnight RV Parking: No
Special Features: Spa.

Colusa Casino Resort & Bingo
3770 Highway 45
Colusa, California 95932
(530) 458-8844
Website: www.colusacasino.com
Map: **#6** (75 miles N. of Sacramento)

Toll-Free Recording: (800) 655-8946
Room Reservations: (877) 869-7829
Rooms: 50 Prices: $109-$129
Suites: 10 Prices: $189-$209
Restaurants: 3 Liquor: Yes
Buffets: B-$6.99 (Sat/Sun) L-$8.95
        D-$12.95/$24.95 (Wed)/ $17.95 (Fri-Sat)
Other Games: BJ, P, TCP, PGP, BG (Fri-Tue)
Overnight RV Parking: Free/RV Dump: No
Special Features: Offers card version of craps.

Coyote Valley Shodakai Casino
7751 N. State Street
Redwood Valley, California 95470
(707) 485-0700
Website: www.coyotevalleycasino.com
Map: **#23** (115 miles N. of San Francisco)

Toll-Free Number: (800) 332-9683
Restaurants: 1 Cafe Liquor: No
Other Games: BJ, BG (Fri-Tue)
Overnight RV Parking: Free/RV Dump: No

Desert Rose Casino
901 County Road 56
Alturas, California 96101
(530) 233-3141
Map: **#27** (250 miles N.E. of Sacramento)

Restaurants: 1 Snack Bar Liquor: Yes
Hours: 10am-11pm/2am (Fri/Sat)
Other Games: BJ, TCP
Overnight RV Parking: Free/RV Dump: No
Senior Discount: Mondays specials from
10am to 5pm if 55 or older

Diamond Mountain Casino
900 Skyline Drive
Susanville, California 96130
(530) 252-1100
Website: www.diamondmountaincasino.com
Map: **#31** (160 Miles N.E. of Sacramento)

Toll-Free Number: (877) 319-8514
Restaurants: 2   Liquor: Yes
Casino Size: 26,000 Square Feet
Other Games: BJ, P
Overnight RV Parking: Free/RV Dump: No
Senior Discount: 15% off in deli if 55 or older
Special Features: New hotel expected to open
in Spring 2008.

Eagle Mountain Casino
P.O. Box 1659
Porterville, California 93258
(559) 788-6220
Website: www.eaglemtncasino.com
Map: **#21** (60 miles S.E. of Fresno)

Toll-Free Number: (800) 903-3353
Restaurants: 2   Liquor: No
Buffets: L-$6.50   D-$10.00 (Fri)/ $8.50 (Sat)
Casino Size: 9,600 Square Feet
Other Games: BJ, P, PGP, BG (Wed-Sun)
Overnight RV Parking: Free/RV Dump: No
Special Features: Food Cout with four fast
Food stations.

Elk Valley Casino
2500 Howland Hill Road
Crescent City, California 95531
(707) 464-1020
Website: www.elkvalleycasino.com
Map: **#7** (84 miles N. of Eureka)

Toll-Free Number: (888) 574-2744
Restaurants: 1   Liquor: Yes
Buffets: D-$15.95 (Wed)
Casino Size: 23,000 Square Feet
Other Games: BJ, P, BG (Thu-Mon)
Overnight RV Parking: Free/RV Dump: No
Senior Discount: $1.99 lunches on Tuesdays.

Fantasy Springs Casino
82-245 Indio Springs Drive
Indio, California 92203
(760) 342-5000
Website: www.fantasyspringsresort.com
Map: **#8** (125 miles E. of Los Angeles)

Toll-Free Number: (800) 827-2WIN
Rooms: 250   Prices: $129-$209
Suites: 11   Prices: $299-$399
Restaurants: 4   Liquor: Yes
Buffets: L-$11.99   D-$17.99/$22.99 (Fri-Sat)
           Brunch-$21.99 (Sun)
Casino Size: 95,000 Square Feet
Other Games: BJ, S21, MB, P, LIR,
           TCP, FCP, BG, OTB
Overnight RV Parking: Free/RV Dump: No
Special Features: 24-lane bowling center.
5,000-seat special events center. Card version
of craps. Golf Course.

Feather Falls Casino
3 Alverda Drive
Oroville, California 95966
(530) 533-3885
Website: www.featherfallscasino.com
Map: **#22** (100 miles N. of Sacramento)

Toll-Free Number: (877) OK-BINGO
Rooms: 74   Prices: $79-$89
Suites: 10   Prices: $180-$280
Restaurants: 2   Liquor: Yes
Buffets: B-$8.95 (Sat/Sun)   L-$7.95
  D-$10.50/$9.99 (Thu)$15.95 (Fri/Sat)
Casino Size: 38,000 Square Feet
Other Games: BJ, P, TCP
Overnight RV Parking: Free/RV Dump: No
Senior Discount: Various on Mon/Wed if 55+

Gold Country Casino
4020 Olive Highway
Oroville, California 95966
(530) 538-4560
Website: www.goldcountrycasino.com
Map: **#22** (100 miles N. of Sacramento)

Toll-Free Number: (800) 334-9400
Rooms: 87   Prices: $99-$139
Restaurants: 3   Liquor: Yes
Buffets: B-$9.99 (Sun)   L-$6.99/$9.99 (Sun)
           D-$9.99/$16.99 (Fri/Sat)
Other Games: BJ, P, TCP, PGP, BG (Wed-Sun)
Overnight RV Parking: Free/RV Dump: No
Special Features: 1,200-seat showroom. Card
version of roulette.

Located just 30 miles N.E. of Sacramento, Thunder Valley Casino is one of the largest casinos in Northern California.

Golden Acorn Casino and Travel Center
1800 Golden Acorn Way
Campo, CA 91906
(619) 938-6000
Website: www.goldenacorncasino.com
Map: **#33** (40 miles S.E. of San Diego)

Toll-Free Number: (866) 794-6244
Restaurants: 1 Liquor: Yes
Other Games: BJ, TCP, CSP
Overnight RV Parking: Free/RV Dump: No
Special Features: 33-acre auto/truck stop and convenience store.

Harrah's Rincon Casino & Resort
33750 Valley Center Road
Valley Center, California 92082
(760) 760-751-3100
Website: www.harrahs.com
Map: **#20** (35 miles N.E. of San Diego)

Toll-Free Number: (877) 777-2457
Rooms: 552 Prices: $89-$169
Suites: 101 Prices: Casino Use Only
Restaurants: 7 Liquor: Yes
Buffets: B-$16.99 (Sat-Sun) L-$13.99
          D-$17.99/$25.99 (Fri-Sun)
Casino Size: 55,000 Square Feet
Other Games: BJ, PGP, MB, P, TCP, LIR
Overnight RV Parking: Free/RV Dump: No

Havasu Landing Resort & Casino
5 Main Street
Havasu Lake, California 92363
(760) 858-4593
Website: www.havasulanding.com
Map: **#18** (200 miles E. of L. A.)

Toll Free Number: (800) 307-3610
Restaurants: 1 Liquor: Yes
Hours: 8:30am-12:30am/2:30am (Fri/Sat)
Other Games: BJ, TCP
Overnight RV Parking: Must use RV park
Casino Size: 6,000 Square Feet
Special Features: Tables open 11:30 am. Marina, RV park ($25 per night), campground rentals. Mobile homes available for daily rental.

Hopland Sho-Ka-Wah Casino
13101 Nakomis Road
Hopland, California 95449
(707) 744-1395
Website: www.shokawah.com
Map: **#23** (100 miles N. of San Francisco)

Toll Free Number: (888) 746-5292
Restaurants: 2 Liquor: Yes
Buffets: B- $5.99 (Sat-Sun)
Other Games: BJ, PGP, TCP, LIR,
          BG (Wed-Sat)
Overnight RV Parking: Free/RV Dump: No

Jackson Rancheria Casino & Hotel
12222 New York Ranch Road
Jackson, California 95642
(209) 223-1677
Website: www.jacksoncasino.com
Map: **#9** (60 miles S.E. of Sacramento)

Toll-Free Number: (800) 822-WINN
Rooms: 126 Price Range: $65-$149
Suites: 20 Price Range: $179-$399
Restaurants: 6 Liquor: No (only with dinner)
Buffets: B-$15.00 (Sat/Sun) L-$10.00 (Mon-Fri)
D-$17.00/$21.00 (Fri-Sat)
Other Games: BJ, PGP, LIR, TCP,
BG (Fri-Mon)
Overnight RV Parking: Free/RV Dump: No
Senior Discount: 10% off buffet if 55 or older
Special Features: 1,500-seat showroom. New
RV park to open summer 2007.

Konocti Vista Casino Resort & Marina
2755 Mission Rancheria Road
Lakeport, California 95453
(707) 262-1900
Website: www.kvcasino.com
Map: **#23** (120 miles N. of San Francisco)

Toll-Free Number: (800) 386-1950
Rooms: 80 Prices: $79-$139
Restaurants: 1 Liquor: Yes
Other Games: BJ, P, TCP, FCP, PGP
Overnight RV Parking: Must use RV park
RV Dump: Free
Special Features: Marina with 80 slips. 74-
space RV park ($30 per night).

La Posta Casino
777 Crestwood Road
Boulevard, California 91905
(619) 824-4100
Website: www.lapostacasino.com
Map: **#33** (60 miles E. of San Diego)

Restaurants: 1 Liquor: No
Hours: 8am-2am (Sun-Thurs)
24-Hours (Fri-Sat)
Other Games: Only Machines
Overnight RV Parking: Yes/RV Dump: No

Lucky Bear Casino
P.O. Box 729
Hoopa, California 95546
(530) 625-5198
Map: **#24** (30 miles N.E. of Eureka)

Restaurants: 1 Snack Bar Liquor: No
Hours: 10am-Mid/1am (Fri/Sat)
Other Games: BJ, P
Overnight RV Parking: No
Special Features: Non-smoking casino.

Lucky 7 Casino
350 N. Indian Road
Smith River, California 95567
(707) 487-7777
Website: www.lucky7casino.com
Map: **#7** (100 miles N. of Eureka)

Toll-Free Number: (866) 777-7170
Restaurants: 1 Liquor: Yes
Other Games: BJ, BG (Sun/Tue/Wed)
Overnight RV Parking: Free/RV Dump: No
Casino Size: 24,000 Square Feet

Mono Wind Casino
37302 Rancheria Lane
Auberry, California 93602
(559) 855-4350
Website: www.monowind.com
Map: **#25** (30 miles N.E. of Fresno)

Restaurants: 1 Liquor: Yes
Other Games: BJ (Thur-Sun 2pm-11:45pm)
Overnight RV Parking: Free/RV Dump: No
Casino Size: 10,000 Square Feet

Morongo Casino Resort and Spa
49750 Seminole Drive
Cabazon, California 92230
(951) 849-3080
Website: www.morongocasinoresort.com
Map: **#3** (90 miles E. of L. A.)]

Toll-Free Number: (800) 252-4499
Rooms: 310 Prices: $99-$249
Suites: 32 Prices: $269-$499
Restaurants: 5 Liquor: Yes
Buffets: L-$13.95 Brunch: $21.95 (Sun)
D-$19.95/$25.95 (Thurs-Sat)
Casino Size: 145,000 Square Feet
Other Games: BJ, P, TCP, LIR, MB, PGP, BG
Overnight RV Parking: Free/RV Dump: Fee
Special Features: Card version of craps.

Paiute Palace Casino
2742 N. Sierra Highway
Bishop, California 93514
(760) 873-4150
Website: www.paiutepalace.com
Map: **#26** (130 miles N.E. of Fresno)

Toll-Free Number: (888) 3-PAIUTE
Restaurants: 1 Liquor: No
Other Games: BJ, P
Overnight RV Parking: Free/RV Dump: No
Senior Discount: 10% off in restaurant if 55+
Special Features: 24-hour gas station and convenience store.

Pala Casino Spa and Resort
11154 Highway 76
Pala, California 92059
(760) 510-5100
Website: www.palacasino.com
Map: **#20** (35 miles N.E. of San Diego)

Toll-Free Number: (877) 946-7252
Room Reservations: (877) 725-2766
Rooms: 425 Prices: $109-$169
Suites: 82 Prices: $139-$270
Restaurants: 7 Liquor: Yes
Buffets: L-$9.99 (Mon-Fri)
          D-$13.99/$19.99 (Fri- Sun)
          Brunch- $12.99 (Sat-Sun)
Other Games: BJ, B, MB, TCP, PGP,
          LIR, CW
Overnight RV Parking: Free (park in west lot)
RV Dump: No
Special Features: Offers card versions of craps and roulette. Fitness center and spa.

Palace Indian Gaming Center
17225 Jersey Avenue
Lemoore, California 93245
(559) 924-7751
Website: www.thepalace.net
Map: **#10** (50 miles S. of Fresno)

Toll-Free Number: (800) 942-6886
Restaurants: 2 Liquor: Yes
Buffets: L-$6.99 (Mon-Thurs)/ $7.99 (Fri)/
          $8.99 (Sat-Sun)
          D-$10.99/ $11.99 (Fri-Sat)
Casino Size: 50,000 Square Feet
Other Games: BJ, P, PGP, LIR, TCP, BG
Overnight RV Parking: Free/RV Dump: No
Senior Discount: 10% off buffet if 55+

Paradise Casino
450 Quechan Drive
Ft Yuma, California 92283
(760) 572-7777
Website: www.paradise-casinos.com
Map: **#37** (170 miles E. of San Diego)

Toll-Free Number: (888) 777-4946
Restaurants: 1 Liquor: Yes
Other Games: BJ, P, BG
Overnight RV Parking: Free/RV Dump: No
Special Features: Part of casino is located across the state border in Arizona. Offers video versions of craps and roulette. 10% off food with slot club card. $1.95 breakfast special.

Pechanga Resort and Casino
45000 Pechanga Parkway
Temecula, California 92592
(951) 693-1819
Website: www.pechanga.com
Map: **#28** (50 miles N. of San Diego)

Toll-Free Number: (877) 711-2946
Room Reservations: (888) PECHANGA
Rooms: 458 Price Range: $119-$309
Suites: 64 Price Range: $179-$750
Restaurants: 8 Liquor: Yes
Buffets: Brunch-$13.49 (Sat/Sun) L-$9.49
          D- $13.99/$20.99 (Fri/Sat)
Other Games: BJ, MB, P, PGP, LIR, TCP, BG
Overnight RV Parking: Must use RV park
RV Dump: $14.00 charge to use
Casino Size: 88,000 Square Feet
Special Features: 168-space RV park ($32 per night/$42 Fri-Sat). Offers card version of craps.

Pit River Casino
20265 Tamarack Avenue
Burney, California 96013
(530) 335-2334
Website: www.pitrivercasino.com
Map: **#29** (190 miles N. of Sacramento)

Toll-Free Number: (888) 245-2992
Restaurants: 1 Snack Bar Liquor: No
Hours: 10am-Midnight/2am (Fri-Sat)
Other Games: BJ, P (Thu-Sat)
Overnight RV Parking: Free/RV Dump: No
Senior Discount: $5 match play and lunch special on Mondays if 55 or older.

Red Earth Casino
3089 Norm Niver Road
Salton City, California 92274
(760) 395-1800
Map: **#39** (114 miles S.E. of Riverside)

Restaurants: 1 Liquor: Yes
Casino Size: 10,000 Square Feet
Other Games: BJ, P, S21
Overnight RV Parking: Free/RV Dump: No

Red Fox Casino & Bingo
300 Cahto Drive
Laytonville, California 95454
(707) 984-6800
Map: **#30** (150 miles N.W. of Sacramento)

Toll-Free Number: (888) 4-RED-FOX
Restaurants: 1 Snack Bar Liquor: No
Hours: 10am-Mid/2am (Fri-Sat)
Overnight RV Parking: Free/RV Dump: No

River Rock Casino
3250 Hwy 128 East
Geyserville, California 95441
(707) 857-2777
Website: www.river-rock-casino.com
Map: **#32** (75 miles N. of San Fran.)

Restaurants: 2 Liquor: Yes
Buffets: Brunch-$12.50 (Sat-Sun) L-$10.50
        D-$10.50/$14.50 (Fri-Sun)
Other Games: BJ, MB, P, PGP, TCP
Overnight RV Parking: No

Robinson Rancheria Resort & Casino
1545 E. Highway 20
Nice, California 95464
(707)275-9000
Website: www.robinsonrancheria.biz
Map: **#11** (100 miles N.W. of Sacramento)

Toll-Free Number: (800) 809-3636
Rooms: 46 Price Range: $69-$129
Suites: 2 Price Range: $175-$295
Restaurants: 2 Liquor: Yes
Buffets: Brunch-$11.95 (Sat-Sun),
        D-$11.95/$18.95 (Fri-Sat)
Casino Size: 37,500 Square Feet
Other Games: BJ, P, PGP, LIR, TCP,
            BG (Sun-Wed)
Overnight RV Parking: Free (one night only)
RV Dump: No
Senior Discount: Various on Wed if 55 or older
Special Features: 60-site RV park ($18/$25 per
night), 2.5 miles from casino.

Rolling Hills Casino
2655 Barham Avenue
Corning, California 96021
(530) 528-3500
Website: www.rollinghillscasino.com
Map: **#36** (115 miles N. of Sacramento)

Toll-Free Number: (888) 331-6400
Rooms: 90 Price Range: $99-$139
Suites: 21 Price Range: $159-$210
Restaurants: 2 Liquor: Yes
Buffet: B-$7.95 L-$9.95
        D-$13.95/$14.95(Fri)
Casino Size: 60,000 Square Feet
Other Games: BJ, PGP, TCP
Overnight RV Parking: Free/RV Dump: No
Senior Discount: 1/2 price buffets Tue/Thu if
50 or older

San Manuel Indian Bingo & Casino
5797 North Victoria Avenue
Highland, California 92346
(909) 864-5050
Website: www.sanmanuel.com
Map: **#12** (65 miles E. of L. A.)

Toll-Free Number: (800) 359-2464
Restaurants: 3 Liquor: Yes
Buffet: L-$9.95
D-$14.95/$21.95(Fri-Sat)
Casino Size: 75,000 Square Feet
Other Games: BJ, MB, P, PGP, LIR, TCP,
FCP, BG (Fri-Wed)
Overnight RV Parking: Free/RV Dump: No
Senior Discount: Special bingo price Fri if 55+
Special Features: Food Court with 3 fast food
dining stations.

Santa Ysabel Resort and Casino
25575 Highway 79
Santa Ysabel, California 92070
(760) 782-0909
Website: santaysabelresortandcasino.com
Map: **#1** (52 miles N.E. of San Diego)

Restaurants: 1 Liquor: Yes
Buffets: Brunch- $11.95 (Sun)
B-$5.99 (Sat-Sun)
L-$8.99 (Sat-Sun)
D-$11.99 (Fri-Sun)
Other Games: BJ, P
Overnight RV Parking: Free/RV Dump: No

Soboba Casino
23333 Soboba Road
San Jacinto, California 92583
(909) 654-2883
Website: www.soboba.net
Map: **#3** (90 miles E. of L. A.)

Toll-Free Number: (866) 4-SOBOBA
Restaurants: 1 Liquor: Yes
Casino Size: 52,000 Square Feet
Other Games: BJ, MB, P, PGP, LIR, TCP, BG
Overnight RV Parking: Free/RV Dump: No

Spa Resort Casino
140 N. Indian Canyon Drive
Palm Springs, California 92262
(760) 323-5865
Website: www.sparesortcasino.com
Map: **#3** (115 miles E. of L. A.)

Toll-Free Number: (800) 258-2WIN
Room Reservations: (800) 854-1279
Rooms: 213 Price Range: $109-$329
Suites: 15 Price Range: $199-$1,700
Restaurants: 5 (1 open 24 hours) Liquor: Yes
Buffets: B-$7.99/$23.99 (Sun) L-$11.99
D-$17.99/$23.99 (Fri-Sat)
Casino Size: 15,000 Square Feet
Other Games: BJ, MB, P, PGP, TCP, FCP
Overnight RV Parking: No
Special Features: Hotel offers hot mineral spa
with massages and facials.

Spotlight 29 Casino
46200 Harrison Place
Coachella, California 92236
(760) 775-5566
Website: www.spotlight29.com
Map: **#8** (130 miles E. of L. A.)

Toll-Free Number: (866) 377-6829
Restaurants: 2 Liquor: Yes
Buffets: D-$8.95 D-$13.95/$16.95 (Fri)
Other Games: BJ, MB, P, PGP, TCP
Overnight RV Parking: Free/RV Dump: No
Special Features: Three fast-food outlets
including McDonald's. 2,200-seat showroom.

Sycuan Resort & Casino
5469 Casino Way
El Cajon, California 92019
(619) 445-6002
Website: www.sycuan.com
Map: **#14** (10 miles E. of San Diego)

Toll-Free Number: (800) 279-2826
Room Reservations: (800) 457-5568
Rooms: 103 Price Range: $120-$185
Suites: 14 Price Range: $150-$3550
Restaurants: 4 Liquor: Yes
Buffets: L-$10.95/$15.95 (Sat/Sun) D-$15.95
Casino Size: 73,000 Square Feet
Other Games: BJ, S21, B, P, PGP, BG
Overnight RV Parking: Free/RV Dump: No
Senior Discount: Various Wed 7-11am if 55+
Special Features: Offers card/tile versions of
roulette and craps. Hotel is three miles from
casino with free shuttle service. Three 18-hole
golf courses. 500-seat showroom.

Table Mountain Casino & Bingo
8184 Table Mountain Road
Friant, California 93626
(559) 822-2485
Website: www.tmcasino.com
Map: **#15** (15 miles N. of Fresno)

Toll-Free Number: (800) 541-3637
Restaurants: 3 Liquor: No
Buffets: L-$10/$11(Sat/Sun)/$13 (Wed/Fri)
          D-$12/$14(Sat/Sun)/$16 (Wed/Fri)
Other Games: BJ, S21, P, PGP, LIR, TCP,
          BG (Wed-Sun)
Overnight RV Parking: Free/RV Dump: No
Senior Discount: $6 lunch buffet Mon/Thu
if 55+

Twin Pine Casino
22223 Highway 29 at Rancheria Road
Middletown, California 95461
(707) 987-0197
Website: www.twinpine.com
Map: **#32** (70 miles W. of Sacramento)

Toll-Free Number: (800) 564-4872
Restaurants: 1 Liquor: No
Other Games: BJ, PGP
Overnight RV Parking: Free/RV Dump: No
Senior Discount: Various Tue mornings 8:30
am-12:00 pm if 55+.

Thunder Valley Casino
1200 Athens Ave
Lincoln, California 95648
(916) 408-7777
Website: www.thundervalleyresort.com
Map: **#35** (35 miles N.E. of Sacramento)

Toll-Free Number: (877) 468-8777
Restaurants: 4 Liquor: Yes
Buffets: Brunch- $16.95 (Sun)
          B- $6.99/$10.99 (Sun)
          L-$9.99
          D-$14.99/$24.99 (Fri)
Other Games: BJ, MB, PGP, LIR, TCP, FCP
Overnight RV Parking: No
Special Features: Affiliated with Station
Casinos of Las Vegas. Five fast-food outlets.

COLORADO

Colorado casinos can be found in the mountain towns of Black Hawk, Central City and Cripple Creek. There are also two Indian casinos (which abide by Colorado's limited gaming rules) in Ignacio and Towaoc.

Gambling is limited in two aspects: one, only electronic games (slots, video poker, video blackjack and video keno) and the table games of poker, blackjack, let it ride and three-card poker are allowed. Two, a single wager cannot exceed $5.

For poker a raise is considered a separate bet. Three raises per round are allowed. On the last round, two players may go "head-to-head" with an unlimited number of raises. Nine varieties of poker are approved for casino play. Texas Hold 'Em, 7-Card Stud and Omaha are the most popular choices.

Blackjack wagers are limited to a $5 maximum, with most casinos allowing a $2 or $3 minimum bet. However, doubles and splits are considered separate bets. Colorado casinos employ Vegas Strip rules and most allow doubling after splits. Since pairs may be split three times (to make up to four hands) it is theoretically possible to bet $40 on what began as a single $5 wager.

Multiple action blackjack is also available in Colorado. Multiple action allows a player to place up to three bets (of up to $5 each) on a single blackjack hand. This hand is then played for three rounds against the same dealer up-card. Several Colorado casinos offer multiple action blackjack.

Here's information, as supplied by Colorado's Division of Gaming, showing the slot machine payback percentages for each city's casinos for the one-year period from July 1, 2006 through June 30, 2007:

	Black Hawk	Central City	Cripple Creek
1¢ Slots	91.51%	91.46%	**91.74%**
5¢ Slots	**93.36%**	**93.36%**	93.35%
25¢ Slots	94.75%	94.76%	**95.16%**
$1 Slots	94.96%	**95.64%**	95.11%
$5 Slots	95.28%	95.03%	**95.45%**
All	93.43%	93.64%	**94.01%**

These numbers reflect the percentage of money returned on each denomination of machine and encompass all electronic machines including video poker and video keno. The best returns for each category are highlighted in bold print.

The maximum hours Colorado casinos can operate are from 8 a.m. until 2 a.m. and the minimum gambling age is 21.

The two major gaming-oriented magazines in Colorado are *The Gambler* and the *Rocky Mountain News Gaming Guide*. Both are free, and available in most casinos. Look in them for ads for casino coupons or fun books. The *Denver Post* Weekend section (published every Friday) also contains coupons and fun book offers for the casinos in Black Hawk and Central City.

For information on visiting Black Hawk or Central City, call (877) 282-8804, or visit their web site at: www.visitbhcc.com. For Cripple Creek information call (877) 858-GOLD.

For general information on Colorado contact the state's tourism board at (800) 433-2656 or www.colorado.com.

Black Hawk

Map Location: **#1** (35 miles west of Denver. Take U.S. 6 through Golden to Hwy 119. Take Hwy 119 to Black Hawk. Another route is I-70 West to exit 244. Turn right onto Hwy. 6. Take Hwy 6 to 119 and into Black Hawk.)

The Lodge at Black Hawk, Colorado Central Station and the Isle of Capri are the only casinos with hotel rooms. The next closest lodging is at Fortune Valley Casino or the Century Casino & Hotel , 3/4-mile up Gregory Street in Central City. Another alternative is the Gold Dust Lodge, on Hwy. 119 about 1.5 miles from the Black Hawk casinos. The Gold Dust features 23 rooms with private baths.

The casinos in Black Hawk and Central City are located one mile apart. The Black Hawk Shuttle Service provides free transportation throughout Black Hawk and Central City.

There are a few bus tour programs operating between the metropolitan Denver area and Black Hawk/Central City. These programs are priced around $15 and usually affiliated with a few casinos that will reimburse a portion of the transportation charge. Check the "Weekend" section of the Friday *Denver Post* and *Rocky Mountain News* for bus tour ads.

All casinos offer electronic games (slots, video poker, video blackjack and video keno). Some casinos also offer: blackjack (BJ), poker (P), let it ride (LIR) and three card poker (TCP).

Ameristar Black Hawk
111 Richman Street
Black Hawk, Colorado 80422
(720) 946-4000
Web Site:www.ameristar.com/blackhawk

Toll-Free Number (866) 667-3386
Restaurants: 4
Buffets: L-$10.95/$15.95 (Sun)
          D-$16.99/$18.99 (Fri/Sat)
Casino Size: 46,161 Square feet
Other Games: BJ, P

Black Hawk Station
141 Gregory Street
Black Hawk, Colorado 80422
(303) 582-5582

Restaurants: 1 (snack bar)
Casino Size: 2,267 Square Feet

Bull Durham Saloon & Casino
110 Main Street
Black Hawk, Colorado 80422
(303) 582-0810
Website: www.bulldurhamcasino.com

Restaurants: 1 (snack bar)
Casino Size: 2,579 Square Feet

Bullwhackers Casino
101 Gregory Street
Black Hawk, Colorado 80422
(303) 271-2500
Website: www.bullwhackers.com

Toll-Free Number: (800) GAM-BULL
Restaurants: 2
Casino Size: 4,944 Square Feet (Bullpen)
Casino Size: 11,911 Square Feet (Bullwhackers)
Senior Discount: Specials on Tue/Wed if 55+
Special Features: Includes **Bullpen Sports** Casino. Bakery.

Canyon Casino
131 Main Street
Black Hawk, Colorado 80422
(303) 777-1111
Website: www.canyoncasino.com

Restaurants: 1
Casino Size: 9,761 Square Feet (Canyon)
Casino Size: 2,429 Square Feet (Grand Plateau)
Special Features: Connected to **Grand Plateau Casino**.

Colorado Central Station Casino
340 Main Street
Black Hawk, Colorado 80422
(303) 582-3000
Website: www.coloradocentralstation.com

Toll-Free Number (800) 843-4753
Rooms: 140 Price Range: $129-$206
Suites: 24 Price Range: $174-$215
Restaurants: 2
Casino Size: 17,613 Square Feet
Other Games: BJ, P
Special Features: Affiliated with Isle of Capri.

Eureka! Casino
211 Gregory Street
Black Hawk, Colorado 80422
(303) 582-1040

Restaurants: 1
Casino Size: 1,902 Square Feet
Special Features: 50¢ strawberry Margarita.

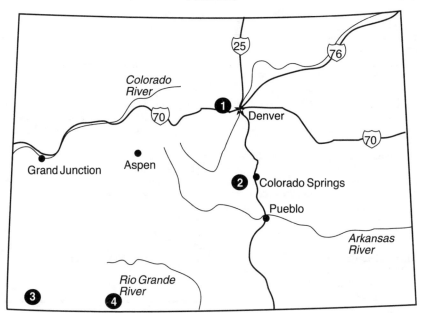

Fitzgeralds Casino
101 Main Street
Black Hawk, Colorado 80422
(303) 582-6162
Website: www.fitzgeraldsbh.com

Toll-Free Number: (800) 538-5825
Restaurants: 1
Casino Size: 10,252 Square Feet
Other Games: BJ, P

Gilpin Hotel Casino
111 Main Street
Black Hawk, Colorado 80422
(303) 582-1133
Website: www.thegilpincasino.com

Restaurants: 2
Other Games: P
Casino Size: 10,615 Square Feet
Senior Discount: Specials on Tue if 50+

Golden Gates Casino
261 Main Street
Black Hawk, Colorado 80422
(303) 582-1650
Website: www.themardigrascasino.com

Casino Size: 7,544 Square Feet (Golden Gates)
Casino Size: 3,985 Square Feet (Golden Gulch)
Other Games: P
Special Features: Connected to **Golden Gulch Casino**.

Isle of Capri Casino - Black Hawk
401 Main Street
Black Hawk, Colorado 80422
(303) 998-7777
Website: www.isleofcapricasino.com

Toll-Free Number (800) 843-4753
Rooms: 107 Price Range: $119-$209
Suites: 130 Price Range: $139-$239
Restaurants: 3
Buffets: B-$7.99 L-$10.99
         D-$15.99/$16.99 (Fri/Sat)
Casino Size: 27,452 Square Feet
Other Games: BJ, TCP, P, LIR

The Lodge Casino at Black Hawk
240 Main Street
Black Hawk, Colorado 80422
(303) 582-1771
Website: www.thelodgecasino.com

Rooms: 47 Price Range: $119-$155
Suites: 3 Price Range: Casino Use Only
Restaurants: 3
Buffets: B-$6.49 L-$10.49$12.99 (Sun)
    D-$15.99
Casino Size: 22,343 Square Feet
OtherGames: BJ,P
Senior Discount: 50% off breakfast and
    lunch buffets Mon/Tue if 50 or older
Special Features: Skybridge to Mardi Gras
Casino. Free valet parking.

Mardi Gras Casino
333 Main Street
Black Hawk, Colorado 80422
(303) 582-5600
Website: www.themardigrascasino.com

Restaurants: 1
Casino Size: 14,133 Square Feet
Other Games: BJ
Special Features: Skybridge to Lodge Casino.

Red Dolly Casino
530 Gregory Street
Black Hawk, Colorado 80422
(303) 582-1100

Restaurants: 1 (snack bar)
Casino Size: 2,439 Square Feet

Riviera Black Hawk Casino
444 Main Street
Black Hawk, Colorado 80422
(303) 582-1000
Website: www.rivierablackhawk.com

Restaurants: 1
Buffet: B-$4.99 L-$10.99/$12.99 (Sat-Sun)
    D-$15.99
Casino Size: 24,812 Square Feet
Other Games: BJ, TCP, P
Senior Discount: 50% off buffet Mon-Wed if 50+

Silver Hawk
100 Chase Street
Black Hawk, Colorado 80422
(303) 271-2500
Website: www.bullwhackers.com

Toll-Free Number: (800) GAM-BULL
Restaurants: 1
Casino Size: 3,670 Square Feet
Senior Discount: Specials on Tue/Wed if 55+

Wild Card Saloon & Casino
112 Main Street
Black Hawk, Colorado 80422
(303) 582-3412

Restaurants: 1
Casino Size: 3,208 Square Feet
Special Features: Grocery store.

Central City

Map location: **#1** (same as Black Hawk).
Central City is located one mile from Black
Hawk. Turn left at the third stoplight on Hwy.
119 and proceed up Gregory Street.

Besides the two casino hotels in Central City
that have rooms, there are also several bed &
breakfasts: Gregory Inn (303-582-5561),
Chateau L'Acadienne (303-582-5209) and
Skye Cottage (303-582-0622).

Century Casino & Hotel
102 Main Street
Central City, Colorado 80427
(303) 582-5050
Website: www.centurycasinos.com

Toll-Free Number: (888) 507-5050
Rooms: 22 Price Range $119-$159
Restaurants: 2
Casino Size: 13,595 Square Feet
Other Games: BJ, P, TCP

Doc Holliday Casino
101 Main Street
Central City, Colorado 80427
(303) 582-1400

Restaurants: 1 Snack Bar
Casino Size: 5,666 Square Feet
Other Games: BJ, P, TCP

Dostal Alley Saloon & Gaming Emporium
1 Dostal Alley
Central City, Colorado 80427
(303) 582-1610

Restaurants: 1 Snack Bar
Casino Size: 741 Square Feet

Famous Bonanza/Easy Street
107 Main Street
(303) 582-5914
Central City, Colorado 80427
Website: www.famousbonanza.com

Toll-Free Number: (866) 339-5825
Restaurants: 1
Casino Size: 4,948 Square Feet (F. Bonanza)
Casino Size: 4,705 Square Feet (Easy Street)
Other Games: BJ, TCP

Fortune Valley Hotel & Casino
321 Gregory Street
Central City, Colorado 80427
(303) 582-0800
Website: www.fortunevalleycasino.com

Toll-Free Number: (800) 924-6646
Room Reservations: (866) 924-6646
Rooms: 118 Price Range $80-$160
Suites: 6 Price Range $160-$210
Restaurants: 2
Buffets: B- $6.49 L-$9.49 Brunch-$11.99
(Sun) D-$14.99/$15.99 (Fri-Sat)
Casino Size: 31,826 Square Feet
Other Games: BJ, P, TCP
Special Features: Tony Roma's restaurant.
Covered parking garage.

Cripple Creek

Map Location: **#2** (47 miles west of Colorado Springs. Take exit 141 at Colorado Springs off I-25. Go west on Hwy. 24 to the town of Divide. Turn left onto Hwy. 67 and go 18 miles to Cripple Creek.)

Cripple Creek has several hotel/casinos the largest of which is the Double Eagle Hotel & Casino. There is also a 67-room motel, Gold King Mountain Inn, located 1/8-mile from the casinos with free shuttle service. For room reservations, call (800) 445-3607.

Many Cripple Creek casinos hand out coupons and Fun Books at their doors. Also check the ads in the *Colorado Springs Gazette*, the *Pueblo Chieftain* and the free tourist magazines. For Cripple Creek tourism information call (877) 858-GOLD or go to www.cripple-creek.co.us

All casinos offer electronic games (slots, video poker, video blackjack and video keno). Some casinos also offer: blackjack (BJ), poker (P), let it ride (LIR) and three card poker (TCP).

Black Diamond Casino
425 E. Bennett Avenue
Cripple Creek, Colorado 80813
(719) 689-2898

Restaurants: 1 (snack bar)
Casino Size: 1,417 Square Feet
Special Features: Real gold vein in wall (upstairs). Video arcade.

Brass Ass Casino
264 E. Bennett Avenue
Cripple Creek, Colorado 80813
(719) 689-2104
Website: www.triplecrowncasinos.com

Restaurants: 1 (snack bar)
Casino Size: 2,627 Square Feet
Special Features: Free hot dogs and popcorn for players. Connected to **Midnight Rose** and **J.P McGill's**. Covered parking garage.

Bronco Billy's Casino
233 E. Bennett Avenue
Cripple Creek, Colorado 80813
(719) 689-2142
Website: www.broncobillyscasino.com

Toll Free Number: (877) 989-2142
Restaurants: 2
Other Games: BJ, P, TCP
Casino Size: 6,151 Square Feet (Bronco's)
Casino Size: 3,556 Square Feet (Buffalo's)
Senior Discount: Specials Mon/Fri 8am-6pm
Special Features: Includes **Buffalo Billy's.**
Free popcorn. Free cookies on weekends. Free
donuts Mon-Thu. 49¢ breakfast.

Colorado Grande Gaming Parlor
300 E. Bennett Avenue
Cripple Creek, Colorado 80813
(719) 689-3517
Website: www.coloradogrande.com

Toll Free Number: (877) 244-9469
Restaurants: 1
Casino Size: 2,911 Square Feet
Senior Discount: Dining discounts if 50+
Special Features: Free cookies on weekends.

Creeker's Casino
274 E. Bennett Avenue
Cripple Creek, Colorado 80813
(719) 689-3239
Website: www.creekerscasino.com

Restaurants: 1
Casino Size: 3,999 Square Feet
Special Features: Wedding chapel.

Double Eagle Hotel & Casino
442 E. Bennett Avenue
Cripple Creek, Colorado 80813
(719) 689-5000
Website: www.decasino.com

Toll-Free Reservations: (800) 711-7234
Rooms: 146 Price Range: $89-$139
Suites: 12 Price Range: $159-$500
Restaurants: 3
Buffets: B-$7.95
        D-$13.95/$22.95 (Fri)/$21.95 (Sat)
Casino Size: 15,889 Square Feet (Double Eagle)
Casino Size: 7,473 Square Feet (Gold Creek)
Other Games: BJ, P
Special Features: Connected to **Gold Creek**
casino. Starbucks. Slot club members get room
discount. Covered parking garage.

Gold Rush Hotel &Casino
209 E. Bennett Avenue
Cripple Creek, Colorado 80813
(719) 689-2646
Website: www.grushcasino.com

Toll-Free Number: (800) 235-8239
Rooms: 13 Price Range: $62-$82
Restaurants: 2
Casino Size: 5,449 Square Feet (Gold Rush)
Casino Size: 1,055 Square Feet (Gold Digger's)
Other Games: BJ, P
Special Features: **Gold Digger's** and **Gold
Rush** are interconnected. 49-cent breakfast.

Imperial Hotel & Casino
123 N. Third Street
Cripple Creek, Colorado 80813
(719) 689-2922
Website: www.imperialcasinohotel.com

Toll-Free Number: (800) 235-2922
Rooms: 29 Price Range: $45-$85
Suites: 2 Price Range: $100-$125
Restaurants: 2
Casino Size: 3,660 Square Feet

Johnny Nolon's Casino
301 E. Bennett Avenue
Cripple Creek, Colorado 80813
(719) 689-2080
Website: www.johnnynolons.com

Restaurants: 2
Casino Size: 5,850 Square Feet

J.P. McGill's Hotel & Casino
232 E. Bennett Avenue
Cripple Creek, Colorado 80813
(719) 689-2446
Website: www.triplecrowncasinos.com

Toll-Free Number: (888) 461-7529
Rooms: 36 Price Range: $89-$109
Suites: 5 Price Range: $179-$220
Restaurants: 1
Casino Size: 7,542 Square Feet
Special Features: Connected to **Midnight
Rose** and **Brass Ass**. 10% room/food discount
for slot club members. Free popcorn for
players. Covered parking garage.

Midnight Rose Hotel & Casino
256 E. Bennett Avenue
Cripple Creek, Colorado 80813
(719) 689-2865
Website: www.triplecrowncasinos.com

Toll-Free Number: (800) 635-5825
Rooms: 19 Price Range: $90-$120
Restaurants: 2
Casino Size: 9,330 Square Feet
Other Games: P
Special Features: Connected to **Brass Ass** and
J.P McGill's. 10% room/food discount for slot
club members. Covered parking garage.

Uncle Sam's Casino
251 E. Bennett Avenue
Cripple Creek, Colorado 80813
(719) 689-2222
Website: www.grushcasino.com

Casino Size: 1,716 Square Feet
Special Features: Free hot dogs for players.
Night club on second floor.

Wild Horse Casino
353 Myers Avenue
Cripple Creek, Colorado 80813
(719) 687-7777
Website: www.thewildhorsecasino.com

Restaurants: 1
Casino Size: 6,123 Square Feet
Other Games: BJ, TCP, LIR, P
Special Features: $1 breakfast 7am-9am daily.

Womacks/Legends Hotel & Casino
200-220 E. Bennett Avenue
Cripple Creek, Colorado 80813
(719) 689-0333
Website: www.womackscasino.com

Toll-Free Number: (888) 966-2257
Rooms: 21 Price Range: $49-$79
Suites: 3 Price Range: $99
Restaurants: 1
Casino Size: 5,494 Square Feet (Womacks)
Casino Size: 4,039 Square Feet (Legends)
Other Games: BJ, P
Special Features: **Womacks** and **Legends** are
interconnected. Rooms for club members only.

Indian Casinos

Sky Ute Casino and Lodge
14826 Highway 172 N.
Ignacio, Colorado 81137
(970) 563-3000
Website: www.skyutecasino.com
Map Location: **#4** (345 miles S.W. of Denver,
20 miles S.E. of Durango)

Toll-Free Number: (888) 842-4180
Room Reservations: (800) 876-7017
Rooms: 36 Price Range: $75-$90
Restaurants: 2 Liquor: No
Hours: 24 Hours Daily
Other Games: BJ, TCP, LIR
        Bingo (Wed/Thu/Sun)
Overnight RV Parking: Free (must park at
        events center)/RV Dump: No
Senior Discount: 10% off room/food if 55+
Special Features: Can stay in RV one mile
away at events center. Southern Ute Cultural
Center and Museum. Free local shuttle.

Ute Mountain Casino & RV Park
3 Weeminuche Drive/P.O. Drawer V
Towaoc, Colorado 81334
(970) 565-8800
Website: www.utemountaincasino.com
Map Location: **#3** (425 miles S.W. of Denver,
11 miles S. of Cortez on Hwys. 160/166)

Toll-Free Number: (800) 258-8007
Hotel Reservations: (888) 565-8837
RV Reservations: (800) 889-5072
Rooms: 70 Price Range: $59-$83
Suites: 20 Price Range: $108-$135
Restaurants: 1 Liquor: No
Buffets: B-$6.95 L-$8.95
        D-$10.95/$19.95 (Fri)
Casino Size: 32,000 Square Feet
Hours: 8am-4am Daily
Other Games: BJ, P
        Keno, Bingo (Fri-Tue)
Overnight RV Parking: Must use RV park
Senior Discount: 15% off non-buffet food if 55+
Special Features: 84-space RV Park ($23 per
night). Ute Tribal Park tours available.

CONNECTICUT

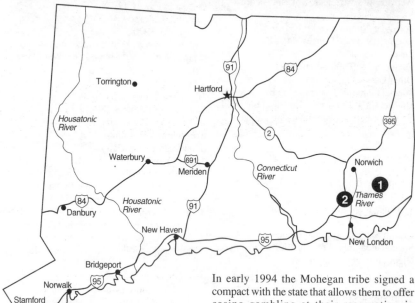

Foxwoods was New England's first casino and it is now the second largest casino in the world.

The Mashantucket Pequot Tribe which operates Foxwoods had to sue the state to allow the casino to open. They argued that since the state legally permitted "Las Vegas Nights," where low-stakes casino games were operated to benefit charities, then the tribe should be entitled to do the same. Eventually, they won their case before the U.S. Supreme Court and began construction of their casino which was financed by a Malaysian conglomerate (after 22 U.S. lenders turned down their loan requests).

When the casino first opened in February 1992, slot machines were not permitted. In January 1993 a deal was made between Governor Weicker and the Pequots which gave the tribe the exclusive right to offer slot machines in return for a yearly payment of 25% of the gross slot revenue. The agreement was subject to cancellation, however, if the state allowed slot machines anywhere else in Connecticut.

In early 1994 the Mohegan tribe signed a compact with the state that allows them to offer casino gambling at their reservation in Uncasville (map location #2). The Pequots gave permission for the Mohegans to have slot machines in their casino. The same 25% of the gross slot revenue payment schedule also applies to the Mohegans. The payment schedules are subject to cancellation, however, if the state legalizes any other form of casino gambling. The Mohegan casino opened in October 1996.

The minimum gambling age at both properties is 18 for bingo and 21 for the casino. Both casinos are open 24 hours. For information on visiting Connecticut call the state's Vacation Center at (800) 282-6863 or visit their website at www.ctbound.org

The games offered at Foxwoods are: blackjack, craps, roulette, baccarat, min-baccarat, big six (money wheel), pai gow poker, pai gow tiles, Caribbean stud poker, Texas Hold' Em bonus poker, Let it Ride, acey-deucey, casino war, chuck-a-luck, Spanish 21, Three-Card poker, Crazy 4 poker and poker; in addition to bingo, keno and pull tabs. There is also a Race Book offering off-track betting on horses, greyhounds and jai-alai.

Foxwoods Resort Casino is the world's second largest casino with over 300,000 square feet of gaming space. The property features three hotels, 35 food outlets, 6 casinos, a high limit casino, a race book, a 3,600-seat bingo room, a new state of the art smoke free World Poker Room™ and more than 7,000 electronic gaming machines.

Foxwoods Resort Casino
Route 2
Mashantucket, Connecticut 06338
(860) 312-3000
Website: www.foxwoods.com
Map Location: **#1** (45 miles S.E. of Hartford; 12 miles N. of I-95 at Mystic). From I-95 take exit 92 to Rt. 2-West, casino is 7 miles ahead. From I-395 take exit 79A to Rt. 2A follow to Rt. 2-East, casino is 2 miles ahead.

Toll-Free Number: (800) FOXWOODS
Hotel Reservations: (800) FOXWOODS
Rooms: 1,398 Price Range: $140-$325
Suites: 183   Price Range: $175-$1,500
Restaurants: 26 (3 open 24 hours)
Buffets: B-$10.50 L-$16.95 D- $19.95
Casino Size: 314,492 Square Feet
Casino Marketing: (800) 99-SLOTS
Overnight RV Parking: Free (self-contained only)/ RV Dump: No
Special Features: Three hotels with pool, Grand Pequot Tower hotel spa and beauty salon, golf. Headliner entertainment, Club BB nightclub. Gift shops. Wampum Rewards Mega Store. Hard Rock Cafe. Wampum Rewards members earn complimentaries at table games, slots, poker and race book. 10% room discount for AAA and AARP members. Two Rees Jones designed golf courses. $1 buffet discount for Wampum Rewards members.

The following information is from Connecticut's Division of Special Revenue regarding Foxwoods' slot payback percentages:

Denomination	Payback %
1¢	87.78
2¢	88.66
5¢	89.87
25¢	91.10
50¢	91.96
$1.00	92.69
$5.00	94.33
$10.00	96.85
$25.00	94.60
$100.00	96.27
Average	**91.28**

These figures reflect the total percentages returned by each denomination of slot machine from July 1, 2006 through June 30, 2007. Foxwoods' total win on its slot machines during that year was slightly more than $805 million and of that amount 25%, or slightly more than $201 million, was paid to the state.

Keep in mind that Foxwoods (as well as Mohegan Sun) doesn't pay any tax on its table games and therefore it isn't required to report the profits on that part of its operation.

The games offered at Connecticut's other casino, Mohegan Sun, are: blackjack, craps, roulette, baccarat, mini-baccarat, pai gow, wheel of fortune, bingo, pai gow poker, Caribbean stud poker, let it ride, Spanish 21, casino war, sic bo and keno. There is also a Race Book offering off-track betting on horses, greyhounds and jai-alai.

Mohegan Sun Casino
1 Mohegan Sun Boulevard
Uncasville, Connecticut 06382
(860) 862-8000
Website: www.mohegansun.com
Map Location: **#2** (Take I-95 Exit 76/I-395 North. Take Exit 79A (Route 2A) East. Less than 1 mile to Mohegan Sun Boulevard)

Toll-Free Number: (888) 226-7711
Room Reservations: (888) 777-7922
Rooms: 1,020 Price Range: $149-$400
Suites: 180 Price Range: $300-$1,000
Restaurants: 29 (3 open 24 hours)
Buffets (Seasons): B-$10.50 L/D-$15.75
Buffets (Sunburst): L/D-$19.00
Casino Size: 295,000 Square Feet
Overnight RV Parking: Free/RV Dump: No
Special Features: Food court with specialty food outlets. Kid's Quest supervised children's activity center. On-site gas station. 30-store shopping arcade.

Here's information from Connecticut's Division of Special Revenue regarding Mohegan Sun's slot payback percentages:

Denomination	Payback %
1/2¢	85.04
1¢	88.68
2¢	89.03
5¢	88.27
25¢	89.74
50¢	90.71
$1.00	92.55
$5.00	93.60
$10.00	96.11
$25.00	95.40
$100.00	95.20
Average	**91.37**

These figures reflect the total percentages returned by each denomination of slot machine from July 1, 2006 through June 30, 2007.

The total win on all of the Mohegan Sun slot machines during that period was slightly more than $916 million and of that amount 25%, or slightly more than $229 million, was paid to the state.

DELAWARE

1 Wilmington

Dover 2

3

Delaware Bay

The minimum gambling age is 21 for slots and 18 for horse racing. For more information on visiting Delaware call the state's tourism office at (800) 441-8846 or visit their web site at: www.delaware.com.

Delaware Park Racetrack & Slots
777 Delaware Park Boulevard
Wilmington, Delaware 19804
(302) 994-2521
Website: www.delpark.com
Map: **#1**

Toll-Free Number: (800) 41-SLOTS
Restaurants: 8
Admission: Free Parking: Free
Valet Parking: $3
Overnight RV Parking: Free/RV Dump: No
Special Features: Live thoroughbred racing mid-April to mid-November. Daily simulcasting of horse racing. Ask for Delaware Park discounted hotel rate at Christiana Hilton (800-348-3133).

Delaware's three pari-mutuel facilities all feature slot machines. Technically, the machines are video lottery terminals (VLT's) because they are operated in conjunction with the Delaware Lottery. Unlike VLT's in other states, however, Delaware's machines pay out in cash. The VLT's also play other games including: video poker, video keno and video blackjack.

By law, all video lottery games must return between 87% and 95% of all wagers on an annual basis. Games can return above 95% but only with the Lottery Director's approval.

According to figures from the Delaware Lottery for the six-month period from January through June, 2007 the average VLT return at Delaware Park was 92.73%, at Dover Downs it was 91.21% and at Midway Slots & Simulcast it was 91.63%.

All casinos are open 24 hours, except for Sundays when they are closed from 6 a.m. to noon. They are also closed on Easter and Christmas.

Dover Downs Slots
1131 N. DuPont Highway
Dover, Delaware 19901
(302) 674-4600
Website: www.doverdowns.com
Map: **#2**

Toll-Free Number: (800) 711-5882
Rooms: 206 Price Range: $125-$250
Suites: 26 Price Range: $195-$805
Restaurants: 4
Buffets: B-$10.00 L-$13.00 D-$16.00
Admission: Free Parking: Free
Valet Parking: $3
Casino Size: 91,000 Square Feet
Overnight RV Parking: Free/RV Dump: Free
          (Not free during NASCAR events)
Special Features: Casino is non-smoking. Live harness racing November through April. Daily simulcasting of horse racing. Comedy Club. Motorsports speedway with NASCAR racing. $2 buffet discount for slot club members.

Midway Slots & Simulcast
Delaware State Fairgrounds
U.S. 13 South
Harrington, Delaware 19952
(302) 398-4920
Website: www.midwayslots.com
Map: **#3** (20 miles S. of Dover)

Toll-Free Number: (888) 88-SLOTS
Restaurants: 3
Buffets: L/D-$12.99/$14.99 (Mon/Wed)
Admission: Free
Parking: Free   Valet Parking: $2
Overnight RV Parking: Free/RV Dump: No
Special Features: Live harness racing April-
June and August-October. Daily simulcasting
of horse racing. $5.99 buffet Fri/Sat 11:30pm
to 2am.

FLORIDA

Florida has three forms of casino gambling: casino boats, Indian casinos and gaming machines at pari-mutuels in one south Florida county.

The casino boats offers gamblers the opportunity to board ships that cruise offshore where casino gambling is legal. From the east coast the boats sail three miles out into the Atlantic Ocean and from the west coast the boats travel nine miles out into the Gulf of Mexico.

A variety of boats are in operation ranging from Port Canaveral's 1,800-passenger, *Ambassador II* cruise ship all the way down to the yacht-sized *SunCruz I* casino boat in Key Largo which carries 149 passengers.

Generally, you will find that the larger ships have more of a variety of things to do besides the gambling, but the cost will be a little higher because of added port/service charges. Most of the ships that sail from the major ports, such as Port Everglades, Port of Palm Beach or Port Canaveral will add port/service charges to the quoted cruise price. Usually, there is also a charge to park your car at the large ports.

Most of the smaller boats which don't dock at the large ports don't have port/service charges added to their cruise prices. Also, most of the smaller boats offer free parking. You will find that almost all of the ships are constantly running price specials so don't be surprised if you call and are quoted a price lower than the regular brochure rates listed here.

Unless otherwise noted, all Florida casino boats offer: blackjack, craps, roulette, slots and video poker. Some casinos also offer: mini-baccarat (MB), poker (P), pai gow poker (PGP), three-card poker (TCP), Caribbean stud poker (CSP), let it ride (LIR), big 6 wheel (B6) bingo (BG) and sports book (SB).

Each casino boat sets its own minimum gambling age: on some boats it's 21 and on others it's 18. The minimum drinking age on all boats is 21. Due to security restrictions, you must present a photo ID at all casino boats or you will not be allowed to board.

For Florida visitor information call (888) 735-2872 or visit their web site at: www.flusa.com. For information on the Florida Keys or Key West call (800) 352-5397 or visit their web site at: www.fla-keys.com.

Daytona Beach

Map: **#12**

SunCruz Casino - Daytona
4880 Front Street
Ponce Inlet, Florida 32127
(386) 322-9600
Web site: www.suncruzcasino.com

Reservation Number: (800) 474-DICE
Gambling Age: 18   Ship's Registry: U.S.A.
Buffets: L-$7.00 D-$10.00
Schedule:
    11:00am - 4:00pm
    7:00pm - Midnight/12:30am (Fri/Sat)
Price: $10
Port Charges: Included
Parking: Free
Casino Size: 18,000 Square Feet
Other Games: MB, P, LIR, TCP
Senior Discount: Free cruise Wed if 50+
Special Features: 560-passenger *SunCruz III* departs from Ponce Inlet near Down the Hatch restaurant. Must be 18 or older to board. Sailing times subject to change due to tide conditions, call ahead for schedule.

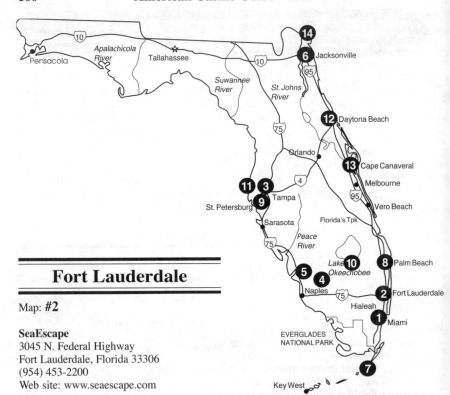

Fort Lauderdale

Map: **#2**

SeaEscape
3045 N. Federal Highway
Fort Lauderdale, Florida 33306
(954) 453-2200
Web site: www.seaescape.com

Reservation Number: (877) SEA-ESCAPE
Gambling Age: 18   Ship's Registry: Bahamas
Food Service: Buffet Included
Schedule:
   11:00am - 4:30pm (Daily)
   7:30pm - 12:30am (Mon-Thu)
   7:30pm - 1:30am (Fri-Sat)
   6:30pm- 11:30pm (Sun)
Prices: Day- $27.95
   Eve- $29.95 (Sun-Thu)/$37.95 (Fri-Sat)
Port Charges: $3 Security Charge: $3
Parking: $8
Other Games: MB, PGP, CSP, TCP, LIR, BG
Senior Discount: $2 off cruise if 55 or older
Special Features: 900-passenger *MV Island Adventure* sails from Port Everglades in Fort Lauderdale. All prices are for advance purchase tickets only - $10 surcharge on tickets purchased at pier. Showroom with live entertainment. Full-service dinner upgrade available. Private cabin rentals. Children's prices offered on day cruises. Must be 21 or older on evening cruises unless accompanied by parent or legal guardian.

Fort Myers Beach

Map: **#5** (40 miles N. of Naples)

Big "M" Casino
450 Harbor Court
Fort Myers Beach, Florida 33931
(239) 765-7529
Web site: www.bigmcasino.com

Toll-Free Number: (888) 373-3521
Gambling Age: 21   Ship's Registry: U.S.A.
Buffets: Brunch-$9.95 L-$9.95 D-$14.95
Schedule: 10:15am - 4:15pm (Daily)
            6:00pm -11:45pm (Daily)
Prices: $10/$20 (Fri/Sat Eve)
Port Charges: Included
Parking: Free (Valet also free)
Other Games: LIR, TCP, No Craps
Special Features: 400-passenger *Big M* sails from Moss Marina next to Snug Harbor on Fort Myers Beach. Closed Mondays from May through December. Must be 21 or older to board. A la carte menu also available. Cashback for slot play.

Jacksonville

Map: **#6**

SunCruz Casino - Jacksonville
4378 Ocean Street
Mayport, Florida 32233
(904) 249-9300
Web site: www.suncruzcasino.com

Toll-Free Number: (800) 474-DICE
Gambling Age: 18   Ship's Registry: U.S.A.
Buffets: L- $7.00 D-$10.00
Schedule
  11:00am - 4:00pm (Mon-Fri)
  11:00am - 4:30pm (Sat)
  11:30am - 5:00pm (Sun)
  7:00pm - 12:00am (Sun-Thu)/12:30 (Sat)
  7:30pm - 1:00am (Fri)
Price: $10
Port Charges: Included   Parking: Free
Other Games: MB, P, CSP, TCP, LIR, B6
Special Features: 600-passenger, *SunCruz VI* departs from Mayport Village. Must be 18 or older to board. A la carte menu also available.

Key Largo

Map: **#7** (50 miles S. of Miami)

SunCruz Casino - Key Largo
99701 Overseas Highway
Key Largo, Florida 33037
(305) 451-0000
Web site: www.suncruzcasino.com

Reservation Number: (800) 474-DICE
Gambling Age: 18   Ship's Registry: U.S.A.
Food Service: Hors d'oeuvres and a la carte
Shuttle Schedule:
 Departs   Noon (Sun)
 Departs   2pm (Wed/Sat)
 Departs   6pm (Mon/Tue)
 Departs   5pm (Thu/Fri)
Price: $10
Port Charges: Included   Parking: Free
Other Games: TCP
Special Features: 149-passenger *SunCruz I* first departs from the Holiday Inn dock in Key Largo at times shown above. The boat then stays offshore and a water taxi shuttles passengers back and forth at differing times. Must be 18 or older to board.

Madeira Beach

Map: #9 (5 miles N. of St. Petersburg)

Treasure Island Casino Cruz
150 John's Pass BoardWalk Place
Madeira Beach, Florida 3370
(727)399-9465
Web site:
www.treasureislandcasinocruz.com

Toll-Free Number: (888) 308-8422
Gambling Age: 18   Ship's Registry: U.S.A.
Buffet: L-$7 D-$10
Schedule:
11:00am - 4:30pm/5:00pm (Sat/Sun/Holidays)
7:00pm - 12:30am/1:00am (Fri/Sat/Holidays)
Price: $10
Port Charges: Included   Parking: Free
Other Games: MB, P, TCP
Special Features: 300-passenger, SunCruz V departs from John's Pass boardwalk. Must be 18 or older to board. A la carte menu also available.

Miami

Map: **#1**

Horizon's Edge Casino Cruises
200 N. Biscayne Boulevard
Miami, Florida 33131
(305) 523-2270
Web site: www.horizonsedge.com

Reservation Number: (800) 582-5932
Gambling Age: 21   Ship's Registry: U.S.A.
Food Service: Buffet Included
  12:00pm - 5:00pm (Daily)
  7:30pm -12:30am/1:00am (Fri/Sat)
Prices: $19.95
Port Charges: Included
Parking: $10 Valet Parking Only
Casino Size: 10,000 Square Feet
Other Games: LIR, TCP
Special Features: 500-passenger *Horizon's Edge* sails from Bayside Marketplace in downtown Miami. Must be 21, or older, to board.

Miami Beach

Map: **#1**

Aquasino South Beach
390 Alton Road Suite B
Miami Beach, FL 33139
(305) 532-0021
Web site: www.aquasinosouthbeach.com

Toll-Free Number: (866) 541-2782
Gambling Age: 21   Ship's Registry: U.S.A.
Food Service: Buffet Included
   12:00pm - 5:00pm (Wed-Sun)
   7:30pm -12:30am/1:00am (Thu-Sat)
Admission Price: $40
Port Charges: Included
Parking: Valet Parking Included in Admission
Casino Size: 10,000 Square Feet
Other Games: MB, LIR, TCP, SB
Special Features: 600-passenger ship sails from Miami Beach Marina. Must be 21, or older, to board.

Palm Beach

Map: **#8**

Palm Beach Princess
One E. 11th Street
Riviera Beach, Florida 33404
(561) 845-2101
Web site: www.pbcasino.com

Reservation Number: (800) 841-7447
Gambling Age: 21   Ship's Registry: Panama
Food Service: Buffet Included
Schedule & Prices:
10:30am - 4:00pm (Mon-Fri) $27/$37 (Sat)
10:30am- 5:00pm (Sun) $37
6:30pm - 11:30pm (Mon-Thu) $27
6:30pm - 11:30pm (Fri/Sat) $37
6:30pm - 11:30pm (Sun) $27
Port Charges: Included
Parking: $5 Valet Parking: $8
Casino Size: 15,000 Square Feet
Other Games: SB, LIR, P, TCP,·BG
Special Features: 850-passenger *Palm Beach Princess* sails from Port of Palm Beach. Private cabin rentals. Children only allowed on day cruises. Must be 21 or older to board on evening cruises. $5 discount for seniors, AAA/AARP members and Florida residents. $5 discount if you book your reservations online.

SunCruz Casino - Palm Beach
One East 11th Street
Riviera Beach, Florida 33404
(561) 842-1889
Web site: www.suncruzcasino.com

Reservation Number: (800) 474-DICE
Gambling Age: 18   Ship's Registry: U.S.A.
Buffets: Included
Schedule:
   11:00am - 4:30pm Daily
   7:30pm -12:15am (Sun-Thurs)
   7:30pm - 12:45am (Fri/Sat)
Prices: Free
Port Charges: Included   Parking: $6
Other Games: MB, P, CSP, LIR, TCP
Special Features: 590-passenger *SunCruz VI* sails from Port of Palm Beach. Must be 18 or older to board. A la carte menu also available.

Port Canaveral

Map: **#13** (60 miles S. of Daytona Beach)

Sterling Casino Lines
Terminal B
Cape Canaveral, Florida 32920
(321) 783-2212
Web site: www.sterlingcasinolines.com

Reservation Number: (800) ROLL-7-11
Gambling Age: 21 Ship's Registry: Bahamas
Buffets: Included
Schedule:
   11:00am - 4:00pm (Daily)
   7:00pm - 12:00am/1am (Fri/Sat)
Price: Free
Port Charges: Included   Parking: Free
Casino Size: 75,000 Square Feet
Other Games: B, MB, LIR
Special Features: 1,800-passenger, *Ambassador II* departs from terminal 2 at Port Canaveral. Free live entertainment in the lounge. Must be 21 or older to board.

SunCruz Casino - Port Canaveral
610 Glen Cheek Drive
Cape Canaveral, Florida 32920
(321) 799-3511
Web site: www.suncruzcasino.com

Toll-Free Number: (800) 474-DICE
Gambling Age: 18   Ship's Registry: U.S.A.
Buffets: L-$7.00 D-$10.00
Schedule
   11:00am - 4:00pm (Mon-Sat)
   11:00am - 4:30pm (Sun)
   7:00pm - 12:00am (Sun-Thu)
   7:00pm - 1:00am (Fri/Sat)
Price: Free
Port Charges: Included   Parking: Free
Other Games: MB, P, CSP, LIR, TCP
Special Features: 1,000-passenger, *SunCruz XII* departs from Port Canaveral. Must be 18 or older to board. A la carte food menu also available.

Port Richey

Map: **#11** (37 miles N.W. of Tampa)

SunCruz Casino - Port Richey
7917 Bayview Street
Port Richey, Florida 34668
(727) 848-3423
Web site: www.portricheycasino.com

Toll-Free Number: (800) 464-3423
Gambling Age: 18   Ship's Registry: U.S.A.
Food Service: A la Carte
Shuttle Schedule:
Departs: 9:30am/11am/3:30pm/7pm
Returns: 3pm/5:30pm/9pm/
            12:30am (1am Fri/Sat)
Price: Free
Port Charges: Included   Parking: Free
Other Games: TCP, CSP
Special Features: 465-passenger *Royal Casino 1* stays offshore and a water taxi shuttles passengers back and forth according to above schedule. Shuttle departs from dock on Pithlachascotee River off of US 19 in Port Richey.

St. Petersburg

Map: **#9**

Casino Royale
151 107th Avenue, Suite F
Treasure Island, FL 33706
Web site: www.casinoroyale21.com
(727) 360-5900

EXPECTED TO OPEN IN LATE 2007. CALL FOR UPDATED INFORMATION.
Reservation Number: (877) 476-9253
Gambling Age: 21   Ship's Registry: U.S.A.
Food Service: A la Carte
Shuttle Schedule: Not set at press time
Price: $10
Port Charges: Included
Other Games: S21, MB, P, PGP, TCP, LIR
Special Features: *Casino Royale* stays offshore and a high-speed catamaran shuttles passengers back and forth from John's Pass, located at 12788 Kingfish Drive in Treasure Island. Must be 21 or older to board.

Indian Casinos

Florida has eight Indian gaming locations. The Seminole Tribe has seven and the eighth is on the Miccosukee Tribe's reservation.

As of August 1, 2007 the only games offered at Indian casinos were Class II games where players compete against each other, rather than against the casino. However, negotiations were underway with the state to allow traditional Class III slots and it is expected that they will be available by late 2007.

The Class II video gaming devices look like slot machines, but are actually bingo games and the spinning reels are for "entertainment purposes only." No public information is available concerning the payback percentages on gaming devices in Florida's Indian casinos.

The other games allowed are: high-stakes bingo, video pull tabs, low-limit poker games (maximum $5 bet, 3 raises per round, no limit to number of rounds) and no-limit poker with a maximum buy-in of $100. Similar poker limits can also be found in many of the state's pari-mutuel facilities (horse tracks, dog tracks, jai-alai frontons and one harness track).

All casinos are open 24 hours (except Brighton and Big Cypress) and all offer bingo except for both Seminole Hard Rock Casinos and the Seminole Casino Coconut Creek. The minimum gambling age is 18 at all Indian casinos.

Big Cypress Casino
30013 Josie Billie Highway
Clewiston, Florida 33440
(863) 983-7245

Map: **#10** (75 miles W. of Palm Beach)

Hours: Noon-Mid Thursday to Sunday Only
Restaurants: Snack Bar
Games: Only Gaming Machines

Brighton Seminole Bingo and Casino
17735 Reservation Road
Okeechobee, Florida 34974
(863) 467-9998
Web site: www.seminolecasinobrighton.com
Map: **#10** (75 miles N.W. of West Palm Beach)

Toll-Free Number: (866) 2-CASINO
Hours: 10am-1am Daily
Restaurants: 1   Liquor: Yes
Casino Size: 24,400 Square Feet
Overnight RV Parking: No
Special Features: Poker starts at 3pm/noon (Sat/Sun).

Hollywood Seminole Gaming
4150 N. State Road 7
Hollywood, Florida 33021
(954) 961-3220
Web site: ww.seminolehollywoodcasino.com
Map: **#2** (1 miles S. of Fort Lauderdale)

Toll-Free Number: (800) 323-5452
Restaurants: 2   Liquor: Yes
Buffets: L-$7.99 D-$8.99
Casino Size: 73,500 Square Feet
Overnight RV Parking: Free/RV Dump: No
Special Features: Located one block south of Hard Rock Hotel & Casino.

Miccosukee Indian Gaming
500 S.W. 177 Avenue
Miami, Florida 33194
(305) 222-4600
Web site: www.miccosukee.com
Map: **#1**

Toll-Free Number: (800) 741-4600
Room Reservations: (877) 242-6464
Rooms: 256 Price Range: $109-$129
Suites: 46 Price Range: $149-$189
Restaurants: 4   Liquor: Yes
Buffets: B-$7.95 L/D-$10.95
Overnight RV Parking: Free/RV Dump: No

Seminole Casino Coconut Creek
5550 NW 40th Street
Coconut Creek, Florida 33073
(954) 977-6700
Web site: www.seminolecoconutcreekcasino.com
Map: **#2**

Toll-Free Number: (866) 2-CASINO
Restaurants: 2   Liquor: Yes
Casino Size: 30,000 Square Feet
Overnight RV Parking: No
Special Features: Free valet parking.

Seminole Casino Immokalee
506 South 1st Street
Immokalee, Florida 33934
(941) 658-1313
Web site: www.theseminolecasino.com
Map: **#4** (35 miles N.E. of Naples)

Toll-Free Number: (800) 218-0007
Restaurants: 1 Liquor: Yes
Casino Size: 22,000 Square Feet

Seminole Hard Rock
Hotel & Casino - Hollywood
1 Seminole Way
Hollywood, Florida 33314
(954) 327-7625
Web site: www.seminolehardrockhollywood.com
Map: **#2** (1 mile S. of Fort Lauderdale)

Toll-Free Number: (866) 502-7529
Room Reservations: (800) 937-0010
Rooms: 437 Price Range: $199-$329
Suites: 63 Price Range: $299-$449
Valet Parking: $7
Restaurants: 4   Liquor: Yes
Buffets: Brunch-$49.95 (Sun)
Casino Size: 130,000 Square Feet
Overnight RV Parking: No
Special Features: Food court. Lagoon-style pool. Health spa. Shopping mall with 20 stores.

The Seminole Hard Rock Hotel & Casino in Hollywood is South Florida's leading entertainment destination. It features a 130,000-square-foot casino, including a poker room, plus a 4-Diamond rated 500-room hotel with a European-style spa. There is also an adjacent complex featuring 24 retail shops, 17 restaurants, 10 nightclubs and a state-of-the-art 6,400-seat Hard Rock Live entertainment venue.

**Seminole Hard Rock
Hotel & Casino - Tampa**
5223 N. Orient Road
Tampa, Florida 33610
(813) 627-7625
Web site: www.hardrockhotelcasinotampa.com
Map: **#3**

Toll-Free Number: (800) 282-7016
Room Reservations: (800) 937-0010
Rooms: 204 Price Range: $169-$229
Suites: 46 Price Range: $195-$395
Restaurants: 2 (1 open 24 hours) Liquor: Yes
Casino Size: 90,000 Square Feet
Overnight RV Parking: Free weekdays only
Special Features: Food court. Health club.

Pari-Mutuels

In early 2005 voters in Broward County (home county of Fort Lauderdale) passed a referendum to allow slot machines at four pari-mutuel facilities within that county.

The first slot facilities opened in late 2006 and two others followed within six months. The fourth facility, Dania Jai-Alai, is not expected to add slots until late 2008.

Florida gaming regulations require a minimum payback of 85% on all gaming machines. From November 15, 2006 through June 30, 2007, the gaming machines at Gulfstream returned 90.50%. From December 28, 2006 through June 30, 2007 the return was 91.13% at Mardi Gras Gaming and from April 14 through June 30, 2007 it was 91.74% at The Isle.

Broward's four pari-mutuel facilities also offer poker games with low stakes similar to the Indian casinos. Admission to all casinos is free and they are allowed to be open a maximum of 16 hours during the week and 24 hours on the weekends.

The minimum gambling age is 18 for pari-mutuel betting or poker and 21 for gaming machines.

Dania Jai-Alai
301 E. Dania Beach Boulevard
Dania Beach, Florida 33004
(954) 920-1511
Website: www.dania-jai-alai.com
Map: #2

Fronton Admission: $1.50
Self-Parking: Free Valet: $3
Restaurants: 1
Overnight RV Parking: No
Special Features: Live jai-alai games Tue-Sat eves and Tue/Sat/Sun afternoons. Daily simulcasting of thoroughbred/harness racing and jai-alai. Slots not expected to open until late 2008.

Gulfstream Park Racing & Casino
901 S. Federal Highway
Hallandale Beach, Florida 33009
(954) 454-7000
Website: www.gulfstreampark.com
Map: #2

Toll-Free Number: (800) 771-TURF
Track Admission: $3/$5 (Fri-Sat)
Parking: Free Valet: Free
Hours 10am-2am Daily
Restaurants: 3
Buffet: D- $16.99/$21.99 (Fri)
Overnight RV Parking: No
Special Features: Live thoroughbred racing Wed-Mon from January through April. Daily simulcasting of thoroughbred racing.

Mardi Gras Racetrak and Gaming Center
831 N. Federal Highway
Hallandale Beach, Florida 33009
(954) 924-3200
Website: www.playmardigras.com
Map: #2

Toll-Free Number: (877) 557-5687
Track Admission: Free
Parking: Free Valet: $7
Hours 10:30am-4:30am/24 Hours (Fri/Sat)
Restaurants: 1
Overnight RV Parking: No
Special Features: Live dog racing daily December through May. Daily simulcasting of dog, thoroughbred and harness races.

The Isle at Pompano Park
1800 S.W. 3rd Street
Pompano Beach, Florida 33069
(954) 972-2000
Website: www.theislepompanopark.com
Map: #2

Toll-Free Number: (800) 843-4753
Track Admission: Free
Self-Parking: Free Valet: $6
Hours 9am-3am/5am (Fri/Sat)
Restaurants: 4
Buffet: B- $16.99 (Sun) L- $11.99
        D- $16.99/ $21.99 (Fri-Sat)
Overnight RV Parking: No
Special Features: Live harness racing Mon/Wed/Fri/Sat eves December through March, Wed/Fri/Sat eves April through November. Daily simulcasting of thoroughbred/harness racing and jai-alai.

GEORGIA

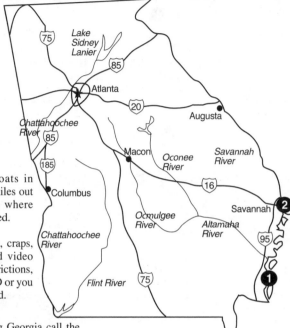

There are two casino boats in Georgia which sail three miles out into international waters where casino gambling is permitted.

Both boats offer blackjack, craps, roulette, poker, slots and video poker. Due to security restrictions, you must present a photo ID or you will not be allowed to board.

For information on visiting Georgia call the state's tourism department at (800) 847-4842 or visit their web site at www.georgia.org.

Emerald Princess II Casino
1 Gisco Point Drive
Brunswick, Georgia 31523
(912) 265-3558
Website: www.emeraldprincesscasino.com
Map Location: **#1** (75 miles S. of Savannah)

Reservation Number: (800) 842-0115
Gambling Age: 21   Parking: Free
Schedule
11:00am - 4:00pm (Fri/Sat)
 1:00pm - 6:00pm (Sun)
 7:00pm - 12:00am (Mon-Thu)
 7:00pm - 1:00am (Fri/Sat)
Price: $10   Port Charges: Included
Special Features: 400-passenger *Emerald Princess II* sails from Gisco Point, at the southern end of the Sidney Lanier Bridge. Soup, salad and sandwich included with cruise. Reservations are required for all cruises. Packages with hotel accommodations are available. No one under 21 permitted to board. Bingo offered on evening cruises.

Diamond Casino
8010 US Highway 80 East
Wilmington Island
Savannah, Georgia 31410
(912) 897-3005
Website: www.diamondcasinosavannah.com
Map Location: **#2**

Reservation Number: (877) 758-2597
Gambling Age: 18   Parking: Free
Food: A la carte menu
Schedule
 12:00pm - 5:00pm (Wed-Sun)
 7:00pm - 12:00am (Sun-Thu)
 7:00pm - 1:00am (Fri/Sat)
Price: $5   Port Charges: Included
Other Games: 3 Card Poker, Let It Ride
Special Features: 500-passenger *Midnight Gambler II* sails from Wilmington Island across from Bull River Marina. $5 admission charge reimbursed with $5 in credit towards gambling, food or drinks.

IDAHO

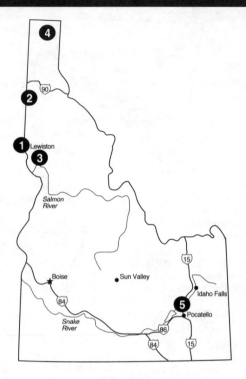

Idaho has six Indian casinos that offer electronic pull-tab machines and other video games. The machines don't pay out in cash. Instead they print out a receipt which must be cashed by a floor attendant or taken to the cashier's cage. Some casinos also offer bingo (BG) and off-track betting (OTB).

The terms of the compact between the tribes and the state do not require any minimum payback percentage that the gaming machines must return to the public.

The minimum gambling age at all casinos is 18 and they are all open 24 hours. For Idaho tourism information call (800) 635-7820 or visit their web site: www.visitid.org

Bannock Peak Casino
1707 W. Country Road
Pocatello, Idaho 83204
(208) 235-1308
Web site: www.sho-ban.com
Map: **#5** (5 miles N. of Pocatello)

Restaurants: 1 Snack Bar Liquor: No
Hours: 6am-12am/1am (Fri/Sat)
Casino Size: 5,000 Square Feet
Other Games: Only gaming machines
Overnight RV Parking: Free/RV Dump: No

Clearwater River Casino
17500 Nez Perce Road
Lewiston, Idaho 83501
(208) 746-5733
Web site: www.crcasino.com
Map: **#1** (250 miles N. of Boise)

Toll-Free Number: (877) 678-7423
Restaurants: 1 Liquor: No
Casino Size: 30,000 Square Feet
Other Games: BG (Fri-Sun)
Overnight RV Parking: Free/RV Dump: No
Special Features: 33-space RV park ($25 per night).

Coeur D'Alene Casino Resort Hotel
U.S. Highway 95/P.O. Box 236
Worley, Idaho 83876
(208) 686-5106
Web site: www.cdacasino.com
Map: **#2** (350 miles N. of Boise)

Toll-Free Number: (800) 523-2464
Rooms: 202 Price Range: $79-$100
Suites: 8 Price Range $150-$400
Restaurants: 4 Liquor: Yes Valet Parking: Free
Buffet: B-$7.99$11.99 (Sat/Sun) L-$11.99
        D-$14.99/$17.99(Fri)/$24.99 (Sat)
Casino Size: 30,000 Square Feet
Other Games: BG (Fri-Sun), OTB
Overnight RV Parking: Free/RV Dump: No
Special Features: 18-hole golf course.

Fort Hall Casino
I-15 Exit 80, PO Box 868
Fort Hall, Idaho 83203
(208) 237-8778
Web site: www.forthallcasino.com
Map: **#5** (14 miles N. of Pocatello)

Toll-Free Number: (800) 497-4231
Restaurants: 1 Snack Bar Liquor: No
Casino Size: 15,000 Square Feet
Other Games: BG (Wed-Sun)
Overnight RV Parking: Must use RV Park
Special Features: 47-space RV park ($20 per night).

It'Se-Ye-Ye Casino
419 Third Street
Kamiah, Idaho 83536
(208) 935-7860
Web site: www.crcasino.com
Map: **#3** (225 miles N. of Boise)

Restaurants: 1 Liquor: No
Hours: 6am-12am/24 Hours (Fri/Sat)
Casino Size: 2,300 Square Feet
Overnight RV Parking: Free/RV Dump: No

Kootenai River Inn Casino and Spa
Kootenai River Plaza
Bonners Ferry, Idaho 83805
(208 267 8511
Web site: www.kootenairiverinn.com
Map: **#4** (450 miles N. of Boise)

Toll-Free Number: (800) 346-5668
Rooms: 47 Price Range: $89-$139
Suites: 4 Price Range $109-$350
Restaurants: 2 Liquor: Yes
Buffets: B-$11.99 (Sun)
Casino Size: 30,000 Square Feet
Other Games: BG (Wed)
Overnight RV Parking: Free/RV Dump: No
Special Features: Hotel is Best Western. Spa.

ILLINOIS

Illinois was the second state to legalize riverboat casinos. Riverboat casinos began operating there in September 1991 with the launching of the first boat: the Alton Belle.

All Illinois riverboats remain dockside and do not cruise. Unlike Mississippi, however, the casinos are not open 24 hours and state law limits the number of gaming licenses to 10.

As of August 2007, there were nine casinos in operation and the 10th license was the subject of a lawsuit. It is unlikely that a 10th casino will open before late 2008.

Here's information from the Illinois Gaming Board showing each casino's average slot payback percentage for the one-year period from June 1, 2006 through May 30, 2007:

CASINO	PAYBACK %
Casino Queen	94.95
Alton Belle	93.87
Grand Victoria	93.63
Rock Island	93.39
Empress	92.38
Harrah's Joliet	92.00
Hollywood	92.14
Par-A-Dice	92.11
Harrah's Metropolis	90.51

These figures reflect the total percentages returned by each casino for all of their electronic machines. As you can see, the Casino Queen returned the most to its slot machine players, while Harrah's in Metropolis returned the least.

The Best Places To Play In The Chicago Area

by John Grochowski

In recent years, the Chicago area had become a welcome oasis for Midwestern video poker players, with Empress in Joliet, Illinois, and four Indiana casinos — Majestic Star, Trump (now Majestic Star II), Resorts and Blue Chip all filling their floors with games that paid in excess of 99 percent with expert play.

Games such as 9-6 Jacks or Better (99.5 percent with expert play), Not So Ugly Deuces (99.7), 9-5 Super Double Bonus (99.6), 8-5 Bonus Poker (99.2) and 9-7-5 Double Bonus (99.1) had become almost commonplace. Regulations in Illinois and Indiana prohibit games that pay more than 100 percent, so the Chicago market never approached the Las Vegas locals market in top-drawer games. Still, Chicagoans used to the volume of 99-percenters close to home were often shocked to find pay tables that didn't match up when they visited the Las Vegas Strip.

Alas, the oasis is drying up. The Chicago market isn't what it was, even a year ago, for video poker play. Majestic Star and Majestic Star II have remnants of the 99-percenters, though it now takes a careful look through the slot floors to find them. Empress, Resorts and Blue Chip have pulled back from the pay table race. There are strong games scattered throughout the area's casinos, but most are at the $1 and up level, and many are on multihand machines such as Triple Play.

There are seven casinos within about a 45-minute drive of Chicago's Loop — in those rare times when traffic is flowing freely. Seven, that is, unless you count Majestic Star and Majestic Star II in Gary, Ind., as separate casinos. They were separate until 2006 when Detroit businessman Donald Barden, owner of the original Majestic Star, bought out Trump Indiana, rechristening the Trump boat "Majestic Star II." The boats are docked in the same harbor, with entrances just across a corridor from each other. and share land-based pavilion facilities with restaurants, a lounge, gift shop and meeting space.

In an extended-area sort of way, the Blue Chip Casino in Michigan City, Indiana, can be regarded as part of the Chicago market, another half-hour or so east of the Gary casinos. Michigan City, with its proximity to the Indiana Dunes, is a recreational hot spot, a favorite for vacationers, and draws a fair amount of business from Chicago. And the land-based Four Winds, which opened in August, 2007, is just 15 minutes from Blue Chip, off the first Michigan exit from Interstate 94.

So that's nine separate operations, even 10 if you count Milwaukee's Potawatomi Bingo Casino, about a 90-minute drive north of Chicago, a land-based Native American casino. Other than Potawatomi and Four Winds, the other casinos in the market must be on water, either on boats or barges, though none actually move. It used to be that the Illinois boats were required to cruise. Customers would buy tickets that cost up to $28 for a two-hour cruise, which consisted of a half-hour boarding period, an hour on the water, and a half-hour disembarking period. No more. There are no more cruises, and there are no admission charges.

On the Indiana side of the Chicago area, Horseshoe in Hammond, Resorts in East Chicago and Trump and Majestic Star in Gary are on large Lake Michigan cruisers. The boats remain in their docks, but are capable of moving. In Illinois, Hollywood in Aurora and Empress and Harrah's, both in Joliet, have moved off their original riverboats, onto dockside barges. Only Grand Victoria in Elgin remains on its original boat, and that remains in dock, too.

There is a movement toward ever bigger and ever more elaborate boats/barges, mimicking the big, land-based casino as much as possible. In early 2006, Blue Chip opened a new boat with 65,000 square feet of gaming space on a single level. Horseshoe is going one better, with a $485 million project for a new boat due to open in 2008 with 100,000 square feet of casino space on one level. That will come as a relief to the tired legs of customers who climb up and down stairs to get to the four gaming levels on the old Horseshoe, and to the lungs of those who are bothered by the smoke in the current, smaller enclosed space.

In Illinois, casinos are smaller, limited by law to 1,200 gaming positions, and the typical mix consists of about 1,100 slots and video poker machines, along with about 30 table games. The only limit in Indiana is that the games must fit on one boat, so the casinos there are much larger — the largest boat, Resorts East Chicago, has more than 1,900 electronic games and 60-plus table games. All the boats are dwarfed by Four Winds, with 3,000 slots and more than 100 tables.

In Indiana, casinos are permitted to remain open 24 hours a day, and they do. In Illinois, 24-hour gaming has never been approved. What about the games? Well, game quality remains tied more to the state of competition than to the state in which a casino floats, and there's enough competition around Chicago that there are some pretty decent opportunities for choosy players.

VIDEO POKER: There are no 100 percent-plus games in the Chicago area. For nearly a decade, Empress Joliet had 10-7 Double Bonus poker, a 100.17-percent game with expert play, and even added a progressive jackpot on dollar games. That changed in 2003 when it moved onto its new barge. Empress bought new gaming equipment for the barge, and in putting video poker on IGT's new game platform, Empress had to get each game re-approved by the Illinois Gaming Board. The board found that 10-7 Double Bonus did not meet its standard that no game may pay more than 100 percent in the long run. Poof! The best deal in the Chicago area was gone.

Savvy players will be able to shop for 99-percent-plus games in the area, though, with Majestic Star having the best remaining selections.

Empress today is a shadow of its former video poker glory, having eliminated all 99-percent-plus single-hand games. Those with the budget for dollar Triple Play/Five Play still can find Not So Ugly Deuces (99.7), 9-6 Jacks or Better (99.5), 8-5 Bonus Poker (99.2) and 9-6 Double Double Bonus (99.0). Check the bartops on the lower level of the two-level barge.

Majestic Star once had dozens of high-paying machines, at levels from nickels to quarters to dollars. There aren't as many good ones now, but if you check the pay tables and find the right machine, the strong pay tables are still there.

For single-hand games, Majestic Star still offers NSU Deuces and 9-6 Jacks or better on both quarter and dollar games. Some machines have them, more don't, so touch the screens and check the pay tables before you play.

Multihand games such as Spin Poker and MultiStrike have retained their strong pay tables in both quarter and dollar versions. There, in addition to the 9-6 Jacks and NSU Deuces, you'll find more unusual games, including 8-5 Super Aces paying 60-for-1 on straight flushes (99.9), 12-4 Double Bonus Deuces Wild (99.8), 9-6 Super Double Bonus (99.7), 9-6 Bonus Deluxe (99.6) and 9-7 Triple Double Bonus (99.6).
Just across the hallway at Majestic Star II, some of the Game Kings in the main video poker room have 9-6 Jacks or Better as a single-hand game. You might also want to check out the nickel 100 Play machines, loaded with NSU Deuces, 9-6 Bonus Deluxe, 9-6 Triple Double Bonus and more.

At Resorts in East Chicago, all that's left of a formerly strong video poker inventory is a bank of $1 9-6 Double Double Bonus machines with progressive jackpots on the royal flush and all four of a kinds. Similarly, Blue Chip in Michigan City, which had made a big upgrade in 2006, fell back to where the only 99-percenters are a single bank of $1 multigame machines with 9-6 Jacks or Better, 8-5 Bonus Poker and 9-7-5 Double Bonus.

Horseshoe in Hammond, Ind., will reward dollar-and-up players who can fade the multihand action, with 8-5-60 Super Aces, NSU Deuces, 9-6 Jacks or Better and 8-5 Bonus Poker on its Triple Play/Five Play and Ten Play machines.

On the Illinois side of the border, Grand Victoria in Elgin has NSU Deuces and 9-6 Jacks on some, but not all, dollar Game Kings. The NSU Deuces also are on Multi Strike games from quarters on up. Hollywood has NSU Deuces on single-hand games in multigame, multidenomination machines at the $1-$2-$5-$10 level and in the high-limit room in $5-$10-$25 machines.

And finally, Four Winds has playable games for dollar players, with dozens of units offering 8-5 Bonus Poker and 9-7-5 Double Bonus. Quarter players will find little of interest here, with pay tables a couple of notches down — 6-5 Bonus Poker and 9-6-4 Double Bonus.

CRAPS: The face of Chicago area craps changed dramatically when Jack Binion's Horseshoe Gaming bought the former Empress Hammond in 1999. The Horseshoe offers 100x odds, and 20x odds have become common among its competitors. Horseshoe caters to big players, and has the highest maximum bets — up to $10,000. Harrah's Entertainment owns Horseshoe now, but has the best craps game in the area.

BLACKJACK: Most games in the Chicago area use either six or eight decks — but at least we haven't seen the movement to 6-5 payoffs on blackjacks that has turned the game into a cash grabber on the Las Vegas Strip. Table minimums are high, especially in Illinois where anything under $15 a hand is rare. In Indiana, you can still find $5 tables at Majestic Star, which also offers the area's only double-deck game..

Harrah's Joliet now stands alone in allowing players to resplit Aces. On most six-deck games the dealer stands on all 17s, you may double after splits and resplit Aces. House edge against a basic strategy player is 0.36 percent. At Empress Joliet, players are no longer permitted to resplit Aces. Games are six decks, double after splits permitted, dealer stands on all 17s. House edge against a basic strategy player: 0.41 percent.

The Empress six-deck game is the same basic game you'll find in Indiana at Majestic Star, Horseshoe, Resorts and Blue Chip. All but Blue Chip have eight-deck tables, too, increasing the house edge to 0.43 percent. Majestic Star has double-deck blackjack, but it's a slightly weaker play than its six-deck games because players are allowed to double down only on two-card totals of 10 or 11. That increases the house edge to 0.53 percent against a basic strategy player.

Hollywood in Aurora has some six-deck tables with $25 minimums that have the same rules as Empress and the Indiana boats, but lower-minimum tables have eight decks and call for the dealer to hit soft 17. House edge on that game is 0.66 percent, making it the weakest blackjack game in the area.

Grand Victoria has the dealer hit soft 17 on its six-deck games, leaving a 0.63 percent house edge on Grand Victoria's six-deck game. North of the border, in Milwaukee, Potawatomi has a six-deck game with the dealer hitting soft 17, double after splits permitted and resplitting pairs restricted so that you can wind up with a total of only three hands. The house edge against a basic strategy player is 0.64 percent.

SLOT MACHINES: Along with the rest of the country, Chicago has seen a great expansion in video bonusing slot games, with the hottest trend being toward lower and lower coin denominations. All Chicago area casinos now have two-cent games, and all except Horseshoe and Grand Victoria have penny slots. Traditional three-reel games remain a big part of the mix at quarters and above.

All slot machines in the area have gone TITO — ticket in, ticket out for easy payouts with no delays for hopper fills or hopper jams.

One thing you'll not find in Illinois or Indiana is million-dollar jackpots. Wide-area progressives such as Megabucks that link several different properties to the same jackpot are illegal in Illinois and Indiana. If you're a jackpot chaser, you'll need to go to Potawatomi in Milwaukee or Four Winds in New Buffalo, which both are on the national Native American link.

Slot payouts tend to be higher in Illinois than in Indiana, from quarters on up, but the Indiana casinos pay as much or more than the Illinois operations in nickels and below. Illinois averages tend to hover around 95 percent on dollars, 93 percent on quarters and 88 percent on nickels, 85 percent on pennies while Indiana returns, are around 94 percent on dollars, 92 percent on quarters and 89 percent on nickels and 86 percent on pennies — with variations from casino to casino, of course.

*John Grochowski writes a weekly syndicated newspaper column on gambling,
hosts a casino radio show on WCKG-FM (105.9) in Chicago and is author of the
"Casino Answer Book" series from Bonus Books.*

Admission is free to all Illinois casinos and, unless otherwise noted, all casinos offer: slots, video poker, blackjack, craps, roulette, Caribbean stud poker and three card poker. Some casinos also offer: let it ride (LIR), baccarat (B), mini-baccarat (MB), poker (P) and pai gow poker (PGP).

If you want to order a drink while playing, be aware that Illinois gaming regulations do not allow casinos to provide free alcoholic beverages. The minimum gambling age is 21.

For more information on visiting Illinois contact the state's Bureau of Tourism at (800) 226-6632 or www.enjoyillinois.com

Argosy's Alton Belle Casino
1 Front Street
Alton, Illinois 62002
(618) 474-7500
Web site: www.argosycasinos.com
Map: **#1** (260 miles S.W. of Chicago. 25 miles N. of St. Louis, MO)

Toll-Free Number: (800) 711-4263
Restaurants: 3
Buffets: L-$9.99 D-$13.95/$18.95 (Thu)
Valet Parking: $5 (Free for slot club members)
Casino Hours: 8am-6am Daily
Casino Size: 23,000 Square Feet
Other Games: LIR
Overnight RV Parking: No
Special Features: Casino features a 1,200-passenger modern yacht and a barge docked on the Mississippi River. 10% off buffets for slot club members.

Argosy's Empress Casino
2300 Empress Drive
Joliet, Illinois 60436
(815) 744-9400
Web site: www.argosycasinos.com
Map: **#2** (43 miles S.W. of Chicago)

Toll-Free Number: (888) 4-EMPRESS
Rooms: 85 Price Range: $79-$120
Suites: 17 Price Range: $109-$129
Casino Hours: 8:30am-6:30am Daily
Restaurants: 3
Buffets: L-$11.99/$14.99 (Sun)
 D-$15.99/$22.99 (Fri)/$17.99 (Sat-Sun)
Valet Parking: Free
Casino Size: 50,000 square feet
Other Games: MB, P
Overnight RV Parking: Must use RV park
Special Features: 2,500-passenger barge
docked on the Des Plaines River. Rooms are
at on-property Empress Hotel. 80-space RV
park ($24-$30 per night).

Casino Queen
200 S. Front Street
E. St. Louis, Illinois 62201
(618) 874-5000
Web site: www.casinoqueen.com
Map: **#6** (290 miles S.W. of Chicago)

Toll-Free Number: (800) 777-0777
Rooms: 150 Price Range: $89-$129
Suites: 7 Price Range: $159-$499
Buffets: B-$7.99 L-$9.99/$11.99 (Sun)
 D-$13.99
Valet Parking: $4
Casino Hours: 9am-7am Daily
Casino Size: 38,000 Square Feet
Other Games: MB, PGP, TCP
Senior Discount: Various Wed 9am-Mid. if 50+
Overnight RV Parking: Must use RV park
Special Features: 2,500-passenger barge
floating in a man-made basin 700 feet from
the Mississippi River. 140-space RV park ($23-
$33 per night). Sports Bar. MetroLink light-
rail station at doorstep. $1 off buffets for slot
club members.

Grand Victoria Casino
250 S. Grove Avenue
Elgin, Illinois 60120
(847) 468-7000
Web site: www.grandvictoriacasino.com
Map: **#4** (41 miles N.W. of Chicago)

Toll Free Number: (888) 508-1900
Restaurants: 4
Buffets: L-$9.99/$21.99 (Sat/Sun)
 D-$12.99/$21.99 (Fri-Sun)
Valet Parking: $5
Casino Hours: 8:30am-6:30am Daily
Casino Size: 29,850 Square Feet
Other Games: B
Overnight RV Parking: No
Senior Discount: $1 off buffets if 65+
Special Features: 1,200-passenger paddle
wheeler-replica docked on the Fox River.

Harrah's Joliet
150 N. Joliet Street
Joliet, Illinois 60432
(815) 740-7800
Web site: www.harrahs.com
Map: **#2** (43 miles S.W. of Chicago)

Toll-Free Number: (800) HARRAHS
Rooms: 200 Price Range: $99-$199
Suites: 4 Price Range: Casino Use Only
Restaurants: 3
Buffets: B- $8.99 L-$12.99/$15.99 (Sat/Sun)
 D-$18.99/$23.99 (Fri)
Valet Parking: $5/Free if hotel guest
Casino Hours: 9am-7am Daily
Casino Size: 39,000 Square Feet
Other Games: MB
Overnight RV Parking: No
Special Features: Casino is on a barge docked
on the Des Plaines River.

Harrah's Metropolis
100 E. Front Street
Metropolis, Illinois 62960
(618) 524-2628
Web site: www.harrahs.com
Map: **#8** (Across from Paducah, KY. Take exit 37 on I-24)

Toll-Free Number: (800) 929-5905
Rooms: 252 Price Range: $99-$299
Suites: 6 Price Range: Casino Use Only
Restaurants: 3
Buffets: L-$10.99/$15.99 (Sat/Sun)
         D-$13.99/$17.99 (Sat/Sun)
Hours: 9am-7am Daily
Valet Parking: $5
Other Games: MB, P, LIR
Casino Size: 30,985 Square Feet
Overnight RV Parking: Free/RV Dump: No
Special Features: 1,300-passenger sidewheeler replica docked on the Ohio River.

Hollywood Casino - Aurora
1 New York Street Bridge
Aurora, Illinois 60506
(630) 801-7000
Web site: www.hollywoodcasinoaurora.com
Map: **#7** (41 miles W. of Chicago)

Toll Free Number: (800) 888-7777
Restaurants: 3
Buffets: L-$11.99 D-$15.99/$18.99 (Fri)
Valet Parking: $5
Casino Hours: 9:30am-4:30am/5:30 (Fri/Sat)
Casino Size: 41,384 Square Feet
Other Games: P
Overnight RV Parking: No
Special Features: Casino is on a barge docked on the Fox River. $3 buffet discount for slot club members.

Jumer's Casino Rock Island
1735 First Avenue
Rock Island, Illinois 61201
(309) 793-4200
Web site: www.jumerscri.com
Map: **#3** (170 miles W. of Chicago)

Toll-Free Number: (800) 477-7747
Restaurants: 1 on boat adjacent to casino
Buffets: B-$6.95 (Sun) L-$6.95 D-$9.95
Valet Parking: Free
Casino Hours: 8am-3am Daily
Casino Size: 17,200 Square Feet
Senior Discount: Free buffet (Mon-Thu) if you
    play a minimum of $200 on slots or buy-in
    for at least $50 and play for a minium of 50
    minutes on tables if 50 or older.
Overnight RV Parking: No
Special Features: 1,200-passenger old-fashioned paddlewheel boat on the Mississippi River. Restaurant is on the *Effie Afton* which is another boat docked next to the casino.

Par-A-Dice Hotel Casino
21 Blackjack Boulevard
East Peoria, Illinois 61611
(309) 698-7711
Web site: www.par-a-dice.com
Map: **#5** (170 miles S.W. of Chicago)

Toll-Free Number: (800) 727-2342
Room Reservations: (800) 547-0711
Rooms: 195 Price Range: $105-$155
Suites 13 Price Range: $175-$500
Restaurants: 3
Buffets: B-$6.95/$12.99 (Sat-Sun)
         L-$9.99/$12.99 (Sat/Sun)
    D-$12.99/$16.99 (Fri)/$18.99 (Sat)/$17.99 (Sun)
Valet Parking: $5
Casino Hours: 9:00am-6:00am Daily
Casino Size: 26,116 Square Feet
Other Games: LIR
Overnight RV Parking: Free/RV Dump: No
Senior Discount: Various Wed 9:30-3:30 if 55+
Special Features: 1,600-passenger modern boat docked on the Illinois River.

INDIANA

In June 1993 Indiana became the sixth state to legalize riverboat gambling. All of the state's riverboat casinos offer dockside gambling and, unless otherwise noted, are open 24 hours and admission is free to all casinos.

Following is information from the Indiana Gaming Commission regarding average slot payout percentages for the one-year period from July 1, 2006 through June 30, 2007:

CASINO	PAYBACK %
Argosy	92.48
Caesars Indiana	91.70
Belterra	91.99
Grand Victoria	91.86
Majestic Star II	92.00
Majestic Star	91.75
Blue Chip	92.16
Horseshoe	91.33
Casino Aztar	91.14
Resorts	90.56
French Lick	91.04

These figures reflect the average percentage returned by each casino for all of their electronic machines including slot machines, video poker, video keno, etc.

Unless otherwise noted, all casinos offer: blackjack, craps, roulette, slots, video poker, video keno and Caribbean stud poker. Optional games include: baccarat (B), mini-baccarat (MB), poker (P), pai gow poker (PGP), three card poker (TCP), four card poker (FCP), Spanish 21 (S21), big 6 wheel (B6) and let it ride (LIR). The minimum gambling age is 21.

If you want to order a drink while playing, be aware that Indiana gaming regulations do not allow casinos to provide free alcoholic beverages.

NOTE: If you happen to win a jackpot of $1,200 or more in Indiana, the casino will withhold 3.4% of your winnings for the Indiana Department of Revenue. You may, however, be able to get *some* of that money refunded by filing a state income tax return. The $1,200 threshold also applies to any cash prizes won in casino drawings or tournaments.

For more information on visiting Indiana call (800) 289-6646 or visit their web site at www.enjoyindiana.com

Argosy Casino & Hotel - Lawrenceburg
777 Argosy Parkway
Lawrenceburg, Indiana 47025
(812) 539-8000
Web site: www.argosy.com/cincinatti
Map: **#3** (95 miles S.E. of Indianapolis)

Toll-Free Number: (888) ARGOSY-7
Rooms: 440 Price Range: $107-$185
Restaurants: 5   Valet Parking: $3
Buffets: B-$7.95 L-$9.95
D-$14.95/$19.95 (Wed/Fri/Sat)
Casino Size: 80,000 Square Feet
Other Games: S21, MB, B6, LIR, P, TCP, PGP, FCP
Overnight RV Parking: Free (only in lot across the street from the casino)/RV Dump: No
Special Features: 4,000-passenger modern yacht docked on the Ohio River. Closest casino to Cincinnati. Reservations are recommended, especially for weekends and holidays.

Belterra Casino Resort and Spa
777 Belterra Drive
Belterra, IN 47020
(812) 427-4008
Web site: www.belterracasino.com
Map: **#1** (35 miles S.W. of Cincinnati, Ohio)

Toll-Free Number: (888) 235-8377
Rooms: 608 Price Range: $89-$189
Suites: Casino use only
Restaurants: 5   Valet Parking: Free
Buffets: B-$7.95/$16.95 (Sun) L-$9.95
D-$15.95
Casino Size: 38,000 Square Feet
Other Games: S21, P, PGP, TCP, LIR
Overnight RV Parking: Free (must park in back rows of parking lot)/RV Dump: No
Special Features: 2,600-passenger sidewheeler docked on the Ohio River. Health club and spa. 18-hole golf course. 1,500-seat showroom. 10x odds on craps.

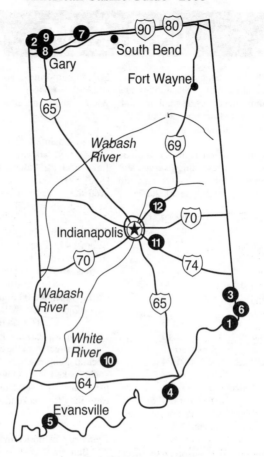

Blue Chip Casino & Hotel
2 Easy Street
Michigan City, Indiana 46360
(219) 879-7711
Web site: www.bluechip-casino.com
Map: **#7** (40 miles E. of Chicago)

Toll-Free Number: (888) 879-7711
Rooms: 180 Price Range: $89-$159
Suites: Casino Use Only
Restaurants: 3   Valet Parking: Free
Buffets: B-$8.99 L-$11.99 D-$18.99
Casino Size: 25,000 Square Feet
Other Games: MB, LIR, P, TCP, FCP
Overnight RV Parking: Free/RV Dump: No
Senior Discount: Various Wed if 55+
Special Features: 2,000-passenger modern
yacht docked in a man-made canal.

Caesars Indiana
11999 Avenue of the Emperors
Elizabeth, Indiana 47117
(812) 969-6000
Web site: www.caesarsindiana.com
Map: **#4** (20 miles S. of New Albany)

Toll-Free Number: (888) 766-2648
Toll-Free Number: (877) 237-6626
Reservation Number: (877) 766-2671
Rooms: 503 Prices: Price Range: $99-$229
Restaurants: 9   Valet Parking: Free
Buffets: B-$8.95/$14.95 (Sat)/$17.95 (Sun)
 L-$9.95 D-$15.95/$20.95 (Tue)/$21.95 (Fri)
Casino Size: 93,000 Square Feet
Other Games: S21, B, MB, P, PGP, LIR, TCP
Overnight RV Parking: Free/RV Dump: No
Special Features: 5,000-passenger sidewheeler
docked on the Ohio River. 18-hole golf course.
Pet kennel.

The 5,000-passenger *Glory of Rome* at Caesars Indiana is the world's largest riverboat casino.

Casino Aztar
421 N.W. Riverside Drive
Evansville, Indiana 47708
(812) 433-4000
Web site: www.casinoaztar.com
Map: **#5** (168 miles S.W. of Indianapolis)

Toll-Free Number: (800) DIAL-FUN
Rooms: 240 Price Range: $84-$118
Suites: 10 Price Range: $149-$225
Restaurants: 5 Valet Parking: Free
Buffets: B-$10.99 L-$12.99
Hours: 8am-5am/24 Hours (Fri/Sat/Holidays)
Casino Size: 47,863 Square Feet
Other Games: S21, P, TCP, FCP, LIR
Overnight RV Parking: No
Senior Discount: Join Club 55, if 55 or older
Special Features: 2,700-passenger paddle-wheeler docked on the Ohio River.

French Lick Springs Resort & Casino
8670 West State Road 56
French Lick, Indiana 47432
(812) 936-9300
Web site: www.frenchlick.com
Map: **#10** (108 miles S. of Indianapolis)

Toll-Free Number: (800) 457-4042
Rooms: 442 Price Range: $129-$269
Restaurants: 7 Valet Parking: Free
Buffets: B-$10 L-$13 D-$20
Casino Size: 84,000 Square Feet
Other Games: P
Overnight RV Parking: Free/RV Dump: No
Special Features: Two 18-hole golf courses. Full-service spa. Six-lane bowling alley.

Grand Victoria Casino & Resort
600 Grand Victoria Drive
Rising Sun, Indiana 47040
(812) 438-1234
Web site: www.grandvictoria.com
Map: **#6** (40 miles S.W. of Cincinnati)

Toll-Free Number: (800) GRAND-11
Rooms: 201 Price Range: $89-$229
Restaurants: 8 Valet Parking: Free
Buffets: B-$7.95 L-$9.95/$13.95 (Sun)
         D-$14.95/$20.95 (Fri/Sat)
Casino Size: 40,000 Square Feet
Other Games: S21, P, LIR, TCP
Overnight RV Parking: Free/RV Dump: No
Senior Discount: Various discounts if 55+
Special Features: 3,000-passenger paddle wheeler docked on Ohio River. Hotel is Hyatt. 18-hole golf course. 1,100-seat showroom.

Horseshoe Casino Hammond
777 Casino Center Drive
Hammond, Indiana 46320
(219) 473-7000
Web site: www.horseshoe.com/hammond
Map: **#2** (10 miles E. of Chicago)

Toll-Free Number: (866) 711-7463
Restaurants: 4
Buffets: B-$9.99/$24.99 (Sun) L-$13.99
         D-$17.99/$24.99 (Fri/Sat)
Valet Parking: $5/$3 with Total Rewards Card
Casino Size: 43,000 Square Feet
Other Games: MB, CSP, TCP
Overnight RV Parking: Free/RV Dump: No
Special Features: 3,000-passenger modern yacht docked on Lake Michigan.

Majestic Star Casinos & Hotel
1 Buffington Harbor Drive
Gary, Indiana 46406
(219) 977-7777
Web site: www.majesticstar.com
Map: **#8** (15 miles E. of Chicago)

Toll-Free Number: (888) 2B-LUCKY
Toll-Free Number: (888) 218-7867
Rooms: 300 Price Range: $99-$129
Restaurants: 6
Buffets: B-$19.99 (Sun) L-$11.99
　　　　D-$17.99/$24.99 (Fri/Sat)
Valet Parking: Free/$5 (Fri-Sun)/$3 for
　　　　slot club members
Casino Size: 43,000 Square Feet
Other Games: S21, MB, PGP, TCP, LIR
Overnight RV Parking: Free/RV Dump: No
Special Features: Two boats: 1,300-passenger
and 2,300-passenger modern yachts docked on
Lake Michigan.

Resorts East Chicago
777 Resorts Boulevard
East Chicago, Indiana 46312
(219) 378-3000
Web site: www.resortseastchicago.com
Map: **#9** (12 miles E. of Chicago)

Toll-Free Number: (877) 496-1777
Hotel Reservations: (866) 711-7799
Rooms: 286 Prices: $119-$179
Suites: 7 Prices: Casino Use Only
Restaurants: 5
Buffets: B-$6.99 L-$11.99
　D-$17.99/$15.99 (Tue)/$24.99 (Fri/Sat)
Valet Parking: $5/ Discounted for club members
Casino Size: 53,000 Square Feet
Other Games: S21, MB, P, TCP
Overnight RV Parking: No
Special Features: 3,750-passenger modern
yacht docked on Lake Michigan.

Pari-Mutuels

In April 2007, the Indiana state legislature
authorized the state's two horse tracks to have
up to 2,000 electronic gaming machines.

It is expected that Indiana Downs will have
their machines in operation by early 2008,
followed by Hoosier Downs in mid-2008. It is
strongly suggested that you call ahead before
visiting these tracks to make sure that the
machines are in operation.

Indiana Downs
4200 N. Michigan Road
Shelbyville, Indiana 46176
(317) 421-0000
Web site: www.indianadowns.com
Map: **#11** (32 miles S.E. of Indianapolis)

Other Games: Only Gaming Machines
Special Features: Thoroughbred horse racing
late April through early July. Harness racing
mid-July through early November. Year-round
simulcasting of thoroughbred and harness
racing.

Hoosier Park
4500 Dan Patch Circle
Anderson, Indiana 46013
(765) 642-7223
Web site: www.hoosierpark.com
Map: **#12** (45 miles N.E. of Indianapolis)

Toll-Free Number: (800) 526-7223
Other Games: Only Gaming Machines
Special Features: Thoroughbred horse racing
early September through late November.
Harness racing early April through late June.
Year-round simulcasting of thoroughbred and
harness racing.

IOWA

Iowa was the first state to legalize riverboat gambling. The boats began operating on April Fools Day in 1991 and passengers were originally limited to $5 per bet with a maximum loss of $200 per person, per cruise.

In early 1994 the Iowa legislature voted to eliminate the gambling restrictions. Additionally, gaming machines were legalized at three of the state's four pari-mutuel facilities. In mid-2004 a provision was added to allow table games at those three tracks. That same year the state also legalized casinos on moored barges that float in man-made basins of water and no longer required the casinos to be on boats. Iowa also has three Indian casinos.

Here's information, as supplied by the Iowa Racing and Gaming Commission, showing the electronic gaming machine payback percentages for all non-Indian locations for the one-year period from July 1, 2006 through June 30, 2007:

LOCATION	PAYBACK %
Prairie Meadows	93.12
Diamond Jo Dubuque	93.02
Dubuque Greyhound	93.02
Isle of Capri - Marquette	92.36
Mississippi Belle II	92.27
Isle of Capri - Bettendorf	92.18
Rhythm City	92.11
Riverside	91.96
Catfish Bend	91.79
Argosy Sioux City	91.70
Wild Rose - Emmetsburg	91.59
Isle of Capri - Waterloo	91.49
Terrible's Lakeside	91.31
Diamond Jo Worth	91.24
Ameristar	91.02
Harrah's	90.93
Horsehoe Council Bluffs	90.77

These figures reflect the total percentages returned by each riverboat casino or pari-mutuel facility for all of its electronic machines including: slots, video poker, video keno, etc.

Admission to all Iowa casinos is free and, unless otherwise noted, all casinos are open 24 hours.

All Iowa casinos offer: blackjack, roulette, craps, slots and video poker. Some casinos also offer: mini-baccarat (MB), poker (P), pai gow poker (PGP), Caribbean stud poker (CSP), let it ride (LIR), big 6 (B6), bingo (BG), keno (K), three card poker (TCP), four card poker (FCP) and Spanish 21 (S21). The minimum gambling age is 21.

NOTE: If you happen to win a jackpot of $1,200 or more in Iowa, the casino will withhold 5% of your winnings for the Iowa Department of Revenue. If you want to try and get that money refunded, you will be required to file a state income tax return and, depending on the details of your return, you *may* get some of the money returned to you. The $1,200 threshold would also apply to any cash prizes won in casino drawings or tournaments.

For more information on visiting Iowa call the state's tourism department at (800) 345-4692 or visit their web site at www.traveliowa.com.

Ameristar Casino Council Bluffs
2200 River Road
Council Bluffs, Iowa 51501
(712) 328-8888
Website: www.ameristarcasinos.com
Map: **#8**

Toll-Free Number: (877) 462-7827
Rooms: 152 Price Range: $119-$249
Suites: 8 Price Range: $225-$275
Restaurants: 4   Valet Parking: Free
Buffets: B-$9.99 (Sat)/$14.99 (Sun)
          L-$9.99 (Mon-Fri) D-$13.99/
          $14.99 (Thu)$15.99 (Sat)/$18.99 (Fri)
Casino Size: 38,500 Square Feet
Other Games: S21, PGP, CSP, LIR, TCP
Overnight RV Parking: Free/RV Dump: No
Senior Discount: Various discounts if 55+
Special Features: 2,700-passenger sidewheeler replica on the Missouri River. Kids Quest supervised children's center.

Argosy Casino - Sioux City
100 Larsen Park Road
Sioux City, Iowa 51101
(712) 294-5600
Website: www.argosy.com/siouxcity
Map: **#3**

Toll-Free Number: (800) 424-0080
Restaurants: 2   Valet Parking: Free
Casino Size: 11,693 Square Feet
Other Games: P, PGP, CSP
Overnight RV Parking: Free/RV Dump: No
Special Features: 1,200-passenger old-
fashioned stern wheeler on the Missouri River.
Comedy Club.

Catfish Bend Casino- Burlington
3001 Wine Gard Ave
Burlington, Iowa 52601
(319) 753-2946
Website: www.catfishbendcasino.com
Map: **#9** (180 miles S.E. of Des Moines)

Toll Free Number: (800) 372-2946
Rooms: 20 Price Range: $89-$109
Suites: 20 Price Range: $159-$259
Restaurants: 4 (1 open 24 hours)
Buffets: B-$5.95 L-$7.95/$8.95 (Sat/Sun)
        D-$9.95
Hours: 8am-2am (Mon)/24 hours (Tue-Sun)
Casino Size: 14,572 Square Feet
Other Games: P, PGP, TCP, FCP
Overnight RV Parking: Free/RV Dump: No

Catfish Bend Casino- Fort Madison
902 Riverview Drive
Fort Madison, Iowa 52627
(319) 372-2946
Website: www.catfishbendcasino.com
Map: **#9** (180 miles S.E. of Des Moines)

Toll Free Number: (800) 372-2946
Restaurants: 2 (1 open 24 hours)
Buffets: Brunch-$14.00 (Sun) L-$7.00
        D-$10.00/$14.00 (Fri)/$11.00 (Sat)
Hours: 8am-2am (Mon)/24 hours (Tue-Sun)
Casino Size: 14,572 Square Feet
Other Games: P, TCP, FCP, PGP
Overnight RV Parking: Free/RV Dump: No
Senior Discount: Various on Thursday if 50+
Special Features: 1,500-passenger paddle
wheeler on the Mississippi River. $3 lunch or
dinner buffet for slot club members on Monday
11am-8pm.

Diamond Jo Casino Dubuque
400 E. Third Street
Dubuque, Iowa 52001
(563) 690-2100
Website: www.diamondjo.com
Map: **#7**

Toll-Free Number: (800) LUCKY-JO
Restaurants: 3   Valet Parking: Free
Buffets: Brunch-$11.95 (Sun)
          D-$15.95 (Fri)/$14.95 (Sat)
Hours: 8am-3am/24 Hours (Fri-Sat)
Casino Size: 17,813 Square Feet
Other Games: P, LIR, TCP, FCP
Overnight RV Parking: Free RV Dump: No
Special Features: 1,600-passenger old-
fashioned steamboat replica on the Mississippi
River.

Diamond Jo Casino Worth
777 Diamond Jo Lane
Northwood, Iowa 50459
(641) 323-7777
Map: **#13** (140 miles N. of Des Moines)

Toll-Free Number: (877) 323-5566
Rooms: 100 Price Range: $90-$150
Restaurants: 1   Valet Parking: Free
Buffets: L-$8.99 D-$12.99
Hours: 8am-3am/24 Hours (Fri-Sat)
Casino Size: 19,322 Square Feet
Other Games: TCP
Overnight RV Parking: Free/RV Dump: No
Special Features: Casino is on a barge. Burger
King and Starbucks.

Harrah's Council Bluffs
One Harrah's Boulevard
Council Bluffs, Iowa 51501
(712) 329-6000
Website: www.harrahs.com
Map: **#8**

Toll Free Number: (800) HARRAHS
Rooms: 240 Price Range: $89-$269
Suites: 11 Price Range Casino Use Only
Restaurants: 4   Valet Parking: Free
Buffets: Brunch-$8.99 (Sat-Sun)
   L-$8.99 (Mon-Fri)
   D-$11.99/$13.99 (Fri-Sat)
Casino Size: 28,006 Square Feet
Other Games: S21, MB, TCP, FCP
Overnight RV Parking: Free/RV Dump: No
Special Features: 2,365-passenger paddle
wheel-replica on the Missouri River.

Isle of Capri Casino - Bettendorf
1821 State Street
Bettendorf, Iowa 52722
(563) 359-7280
Website: www.isleofcapricasino.com
Map: **#2**

Toll-Free Number: (800) 724-5825
Rooms: 220 Price Range: $80-$110
Suites: 36 Price Range $109-$185
Restaurants: 4   Valet Parking: Free
Buffets: B-$6.99 L-$8.99 Brunch-$13.99
          D-$13.99/$14.99 (Fri-Sun)
Other Games: P, PGP, CSP, TCP
Casino Size: 28,298 Square Feet
Overnight RV Parking: Free/RV Dump: No
Senior Discount: Various on Tue/Thu if 50+
Special Features: 2,500-passenger old-
fashioned paddle wheeler on the Mississippi
River. 53-slip marina.

Isle of Capri Casino - Marquette
100 Anti Monopoly Street
Marquette, Iowa 52158
(563) 873-3531
Website: www.isleofcapricasino.com
Map: **#10** (60 miles N. of Dubuque)

Toll-Free Number: (800) 4-YOU-BET
Rooms: 22 Price Range: $89
Suites: 3 Price Range: $125
Restaurants: 2   Valet Parking: Free
Buffets: B-$4.99/$6.99 (Sat) L-$7.99
          Brunch-$9.99 (Sun)
          D-$10.99/$14.99 (Fri/Sat)
Hours: 9am-3am/24 Hours (Fri/Sat)
Other Games: P, LIR, TCP, FCP
Casino Size: 18,747 Square Feet
Overnight RV Parking: Free/RV Dump: No
Senior Discount: Various Tue/Thu if 50+
          always10% off buffet if 50 or older
Special Features: 1,200-passenger paddle
wheeler on the Mississippi River.

Isle of Capri Casino - Waterloo
777 Isle of Capri Boulevard
Waterloo, Iowa 52701
(319)833-4753
Website: www.theislewaterloo.com
Map: **#11** (90 miles W. of Dubuque)

Toll-Free Number: (800) THE ISLE
Rooms: 170 Price Range: $89-$119
Suites: 27 Price Range: $119-$149
Restaurants: 3
Buffets: B-$7.95 L-$9.95
        Brunch-$14.95 (Sun)
        D-$15.95/$17.99 (Fri/Sat)
Other Games: P, TCP, PGP
Casino Size: 35,000 Square Feet
Overnight RV Parking: Free/RV Dump: No
Senior Discount: Various Tue/Thu if 50+
        always10% off buffet if 50 or older
Special Features: 1,200-passenger paddle
wheeler on the Mississippi River.

Mississippi Belle II
311 Riverview Drive
Clinton, Iowa 52733
(563) 243-9000
Website: www.belle2casino.com
Map: **#1** (83 miles E. of Cedar Rapids)

Toll-Free Number: (800) 457-9975
Restaurants: 2   Valet Parking: Not Offered
Buffets: B-$9.00 (Sat/Sun) L-$9.00
  D-$6.00 (Mon)/$12.00 (Wed/Thurs/Sun)/
  $14.00 (Sat)/ $15.00 (Fri)
Hours: 9am-2am/4am (Fri/Sat)
Casino Size: 9,952 Square Feet
Other Games: CSP, PGP, TCP, LIR
Overnight RV Parking: Free/RV Dump: No
Special Features: 1,000-passenger old-
fashioned paddle wheeler on the Mississippi
River. Offers Stay & Play packages with local
motels/hotels. New land-based "Wild Rose
Casino and Resort" is being built on current
site and expected to open in mid-2008.

Rhythm City Casino
101 West River Drive
Davenport, Iowa 52801
(319) 328-8000
Website: www.rhythmcitycasino.com
Map: **#2** (80 miles S.E. of Cedar Rapids)

Toll-Free Number: (800) BOAT-711
Restaurants: 2   Valet Parking: Free
Buffets: B-$5.99 L-$8.99/$12.99 (Sun)
        D-$12.99
Casino Size: 32,862 Square Feet
Other Games: PGP, TCP, FCP
Overnight RV Parking: Free/RV Dump: No
Senior Discount: Various Mon/Wed if 50+
Special Features: 2,200-passenger riverboat on
the Mississippi River. Affiliated with Isle of
Capri Casinos.

Riverside Casino & Golf Resort
3184 Highway 22
Riverside, Iowa 52327
(319) 648-1234
Website: www.riversideresortandcasino.com
Map: **#14** (81 miles W. of Davenport)

Toll-Free Number: (877) 677-3456
Rooms: 200 Price Range: $90-$200
Restaurants: 2   Valet Parking: Free
Buffets: B-$7.99 L-$9.99/$14.99 (Sat)
Brunch- $14.99 (Sun) D-$14.99
Casino Size: 60,000 Square Feet
Overnight RV Parking: Free/RV Dump: No
Other Games: P, PGP, CSP
Special Features: Casino is on a barge. 18-hole
golf course. 20-space RV park. 1,200-seat
showroom.

Terrible's Lakeside Casino
777 Casino Drive
Osceola, Iowa 50213
(641) 342-9511
Website: www.terribleherbst.com
Map: **#12** (50 miles S. of Des Moines)

Toll-Free Number: (877) 477-5253
Suites: 63   Price: $79-$159
Restaurants: 2   Valet Parking: Free
Buffets: B-$5.99 L-$7.99 Brunch-$11.99
(Sun) D-$9.99/$13.99 (Fri-Sat)
Casino Size: 25,000 Square Feet
Other Games: P, PGP, TCP
Overnight RV Parking: Free/RV Dump: No
Senior Discount: Various on Mon/Wed if 50+
Special Features: 1,500-passenger old-
fashioned paddle wheeler on West Lake. 47-
space RV park ($20 per night). Fishing/boating
dock.

Wild Rose Casino & Resort
777 Main Street
Emmetsburg, Iowa 50536
(712) 852-3400
Website: www.wildroseresorts.com
Map: **#12** (120 miles N.E. of Sioux City)

Toll-Free Number: (877) 720-7673
Rooms: 62 Price Range: $69-$99
Suites: 8 Price Range: $99-$129
Restaurants: 2   Valet Parking: Free
Buffets: B-$5.95 L-$7.95
        Brunch -$9.95 (Tue/Sun)
        D-$10.95/$13.95 (Fri/Sat)
Hours: 8am-2am Hours (Fri/Sat)
Casino Size: 28,000 Square Feet
Other Games: P, PGP
Senior Discount: Various Tue if 55+
Overnight RV Parking: Must use RV park
Special Features: Casino is on a barge. $2 off
buffets for slot club members. 68-space RV
park ($15 per night).

Indian Casinos

Casino Omaha
1 Blackbird Bend Boulevard
Onawa, Iowa 51040
(712) 423-3700
Map: **#4** (30 miles S. of Sioux City, 60 miles
N. of Omaha, 4 miles W. of I-29 at exit 112)

Toll-Free Number: (800) 858-U-BET
Restaurants: 1 Liquor: Yes Valet Park: None
Buffets: B-$9.95 (Sat/Sun) L-$7.99
        D-$9.99/$14.99 (Fri)/$12.99 (Sat-Sun)
Hours: 8am-2am/24 Hours
Overnight RV Parking: Free/RV Dump: No
Casino Size: 30,000 Square Feet

Meskwaki Bingo Casino Hotel
1504 305th Street
Tama, Iowa 52339
(641) 484-2108
Website: www.meskwaki.com
Map: **#5** (40 miles W. of Cedar Rapids)

Toll-Free Number: (800) 728-4263
Rooms: 390 Price Range: $55-$99
Suites: 14 Price Range: $185-$250
Restaurants: 4 Liquor: No   Valet Park: Free
Buffets: B-$6.95/$7.95 (Sat-Sun) L-$8.95
        Brunch-$10.95 (Sun) D-$10.95/$11.95
        (Thurs)/$17.95 (Fri)/$14.25 (Sat)
Other Games: S21, MB, P, PGP, LIR, TCP
        K, BG, Off-Track Betting
Overnight RV Parking: Must Use RV Park
Senior Discount: $1 off buffet if 55+
Special Features: 50-space RV park ($15 per
night).

WinnaVegas Casino
1500 330th Street
Sloan, Iowa 51055
(712) 428-9466
Website: www.winnavegas.biz
Map: **#6** (20 miles S. of Sioux City)

Toll-Free Number: (800) 468-9466
Restaurants: 1 Liquor: Yes Valet Park: Free
Buffets: L-$5.95 D-$7.95/$10.95 (Fri)
Other Games: S21, P, LIR, BG
Overnight RV Parking: Free/RV Dump: No
Special Features: 20-space RV park ($7 per
night).

Pari-Mutuels

Horseshoe Casino - Council Bluffs
2701 23rd Avenue
Council Bluffs, Iowa 51501
(712) 323-2500
Website: www.horseshoe.com/councilbluffs
Map: **#8** (102 miles S. of Sioux City)

Toll-Free Number: (877) 771-7463
Restaurants: 3   Valet Parking: Free
Buffets: L-$10.99/$12.99 (Sun)
        D-$13.99/$15.99 (Fri/Sat)
Casino Size: 68,000 Square Feet
Other Games: P, PGP, CSP
Overnight RV Parking: Free/RV Dump: No
Special Features: Live dog racing (Tue-Sun).
Daily horse and greyhound race simulcasting.
Free shuttle service from local hotels.
Affiliated with Harrah's. 100x odds on craps.
New 158-room hotel expected to open by mid-2008.

Dubuque Greyhound Park & Casino
1855 Greyhound Park Road
Dubuque, Iowa 52001
(563) 582-3647
Website: www.dgpc.com
Map: **#7**

Toll-Free Number: (800) 373-3647
Restaurants: 2   Valet Parking: Free
Buffets: B-$13.50 (Sun)
        L-$10.95 (Wed/Sat) D-$16.95 (Fri/Sat)
Hours: 8am-3am/24 Hours (Fri/Sat)
Casino Size: 29,000 Square Feet
Other Games: LIR, TCP, FCP, P
Overnight RV Parking: Free/RV Dump: No
Senior Discount: Various specials Wed if 55+
Special Features: Live greyhound racing (Wed-Sun) from May through October. Greyhound, harness and thoroughbred simulcasting all year.

Prairie Meadows Racetrack & Casino
1 Prairie Meadows Drive
Altoona, Iowa 50009
(515) 967-1000
Website: www.prairiemeadows.com
Map: **#11** (5 miles E. of Des Moines)

Toll-Free Number: (800) 325-9015
Restaurants: 1   Valet Parking: Free
Buffets: $13.95 (Fri/Sat)
Casino Size: 39,324 Square Feet
Other Games: MB, P, PGP, TCP
Overnight RV Parking: No
Senior Discount: Various specials if 55+
Special Features: Live thoroughbred and quarter-horse racing April through October. Daily simulcasting of dog and horse racing

KANSAS

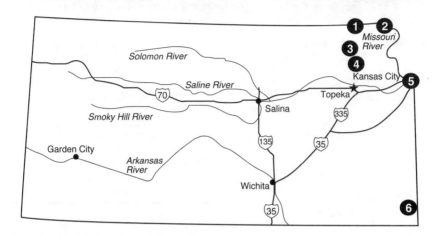

There are four Indian tribes in Kansas with casinos. According to officials at the Kansas State Gaming Agency, the terms of the state's compacts with the tribes regarding the minimum payback amounts on their machines are not a matter of public record and no information can be released.

Unless otherwise noted, all Kansas Indian casinos are open 24 hours and offer the following games: blackjack, craps, roulette, slots and video poker. Other games include: poker (P), Caribbean stud poker (CSP), let it ride (LIR), three card poker (TCP) and bingo (BG). The minimum gambling age is 21.

In April 2007 the Kansas legislature authorized local referendums in several counties to allow slots at three pari-mutuel race tracks and four state-run casinos. The slots were approved at only two of the three tracks and they are expected to have the slots in operation by mid-2008.

State-run casinos were approved for Wyandotte County (home to Kansas City), Ford County and two other areas in south-central and southeastern Kansas. The earliest any of the the state-run casinos will open is early 2009.

For more information on visiting Kansas call the state's tourism department at (800) 2-KANSAS or visit their web site at www.visitks.com

Casino White Cloud
777 Jackpot Drive
White Cloud, Kansas 66094
(785) 595-3430
Map: **#2** (70 miles N.E. of Topeka)

Toll-Free Number: (877) 652-6115
Restaurants: 1   Liquor: Yes   Valet Parking: No
Buffets: L-$6.95 D-$8.00
Casino Size: 21,000 Square Feet
Casino Hours: 9am-1am/3am (Fri/Sat)
Other Games: BG, No Craps, No Roulette
Overnight RV Parking: Free/RV Dump: No

Golden Eagle Casino
1121 Goldfinch Road
Horton, Kansas 66439
(785) 486-6601
Map: **#3** (45 miles N. of Topeka)
Website: www.goldeneaglecasino.com

Toll-Free Number: (888) 464-5825
Restaurants: 2 Liquor: No Valet Parking: No
Buffets: B-$6.95 (Sat/Sun) L-$7.95
 D-$9.95/$12.95(Thu)/$10.95 (Fri) $11.95 (Sat)
Other Games: P, LIR, BG (Wed-Sun)
Overnight RV Parking: Free/RV Dump: No
Senior Discount: Various Thu 11am-4pm if 55+
Special Features: RV hookups available ($10
per night).

Harrah's Prairie Band Casino and Hotel
12305 150th Road
Mayetta, Kansas 66509
(785) 966-7777
Website: www.pbpgaming.com
Map: **#4** (17 miles N. of Topeka)

Toll-Free Number: (888) 727-4946
Rooms: 290 Price Range: $69-$229
Suites: 8 Price Range: Casino Use Only
Restaurants: 3 Liquor: Yes Valet Parking: Free
Buffets: B-$7.99 L-$8.99/$9.99 (Sun)
        D-$12.99/$14.99 (Wed-Sat)
Casino Size: 33,000 Square Feet
Other Games: MB, P, PGP, LIR, TCP
Overnight RV Parking: Must use RV park
Special Features: 67-space RV park ($20-$30
per night).

Sac & Fox Casino
1322 U.S. Highway 75
Powhattan, Kansas 66527
(785)-467-8000
Map: **#1** (60 miles N. of Topeka)
Website: www.sacandfoxcasino.com

Toll-Free Number: (800) 990-2946
Restaurant: 3 Liquor: Yes Valet Parking: No
Buffets: B-$5.95/$9.95 (Sun) L-$7.95
        D-$9.95/$15.95 (Fri)/$10.95 (Sat)
Casino Size: 40,000 Square Feet
Other Games: LIR, TCP
Overnight RV Parking: Free/RV Dump: No
Senior Discount: $1 off meals if 55 or older
Special Features: 24-hour truck stop. Golf
driving range. 12-space RV park ($10 per
night).

Pari-Mutuels

Slot machines are expected to be in operation
at two Kansas pari-mutuel tracks by mid-2008.

The Woodlands
9700 Leavenworth Rd
Kansas City, Kansas 66109
(913) 299-9797
Website: www.woodlandskc.com
Map: **#5**

Toll-Free Number: (800) 695-7223
Restaurants: 4
Special Features: Live dog racing Thu-Mon
all year long. Live horse racing late September
to late October. Daily simulcast of dog and
horse racing.

Camptown Greyhound Park
313 S. Highwya 69
Frontenac, Kansas 66763
(620) 230-0022
Map: **#6** (125 miles S. of Kansas City)

Restaurants: 1
Special Features: Closed at press time, but
expected to reopen in early 2008.

LOUISIANA

Louisiana was the fourth state to approve riverboat casino gambling and its 1991 gambling law allows a maximum of 15 boats statewide. In 1992 a provision was added for one land-based casino in New Orleans.

The state also has three land-based Indian casinos and four gaming machines-only casinos located at pari-mutuel facilities. Additionally, video poker is permitted at Louisiana truck stops, OTB's and bars/taverns in 31 of the state's 64 parishes (counties). All riverboat casinos in Louisiana are required to remain dockside and all are open 24 hours.

Gaming regulations require that gaming machines in casinos be programmed to pay back no less than 80% and no more than 99.9%. For video gaming machines at locations other than casinos the law requires a minimum return of 80% and a maximum return of 94%.

Louisiana gaming statistics are not broken down by individual properties. Rather, they are classified by region: Baton Rouge (BR), Lake Charles (LC), New Orleans (NO) and Shreveport/Bossier City (SB).

The Baton Rouge casinos consist of the Belle of Baton Rouge,Casino Rouge and Evangeline Downs. The Lake Charles casinos include: Isle of Capri, L' auberge du Lac and Delta Downs. New Orleans area casinos are: Bally's, Boomtown, Harrah's (landbased) and Treasure Chest. The Shreveport/Bossier city casinos include: Sam's Town, Edlorado, Boomtown, DiamondJacks (formerly Isle of Capri), Horseshoe and Harrah's Louisiana Downs.

Here's information, as supplied by the Louisiana State Police-Riverboat Gaming Section, showing the average electronic machine payback percentages for each area's casinos for the 12-month period from June, 2006 through May, 2007:

	BR	**LC**	**NO**	**SB**
1¢	**89.9%**	89.5%	89.3%	89.0%
5¢	**91.1%**	90.2%	**91.1%**	90.8%
25¢	**93.3%**	92.3%	93.0%	92.5%
$1	**93.9%**	93.4%	**93.9%**	93.7%
$5	**95.1%**	94.7%	94.5%	93.8%
All	**92.1%**	92.0%	92.0%	91.9%

These numbers reflect the percentage of money returned on each denomination of machine and encompass all electronic machines including video poker and video keno. The best returns for each category are highlighted in bold print and you can see that the Baton Rouge area casinos offered the best returns in most categories.

NOTE: If you happen to win a jackpot of $1,200 or more in Louisiana, the casino will withhold 6% of your winnings for the Louisiana Department of Revenue. If you want to try and get that money refunded, you will be required to file a state income tax return and, depending on the details of your return, you *may* get some of the money returned to you. The $1,200 threshold would also apply to any cash prizes won in casino drawings or tournaments.

All casinos offer: blackjack, craps, roulette, slots and video poker. Optional games include: Spanish 21 (S21), baccarat (B), mini-baccarat (MB), poker (P), Caribbean stud poker (CSP), pai gow poker (PGP), let it ride (LIR), casino war (CW), three-card poker (TCP), four card (FCP), big 6 wheel (B6), keno (K) and bingo (BG). The minimum gambling age is 21 for casino gaming and 18 for pari-mutuel betting.

For more information on visiting Louisiana call the state's tourism department at (800) 633-6970 or visit www.louisianatravel.com

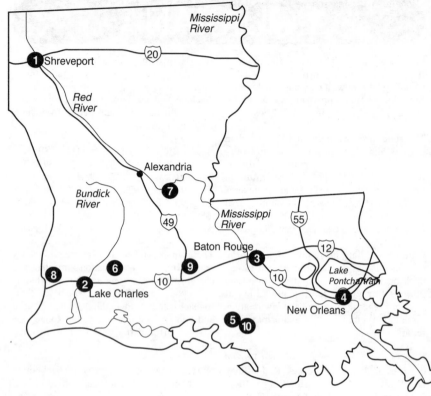

Amelia Belle Casino
500 Lake Palourde Rd
Amelia, Louisiana 70340
(985) 384-6044
Website: www.ameliabellecasino.com
Map: **#10** (75 miles S. of Baton Rouge)

Toll-Free Number: 1-888-777-1143
Restaurants: 2
Buffets: L- $7.95/$10.95 (Sat/Sun) D- $10.95
Casino Size: 30,000 Square Feet
Other Games: P, CSP, PGP, LIR, TCP
Overnight RV Parking: No
Special Features: 1,200-passenger paddle
wheeler on Bayou Boeuf.

Belle of Baton Rouge
103 France Street
Baton Rouge, Louisiana 70802
(225) 378-6000
Website: www.belleofbatonrouge.com
Map: **#3**

Toll-Free Number: (800) 676-4847
Restaurants: 4   Valet Parking: $10
Buffets: B-$10.95 L-$12.95/$19.95 (Sun)
          D-$19.95 (Fri/Sat Only)
Casino Size: 29,000 Square Feet
Other Games: S21, P, CSP, TCP
Overnight RV Parking: No
Senior Discount: 2-for-1 buffet Mon-Thu
          if 50 or older
Special Features: 1,500-passenger paddle
wheeler on the Mississippi River. 300-room
Sheraton Hotel is adjacent to casino (800-325-
3535). 10% off food/drink for slot club
members.

Boomtown Casino & Hotel Bossier City
300 Riverside Drive
Bossier City, Louisiana 71171
(318) 746-0711
Website: www.boomtownbossier.com
Map: **#1** (across the Red River From Shreveport)

Toll-Free Number: (866) 462-8696
Rooms: 100 Price Range: $109-$129
Suites: 88 Price Range: $129-$159
Restaurants: 4 Valet Parking: Free
Buffets: B-$7.99/$24.99 (Sun) L-$9.99
    D-$12.99/$17.99(Thurs)/$19.99 (Fri-Sat)
Casino Size: 28,000 Square Feet
Other Games: S21, MB, CSP, LIR, TCP
Overnight RV Parking: No
Senior Discount: Various on Wednesdays + 25% off food/retail purchases.
Special Features: 1,925-passenger paddle wheeler on the Red River. $1 off buffets for slot club members.

Boomtown Casino New Orleans
4132 Peters Road
Harvey, Louisiana 70058
(504) 366-7711
Website: www.boomtownneworleans.com
Map: **#4** (a suburb of New Orleans)

Toll-Free Number: (800) 366-7711
Restaurants: 4 Valet Parking: Free
Buffets: L-$9.95/$14.95 (Sun)
        D-$12.95/$16.95 (Thu)
        $19.95 (Fri)/$27.95 (Sat)
Casino Size: 30,000 Square Feet
Other Games: MB, P, PGP, TCP
Overnight RV Parking: Free/RV Dump: No
Senior Discount: $2 off buffets if 55 or older
Special Features: 1,600-passenger paddle wheeler on the Harvey Canal. Family arcade. New 200-room hotel expected to open late 2008.

Eldorado Casino Shreveport
451 Clyde Fant Parkway
Shreveport, Louisiana 71101
(318) 220-0981
Website: www.eldoradoshreveport.com
Map: **#1**

Hotel Reservations: (877) 602-0711
Suites: 403 Price Range: $135-$250
Restaurants: 4 Valet Parking: Free
Buffet: B-$13.50 (Sat-Sun) L-$10.99
        D-$14.99/$13.50 (Tue)/$19.99 (Fri)
Casino Size: 29,607 Square Feet
Other Games: MB, CW, P, PGP,
        CSP, LIR, TCP
Overnight RV Parking: No
Special Features: 1,500-passenger paddle wheeler on the Red River.

Harrah's New Orleans
Canal at the River
New Orleans, Louisiana 70130
(504) 533-6000
Website: www.harrahs.com
Map: **#4**

Toll-Free Number: (800) 847-5299
Toll-Free Number: (800) HARRAHS
Suites: 450 Price Range: $160-$860
Restaurants: 4
Buffet: B-$9.99 L-$12.99/$27.99 (Sun)
        D-$27.99/$29.99 (Fri/Sat)
Valet Parking: $10 first two hours/$5 for each
        additional two hours/$25 maximum
        (Free for Diamond and Platinum members)
Casino Size: 115,000 Square Feet
Other Games: B, MB, P, PGP, CSP, LIR,
        TCP, FCP, B6
Overnight RV Parking: No
Senior Discount: Mon-Thu buffet discounts ($2 off breakfast/$3 off lunch) if 65+
Special Features: Landbased casino. Five themed gaming areas. Fast food court. Daily live jazz music. Self-parking costs $5 to $25 depending on length of stay. Slot club members playing for minimum of 30 minutes can get validated for up to 24 hours of free parking.

Hollywood Casino- Baton Rouge
1717 River Road North
Baton Rouge, Louisiana 70802
(225) 381-7777
Website: www.casinorouge.com
Map: **#3**

Toll-Free Number: (800) 44-ROUGE
Restaurants: 4   Valet Parking: Free
Buffets: L-$9.95/$16.95 (Sun)
        D-$12.95/$16.95 (Fri-Sat)
Casino Size: 28,146 Square Feet
Other Games: P, PGP, TCP
Overnight RV Parking: Free/RV Dump: No
Special Features: 1,500-passenger paddle
wheeler on the Mississippi River.

Horseshoe Casino Hotel - Bossier City
711 Horseshoe Boulevard
Bossier City, Louisiana 71111
(318) 742-0711
Website: www.horseshoe.com
Map: **#1** (across the Red River from
Shreveport)

Toll-Free Number: (800) 895-0711
Suites: 606 Price Range: $95-$295
Restaurants: 4   Valet Parking: Free
Buffets: L-$12.95 D-$18.95/$20.95 (Fri/Sat)
Other Games: MB, P, CSP, TCP
Casino Size: 29,500 Square Feet
Overnight RV Parking: Free/RV Dump: No
Senior Discount: 10% buffet discount if 55+
Special Features: 2,930-passenger paddle
wheeler on the Red River. Affiliated with
Harrah's.

DiamondJacks Casino - Bossier City
711 Isle of Capri Boulevard
Bossier City, Louisiana 71111
(318) 678-7777
Website: www.diamondjacks.com
Map: **#1** (across the Red River from
Shreveport)

Toll-Free Number: (866) 552-9629
Suites: 570 Price Range: $109-$179
Restaurants: 3   Valet Parking: Free
Buffets: B-$7.99 L-$10.99 D-$14.99
Casino Size: 30,000 Square Feet
Other Games: MB, PGP, CSP, TCP,
          FCP LIR, K
Overnight RV Parking: Must use RV park
Special Features: 1,650-passenger paddle
wheeler on the Red River. 32-space RV park
($30/$35 Fri-Sat). Supervised childcare center.
1,200-seat showroom.

Isle of Capri - Lake Charles
100 Westlake Avenue
Westlake, Louisiana 70669
(337) 430-0711
Website: www.isleofcapricasino.com
Map: **#2** (220 miles W. of New Orleans)

Toll-Free Number: (800) THE-ISLE
Inn Rooms: 241 Price Range: $59-$109
Suite Rooms: 252 Price Range: $139-$299
Restaurants: 5   Valet Parking: Free
Buffets: B-$6.99 L-$10.99 D-$16.99
Casino Size: 48,900 Square Feet
Other Games: MB, P, PGP, CSP, TCP, LIR, B6
Overnight RV Parking: Must use RV park
Senior Discount: Various Tue if 50+
Special Features: Two 1,200-passenger paddle
wheelers on Lake Charles. 8-space RV park
($10 per night).

L'auberge du Lac Hotel & Casino
3202 Nelson Road
Lake Charles, Louisiana 70601
(337) 475-2900
Website: www.ldlcasino.com
Map: **#2** (220 miles W. of New Orleans)

Toll-Free Number: (866) 580-7444
Rooms: 636 Price Range: $149-$349
Suites: 99 Price Range: $199-$750
Restaurants: 5   Valet Parking: Free
Buffet: L-$12.99 D-$16.99/$25.99 (Thurs-
        Sat)/$18.99 (Sun)
Casino Size: 30,000 Square Feet
Other Games: MB, PGP, CSP, LIR, TCP
Overnight RV Parking: Must use RV park.
Special Features: 18-hole golf course. Spa.
Pool with lazy river ride. 1,500-seat event
center. 13-space RV park ($45 per night).

Sam's Town Hotel & Casino Shreveport
315 Clyde Fant Parkway
Shreveport, Louisiana 71101
(318) 424-7777
Website: www.samstownshreveport.com
Map: **#1**

Toll-Free Number: (866) 861-0711
Rooms: 514 Price Range: $79-$229
Restaurants: 3   Valet Parking: Free
Buffet: B-$13.99/$12.99 (Sat)
  L/D-$13.99/$14.99 (Sat-Sun)/$15.99 (Wed-Fri)
Casino Size: 30,000 Square Feet
Other Games: MB, LIR, TCP
Overnight RV Parking: No
Special Features: 1,650-passenger paddle
wheeler on the Red River.

Treasure Chest Casino
5050 Williams Boulevard
Kenner, Louisiana 70065
(504) 443-8000
Website: www.treasurechest.com
Map: **#4** (a suburb of New Orleans)

Toll-Free Number: (800) 298-0711
Restaurants: 2   Valet Parking: $5
Buffet: D- $19.95/$24.95 (Fri/Sat)
Casino Hours: 11am-3am/5am (Fri/Sat)
Casino Size: 25,767 Square Feet
Other Games: MB, PGP, TCP, FCP
Overnight RV Parking: No
Senior Discount: If 50+ join Treasured Friends
Special Features: 1,900-passenger paddle
wheeler on Lake Pontchartrain.

Indian Casinos

Coushatta Casino Resort
777 Coushatta Drive
Kinder Louisiana 70648
(318) 738-7300
Website: www.coushattacasinoresort.com
Map: **#6** (35 miles N.E. of Lake Charles)

Toll-Free Number: (800) 584-7263
Room Reservations: (888) 774-7263
Hotel Rooms: 118 Price Range: $109-$129
Suites: 90 Price Range: Casino Use Only
Inn Rooms: 195 Price Range: $79-$99
Lodge Rooms: 92 Price Range: $79-$99
Restaurants: 6 Liquor: Yes Valet Park: Free
Buffets: B-$7.25 L-$12.00/$13.99 (Sun)
        D-$13.99/$21.99 (Fri/Sat)
Casino Size: 100,000 Square Feet
Other Games: MB, P, PGP, TCP, FCP
Overnight RV Parking: Must use RV Park
Special Features: Land-based casino. 100-
space RV park ($17/$22 Fri-Sat). Video arcade.
Kids Quest childcare center. 18-hole golf
course.

Cypress Bayou Casino
P.O. Box 519
Charenton, Louisiana 70523
(318) 923-7284
Website: www.cypressbayou.com
Map: **#5** (75 miles S. of Baton Rouge)

Toll-Free Number: (800) 284-4386
Restaurants: 3 Liquor: Yes Valet Parking: Free
Casino Size: 125,000 Square Feet
Other Games: CSP, LIR, TCP, B6
Overnight RV Parking: Free/RV Dump: No
Special Features: Land-based casino. Gift
shop. Cigar bar. 12-space RV park ($10 per
night).

Paragon Casino Resort
711 Paragon Place
Marksville, Louisiana 71351
(318) 253-1946
Website: www.paragoncasinoresort.com
Map: **#7** (30 miles S.E. of Alexandria)

Toll-Free Number: (800) 946-1946
Rooms: 335 Price Range: $73-$129
Suites: 57 Price Range: $103-$343
Restaurants: 6 Liquor: Yes Valet Parking: Free
Buffets: B-$7.99 L-$9.99/$12.99 (Sun)
          D-$14.99/ $18.99 (Fri/Sat)
Casino Size: 74,120 Square Feet
Other Games: P, CSP, LIR, TCP, FCP
Overnight RV Parking: Must use RV park
Special Features: Land-based casino. 185-space RV Park ($13/$16 Fri-Sat). Video arcade. Kids Quest childcare center. 18-hole golf course.

Pari-Mutuels

Delta Downs Racetrack & Casino
2717 Highway 3063
Vinton, Louisiana 70668
(337) 589-7441
Website: www.deltadowns.com
Map: **#8** (20 miles W. of Lake Charles)

Toll-Free Number: (800) 589-7441
Room Reservations: (888) 332-7829
Rooms: 203 Price Range: $65-$134
Suites: 33 Price Range: Casino use only
Restaurants: 2   Valet Parking: Free
Buffets: B- $13.99 (Sun)
        L-$10.99/$19.99 (Sat)
        D-$14.99/$19.99 (Fri/Sat)
Other Games: Only machines
Overnight RV Parking: Free/RV Dump: No
Special Features: Live thoroughbred and quarter-horse racing (Thu-Sun) early October through mid-July. Daily simulcasting of horse racing.

Evangeline Downs Racetrack & Casino
2235 Creswell Lane Extension
Opelousas, Louisiana 70570
(337) 896-7223
Website: www.evangelinedowns.com
Map: **#9** (30 miles W. of Baton Rouge)

Toll-Free Number: (866) 472-2466
Restaurants: 3   Valet Parking: Free
Buffets: L-$6.99 D-$9.99/$16.99 (Fri)
Casino Size: 72,120 Square Feet
Other Games: Only machines
Overnight RV Parking: Free/RV Dump: No
Senior Discount: Various Tue if 50 or older
Special Features: Live thoroughbred and quarter-horse racing (Wed-Sat) April through November. Daily simulcasting of horse racing.

Fair Grounds Racecourse
1751 Gentilly Boulevard
New Orleans, Louisiana 70119
(504) 944-5515
Website: www.fairgroundsracecourse.com
Map: **#4**

Restaurants: 1   Valet Parking: $5
Other Games: Only machines
Overnight RV Parking: Free/RV Dump: No
Special Features: Live thoroughbred racing November through March.

Harrah's Louisiana Downs
8000 E. Texas Street
Bossier City, Louisiana 71111
(318) 742-5555
Website: www.harrahs.com
Map: **#1**

Toll-Free Number: (800) HARRAHS
Restaurants: 5   Valet Parking: Free
Buffets: B-$7.99 (Tue-Thu/Sat-Sun)
     L-$9.99/$12.99 (Sun)
     D-$12.99/$15.99 (Thu/Sat)/$16.99 (Fri)
Other Games: Only machines
Overnight RV Parking: Free/RV Dump: No
Senior Discount: Various Tue if 50 or older
Special Features: Live thoroughbred racing (Thu-Sun) late April through early October. Live quarter-horse racing racing (Sat-Wed) late October through November. Daily simulcasting of horse racing. 249-room Springhill Suites expected to open by early 2008.

MAINE

In early 2004 the Maine legislature authorized slot machines to be placed at Bangor Raceway and that facility opened in November 2005.

Gaming regulations require a minimum return of 89% on all machines and the games offered include: slots, video poker and video blackjack.

During the 6-month period from January through June 2007, the avergae return on gaming machines was 93.01%

The minimum gambling age is 21 for slots and 18 for pari-mutuel wagering.

For more information on visiting Maine call their Office of Tourism at (888) 624-6345 or visit their website at www.visitmaine.com.

Hollywood Slots at Bangor
427 Main Street
Bangor, Maine 04402
(207) 262-6146
Website: www.hollywoodslotsatbangor.com
Map: **#1**

Toll-Free Number: (877) 779-7771
Admission: Free   Parking: Free
Restaurants: 1
Hours: 9am-1am/2am (Fri/Sat)
          Noon-1am (Sun)
Special Features: Live harness racing day and evenings from late May through late July. Daily simulcasting of horse and harness racing.

MASSACHUSETTS

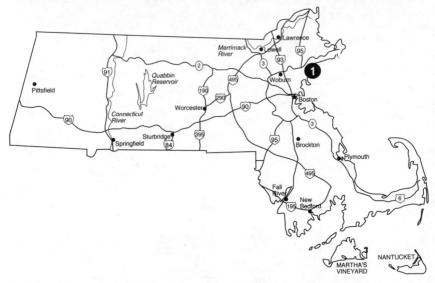

There is one casino boat in Massachusetts which sails three miles out into international waters where casino gambling is permitted. All passengers must present a photo ID or they will not be allowed to board.

The games offered include: blackjack, craps, roulette, poker, three-card poker, let it ride, slots, video poker and bingo.

For information on visiting Massachusetts call (800) 447-MASS or visit their web site at www.massvacation.com.

Horizon's Edge Casino Cruises
76 Marine Boulevard
Lynn, Massachusetts 01905
(781) 581-7733
Website: www.horizonsedge.com
Map: **#1** (11 miles N.E. of Boston)

Toll-Free Reservations: (800) 582-5932
Gambling Age: 21
Ship's Registry: U.S.
Buffets: Included
Schedule:
    11:00am - 5:00pm
    6:30pm - 12:00am
    7:00pm -12:30am (Fri)
    7:00pm -1:00am (Sat)
Prices: $27 (Mon-Fri Day/Sun-Thu Eve)
        $37 (Sat-Sun Day/Fri-Sat Eve)
Port Charges: Included
Parking: Free
Senior Discount: $5 discount Mon-Fri if 55+
Special Features: 490-passenger *Horizon's Edge* sails from Marina off of Lynnway in Lynn. 2-for-1 admisssion Monday day/eve sailings. No one under 21 permitted to board.

MICHIGAN

One of Michigan's most popular casinos is actually in Canada. It's Casino Windsor in Ontario which is just across the river from downtown Detroit.

All winnings are paid in Canadian currency and the minimum gambling age is 19. The casino is open 24 hours and offers the following games: blackjack, Spanish 21, craps, roulette, baccarat, mini-baccarat, big six wheel, pai-gow poker, Caribbean stud poker, three-card poker and let it ride.

Casino Windsor
377 Riverside Drive East
Windsor, Ontario N9A 7H7
(519) 258-7878
Website: www.casinowindsor.com
Map: **#12**

**NAME WILL CHANGE TO
CAESARS WINDSOR IN MID-2008**
PRICES ARE IN CANADIAN DOLLARS
Toll-Free Number: (800) 991-7777
Room Reservations: (800) 991-8888
Rooms: 349 Price Range: $125-$300
Suites: 40 Price Range: $250-$1,000
Restaurants: 4 (1 open 24 hours)
Buffets: L-$16.95/$18.95 (Sun) D-$21.95
Valet Parking: Free
Casino Size: 100,000 Square Feet
Casino Marketing: (800) 881-7777
Overnight RV Parking: Free/RV Dump: No
Special Features: Entire casino is non-smoking.

The only non-Indian casinos in Michigan are located in downtown Detroit. All three are open 24 hours and offer the following games: blackjack, craps, roulette, baccarat, mini-baccarat, Caribbean stud poker, three-card poker, pai gow poker, let it ride, big 6 wheel and casino war. No public information is available about the payback percentages on Detroit's gaming machines.

The minimum gambling age at all Detroit casinos is 21 and all three casinos offer free valet parking.

Greektown Casino
555 E. Lafayette Boulevard
Detroit, Michigan 48226
(313) 223-2999
Website: www.greektowncasino.com
Map: **#12**

Toll free Number: (888) 771-4386
Restaurants: 2
Casino Size: 75,000 Square Feet
Other Games: Poker
Overnight RV Parking: No

MGM Grand Detroit Casino
1777 Third St.
Detroit, Michigan 48226
(313) 393-7777
Website: detroit.mgmgrand.com
Map: **#12**

Toll-Free Number: (877) 888-2121
Room Reservations: (800) 991-8888
Rooms: 335 Price Range: $299-$450
Suites: 65 Price Range: $499-$3,000
Restaurants: 4 (1 open 24 hours)
Buffets: L-$14.95/$18.95 (Sat)/$12.95 (Sun)
 D-$17.95/$29.95 (Fri)/$22.95 (Sat)/$18.95 (Sun)
Casino Size: 75,000 Square Feet
Other Games: Spanish 21
Overnight RV Parking: No

MotorCity Casino
2901 Grand River Avenue
Detroit, Michigan 48201
(313) 237-7711
Website: www.motorcitycasino.com
Map: **#12**

Toll-Free Number: (877) 777-0711
Restaurants: 4 (1 open 24 hours)
Buffets: L-$17.00 D-$21.00/$31.00 (Fri)
Casino Size: 75,000 Square Feet
Other Games: Spanish 21
Overnight RV Parking: Free/RV Dump: No
Special Features: New 400-room hotel expected to open by early 2008.

Indian casinos in Michigan are not required to release information on their slot machine payback percentages. However, according to officials at the Michigan Gaming Control Board, which is responsible for overseeing the tribal-state compacts, "the machines must meet the minimum standards for machines in Nevada or New Jersey." In Nevada the minimum return is 75% and in New Jersey it's 83%. Therefore, Michigan's Indian casinos must return at least 75% in order to comply with the law.

Unless otherwise noted, all Indian casinos in Michigan are open 24 hours and offer the following games: blackjack, craps, roulette, slots and video poker. Other games offered include: Spanish 21 (S21), craps (C), roulette (R), baccarat (B), mini-baccarat (MB), poker (P), Caribbean stud poker (CSP), let it ride (LIR), three-card poker (TCP), four-card poker (FCP), keno (K) and bingo (BG).

The minimum gambling age is 21 at all Indian casinos except for the following seven where it's 18: Leelanau Sands, Turtle Creek, Chip-In's, Ojibwa, Ojibwa II, Lac Vieux and Soaring Eagle. Valet parking is free at all casinos.

For more information on visiting Michigan call the state's department of tourism at (800) 543-2937 or go to www.michigan.org.

Bay Mills Resort & Casino
11386 Lakeshore Drive
Brimley, Michigan 49715
(906) 248-3715
Website: www.4baymills.com
Map: **#3** (12 miles S.W. of Sault Ste. Marie)

Toll-Free Number: (888) 422-9645
Rooms: 142 Price Range: $69-$119
Suites: 4 Price Range: $150-$200
Restaurants: 3 (1 open 24 hours) Liquor: Yes
Buffets: B-$6.49 L-$7.99
         D-$12.99/$15.99 (Tue/Thu/Sat)
Casino Size: 15,000 Square Feet
Other Games: P, CSP, LIR, TCP
Overnight RV Parking: Must use RV park
Senior Discount: Various Wed 7:30am-2pm if 50+
Special Features: Free shuttle to King's Club and Kewadin casinos. 76-space RV park ($15/$20 with hookups). 18-hole golf course.

Chip-In's Island Resort & Casino
P.O. Box 351
Harris, Michigan 49845
(906) 466-2941
Website: www.chipincasino.com
Map: **#1** (13 miles W. of Escanaba on Hwy. 41)

Toll-Free Number: (800) 682-6040
Rooms: 102 Price Range: $69-$99
Suites: 11 Price Range: $150-$200
Restaurants: 3 Liquor: Yes
Casino Size: 135,000 Square Feet
Overnight RV Parking: Must use RV park
Other Games: S21, P, TCP, FCP, LIR, K, BG
Special Features: 53-space RV park ($15 per night).

Four Winds Casino
11111 Wilson Rd.
New Buffalo, MI 49117
(269) 926-4500
Website: www.fourwindscasino.com
Map: **#17** (75 miles E. of Chicago)

Toll-Free Number: (866) 494-6371
Rooms: 129 Price Range: $129-$249
Suites: 36 Price Range: $249-$949
Restaurants: 6 Liquor: Yes
Casino Size: 130,000 Square Feet
Overnight RV Parking: Free/RV Dump: No
Other Games: MB, P, LIR, TCP, PGP

Kewadin Casino - Christmas
N7761 Candy Cane Lane
Munising, Michigan 49862
(906) 387-5475
Website: www.kewadin.com
Map: **#9** (40 miles E. of Marquette)

Toll-Free Number: (800) KEWADIN
Restaurants: 1 Liquor: Yes
Hours: 8am-3am Daily
Valet Parking: Not offered
Casino Size: 3,060 Square Feet
Other Games: LIR, TCP, No craps/roulette
Overnight RV Parking: Free/RV Dump: No
Special Features: Free local-area shuttle service.

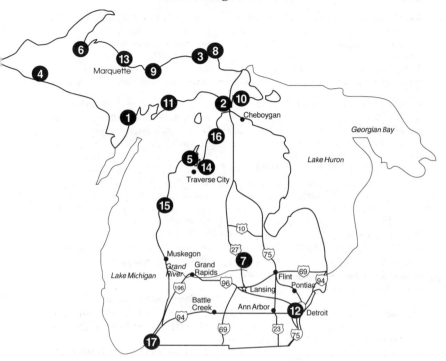

Kewadin Casino - Hessel
3 Mile Road, Box 789
Hessel, Michigan 49745
(906) 484-2903
Website: www.kewadin.com
Map: **#10** (20 miles N.E. of St. Ignace)

Toll-Free Number: (800) KEWADIN
Restaurants: 1 Deli Liquor: Yes
Valet Parking: Not offered
Hours: 8am-12am Daily
Casino Size: 6,500 Square Feet
Other Games: Only gaming machines
Overnight RV Parking: Free/RV Dump: No
Special Features: Free local-area shuttle
service.

Kewadin Casino - Manistique
US 2 East, Rte 1, Box 1533D
Manistique, Michigan 49854
(906) 341-5510
Website: www.kewadin.com
Map: **#11** (95 miles S.E. of Marquette)

Toll-Free Number: (800) KEWADIN
Restaurants: 1 Deli Liquor: Yes
Valet Parking: Not offered
Hours: 8am-3am Daily
Casino Size: 25,000 Square Feet
Other Games: LIR, TCP, K, BG, No Craps
Overnight RV Parking: Free/RV Dump: No
Senior Discount: Various Wed 8am-7pm if 50+
Special Features: 40-space RV park open May-
October ($18 per night). Free shuttle service
from local motels.

Kewadin Casino Hotel - Sault Ste. Marie
2186 Shunk Road
Sault Ste. Marie, Michigan 49783
(906) 632-0530
Website: www.kewadin.com
Map: **#8**

Toll-Free Number: (800) KEWADIN
Rooms: 300 Price Range: $69-$95
Suites: 20 Price Range: $95-$142
Restaurants: 2 Liquor: Yes
Buffets: B-$6.25/$10.50 (Sun) L-$9.50
    D-$12.50/$15.50 (Fri)/$17.50 (Mon/Sat)
Casino Size: 85,123 Square Feet
Other Games: P, CSP, LIR, TCP, K, BG
Overnight RV Parking: Must use RV park
Senior Discount: Various Thu 7am-7pm if 50+
Special Features: Free shuttle to local motels
and airport. 75-space RV park ($12 per night).

Kewadin Casino - St. Ignace
3039 Mackinaw Trail
St. Ignace, Michigan 49781
(906) 643-7071
Website: www.kewadin.com
Map: **#2** (50 miles S. of Sault Ste. Marie)

Toll-Free Number: (800) KEWADIN
Restaurants: 1 Deli Liquor: Yes
Buffets: B-$6.25 L-$9.50
         D-$12.50/$17.50 (Mon/Sat)
Casino Size: 56,168 Square Feet
Other Games: S21, P, LIR, TCP, FCP, K
Overnight RV Parking: Free/RV Dump: No
Senior Discount: Various Thu 7am-7pm if 50+
Special Features: Local motels/hotels offer
packages with free shuttle service. Sports bar.

Kings Club Casino
12140 W. Lakeshore Drive
Brimley, Michigan 49715
(906) 248-3700
Website: www.4baymills.com
Map: **#3** (12 miles S.W. of Sault Ste. Marie)

Toll-Free Number: (888) 422-9645
Restaurants: 3 Liquor: Yes
Valet Parking: Not offered
Casino Size: 6,500 Square Feet
Other Games: Only gaming machines
Overnight RV Parking: Must use RV park
Senior Discount: Various Tue 10am-10pm if 50+
Special Features: Two miles from, and
affiliated with, Bay Mills Resort & Casino. 75-
space RV park ($15/$20 w/hookup) at Bay
Mills.

Lac Vieux Desert Casino
N 5384 US 45 North
Watersmeet, Michigan 49969
(906) 358-4226
Website: www.lacvieuxdesert.com
Map: **#4** (49 miles S.E. of Ironwood)

Toll-Free Number: (800) 583-3599
Room Reservations: (800) 895-2505
Rooms: 107 Price Range: $70-$80
Suites: 25 Price Range: $100-$150
Restaurants: 1 Liquor: Yes
Buffets: D-$17.95 (Fri/Sat)
Valet Parking: Not offered
Casino Size: 25,000 Square Feet
Other Games: LIR, P (Thu-Sun), BG
Overnight RV Parking: Must use RV park
Senior Discount: Various Tuesdays if 55+
Special Features: 9-hole golf course. 14-space
RV park ($5 per night).

Leelanau Sands Casino
2521 N.W. Bayshore Drive
Sutton's Bay, Michigan 49682
(231) 271-4104
Website: www.casino2win.com
Map: **#5** (4 miles N. of Sutton's Bay)

Toll-Free Number: (800) 922-2946
Room Reservations: (800) 930-3008
Rooms: 51 Price Range: $79-$99
Suites: 2 Price Range: $109-$119
Restaurants: 1 Liquor: Yes
Buffets: Brunch-$11.95 (Sun)
Casino Size: 72,000 Square Feet
Hours: 8am-2am Daily
Other Games: CSP, LIR, P, TCP, FCP,
              BG (Wed/Thu/Fri/Sun)
Overnight RV Parking: Free/RV Dump: No
Senior Discount: Various on Thu if 55+
Special Features: RV hook-ups available for
$10 per night.

Little River Casino
2700 Orchard Drive
Manistee, Michigan 49660
(231) 723-1535
Website: www.littlerivercasinos.com
Map: **#15** (60 miles S.W of Traverse City)

Toll-Free Number: (888) 568-2244
Toll-Free Number: (866) 466-7338
Rooms: 271 Price Range: $99-$169
Suites: 20 Price Range: $199-$279

Restaurants: 3 Liquor: Yes
Buffets: B-$6.99 D-$9.99/$19.99 (Fri/Sat)
Casino Size: 75,000 Square Feet
Other Games: P, LIR, CSP, TCP
Senior Discount: Various if you sign up for Senior Slot Club. Must be 55+.
Overnight RV Parking: Free/RV Dump: Free
Special Features: 95-space RV park open April-November ($18/$20 per night).

Odawa Casino Resort
1760 Lears Road
Petoskey, Michigan 49770
(231) 439-9100
Website: www.odawacasino.com
Map: **#16** (50 miles S.W of Cheboygan)

Toll-Free Number: (877) 442-6464
Rooms: 127 Price Range: $79-$129
Suites: 10 Price Range- $109-$159
Restaurants: 4 Liquor: Yes
Buffets: B-$9.95 L-$12.95 D-$18.95
Casino Size: 33,000 Square Feet
Hours: 8am-4am Daily
Other Games: LIR, TCP
Overnight RV Parking: Free/RV Dump: No
Senior Discount: Various Wed 8am-8pm if 55+
Special Features: Hotel is 1/4-mile from casino and rooms offer views of Little Traverse Bay. Free shuttle service to/from local hotels.

Ojibwa Casino Resort - Baraga
797 Michigan Avenue
Baraga, Michigan 49908
(906) 353-6333
Website: www.ojibwacasino.com
Map: **#6** (30 miles S. of Houghton)

Toll-Free Number: (800) 323-8045
Rooms: 78 Price Range: $60-$75
Suites: 2 Price Range: $69-$85
Restaurants: 1 Liquor: Yes
Buffets: B-$12.95 (Sun) L-$7.95
         D-$15.95 (Fri/Sat)
Casino Size: 17,000 Square Feet
Other Games: P (Thu-Sat), TCP,
         BG (Mon/Tue/Thu)
Overnight RV Parking: Must use RV park
Senior Discount: Various Mon 10am-5pm if 55+
Special Features: 12-space RV Park ($10 per night). 8-lane bowling alley. Table games open noon-2am/4am (Fri/Sat).

Ojibwa Casino - Marquette
105 Acre Trail
Marquette, Michigan 49855
(906) 249-4200
Website: www.ojibwacasino.com
Map: **#13**

Toll-Free Number: (888) 560-9905
Restaurants: 1 Snack Bar Liquor: Yes
Valet Parking: Not offered
Other Games: LIR
Overnight RV Parking: Free/RV Dump: No
Senior Discount: Various Mon 10am-5pm if 55+
Special features: 7-space RV Park (Free). Table games open noon-2am/4am (Fri/Sat).

Soaring Eagle Casino & Resort
6800 E Soaring Eagle Boulevard
Mount Pleasant, Michigan 48858
(517) 775-5777
Website: www.soaringeaglecasino.com
Map: **#7** (65 miles N. of Lansing)

Toll-Free Number: (888) 7-EAGLE-7
Room Reservations: (877) 2-EAGLE-2
Rooms: 491 Price Range: $129-$199
Suites: 21 Price Range: $199-$399
Restaurants: 5 Liquor: Yes
Buffets: B-$8.75 L/D-$15.75/$19.75 (Mon/Wed)
Casino Size: 150,000 Square Feet
Other Games: P, CSP, LIR, TCP,
         BG (Wed-Sun), B6
Overnight RV Parking: Free/RV Dump: No
Special Features: Casino is in two separate buildings. Kid's Quest childcare center. Video arcade. Gift shop. Art gallery.

Turtle Creek Casino
7741 M-72 East
Williamsburg, Michigan 49690
(231) 534-8888
Website: www.casino2win.com
Map: **#14** (8 miles E. of Traverse City)

Toll-Free Number: (888) 777-8946
Restaurants: 2 Liquor: Yes
Casino Size: 29,000 Square Feet
Other Games: TCP, FCP, LIR
Overnight RV Parking: Free/RV Dump: No

MINNESOTA

All Minnesota casinos are located on Indian reservations and under a compact reached with the state the only table games permitted are card games such as blackjack and poker. Additionally, the only kind of slots allowed are the electronic video variety. Therefore, you will not find any mechanical slots that have traditional reels - only video screens.

According to the terms of the compact between the state and the tribes, however, the minimum and maximum payouts are regulated as follows: video poker and video blackjack - 83% to 98%, slot machines - 80% to 95%, keno - 75% to 95%. Each tribe is free to set its machines to pay back anywhere within those limits and the tribes do not not release any information regarding their slot machine percentage paybacks.

The hours of operation are listed for those casinos that are not open on a 24-hour basis. Unless otherwise noted, all casinos offer: video slots, video poker, video keno and blackjack. Optional games include: poker (P), Caribbean stud poker (CSP), pai gow poker (PGP), three-card poker (TCP), let it ride (LIR) and bingo (BG).

The minimum gambling age is 18 at all casinos. Valet parking is free at all casinos except Jackpot Junction and Mystic Lake. For more information on visiting Minnesota call the state's office of tourism at (800) 657-3700 or go to www.exploreminnesota.com.

Black Bear Casino & Hotel
1785 Highway 210
Carlton, Minnesota 55718
(218) 878-2327
Website: www.blackbearcasinohotel.com
Map: **#1** (130 miles N. of Twin Cities)

Toll-Free Number: (888) 771-0777
Reservation Number: (800) 553-0022
Rooms: 158 Price Range: $45-$115
Suites: 60 Price Range: $65-$185
Restaurants: 2 Liquor: Yes
Buffets: B-$3.95 L-$6.95/$9.95 (Sun)
          D-$11.95/$17.95 (Thu)

Casino Size: 65,000 Square Feet
Other Games: P, BG
Overnight RV Parking: Free/RV Dump: No
Special Features: Hotel is connected to casino by a skywalk.

Fond-du-Luth Casino
129 E. Superior Street
Duluth, Minnesota 55802
(218) 722-0280
Website: www.fondduluthcasino.com
Map: **#3** (150 miles N.E. of Twin Cities)

Toll-Free Number: (800) 873-0280
Restaurants: 2 Snack Bars Liquor: Yes
Casino Size: 20,000 Square Feet
Other Games: Only Blackjack and Slots
Overnight RV Parking: No
Senior Discount: Various specials Mon-Wed
          10am to 6pm if 55 or older
Special Features: One hour free parking in lot adjacent to casino (must be validated in casino). Free shuttle to/from Black Bear Casino.

Fortune Bay Resort/Casino
1430 Bois Forte Road
Tower, Minnesota 55790
(218) 753-6400
Website: www.fortunebay.com
Map: **#4** (150 miles N.E. of Twin Cities. 24 miles N.E. of Virginia, MN on the S. shore of Lake Vermilion)

Toll-Free Number: (800) 992-7529
Hotel Reservations: (800) 555-1714
Rooms: 83 Price Range: $69-$109
Suites: 33 Price Range: $89-$189
Restaurants: 4   Liquor: Yes Valet: Free
Buffets: B-$5.95 (Sat/Sun)
          D-$12.95
Casino Size: 17,000 Square Feet
Other Games: P, BG (Wed-Sun)
Overnight RV Parking: Must use RV park
Senior Discount: Specials Mon/Thu if 55+
Special Features: Located on S.E. shore of Lake Vermilion. 84-slip marina. 36-space RV Park ($25/$30 w/hookup). Snowmobile and hiking trails. 18-hole golf course.

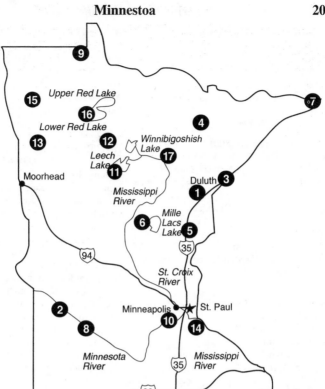

Grand Casino Hinckley
777 Lady Luck Drive
Hinckley, Minnesota 55037
(320) 384-7777
Website: www.grandcasinosmn.com
Map: **#5** (75 miles N. of Twin Cities. One mile E. of I-35's Hinckley exit on Hwy. 48)

Toll-Free Number: (800) 472-6321
Hotel/RV/Chalet Reservations: (800) 995-4726
Rooms: 485 Price Range: $65-$93 (Hotel)
        Price Range: $55-$85 (Inn)
        Price Range: $55-$93 (Chalet)
Suites: 52 Price Range: $99-$195
Restaurants: 5 Liquor: Yes Valet: Free
Buffets: L-$8.49 Brunch-$9.99 (Sat/Sun) D-$11.99 (Wed)/$19.99 (Tues)/$15.99 (Thurs)/$13.99(Fri/Sat)/$17.99 (Sun)
Casino Size: 54,800 Square Feet
Other Games: P, BG (Thu-Mon)
Overnight RV Parking: Must use RV park
Casino Marketing: (800) 472-6321
Special Features: 222-space RV park ($20 per night/$23 Fri/Sat). Kid's Quest childcare center. 18-hole golf course. Free pet kennel.

Grand Casino Mille Lacs
777 Grand Avenue
Onamia, Minnesota 56359
(320) 532-7777
Website: www.grandcasinosmn.com
Map: **#6** (90 miles N. of Twin Cities. On Highway 169 on the W. shore of Lake Mille Lacs)

Toll-Free Number: (800) 626-5825
Room Reservations: (800) HOTEL-17
Rooms: 284 Price Range: $49-$109
Suites: 14 Price Range: $139-$349
Restaurants: 4 Liquor: No
Buffets: L-$7.98 Brunch-$9.99 (Sat/Sun)
  D-$17.99 (Mon)/$12.99 (Tues/Thurs)/$15.99 (Wed)/$19.99 (Fri)/$13.99 (Sat/Sun)
Casino Size: 42,000 Square Feet
Other Games: P, BG
Overnight RV Parking: Free/RV Dump: No
Casino Marketing: (800) GRAND-76
Special Features: Resort has two hotels (one is off-property). Kid's Quest childcare center. Free pet kennel.

Grand Portage Lodge & Casino
P.O. Box 233
Grand Portage, Minnesota 55605
(218) 475-2401
Website: www.grandportage.com
Map: **#7** (N.E. tip of Minnesota. 300 miles N. of Twin Cities. On Highway 61, five miles from the Canadian border)

Reservation Number: (800) 543-1384
Rooms: 90 Price Range: $85-$115
Suites: 10 Price Range: $165-$185
Restaurants: 2 Liquor: Yes Valet Parking: No
Casino Size: 15,268 Square Feet
Other Games: BG, No Blackjack
Overnight RV Parking: Must use RV park
Special Features: On shore of Lake Superior. Hiking, skiing and snowmobile trails. Gift shop. Marina. 10-space RV park open June-Sept ($24 per night).

Jackpot Junction Casino Hotel
P.O. Box 420
Morton, Minnesota 56270
(507) 644-3000
Website: www.jackpotjunction.com
Map: **#8** (110 miles S.W. of Twin Cities)

Toll-Free Number: (800) WIN-CASH
Rooms: 253 Price Range: $65-$79
Suites: 23 Price Range: $105-$190
Restaurants: 4 (1 open 24 hours) Liquor: Yes
Buffets: B-$4.99/$7.99 (Sat) L-$9.99
Brunch-$11.99 (Sun) D-$11.99/$16.99 (Thurs)
Valet Parking: Not Offered
Other Games: P, PGP, TCP, LIR, BG
Senior Discount: 25% off Wed lunch or dinner buffets if 55+
Overnight RV Parking: Must use RV park
Special Features: 40-space RV park ($15 per night/$20 Fri-Sat). Kids Quest childcare center. 18-hole golf course. Gift shop.

Little Six Casino
2354 Sioux Trail N.W.
Prior Lake, Minnesota 55372
(952) 445-9000 (Mystic Lake)
Website: www.littlesixcasino.com
Map: **#10** (25 miles S.W. of Twin Cities. On County Road 83)

Toll-Free: (800) 262-7799 (Mystic Lake)
Restaurants: 1 Liquor: No
Hours: 10am-4am/24 hours (Fri-Mon)
Special Features: 1/4-mile north of Mystic Lake Casino.

Mystic Lake Casino Hotel
2400 Mystic Lake Boulevard
Prior Lake, Minnesota 55372
(952) 445-9000
Website: www.mysticlake.com
Map: **#10** (25 miles S.W. of Twin Cities. On County Road 83, 3 miles S. of Hwy 169)

Toll-Free Number: (800) 262-7799
Hotel Reservations: (800) 813-7349
RV Reservations: (800) 653-2267
Rooms: 400 Price Range: $79-$135
Suites: 16 Price Range: $129-$375
Restaurants: 4 Liquor: No
Buffets: L-$9.95/$13.95 (Sat/Sun)
            D-$16.95/$22.95 (Wed)
Valet Parking: $3
Casino Size: 102,000 Square Feet
Other Games: BG
Overnight RV Parking: Free/RV Dump: No
Senior Discount: Various Tue 8am-11am if 55+
Special Features: Free shuttle bus service from Twin Cities area. Also has a second casino - Dakota Country with 45,000-square-feet of gaming space. 122-space RV park ($30 per night spring/summer, $21 fall/winter). Health club. Childcare facility.

Northern Lights Casino
6800 Y Frontage Rd NW
Walker, Minnesota 56484
(218) 547-2744
Website: www.northernlightscasino.com
Map: **#11** (175 miles N. of the Twin Cities. Near the S. shore of Lake Leech four miles S. of Walker, MN at the junction of Highways 371 & 200)

Toll-Free Number: (800) 252-7529
Toll-Free Number: (877) 544-4879
Room Reservations: (866) 652-4683
Rooms: 105 Price Range: $70-$135
Suites: 4 Price Range: $132-$165
Restaurants: 3 Liquor: Yes
Buffets: L-$6.95/$5.95 (Mon)
            Brunch-$7.95 (Sat)/$8.95 (Sun)
            D-$8.95/$18.95 (Thu)/$13.50(Fri/Sat)
Casino Size: 40,000 Square Feet
Other Games: P
Overnight RV Parking: Free/RV Dump: No
Senior Discount: Various Thu 10am-6:30pm
            and Mon 8am-12am if 50+
Special Features: 90-foot dome simulates star constellations. 20% room discount for slot club members. Free comedy show Tue at 7pm.

Palace Casino Hotel
6280 Upper Cass Frontage Rd NW
Cass Lake, Minnesota 56633
(218) 335-7000
Website: www.palacecasinohotel.com
Map: **#12** (220 miles N.W. of Twin Cities)

Toll-Free Number: (877) 9-PALACE
Room Reservations: (800) 442-3910
Rooms: 64 Price Range: $49-$69
Suites: 16 Price Range $59-$79
Restaurants: 2 Liquor: No
Casino Size: 30,000 Square Feet
Other Games: P, BG (Thu-Sun)
Overnight RV Parking: Free/RV Dump: Free
Senior Discount: Various Wed 9am-9pm if 50+
Special Features: 15-space RV park offers free
parking and hookup.

Prairie's Edge Casino Resort
5616 Prairie's Edge Lane
Granite Falls, Minnesota 56241
(320) 564-2121
Website: www.prairiesedgecasino.com
Map: **#2** (110 miles W. of Twin Cities. Five
miles S.E. of Granite Falls on Highway 67 E.)

Toll-Free Number: (866) 293-2121
Rooms: 79 Price Range: $49-$89
Suites: 10 Price Range: $129-$169
Restaurants: 2 Liquor: Yes
Buffets: Brunch-$8.95 (Sun)
          D-$8.95/$9.95 (Sat)
Valet Parking: Not Offered
Casino Size: 36,000 Square Feet
Other Games: P
Overnight RV Parking: Free/RV Dump: No
Special Features: 55-space RV park ($16 per
night/$24 w/hookups). Convenience store.
Non-smoking slot area.

Seven Clans Casino Red Lake
Highway 1 East
Red Lake, MN 56671
(218) 679-2500
Web: www.sevenclanscasino.com
Map: **#16** (31 miles N. of Bemidji)

Toll-Free Number: (888) 679-2501
Restaurants: 1 Liquor: No
Valet Parking: Not Offered
Casino Size: 19,875 Square Feet
Casino Hours: 10am-1am/9am-2am (Thu-Sun)
Overnight RV Parking: Free/RV Dump: No
Senior Discount: Special Mon 10am-7pm if 55+

Seven Clans Casino Thief River Falls
Rt 3, Box 168A
Thief River Falls, Minnesota 56701
(218) 681-4062
Website: www.sevenclanscasino.com/trf.html
Map: **#15** (275 miles N.W. of Minneapolis)

Toll-Free Number: (800) 881-0712
Room Reservations: (866) 255-7848
Suites: 151 Price Range: $69-$99
Restaurants: 1 Liquor: No
Buffets: B-$7.95 L-$8.95 D-$8.95
Valet Parking: Not Offered
Casino Size: 16,000 Square Feet
Other Games: P
Overnight RV Parking: Free/RV Dump: No
Senior Discount: Various Tue 7am-7pm and
          10% off food at all times if 55+
Special features: Indoor water park. Malt shop.

Seven Clans Casino Warroad
1012 E. Lake Street
Warroad, MN 56763
(218) 386-3381
Website: www.sevenclanscasino.com
Map: **#9** (400 miles N.W. of Twin Cities)

Toll-Free Number: (800) 815-8293
Room Reservations: (888) 714-5514
Rooms: 34 Price Range: $49-$66
Suites: 7 Price Range: $90-$100
Restaurants: 1 Liquor: No
Casino Size: 13,608 Square Feet
Overnight RV Parking: Free/RV Dump: No
Senior Discount: Various Thu 8am-6pm if 55+
Special Features: Hotel is Super 8 located one
mile from casino with free shuttle service
provided.

Shooting Star Casino Hotel
777 Casino Boulevard
Mahnomen, Minnesota 56557
(218) 935-2701
Website: www.starcasino.com
Map: **#13** (250 miles N.W. of Twin Cities)

Room Reservations: (800) 453-STAR
Rooms: 360 Price Range: $69-$99
Suites: 30 Price Range: $99-$115
Restaurants: 4 Liquor: Yes
Buffets: B-$4.99 L-$6.99/$9.99 (Sun)
        D-$8.99/$14.99 (Fri)/$11.99 (Sat)
Other Games: P, BG
Overnight RV Parking: Must use RV park
Senior Discount: $5 off room if 50 or older
Special Features: 47-space RV park ($19 per
night). Childcare facility for children up to 12
years of age.

Treasure Island Resort Casino
5734 Sturgeon Lake Road
Red Wing, Minnesota 55066
(651) 388-6300
Website: www.treasureislandcasino.com
Map: **#14** (40 miles S.E. of Twin Cities.
Halfway between Hastings and Red Wing, off
Highway 61 on County Road 18)

Toll-Free Number: (800) 222-7077
Room/RV Reservations: (888) 867-7829
Restaurants: 4 Liquor: Yes
Rooms: 250 Price Range: $79-$119
Suites: 28 Price Range: $179-$269
Buffets: Brunch-$11.99 (Sat-Sun) L-$8.99
        D-$12.99/$19.99 (Thu)/$14.99 (Fri/Sat)
Valet Parking: $3
Casino Size: 110,000 Square Feet
Other Games: P, BG
Overnight RV Parking: Free/RV Dump: No
Senior Discount: First Wednesday of each
    month 10am-2pm get coupon book if 55+
Special Features: 95-space RV park open
April-October ($18 per night/13 amp $20 per
night/50amp). 137-slip marina. Dinner and
sightseeing cruises. Childcare facility for
children up to 12 years of age.

White Oak Casino
45830 US Hwy 2
Deer River, MN 56636
(218) 246-9600
Website: www.whiteoakcasino.com
Map: **#17** (5 miles N.W. of Grand Rapids)

Toll-Free Number: (800) 653-2412
Restaurants: 1 Snack Bar Liquor: Yes
Casino Size: 11,000 Square Feet
Other Games: P
Overnight RV Parking: Free/RV Dump: No
Senior Discount: Various Tue 10am-6pm if
50+

Pari-Mutuel

Minnesota has one racetrack that offers the
card games of blackjack, poker, pai gow poker,
let it ride, Caribbean stud poker three card poker
and four card poker.

The completely nonsmoking card room is
open 24 hours and admission is free. Players
must pay a commission to the card room on
each hand played for all games except regular
poker, where a rake is taken from each pot.
The minimum gambling age is 18.

Canterbury Park
1100 Canterbury Road
Shakopee, Minnesota 55379
(952) 445-7223
Website: www.canterburypark.com
Map: **#10** (22 miles S.W. of Twin Cities)

Horse Track Toll-Free: (800) 340-6361
Card Room Toll-Free: (866) 667-6537
Admission: $5 (for horse racing)
Admission: Free (for card room)
Self-Parking: Free   Valet Parking: $6
Restaurants: 2
Casino Size: 18,000 Square Feet
Overnight RV Parking: No
Special Features: Live horse racing Mid-May
through early September. Daily simulcasting.
Free shuttle service to/from Mall of America.

MISSISSIPPI

Mississippi was the third state to legalize riverboat gambling when it was approved by that state's legislature in 1990. The law restricts casinos to coast waters (including the Bay of St. Louis and the Back Bay of Biloxi) along the Mississippi River and in navigable waters of counties that border the river.

Mississippi law also requires that riverboats be permanently moored at the dock and they are not permitted to cruise. This allows the riverboats to offer 24-hour dockside gambling. The Isle of Capri in Biloxi was the first casino to open on August 1, 1992 followed one month later by The President.

Since the law does not require that the floating vessel actually resemble a boat, almost all of the casinos are built on barges. This gives them the appearance of a land-based building, rather than a riverboat. Due to the destruction caused by Hurricane Katrina in August 2006, the Mississippi legislature authorized the state's gulf coast casinos to be rebuilt on land within 800-feet of the shoreline and some casinos have been rebuilt in that manner.

The Mississippi Gaming Commission does not break down its slot statistics by individual properties. Rather, they are classified by region. The **Coastal** region includes Biloxi, Gulfport and Bay Saint Louis. The **North** region includes Tunica, Greenville and Lula. The **Central** region includes Vicksburg and Natchez.

With that in mind here's information, as supplied by the Mississippi Gaming Commission, showing the machine payback percentages for each area's casinos for the one-year period from June 1, 2006 through May 31, 2007:

These numbers reflect the percentage of money returned on each denomination of machine and encompass all electronic machines including video poker and video keno. The best returns for each category are highlighted in bold print and you can see that all of the gaming areas offer rather similar returns on their machines.

Mississippi is one of the few states that breaks down its progressive machine statistics separately and you can see that the return is always less on machines with progressive jackpots.

Unless otherwise noted, all casinos are open 24 hours and offer: slots, video poker, blackjack, craps, roulette and three card poker. Other game listings include: Spanish 21 (S21), baccarat (B), mini-baccarat (MB), poker (P), pai gow poker (PGP), let it ride (LIR), Caribbean stud poker (CSP), big six wheel (B6), casino war (CW) and keno (K). The minimum gambling age is 21 and there is no charge for valet parking at those casinos offering it.

NOTE: If you happen to win a jackpot of $1,200 or more in Mississippi, the casino will deduct 3% of your winnings and pay it to the Mississippi Tax Commission as a gambling tax. The tax is nonrefundable and the $1,200 threshold would also apply to any cash prizes won in casino drawings or tournaments.

For more information on visiting Mississippi call the state's tourism department at (866) SEE-MISS or go to: www.visitmisissippi.com

For Biloxi tourism information call (800) 237-9493 or go to: www.gulfcoast.org. For Tunica tourism information call (888) 4-TUNICA or go to: www.tunicamiss.com

	Coastal	North	Central
5¢ Slots	**92.25%**	90.74%	92.88%
5¢ Prog.	**89.21%**	88.64%	89.03%
25¢ Slots	**94.54%**	93.21%	93.15%
25¢ Prog.	90.11%	**90.69%**	89.04%
$1 Slots	94.87%	94.64%	**95.54%**
$1 Prog.	**92.22%**	91.73%	90.95%
$5 Slots	**95.30%**	94.97%	94.93%
All	**93.31%**	93.00%	93.20%

Bay St. Louis

Map: **#2** (on St. Louis Bay, 40 miles E. of New Orleans)

Hollywood Casino Bay St. Louis
711 Hollywood Boulevard
Bay St. Louis, Mississippi 39520
(228) 467-9257
Website: www.hollywoodcasinobsl.com

Toll-Free Number: (866) 758-2591
Rooms: 498 Price Range: $99-$179
Suites: 78 Price Range: Casino Use Only
Restaurants: 2 (1 open 24 hours)
Buffets: B- $9.99 (Mon-Fri)
 L-$9.99 (Mon-Fri) Brunch-$17.99 (Sat-Sun)
 D-$17.99 (Mon-Thurs)
Casino Size: 40,000
Overnight RV Parking: Must use RV park
Special Features: 100 hookup RV Park ($28 per night). 18-hole golf course.

Biloxi

Map: **#1** (On the Gulf of Mexico, 80 miles E. of New Orleans)

Beau Rivage
875 Beach Boulevard
Biloxi, Mississippi 39530
(228) 386-7111
Website: www.beaurivageresort.com

Toll-Free Number: (888) 750-7111
Room Reservations: (888) 56-ROOMS
Rooms: 1,740 Price Range: $109-$229
Suites: 95 Price Range: $295-$375
Restaurants: 4 (1 open 24 hours) Valet: Free
Buffets: B- $9.99 L-$11.99
 D-$19.99/$24.99 (Fri/Sat)
Casino Size: 71,669 Square Feet
Other Games: MB, PGP, P
Overnight RV Parking: Free/RV Dunp: Np
Casino Marketing: (888) 567-2328
Special Features: Casino is on a barge. 18-hole golf course. Spa. Beauty salon. 13-store shopping arcade.

Boomtown Casino - Biloxi
676 Bayview Avenue
Biloxi, Mississippi 39530
(228) 435-7000
Website: www.boomtownbiloxi.com

Toll-Free Number: (800) 627-0777
Restaurants: 2 (1 open 24 hours) Valet: Free
Buffets: B-$7.95 L-$9.95
 D-$16.95/$19.95 (fri-Sun)
Casino Size: 51,665 Square Feet
Other Games: P
Overnight RV Parking: Free/RV Dump: No
Special Features: Casino is on a barge.

Grand Casino Resort Biloxi
265 Beach Boulevard
Biloxi, Mississippi 39530
(228) 436-2946
Website: www.grandbiloxi.com

Toll-Free Number: (800) 946-2946
Rooms: 500 Price Range: $159-$429
Suites: 40 Price Range: Casino Use Only
Restaurants: 3 (1 open 24 hours)
Buffets: B-$9.99 L-$11.99 D-$21.99
Casino Size: 27,610
Other Games: MB, PGP, TCP, FCP
Overnight RV Parking: Free/RV Dump: No
Special Features: Land-based casino. 18-hole golf course. Spa. Beauty salon.

Hard Rock Hotel & Casino - Biloxi
777 Beach Boulevard
Biloxi, Mississippi 39530
(228) 374-7625
Website: www.hardrockbiloxi.com

Toll-Free Number: (877) 877-6256
Rooms: 306 Prices: $139-$189
Suites: 64 Prices: $229-$529
Restaurants: 4 (1 open 24 hours)
Buffets: L-$12.99 Brunch-$19.99 (Sat/Sun)
 D-$15.99/$21.99 (Wed/Fri/Sat)
Casino Size: 48,500 Square Feet
Other Games: MB, P, PGP
Special Features: Casino is on a barge. Spa. Nightclub. Collection of rock and roll memorabilia on display.

The Best Places To Play On The Gulf Coast
(Biloxi and Gulfport Only)

Roulette - The house edge on a single-zero wheel cuts the house edge from 5.26% down to a more reasonable 2.70%. Unfortunately, there are no casinos on the Gulf Coast that offer single-zero roulette.

Craps - IP is the most liberal of all gulf coast casinos by offering 20X odds on its craps games. All other casinos offer 10X odds, except for Boomtown which limits players to 5X odds.

Blackjack - Gulf Coast casinos offer some of the best blackjack outside of Nevada and, unlike most Nevada casinos, there are only two games where the dealer hits soft 17. This rule is advantageous for the player by .20%. All of the recommendations in this section apply to players using perfect basic strategy for each particular game.

Eight casinos offer a single-deck game, but all should be avoided because they all pay less than the standard 3-to-2 for winning blackjacks. The casino edge in all of these games is more than 1.20%.

Boomtown, Grand, Palace and Treasure Bay are tied for the best double-deck game, with the following rules: double down on any first two cards, re-split any pair (including aces) and doubling allowed after splitting. This works out to a casino edge of just .14%. Next best are Beau Rivage, Hard Rock, IP, Island View and Isle of Capri which have similar rules, except they don't allow the resplitting of aces which brings the casino edge up to .19%.

Boomtown and Island View have a four-deck game which is dealt from a continuous shuffling machine (CSM). The rules are identical to the above .14% two-deck game, but it's four decks, with a resulting casino advantage of .29%. The same game, with the addition of late surrender, is available at Beau Rivage and the advantage is lessened to .22%.

For six-deck shoe games the best place to play is Beau Rivage which allows doubling down on any first two cards, doubling after splitting, late surrender and resplitting of aces. The casino advantage in this game is .26%. You should be careful, however, because some other tables offering this game at Beau Rivage will hit soft 17 and this raises the casino advantage to .46%

All other casinos, except for Isle of Capri, offer the same rules as Beau Rivage with the exception of late surrender. The edge in these games is .34%. The Isle won't let you resplit aces and that brings the casino advantage up to .41%

Only the Grand and Isle of Capri have eight-deck games. It's best to avoid them, however, because the six-deck games offer lower casino advantages.

Video Poker - Some of the best video poker games on the Gulf Coast for lower limit players are 10/6 Double Double Bonus (99.9%), 9/6 Jacks or Better (99.5%), 8/5 Bonus Poker (99.2%) and 8/5 Bonus Poker Aces and Faces (99.3%). The only difference between regular Bons Poker and the Aces/Faces version is that in the regular version you are given 40 coins for four-of-a-kind in 2's, 3's or 4's, but in the Aces/Faces variation you get 40 coins for four-of-a-kind in Jacks, Queens or Kings.

Quarter and $1 9/6 Jacks or Better games can be found at IP, Isle of Capri and Island View casinos. IP and Island View also offer them in 50-cent denominations. $1 progressives are available at the Grand and Island View.

10/6 Double Double Bonus is offered at the Beau Rivage for quarter, 50-cent and $1 players. At the $5 and $10 level, the game can be found at IP.

8/5 Bonus Poker is available for quarter players at the Isle of Capri. The IP also has it for quarters and half-dollars. At the $1 level, Bonus Poker can be found at both of the previous properties, plus the Palace. IP and the Palce also offer the game for $5 players.

The slightly better Aces and Faces version of of 8/5 Bonus Poker is available for quarter, 50-cent and $1 players at the Grand, while the IP also has it for $1 players.

For Deuces Wild players the Palace has $1 and $5 versions of 16/10 Not-So-Ugly Deuces with a payback of 99.73%.

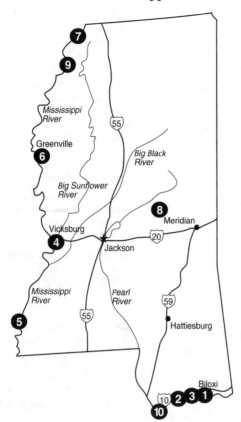

IP Hotel & Casino
850 Bayview Avenue
Biloxi, Mississippi 39530
(228) 436-3000
Website: www.ipbiloxi.com

Toll-Free Number: (888) 946-2847
Room Reservations: (800) 634-6441
Rooms: 1,088 Price Range: $129-$229
Suites: 14 Price Range: $199-$475
Restaurants: 3 (1 open 24 hours)
Buffets: B-$9.95 L-$11.95
      D-$19.95/$25.95 (Fri-Sat)
Casino Size: 66,768 Square Feet
Other Games: MB, P, PGP, CSP, LIR
Overnight RV Parking: Free/RV Dump: No
Special Features: Casino is on a barge. Six-screen movie theater. Health spa.

Isle of Capri Casino & Hotel - Biloxi
151 Beach Boulevard
Biloxi, Mississippi 39530
(228) 436-4753
Website: www.isleofcapricasino.com/Biloxi

Toll-Free Number: (800) 843-4753
Rooms: 541 Price Range: $99-$159
Suites: 200 Price Range: $119-$199
Restaurants: 4 (1 open 24 hours)
Buffets: B-$7.25/$ L-$9.75 D-$17.95
Casino Size: 57,252 Square Feet
Other Games: PGP
Overnight RV Parking: No
Senior Discount: Various on Tue/Thu if 50+
Special Features: Land-based casino. Spa. Beauty salon. Golf packages offered.

Palace Casino Resort
158 Howard Avenue
Biloxi, Mississippi 39530
(228) 432-8888
Website: www.palacecasinoresort.com

Toll-Free Number: (800) PALACE-9
Rooms: 234 Price Range: $89-$169
Suites: 14 Price Range: $500
Restaurants: 2 (1 open 24 hours) Valet: Free
Buffets: B-$6.99 L-$9.99 D-$16.99
Casino Size: 26,260 Square Feet
Other Games: PGP
Overnight RV Parking: No
Senior Discount: Various on Thu if 50+
Special Features: Land-based casino. 10-slip marina.

Treasure Bay Casino and Hotel
1980 Beach Boulevard
Biloxi, Mississippi 39531
(228) 385-6000
Website: www.treasurebay.com

Toll-Free Number: (800) 747-2839
Restaurants: 1 (1 open 24 hours) Valet: Free
Buffets: B-$9.00 L-$11.00 D-$20.00
Casino Size: 6,817 Square Feet
Other Games: PGP, CSP, LIR
Overnight RV Parking: No
Special Features: Land-based casino. 249-room hotel expected to open by early 2008.

Greenville

Map: **#6** (On the Mississippi River, 121 miles N.W. of Jackson)

Bayou Caddy's Jubilee Casino
242 S. Walnut Street
Greenville, Mississippi 38701
(662) 335-1111

Restaurants: 3 Valet Parking: No
Casino Size: 28,500 Square Feet
Other Games: CSP
Overnight RV Parking: Free/RV Dump: No

Lighthouse Point Casino
199 N. Lakefront Road
Greenville, Mississippi 38701
(662) 334-7711
Website: www.lighthouse-casino.com

Toll-Free Number: (800) 878-1777
Hotel Reservations: (800) 228-2800
Restaurants: 1 Valet Parking: No
Casino Size: 22,000 Square Feet
Other Games: No three card poker
Overnight RV Parking: Free/Dump: No
Special Features: Casino is on paddlewheel er..

Gulfport

Map: **#3** (On the Gulf of Mexico, 70 miles E. of New Orleans)

Island View Casino Resort
3300 W. Beach Boulevard
Gulfport, Mississippi 39501
(228) 314-2100
Website: www.islandviewcasino.com

Toll-Free Number: (800) 817-9089
Rooms: 600 Price Range: $109-$189
Restaurants: 3 (1 open 24 hours) Valet: Free
Buffets: B-$7.99 L-$9.99 D-$17.99
Other Games: MB, LIR
Casino Size: 28,938 Square Feet
Overnight RV Parking: Free/RV Dump: No
Special Features: Land-based casino.

Lula

Map **#9** (On the Mississippi River, 70 miles S. of Memphis, TN)

Isle of Capri Casino & Hotel - Lula
777 Isle of Capri Parkway
Lula, Mississippi 38644
(662) 363-4600
Website: www.isleofcapricasino.com

Toll-Free Number: (800) 789-5825
Toll-Free Number: (800) THE-ISLE
Rooms: 485 Price Range: $29-$99
Suites: 40 Price Range: Casino Use Only
Restaurants: 3
Buffets: B-$10.69/$8.55 (Fri/Sat) L-$10.69
　　　　D-$10.69/$19.25 (Fri/Sat)
Casino Size: 63,500 Square Feet
Overnight RV Parking: $14.95 per night
Senior Discount: Various on Mon/Wed if 50+
Special Features: Video arcade. Fitness center.

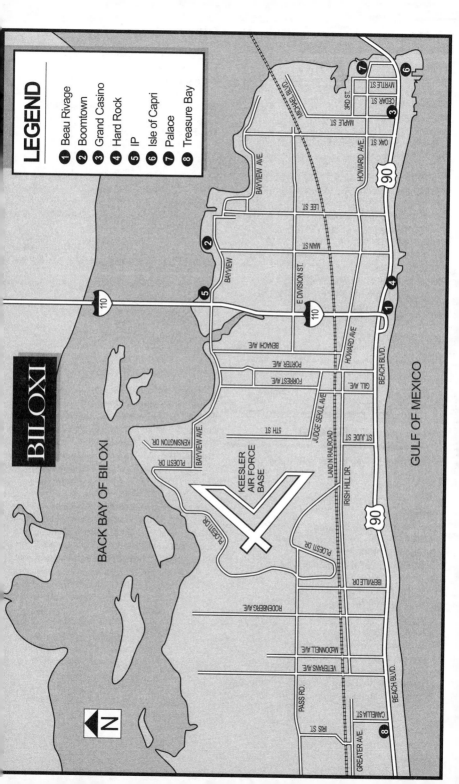

Natchez

Map: **#5** (on the Mississippi River, 102 miles S.W. of Jackson)

Isle of Capri Casino & Hotel - Natchez
53 Silver Street
Natchez, Mississippi 39120
(601) 445-0605
Website: www.isleofcapricasino.com

Toll-Free Number: (800) 722-LUCK
Toll-Free Number: (800) THE-ISLE
Rooms: 138 Price Range: $69-$129
Suites: 5 Price Range: Casino Use Only
Restaurants: 2
Buffets: B: $6.99 (Sat/Sun) L-$7.99
    D-$11.99/$16.99 (Fri/Sat)/$13.99 (Sun)
Casino Size: 17,634 Square Feet
Other Games: P
Overnight RV Parking: No
Senior Discount: Various on Tue/Thu if 50+
Special Features: Casino is built on barge that resembles 1860s paddlewheeler. Hotel is across street with free shuttle service to/from casino.

Tunica

Map: **#7** (on the Mississippi River, 28 miles S. of Memphis, TN)

Bally's Tunica
1450 Bally's Boulevard
Robinsonville, Mississippi 38664
(662) 357-1500
Website: www.ballystunica.com

Toll-Free Number: (800) 382-2559
Rooms: 235 Price Range: $59-$129
Suites: 8 Price Range: Casino Use Only
Restaurants: 3
Buffets: L-$8.75
Casino Size: 46,545 Square Feet
Other Games: CSP
Overnight RV Parking: Free/RV Dump: No
Special Features: Refrigerators in every room.

Fitzgeralds Casino/Hotel
711 Lucky Lane
Robinsonville, Mississippi 38664
(662) 363-5825
Website: www.fitzgeraldstunica.com

Toll-Free Number: (800) 766-LUCK
Room Reservations: (888) 766-LUCK
Rooms: 507 Price Range: $69-$139
Suites: 70 Price Range: Casino Use Only
Restaurants: 3   Valet Parking: Free
Buffets: B-$4.95 L-$8.95
    D-$12.95/$17.95 (Fri)/$14.95 (Sat)
Casino Size: 38,088 Square Feet
Other Games: CSP
Overnight RV Parking: Free/RV Dump: No
Special Features: Indoor pool and spa. Sports pub.

Gold Strike Casino Resort
100 Casino Center Drive
Robinsonville, Mississippi 38664
(662) 357-1111
Website: www.goldstrikemississippi.com

Toll-Free Number: (888) 24K-PLAY
Room Reservations: (866) 245-7511
Rooms: 1,130 Price Range: $79-$169
Suites: 70 Price Range: $175-$229
Restaurants: 3   Valet Parking: Free
Buffets: B-$7.99 L-$9.99
    Brunch-$12.99 (Sat/Sun)
    D-$14.99/$18.99 (Fri/Sun)
Casino Size: 50,486 Square Feet
Other Games: MB, P, PGP, CSP, LIR
Overnight RV Parking: Free/RV Dump: No
Special Features: Food court with three fast-food restaurants. Health spa. Starbucks. Suites only available through casino host on Fri/Sat.

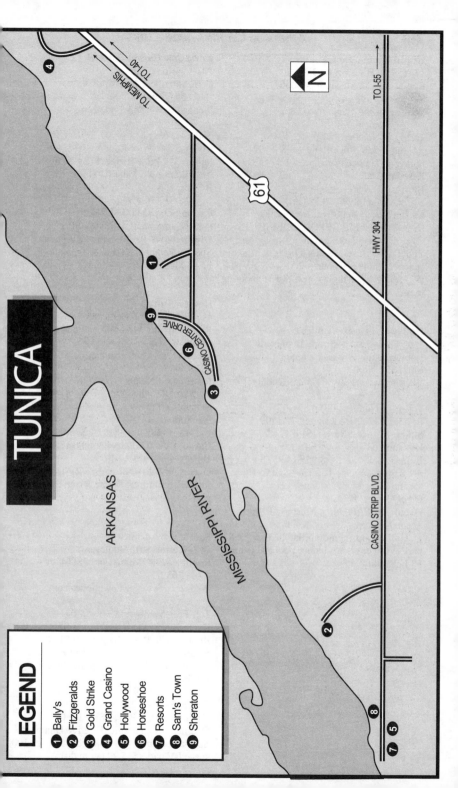

Grand Casino Tunica
13615 Old Highway 61 N.
Robinsonville, Mississippi 38664
(662) 363-2788
Website: www.grandtunica.com

Toll-Free Number: (800) 946-4946
Rooms: 1,356 Price Range: $39-$199
Suites: 117 Price Range: $249-$999
Restaurants: 8
Buffets: B-$7.99 L-$9.99
      D-$14.99/$19.99 (Fri)
Casino Size: 136,000 Square Feet
Other Games: MB, P, PGP, CSP, LIR
Overnight RV Parking: No
Special Features: Kid's Quest childcare center. 18-hole golf course. 200-space RV park ($17 to $25 per night). Spa. Sport shooting range.

Hollywood Casino Tunica
1150 Casino Strip Resorts Boulevard
Robinsonville, Mississippi 38664
(662) 357-7700
Website: www.hollywoodtunica.com

Toll-Free Number: (800) 871-0711
Rooms: 437 Price Range: $79-$199
Suites: 57 Price Range: $149-$349
Restaurants: 3
Buffets: B-$7.50 L-$8.95/$14.95 (Sun)
  D-$14.95/$17.95 (Tue/Thu)/$19.95 (Fri)
Casino Size: 54,000 Square Feet
Other Games: P, CSP
Overnight RV Parking: Must use RV park
Special Features: Casino features a collection of Hollywood memorabilia. 123-space RV park ($18 per night). Indoor pool and jacuzzi. 18-hole golf course.

Horseshoe Casino & Hotel
1021 Casino Center Drive
Robinsonville, Mississippi 38664
(662) 357-5500
Website: www.horseshoe.com

Toll-Free Number: (800) 303-7463
Rooms: 200 Price Range: $79-$199
Suites: 311 Price Range: $129-$479
Restaurants: 5   Valet Parking: Free
Buffets: B-$8.99 L-$9.99/$16.49 (Sun)
      D-$16.99/$23.99 (Fri)/$19.99 (Sat)
Casino Size: 63,000 Square Feet
Other Games: MB, P, PGP, CSP, LIR
Overnight RV Parking: Free/RV Dump: No
Special Features: Blues & Legends Hall of Fame Museum. Bluesville Nightclub.

Resorts Tunica
1100 Casino Strip Boulevard
Robinsonville, Mississippi 38664
(662) 363-7777
Website: www.resortstunica.com

Reservation Number: (866) 676-7070
Rooms: 182 Price Range: $49-$149
Suites: 19 Price Range: Casino Use Only
Restaurants: 4
Buffets: L-$8.99 D-$12.99/$15.99 (Sat)
Casino Size: 35,000 Square Feet
Other Games: CSP, LIR
Overnight RV Parking: Free/RV Dump: Free
Special Features: 18-hole River Bend Links golf course is adjacent to property.

Sam's Town Tunica
1477 Casino Strip Boulevard
Robinsonville, Mississippi 38664
(662) 363-0711
Website: www.samstowntunica.com

Toll-Free Number: (800) 456-0711
Room Reservations: (800) 946-0711
Rooms: 850 Price Range: $59-$149
Suites: 44 Price Range: $99-$199
Restaurants: 4   Valet Parking: Free
Buffets: B-$7.95 L-$8.95/$10.95 (Fri/Sat)
      D-$14.95/$18.99 (Fri/Sat)
Casino Size: 74,210 Square Feet
Other Games: P, PGP, CSP, LIR, K
Overnight RV Parking: Free/RV Dump: No
Special Features: 18-hole golf course. 100-space RV park ($15.99 per night).

The Best Places To Play in Tunica

Roulette - The house edge on a single-zero wheel cuts the house edge from 5.26% down to a more reasonable 2.70%. Unfortunately, there are no casinos in Tunica that offer single-zero roulette

Craps - The Horseshoe is the only casino in Tunica to offer 100X odds. All others offer 20X odds. Five casinos pay triple (rather than double) on 12 in the field, which cuts the house edge on this bet in half from 5.6 percent to 2.8 percent. The five casinos offering this slightly better field bet are: Hollywood, Horseshoe, Gold Strike, Sam's Town, and Fitzgeralds.

Blackjack - The blackjack games in Tunica are most similar to those offered in downtown Las Vegas. Most casinos offer both single and double-deck games, as well as six-deck shoe games. That's good. The bad part, however, is that dealers hit soft 17 at all games. This results in an extra advantage for the house of .20%. All of the following recommendations apply to players using perfect basic strategy for each particular game.

The best one-deck games can be found at Fitzgeralds, the Grand and Horseshoe. They all allow doubling down on any two cards and resplitting any pair (including aces) which results in a casino advantage of just .15%

At Gold Strike and Sam's Town they offer a game identical to the above except they won't allow you to resplit aces and this results in a slightly higher house edge of .18%. Be aware that Bally's and Sheraton offer some single-deck games that pay 6-to-5, or even-money, for blackjack rather than the standard 3-to-2. These games should be avoided as they have a casino advantage of greater than 1.20%.

Bally's, Fitzgeralds, Gold Strike, Grand, Hollywood, Horseshoe and Sheraton are the best places to play double-deck because their games have the following rules: double down on any first two cards, resplit any pair (including aces), and double down after split. This works out to a casino edge of .35%.

Tunica's remaining two casinos: Resorts and Sam's Town, both offer the next best game. The only rule change from the previous one is that you aren't allowed to resplit aces and the casino edge in this game is .40%.

The best six-deck games can be found at Bally's, Fitzgeralds, Gold Strike, Grand, Hollywood, Horseshoe and Sheraton which all have rules identical to their two-deck games. The casino advantage in this game is .56%.

The two remaining six-deck games are those offered at Resorts and Sam's Town. Both offer a game with a slightly higher casino edge of .63% because they won't allow you to resplit aces.

Video Poker -Some of the best video poker games in Tunica for lower limit players are 10/6 Double Double Bonus (99.9%), 9/6 Jacks or Better (99.5%), 8/5 Bonus Poker (99.2%) and 8/5 Bonus Poker Aces and Faces (99.3%). The only difference between regular Bons Poker and the Aces/Faces version is that in the regular version you are given 40 coins for four-of-a-kind in 2's, 3's or 4's, but in the Aces/Faces variation you get 40 coins for four-of-a-kind in Jacks, Queens or Kings.

9/6 Jacks or Better can be found in most of Tunica's casinos, with the main exceptions being the Horseshoe and Bally's. Fitzgerald's has it in quarters in single-line games and in Triple Play/Five Play and 50 Play. Sam's Town, Gold Strike and Resorts offer it in quarters, 50-cents and dollars. Hollywood has quarters in single games, and $1 and $5 in Triple Play/Five Play. Grand has it in $5, $10 and $25 denominations. Sheraton has the widest range, from a pennies (100 coin) game on up through $5.

For those of you who like 8/5 Aces & Faces, Bally's has it in 50-cent and dollar games. The Grand also has it in dollars. Regular 8/5 Bonus Poker can be found for quarters at Gold Strike, for quarters, 50 cents, $1 and $5 at Sheraton, plus Resorts has it with a progressive jackpot for $1 players.

For Deuces Wild players, there is Not-So-Ugly Deuces (99.7%) in town, at Fitzgerald's in quarter Triple Play/Five Play and quarter Fifty Play machines.

10/6 Double Double Bonus can only be found at Hollywood which has just one quarter machine and two 50-cent machines.

Sheraton Casino & Hotel
1107 Casino Center Drive
Robinsonville, Mississippi 38664
(662) 363-4900
Website: www.caesars.com/Sheraton/Tunica

Toll-Free Number: (800) 391-3777
Suites: 140 Price Range: $59-$319
Restaurants: 3 Valet Parking: Free
Buffets: Brunch-$7.99 (Sun) L-$7.99
       D-$7.99/$12.99 (Wed-Sun)
Casino Size: 32,800 Square Feet
Other Games: CSP, LIR
Overnight RV Parking: Free/RV Dump: No
Special Features: All suite hotel with jacuzzi in every room. Spa and fitness center.

Vicksburg

Map: **#4** (on the Mississippi River, 44 miles W. of Jackson)

Vicksburg is one of the most historic cities in the South and is most famous for its National Military Park where 17,000 Union soldiers are buried. The Park is America's best-preserved Civil War battlefield and you can take a 16-mile drive through the 1,858-acre Park on a self-guided tour. In the Park you can also see the U.S.S. Cairo, the only salvaged Union Ironclad. Admission to the Park is $8 per car and allows unlimited returns for seven days.

There are about 12 historic homes in Vicksburg that are open to the public for narrated tours. Admission prices are $6 for adults and $4 for children 12 and under. Some of the homes also function as Bed and Breakfasts and rooms can be rented for overnight stays.

For more information on visiting Vicksburg call the city's Convention and Visitors Bureau at (800) 221-3536, or visit their web site at: www.vicksburgcvb.org

Ameristar Casino Hotel - Vicksburg
4146 Washington Street
Vicksburg, Mississippi 39180
(601) 638-1000
Website: www.ameristarcasinos.com

Reservation Number: (800) 700-7770
Rooms: 146 Price Range: $71-$121
Suites: 4 Price Range: $131-$191
Restaurants: 3
Buffets: B-$5.99 L-$9.99 Brunch-$14.99 (Sun)
       D-$12.99/$21.99 (Fri/Sat)
Casino Size: 44,503 Square Feet
Other Games: S21, CSP, LIR
Overnight RV Parking: Free/RV Dump: No

Horizon Casino Hotel
1310 Mulberry Street
Vicksburg, Mississippi 39180
(601) 636-3423
Website: www.horizonvicksburg.com

Toll-Free Number: (800) 843-2343
Rooms: 101 Price Range: $59-$99
Suites: 16 Price Range: $119-$149
Restaurants: 3
Buffets: B-$5.99/$7.99 (Sat/Sun)
       L-$7.99/$11.99 (Sun)
       D-$10.99/$12.99 (Fri/Sat)
Casino Size: 20,999 Square Feet
Other Games: P
Overnight RV Parking: Free/RV Dump: No
Special Features: Casino is on 1,200-passenger paddlewheel riverboat.

DiamondJacks Casino - Vicksburg
3990 Washington Street
Vicksburg, Mississippi 39180
(601) 636-5700
Website: www.diamondjacks.com

Toll-Free Number: (877) 711-0677
Rooms: 60 Price Range: $79-$100
Suites: 62 Price Range: $160-$200
Restaurants: 3 Valet Parking: Free
Buffets: B-$5.99 L-$8.99
       D-$11.99/$20.99 (Fri/Sat)
Casino Size: 32,000 Square Feet
Other Games: CSP
Overnight RV Parking: Must use RV park
Special Features: 67-space RV park ($16 per night).

Rainbow Hotel Casino
1380 Warrenton Road
Vicksburg, Mississippi 39182
(601) 636-7575
Website: www.rainbowcasino.com

Toll-Free Number: (800) 503-3777
Room Reservations: (800) 434-5800
Rooms: 82 Price Range: $89-$110
Suites: 7 Price Range: $149-$219
Restaurants: 1
Buffets: L-$7.99 D-$10.99/$17.99 (Fri/Sat)
Casino Size: 25,000 Square Feet
Other Games: No Roulette
Overnight RV Parking: No
Special Features: Hotel is Amerihost Inn.

Waveland

Map: **#10** (45 miles W. of Biloxi)

Silver Slipper Casino
5000 South Beach Boulevard
Bay St. Louis, Mississippi 39520
(228) 396-5943
Website: www.silverslipper-ms.com

Toll-Free Number: (866) 775-4773
Restaurants: 3 (1 open 24 hours)
Buffets: L-$9.95 Brunch-$17.95
          D-$17.95/$19.95 (Fri-Sat)
Casino Size: 36,826 Square Feet
Special Features: Land-based casino.

Indian Casino

Pearl River Resort
Highway 16 West
Philadelphia, Mississippi 39350
(601) 650-1234
Website: www.pearlriverresort.com
Map: **#8** (81 miles N.E. of Jackson)

Toll-Free Number: (800) 557-0711
Room Reservations (866) 44-PEARL
Silver Star Rooms: 420 Prices: $69-$159
Silver Star Suites: 75 Prices: $189-$780
Golden Moon Rooms: 427 Prices: $69-$199
Golden Moon Suites: 145 Prices: $239-$800
Restaurants: 12 Liquor: Yes Valet: Free
Silver Star Buffet: L-$6.49/$12.49 (Sun)
          D-$10.49
Golden Moon Buffet: B-$8.55 (Mon)
          L-$8.49 D-$11.99
Silver Star Casino Size: 90,000 Square Feet
Golden Moon Casino Size: 90,000 Square Feet
Other Games: MB, P, CSP, B6
Overnight RV Parking: Free/RV Dump: No
Special Features: Two separate land-based
hotel/casinos across the street from each other.
18-hole golf course. 15-acre water park. Health
spa. Beauty salon. Shopping arcade with nine
stores.

MISSOURI

In November, 1992 Missouri voters approved a state-wide referendum to allow riverboat gambling. That made Missouri the fifth state to approve this form of gambling.

There is no limit to the number of licenses that may be issued by the state's gaming commission and all boats remain dockside. Since the boats are not required to cruise, almost all casinos are built on a barge which gives them the appearance of a land-based building, rather than a riverboat.

When Missouri's riverboat casinos first began operating they were required to cruise and they all conducted two-hour gaming sessions with a $500 loss-limit on each session. In early 2000 the law was changed to allow continuous boardings and cruising was no longer required. However, the state's loss limit provision is still in force and you are not allowed to lose more than $500 within a two-hour period. All casinos base that two-hour period beginning on even hour times: 12-2, 2-4, 4-6, 6-8, 8-10, 10-12.

When you first enter a casino you must present an ID to receive a slot club card which will be used to track your chip and/or slot token purchases. Once you have purchased $500 worth of chips or tokens you will not be able to buy anymore until the beginning of the next even hour. There is no limit on winnings.

Admission is free to all Missouri casinos except for the President which charges $2 for first-time visitors and then allows free admission for all subsequent visits.

Unlike dockside gaming in Mississippi, most Missouri casinos are not open 24 hours and the hours of operation are listed for each casino.

Here's information from the Missouri Gaming Commission regarding the payback percentages for each casino's electronic machines for the 12-month period from June 1, 2006 through May 31, 2007:

CASINO	PAYBACK %
President	92.3
Isle of Capri - Boonville	92.1
Argosy	91.9
Terrible's St. Jo	91.9
Isle of Capri K.C.	91.9
Harrah's K.C.	91.8
Harrah's M.H.	91.6
Terrible's Mark Twain	91.5
Ameristar-K.C.	91.4
Ameristar-St. Charles	91.4
Aztar	89.8

These figures reflect the total percentages returned by each casino for all of their electronic machines including slot machines, video poker, video keno, etc.

Unless otherwise noted, all casinos offer: slots, video poker, craps, blackjack, roulette and Caribbean stud poker. Optional games include: baccarat (B), mini-baccarat (MB), poker (P), pai gow poker (PGP), let it ride (LIR), Spanish 21 (S21), three-card poker (TCP) and four card poker (FCP).

If you want to order a drink while playing, be aware that Missouri gaming regulations do not allow casinos to provide free alcoholic beverages. The minimum gambling age is 21.

NOTE: If you happen to win a jackpot of $1,200 or more in Missouri, the casino will withhold 4% of your winnings for the Missouri Department of Revenue. If you want to try and get that money refunded, you will be required to file a state income tax return and, depending on the details of your return, you *may* get some of the money returned to you. The $1,200 threshold would also apply to any cash prizes won in casino drawings or tournaments.

For more information on visiting Missouri call the state's Travel Center at (800) 877-1234 or go to: www.visitmo.com

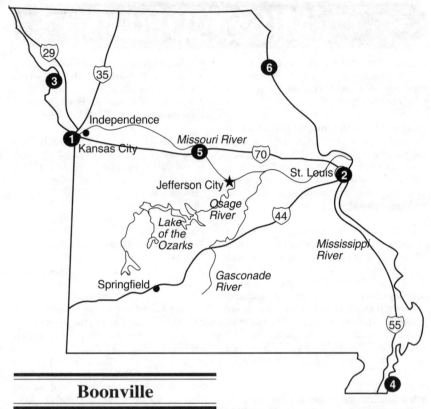

Boonville

Map: **#5** (100 miles E. of Kansas City)

Isle of Capri Casino - Boonville
100 Isle of Capri Boulevard
Boonville, Missouri 65233
(660) 882-1200
Website: www.isleofcapricasino.com

Toll-Free Number: (800) 843-4753
Rooms: 113 Price Range: $99-$139
Suites: 27 Price Range: $139-$179
Restaurants: 3   Valet Parking: Free
Buffets: B-$6.99/$7.99 (Sat/Sun) L-$8.99
Brunch-$10.99 D-$12.99/$16.99 (Sun/Wed/
Fri/$17.00 (Sat)
Hours: 8am-5am/24 Hours (Fri/Sat)
Casino Size: 28,000 Square Feet
Other Games: P, TCP, LIR
Overnight RV Parking: Free/RV Dump: No
Senior Discount: Various on Tue/Thu if 50+
Special Features: 600-passenger barge on the
Missouri River.

Caruthersville

Map: **#4** (200 miles S. of St. Louis)

Casino Aztar
777 East Third Street
Caruthersville, Missouri 63830
(573) 333-6000
Website: www.casinoaztarmo.com

Toll-Free Number (800) 679-4945
Restaurants: 1   Valet Parking: $2
Buffets: D-$12.99 (Sat)/$7.49 (Sun)
Hours: 9am-3am/24 hrs (Fri/Sat)
Casino Size: 18,480 Square Feet
Other Games: TCP
Overnight RV Parking: Free/RV Dump: Free
Senior Discount: Free valet parking if 55+
Special Features: 875-passenger sternwheeler
on the Mississippi River. 27-space RV park
($20 per night). 1,000-seat amphitheater.

The Best Places To Play Blackjack in Kansas City

All Missouri casinos "hit" soft 17. This is slightly more advantageous for the casino than "standing" on soft 17 and it adds an extra .20% to the casino's mathematical edge in all blackjack games.

The only single-deck blackjack game in Kansas City is offered at the Argosy, but since blackjacks in this game only pay 6-to-5, rather than the traditional 7.5-to-5, this results in an overall casino advantage of about 1.5% and it's best to avoid this game.

The Isle of Capri offers the best two-deck game. It has a .35% casino advantage against a basic strategy player and the rules are: dealer hits soft 17 (ace and six), double down on any two cards, split and re-split any pair (including aces), and double allowed after splitting.

Next best are Argosy, Ameristar and Harrah's which all offer the same game, with the exception of allowing aces to be re-split. The casino advantage in this game is .40%

All four Kansas City casinos offer an identical six-deck game with the following rules: dealer hits soft 17 (ace and six), double down on any two cards, split and re-split any pair (including aces), and double allowed after splitting. The casino's mathematical edge against a perfect basic strategy player in this game is .56%.

Kansas City

Map: **#1**

Ameristar Casino Hotel Kansas City
3200 North Ameristar Drive
Kansas City, Missouri 64161
(816) 414-7000
Website: www.ameristarcasinos.com/kc

Toll-Free Number: (800) 499-4961
Rooms: 142 Price Range: $149-$249
Suites: 42 Price Range: $169-$529
Restaurants: 14   Valet Parking: $5
Buffets: L-$11.99/$15.99 (Sat/Sun)
 D-$15.99/$19.99 (Thu/Sat)/$22.99 (Tue/Fri)
Hours: 8am-5am/24 Hours (Fri/Sat)
Casino Size: 140,000 Square Feet
Other Games: MB, P, PGP, FCP, TCP, LIR
Overnight RV Parking: Free/RV Dump: No
Special Features: 4,000-passenger barge adjacent to the Missouri River. 41-screen Sports Pub. 18-screen movie theater complex. Burger King. 1,384-seat event center.

Argosy Casino
777 N.W. Argosy Parkway
Riverside, Missouri 64150
(816) 746-3100
Website: www.argosy.com/kansascity

Toll-Free Number: (800) 270-7711
Rooms: 250 Price Range: $134-$159
Suites: 8 Price Range: $650
Restaurants: 5   Valet Parking: $4
Buffets: B-$8.99 L-$10.99/$14.99 (Sun)
         D-$14.99/$23.99 (Wed-Sat)
Hours: 8am-5am/24 Hours (Fri/Sat)
Casino Size: 62,000 Square Feet
Other Games: S21, MB, P, PGP, LIR, TCP
Overnight RV Parking: Free/RV Dump: No
Special Features: 4,675-passenger single-deck Mediterranean-themed barge adjacent to the Missouri River.

Harrah's North Kansas City
One Riverboat Drive
N. Kansas City, Missouri 64116
(816) 472-7777
Website: www.harrahs.com

Toll-Free Number: (800) HARRAHS
Rooms: 350 Price Range: $119-$199
Suites: 42 Price Range: $119-$279
Restaurants: 5   Valet Parking: $5
Buffets: B-$7.99 L-$9.99/$13.99 (Sat/Sun)
        D-$14.99 (Mon/Sat)/$21.99 (Tues)/
$20.99 (Wed/Fri)/$19.99 (Thurs)/$17.99 (Sun)
Hours: 8am-5am/24 Hours (Fri/Sat)
Casino Size: 60,100 Square Feet
Other Games: MB, P, PGP, TCP, LIR
Senior Discount: Various if 50 or older
Overnight RV Parking: Free/RV Dump: No
Special Features: 1,700-passenger two-deck
barge adjacent to the Missouri River.

Isle of Capri Casino - Kansas City
1800 E. Front Street
Kansas City, Missouri 64120
(816) 855-7777
Website: www.isleofcapricasino.com

Toll-Free Number: (800) 843-4753
Restaurants: 4   Valet Parking: Free
Buffets: B-$6.99 L-$9.99
        D-$13.99/$16.99 (Fri/Sat)
Hours: 8am-5am/24 Hours (Fri/Sat)
Casino Size: 30,000 Square Feet
Other Games: P, PGP, TCP
Overnight RV Parking: Free/RV Dump: No
Senior Discount: Various specials Thu if 50+
Special Features: 2,000-passenger two-deck
Caribbean-themed barge docked in a man-
made lake fed by the Missouri River.

La Grange

Map: **#6** (150 miles N.W. of St. Louis)

Terrible's Mark Twain Casino
104 Pierce Street
La Grange, Missouri 63348
(573) 655-4770
Website: www.terribleherbst.com

Toll-Free Number: (866) 454-5825
Restaurants: 1   Valet Parking: Not Offered
Hours: 8am-2am/4am (Fri/Sat)
Casino Size: 18,000 Square Feet
Other Games: No CSP
Overnight RV Parking: Must use RV park
Special Features: 600-passenger barge on the
Mississippi River. 8-space RV park ($5 per
night). Gift shop.

St. Joseph

Map: **#3** (55 miles N. of Kansas City)

Terrible's St. Jo Frontier Casino
77 Francis Street
St. Joseph, Missouri 64501
(816) 279-5514
Website: www.terribleherbst.com

Toll-Free Number: (800) 888-2946
Restaurants: 3   Valet Parking: Not Offered
Buffets: B-$5.99 L-$7.49
        D-$10.99/$13.99 (Tue)
Hours: 8am-2am/4am (Fri/Sat)
Casino Size: 18,000 Square Feet
Other Games: TCP, No CSP
Overnight RV Parking: Free/RV Dump: No
Senior Discount: 50% off breakfast buffet
                Tue/Thu if 55 or older
Special   Features: 1,146-passenger
paddlewheel boat adjacent to the Missouri
River. Gift shop.

The Best Places To Play Blackjack in St. Louis

All Missouri casinos "hit" soft 17. This is slightly more advantageous for the casino than "standing" on soft 17 and it adds an extra .20% to the casino's mathematical edge in all blackjack games. In St. Louis, however, the Casino Queen in nearby E. St. Louis, Illinois stands on soft 17.

The best two-deck game is offered at Ameristar with these rules: double down on any two cards, split and re-split any pair (except aces), and double allowed after splitting. The casino advantage is .40%. A similar game is offered by Harrah's with two rule changes: no doubling after splitting and doubling down is limited to two-card totals of 9 or more. The casino advantage is .65%.

All three St. Louis City casinos offer an identical six-deck game with the following rules: double down on any two cards, split and re-split any pair (including aces), and double allowed after splitting. The casino's mathematical edge against a perfect basic strategy player in this game is .56%. The same game is offered at the Casino Queen in E. St Louis, Illinois, but the house stands on soft 17 in that game and it lowers the casino advantage to .35%.

St. Louis

Map: **#2**

Pinnacle Entertainment is building a new casino in the St. Louis area.

The St. Louis River City Casino will be located in Lemay, about 10 miles south of St. Louis. It will feature a 90,000-square-foot casino, a 100-room hotel, plus many non-gaming amenities, including a new county park with softball and soccer fields, an outdoor concert amphitheater, an indoor ice skating rink, a retail/entertainment center, a multiplex movie theater, and a bowling alley. It is expected to open in late 2008. For more current information, visit the company's web site at www.pinnaclestlouis.com

In addition to the four St. Louis-area casinos listed below, the Casino Queen in E. St. Louis, Illinois is also a nearby casino. It is located on the other side of the Mississippi river from downtown St. Louis. Additionally, the Alton Belle in Alton, Illinois is about 25 miles north of St. Louis. Both Illinois casinos are not restricted by the $500 loss limit (per two-hours) that is in effect in Missouri casinos.

Ameristar Casino St. Charles
P.O. Box 720
St. Charles, Missouri 63302
(314) 949-4300
Website: www.ameristarcasinos.com/stcharles

Toll-Free Number: (800) 325-7777
Restaurants: 7   Valet Parking: $5
Buffets: L-$11.99/$15.99 (Sat/Sun)
      D-$16.99/$19.99 (Sat)/$21.99 (Tue/Fri)
Hours: 8am-5am/24 Hours (Fri/Sat)
Casino Size: 130,000 Square Feet
Other Games: FCP, TCP
Overnight RV Parking: No
Senior Discount: Various Mon-Thu if 55 or older
Special Features: 2,000-passenger barge on the Missouri River. New 400-room all suite hotel expected to open by early 2008.

Harrah's St. Louis
777 Casino Center Drive
Maryland Heights, Missouri 63043
(314) 770-8100
Website: www.harrahs.com

Toll-Free Number: (800) HARRAHS
Rooms: 455 Price Range: $109-$199
Suites: 47 Price Range: $169-$399
Restaurants: 7 Valet Parking: $5
Buffets: B-$7.99 L-$10.99/$14.99 (Sat/Sun)
        D-$15.99/$18.99 (Thu/Fri)
Hours: 8am-5am/24 Hours (Fri-Sun)
Casino Size: 120,000 Square Feet Total
Other Games: S21, MB, P, PGP, TCP, LIR
Overnight RV Parking: Free/RV Dump: No
Senior Discount: Various Tue/Fri if 50 or older
Special Features: Two 3,200-passenger barges
on the Missouri River.

Lumière Place Casino Resort
727 North First Street
St. Louis, Missouri 63102
(314) 450-5000
Website: www.lumiereplace.com

Rooms: 200 Price Range: $109-$199
Restaurants: 5   Valet Parking: Free
Buffets: NOT SET AT PRESS TIME
Hours: 8am-4am/24 Hours (Fri/Sat)
Casino Size: 75,000 Square Feet
Special Features: 2,500-passenger barge
floating in a man-made canal 700 feet from
the Mississippi River.

President Casino - St. Louis
800 North First Street
St. Louis, Missouri 63102
(314) 622-3000
Website: www.presidentcasino.com

Toll-Free Number: (800) 772-3647
Restaurants: 2   Valet Parking: Free
Buffets: L-$8.99/$11.95 (Sun) D-$11.99
Hours: 8am-4am/24 Hours (Fri/Sat)
Admission: $2 (First-time visit only)
Casino Size: 58,000 Square Feet
Other Games: S21, TCP, No CSP
Overnight RV Parking: No
Senior Discount: Various on Thu if 50 or older
Special Features: 2,500-passenger, art deco
riverboat on the Mississippi River near the
Gateway Arch. Free shuttle service to and from
all downtown hotels. One block from Laclede's
Landing Metro Link Light Rail Station.

MONTANA

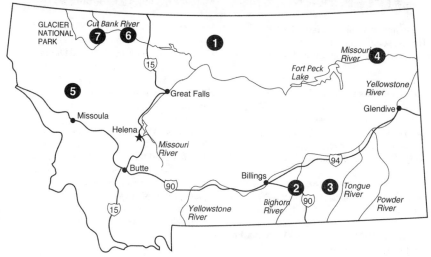

Montana law permits bars and taverns to have up to 20 video gaming devices that play video poker, video keno, or video bingo. These machines are operated in partnership with the state and are not permitted to pay out in cash; instead, they print out a receipt which must be taken to a cashier. The maximum bet on these machines is $2 and the maximum payout is limited to $800. Montana gaming regulations require these machines to return a minimum of 80%.

All of Montana's Indian casinos offer Class II video gaming devices that look like slot machines, but are actually bingo games and the spinning reels are for "entertainment purposes only."

One Indian casino, Glacier Peaks Casino & Racetrack, also offers player-banked versions of blackjack and mini-baccarat where each player must pay a commission to the house for each bet that is made. They also offer bingo-based versions of craps and roulette.

The maximum bet on these machines is $5 and the maximum payout is capped at $1,500. According to Montana's Gambling Control Division, there are no minimum payback percentages required for gaming machines on Indian reservations. The minimum gambling age is 18.

For Montana tourism information call (800) VISIT-MT or go to: www.visitmt.com

Charging Horse Casino
P.O. Box 1259
Lame Deer, Montana 59043
(406) 477-6677
Map: **#3** (90 miles S.E. of Billings on Hwy. 212)

Restaurants: 1 Liquor: No
Hours: 8am-2am Daily
Overnight RV Parking: Free/RV Dump: No

Discovery Lodge Casino
1 Tree Lane
Cut Bank, Montana 59427
(406) 873-2885
Map: **#6** (35 miles E. of Browning)

Restaurants: 1 Snack Bar Liquor: No
Hours: 10:30am-11:30pm Daily
Overnight RV Parking: Free/RV Dump: Free

Four C's Cafe & Casino
Rocky Boy Route, Box 544
Box Elder, Montana 59521
(406) 395-4863
Map: **#1** (75 miles N.E. of Great Falls)

Restaurants: 1 Liquor: No
Hours: 10am-12am/2am (Thu-Sat)
Overnight RV Parking: Free/RV Dump: No

Glacier Peaks Casino
209 N. Piegan Street
Browning, Montana 59417
(406) 338-2274
Website: www.glaciercash.com
Map: **#7** (140 miles N.W of Great Falls)

Toll-Free: (888) 848-8188
Restaurants: 1 Snack Bar Liquor: No
Hours: 10:00am-2:00am Daily
Other Games: Bingo (Wed-Fri)
Overnight RV Parking: Free/RV Dump: Free

KwaTaqNuk Casino Resort
303 Highway 93
E. Polson, Montana 59860
(406) 883-3636
Website: www.kwataqnuk.com
Map: **#5** (65 miles N. Of Missoula)

Room Reservations: (800) 882-6363
Rooms: 112 Price Range: $79-$135
Restaurants: 1 Liquor: Yes
Hours: 24 Hours Daily
Overnight RV Parking: Free/RV Dump: Free
Special Features: Hotel is Best Western. Two
casinos, one is nonsmoking.

Little Big Horn Casino
P.O. Box 580
Crow Agency, Montana 59022
(406) 638-4000
Map: **#2** (65 miles S.E. of Billings)

Restaurants: 1 Liquor: No
Hours: 8am-2am/4am (Thurs-/Sat)
Overnight RV Parking: Free/RV Dump: No

Silver Wolf Casino
Highway 25 East
P.O. Box 726
Wolf Point, Montana 59201
(406) 653-3475
Map: **#4** (180 miles N.E of Billings)

Restaurants: 1 Snack Bar Liquor: No
Hours: 10am-Mid Daily
Other Games: Bingo
Overnight RV Parking: Free/RV Dump: No

NEVADA

All Nevada casinos are open 24 hours and, unless otherwise noted, offer: slots, video poker, craps, blackjack, and roulette. The minimum gambling age is 21.

For Nevada tourism information call (800) 237-0774 or go to: www.travelnevada.com.

Other games in the casino listings include: sports book (SB), race book (RB), Spanish 21 (S21), baccarat (B), mini-baccarat (MB), pai gow (PG), poker (P), pai gow poker (PGP), Caribbean stud poker (CSP), let it ride (LIR), three-card poker (TCP), four card poker (FCP), sic bo (SIC), keno (K), big 6 wheel (B6) and bingo (BG).

Amargosa Valley

Map Location: **#8** (91 miles N.W. of Las Vegas on Hwy. 95)

Longstreet Hotel Casino RV Resort
Route 373, HCR 70
Amargosa Valley, Nevada 89020
(775) 372-1777
Website: www.longstreetcasino.com

Rooms: 59 Price Range: $79-$109
Restaurants: 1
Other Games: No table games
Overnight RV Parking: Free/RV Dump: Free
Senior Discount: 10% off food if 55 or older
Special Features: 50-space RV Park ($22 per night). 24-hour convenience store.

Battle Mountain

Map Location: **#9** (215 mile N.E. of Reno on I-80)

Nevada Hotel & Casino
8 E. Front Street
Battle Mountain, Nevada 89820
(775) 635-2453

Restaurants: 1
Casino Size: 840 Square Feet
Other Games: No craps or roulette
Overnight RV Parking: No

Beatty

Map Location: **#10** (120 miles N.W. of Las Vegas on Hwy. 95)

Stagecoach Hotel & Casino
P.O. Box 836
Beatty, Nevada 89003
(775) 553-2419

Reservation Number: (800) 4-BIG-WIN
Rooms: 50 Price Range: $35-$51
Restaurants: 2 (1 open 24 hours)
Casino Size: 8,810 Square Feet
Other Games: SB, RB, P, B6, No roulette
Overnight RV Parking: Free/RV Dump: No
Special Features: Swimming pool and Jacuzzi. Seven miles from Rhyolite ghost town. RV Park ($15 a night).

Boulder City

Map Location: **#11** (22 miles S.E. of Las Vegas on Hwy. 93)

Hacienda Hotel & Casino
U.S. Highway 93
Boulder City, Nevada 89005
(702) 293-5000
Website: www.haciendaonline.com

Reservation Number: (800) 245-6380
Rooms: 360 Price Range: $60-$100
Suites: 18 Price Range: $90-$160
Restaurants: 3 (1 open 24 hours)
Buffets: B-$5.95 L-$5.99/$7.99 (Sun)
        D-$8.95/$6.95 (Mon/Thu)
        D-$14.95/(Fri)/$10.95 (Sat-Sun)
Casino Size: 19,300 Square Feet
Other Games: SB, RB, P
Overnight RV Parking: No

Carson City

Map Location: **#7** (32 miles S. of Reno on Hwy. 395)

Carson Nugget
507 N. Carson Street
Carson City, Nevada 89701
(775) 882-1626
Website: www.ccnugget.com

Toll-Free Number: (800) 426-5239
Reservation Number: (800) 338-7760
Rooms: 82 Price Range: $49
Restaurants: 5 (1 open 24 hours)
Buffets: B-$6.50 (Sat) L-$6.50/$8.50 (Sun)
        D-$8.50/$14.50 (Fri)
Casino Size: 24,853 Square Feet
Other Games: SB, RB, P, TCP, K, BG
Overnight RV Parking: Free/RV Dump: No
Senior Discount: 15-20% off food if 50+
Special Features: Rare gold display. Free supervised childcare center. Rooms are one block away from casino.

Carson Station Hotel Casino
900 S. Carson Street
Carson City, Nevada 89702
(775) 883-0900
Website: www.carsonstation.com

Toll-Free Number: (800) 501-2929
Rooms: 92   Price Range: $58-$79
Suites: 3   Price Range: $95-$115
Restaurants: 2 (1 open 24 hours)
Casino Size: 12,750 Square Feet
Other Games: SB, RB, TCP, K, No Roulette
Overnight RV Parking: No
Special Features: Hotel is Best Western.

Casino Fandango
3800 S. Carson Street
Carson City, Nevada 89005
(775) 885-7000
Website: www.casinofandango.com

Restaurants: 3
Casino Size: 30,930 Square Feet
Buffets: Brunch-$10.99/$14.99 (Sat/Sun)
        D-$13.49 (Wed/Thu/Sun)/$20.99 (Fri/Sat)
Other Games: SB, RB, P, PG, TCP, K
Overnight RV Parking: Free/RV Dump: No

Gold Dust West
2171 Highway 50 East
Carson City, Nevada 89701
(775) 885-9000
http://www.gdwcasino.com

Toll-Free Number: (877) 519-5567
Rooms: 148 Price Range: $81-$115
Suites: 22 Price Range: $100-$175
Restaurants: 2 (1 open 24 hours)
Casino Size: 12,000 Square Feet
Other Games: SB, RB, P, TCP,
Overnight RV Parking: Must use RV park
Senior Discount: 10% off food if 55 or older
Special Features: Hotel is Best Western. 48-space RV park ($14 winter/$24 summer). 32-lane bowling center.

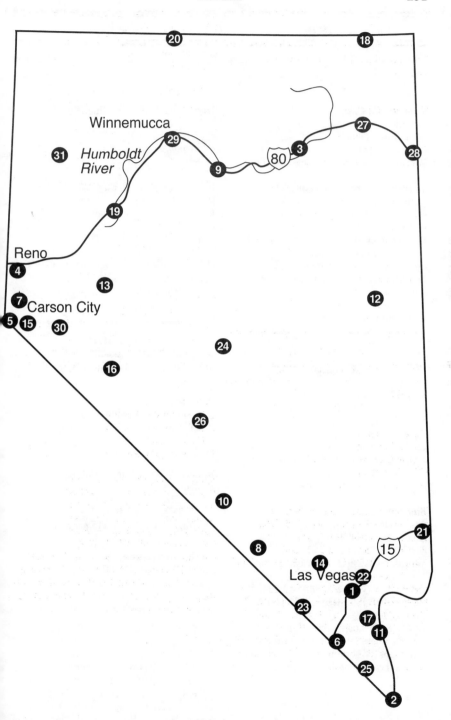

Elko

Map Location: **#3** (289 miles N.E. of Reno on I-80)

Commercial Casino
345 4th Street
Elko, Nevada 89801
(775) 738-3181
Website: www.commercialcasinos.com

Toll-Free Number: (800) 648-2345
Restaurants: 2 (1 open 24 hours)
Casino Size: 6,440 Square Feet
Other Games: No table games
Overnight RV Parking: Yes/RV Dump: No
Special Features: Oldest continually operating casino in Nevada. 10-foot-tall stuffed polar bear in casino. Large gunfighter art collection.

Red Lion Inn & Casino
2065 Idaho Street
Elko, Nevada 89801
(775) 738-2111
Website: www.redlioncasino.com

Reservation Number: (800) 545-0044
Rooms: 223 Price Range: $89-$119
Suites: 2 Price Range: $259
Restaurants: 2 (1 open 24 hours)
Casino Size: 20,350 Square Feet
Other Games: SB, RB, P, TCP, K
Overnight RV Parking: No

Stockmen's Hotel & Casino
340 Commercial Street
Elko, Nevada 89801
(775) 738-5141
Website: www.stockmenscasinos.com

Reservation Number: (800) 648-2345
Rooms: 141 Price Range: $31-$60
Restaurants: 2
Casino Size: 7,030 Square Feet
Other Games: SB, TCP, No roulette
Overnight RV Parking: Free/RV Dump: No
Special Features: 24-hour shuttle service.

Ely

Map Location: **#12** (317 miles E. of Reno on Hwy. 50)

Hotel Nevada & Gambling Hall
501 Aultman Street
Ely, Nevada 89301
(775) 289-6665
Website: www.hotelnevada.com

Reservation Number: (888) 406-3055
Rooms: 45 Price Range: $30-$85
Restaurants: 1 (open 24 hours)
Casino Size: 3,730 Square Feet
Other Games: SB, RB P, TCP,
              No craps or roulette
Overnight RV Parking: Free RV Dump: No
Special Features: Historical display of mining, ranching and railroad artifacts.

Fallon

Map Location: **#13** (61 miles E. of Reno on Hwy. 50)

Bonanza Inn & Casino
855 W. Williams Avenue
Fallon, Nevada 89406
(775) 423-6031

Rooms: 74 Price Range: $50-$60
Restaurants: 1
Casino Size: 5,830 Square Feet
Other Games: SB, RB, K, No Table Games
Overnight RV Parking: $15 per night

Stockman's Casino
1560 W. Williams Avenue
Fallon, Nevada 89406
(775) 423-2117
Website: www.stockmanscasino.com

Holiday Inn Reservations: (888) 465-4329
Rooms: 98 Price Range: $79-$89
Suites: 8 Price Range: $109-$139
Restaurants: 2 (1 open 24 hours)
Casino Size: 8,365 Square Feet
Other Games: K, No roulette or craps
Overnight RV Parking: Free/RV Dump: No
Special Features: Hotel is Holiday Inn Express.

Gardnerville

Map Location: **#15** (45 miles S. of Reno on Hwy. 395)

Sharkey's Nugget
1440 Highway 395N
Gardnerville, Nevada 89410
(775) 782-3133

Restaurants: 1
Casino Size: 4,650 Square Feet
Other Games: SB, RB, No craps or roulette
Overnight RV Parking: No
Senior Discount: 10% off food if 50 or older
Special Features: Blackjack played 5pm-1am (Wed/Fri/Sat) and 10am-6pm (Sun).

Topaz Lodge & Casino
1979 Highway 395 South
Gardnerville, Nevada 89410
(775) 266-3338
Website: www.topazlodge.com

RV/Room Reservations: (800) 962-0732
Rooms: 59   Price Range: $65-$85
Restaurants: 3 (1 open 24 hours)
Buffets: D-$19.95 (Fri)/$10.95 (Sat)
Casino Size: 12,800 Square Feet
Other Games: SB, RB, BG, P, TCP, No roulette
Overnight RV Parking: Must use RV park
Special Features: 60-space RV park ($27 per night).

Gerlach

Map Location: **#31** (107 miles N.E. of Reno)

Bruno's Country Club
445 Main Street
Gerlach, Nevada
(775) 557-2220

Rooms: 40 Price Range: $35-$65
Restaurants: 1
Other Games: No table games
Overnight RV Parking: No

Hawthorne

Map Location: **#16** (138 miles S.E. of Reno on Hwy. 95)

El Capitan Resort Casino
540 F Street
Hawthorne, Nevada 89415
(775) 945-3321
Website: www.elcapitanresortcasino.com

Toll Free: (800) 922-2311
Rooms: 103 Price Range: $50-$55
Restaurants: 1 (open 24 hours)
Casino Size: 10,000 Square Feet
Other Games: SB, RB, No craps or roulette
Overnight RV Parking: Free/RV Dump: No

Henderson

Map Location: **#17** (15 miles S.E. of Las Vegas on Hwy. 93)

Barley's Casino & Brewing Co.
4500 E. Sunset Road #30
Henderson, Nevada 89014
(702) 458-2739
Website: www.barleys.com

Restaurants: 3
Casino Size: 5,190 Square Feet
Other Games: SB, No table games
Overnight RV Parking: No
Special Features: Located in a strip mall. Six varieties of beer micro-brewed on the premises.

Casino MonteLago
8 Strata di Villaggio
Henderson, NV 89011
(702) 939-8888
Website: www.casinomontelago.com

Toll Free Number: (877) 553-3555
Restaurants: 2 (1 open 24 hours)
Casino Size: 22,000 Square Feet
Other Games: SB, RB
Overnight RV Parking: No

The Green Valley Ranch Resort, Casino and Spa in Henderson is
one of the most popular "locals" casinos in the greater Las Vegas area.

Eldorado Casino
140 Water Street
Henderson, Nevada 89015
(702) 564-1811
Website: www.eldoradocasino.com

Restaurants: 2
Casino Size: 17,756 Square Feet
Other Games: SB, K, BG
Overnight RV Parking: No

Fiesta Henderson Casino Hotel
777 West Lake Mead Drive
Henderson, Nevada 89015
(702) 558-7000
Website: henderson.fiesta.com

Toll-Free Number: (866) 469-7666
Rooms: 224 Price Range: $35-$109
Suites: 8 Price Range: $135-$259
Restaurants: 4 (1 open 24 hours)
Buffets: L-$7.99/$12.99 (Sat/Sun)
        D-$9.99/$10.99 (Fri-Sun)
Casino Size: 39,760 Square Feet
Other Games: SB, RB, P, PGP, TCP, K, BG
Overnight RV Parking: No
Senior Discount: Join Fun Club if 50 or older

Green Valley Ranch Resort
2300 Paseo Verde Drive
Henderson, Nevada 89012
(702) 617-7777
Website: www.greenvalleyranchresort.com

Room Reservations: (866) 782-9487
Rooms: 200 Price Range: $149-$364
Suites: 45 Price Range: $399-$3,000
Restaurants: 8 (1 open 24 hours)
Buffets: B-$8.99/$18.99 (Sat/Sun) L-$10.99
        D-$17.99/$18.99 (Fri-Sun)
Casino Size: 110,739 Square Feet
Other Games: SB, RB, B, MB, P, PGP, LIR, TCP
Overnight RV Parking: No

Jokers Wild
920 N. Boulder Highway
Henderson, Nevada 89015
(702) 564-8100
Website: www.jokerswildcasino.com

Restaurants: 2 (1 open 24 hours)
Casino Size: 23,698 Square Feet
Other Games: SB, P, K
Overnight RV Parking: No
Senior Discount: $1 off dinner if 55 or older

Klondike Sunset Casino
444 West Sunset
Henderson, Nevada 89015
(702) 568-7575

Restaurants: 1
Casino Size: 7,700 Square Feet
Other Games: SB, RB, No craps
Overnight RV Parking: No

Magic Star Casino
2000 S. Boulder Highway
Henderson, Nevada 89015
(702) 558-6454

Restaurants: 1
Casino Size: 6,500 Square Feet
Other Games: SB, No table games
Overnight RV Parking: No

Railroad Pass Hotel & Casino
2800 S. Boulder Highway
Henderson, Nevada 89015
(702) 294-5000
Website: www.railroadpass.com

Toll-Free Number: (800) 654-0877
Rooms: 100 Price Range: $39-$69
Suites: 20 Price Range: $69-$99
Restaurants: 3 (1 open 24 hours)
Buffets: B-$8.99 (Sat/Sun) L-$5.99
        D-$7.99/$14.99 (Fri)/$9.49 (Sat)
Casino Size: 12,803 Square Feet
Other Games: SB, RB, P, No roulette
Overnight RV Parking: No
Senior Discount: Food discount Mon if 55+

Skyline Restaurant & Casino
1741 N. Boulder Highway
Henderson, Nevada 89015
(702) 565-9116

Restaurants: 1
Casino Size: 9,000 Square Feet
Other Games: SB, RB, No craps or roulette
Overnight RV Parking: No

Sunset Station Hotel and Casino
1301 W. Sunset Road
Henderson, Nevada 89014
(702) 547-7777
Website: www.sunsetstation.com

Toll-Free Number: (888) 319-4655
Reservation Number: (888) 786-7389
Rooms: 448 Price Range: $69-$179
Suites: 18 Price Range: $99-$209
Restaurants: 12 (1 open 24 hours)
Buffets: B-$7.99 L-$7.99
        Brunch-$12.99 (Sat/Sun) D-$12.99
Casino Size: 89,443 Square Feet
Other Games: SB, RB, MB, P, PGP,
        LIR, TCP, K, BG
Overnight RV Parking: No
Senior Discount: Mon-Fri Lunch buffet
        discount if 55+
Special Features: 13-screen movie theater.
Kid's Quest childcare center. Hooter's sports
bar. Food Court with eight fast food stations.
Bowling Alley.

Indian Springs

Map Location: **#14** (35 miles N.W. of Las
Vegas on Hwy. 95)

Indian Springs Casino
372 Tonopah Highway
Indian Springs, Nevada 89018
(702) 879-3456
Website: www.dirtymoe.com

Reservation Number: (877) 977-7746
Restaurants: 1 (open 24 hours)
Rooms: 45 Price Range: $37-$49
Casino Size: 2,300 Square Feet
Other Games: P, No craps or roulette
Overnight RV Parking: Must use RV park
Special Features: 58-space RV park ($16 per
night). Convenience store.

Jackpot

Map Location: **#18** (Just S. of the Idaho border on Hwy. 93)

Barton's Club 93
Highway 93
Jackpot, Nevada 89825
(775) 755-2341
Website: www.bartonsclub93.com

Toll-Free Number: (800) 258-2937
Rooms: 98 Price Range: $28-$60
Suites: 4 Price Range: $89-$124
Restaurants: 2
Buffets: B-$7.93 (Sat/Sun) D-$6.93 (Wed)/
        $7.93(Thu)/$14.93(Fri)/$13.93 (Sat)/
        $8.93 (Sun)
Casino Size: 9,550 Square Feet
Other Games: P, LIR, TCP
Overnight RV Parking: No

Cactus Pete's Resort Casino
1385 Highway 93
Jackpot, Nevada 89825
(775) 755-2321
Website: www.ameristarcasinos.com

Reservation Number: (800) 821-1103
Rooms: 272 Price Range: $62-$126
Suites: 28 Price Range: $112-$180
Restaurants: 4 (1 open 24 hours)
Buffets: Brunch-$11.99 (Sat)/$14.99 (Sun)
        D-$11.99/$17.99 (Fri/Sat)
Casino Size: 25,351 Square Feet
Other Games: SB, RB, P, TCP, LIR, K
Overnight RV Parking: Must use RV park
Special Features: 91-space RV park ($17 per night). Every Wed 5pm-11pm two restaurants are half-price. 18-hole golf course. Beauty Salon, Ampitheatre, and Tennis Courts.

Horseshu Hotel & Casino
Highway 93
Jackpot, Nevada 89825
(702) 755-7777
Website: www.ameristarcasinos.com

Reservation Number: (800) 432-0051
Rooms: 110 Price Range: $40-$90
Suites: 10 Price Range: $60-$150
Restaurants: 1
Casino Size: 3,377 Square Feet
Other Games: No roulette or craps
Overnight RV Parking: No

Jean

Map Location: **#6** (22 miles S.W. of Las Vegas on I-15; 12 miles from the California border)

Gold Strike Hotel & Gambling Hall
1 Main Street/P.O. Box 19278
Jean, Nevada 89019
(702) 477-5000
Website: www.stopatjean.com

Reservation Number: (800) 634-1359
Rooms: 800 Price Range: $35-$89
Suites: 13 Price Range: $59-$119
Restaurants: 3 (1 open 24 hours)
Buffets: B-$6.99 (Sat/Sun) L-$6.99
        D-$7.99/$9.99 (Fri)
Casino Size: 37,006 Square Feet
Other Games: SB, RB, CSP
Overnight RV Parking: No
Special Features: Free shuttle to Nevada Landing. $6.99 prime rib dinner served 24 hours. Burger King.

Lake Tahoe

Map Location: **#5** (directly on the Nevada/California border; 98 miles northeast of Sacramento and 58 miles southwest of Reno).

The area is best known for its many recreational activities with skiing in the winter and water sports in the summer. Lake Tahoe Airport is located at the south end of the basin. The next closest airport is in Reno with regularly scheduled shuttle service by bus. Incline Village and Crystal Bay are on the north shore of Lake Tahoe, while Stateline is located on the south shore. For South Lake Tahoe information call the Lake Tahoe Visitors Authority at (800) AT-TAHOE and for North Lake Tahoe information call the Incline Village/Crystal Bay Convention & Visitors Authority at (800) GO-TAHOE.

Here's information, as supplied by Nevada's State Gaming Control Board, showing the slot machine payback percentages for all of the south shore casinos for the fiscal year beginning July 1, 2006 and ending June 30, 2007:

Denomination	Payback %
1¢ Slots	89.02
5¢ Slots	92.33
25¢ Slots	92.52
$1 Slots	94.41
$1 Megabucks	88.83
$5 Slots	95.02
$25 Slots	94.23
All Slots	93.02

And here's that same information for the north shore casinos:

Denomination	Payback %
1¢ Slots	91.37
5¢ Slots	91.90
25¢ Slots	93.93
$1 Slots	93.72
$1 Megabucks	87.55
$5 Slots	94.78
All Slots	94.27

These numbers reflect the percentage of money returned to the players on each denomination of machine. All electronic machines including slots, video poker and video keno are included in these numbers.

Optional games in the casino listings include: sports book (SB), race book (RB), Spanish 21 (S21), baccarat (B), mini-baccarat (MB), poker (P), pai gow poker (PGP), Caribbean stud poker (CSP), let it ride (LIR), three-card poker (TCP), four card poker (FCP), keno (K) and bingo (BG).

Bill's Casino

U.S. Highway 50
Stateline, Nevada 89449
(775) 588-6611
Website: www.harrahs.com

Restaurants: 1 (open 24 hours)
Casino Size: 18,000 Square Feet
Special Features: Adjacent to, and owned by, Harrah's. Completely non-smoking. Hot dog and a beer for $2.50

Cal-Neva Resort Spa & Casino

2 Stateline Road
Crystal Bay, Nevada 89402
(775) 832-4000
Website: www.calnevaresort.com

Reservation Number: (800) CAL-NEVA
Rooms: 199 Price Range: $149-$189
Suites: 18 Price Range: $229-$329
Restaurants: 1
Casino Size: 15,000 Square Feet
Other Games: No craps
Overnight RV Parking: No
Special Features: Straddles California/Nevada state line on north shore of Lake Tahoe. European Spa. Three wedding chapels. Florist. Photo studio. Bridal boutique. Gift shop. Airport shuttle. Internet cafe.

Crystal Bay Club Casino

14 State Route 28
Crystal Bay, Nevada 89402
(775) 833-6333
Website: www.crystalbaycasino.com

Restaurants 2 (1 open 24 hours)
Casino Size: 13,034 Square Feet
Other Games: RB, SB, TCP
Overnight RV Parking: No
Senior Discount: 15% off food if 60 or older

Harrah's Lake Tahoe

Highway 50/P.O. Box 8
Stateline, Nevada 89449
(775) 588-6611
Website: www.harrahs.com

Reservation Number: (800) HARRAHS
Rooms: 463 Price Range: $99-$249
Suites: 62 Price Range: $129-$800
Restaurants: 4
Buffets: B-$10.99/$15.99 (Sat)$18.99 (Sun)
 L-$11.99 D-$17.99/$24.99 (Fri/Sat)/$18.99 (Sun)
Casino Size: 56,600 Square Feet
Other Games: SB, B, MB, PG, PGP,
 LIR, TCP, K
Overnight RV Parking: No
Special Features: On south shore of Lake Tahoe. Health club. Pet kennel. Lake cruises.

Harveys Resort Hotel/Casino - Lake Tahoe
Highway 50
Stateline, Nevada 89449
(775) 588-2411
Website: www.harveys.com

Toll-Free Number: (800) 553-1022
Reservation Number: (800) HARVEYS
Rooms: 704 Price Range: $159-$359
Suites: 36 Price Range: $250-$679
Restaurants: 8 (1 open 24 hours)
Casino Size: 44,070 Square Feet
Other Games: SB, RB, B, MB, P,
                          PGP, LIR, TCP, B6, K
Overnight RV Parking: No
Special Features: On south shore of Lake
Tahoe. 2,000-seat amphitheater. Comedy Club.
Hard Rock Cafe. Owned by Harrah's.

Hyatt Regency Lake Tahoe
Resort & Casino
P.O. Box 3239
Incline Village, Nevada 89450
(775) 832-1234
Website: www.laketahoehyatt.com

Toll-Free Number: (800) 553-3288
Hyatt Reservations: (800) 233-1234
Rooms: 412 Price Range: $179-$415
Suites: 48 Price Range: $529-$1,400
Restaurants: 4 (1 open 24 hours)
Buffets: B-$21 D-$30 (Fri)/$28 (Sat)
Casino Size: 18,900 Square Feet
Other Games: SB, P, LIR, TCP
Overnight RV Parking: No
Senior Discount: Food/room discounts if 62+
Special Features: On north shore of Lake
Tahoe. Two Robert Trent Jones golf courses.

Lake Tahoe Horizon
50 Highway 50/P.O. Box C
Lake Tahoe, Nevada 89449
(775) 588-6211
Website: www.horizoncasino.com

Toll-Free Number: (800) 322-7723
Reservation Number: (800) 648-3322
Rooms: 519 Price Range: $79-$229
Suites: 20 Price Range: $359-$650
Restaurants: 5
Buffets: B-$13.95 (Sun)
             D-$11.95/$14.95 (Fri/Sat)
Casino Size: 39,689 Square Feet

Other Games: PGP, LIR, TCP
Overnight RV Parking: Free (4 nights max)
Special Features: On south shore of Lake
Tahoe. Outdoor heated pool with 3 hot tubs.
Wedding chapel. Video arcade. Baskin-
Robbins.

Lakeside Inn and Casino
Highway 50 at Kingsbury Grade
Stateline, Nevada 89449
(775) 588-7777
Website: www.lakesideinn.com

Toll-Free Number: (800) 523-1291
Room Reservations: (800) 624-7980
Rooms: 124 Price Range: $79-$149
Suites: 8   Price Range: $99-$299
Restaurants: 2 (1 open 24 hours)
Casino Size: 18,195 Square Feet
Other Games: SB, RB, P, TCP, K
Overnight RV Parking: No
Senior Discount: Various if 55 or older
Special Features: On south shore of Lake
Tahoe. $2.99 breakfast 11pm-11am. $10.50
prime rib dinner 4pm-10pm. Specials for
birthday celebrants. $2 drinks at all times.

Montbleu Resort Casino & Spa
55 Highway 50
Stateline, Nevada 89449
(775) 588-3515
Website: www.montbluresort.com

Toll-Free Number: (888) 829-7630
Reservation Number: (800) 648-3353
Rooms: 403 Price Range: $129-$299
Suites: 37 Price Range: $379-$999
Restaurants: 4 (1 open 24 hours)
Buffets: D-$23.99
Casino Size: 40,500 Square Feet
Other Games: SB, RB, MB, P, LIR, TCP
Overnight RV Parking: No
Special Features: On south shore of Lake
Tahoe. Health spa.

See the Reno, Nevada
section for a story on
"The Best Places
to Gamble in
Reno/Tahoe."

Tahoe Biltmore Lodge & Casino
#5 Highway 28/P.O. Box 115
Crystal Bay, Nevada 89402
(775) 831-0660
Website: www.tahoebiltmore.com

Reservation Number: (800) BILTMOR
Rooms: 92 Price Range: $59-$119
Suites: 7 Price Range: $139-$179
Restaurants: 2 (1 open 24 hours)
Casino Size: 10,480 Square Feet
Other Games: SB, RB
Overnight RV Parking: Free/RV Dump: No
Senior Discount: Various if 55 or older
Special Features: On north shore of Lake
Tahoe. $1.99 breakfast special. $5.95 prime
rib dinner.

Las Vegas

Map Location: **#1**

Las Vegas is truly the casino capital of the
world! While many years ago the city may
have had a reputation as an "adult playground"
run by "shady characters," today's Las Vegas
features many world-class facilities run by
some of America's most familiar corporate
names.

Las Vegas has more hotel rooms - 132,000 -
than any other city in the U.S. and it attracts
more than 39 million visitors each year. The
abundance of casinos in Las Vegas forces them
to compete for customers in a variety of ways
and thus, there are always great bargains to be
had, but only if you know where to look.

Las Vegas Advisor newsletter publisher,
Anthony Curtis is the city's resident expert
on where to find the best deals. His monthly
12-page publication is always chock full of
powerful, money-saving, profit-making, and
vacation-enhancing tips for the Las Vegas
visitor. Visit his Web site at
www.LasVegasAdvisor.com to find a wealth
of information on Las Vegas happenings. Here
are some of Anthony's thoughts on the Best
of Las Vegas:

Best Las Vegas Bargain
Shrimp Cocktail, 99¢, Golden Gate

The Golden Gate's 99¢ shrimp cocktail is not
only the current best bargain in town, it's been
one of the best for more than 40 years. The
six-ounce sundae glass full of shrimp was
introduced back in 1957 for 50¢ and remained
at that price until it was raised to 99¢ in 1991.
All shrimp. No filler. Served 11 am to 2 am
daily.

Best Loss Leader
$1 Michelob, Casino Royale

You can still get an ice-cold beer on the Strip
for a buck. The center-Strip Casino Royale
offers $1 Michelob in the bottle 24 hours a
day. You can also get two flavors of frozen
margaritas for a buck apiece. In case
something changes here, Slots A Fun right
down the street usually sells bottled imports
in the $1 to $1.50 range.

Best Lounge Entertainment
Casbar Lounge, Sahara

The Sahara is changing hands and is destined
to become one of the hip hangouts on the
Strip, but the retro Casbar Lounge still jams
nightly. The action kicks off at about 8 pm
and runs till the end of the 1 am show (one-
drink minimum). The Casbar remains the
perfect throwback to the heyday of the Las
Vegas lounges.

Best Breakfast
Steak & Eggs $2.99, Arizona Charlie's
Decatur

This sirloin steak, two eggs, potatoes, and
toast is served 24 hours a day, 7 days week,
and has been for a decade. If you don't feel
like standing in the usual long line, check the
20-seat counter, where seats turn over quickly.
There's also ham & eggs for the same price.

Best Buffet
Spice Market $13.99-$24.99, Aladdin

In numerous surveys conducted at LasVegasAdvisor.com, the pricy "gourmet buffets" out-poll the value-oriented "superbuffets." The competing gourmet buffets at Paris, Bellagio, Mirage, and Treasure Island are each spectacular in their own right, but the Aladdin's Spice Market takes top honors. This buffet has always had one of the best selections of vegetables in town, and for dinner you can get king crab legs daily, plus lamb skewers at the good Middle Eastern station.

Best Sunday Brunch
Bally's, $65

A vacation-topping Sunday brunch is the perfect Las Vegas splurge, and the epic Sterling Brunch at Bally's is as good as it gets. Despite being the highest-priced spread in town, the Sterling Brunch still qualifies as a bargain, offering sushi, oysters and clams, lobster tail, prime meats, and fantastic desserts, including goblets of fresh berries. The brand of champagne changes, but it's always a step or two above that served at the other brunches in town.

Best Meal
Steak Dinner, $4.95, Ellis Island

Carrying on the tradition of the legendary Las Vegas steak dinners is the Ellis Island "filet-cut" sirloin. This complete dinner comes with choice of soup or salad, vegetable, baked potato, and dinner rolls for just $4.95. The 10-ounce steak is thick, so it can be cooked perfectly to specifications. Though available 24 hours a day seven days a week in the cafe, this great dinner is listed nowhere on the menu; you have to ask for it.

Best Show
Comedy Stop, Tropicana, $19.95

The "Comedy Stop" at the Trop is the best of Las Vegas' comedy clubs, and is still one of the least expensive shows in town. See great comedians night after night, and get $5 off with coupons that appear regularly in the freebie magazines.

Best Free Spectacle
Fremont Street Experience

With its 12.5 million light-emitting diodes, the Fremont Experience light show remains at the forefront of Las Vegas' formidable free-spectacle roster. The show runs five times per night, beginning when it gets dark. Afterward you can explore the downtown hotels and a revamped Fremont East entertainment district.

Best Funbook
Stratosphere, Free

The best funbook in town is available at the Stratosphere. It comes with gambling coupons with an expected value of about $15, or $20 if you use a $5 poker buy-in bonus. You can get one per week with a valid ID, out-of-state or local.

Unlike New Jersey, the Nevada Gaming Control Board does not break down its slot statistics by individual properties. Rather, they are classified by area.

The annual gaming revenue report breaks the Las Vegas market down into two major tourist areas: the Strip and downtown. There is also a very large locals market in Las Vegas and those casinos are shown in the gaming revenue report as the Boulder Strip and North Las Vegas areas.

When choosing where to do your slot gambling, you may want to keep in mind the following slot payback percentages for Nevada's fiscal year beginning July 1, 2006 and ending June 30, 2007:

1¢ Slot Machines
The Strip - 88.80%
Downtown - 89.21%
Boulder Strip - 89.86%
N. Las Vegas - 90.25%

5¢ Slot Machines
The Strip - 88.79%
Downtown - 91.30%
Boulder Strip - 94.44%
N. Las Vegas - 94.07%

25¢ Slot Machines
The Strip - 91.36%
Downtown - 94.60%
Boulder Strip - 96.40%
N. Las Vegas - 96.14%

$1 Slot Machines
The Strip - 93.56%
Downtown - 95.31%
Boulder Strip - 96.26%
N. Las Vegas - 96.89%

$1 Megabucks Machines
The Strip - 88.02%
Downtown - 88.08%
Boulder Strip - 88.03%
N. Las Vegas - 87.07%

$5 Slot Machines
The Strip - 94.60%
Downtown - 94.51%
Boulder Strip - 95.89%
N. Las Vegas - 96.83%

$25 Slot Machines
The Strip - 96.50%
Downtown - 97.80%
Boulder Strip - 93.81%
N. Las Vegas - N/A

All Slot Machines
The Strip - 93.19%
Downtown - 93.59%
Boulder Strip - 94.85%
N. Las Vegas - 94.50%

These numbers reflect the percentage of money returned to the players on each denomination of machine. All electronic machines including slots, video poker and video keno are included in these numbers and the highest-paying returns are shown in bold print.

As you can see, the machines in downtown Las Vegas pay out slightly more than those located on the Las Vegas Strip.

Returns even better than the downtown casinos can be found at some of the other locals casinos along Boulder Highway such as Boulder Station and Sam's Town and also in the North Las Vegas area which would include the Fiesta, Santa Fe and Texas Station casinos. Not only are those numbers among the best returns in the Las Vegas area, they are among the best payback percentages for anywhere in the United States.

This information is pretty well known by the locals and that's why many of them do their slot gambling away from the Strip unless they are drawn by a special slot club benefit or promotion.

One area where the Strip casinos usually offer an advantage over the locals casinos is in the game of blackjack. You will find that all downtown, North Las Vegas and Boulder Strip casinos will "hit" a soft 17 (a total of 17 with an ace counted as 11 rather than one). This is a slight disadvantage (-0.20%) for the player and many Strip casinos do not hit soft 17.

As mentioned before, one of the best sources for finding out about the best "deals" on a current basis in the Las Vegas area is the *Las Vegas Advisor*. It is a 12-page monthly newsletter published by gaming expert Anthony Curtis. *Las Vegas Advisor* accepts no advertising and each issue objectively analyzes the best values in lodging, dining, entertainment and gambling to help you get the most for your money when visiting Las Vegas. The newsletter is especially well known for its "Top Ten Values" column which is often quoted by major travel publications. Each subscription also comes with a benefit package valued at more than $800.

There are many free tourist magazines that run coupon offers for casino fun books or special deals. Some sample titles are: *Tour Guide, Showbiz, What's On In Las Vegas, Best Read Guide* and *Today in Las Vegas*. All of these magazines are usually available in the hotel/ motel lobbies or in the rooms themselves. If a fun book listing in this section says to look for an ad in a magazine, then it can probably be found in one of these publications.

If you are driving an RV to Las Vegas and want to stay overnight for free in a casino parking lot the only casino that will alow you to do that is Bally's.

For Nevada tourism information call (800) NEVADA-8. For Las Vegas information call the city's Convention & Visitors Authority at (702) 892-0711, or visit their web site at: www.lasvegas24hours.com.

Other games in the casino listings include: sports book (SB), race book (RB), Spanish 21 (S21), baccarat (B), mini-baccarat (MB), pai gow (PG), poker (P), pai gow poker (PGP), Caribbean stud poker (CSP), let it ride (LIR), three-card poker (TCP), four card poker (FCP), red dog (RD), big 6 wheel (B6), sic bo (SIC), keno (K) and bingo (BG).

Arizona Charlie's - Boulder

4575 Boulder Highway
Las Vegas, Nevada 89121
(702) 951-9000
Website: www.azcharlies.com

Reservation Number: (888) 236-9066
RV Reservations: (800) 970-7280
Rooms: 300 Price Range: $50-$70
Restaurants: 3 (1 open 24 hours)
Buffets: B-$5.29 L-$6.75
       D-$8.75/$11.99 (Tue/Thurs)
Casino Size: 40,398 Square Feet
Other Games: SB, RB, PGP, BG
Senior Discount: 10% off buffets if 55 or older
Special Features: 239-space RV park ($21 to $33 per night). $2.99 steak & eggs special served 24 hours in Sourdough Cafe.

Arizona Charlie's - Decatur

740 S. Decatur Boulevard
Las Vegas, Nevada 89107
(702) 258-5200
Website: www.azcharlies.com

Reservation Number: (800) 342-2695
Rooms: 245 Price Range: $60-$100
Suites: 10 Price Range: $120-$160
Restaurants: 5 (1 open 24 hours)
Buffets: B-$5.99 L-$6.99/$9.99 (Sun) D-$8.99
Casino Size: 53,727 Square Feet
Other Games: SB, RB, P, PGP, K, BG
Senior Discount: 10% off buffets if 55 or older
Special Features: Video arcade. $2.99 steak & eggs special served 24 hours in Sourdough Cafe.

Bally's Las Vegas

3645 Las Vegas Blvd. South
Las Vegas, Nevada 89109
(702) 739-4111
Website: www.ballyslv.com

Toll-Free Number: (800) 7-BALLYS
Reservation Number: (888) 215-1078
Rooms: 2,814 Price Range: $69-$220
Suites: 265 Price Range: $185-$525
Restaurants: 6 (1 open 24 hours)
Buffets: B-$13.99 L-$15.99 D-$19.99
              Brunch-$19.99 (Sun)
Casino Size: 139,251 Square Feet
Other Games: SB, RB, B, MB, P, PG,
             PGP, CSP, LIR, TCP, K, B6
Overnight RV Parking: Free/RV Dump: No
Senior Discount: 15% off rooms if 50 or older
Special Features: 20 retail stores. "Jubilee" stage show.

The Best Places To Play In Las Vegas

Roulette - There are 13 casinos in Las Vegas that offer single-zero roulette. At seven of the casinos (Caesars, Las Vegas Hilton, Monte Carlo, Nevada Palace, Paris, Stratosphere and Venetian) the game has a 2.70% edge as compared to the usual 5.26% edge on a double-zero roulette wheel. At the other six casinos (Bellagio, Mandalay Bay, MGM Grand, Mirage, Rio and Wynn), the advantage is lowered to 1.35% on even-money bets because if zero comes in you only lose half of your bet. The lowest minimum ($2) can be found at Nevada Palace and 25-cent chips are offered. Be aware that all of the other casinos offer single-zero wheels at just some of their roulette games and not all of them. The Stratosphere offers $5 or $10 minimum bets and the minimum bet is at least $25 at all of the other Strip casinos (sometimes $10 during the day). The minimum is $100 at Bellagio, Las Vegas Hilton and Mandalay Bay.

Craps - Only one casino allows up to 100x odds on its craps tables: Casino Royale (minimum bet is $3). Next best are Sam's Town and Main Street Station at 20X odds.

Blackjack - All recommendations in this section apply to basic strategy players. For single-deck games you should always look for casinos that pay the standard 3-to-2 for blackjacks. A recent trend is for many casinos to only pay 6-to-5 for blackjack and this increases the casino edge tremendously. The casino advantage in these games is around 1.5% and they should be avoided. Many casinos also offer a blackjack game called Super Fun 21. This is another game that should be avoided as the casino advantage is .94%.

The best single-deck games can be found at three casinos which offer the following rules: dealer hits soft 17, double down on any first two cards, split any pair, re-split any pair (except aces), and no doubling after splitting. The casino edge in this game is .18% and it's offered at El Cortez, Four Queens and the Western. Minimum bets are $2 to $10.

The best double-deck game in Las Vegas is offered at eight casinos with the following rules: dealer stands on soft 17, double down on any first two cards, re-split any pair (except aces) and doubling allowed after splitting. The casinos that offer it are: Venetian, Bellagio, Mirage, Luxor, New York New York, Wynn Las Vegas, MGM Grand and Treasure Island. The casino edge in these games is .19%. Unfortunately, all of these casinos will require higher minimum bets (usually $50 and up).

The next best two-deckers can be found at 11 "locals" casinos that have the same rules as above, with two exceptions: the dealer hits soft 17 and you are allowed to resplit aces. The casino advantage is .35% and the game can be found at: Arizona Charlie's Boulder, Boulder Station, Green Valley Ranch, Opera House, Palace Station, Red Rock, Santa Fe Station, Silver Nugget, Sunset Stattion, Texas Station and Wild Wild West. The minimum bet at these casinos is usually $5.

For six-deck shoe games the best casinos have these rules: dealer stands on soft 17, double after split allowed, late surrender offered and resplitting of aces allowed. The casino edge in this game works out to .26% and you can find it at many major casinos: Bellagio, Luxor, Palms, Monte Carlo, Green Valley Ranch, Red Rock, Mandalay Bay, MGM Grand, Mirage, New York New York, Hard Rock, Treasure Island, Caesars Palace, Wynn Las Vegas and the Venetian. The minimum bet at most of these casinos is $50 or $100, but MGM Grand and Monte Carlo have $10 minimums.

Almost all of these casinos also offer this same game with identical rules except that they will hit soft 17. The minimums in this game are lower ($5 or $10) but the casino's mathematical edge is raised to .46%. Luxor, Palms, MGM Grand, Mirage, New York New York, Monte Carlo and Venetian, also offer an eight-deck game with the same rules as the .26% six-deck game. The casino advantage in this eight-deck game is .49%.

Video Poker - The correct answer to the question "where is the best place to play?" will vary, depending on who you are and what's important to you. Las Vegas residents are pretty focused on finding the best games, while visitors with families in tow hope to find upscale resorts that mail good free room offers. This article focuses on the latter group.

The overall quality of Vegas video poker has declined significantly over the last few years. Once the undisputed Mecca of video poker enthusiasts, players are now generally better off visiting Reno or Laughlin.

Particularly hard-hit has been the Strip itself. Former mainstays like New York-New York, Bally's and Paris have all been transformed into mediocre plays. The Stardust is now just dust. The New Frontier is no more. Caesars has succumbed to the Harrah's policy of tightening its games to the maximum extent possible (thus ensuring that you will lose more quickly, leaving more time for shopping). However, due to the sheer magnitude of choices available, great plays for visitors still exist, even on the Strip.

Low-rollers will find some scraps at the old properties. The Stratosphere has a handful of 25c 10/7 Double Bonus (100.1%) and 15/8 loose deuces (100.0%) near the buffet, and also mails great room offers to low-rollers. The Riviera features easy comps and room offers. The Tropicana still has a couple of aging 25c full-pay Deuces (100.7%) machines and excellent room offers. The best plays for low-rollers are downtown, especially at Main Street Station, with its good collection of quarter machines (especially the six multidenom machines in the valet entrance area against the wall that contain full-pay Deuces), plus their 4-of-a-kind promo, and endless free room offers.

Oddly, the three premier plays for dollar players are at the four premier properties of the entire strip. The Venetian has a handful of multigames with $1 9/6 (99.5%) Jacks or Better just outside their high roller area, and 8/5 Bonus (99.2%) in dollars and up, but the main attractions here are the excellent free room offers to the most luxurious standard rooms on the Strip. The Bellagio has plenty of $2 and up 9/6 Jacks and again, surprisingly good room offers. Wynn Las Vegas has an excellent selection of 9/6 Jacks and while comps are difficult, room offers are pretty good.

Four of the newest off-strip casinos offer an odd combination of great low-roller plays and luxurious (but hard-to-comp) accommodations. Casino Montelago features multigames full of great 100%+ 25c games in a tranquil, isolated Mediterranean-like "Village" on Lake Las Vegas, 20 miles east of the strip. Green Valley Ranch has plenty of similar plays in their "Optimum Play" multigames and is only a few minutes from the strip. The Palms has some of the best games in town (especially their bank of 25c 15/9/5 deuces by the north door with a progressive for the royal flush) and is only a mile west of the strip. The gorgeous (albeit distant) Red Rock casino offers some good games in the banks with signs that say "optimum play". The only downside to these properties is the likelihood that you will wind up paying (and paying quite a bit) for your room, as free-room offers at all four properties are rare.

Other worthwhile plays for low-rolling visitors include: Terrible's (9/6 Jacks and great room offers). El Cortez, Four Queens, and Las Vegas Club have great low-roller VP and room offers, but are housed in aging downtown properties with little to do besides gamble. Boulder Station, Sam's Town, and Fiesta Henderson (strong low roller plays, albeit on the "Boulder Strip"). The new South Point casino offers a strong inventory and early indications are that they are generous with free rooms and food. The refurbished Silverton has a decent collection of progressives. Gold Coast and Suncoast have recently re-introduced a couple of banks of 25c full-pay Deuces and are generous with free room offers.

Free Things To See In Las Vegas!

Masquerade Village

The Masquerade Show in the Sky is a $25-million extravaganza in the sky and on the stage at the Rio Hotel & Casino. Five floats travel on an overhead track above the casino, while numerous dancers, musicians, aerialists and stiltwalkers perform on stage, or from attractions that drop from the ceiling or from circular lifts rising from the floor.

There are four differently themed shows on a rotating schedule daily at 3, 4, 5, 6:30, 7:30, 8:30, and 9:30 p.m.

Bellagio
3600 Las Vegas Blvd. South
Las Vegas, Nevada 89109
(702) 693-7111
Website: www.bellagioresort.com

Reservation Number: (888) 987-6667
Rooms: 2,688 Price Range: $169-$499
Suites: 308 Price Range: $359-$5,500
Restaurants: 13 (2 open 24 hours)
Buffets: B-$14.95/$23.95 (Sat/Sun)
          L-$19.95 D-$27.95/$33.95 (Fri/Sat)
Casino Size: 159,760 Square Feet
Other Games: SB, RB, B, MB, P, PG, PGP,
          CSP, LIR, TCP, K, B6
Special Features: Lake with nightly light and water show. Shopping mall. Two wedding chapels. Beauty salon and spa. Cirque du Soleil's "O" stage show.

Bill's Gambling Hall & Saloon
3595 Las Vegas Blvd. South
Las Vegas, Nevada 89109
(702) 737-2100
Website: www.billslasvegas.com

Reservation Number: (866) 245-5745
Rooms: 200 Price Range: $49-$179
Suites: 12 Price Range: $195-$275
Restaurants: 2 (1 open 24 hours)
Casino Size: 32,000 Square Feet
Other Games: SB, RB, TCP, PGP
Special Features: Located where Flamingo meets the Strip. Home of Big Elvis.

Binion's Gambling Hall and Hotel
128 E. Fremont Street
Las Vegas, Nevada 89101
(702) 382-1600
Website: www.binions.com

Toll-Free Number: (800) 937-6537
Reservation Number: (800) 622-6468
Rooms: 300 Price Range: $19-$109
Suites: 34 Price Range: $109-$129
Restaurants: 3 (1 open 24 hours)
Casino Size: 87,000 Square Feet
Other Games: SB, RB, MB, P, PGP, LIR,
          TCP, B6, K
Special Features: Steak House on 24th floor offers panoramic views of Las Vegas. $1.99 ham and eggs breakfast special 12am-6am.

Boulder Station Hotel & Casino
4111 Boulder Highway
Las Vegas, Nevada 89121
(702) 432-7777
Website: www.stationcasinos.com

Toll-Free Number: (800) 981-5577
Reservation Number: (800) 683-7777
Rooms: 300 Price Range: $45-$149
Restaurants: 13 (1 open 24 hours)
Buffets: B-$5.99 L-$7.99/$10.99 (Sat/Sun)
          D-$10.99/$11.99 (Fri/Sat)
Casino Size: 89,443 Square Feet
Other Games: SB, RB, MB, P, PGP, TCP, K, BG
Special Features: 11-screen movie complex. Kid Quest childcare center. $1 buffet discount for slot club members. Live entertainment in Railhead. 12,000-square-feet of meeting space.

Caesars Palace
3570 Las Vegas Blvd. South
Las Vegas, Nevada 89109
(702) 731-7110
Website: www.caesars.com

Toll-Free Number: (800) 634-6001
Reservation Number: (800) 634-6661
Rooms: 3,349 Price Range: $140-$379
Petite Suites: 242 Price Range: $220-$600
Suites: 157 Price Range: $750-$1,250
Restaurants: 12 (1 open 24 hours)
Buffets: B-$15.50 L-$17.50/$23.50 (Sat/Sun)
     D-$23.50
Casino Size: 176,573 Square Feet
Other Games: SB, RB, B, MB, PG, P
     PGP, CSP, LIR, TCP, B6, K
Special Features: Health spa. Beauty salon. Shopping mall with 125 stores and interactive attractions. "Celine Dion" and "Elton John" stage shows.

California Hotel & Casino
12 Ogden Avenue
Las Vegas, Nevada 89101
(702) 385-1222
Website: www.thecal.com

Reservation Number: (800) 634-6505
Rooms: 781 Price Range: $40-$110
Suites: 74 Price Range: Casino Use Only
Restaurants: 4 (1 open 24 hours)
Casino Size: 35,848 Square Feet
Other Games: SB, PGP, LIR, TCP, K
Special Features: 93-space RV park ($14 per night). Offers charter packages from Hawaii.

Casino Royale & Hotel
3411 Las Vegas Blvd. South
Las Vegas, Nevada 89109
(702) 737-3500
Website: www.casinoroyalehotel.com

Toll-Free Number: (800) 854-7666
Rooms: 151 Price Range: $99-$119
Suites: 3 Price Range: $169-$199
Restaurants: 3 (1 open 24 hours)
Casino Size: 17,500 Square Feet
Other Games: TCP, CSP
Special Features: Outback, Denny's and Subway. Refrigerator in every room. 100x odds on craps.

Circus Circus Hotel & Casino
2880 Las Vegas Blvd. South
Las Vegas, Nevada 89109
(702) 734-0410
Website: www.circuscircus.com

Toll-Free Number: (800) 634-3450
Room Reservations: (877) 224-7287
RV Reservations: (800) 562-7270
Rooms: 3,770 Price Range: $39-$125
Suites: 122 Price Range: $99-$278
Restaurants: 9 (2 open 24 hours)
Buffets: B-$9.99 L-$11.99 D-$12.99
Casino Size: 107,195 Square Feet
Other Games: SB, RB, P, PGP,
     CSP, LIR, TCP, B6
Special Features: Free circus acts 11 am-midnight. 400-space KOA RV park ($22 to $42 per night). Wedding chapel. Midway and arcade games. Indoor theme park.

El Cortez Hotel & Casino
600 E. Fremont Street
Las Vegas, Nevada 89101
(702) 385-5200
Website: www.elcortezhotelcasino.com

Reservation Number: (800) 634-6703
Rooms: 299 Price Range: $27-$119
Suites: 10 Price Range: $89-$179
Restaurants: 2 (1 open 24 hours)
Casino Size: 45,300 Square Feet
Other Games: SB, RB, MB, P, PGP, TCP, K
Special Features: Video arcade. Gift shop and ice cream parlor. Barber shop. Beauty salon.

Ellis Island Casino
4178 Koval Lane
Las Vegas, Nevada 89109
(702) 733-8901
Website: www.ellisislandcasino.com

Restaurants: 1 (open 24 hours)
Casino Size: 12,466 Square Feet
Other Games: SB, RB
Special Features: Super 8 Motel next door. Microbrewery. $4.95 steak dinner (not on menu, must ask for it).

The Best Vegas Values

By H. Scot Krause

Welcome to "Vegas Values!" For those of you who may be unfamiliar with the title, it's an exclusive weekly column found only at: *www.americancasinoguide.com*, the companion website to this book. The column is updated weekly with what we consider to be some of the best, current entertainment, gambling and dining values, and promotions located throughout Las Vegas. Tune in and click on every week beginning Sunday for the latest news and information for the upcoming week, along with a steady, growing list of ongoing promotions. Listed below are examples and excerpts from the "Vegas Values" column. We hope at least some of the listings are enlightening for you and will help you enjoy your Las Vegas vacation a little more by taking advantage of these promotions and specials. Remember, promotions are subject to change and may be cancelled at anytime. Call ahead to verify before making a special trip.

Arizona Charlie's Decatur or Arizona Charlie's Boulder: Launched a new member promotion in 2007 that reimburses new slot club members' losses up to $100 on their first day of play when they sign up for a new player card. New Ultimate Rewards enrollees can sign up for an Ultimate Rewards card and play slots until midnight of the same day. At the end of their play, they go to the cage and let the attendant know they are finished playing. If they have lost at least $5, those losses will be reimbursed up to a maximum of $100.

Binion's Gambling Hall: Offering $10 in Free Play when you sign up for Binion's Club as a first-time new member.

California: The Market Street Cafe offers a daily Prime Rib Special (served from 4:00 p.m. to 11:00 p.m.) that includes salad bar, entree, potato, vegetable, and cherries jubilee over ice cream for dessert for just $6.99. Super deal!

Circus-Circus: Offers "Win Cards." Pick up a coupon at the One Club to receive $15 in non-negotiable chips for $10 to be used at the table games. The FREE set of Win Cards will help you learn to play the games. The offer is limited to one per person.

Ellis Island: Best steak deal in Las Vegas! $4.95 complete steak dinner available 24/7. It's not on the menu. Ask your server for it!

El Cortez: Out-of-state visitors can request a coupon Funbook from the El Cortez by e-mail. Send request to: webreservations@exber.net The book includes six coupons including a $5 dining credit and a $5 blackjack matchplay coupon.

Fitzgeralds: You can receive 500 cash-back points within 14 days of your birthday (before or after). Simply insert cash into any slot machine on the casino floor, earn at least one point, and 500 points will automatically be added to your account.

Four Queens: New members signing up for the Royal Player's Club receive a FREE t-shirt with 40 points earned within the first 24 hours of play.

Gold Coast: They have long offered one of the best steak specials in all of Las Vegas. It's a huge Texas T-Bone that includes potato, onion rings, Texas toast, baked beans and a 16 oz. draft beer, all for $10.95. It's available 24 hours in the Monterey Room (coffee shop).

Golden Gate: 99-cent shrimp cocktail. It comes in a tulip cocktail glass with lemon, crackers, and a tangy homemade sauce. It's served at the Deli in the back of the casino from 11 am to 3 am daily.

Hard Rock: Offers $30 for $20 Win Cards. Buy in for $20, get a set of Win Cards (basic explanation/strategy for table games) and $30 in non-negotiable chips. First time Win Cards have ever been offered for more than the standard $15 for $10 deal. Offer is available once per year.

Main Street Station: An often-overlooked promotion called "Score with Four" continues year after year. Hit any 4-of-a-kind, straight flush, royal flush or 300-coin slot win and receive a scratch card for additional cash. Most of the scratch cards are of the $1.00 to $5.00 variety, but they do offer cards valued at $20, $50 and $100, as well as rare $5,000 cards.

Nevada Palace: They offer the best birthday promotion in the city, especially if you are a player. Report to the Player's Circle promotion booth on your birthday and receive a FREE T-shirt, Coffee mug and a prize balloon. You will also receive a voucher valid for double pay if you hit a royal flush on your special day and another coupon voucher good for an extra 10% bonus on all hand paid jackpots that day. $5 blackjacks also pay double on your birthday. If you return the following day, you'll receive a second prize balloon that may include anything from coin bonuses to hotel stays, gifts and even possibly a leather jacket.

Poker Palace: Birthday special: Club members with at least 1,500 lifetime points get a FREE dinner for two. Can be used anytime during the month of your birthday.

Sam's Town: Willy & Jose's birthday special is a FREE T-Shirt, FREE Margarita and a FREE Desert with a $9.99 entrée purchase on your birthday.

Santa Fe Station: Ongoing Birthday Promotion: FREE $25 table games bet if you stop in and play on your birthday! (Must show a valid I.D. directly at the Pit) Not a matchplay…just a free $25 bet!

Station Casinos (Boulder Station, Palace Station, Sunset Station, Texas Station, Green Valley Ranch, Red Rock Resort or Santa Fe Station): Sign up as a new member for a Boarding Pass slot club card and receive FREE Slot Play! Visit the slot club booth to pick up a player's card and set your PIN. You will automatically receive free cash slot play (minimum $5) for an amount up to $500 on your new card. Insert your card and enter your PIN in any slot or video poker machine to activate your free play cash. Promotion is for new slot club members only.

Remember, when visiting Las Vegas, the 2008 American Casino Guide Books are also available in the following casino gift shops in Las Vegas: all Station Casinos, both Fiesta Casinos, Wild, Wild West, Terrible's Casino and the Cannery Casino. The price is $16.95. Players may use their points to purchase books.

That's it for this edition...Luck, royals, good food and jackpots to all...

H. Scot Krause is a freelance writer and researcher, originally from Cleveland, Ohio.
He is a thirteen-year resident of Las Vegas raising his 5-year old son, Zachary.
Scot reports, researches, and writes about casino games, events and promotions for
The American Casino Guide as well as other publications and marketing/consulting firms.

Free Things To See In Las Vegas!

Sirens of TI Show

The front of the Treasure Island (TI) Resort features the Sirens of TI live-action show, where sexy females battle it out with a band of renegade male pirates in a modern interpretation of the Battle of Buccaneer Bay.

Shows nightly at 7, 8:30, 10 and 11:30p.m. Lines start forming in front about 45 minutes before showtime. VIP viewing is offered in the front area for TI hotel guests who show their room key. The show is always subject to cancellation due to weather conditions. If it's a windy day, you may want to call ahead to verify that that the show hasn't been canceled.

Excalibur Hotel/Casino
3850 Las Vegas Blvd. South
Las Vegas, Nevada 89109
(702) 597-7777
Website: www.excaliburcasino.com

Reservation Number: (800) 937-7777
Rooms: 4,008 Price Range: $59-$159
Suites: 46 Price Range: $109-$389
Restaurants: 5 (1 open 24 hours)
Buffets: B-$10.99 L-$12.99/$14.99 (Sun)
          D-$15.99
Casino Size: 97,781 Square Feet
Other Games: SB, RB, MB, P, PGP,
             CSP, LIR, TCP, B6, K
Special Features: Canterbury wedding chapel. Strolling Renaissance entertainers. Video arcade and midway games. Nightly "Tournament of Kings" dinner show.

Fiesta Casino Hotel
See North Las Vegas section

Fitzgeralds Las Vegas
301 Fremont Street
Las Vegas, Nevada 89101
(702) 388-2400
Website: www.fitzgeralds.com

Reservation Number: (800) 274-5825
Rooms: 624 Price Range: $45-$89

Suites: 14 Price Range: $119-$250
Restaurants: 4 (1 open 24 hours)
Buffets: B/L-$6.99/$8.99 (Sat/Sun)
          D-$9.99/$13.99 (Fri)/$12.99 (Sat)
Casino Size: 42,251 Square Feet
Other Games: S21, LIR, CSP, PGP, P, TCP, K
Special Features: Fast food court with McDonald's and Krispy Kreme.

Flamingo Las Vegas
3555 Las Vegas Blvd. South
Las Vegas, Nevada 89109
(702) 733-3111
Website: www.flamingolasvegas.com

Reservation Number: (800) 732-2111
Rooms: 3,545 Price Range: $175-$249
Suites: 215 Price Range: $360-$775
Restaurants: 8 (1 open 24 hours)
Buffets: B-$13.99 L-$15.99/$17.99 (Sat/Sun)
          D-$19.99
Casino Size: 73,147 Square Feet
Casino Marketing: (800) 225-4882
Other Games: SB, RB, MB, P, PG, PGP,
             CSP, LIR, TCP, B6, K
Special Features: Health Spa. Shopping arcade. Jimmy Buffet's Margaritaville restaurant. "Toni Braxton" stage show.

Four Queens Hotel/Casino
202 Fremont Street
Las Vegas, Nevada 89101
(702) 385-4011
Website: www.fourqueens.com

Reservation Number: (800) 634-6045
Rooms: 690 Price Range: $34-$134
Suites: 48 Price Range: $79-$240
Restaurants: 3 (1 open 24 hours)
Casino Size: 27,389 Square Feet
Other Games: SB, RB, PGP, LIR, TCP, K
Special Features: 99¢ shrimp cocktail.

Fremont Hotel & Casino
200 E. Fremont Street
Las Vegas, Nevada 89101
(702) 385-3232
Website: www.fremontcasino.com

Toll-Free Number: (800) 634-6460
Reservation Number: (800) 634-6182
Rooms: 428 Price Range: $90-$120
Suites: 24 Price Range: Casino Use Only
Restaurants: 4 (1 open 24 hours)
Buffets: B-$5.79 L-$6.49/$9.99 (Sat/Sun)
    D-$9.99/$12.99 (Wed/Sat)/$15.99 (Sun/Tue/Fri)
Casino Size: 30,244 Square Feet
Other Games: SB, RB, PGP, LIR, TCP, K
Special Features: 99¢ shrimp cocktail at snack bar. Tony Roma's restaurant.

Gold Coast Hotel & Casino
4000 W. Flamingo Road
Las Vegas, Nevada 89103
(702) 367-7111
Website: www.goldcoastcasino.com

Toll-Free Number: (888) 402-6278
Rooms: 750 Price Range: $45-$165
Suites: 27 Price Range: $175-$250
Restaurants: 6 (1 open 24 hours)
Buffets: B-$6.95/$12.95 (Sun) L-$8.45
    D-$12.95/$13.95 (Sun)/$17.45 (Thu)
Casino Size: 85,545 Square Feet
Other Games: SB, RB, MB, P, PGP, TCP, K, BG
Special Features: 70-lane bowling center. Showroom. Free childcare. $9.95 Texas T-bone steak special in coffee shop.

Golden Gate Hotel & Casino
One Fremont Street
Las Vegas, Nevada 89101
(702) 385-1906
Website: www.goldengatecasino.com

Reservation Number: (800) 426-1906
Rooms: 106 Price Range: $45-$70
Restaurants: 2 (2 open 24 hours)
Casino Size: 9,090 Square Feet
Other Games: SB, RB
Special Features: 99¢ shrimp cocktail. Oldest hotel in Vegas (opened 1906).

The Golden Nugget
129 E. Fremont Street
Las Vegas, Nevada 89101
(702) 385-7111
Website: www.goldennugget.com

Toll-Free Number: (800) 634-3403
Reservation Number: (800) 634-3454
Rooms: 1,805 Price Range: $59-$169
Suites: 102 Price Range: $175-$750
Restaurants: 5 (1 open 24 hours)
Buffets: B-$8.99/$16.99 (Sat/Sun) L-$9.99
    D-$16.99/$19.99 (Fri-Sun)
Casino Size: 35,780 Square Feet
Other Games: SB, RB, MB, P, PGP, CSP
    LIR, TCP, B6, K
Special Features: World's largest gold nugget (61 pounds) on display. Health spa.

Hard Rock Hotel & Casino
4455 Paradise Road
Las Vegas, Nevada 89109
(702) 693-5000
Website: www.hardrockhotel.com

Toll-Free Number: (800) HRD-ROCK
Rooms: 340 Price Range: $109-$279
Suites: 28 Price Range: $399-$519
Restaurants: 2 (1 open 24 hours)
Casino Size: 30,000 Square Feet
Other Games: SB, RB, B, MB, PGP,
    CSP, LIR, TCP, B6
Special Features: Rock and Roll memorabilia display. Beach Club with cabanas and sandy beaches. Lagoon with underwater music.

Free Things To See In Las Vegas!

Fremont Street Experience

This $70 million computer-generated sound and light show takes place 90 feet in the sky over a pedestrian mall stretching four city blocks in downtown Las Vegas and in mid-2004 the entire system was upgraded with new LED modules to provide even crisper and clearer images. It's like watching the world's largest plasma TV with larger-than-life animations, integrated live video feeds, and synchronized music.

There are five differently themed shows nightly. Starting times vary, beginning at dusk, but then begin on the start of each hour through midnight.

Harrah's Las Vegas
3475 Las Vegas Blvd. South
Las Vegas, Nevada 89109
(702) 369-5000
Website: www.harrahs.com

Toll-Free Number: (800) 392-9002
Reservation Number: (800) HARRAHS
Rooms: 2,672 Price Range: $49-$270
Suites: 94 Price Range: $250-$595
Restaurants: 8 (1 open 24 hours)
Buffets: B-$14.99/$19.99 (Sat/Sun)
        L-$16.99 D-$22.99
Casino Size: 90,637 Square Feet
Other Games: SB, RB, B, MB, P, PG, PGP,
              CSP, LIR, TCP, B6, K
Special Features: Mardi Gras-themed casino. "Rita Rudner" comedy show. Improv Comedy Club. "Mac King" stage show.

Hooters Casino Hotel
115 East Tropicana Avenue
Las Vegas, Nevada 89109
(702) 739-9000
Website: www.hooterscasinohotel.com

Toll-Free Number: (866) LV-HOOTS
Rooms: 694 Price Range: $59-$149
Suites: 17 Price Range: $249-$500
Restaurants: 6 (1 open 24 hours)
Casino Size: 27,546 Square Feet
Other Games: SB, LIR, P, PGP, TCP
Special Features: Dan Marino's restaurant.

Imperial Palace Hotel & Casino
3535 Las Vegas Blvd. South
Las Vegas, Nevada 89109
(702) 731-3311
Website: www.imperialpalace.com

Toll-Free Number: (800) 351-7400
Reservation Number: (800) 634-6441
Rooms: 2,415 Price Range: $59-$300
Suites: 225 Price Range: $129-$395
Restaurants: 9 (1 open 24 hours)
Buffets: B-$9.99 L-$11.99/$12.99(Sat/Sun)
        D-$14.99
Casino Size: 75,000 Square Feet
Other Games: SB, RB, P, PGP, LIR, TCP, B6, K
Special Features: The Auto Collections (admission charge). The Spa. Wedding chapel.

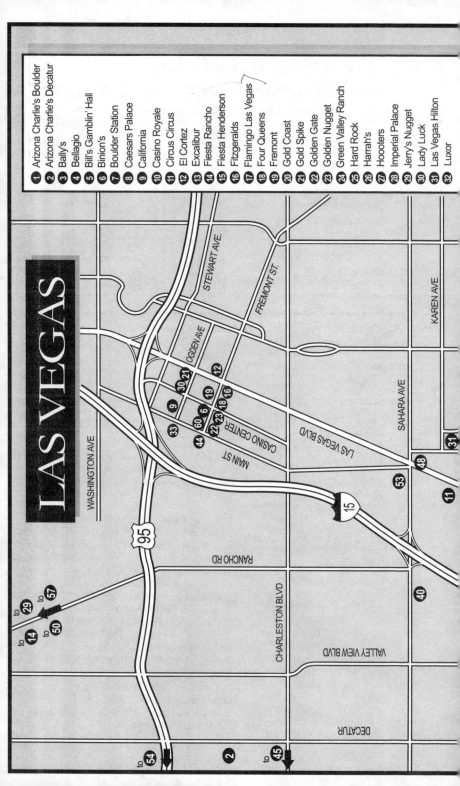

LAS VEGAS

1. Arizona Charlie's Boulder
2. Arizona Charlie's Decatur
3. Bally's
4. Bellagio
5. Bill's Gamblin' Hall
6. Binion's
7. Boulder Station
8. Caesars Palace
9. California
10. Casino Royale
11. Circus Circus
12. El Cortez
13. Excalibur
14. Fiesta Rancho
15. Fiesta Henderson
16. Fitzgeralds
17. Flamingo Las Vegas
18. Four Queens
19. Fremont
20. Gold Coast
21. Gold Spike
22. Golden Gate
23. Golden Nugget
24. Green Valley Ranch
25. Hard Rock
26. Harrah's
27. Hoooters
28. Imperial Palace
29. Jerry's Nugget
30. Lady Luck
31. Las Vegas Hilton
32. Luxor

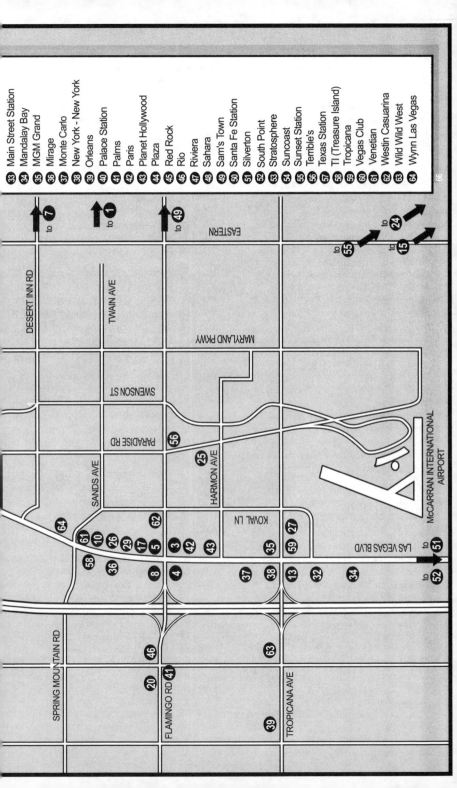

33 Main Street Station
34 Mandalay Bay
35 MGM Grand
36 Mirage
37 Monte Carlo
38 New York - New York
39 Orleans
40 Palace Station
41 Palms
42 Paris
43 Planet Hollywood
44 Plaza
45 Red Rock
46 Rio
47 Riviera
48 Sahara
49 Sam's Town
50 Santa Fe Station
51 Silverton
52 South Point
53 Stratosphere
54 Suncoast
55 Sunset Station
56 Terrible's
57 Texas Station
58 TI (Treasure Island)
59 Tropicana
60 Vegas Club
61 Venetian
62 Westin Casuarina
63 Wild Wild West
64 Wynn Las Vegas

Jerry's Nugget
See North Las Vegas section

Lady Luck Casino Hotel
206 N. Third Street
Las Vegas, Nevada 89101
(702) 477-3000
Website: www.ladylucklv.com

CLOSED - EXPECTED TO REOPEN SPRING 2008
Toll-Free Number: (800) 523-9582
Room Reservations: (800) LADY-LUCK
Rooms: 792 Price Range: $39-$150
Suites: 134 Price Range: $55-$500
Restaurants: 4 (2 open 24 hours)
Buffets: B-$6.95 D-$10.95/$15.95 (Fri)
Casino Size: 23,000 Square Feet
Casino Marketing: (800) 634-6580
Other Games: SB, RB, PGP, LIR, TCP

Las Vegas Auto/Truck Plaza
8050 S. Industrial Road
Las Vegas, Nevada 89118
(702) 361-1176

Restaurants: 1 (Open 24 hours)
Casino Size: 1,700 Square Feet
Other Games: TCP, No craps or roulette
Special Features: Players Club gives table
players comps/discounts in stores and
restaurants.

Las Vegas Hilton
3000 Paradise Road
Las Vegas, Nevada 89109
(702) 732-5111
Website: www.lvhilton.com

Reservation Number: (800) 732-7117
Rooms: 2,956 Price Range: $69-$199
Suites: 305 Price Range: $250-$1,750
Restaurants: 14 (1 open 24 hours)
Buffets: B-$11.99/$16.99 (Sat/Sun)
       L-$12.99 D-$16.99
Casino Size: 78,440 Square Feet
Other Games: SB, RB, B, MB, P, PG, PGP,
             LIR, TCP, B6
Casino Marketing: (800) 457-3307
Special Features: *Star Trek: The Experience* -
an interactive adventure. "Barry Manilow"
stage show. World's largest race and sports
book. Health club. Jogging track.

Longhorn Casino
5288 Boulder Highway
Las Vegas, Nevada 89122
(702) 435-9170

Toll-Free Number: (800) 825-0880
Restaurants: 1 (open 24 hours)
Casino Size: 4,825 Square Feet
Other Games: SB, RB, No craps or roulette

Luxor Las Vegas
3900 Las Vegas Blvd. South
Las Vegas, Nevada 89119
(702) 262-4000
Website: www.luxor.com

Reservation Number (800) 288-1000
Pyramid Rooms: 1,948 Price Range: $79-$249
Pyramid Suites 237 Price Range: $155-$359
Tower Rooms: 2,256 Price Range: $99-$269
Tower Suites 236 Price Range: $169-$409
Restaurants: 9 (1 open 24 hours)
Buffets: B-$11.99 L-$13.99 D-$19.99
Casino Size: 98,581 Square Feet
Other Games: SB, RB, MB, P, PGP, SIC,
             LIR, TCP, B6
Casino Marketing: (800) 956-0289
Special Features: 30-story pyramid-shaped
hotel with Egyptian theme. King Tut museum.
"Carrot Top" comedy show. IMAX theater.

Main Street Station Hotel & Casino
200 N. Main Street
Las Vegas, Nevada 89101
(702) 387-1896
Website: www.mainstreetcasino.com

Toll-Free Number: (800) 713-8933
Reservation Number: (800) 465-0711
Rooms: 406 Price Range: $40-$120
Suites: 14 Price Range: Casino Use Only
Restaurants: 4 (1 open 24 hours)
Buffets: B-$5.99/$9.95 (Sun) L-$7.89
    D-$10.99/$15.99(Fri/Sat)/$13.29 (Tue/Thu)
Casino Size: 26,918 Square Feet
Other Games: PGP, LIR, TCP
Special Features: 99-space RV park ($14/$19
per night).

Free Things To See In Las Vegas!

MGM Grand's $9 million Lion Habitat is located inside the property near the entertainment dome and it showcases up to five lions daily.

The Habitat is open 11 a.m. to 10 p.m. daily and features four separate waterfalls, overhangs, a pond and Acacia trees. There are numerous viewing areas that allow you to get an upclose view of the lions, including overhead and beneath you on the walkway.

The Habitat has a retail souvenir shop and, for a $25 fee, you can have your photo taken with a lion cub during the hours of 11am-1pm or 3pm-4pm. For more information on the Lion Habitat, call the MGM Grand at (800) 929-1111, or visit their web site at www.mgmgrand.com

Mandalay Bay
3950 Las Vegas Blvd. South
Las Vegas, Nevada 89109
(702) 632-7777
Web Site: www.mandalaybay.com

Reservation Number: (877) 632-7000
Rooms: 3,220 Price Range: $109-$429
Suites: 424 Price Range: $139-$589
Restaurants: 16 (1 open 24 hours)
Buffets: B-$15.99/$26.99 (Sun)
L-$19.99 D-$26.99
Casino Size: 157,024 Square Feet
Other Games: SB, RB, B, MB, P, PG, PGP,
LIR, TCP, B6
Special Features: 424-room Four Seasons Hotel on 35th-39th floors. *House of Blues* restaurant. Sand and surf beach with lazy river ride. Shark Reef exhibit (admission charge). Spa. "Mama Mia" stage show.

MGM Grand Hotel Casino
3799 Las Vegas Blvd. South
Las Vegas, Nevada 89109
(702) 891-1111
Web-Site: www.mgmgrand.com

Toll-Free Number: (800) 929-1111
Reservation Number: (800) 646-7787
Skyloft Reservations: (877) 646-5638
Rooms: 5,005 Price Range: $89-$329
Suites: 752 Price Range: $169-$900
Skylofts: 51 Price Range: $800-$10,000
Restaurants: 8 (1 open 24 hours)
Buffets: B-$13.99 L-$15.49/$21.45 (Sat/Sun)
D-$25.99/$27.99 (Fri/Sat)
Casino Size: 156,023 Square Feet
Other Games: SB, RB, B, MB, PG, PGP,
P, LIR, TCP, B6
Special Features: World's largest hotel. Comedy Club. Rainforest Cafe. Midway games and arcade. Free lion habitat exhibit. Cirque du Soleil "Ka" stage show. "La Femme" stage show.

The Mirage
3400 Las Vegas Blvd. South
Las Vegas, Nevada 89109
(702) 791-7111
Website: www.themirage.com

Reservation Number: (800) 627-6667
Rooms: 3,044 Price Range: $79-$399
Suites: 281 Price Range: $299-$1,500
Restaurants: 11 (1 open 24 hours)
Buffets: B-$12.50/$20.50 (Sat/Sun) L-$17.95
        D-$22.50
Casino Size: 95,900 Square Feet
Other Games: SB, RB, B, MB, PG, P,
            PGP, LIR, TCP, B6
Special Features: Siegfried & Roy's Secret
Garden and Dolphin Habitat (admission
charge). Aquarium display at check-in desk.
Royal white tiger habitat viewing area (free).
Simulated volcano with periodic "eruptions."
"Danny Gans" stage show. Cirque du Soleil's
"Love" stage show.

Monte Carlo Resort & Casino
3770 Las Vegas Blvd. South
Las Vegas, Nevada 89109
(702) 730-7777
Website: www.montecarlo.com

Reservation Number: (800) 311-8999
Rooms: 3,002 Price Range: $49-$259
Suites: 259 Price Range: $139-$489
Restaurants: 7 (1 open 24 hours)
Buffets: B-$12.25/$19.50 (Sun)
        L-$14.25 D-$19.50
Casino Size: 84,000 Square Feet
Other Games: SB, RB, MB, P, PGP,
           CSP, LIR, TCP, B6
Special Features: Food court with McDonald's,
Nathan's, Sbarro's, Haagen Daz and bagel
shop. Microbrewery. Pool with lazy river ride.
Health spa. "Lance Burton, Master Magician"
stage show.

Nevada Palace Hotel & Casino
5255 Boulder Highway
Las Vegas, Nevada 89122
(702) 458-8810
Website: www.nvpalace.com

Reservation Number: (800) 634-6283
Rooms: 210 Price Range: $50-$65
Restaurants: 2 (1 open 24 hours)
Buffets: B-$5.49 (Sat)/$5.99 (Sun)
        D-$6.99/$11.99 (Fri)/$8.99 (Sat/Sun)
Casino Size: 15,000 Square Feet
Other Games: SB, K
Senior Discount: Food discounts if 55 or older
Special Features: 168-space RV park ($15 per
night).

New York-New York Hotel & Casino
3790 Las Vegas Blvd. South
Las Vegas, Nevada 89109
(702) 740-6969
Website: www.nynyhotelcasino.com

Reservation Number: (800) 693-6763
Rooms: 2,024 Price Range: $89-$270
Suites: 12 Price Range: Casino Use Only
Restaurants: 11 (1 open 24 hours)
Casino Size: 64,269 Square Feet
Other Games: SB, RB, MB, PGP, SIC
           CSP, LIR, TCP, B6
Special Features: Replica Statue of Liberty and
Empire State Building. *Manhattan Express*
roller coaster. *ESPN Zone* restaurant. Cirque
du Soleil's "Zumanity" stage show.

Free Things To See In Las Vegas!

The Fountains at Bellagio

More than one thousand fountains dance in front of the Bellagio hotel, creating a union of water, music and light. The display spans more than 1,000 feet, with water soaring as high as 240 feet. The fountains are choreographed to music ranging from classical and operatic pieces to songs from Broadway shows.

Showtimes are every 30 minutes from 3 p.m (noon on Sat/Sun) until 8 p.m. After 8p.m. the shows start every 15 minutes until midnight. A list of all musical selections is available on the Bellagio web site at: www.bellagio.com

The Orleans Hotel & Casino
4500 W. Tropicana Avenue
Las Vegas, Nevada 89103
(702) 365-7111
Website: www.orleanscasino.com

Reservation Number: (800) ORLEANS
Rooms: 1,828 Price Range: $49-$159
Suites: 58 Price Range: $249-$499
Restaurants: 9 (1 open 24 hours)
Buffets: B-$6.95/$13.95 (Sun) L-$8.95
       D-$13.95/$17.95 (Mon)/$14.95 (Wed)
Casino Size: 137,000 Square Feet
Other Games: SB, RB, MB, P, PGP, LIR, TCP, K
Special Features: 70-lane bowling center. 18-screen movie theater. Kids Tyme childcare. 9,000-seat arena. Free shuttle to Gold Coast and Barabary Coast.

O'Sheas Casino
3555 Las Vegas Blvd. South
Las Vegas, Nevada 89109
(702) 697-2767

Toll-Free: (800) 329-3232 ask for O'Shea's
Other Games: LIR
Special Features: Property is part of the Flamingo. Burger King. "Vinnie Favorito" comedy show.

Palace Station Hotel & Casino
2411 West Sahara Avenue
Las Vegas, Nevada 89102
(702) 367-2411
Website: www.palacestation.com

Reservation Number: (800) 544-2411
Rooms: 949 Price Range: $39-$119
Suites: 82 Price Range: $79-$149
Restaurants: 5 (1 open 24 hours)
Buffets: B-$6.99/$9.99 (Sat/Sun) L-$7.99
       D-$9.99
Casino Size: 84,000 Square Feet
Other Games: SB, RB, MB, PG, P, PGP, SIC
             LIR, TCP, K, BG

The Palms
4321 Flamingo Road
Las Vegas, Nevada 89103
(702) 942-7777
Website: www.thepalmslasvegas.com

Toll Free Number: (866) 942-7777
Reservation Number: (866) 942-7770
Rooms: 447 Price Range: $89-$359
Suites: 60 Price Range: $139-$389
Specialty Suites: 9 Prices: $2,500-$40,000
Restaurants: 7 (1 open 24 hours)
Buffets: B-$7.99/$16.99 (Sun) L-$9.99
       D-$16.99
Casino Size: 55,689 Square Feet
Other Games: SB, RB, B, MB, P, PGP,
             LIR, TCP, B6
Special Features: 14-theater cineplex. IMAX theater. Tattoo shop. Kid's Quest childcare center. Recording studio. Playboy store.

Paris Casino Resort
3655 Las Vegas Blvd. South
Las Vegas, Nevada 89109
(702) 946-7000
Website: www.parislasvegas.com

Reservation Number: (888) BON-JOUR
Rooms: 2,916 Price Range: $99-$359
Suites: 300 Price Range: $350-$1,500
Restaurants: 7 (1 open 24 hours)
Buffets: B-$14.99/$24.99 (Sun)
　　　　 L-$17.99 D-$24.99
Casino Size: 66,451 Square Feet
Other Games: SB, RB, MB, PGP, CSP, LIR, K
Special Features: Replicas of Paris landmarks.
50-story Eiffel Tower with restaurant/
observation deck. "The Producers" stage show.

Planet Hollywood
3667 Las Vegas Boulevard S.
Las Vegas, Nevada 89109
(702) 785-5555
Website: www.planethollywoodresort.com

Reservation Number: (877) 333-9474
Rooms: 1,878 Price Range: $99-$299
Parlor Rooms: 466 Price Range: $279-$349
Suites: 223   Price Range: $299-$629
Restaurants: 5 (1 open 24 hours)
Buffets: B-$12.99/$20.99 (Sat/Sun)
　　　　 L-$15.99 D-$24.99
Casino Size: 102,916 Square Feet
Other Games: SB, RB, MB, P, PG, PGP,
　　　　　　　 CSP, LIR, TCP, K, B6
Special Features: 130-store retail mall. 7,000-
seat Theater of the Performing Arts. Health spa
and salon.

Plaza Hotel & Casino
1 Main Street
Las Vegas, Nevada 89101
(702) 386-2110
Website: www.plazahotelcasino.com

Reservation Number: (800) 634-6575
Rooms: 1,037 Price Range: $29-$109
Suites: 60   Price Range: $79-$169
Restaurants: 3 (1 open 24 hours)
Buffets: B/L/D-$7.77
Casino Size: 58,660 Square Feet
Other Games: SB, RB, MB, P, PGP,
　　　　　　　 LIR, TCP, K, BG
Special Features: Domed Center Stage
restaurant offers full view of Fremont Street
Experience.

Rampart Casino
221 N. Rampart Boulevard
Las Vegas, Nevada 89128
(702) 507-5900
Website: www.rampartcasino.com

Toll-Free Number: (866) 999-4899
Reservation Number: (877) 869-8777
Rooms: 440 Price Range: $179-$199
Suites: 70 Price Range: $229-$449
Restaurants: 6 (1 open 24 hours)
Buffets: L-$8.99/$12.99 (Sun)
　D-$11.99/$14.99 (Tue)/$17.99 (Thu)/$13.99 (Sat)
Casino Size: 56,750 Square Feet
Other Games: SB, RB, PGP, TCP, K
Special Features: Hotel is JW Marriott. Golf
course. Spa.

Red Rock Resort Spa Casino
10973 W. Charleston Boulevard
Las Vegas, Nevada 89135
(702) 797-7777
Website: www.redrockstation.com

Rooms: 366 Price Range: $129-$499
Suites: 48 Price Range: $499-$950
Restaurants: 10 (1 open 24 hours)
Buffets: B-$8.99/$20.99 (Sat/Sun)
　　　　 L-$10.99 D-$17.99/$20.99 (Fri/Sat)
Casino Size: 119,309 Square Feet
Other Games: SB, RB, MB, P, PGP, TCP,
　　　　　　　 LIR, K, BG
Special Features: 16-screen movie complex.
Childcare center. Full-service spa.

Rio Suites Hotel & Casino
3700 W. Flamingo Road
Las Vegas, Nevada 89103
(702) 252-7777
Website: www.playrio.com

Reservation Number: (800) PLAY RIO
Suites: 2,563 Price Range: $100-$240
Restaurants: 14 (1 open 24 hours)
Buffets: B-$13.99/$23.99 (Sat/Sun)
　　　　 L-$16.99 D-$23.99
Seafood Buffet: D-$34.99 (opens 4pm)
Casino Size: 117,330 Square Feet
Other Games: SB, RB, B, MB, P, PG, PGP,
　　　　　　　 CSP, LIR, TCP, B6, K
Overnight RV Parking: Free/RV Dump: No
Special Features: Masquerade Village area
offers free "Masquerade Show in the Sky"
daily at 3:00, 4:00, 5:00, 6:30, 7:30, 8:30 and
9:30 20-store shopping mall. Three wedding
chapels. "Penn and Teller" stage show.

More FREE Things to See in Las Vegas

By H. Scot Krause

Las Vegas attracts over 35 million visitors every year and seeing the sights and free attractions are still some of the "best bets" anywhere in the world. While "old Vegas" and the lure of cheap buffets is disappearing, since the mid 90's, the grandeur of the attractions is the new lure that entices guests to visit the city and enjoy its splendor— much of it for FREE!

In no particular order, we start at The Bellagio Hotel and Casino, one of the largest premier megaresorts on the Strip. From the outside, Bellagio's world-famous fountains entertain guests with a dazzling water and light show that combines opera, classical and whimsical music with carefully choreographed movements.

Once inside, just beyond Bellagio's gracious lobby, which in itself is another sight to behold with sculptures and marble galore, lies the Conservatory & Botanical Gardens, a kaleidoscope for your senses. Each season these magnificent gardens take on an entirely new look, abounding in fragrance, texture and color. Row upon row of exotic plants and flowers weave a glorious tapestry displaying the unique highlights of every season and holiday. The display is open 24 hours a day.

With its amazing columns and pillars, just strolling the grounds at Caesars Palace is an awesome sight, but the Forum Shops and shows are a huge attraction. The Fall of Atlantis fountain show features animatronic figures fighting for control of Atlantis in this exciting production. An amazing salt water aquarium comprises the show's platform and you can watch as a diver feeds the tropical puffers, flounder, sharks and the rest of the aquarium's inhabitants at various times each day. On the west end of the mall is the Festival Fountain show where visitors are entertained by the Greek gods Bacchus, Venus, Apollo and Plutus in animatronic form, holding the audience spellbound with a fantastic laser, water and light show.

Crowding in on the wooden planks at the front entrance of TI (Treasure Island), sightseers are treated to the free Sirens of TI show nightly. The outdoor spectacle is a 17th century clash between a group of beautiful, tempting sirens and a band of renegade pirates. With their mesmerizing and powerful song, the Sirens lure the pirates to their cove, stir up a tempest strong enough to sink a ship, and transform Sirens' Cove into a 21st century party.

Every 15 minutes from usually starting around 8:00 p.m. (depending on the time of year) to midnight, the earth shakes and flames shoot into the night sky spewing smoke and fire 100 feet above the waters below, transforming a tranquil waterfall into spectacular streams of molten lava. The volcano at The Mirage has been a Las Vegas signature attraction since the resort opened in 1989, mesmerizing spectators with it thunderous, fiery display. The volcano, situated on three water-covered acres, is 54 feet high and circulates 119,000 gallons of water per minute. The show may be cancelled during times of high winds or inclement weather.

Bringing the kids? Or just feel like a kid again yourself? How about free high wire and live circus acts all for free? Billed as the "World's Largest Permanent Circus" a variety of world renowned live circus acts perform every half hour from 11:00 a.m. to midnight on the carnival midway at Circus Circus Hotel and Casino.

The Auto Collections at the Imperial Palace Hotel & Casino is the world's largest and finest selection of antique, classic, muscle and special interest automobiles on display. Additionally, all vehicles (unless otherwise noted) are for sale. The collection is located on the fifth floor of the self-parking garage and is open daily from 9:30 a.m. to 9:30 p.m. While technically the attraction is not free (general admission is $6.95 for adults and $5.95 for seniors) it is a great low-cost bargain and there are usually 2-for-1 or discount coupons found in many of the tourist publications around town.

Be part of the free "Piano Bar" show at Harrah's Las Vegas nightly. Keyboarding extraordinaires battle it out for the best-played piano music as judged by you, the audience. It's always a good time atmosphere. And just outside the doors of the lounge is Harrah's Carnival Court featuring entertainment and some of the world's finest flair bartenders. Masterful mixologists create colorful and potent concoctions while they entertain the thirsty crowds. Other flair bartenders can be seen at the Ghost Bar at The Palms Hotel & Casino, Kahunaville at TI, Studio 54 at the MGM Grand and the Voodoo Lounge at the Rio Hotel & Casino.

The aquarium in the lobby of the Mandalay Bay Hotel is a sight to behold. The 12,200-gallon saltwater tank is a preview to what can be seen in the 1 million gallon Shark Reef at Mandalay Bay exhibit located near the South convention center.

The open-air home of magician's Siegfried & Roy's Royal White Tigers is available for public viewing throughout the day and evening at The Mirage Casino Hotel. Siegfried & Roy have dedicated their lives to preserving these rare animals, and their efforts have helped save them from total extinction. The Tiger Habitat contains many features designed to enhance the comfort of the animals and provide spectacular viewing for guests. The open-air environment features a swimming pool with fountains and simulated mountain terrain for the tigers' enjoyment and the public's entertainment.

Just off the Strip, west on Flamingo, the Rio Suite Hotel and Casino offers a very popular free attraction with its Masquerade Show in the Sky. Experience the excitement of Brazil's Carnivale and see one of Las Vegas' best totally free shows!

The Show in the Sky performs seven times daily in the Rio's Masquerade Village, featuring state-of-the-art floats that suspend from the ceiling and parade above the casino floor.

The Rio also features one-of-a-kind "BevErtainment", a concept that combines Las Vegas' most recognizable icons, the cocktail server and the entertainer. Glamorous entertainers traverse the casino floor not only taking drink orders, but also periodically pausing to grace strategically-placed stages for 90-second live performances. Some sing, some dance — they have their own styles and abilities; yet they all have one thing in common: they serve beverages swiftly, and with a smile.

H. Scot Krause is a freelance writer and researcher, originally from Cleveland, Ohio. He is a thirteen-year resident of Las Vegas raising his 5-year old son, Zachary. Scot reports, researches, and writes about casino games, events and promotions for The American Casino Guide as well as other publications and marketing/consulting firms.

This article is re-printed with permission from Casino Player magazine, May, 2007 issue.

Riviera Hotel & Casino
2901 Las Vegas Blvd. South
Las Vegas, Nevada 89109
(702) 734-5110
Website: www.rivierahotel.com

Toll-Free Number: (800) 634-3420
Reservation Number: (800) 634-6753
Rooms: 2,100 Price Range: $99-$139
Suites: 154 Price Range: $299-$399
Restaurants: 5 (1 open 24 hours)
Buffets: B-$10.99/$13.99 (Sat/Sun)
    L-$11.99 D-$14.99
Casino Size: 109,800 Square Feet
Other Games: SB, RB, MB, P, PGP, CSP
    LIR, TCP, B6
Special Features: Burger King, Pizza Hut, Panda Express and Quizno's Subs. Three stage shows: "Ice," "La Cage" and "Crazy Girls." Comedy Club.

Sahara Hotel & Casino
2535 Las Vegas Blvd. South
Las Vegas, Nevada 89109
(702) 737-2111
Website: www.saharavegas.com

Toll-Free Number: (800) 634-6010
Reservation Number: (800) 634-6666
Rooms: 1,730 Price Range: $49-$149
Suites: 100 Price Range: $142-$240
Restaurants: 5 (1 open 24 hours)
Buffets: B-$8.99 L-$9.99/$11.99 (Sat/Sun)
    D-$10.99 (Sat-Sun)
Casino Size: 45,290 Square Feet
Other Games: P, PGP, LIR, TCP, B6, K
Special Features: Monorail station. *NASCAR* Cafe. *Las Vegas Cyber Speedway* with roller coaster and race car simulator. The "Platters, Drifters, Coasters;" "Matsuri;" and "Amazing Johnathan" stage shows. Wedding chapel. $1 off buffets for slot club members.

Sam's Town Hotel & Gambling Hall
5111 Boulder Highway
Las Vegas, Nevada 89122
(702) 456-7777
Website: www.samstown.com

Toll-Free Number: (800) 897-8696
Reservation Number: (800) 634-6371
Rooms: 620 Price Range: $35-$129
Suites: 30 Price Range: $119-$275
Restaurants: 6 (1 open 24 hours)
Buffets: B-$5.99/$9.99 (Sat/Sun) L-$7.99
 D-$10.99/$11.99 (Wed)/$17.99 (Fri)/$13.99 (Sat)
Casino Size: 118,000 Square Feet
Other Games: SB, RB, P, PGP,
                LIR, TCP, K, BG
Special Features: 500-space RV park ($22 to
$27 per night). Indoor promenade with free
laser-light show. 24-hour 56-lane bowling
center. 18-theater cinema complex. Childcare
center. $1 buffet discount for slot club
members.

Santa Fe Station Hotel & Casino
4949 North Rancho Drive
Las Vegas, Nevada 89130
(702) 658-4900
Website: www.santafestationlasvegas.com

Toll Free Number: (866) 767-7770
Reservation Number: (866) 767-7771
Rooms: 200 Price Range: $79-$179
Restaurants: 3 (1 open 24 hours)
Buffets: B-$7.99/$13.99 (Sat/Saun) L-$9.99
         D-$13.99
Casino Size: 116,375 Square Feet
Other Games: SB, RB, MB, P, PGP, TCP, K, BG
Special Features: 60-lane bowling center. 16-
screen cinema. Live entertainment. Kid's
Quest childcare center.

Silver Saddle Saloon
2501 E. Charleston Boulevard
Las Vegas, Nevada 89104
(702) 474-2900

Restaurants: 1
Other Games: No craps or roulette. Blackjack
only played 4pm-4am (Fri)/9am-6am (Sat/
Sun)

Silverton Casino Hotel Lodge
3333 Blue Diamond Road
Las Vegas, Nevada 89139
(702) 263-7777
Website: www.silvertoncasino.com

Toll-Free Number: (800) 588-7711
Room/RV Reservations: (866) 946-4373
Rooms: 292 Price Range: $79-$119
Suites: 8 Price Range: $269-$359
Restaurants: 5 (1 open 24 hours)
Buffets: L-$8.99/$13.99 (Sat/Sun)
         D-$13.99/$16.99 (Fri/Sat)
Casino Size: 44,640 Square Feet
Other Games: SB, RB, MB, P, PGP, TCP, K

Slots-A-Fun Casino
2890 Las Vegas Blvd. South
Las Vegas, Nevada 89109
(702) 794-3814

Toll-Free Number: (800) 354-1232
Restaurants: 1 Subway Sandwich Shop
Casino Size: 16,733 Square Feet
Other Games: LIR, TCP
Special Features: $.99 1/4-pound hot dog. $1
blackjack and craps. 50-cent roulette.

South Point Hotel and Casino
9777 Las Vegas Blvd. South
Las Vegas, Nevada 89123
(702) 796-7111
Website: www.southpointcasino.com

Toll-Free Number: (866) 796-7111
Rooms: 1,325 Price Range: $69-$139
Suites: 25 Price Range: $219-$700
Restaurants: 6 (1 open 24 hours)
Buffets: B-$6.45 L-$7.45/$11.95 (Sun)
         D-$12.95/$13.95 (Mon)/$16.95 (Wed)
Casino Size: 96,400 Square Feet
Other Games: SB, RB, MB, P, PGP, TCP, BG
Special Features: 16-screen movie complex.
Equestrian center with 4,400-seat arena and
1,200 stalls. 64-lane bowling center. Kid's
Tyme childcare facility. Health spa.

Stratosphere Hotel & Casino
2000 Las Vegas Blvd. South
Las Vegas, Nevada 89104
(702) 380-7777
Website: www.stratospherehotel.com

Reservation Number: (800) 99-TOWER
Rooms: 2,444 Price Range: $39-$139
Suites: 250 Price Range: $119-$209
Restaurants: 8 (1 open 24 hours)
Buffets: B/L-$10.25/$11.25(Fri/Sat)/$14.25
    (Sun) D-$14.25/$18.25 (Fri)
Casino Size: 55,784 Square Feet
Other Games: SB, RB, MB, P, PGP, CSP,
    LIR, TCP, B6
Senior Discount: Tower discount if 55+
Special Features: 135-story observation tower
(admission charge). Revolving restaurant at top
of tower. 50 retail stores. Kid's Quest childcare
center. "American Superstars" and "Bite" stage
shows.

Suncoast Hotel and Casino
9090 Alta Drive
Las Vegas, Nevada 89145
(702) 636-7111
Website: www.suncoastcasino.com

Toll-Free Number: (866) 636-7111
Rooms: 432 Price Range: $70-$150
Suites: 40 Price Range: $185-$265
Restaurants: 6 (1 open 24 hours)
Buffets: B-$6.45/ $12.95 (Sun) L-$8.95
    D-$12.95/ $13.95 (Tue)/ $17.95 (Fri)
Casino Size: 94,938 Square Feet
Other Games: SB, RB, MB, P, PGP, TCP, BG
Special Features: 64-lane bowling center. 16-
screen movie theater. Kids Tyme childcare.
Seattle's Best Coffee. Free shuttles to airport ,
Strip and other Coast properties.

Sunset Station
See Henderson section

Terrible's Hotel and Casino
4100 Paradise Road
Las Vegas, Nevada 89156
(702) 733-7000
Website: www.terribleherbst.com

Reservation Number: (800) 640-9777
Rooms: 370 Price Range: $59-$99
Restaurants: 2 (1 open 24 hours)
Buffets: B: $4.99/$8.99 (Sun)
    L-$6.99 D-$9.99/$12.99 (Thu)
Casino Size: 28,266 Square Feet
Other Games: SP, RB, K, BG

Texas Station
See North Las Vegas section

Treasure Island (TI)
3300 Las Vegas Blvd. South
Las Vegas, Nevada 89109
(702) 894-7111
Website: www.treasureisland.com

Reservation Number: (800) 944-7444
Rooms: 2,665 Price Range: $89-$299
Suites: 220 Price Range: $159-$999
Restaurants: 8 (2 open 24 hours)
Buffets: B-$12.00 L-$15.00
    Brunch-$15.00 (Sat)/$18. 00 (Sun)
    D-$20.00/$26.00 (Fri/Sat)
Casino Size: 55,680 Square Feet
Other Games: SB, RB, B, MB, P, PG, PGP,
    LIR, TCP, B6, K
Casino Marketing: (800) 944-3777
Special Features: *Sirens of TI* live-action show
every 90 minutes from 7:00pm until 11:30pm.
Health spa/salon. Two wedding chapels. Ben
&Jerry's. Starbucks. Krispy Kreme. Cirque du
Soleil's "Mystere" stage show. Indoor/outdoor
nightclub.

Tropicana Resort & Casino
3801 Las Vegas Blvd. South
Las Vegas, Nevada 89109
(702) 739-2222
Website: www.tropicanalv.com

Reservation Number: (888) 826-8767
Rooms: 1,877 Price Range: $45-$159
Suites: 115   Price Range: $215-$330
Restaurants: 5 (1 open 24 hours)
Buffets: B-$10.99/$16.25 (Sat/Sun) L-$11.99
        D-$15.50
Casino Size: 62,011 Square Feet
Other Games: SB, RB, P, LIR, TCP
Senior Discount: Various if 65 or older
Special Features: Wedding chapel. Seasonal swim-up blackjack table. "Folies Bergere" and "Extreme Magic" stage shows. Comedy club.

Tuscany Suites & Casino
255 East Flamingo Road
Las Vegas, Nevada 89109
(702) 893-8933
Website: www.tuscanylasvegas.com

Reservation Number: (877) 887-2261
Suites: 760 Price Range: $109-$139
Restaurants: 5 (1 open 24 hours)
Casino Size: 54,066 Square Feet
Other Games: SB, RB, P
Special Features: All suite hotel. Wedding chapel.

Vegas Club Hotel & Casino
18 E. Fremont Street
Las Vegas, Nevada 89101
(702) 385-1664
Website: www.vegasclubcasino.net

Reservation Number: (800) 634-6532
Rooms: 410 Price Range: $54-$94
Restaurants: 4 (1 open 24 hours)
Buffets: B/L/D-$7.77
Casino Size: 3,431 Square Feet
Other Games: PGP, TCP
Special Features: Sports themed-casino with large collection of sports memorabilia.

The Venetian Resort Hotel Casino
3355 Las Vegas Blvd. South
Las Vegas, Nevada 89109
(702) 414-1000
Website: www.venetian.com

Reservation Number: (888) 283-6423
Suites: 4,046 Price Range: $179-$2,500
Restaurants: 17 (1 open 24 hours)
Casino Size: 103,474 Square Feet
Other Games: SB, RB, B, MB, P, PG,
              PGP, CSP, LIR, TCP, B6
Special Features: Recreates city of Venice with canals, gondoliers and replica Campanile Tower, St. Mark's Square, Doge's Palace and Rialto Bridge. 90 retail stores. Madame Tussaud's Wax Museum. Guggenheim/ Hermitage Museum. Canyon Ranch Spa. "Blue Man Group" and "Phantom"stage shows.

Western Hotel & Casino
899 East Fremont Street
Las Vegas, Nevada 89101
(702) 384-4620
Website: www.westernhotelcasino.com

RV/Room Reservations: (866) 937-8777
Restaurants: 1 (open 24 hours)
Casino Size: 8,925
Other Games: No craps
Special Features: 69-space RV park ($15 per night).

Westin Casuarina Hotel & Casino
160 East Flamingo Road
Las Vegas, Nevada 89109
(702) 836-5900
Website: www.starwood.com

Westin Reservations: (800) 228-3000
Rooms: 816 Price Range: $199-$224
Suites: 10 Price Range: $299-$549
Restaurants: 1 (open 24 hours)
Buffets: B-$12.95
Casino Size: 13,500 Square Feet
Other Games: TCP

Wild Wild West Casino
3330 West Tropicana Avenue
Las Vegas, Nevada 89103
(702) 740-0000
Website: www.wwwesthotelcasino.com

Reservation Number: (800) 634-3488
Rooms: 262 Price Range: $39-$109
Restaurants: 1 (open 24 hours)
Casino Size: 3,350 Square Feet
Other Games: SB
Special Features: Part of Station Casinos group. Discount smoke shop. 15-acre truck plaza.

Wynn Las Vegas
3145 Las Vegas Blvd. South
Las Vegas, Nevada 89109
(702) 770-7000
Website: www.wynnlasvegas.com

Toll-Free Number: (888) 320-WYNN
Rooms: 2,359 Prices: $199-$549
Suites: 351 Prices: $450-$1,050
Restaurants: 18 (2 open 24 hours)
Buffets: B-$17.95/$34.95 (Sat/Sun) L-$21.95
    D-$33.95/$37.95 (Fri/Sat)
Casino Size: 109,900 Square Feet
Other Games: SB, RB, B, MB, P, PG,
        PGP, CSP, LIR, TCP, B6, K
Special Features: 150-foot man-made mountain with five-story waterfall. 18-hole golf course. Full-service Ferrari and Maserati dealership. "Le Reve" and "Spamalot" stage shows. Spa and salon.

Laughlin

Map location: **#2** (on the Colorado River, 100 miles south of Las Vegas and directly across the river from Bullhead City, Arizona)

Laughlin is named after Don Laughlin, who owns the Riverside Hotel & Casino and originally settled there in 1966. The area offers many water sport activities on the Colorado River as well as at nearby Lake Mojave.

For Laughlin tourism information call: (800) 4-LAUGHLIN. You can also visit their Website at: www.visitlaughlin.com.

Here's information, as supplied by Nevada's State Gaming Control Board, showing the slot machine payback percentages for all of Laughlin's casinos for the fiscal year beginning July 1, 2006 and ending June 30, 2007:

Denomination	Payback %
1¢ Slots	89.25
5¢ Slots	90.75
25¢ Slots	94.64
$1 Slots	95.32
$1 Megabucks	88.17
$5 Slots	95.98
$25 Slots	95.03
All Slots	93.35

These numbers reflect the percentage of money returned to the players on each denomination of machine. All electronic machines including slots, video poker and video keno are included in these numbers.

Optional games in the casino listings include: sports book (SB), race book (RB), Spanish 21 (S21), baccarat (B), mini-baccarat (MB), poker (P), pai gow poker (PGP), Caribbean stud poker (CSP), let it ride (LIR), three-card poker (TCP), four card poker (FCP), keno (K), sic bo (SIC), big 6 wheel (B6) and bingo (BG).

Aquarius Casino Resort
1900 S. Casino Drive
Laughlin, Nevada 89029
(702) 298-5111
Website: www.aquariuscasinoresort.com

Reservation Number: (800) 435-8469
Rooms: 1,900 Price Range: $30-$70
Suites: 90   Price Range: $96-$200
Restaurants: 11 (1 open 24 hours)
Buffets: B-$6.99 L-$7.99 D-$10.99/$13.99 (Sun)
Casino Size: 57,070 Square Feet
Other Games: RB, MB, P, PGP,
              LIR, TCP, B6, K
Overnight RV Parking: No
Special Features: Burger King. Subway shop.
Panda Express. 3,300-seat amphitheater.

Colorado Belle Hotel Casino & Microbrewery
2100 S. Casino Drive
Laughlin, Nevada 89029
(702) 298-4000
Website: www.coloradobelle.com

Reservation Number: (800) 477-4837
Rooms: 1,124 Price Range: $23-$95
Suites: 49   Price Range: $125-$175
Restaurants: 6
Buffets: B-$10.99(Sat/Sun) L-$8.99 (Wed-Fri)
        D-$12.99/$18.99 (Fri)/$16.99 (Sat)
Casino Size: 47,680 Square Feet
Other Games: SB, P, PGP, CSP, TCP, LIR, K
Overnight RV Parking: No
Special Features: Video arcade. Sand beach.
Microbrewery. Spa. Krispy Kreme.

Don Laughlin's
Riverside Resort Hotel & Casino
1650 S. Casino Drive
Laughlin, Nevada 89029
(702) 298-2535
Website: www.riversideresort.com

Reservation Number: (800) 227-3849
Rooms: 1,405 Price Range: $42-$199
Executive Rooms: 93 Price Range: $89-$699
Restaurants: 7 (2 open 24 hours)
Buffets: B-$7.49 L-$7.99/$13.99 (Sun)
        D-$10.99/$13.99 (Fri)
Casino Size: 86,106 Square Feet
Other Games: SB, RB, P, PG, LIR,
              TCP, FCP, K, BG
Overnight RV Parking: Must use RV park
Special Features: 740-space RV park ($22 per
night). Six-screen cinema. Free car exhibit. 34-
lane bowling center. Childcare center.

Edgewater Hotel Casino
2020 S. Casino Drive
Laughlin, Nevada 89029
(702) 298-2453
Website: www.edgewater-casino.com

Toll-Free Number: (800) 289-8777
Reservation Number: (800) 677-4837
Rooms: 1,420 Price Range: $26-$75
Suites: 23 Price Range: $100-$195
Restaurants: 4
Buffets: B-$6.99 L-$8.99/$10.99 (Sat/Sun)
        D-$12.99/$18.99 (Fri)/$16.99 (Sat)
Casino Size: 54,208 Square Feet
Other Games: SB, RB, P, PGP, TCP, LIR, K, BG
Overnight RV Parking: No
Senior Discount: Room discount if 55 or older
Special Features: $1.29 shrimp cocktail.
Krispy Kreme, McDonald's and Dairy Queen.

Golden Nugget Laughlin
2300 S. Casino Drive
Laughlin, Nevada 89029
(702) 298-7111
Website: www.goldennugget.com

Reservation Number: (800) 237-1739
Rooms: 300 Price Range: $29-$85
Suites: 4 Price Range: $150-$300
Restaurants: 5 (1 open 24 hours)
Casino Size: 32,600 Square Feet
Other Games: SB, RB, PG, TCP, K
Casino Marketing: (800) 955-7568
Overnight RV Parking: Free/RV Dump: No
Special Features: Suites must be booked
through casino marketing. Gift shop.

Harrah's Laughlin Casino & Hotel
2900 S. Casino Drive
Laughlin, Nevada 89029
(702) 298-4600
Website: www.harrahslaughlin.com

Reservation Number: (800) HARRAHS
Rooms: 1,451 Price Range: $37-$107
Suites: 115 Price Range: Casino Use Only
Restaurants: 4 (1 open 24 hours)
Buffets: Brunch-$11.79 (Daily) D-$14.79
Casino Size: 47,000 Square Feet
Other Games: SB, RB, P, PGP, TCP, LIR, K
Overnight RV Parking: No
Special Features: Salon and day spa. Beach
and pools. 300-seat showroom. 3,000-seat
amphitheater. McDonald's. Baskin-Robbins.
Cinnabon. Starbucks.

Pioneer Hotel & Gambling Hall
2200 S. Casino Drive
Laughlin, Nevada 89029
(702) 298-2442
Website: www.pioneerlaughlin.com

Reservation Number: (800) 634-3469
Rooms: 416 Price Range: $25-$85
Suites: 20 Price Range: $60-$90
Restaurants: 2 (1 open 24 hours)
Buffets: B-$5.95 L-$6.95/$12.95 (Fri)/$8.95
      (Sun) D-$8.95/$12.95 (Fri)/$8.95 (Sun)
Casino Size: 19,500 Square Feet
Other Games: LIR, P, TCP, K
Overnight RV Parking: Free/RV Dump: No
Special Features: Western-themed casino.
Western wear store. Liquor/cigarette store.

Ramada Express Hotel & Casino
2121 S. Casino Drive
Laughlin, Nevada 89029
(702) 298-4200
Website: www.ramadaexpress.com

Toll-Free Number: (800) 243-6846
Rooms: 1,501 Price Range: $29-$79
Suites: 55 Price Range: $89-$119
Restaurants: 5 (1 open 24 hours)
Buffets: B-$6.99 D-$9.99
Casino Size: 44,702 Square Feet
Other Games: SB, RB, P, PGP, TCP, LIR
Casino Marketing: (800) 343-4533
Overnight RV Parking: Free/RV Dump: No
Special Features: Display of railroad antiques
and memorabilia. Free train rides (10am-5pm
Sat-Wed). Train-shaped swimming pool.

River Palms Resort Casino
2700 S. Casino Drive
Laughlin, Nevada 89029
(702) 298-2242
Website: www.rvrpalm.com
Toll-Free Number: (800) 835-7904
Reservation Number: (800) 835-7903
Rooms: 995 Price Range: $27-$75
Suites: 8 Price Range: $55-$350
Restaurants: 7 (1 open 24 hours)
Buffets: B-$5.99/$7.99 (Sun) L-$6.99
      D-$9.99/$11.99 (Fri/Sat)
Casino Size: 60,950 Square Feet
Other Games: SB, P, PGP, TCP, LIR, BG
Overnight RV Parking: Free/RV Dump: No
Special Features: Health spa.

Lovelock

Map Location: **#19** (92 miles N.E. of Reno
on I-80)

Sturgeon's Casino
1420 Cornell Avenue
Lovelock, Nevada 89419
(775) 273-2971
Website: www.ramada.com

Toll-Free Number: (888) 234-6835
Rooms: 74 Price Range: $59-$70
Spa Rooms: 2 Price Range: $89-$100
Restaurants: 1
Casino Size: 9,100 Square Feet
Other Games: SB, RB, BG, No table games
Overnight RV Parking: Free/RV Dump: No
Special Features: Hotel is Ramada Inn.

McDermitt

Map Location: **#20** (Just S. of the Oregon
border on Hwy. 95)

Say When
P.O. Box 375
McDermitt, Nevada 89421
(775) 532-8515

Restaurants: 1
Casino Size: 5,940 Square Feet
Other Games: No table games
Overnight RV Parking: Free/RV Dump: No

Mesquite

Map Location: **#21** (77 miles N.E. of Las Vegas on I-15 at the Arizona border)

Here's information, as supplied by Nevada's State Gaming Control Board, showing the slot machine payback percentages for all of the Mesquite area casinos for the fiscal year beginning July 1, 2006 and ending June 30, 2007:

Denomination	Payback %
1¢ Slots	89.50
5¢ Slots	94.11
25¢ Slots	94.45
$1 Slots	95.35
$1 Megabucks	89.05
$5 Slots	95.52
All Slots	93.77

These numbers reflect the percentage of money returned on each denomination of machine and encompass all electronic machines including slots, video poker and video keno.

CasaBlanca Hotel-Casino-Golf-Spa

950 W. Mesquite Boulevard
Mesquite, Nevada 89027
(702) 346-7259
Website: www.casablancaresort.com

Reservation Number: (800) 459-7529
Rooms: 500 Price Range: $49-$129
Suites: 18 Price Range: $69-$249
Restaurants: 3 (1 open 24 hours)
Buffets: B-$5.99/$8.99 (Sun) L-$6.99
    D-$10.99/$14.99 (Fri-Sat)
Casino Size: 27,000 Square Feet
Other Games: SB, RB, PGP, TCP
Overnight RV Parking: Must use RV park
Special Features: 45-space RV park ($15 per night). 18-hole golf course. Health spa.

Eureka Casino & Hotel

275 Mesa Boulevard
Mesquite, Nevada 89027
(702) 346-4600
Website: www.eurekamesquite.com

Reservation Number: (800) 346-4611
Rooms: 192 Price Range: $49-$99
Suites: 18 Price Range: $99-$249
Restaurants: 2 (1 open 24 hours)
Buffets: B-$6.99/$9.99 (Sat-Sun) L-$7.99
    D-$10.99 (Sun-Thurs)/$16.99 (Fri)/
    $12.99 (Sat)
Casino Size: 31,612 Square Feet
Other Games: SB, RB, P, PGP, TCP, LIR, BG
Overnight RV Parking: No

Oasis Resort•Casino•Golf•Spa

P.O. Box 360
Mesquite, Nevada 89024
(702) 346-5232
Website: www.oasisresort.com

Reservation Number: (800) 21-OASIS
Rooms: 1,000 Price Range: $40-$89
Suites: 100 Price Range: $79-$139
Restaurants: 3 (1 open 24 hours)
Buffets: B-$6.99/$9.99 (Sun)
    L-$7.99 D-$10.99/$15.99(Fri/Sat)
Casino Size: 30,000 Square Feet
Other Games: SB, RB, P, PGP, TCP, LIR
Overnight RV Parking: Must use RV park
Special Features: 50-space RV park ($16 per night). 18-hole golf course. Wagon trail rides. Shotgun sports club. Health club and spa.

Virgin River Hotel/Casino/Bingo

100 Pioneer Boulevard
Mesquite, Nevada 89027
(702) 346-7777
Website: www.virginriver.com

Reservation Number: (800) 346-7721
Rooms: 720 Price Range: $30-$79
Suites: 2 Price Range: $250
Restaurants: 2 (1 open 24 hours)
Buffets: B-$6.99/$7.49 (Sat/Sun) L-$7.99
    D-$9.99 (Mon-Fri)/$11.99 (Sat)/$12.99 (Sun)
Casino Size: 37,000 Square Feet
Other Games: SB, RB, P, PGP, TCP, K, BG
Overnight RV Parking: Must use RV park
Special Features: 34-space RV park ($16 per night). 24-lane bowling center. Four movie theaters.

Minden

Map Location: **#15** (42 miles S. of Reno on Hwy. 395)

Carson Valley Inn
1627 Highway 395 N.
Minden, Nevada 89423
(775) 782-9711
Website: www.cvinn.com

Reservation Number: (800) 321-6983
Hotel Rooms: 146 Price Range: $59-$109
Hotel Suites: 7 Price Range: $129-$189
Lodge Rooms: 75 Price Range: $49-$89
Restaurants: 4 (1 open 24 hours)
Casino Size: 21,260 Square Feet
Other Games: SB, RB, P, TCP, K
Overnight RV Parking: Free/Dump; $5
Senior Discount: Various discounts if 50+
Special Features: 59-space RV park ($22 winter/$27 summer). 24-hour convenience store. Wedding chapel. Childcare center.

N. Las Vegas

Map Location: **#22** (5 miles N.E. of the Las Vegas Strip on Las Vegas Blvd. N.)

Barcelona Hotel & Casino
5011 E. Craig Road
N. Las Vegas, Nevada 89115
(702) 644-6300
Website: www.barcelonalasvegas.com

Toll-Free Number: (800) 223-6330
Rooms: 178 Price Range: $42-$89
Restaurants: 1 (open 24 hours)
Casino Size: 2,220 Square Feet
Other Games: SB, RB, No craps
Overnight RV Parking: No
Senior Discount: $5 off room if 62 or older
Special Features: Weekly/monthly room rates.

Bighorn Casino
3016 E. Lake Mead Boulevard
N. Las Vegas, Nevada 89030
(702) 642-1940

Restaurants: 1
Casino Size: 3,740 Square Feet
Other Games: SB, RB No craps or roulette
Overnight RV Parking: No

Cannery Hotel & Casino
2121 E Craig Road
N. Las Vegas, Nevada 89030
(702) 507-5700
Website: www.cannerycasinos.com

Toll-Free Number: (866) 999-4899
Rooms: 201 Price Range: $69-$134
Restaurants: 4 (1 open 24 hours)
Buffets: B- $9.99 (Sat-Sun)
L- $7.99 (Mon-Fri)
D-$11.99/$17.99(Thu)
Casino Size: 80,375 Square Feet
Other Games: SB, RB, P, PGP, BG
Overnight RV Parking: No
Special Features: Property is themed to resemble a 1940's canning factory.

Fiesta Casino Hotel
2400 N. Rancho Drive
N. Las Vegas, Nevada 89130
(702) 631-7000
Website: rancho.fiestacasino.com

Reservation Number: (800) 731-7333
Rooms: 100 Price Range: $39-$149
Restaurants: 7 (1 open 24 hours)
Buffets: Brunch-$10.99 (Sat/Sun) L-$7.99
D-$9.99/$10.99 (Fri/Sat)
Casino Size: 59,951 Square Feet
Other Games: SB, RB, P, PGP, K, BG
Overnight RV Parking: Yes/Dump: No
Senior Discount: Join Fiesta 50 for discounts
Special Features: Ice skating arena. Drive-through sports book. Coffee bar. Smoke shop. Buffet discount for slot club members.

Jerry's Nugget
1821 Las Vegas Blvd. North
N. Las Vegas, Nevada 89030
(702) 399-3000
Website: www.jerrysnugget.com

Restaurants: 2
Casino Size: 33,101 Square Feet
Other Games: SB, RB, K, BG
Overnight RV Parking: No
Special Features: Bakery.

Opera House Saloon & Casino
2542 Las Vegas Blvd. North
N. Las Vegas, Nevada 89030
(702) 649-8801

Restaurants: 1
Casino Size: 4,420 Square Feet
Other Games: BG, No craps or roulette
Overnight RV Parking: No

The Poker Palace
2757 Las Vegas Blvd. North
N. Las Vegas, Nevada 89030
(702) 649-3799

Restaurants: 1
Casino Size: 26,000 Square Feet
Other Games: SB, RB, P, BG,
            No craps or roulette
Overnight RV Parking: No

Ramada Inn Speedway Casino
3227 Civic Center Drive
N. Las Vegas, Nevada 89030
(702) 399-3297
Website: www.ramada.com

Reservation Number: (877) 333-9291
Rooms: 92 Price Range: $49-$89
Suites: 3   Price Range: $119-$129
Restaurants: 1 (open 24 hours)
Casino Size: 14,680 Square Feet
Other Games: SB, RB, P
Overnight RV Parking: No
Special Features: Closest hotel/casino to Las
Vegas Motor Speedway.

Silver Nugget
2140 Las Vegas Blvd. North
N. Las Vegas, Nevada 89030
(702) 399-1111
Website: www.silvernuggetcasino.net

Restaurants: 1
Casino Size: 18,100 Square Feet
Other Games: SB, RB, BG, No roulette or craps
Overnight RV Parking: Must use RV park
Senior Discount: 10% off food if 55 or older
Special Features: 152-space RV park ($18 per
night). 24-lane bowling center.

Texas Station
2101 Texas Star Lane
N. Las Vegas, Nevada 89032
(702) 631-1000
Website: www.texasstation.com

Toll-Free Number: (800) 654-8804
Reservation Number: (800) 654-8888
Rooms: 200 Price Range: $49-$169
Restaurants: 5 (1 open 24 hours)
Buffets: B-$5.99/$10.99 (Sat/Sun)
        L-$7.99 D-$9.99/$10.99 (Fri-Sun)
Casino Size: 123,045 Square Feet
Other Games: SB, RB, P, PGP, LIR,
            TCP, K, BG
Overnight RV Parking: No
Senior Discount: Various if 55 or older
Special Features: 18-screen movie theater. 60-
lane bowling center. Kids Quest childcare
center. Food court. Wedding chapels. Video
arcade. 2,000-seat events center. Buffet
discount for slot club members.

Wildfire Casino
1901 N. Rancho Drive
N. Las Vegas, NV 89106
(702) 648-3801
Website: www.wildfirecasinolasvegas.com

Restaurants: 1 (open 24 hours)
Casino Size: 6,800 Square Feet
Other Games: SB, RB, No table games
Overnight RV Parking: No
Special Features: Part of Station Casinos
group.

Pahrump

Map Location: **#23** (59 miles W. of Las Vegas on Hwy. 160)

Pahrump Nugget Hotel & Gambling Hall
681 S. Highway 160
Pahrump, Nevada 89048
(775) 751-6500
Website: www.pahrumpnugget.com

Toll Free Number: (866) 751-6500
Rooms: 70 Price Range: $49-$110
Restaurants: 3 (1 open 24 hours)
Buffets: Brunch-$6.99 (Sat/Sun)
D-$8.99/$13.99 (Fri)
Casino Size: 20,471 Square Feet
Other Games: SB, P, LIR, TCP, BG
Overnight RV Parking: No
Senior Discount: $6.45 Dinner Buffet (Sat-Thurs)
Special Features: 24-lane bowling center. Video arcade. Supervised childcare center. Food court with Dairy Queen and sub shop.

Saddle West Hotel/Casino & RV Park
1220 S. Highway 160
Pahrump, Nevada 89048
(775) 727-1111
Website: www.saddlewest.com

Reservation Number: (800) 433-3987
Rooms: 148 Price Range: $39-$90
Suites: 10 Price Range: $89-$129
Restaurants: 2 (1 open 24 hours)
Buffets: B-$7.95 (Sat/Sun)
L-$9.95/$11.95 (Sat-Sun)
D-$10.95/$13.95 (Fri)/$12.95 (Sat)
Casino Size: 18,457 Square Feet
Other Games: SB, RB, BG, No roulette
Overnight RV Parking: Free/RV Dump: No
Senior Discount: 10% on food/rooms if 55+
Special Features: 80-space RV park ($22 per night). Closest casino to Death Valley Park.

Terrible's Lakeside Casino & RV Park
5870 S. Homestead Road
Pahrump, Nevada 89048
(775) 751-7770
Website: www.terribleherbst.com

Toll Free Number: (888) 558-5253
Restaurants: 1
Buffets: B-$3.99 L-$4.99
D-$5.99/$6.99 (Fri/Sat)
Casino Size: 12,122 Square Feet
Other Games: SB, P, K, BG, No craps or roulette
Overnight RV Parking: Must use RV park
Senior Discount: 10% off buffets if 55 or older
Special Features: 159-space RV park (May-August: $24/$29 (Fri/Sat)/Sept-April: $26/$36 (Fri/Sat). General store and gas station.

Terrible's Pahrump
771 Frontage Road
Pahrump, Nevada 89048
(775) 751-7777
Website: www.terribleherbst.com

Toll Free Number: (888) 837-7425
Restaurants: 1
Casino Size: 10,690 Square Feet
Other Games: SB, RB, P, K, BG, No roulette
Overnight RV Parking: Free/RV Dump: No
Special Features: Blimpie's, Pizza Hut and Baskin-Robbins food outlets. General store and Chevron gas station.

Primm

Map Location: **#6** (25 miles S.W. of Las Vegas on I-15; 9 miles from the California border)

Buffalo Bill's Resort & Casino
31700 Las Vegas Blvd S.
Primm, Nevada 89019
(702) 382-1212
Website: www.primadonna.com

Toll-Free Number: (800) FUN-STOP
Rooms: 1,242 Price Range: $38-$69
Suites: 15 Price Range: $139-$205
Restaurants: 5 (1 open 24 hours)
Buffets: B-$7.95/$8.95 (Sun) L-$8.95 D-$9.95
Casino Size: 62,130 Square Feet
Other Games: SB, RB, P, PGP, LIR,
           TCP, B6, K, BG
Overnight RV Parking: Free/RV Dump: No
Special Features: 3 Roller coasters. Flume ride. Two water slides. Movie theater. Video Arcade. 6,500-seat arena. Train shuttle connects to Whiskey Pete's and Primm Valley.

Primm Valley Resort & Casino
31900 Las Vegas Blvd S.
Primm, Nevada 89019
(702) 382-1212
Website: www.primadonna.com

Reservation Number: (800) FUN-STOP
Rooms: 661 Price Range: $43-$75
Suites: 31 Price Range: $129-$205
Restaurants: 3 (1 open 24 hours)
Buffets: B-$6.95/$8.95 (Sat/Sun) L-$8.95
         D-$9.95
Casino Size: 38,049 Square Feet
Other Games: SB, RB, PGP, LIR,
           TCP, K, BG
Overnight RV Parking: Free/RV Dump: No
Special Features: Free monorail to Whiskey Pete's. Al Capone's car and Bonnie & Clyde's "death" car on display. Free monorail service to Primm Valley.

Whiskey Pete's Hotel & Casino
100 W. Primm Boulevard
Primm, Nevada 89019
(702) 382-1212
Website: www.primadonna.com

Reservation Number: (800) FUN-STOP
Rooms: 777 Price Range: $32-$55
Suites: 4 Price Range: $149-$209
Restaurants: 4 (1 open 24 hours)
Buffets: B-$7.95 L-$7.95
         D-$9.95/$10.95 (Fri)
Casino Size: 36,400 Square Feet
Other Games: SB, RB, LIR, TCP, K
Overnight RV Parking: Free/RV Dump: No

Reno

Map Location: **#4** (near the California border, 58 miles N.E. of Lake Tahoe and 32 miles N. of Carson City).

Reno may be best known for its neon arch on Virginia Street which welcomes visitors to "The Biggest Little City in the World." The current arch is actually the fourth one since the original arch was built in 1927. The area also houses the nation's largest car collection at the National Automobile Museum.

For Reno information call the Reno/Sparks Convention & Visitors Authority at (800) FOR-RENO or go to their website at: www.renolaketahoe.com.

Overnight parking of an RV in a casino parking lot is prohibited in Reno.

Here's information, as supplied by Nevada's State Gaming Control Board, showing the slot machine payback percentages for all of the Reno area casinos for the fiscal year beginning July 1, 2006 and ending June 30, 2007:

Denomination	Payback %
1¢ Slots	91.76
5¢ Slots	93.45
25¢ Slots	92.96
$1 Slots	95.84
$1 Megabucks	91.51
$5 Slots	95.82
$25 Slots	95.14
All Slots	94.85

The arch in downtown Reno that welcomes visitors to "The Biggest Little City in the World" is the city's most famous landmark.

These numbers reflect the percentage of money returned on each denomination of machine and encompass all electronic machines including slots, video poker and video keno.

Optional games in the casino listings include: sports book (SB), race book (RB), Spanish 21 (S21), baccarat (B), mini-baccarat (MB), pai gow (PG), poker (P), pai gow poker (PGP), Caribbean stud poker (CSP), let it ride (LIR), three-card poker (TCP), four card poker (FCP), big 6 wheel (B6), keno (K) and bingo (BG).

Atlantis Casino Resort
3800 S. Virginia Street
Reno, Nevada 89502
(775) 825-4700
Website: www.atlantiscasino.com

Reservation Number: (800) 723-6500
Rooms: 975 Price Range: $38-$248
Suites: 120 Price Range: $138-$498
Restaurants: 8 (1 open 24 hours)
Buffets: B-$9.99/$10.99 (Sat) $17.99 (Sun)
 L-$10.99/$11.99 (Sat) D-$8.99
 $26.99 (Fri) $25.99 (Sat)/$10.99 (Wed)
Casino Size: 51,000 Square Feet
Other Games: SB, RB, P, PGP, LIR, TCP, K
Senior Discount: 10% off buffet if 55 or older
Special Features: Health spa and salon.

Bonanza Casino
4720 N. Virginia Street
Reno, Nevada 89506
(775) 323-2724
Website: www.bonanzacasino.com

Restaurants: 2 (1 open 24 hours)
Buffets: B-$10.95 (Sat)/$10.95 (Sun)
 L-$8.95 D-$10.95/$13.95 (Fri/Sat)
Casino Size: 12,583 Square Feet
Other Games: SB, RB, P, K

Bordertown Casino RV Resort
19575 Highway 395 N.
Reno, Nevada 89506
(775) 972-1309
Website: www.bordertowncasinorv.com

Toll-Free Number: (800) 443-4383
RV Reservations: (800) 218-9339
Restaurants: 2
Casino Size: 4,600 Square Feet
Other Games: SB, RB, No craps or roulette
Special Features: 50-space RV park ($30 per night). Gas station/convenience store. Located 15 miles N. of downtown Reno.

Circus Circus Hotel Casino/Reno
500 N. Sierra Street
Reno, Nevada 89503
(775) 329-0711
Website: www.circusreno.com

Toll-Free Number: (888) 682-0147
Reservation Number: (800) 648-5010
Rooms: 1,464 Price Range: $50-$180
Suites: 108   Price Range: $70-$220
Restaurants: 6 (1 open 24 hours)
Buffets: B-$7.50/$8.95 (Sat/Sun) L-$8.50
        D-$12.50/$16.50 (Fri/Sat)
Casino Size: 71,759 Square Feet
Other Games: SB, RB, MB, P, PGP,
            TCP, LIR, B6, K
Special Features: Free circus acts. Carnival
games. 24-hour gift shop/liquor store.

Club Cal-Neva/Virginian Hotel and Casino
38 E. Second Street
Reno, Nevada 89505
(775) 323-1046
Website: www.clubcalneva.com

Toll-Free Number (877) 777-7303
Rooms: 303 Price Range: $54-$99
Suites: 6 Price Range: $119-$249
Restaurants: 5 (1 open 24 hours)
Casino Size: 43,260 Square Feet
Other Games: P, PGP, LIR, TCP, K
Special Features: Hot dog and a beer for $2.50.

Diamond's Casino at Holiday Inn
1010 E. 6th Street
Reno, Nevada 89512
(775) 786-5151

Holiday Inn Reservations: (888) 465-4329
Rooms: 280 Price Range: $89-$109
Suites: 6 Price Range: $99-$189
Restaurants: 2 (1 open 24 hours)
Casino Size: 10,000 Square Feet
Other Games: SB, RB, No roulette or craps
Special Features: Rooms are at Holiday Inn
which is next door.

Eldorado Hotel Casino
345 N. Virginia Street
Reno, Nevada 89501
(775) 786-5700
Website: www.eldoradoreno.com

Toll-Free Number: (800) 648-4597
Reservation Number: (800) 648-5966
Rooms: 817 Price Range: $59-$139
Suites: 127 Price Range: $139-$450
Restaurants: 8 (1 open 24 hours)
Buffets: B-$8.99/$10.99 (Sat)/$12.99 (Sun)
        L-$9.99 D-$14.99/$19.99 (Fri/Sat)
Casino Size: 76,500 Square Feet
Other Games: SB, RB, MB, PG, P, PGP,
            LIR, TCP, B6, K
Senior Discount: Food discounts if 60 or older
Special Features: In-house coffee roasting.
Pasta shop. Microbrewery. Bakery. Butcher
shop. Gelato factory. Video arcade.

Fitzgeralds Casino/Hotel - Reno
255 N. Virginia Street
Reno, Nevada 89504
(775) 785-3300
Website: www.fitzgeraldsreno.com

Toll-Free Number: (800) 535-LUCK
Room Reservations: (800) 648-5022
Rooms: 351 Price Range: $36-$122
Suites: 8 Price Range: $98-$240
Restaurants: 3 (1 open 24 hours)
Buffets: B-$6.95/$8.49 (Sat)/$9.49 (Sun)
        L-$7.59/$8.49 (Sat)/$9.49 (Sun)
        D-$10.89/$11.89 (Sat)
Casino Size: 26,380 Square Feet
Other Games: SB, RB, TCP, K
Special Features: Irish-themed casino. $8.95
prime rib dinner special.

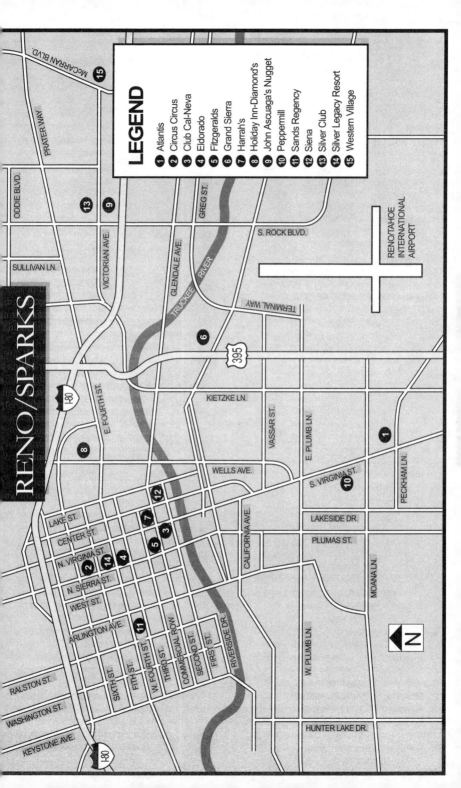

RENO/SPARKS

LEGEND

1. Atlantis
2. Circus Circus
3. Club Cal-Neva
4. Eldorado
5. Fitzgeralds
6. Grand Sierra
7. Harrah's
8. Holiday Inn-Diamond's
9. John Ascuaga's Nugget
10. Peppermill
11. Sands Regency
12. Siena
13. Silver Club
14. Silver Legacy Resort
15. Western Village

Grand Sierra Resort & Casino
2500 E. Second Street
Reno, Nevada 89595
(775) 789-2000
Website: www.grandsierraresort.com

Room Reservations: (800) 501-2651
RV Reservations: (888) 562-5698
Rooms: 1,847 Price Range: $70-$375
Suites: 154 Price Range: $249-$899
Restaurants: 10 (1 open 24 hours)
Buffets: B-$9.99 L-$11.99 D-$16.99
Casino Size: 117,400 Square Feet
Other Games: SB, RB, MB, P, PG, PGP,
LIR, TCP, B6, K
Senior Discount: Various if 55 or older
Special Features: Two movie theaters. 50-lane bowling center. 174-space RV park ($40-$52 summer/$28-$35 winter). 50-lane bowling center. Health club. Shopping mall. Family amusement center. Laketop golf driving range. Indoor simulated golf.

Harrah's Reno
219 N. Center Street
Reno, Nevada 89501
(775) 786-3232
Website: www.harrahsreno.com

Toll-Free Number: (800) 423-1121
Reservation Number: (800) HARRAHS
Rooms: 886 Price Range: $65-$215
Suites: 60 Price Range: Casino use only
Restaurants: 7 (1 open 24 hours)
Buffets: B-$8.99 L-$10.99
    Brunch-$12.99(Sat/Sun)
    D-$13.99/$18.99 (Sat/Sun)/$15.99 (Sun)
Casino Size: 45,200 Square Feet
Other Games: SB, RB, B, MB, P, PG,
PGP, LIR, TCP, K
Special Features: Improv Comedy Club.

Peppermill Hotel Casino Reno
2707 S. Virginia Street
Reno, Nevada 89502
(775) 826-2121
Website: www.peppermillreno.com

Toll-Free Number: (800) 648-6992
Reservation Number: (800) 282-2444
Rooms: 1,070 Price Range: $56-$189
Suites: 185 Price Range: $119-$259
Restaurants: 6 (1 open 24 hours)
Buffets: B-$8.99/$16.99 (Sun)/$10.99 (Sat)
    L-$9.99/$11.99 (Sat)

D-$15.99/$26.99 (Fri)/$24.99 (Sat
Casino Size: 69,978 Square Feet
Other Games: SB, RB, MB, PG, P, PGP,
LIR, TCP, K
Senior Discount: Various discounts if 55+

The Sands Regency Hotel Casino
345 North Arlington Avenue
Reno, Nevada 89501
(775) 348-2200
Website: www.sandsregency.com

Reservation Number: (800) 648-3553
Rooms: 811 Price Range: $39-$89
Suites: 27 Price Range: $109-$289
Restaurants: 3 (1 open 24 hours)
Buffets: D-$11.99
Casino Size: 29,000 Square Feet
Other Games: SB, RB, P, LIR, PGP, TCP, K, BG
Special Features: Arby's. Tony Roma's.

Siena Hotel Spa Casino
1 S. Lake Street
Reno, Nevada 89501
(775) 337-6260
Website: www.sienareno.com

Toll-Free Number: (877) 743-6233
Rooms: 214 Price Range: $89-$199
Suites: 27 Price Range: $129-$649
Restaurants: 3 (1 open 24 hours)
Buffets: B-$24.95 (Sun)
Casino Size: 21,050 Square Feet
Other Games: SB, RB, PGP, TCP, K
Special Features: Health spa.

Silver Legacy Resort Casino
407 N. Virginia Street
Reno, Nevada 89501
(775) 325-7401
Website: www.silverlegacy.com

Toll-Free Number: (800) 687-7733
Reservation Number: (800) 687-8733
Rooms: 1,720 Price Range: $59-$169
Suites: 150 Price Range: $95-$250
Restaurants: 5 (1 open 24 hours)
Buffets: B-$8.99/$12.99 (Sat/Sun)
    L-$9.99 D-$14.99/$19.99 (Fri/Sat)
Casino Size: 88,400 Square Feet
Other Games: SB, RB, B, PG, PGP,
LIR, TCP, B6, K
Special Features: Simulated mining machine above casino floor. Comedy club. Rum bar.

The Best Places To Play in Reno/Tahoe

Roulette - The house edge on a single-zero wheel cuts the house edge from 5.26% down to a more reasonable 2.70%. Unfortunately, there are no casinos in Reno/Tahoe that offer single-zero roulette

Craps - Almost all Reno/Tahoe area casino offer double odds on their crap games. The casinos offering the highest odds are the Siena and Sands Regency in Reno, plus the Lakeside Inn in Lake Tahoe which all offer 10X odds.

Blackjack - There's good news and bad news for blackjack players in Northern Nevada. The good news is that there is an abundance of single-deck and double-deck games available. The bad news though is that all casinos in the Reno/Tahoe area hit soft 17. This results in a slightly higher advantage (.20%) for the casinos. Additionally, some casinos may also restrict your double-downs to two-card totals of 10 or 11 only. The following recommendations apply to basic strategy players.

For single-deck games you should always look for casinos that pay the standard 3-to-2 for blackjacks. Some casinos only pay 6-to-5 for blackjack and this increases the casino edge tremendously. The casino advantage in these games is around 1.5% and they should be avoided. Many casinos also offer a blackjack game called Super Fun 21. This is another game that should be avoided as the casino advantage is .94%.

The best single-deck game is at the Alamo Travel Center in Sparks which has the following rules: double down on any first two cards, split any pair, resplit any pair, late surrender, and they will count a "six-card Charlie" as an automatic winner. The casino edge here is .10%.

Next best are seven casinos that offer single-deck with the basic Northern Nevada rules: double down on any first two cards, split any pair and resplit any pair (except aces): Baldini's, Boomtown, John Ascuaga's Nugget, Siena, Rail City, Western Village and Silver Club. The casino edge here is .18%. (NOTE: There are numerous casinos that offer a game similar to this one except they will only allow you to double down on totals of 10 or more. This raises the casino edge in this game to .44%)

There are seven casinos that tie for best place to play double-deck blackjack: Peppermill, Silver Legacy, Atlantis, Grand Sierra, Eldorado, Club Cal-Neva and John Ascuaga's Nugget. Their two-deck games have the following rules: double down on any first two cards, split any pair, and resplit any pair (except aces). This works out to a casino edge of .53%

The best six-deck games can be found at six Lake Tahoe casinos: Crystal Bay Club, Harrah's, Harvey's, Hyatt Regency, Lakeside Inn and MontBleu. The game's edge is .56% with these rules: double down on any two cards, split any pair, resplit any pair (including aces) and double allowed after split.

If you take away resplitting of aces from the previously mentioned rules you have a game with a casino edge of .63% which is offered in Reno at Atlantis, Grand Sierra, John Ascuaga's Nugget and the Peppermill. It's also offered in Lake Tahoe at the Horizon.

Video Poker - Smart video poker players know that the three best varieties of machines to look for are: 9/6 Jacks or Better, 10/7 Double Bonus and full-pay Deuces Wild. By only playing these three kinds of machines, playing the maximum coin and using perfect strategy you can achieve, theoretically, the following payback percentages: 99.54% on 9/6 Jacks or Better, 100.17% on 10/7 Double Bonus and 100.76% on full-pay Deuces Wild.

Good video poker opportunities are available in Northern Nevada, with the exception of full-pay Deuces Wild, which is hard to find. A slightly lesser-paying version, known as Not So Ugly Deuces (NSUD), which returns 99.73%, however, is widely available.

In North Lake Tahoe the Biltmore has 9/6 Jacks or Better in quarters through dollars, with multi-point days and easy comps. The Crystal Bay club offers 10/7 Double Bonus in quarters through dollars with multi-point days. Hyatt Regency is easily the nicest hotel at Lake Tahoe and one of the best in Nevada. The best game is the dollar 9/5 Jacks progressive with very good comps there.

At the south end of the lake, Bill's has a couple of machines with full-pay Deuces, 10/7 Double Bonus and 10/6 Double Double Bonus in the dime denomination. They also have 9/6 Jacks in quarters – lots of them, but no slot club. Harrah's best games are Triple Plays with dollar/two-dollar Jacks. Also some high-limit Jacks and a couple dozen machines with 8/5 Bonus Poker in a variety of denominations – quarters through $2.

Across the street at Harvey's, the Jacks are more expensive – $5 and up while the Bonus Poker is similar to Harrah's including 50-Plays at quarters through $1. Lakeside has quarter Pick'em, while the Horizon has dollar NSU Deuces and 9/6 Jacks. Montbleu (formerly Caesar's Tahoe) has 9/6 Jacks in dollars through five-dollars.

In Reno, Atlantis has a huge VP inventory featuring $1Dollar Pick'em (99.95%) and NSUD in a variety of denominations. Boomtown has 10/7 Double Bonus, NSUD and 9/6 Jacks for $1 through $5, as well as quarter Jacks (including Triple Play). Circus Circus has quarter Pick'em, NSUD for $1 and $2, plus penny 9/6 Jacks in Hundred-Plays.

Club Cal Neva has 10/7 Double Bonus, Pick'em, NSUD and 9/6 Jacks in a variety of denominations. The Eldorado has one of the best inventories with 10/7 Double Bonus, NSUD and 9/6 Jacks in a wide range of denominations. Grand Sierra has NSUD in Multi-plays from $1 through $5 and 9/6 Jacks in a variety of denominations. Harrah's has 9/6 Jacks for $1 and up. Peppermill has 25-cent 10/7 Double Bonus in quarters, plus NSUD and 9/6 Jacks in a variety of denominations.

Sands Regency has 25-cent NSUD, while Siena has 50-cent and $1 NSUD, plus a variety of 9/6 Jacks. Silver Legacy has full pay Deuces Wild, 10/7 Double Bonus and 9/6/90 Jacks in nickel and dime 100-Plays. Western Village has 10/7 Double Bonus, as well as NSUD and 9/6 Jacks or Better all over the place and in all kinds of denominations and platforms.

Searchlight

Map Location: **#25** (58 miles S. of Las Vegas on Hwy. 95)

Searchlight Nugget Casino
100 N. Highway 95
Searchlight, Nevada 89046
(702) 297-1201

Casino Size: 3,260 Square Feet
Other Games: P, No craps or roulette
Overnight RV Parking: Free/RV Dump: No

Sparks

Map Location: **#4** (Sparks is a suburb of Reno and is located one mile east of Reno on I-80)

Here's information, from Nevada's Gaming Control Board, showing the slot machine payback percentages for all of the Sparks area casinos for the fiscal year beginning July 1, 2006 and ending June 30, 2007:

Denomination	Payback %
1¢ Slots	93.07
5¢ Slots	94.54
25¢ Slots	95.33
$1 Slots	96.27
$1 Megabucks	88.26
$5 Slots	96.31
All Slots	95.28

These numbers reflect the percentage of money returned on each denomination of machine and encompass all electronic machines including slots, video poker and video keno.

Alamo Travel Center
1959 East Greg Street
Sparks, Nevada 89431
(775) 355-8888
Website: www.thealamo.com

Super 8 Room Reservations: (800) 800-8000
Rooms: 64 Price Range: $69-$89
Suites: 7 Price Range: $95-$169
Restaurants: 1 (open 24 hours)
Casino Size: 7,150 Square Feet
Other Games: SB, RB, P, No roulette
Overnight RV Parking: Free/RV Dump: No
Special Features: Motel is Super 8. Truck stop. Video arcade. Post office and gas station.

Baldini's Sports Casino
865 South Rock Boulevard
Sparks, Nevada 89431
(775) 358-0116
Website: www.baldinissportscasino.com

Restaurants: 4 (1 open 24 hours)
Buffets: B- $8.58/ $18.02 (Sat-Sun
        D-$10.73/$18.02(Fri-Sun)
Casino Size: 42,900 Square Feet
Other Games: SB, RB, P, TCP, K
        No craps or roulette
Overnight RV Parking: Free/RV Dump: No
Senior Discount: 15% off food if 55 or older
Special Features: Convenience store. Gas station. Free six-pack of Pepsi awarded with natural 4-of-a-kind, or better, in video poker with maximum coins bet. All single-deck blackjack.

John Ascuaga's Nugget
1100 Nugget Avenue
Sparks, Nevada 89431
(775) 356-3300
Website: www.janugget.com

Toll-Free Number: (800) 648-1177
Rooms: 1,450 Price Range: $59-$155
Suites: 150 Price Range: $109-$295
Restaurants: 8 (1 open 24 hours)
Buffets: B-$9.50 (Sat)/$12.95 (Sun) L-$8.99
        D-$14.99 /$19.95 (Fri-Sun)
Casino Size: 82,600 Square Feet
Overnight RV Parking: Free (3 day maximum)
        RV Dump: No
Other Games: SB, RB, P, PGP, LIR, TCP, K, BG
Special Features: Wedding chapel. Health club.

Rail City Casino
2121 Victorian Avenue
Sparks, Nevada 89431
(775) 359-9440
Website: www.railcity.com

Restaurants: 1
Buffets: B/L-$5.95 (Mon-Fri) D-$6.95/$9.95 (Fri)
Casino Size: 18,120 Square Feet
Other Games: SB, RB, P, K, No craps or roulette
Overnight RV Parking: No
Senior Discount: 20% off buffet if 50 or older

Silver Club Hotel/Casino
1040 Victorian Avenue
Sparks, Nevada 89432
(775) 358-4771
Website: www.silverclub.com

Reservation Number: (800) 905-7774
Rooms: 204 Price Range: $39-$79
Suites: 8 Price Range: $90-$225
Restaurants: 4 (1 open 24 hours)
Buffets: B- $6.95 (Sun) D-$9.25 (Thu-Mon)
Casino Size: 16,214 Square Feet
Other Games: SB, RB, TCP, K
Overnight RV Parking: No
Senior Discount: 10% off food if 55 or older

Western Village Inn & Casino
815 Nichols Boulevard
Sparks, Nevada 89432
(775) 331-1069

Reservation Number: (800) 648-1170
Rooms: 280 Price Range: $41-$41
Suites: 5 Price Range: $155-$175
Restaurants: 3 (1 open 24 hours)
Casino Size: 26,973 Square Feet
Other Games: SB
Overnight RV Parking: Free/RV Dump: No
Senior Discount: Room discount if 55 or older

Tonopah

Map Location: **#26** (200 miles N.W. of Las Vegas on Hwy. 95 where it meets Hwy. 6)

Tonopah Station House
1137 S. Main Street
Tonopah, Nevada 89049
(775) 482-9777

Ramada Reservations: (800) 272-6232
Rooms: 75 Price Range: $58-$78
Suites: 3 Price Range: $75-$125
Restaurants: 1 (open 24 hours)
Casino Size: 10,500 Square Feet
Other Games: No table games
Overnight RV Parking: Free/RV Dump: No
Special Features: 20-space RV park ($18 per night). Hotel is Ramada Inn.

Verdi

Map Location: **#4** (4 miles W. of Reno on I-80 at the California border)

Boomtown Hotel & Casino
P.O. Box 399
Verdi, Nevada 89439
(775) 345-6000
Website: www.boomtownreno.com

Toll-Free Number: (800) 648-3790
Room/RV Reservations: (877) 626-6686
Rooms: 318 Price Range: $69-$165
Suites: 20 Price Range: $115-$279
Restaurants: 4 (1 open 24 hours)
Buffets: B/L-$8.99/$11.99 (Fri-Sun)
         D-$12.99/$25.99 (Fri-Sun)
Casino Size: 39,650 Square Feet
Other Games: SB, RB, P, PGP, TCP, LIR, K
Overnight RV Parking: Free/RV Dump: No
Special Features: 203-space RV park ($30 per night). 24-hour mini-mart. Indoor family fun center with rides and arcade games. Free shuttle to/from Reno.

Wells

Map Location: **#27** (338 miles N.E. of Reno on I-80)

Four Way Bar/Cafe & Casino
U.S. 93 & Interstate 80
Wells, Nevada 89835
(775) 752-3344

Restaurants: 1
Casino Size: 5,000 Square Feet
Other Games: No craps or roulette
Overnight RV Parking: Free/RV Dump: No

W. Wendover

Map Location: **#28** (Just W. of the Utah border on I-80)

Here's information, as supplied by Nevada's State Gaming Control Board, showing the slot machine payback percentages for all of the Wendover area casinos for the fiscal year beginning July 1, 2006 and ending June 30, 2007:

Denomination	Payback %
1¢ Slots	93.26
5¢ Slots	92.16
25¢ Slots	92.99
$1 Slots	96.19
$1 Megabucks	87.23
$5 Slots	97.14
$25 Slots	97.04
All Slots	94.68

These numbers reflect the percentage of money returned on each denomination of machine and encompass all electronic machines including slots, video poker and video keno.

Montego Bay Casino Resort
100 Wendover Boulevard
W. Wendover, Nevada 89883
(775) 664-9100
Website: www.montegobaywendover.com

Toll-Free Number: (877) 666-8346
Reservation Number: (800) 537-0207
Rooms: 437 Price Range: $60-$140
Suites: 52 Price Range: $80-$205
Restaurants: 2 (1 open 24 hours)
Buffets: B-$8.95 L-$12.95
         Brunch-$14.95 (Sat/Sun)
         D-$15.95/$22.95 (Fri)/$18.95 (Sat)
Casino Size: 49,400 Square Feet
Other Games: SB, RB, P, PGP, TCP
Overnight RV Parking: Free/RV Dump: No
Senior Discount: $2 buffet discount if 55+
Special Features: Connected by sky bridge to Wendover Nugget. Liquor Store. Golf packages.

Peppermill Inn & Casino
680 Wendover Boulevard
W. Wendover, Nevada 89883
(775) 664-2255
Website: www.peppermillwendover.com

Reservation Number: (800) 648-9660
Rooms: 302 Price Range: $55-$120
Suites: 42 Price Range: $75-$225
Restaurants: 2 (1 open 24 hours)
Buffets: B-$8.95 L-$12.95
         Brunch-$14.95 (Sat/Sun)
         D-$15.95/$22.95 (Fri)/$18.95 (Sat)
Casino Size: 30,577 Square Feet
Other Games: PGP, LIR, TCP, K
Overnight RV Parking: Free/RV Dump: No
Senior Discount: $2 buffet discount if 55+

Rainbow Hotel Casino
1045 Wendover Boulevard
W. Wendover, Nevada 89883
(775) 664-4000
Website: www.rainbowwendover.com

Toll-Free Number: (800) 217-0049
Rooms: 379 Price Range: $55-$120
Suites: 50 Price Range: $75-$175
Restaurants: 3 (1 open 24 hours)
Buffets: B-$8.95 L-$12.95 B
         Brunch-$14.95 (Sat/Sun)
         D-$15.95/$22.95 (Fri)/$18.95 (Sat)
Casino Size: 51,060 Square Feet
Other Games: SB, RB, P, PGP, LIR, TCP
Overnight RV Parking: Free/RV Dump: No
Senior Discount: $2 buffet discount if 55+

Red Garter Hotel & Casino
P.O. Box 2399
W. Wendover, Nevada 89883
(775) 664-3315
Website: www.redgartercasino.com

Toll-Free Number: (800) 982-2111
Rooms: 46 Price Range: $22-$60
Restaurants: 1 (open 24 hours)
Buffets: D-$7.95 (Sun)
Casino Size: 30,000 Square Feet
Other Games: SB, TCP
Overnight RV Parking: No

Wendover Nugget Hotel & Casino
101 Wendover Boulevard
W. Wendover, Nevada 89883
(775) 664-2221
Website: www.wendovernugget.com

Toll-Free Number: (800) 848-7300
Rooms: 500 Price Range: $45-$109
Suites: 60 Price Range: $60-$200
Restaurants: 3 (1 open 24 hours)
Buffets: Brunch-$13.95 (Sat/Sun) L-$11.95
    D-$14.95/$21.95 (Fri)/$18.95 (Sat)
Casino Size: 40,089 Square Feet
Other Games: SB, RB, P, TCP, B6, K
Overnight RV Parking: Free/RV Dump: No
Senior Discount: Room/food discounts if 55+
Special Features: 56-space RV park ($17 per
night). Sky bridge to Montego Bay.

Winners Hotel/Casino
185 W. Winnemucca Boulevard
Winnemucca, Nevada 89445
(775) 623-2511
Website: www.winnerscasino.com

Reservation Number: (800) 648-4770
Rooms: 123 Price Range: $35-$60
Suites: 3 Price Range: $69-$89
Restaurants: 2 (1 open 24 hours)
Buffets: B-$6.49 (Sat/Sun) D-$14.95 (Fri)
Casino Size: 11,240 Square Feet
Other Games: SB, RB, P, TCP
Overnight RV Parking: Free/ Dump: No
Senior Discount: Room discount if 55+
Special Features: Courtesy car service. Gift
shop. Video arcade.

Winnemucca

Map Location: **#29** (164 miles N.E. of Reno
on I-80)

Model T Hotel/Casino/RV Park
1130 W. Winnemucca Blvd.
Winnemucca, Nevada 89446
(775) 623-2588
Website: www.modelt.com

Reservation Number: (800) 645-5658
Rooms: 75 Price Range: $40-$85
Restaurants: 4 (1 open 24 hours)
Casino Size: 9,482 Square Feet
Other Games: SB, RB, No craps or roulette
Overnight RV Parking: Free/RV Dump: No
Special Features: Hotel is Quality Inn. 58-
space RV park ($22 per night). Taco Bell. Ice
cream shop. Gourmet coffee shop.

Red Lion Inn & Casino
741 W. Winnemucca Boulevard
Winnemucca, Nevada 89445
(775) 623-2565
Website: www.redlionwinn.com

Reservation Number: (800) 633-6435
Rooms: 100 Price Range: $89-$139
Suites: 7 Price Range: $119-$170
Restaurants: 1 (open 24 hours)
Casino Size: 20,350 Square Feet
Other Games: SB, RB, No craps or roulette
Overnight RV Parking: No

Yerington

Map Location: **#30** (60 miles S.E. of Reno
on Hwy. Alt. 95)

Casino West
11 N. Main Street
Yerington, Nevada 89447
(775) 463-2481
Website: www.casino-west.net

Reservation Number: (800) 227-4661
Rooms: 49 Price Range: $46-$50
Suites: 29 Price Range: $55-59
Restaurants: 1 (open 24 hours)
Buffets: D- $12.95 (Fri)/$7.50 (Sat-Sun)
Casino Size: 4,950 Square Feet
Other Games: P, No craps or roulette
Overnight RV Parking: Must use RV park
Senior Discount: Room discounts if 55+
Special Features: 5-space RV park ($7 per
night). Movie theater. 12-lane bowling alley.

Indian Casino

Avi Resort & Casino
10000 Aha Macav Parkway
Laughlin, Nevada 89029
(702) 535-5555
Website: www.avicasino.com
Map Location: **#2**

Toll-Free Number: (800) AVI-2-WIN
Rooms: 426 Price Range: $42-$65
Suites: 29 Price Range: $120-$175
Restaurants: 3 (1 open 24 hours)
Buffets: B-$6.99/$7.99 (Sat/Sun) L-$7.49
      D-$10.99/$13.49 (Fri)/$11.49 (Sat)
Casino Size: 25,000 Square Feet
Other Games: SB, RB, P, TCP, LIR, K, BG
Overnight RV Parking: Free/RV Dump: No
Special Features: 260-space RV park ($19
May-Oct/$23 Nov-April). On Colorado River
with boat dock, launch and private beach.
Baskin-Robbins. Subway. 8-screen cinema.
Smoke shop. Kid's Quest childcare center.

NEW JERSEY

Map Location: **#1** (on the Atlantic Ocean in southeast NJ, 130 miles south of New York City and 60 miles southeast of Philadelphia)

Once a major tourist destination that was world-famous for its steel pier and boardwalk, Atlantic City gradually fell into decline and casino gambling was seen as its salvation when voters approved it there in 1976.

The first casino (Resorts International) opened to "standing-room-only" crowds in 1978. Since then 11 more casinos have opened and all but three are located along the boardwalk. Those three, Borgata, Harrah's and Trump Marina, are located in the Marina section.

In mid-1997 Bally's Wild Wild West casino (Atlantic City's first themed casino) opened, but due to a quirk in the licensing law, this casino is only considered part of Bally's and not a separate casino. Additionally, in late 2002, the Claridge Casino Hotel formally joined Bally's as "The Claridge Tower" and it is no longer considered a separate casino.

If you fly into Atlantic City it's a 14-mile drive from the airport to the casinos and there are only two choices of transportation. The taxi charges are regulated and it's a flat $27 to any casino. That price include all tolls and luggage.

The other option is a rental car and the only three rental car companies at the airport are Hertz, Avis and Budget. Rental rates are in the range of $60-$70 per day but you can usually get a discount on those rates by booking online or using a coupon. In addition to the rental cost there's about another 22% in taxes and fees.

There is a charge of $3 to $5 per 24 hours (6 a.m. to 6 a.m.) for parking in a garage at any casino in Atlantic City. Whenever you pay the fee you are issued a receipt which you can then use to park for free at *one* other casino. When you leave the second garage you have to give them the receipt from the first garage.

For transportation among the casinos there are two options, besides taxis. A 24-hour jitney service makes stops along Pacific Avenue and will drop you off by any casino including those

in the Marina. The jitneys are very efficient and you will probably never have a wait of more than five minutes for one to arrive.

The cost for one ride is $2.00 per person. Frequent rider tickets are offered for $17.50 per 10 rides and senior citizens, 65 or older, can buy 10 rides for $6. For jitney information call (877) 92-TRAIN.

On the Atlantic City Boardwalk itself, there are the famous rolling chairs. These are covered two-seater wicker chairs on wheels that are pushed by an attendant as he walks you to your destination. The posted rates are the same for all chairs, but some of the drivers are willing negotiate a better price, The charges are: $5 for up to five blocks; $10 for six to 12 blocks; $15 for 13 to 21 blocks; and $20 for 22 to 32 blocks. For more information on rolling chairs call (609) 347-7500 or (609) 344-1702.

ATLANTIC CITY

LEGEND

1 Atlantic City Hilton
2 Bally's Atlantic City
3 Borgata
4 Caesars
5 Claridge
6 Harrah's
7 Resorts
8 Showboat
9 Tropicana
10 Trump Marina
11 Trump Plaza
12 Trump Taj Mahal
13 Wild Wild West

Following is information from the New Jersey Casino Control Commission regarding average slot payout percentages for the 12-month period from July 1, 2006 through June 30, 2007:

CASINO	PAYBACK %
Borgata	92.6
Trump Plaza	92.0
Trump Taj Mahal	91.8
Harrah's	91.8
Harrah's	91.8
A.C. Hilton	91.7
Trump Marina	91.7
Tropicana	91.5
Resorts	91.4
Bally's A.C.	91.0
Caesars	91.0
Showboat	90.6

These figures reflect the total percentages returned by each casino for all of their electronic machines which includes slot machines, video poker, etc.

All Atlantic City casinos are open 24 hours and, unless otherwise noted, the games offered at every casino are: slots, video poker, craps, blackjack, Spanish 21, roulette, baccarat, mini-baccarat, poker, Caribbean stud poker, three card poker, four card poker, Texas hold'em bonus poker, let it ride, pai gow tiles and pai gow poker. Additional games offered include: sic bo (SB), keno (K), off-track betting (OTB), and big six wheel (B6). The minimum gambling age is 21.

For more information on visiting New Jersey you can contact the state's Travel & Tourism Department at (800) 537-7397 or go to: www.visitnj.com.

For information only on Atlantic City call (800) VISIT-NJ or go to their web site at: www.atlanticcitynj.com.

Atlantic City Hilton Casino Resort
Boston Avenue & The Boardwalk
Atlantic City, New Jersey 08401
(609) 347-7111
Website: www.hiltonac.com

Reservation Number: (800) 257-8677
Rooms: 604 Price Range: $150-$365
Suites: 200 Price Range: $220-$600
Restaurants: 7   Valet Parking: $3
Buffets: L/D-$18.75
Casino Size: 69,422 Square Feet
Other Games: No off-track betting
Casino Marketing: (800) 843-4726
Special Features: 1,200-seat theater. Unisex salon. Spa. Beach bar.

Bally's Atlantic City
Park Place and the Boardwalk
Atlantic City, New Jersey 08401
(609) 340-2000
Website: www.ballysac.com

Toll-Free Number: (800) 772-7777
Reservation Number: (800) 225-5977
Rooms: 1,611 Price Range: $99-$389
Suites: 146 Price Range: $210-$620
Restaurants: 18   Valet Parking: $5
Buffets (Bally's): B-$11.99 (Sat/Sun)
           L/D-$13.99/$17.99 (Sat/Sun)
Buffets (W.W. West): L-$15.99 D-$20.99
Casino Size 225,940 Square Feet
Other Games: SB, B6, K
Special Features: Southern walkway connects to Wild Wild West casino. Northern walkway connects to Claridge casino and hotel.

Borgata Hotel Casino And Spa
One Borgata Way
Atlantic City, NJ 08401
(609) 317-1000
Website: www.theborgata.com

Toll-Free Number: (866) 692-6742
Rooms: 1,600 Prices Range: $169-$429
Suites: 400 Price Range: $299-$1,000
Restaurants: 11   Valet Parking: $5
Buffets: B-$13.95/$21.95 (Sun)
           L-$17.95 D-$27.95
Casino Size: 160,414 Square Feet
Other Games: B6
Special Features: 3,700-seat events center. 1,000-seat music theater. Comedy club. Health spa. Barbershop. Hair and nail salon. New 800-room hotel to open by early 2008.

The Best Places To Play in Atlantic City

Blackjack: Some Atlantic City casinos offer a single-deck blackjack game. The problem is that these single-deck games only pay 6-to-5 when you get a blackjack (rather than the standard 7.5-to-5) and this raises the casino advantage in this game to 1.58%, Don't play this game!

Other than that single-deck variation, the blackjack games offered at Atlantic City casinos are pretty much all the same: eight-deck shoe games with double down on any first two cards, dealer stands on soft 17, pairs can be split up to three times and doubling after splitting is allowed. This works out to a casino edge of .44% against a player using perfect basic strategy and every casino in Atlantic City, except for Baorgata, offers this game. Borgata only offers six-deck games in their casino(except for Spanish 21) and this results in a slightly lower mathematical advantage of .42%. The Tropicana has a rule variation on the above game because they don't allow resplitting of pairs and that brings the house advantage up to .48%.

If you're willing to make higher minimum bets you can find slightly better games. Most casinos offer six-deck games with minimum bets of $25, $50 or $100 per hand (Borgata has $10 minimums during the day). A six-deck game, with the standard Atlantic City rules in effect, lowers the casino edge from .44% to .42% and it is offered at every casino in the city, except for Wild Wild West and Trump Marina which actually offers the city's best six-deck game. The Marina adds late surrender to the above ruleswhihc brings their advantage down to .34%. The minimum bet is $50.

Roulette: When choosing roulette games it's usually best to play in a casino offering a single-zero wheel because the casino advantage is 2.70% versus a double-zero wheel which has a 5.26% advantage. However, that situation is somewhat different in Atlantic City because of certain gaming regulations.

On double-zero wheels the casinos can only take one-half of a wager on even-money bets (odd/even, red/black, 1-18/19-36) when zero or double-zero is the winning number. This lowers the casino edge on these particular bets to 2.63%, while the edge on all other bets remains at 5.26%. This rule is not in effect on single-zero wheels and virtually all bets on that game have a 2.70% house edge.

There are eight casinos that have single-zero roulette wheels: Harrah's, Trump Marina, Bally's, Borgata, Trump Taj Mahal, Hilton, Tropicana and Caesars. You should be aware, however, that almost all of these games are only open on weekends (or by special request) and they require $25 minimum bets ($50 at Plaza, $100 at Taj Mahal).

Craps: Resorts, Taj Mahal, Tropicana, Trump Marina and the Hilton all offer five times odds on all of their crap games ($10 minimum). The Claridge offers five times odds on some, but not all, of their games.

Video Poker: The best game to be found in Atlantic City is full-pay Pick 'em Poker (99.15 percent) at Bally's and also found in quarters on the first level of the Claridge section. All other Pick 'em games in Atlantic City are short pay. Avoid them.

Quarter Games – The best widely available game in Atlantic City is 9/6 Jacks or Better (99.54 percent). The game is found most abundantly at Trump Plaza, (mostly in the smoking section just up the escalator, but a couple of banks in non-smoking near the parking garage end), Showboat (the non-smoking House of Blues section near the Boardwalk and about half a dozen in the smoking area) and the Borgata (at the B-bar for smokers and scattered around the casino for non-smokers). The Borgata also has several Multi Strike machines with 9/6 Jacks located near the entrance to the buffet. Caesars also has a bank of slow-moving progressive slant-tops near the Toga bar and a bank of uprights near the Boardwalk entrance. You can find a few full-pay Jacks or Better machines at Harrah's and Bally's and one at Trump Marina. But be forewarned, most casinos have recently scaled back the comps and cashback they offer to people who primarily play this game. The Tropicana has four full-pay Double Joker machines (look for Sigma machines, not IGT), but only when you play 10 coins. If you play less than 10 coins then the machine only pays 500 per coin on the royal rather than 800.

The best place for 8/5 Bonus Poker (99.16 percent) is Resorts, scattered in multi-game machines throughout the casino. For more action, Bally's has three banks of 8/5 Bonus triple-play progressives, two of them in the Park Place casino and one in the Wild, Wild West. The Hilton also has one bank of 13 triple-play progressives.

Double-Bonus players will want to head to the Showboat or Trump Plaza. There are plentiful games of 9/7 Aces and Faces Double Bonus (99.2 percent) in multi-game machines at the Showboat. Trump Plaza has lots of 9/7 Double Bonus (99.11 percent), also in multi-game machines. For an interesting twist, look for the quarter Double Bonus-Double Jackpot (100.09 percent) games found in Showboat and Harrah's. It is a 9-6-5 game with a whopping 8,000 coins for the royal flush. They'll be in Bally's Game Makers with the green face glass.

Dollar Games- The best play for dollar players is at Bally's, with dollar progressive 9/6 Jacks or Better and 8/5 Bonus Poker games in its Park Place poker section. Every other casino except for the Hilton has 9/6 Jacks or Better in dollars, with the largest number at the Borgata. Look in or near the high-limit area, except at the Tropicana, where the full-pay dollar machines are in a walkway between the two main playing areas.

Bally's has a full-pay triple play Double Joker game in its Gold Room along with triple play 9/6.Trump Plaza offers plenty of 9/7 Double Bonus in dollars, and you can find dollar 9/7 Aces and Faces Double Bonus at the Showboat. If you want to play 9/6 Jacks or Better at the $5 or higher level, it's in every high-limit slot room in town.

Caesars Atlantic City
2100 Pacific Avenue
Atlantic City, New Jersey 08401
(609) 348-4411
Website: www.caesarsac.com

Toll-Free Number: (800) 443-0104
Reservation Number: (800) 524-2867
Rooms: 1,479 Price Range: $125-$450
Suites: 198 Price Range: $195-$800
Restaurants: 12 Valet Park: $10/$20 (Fri-Sun)
Buffets: B-$12.99/$17.99 (Sat/Sun)
          L-$17.99/$24.99 (Fri-Sun)
          D-$21.99/$24.99 (Fri-Sun)
Casino Size: 140,011 Square Feet
Casino Marketing: (800) 367-3767
Other Games: SB, B6, K
Special Features: Roman themed hotel and casino. Health spa. Shopping arcade. Unisex beauty salon.

Harrah's Casino Hotel
777 Harrah's Boulevard
Atlantic City, New Jersey 08401
(609) 441-5000
Website: www.harrahs.com

Reservation Number: (800) 2-HARRAH
Rooms: 1,310 Price Range: $79-$359
Suites: 316 Price Range: Casino Use Only
Restaurants: 8 Valet Parking: $5
Buffets: B-$14.99 (Sat/Sun)
          D-$21.99/$26.99 (Fri-Sun)
Casino Size: 147,077 Square Feet
Other Games: K, No off-track betting
·   No pai gow tiles
Special Features: 65-slip marina. Beauty salon. Miniature golf course (in season).

Resorts Atlantic City
1133 Boardwalk
Atlantic City, New Jersey 08401
(609) 344-6000
Website: www.resortsac.com

Toll-Free Number: (800) 336-6378
Reservation Number: (800) 334-6378
Rooms: 879 Price Range: $119-$375
Suites: 79 Price Range: $250-$1,000
Restaurants: 10 Valet Park: $4/$10 (Fri-Sun)
Buffets: L/D-$18.75
Casino Size: 100,138 Square Feet
Casino Marketing: (800) 438-7424
Special Features: Indoor/outdoor pools. Health spa. 1,350-seat theater. Comedy club. Beachfront bar. $3 buffet discount for slot club members.

Showboat Casino-Hotel
801 Boardwalk
Atlantic City, New Jersey 08401
(609) 343-4000
Website: www.harrahs.com

Reservation Number: (800) 621-0200
Rooms: 1,181 Price Range: $99-$249
Suites: 128 Price Range: Casino Use Only
Restaurants: 7 Valet Park: $5/$10 (Fri-Sun)
Buffets: L-$17.99 D-$21.99
Casino Size: 140,264 Square Feet
Other Games: B6
Special Features: New Orleans-themed casino.

Tropicana Casino & Resort
Brighton Avenue and the Boardwalk
Atlantic City, New Jersey 08401
(609) 340-4000
Website: www.tropicana.net

Toll-Free Number: (800) THE-TROP
Reservation Number: (800) 338-5553
Rooms: 1,426 Price Range: $99-$300
Suites: 340 Price Range: $155-$675
Restaurants: 16 Valet Park: $5/$10 (Fri-Sun)
Buffets: B-$15.99 L/D-$21.99
Casino Size: 147,248 Square Feet
Other Games: B6
Special Features: Features "The Quarter," a dining/entertainment complex with 30 stores.

Trump Marina Hotel Casino
Huron Avenue & Brigantine Boulevard
Atlantic City, New Jersey 08401
(609) 441-2000
Website: www.trumpmarina.com

Reservation Number: (800) 365-8786
Toll-Free Number (800) 777-1177
Rooms: 568 Price Range: $99-$359
Suites: 160 Price Range: $175-$650
Restaurants: 7 Valet Parking: $5
Buffets: B-$11.99 L/D-$17.99
Casino Size: 79,676 Square Feet
Other Games: No poker
Casino Marketing: (800) 777-8477
Special Features: Adjacent to marina with 640 slips. 3-acre recreation deck with pools, jogging track, tennis courts, miniature golf course and health club. 1,500-seat event center.

Trump Plaza Hotel and Casino
The Boardwalk at Mississippi Avenue
Atlantic City, New Jersey 08401
(609) 441-6000
Website: www.trumpplaza.com

Reservation Number: (800) 677-7378
Rooms: 762 Price Range: $135-$425
Suites: 142 Price Range: $250-$575
Restaurants: 9 Valet Parking: $5
Buffets: L/D-$15.95/$18.95 (Fri-Sun)
Casino Size: 96,656 Square Feet
Other Games: SB, B6, No poker
        No off-track betting
Casino Marketing: (800) 677-0711
Special Features: Health spa. Indoor pool. Rainforest Cafe. Beach bar.

Trump Taj Mahal Casino Resort
1000 Boardwalk at Virginia Avenue
Atlantic City, New Jersey 08401
(609) 449-1000
Website: www.trumptaj.com

Reservation Number: (800) 825-8888
Rooms: 1,013 Price Range: $150-$450
Suites: 237 Price Range: $350-$600
Restaurants: 11 Valet Parking: $5
Buffets: B-$10.95 L/$17.95 D-$18.95
Casino Size: 161,245 Square Feet
Casino Marketing: (800) 234-5678
Other Games: SB, B6, K
Special Features: Health spa. Hard Rock cafe. 5,000-seat event center. 1,400-seat showroom.

NEW MEXICO

New Mexico's Indian casinos offer an assortment of table games and electronic gaming machines. Additionally, slot machines are allowed at the state's racetracks as well as at about 40 various fraternal and veterans clubs.

New Mexico gaming regulations require that electronic machines at racetracks and fraternal/veterans organizations return a minimum of 80% to a maximum of 96%.

New Mexico's Indian tribes do not make their slot machine payback percentages a matter of public record but the terms of the compact between the state and the tribes require all electronic gaming machines to return a minimum of 80%.

Unless otherwise noted, all New Mexico Indian casinos are open 24 hours and offer: blackjack, craps, roulette, video slots and video poker. Some casinos also offer: Spanish 21 (S21), mini-baccarat (MB), poker (P), pai gow poker (PGP), three card poker (TCP), four card poker (FCP), Caribbean stud poker (CSP), let it ride (LIR), casino war (CW), big 6 wheel (B6), keno (K), bingo (BG) and off track betting (OTB). The minimum gambling age is 21 for the casinos and 18 for bingo or pari-mutuel betting.

Please note that all New Mexico casinos are prohibited from serving alcohol on the casino floor. If a casino serves alcohol it can only be consumed at the bar and not in the casino itself.

For information on visiting New Mexico call the state's tourism department at (800) 733-6396 or go to: www.newmexico.org.

Apache Nugget Casino
PO Box 650
Dulce, New Mexico 87528
(505) 289-2486
Website: www.apachenugget.com
Map: **#15** (on Jicarilla reservation at intersection of Hwys 550 and 537 near Cuba)

Restaurants: 1 Liquor: No
Other Games: Only gaming machines
Hours: 9am-2am/24 Hours (Fri/Sat)
Casino Size: 12,000 Square Feet
Overnight RV Parking: Free/RV Dump: No

Best Western Jicarilla Inn and Casino
U.S. Highway 64
Dulce, New Mexico 87529
(505) 759-3663
Website: www.apachenugget.com
Map: **#12** (95 miles N.W. of Santa Fe)

Room Reservations: (800) 428-2627
Rooms: 43 Price Range: $75-$95
Restaurants: 1 Liquor: Yes
Hours: 9am-1am/2am (Fri/Sat)/12am (Sun)

Big Rock Casino Bowl
419 N. Riverside Drive
Espanola, New Mexico 87532
(505) 747-3100
Website: www.bigrockcasino.com
Map: **#7** (25 miles N. of Santa Fe)

Toll-Free Number: (866) 244-7625
Restaurants: 2 Liquor: Yes
Hours: 8am-4am/24 Hours (Fri/Sat)
Overnight RV Parking: Free/RV Dump: No
Special Features: 24-lane bowling center. $1.99 breakfast special Sat/Sun if slot club member.

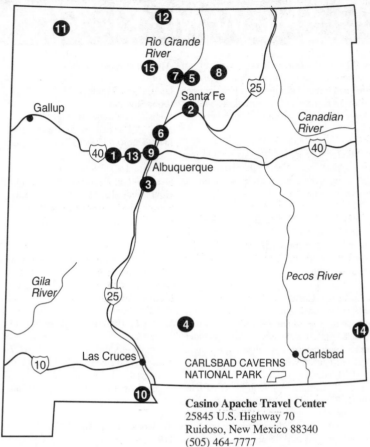

Camel Rock Casino
17486-A Highway 84/285
Santa Fe, New Mexico 87504
(505) 984-8414
Website: www.camelrockcasino.com
Map: **#2**

Toll-Free Number: (800) GO-CAMEL
Restaurants: 1   Liquor: No
Buffets: Brunch- $10.00 (Sun)
       B-$3.00 (Mon-Wed)
       L-$9.00 D-$9.00/$15.00 (Fri/Sun)
Hours: 8am-4am/24 Hours (Thurs-Sat)
Casino Size: 60,000 Square Feet
Other Games: TCP, No craps
Overnight RV Parking: Free/RV Dump: No
Senior Discount: Various on Thursday if 55+

Casino Apache Travel Center
25845 U.S. Highway 70
Ruidoso, New Mexico 88340
(505) 464-7777
Map: **#4** (90 miles N.E. of Las Cruces)

Restaurants: 1 Liquor: Yes
Hours: 8am-4am daily
Casino Size: 10,000 Square Feet
Other Games: No craps
Overnight RV Parking: Free/RV Dump: No
Special Features: Free shuttle service to Inn
of the Mountain Gods Casino. Truck stop.
Discount smoke shop.

Casino Express
14500 Central Avenue
Albuquerque, New Mexico 87120
(505) 552-7777
Map: **#3** (I-40 at exit 140)

Toll-Free Number: (866) 352-7866
Hours: 8am-4am/24 Hours (Thu-Sat)
Other Games: Only gaming machines
Overnight RV Parking: Free/RV Dump: No

Cities of Gold Casino Hotel
10-B Cities of Gold Road
Santa Fe, New Mexico 87501
(505) 455-3313
Website: www.citiesofgold.com
Map: **#2** (Intersection of Hwys 84/285/502)

Toll-Free Number: (800) 455-3313
Room Reservations: (877) 455-0515
Rooms: 122 Price Range: $65-$109
Suites: 2 Price Range: $136
Restaurants: 3 Liquor: Yes
Buffets: B-$5.00 L-$7.00 D-$8.50/$13.99 (Sun)
Hours: 8am-4am/24 hours (Fri/Sat)
Casino Size: 40,000 Square Feet
Other Games: P, BG
Overnight RV Parking: Free/RV Dump: No
Special Features: They also operate the Cities of Gold Sports Bar which is one block away from main casino. Liquor is served there but they only have slots and OTB - no table games. 27-hole golf course.

Dancing Eagle Casino and RV Park
Interstate 40, Exit 108
Casa Blanca, New Mexico 87007
(505) 552-1111
Website: www.dancingeaglecasino.com
Map: **#1** (40 miles W. of Albuquerque)

Toll-Free Number: (877) 440-9969
Restaurants: 1 Liquor: No
Hours: 8am-4am/24 Hours (Thu-Sun)
Casino Size: 21,266 Square Feet
Other Games: TCP, No craps
Overnight RV Parking: Free/RV Dump: No
Special Features: Located on I-40 at exit 108. Truck stop. 35-space RV park ($20 per night/ $10 for slot club members).

Inn of the Mountain Gods Resort & Casino
277 Carrizo Canyon Road
Mescalero, New Mexico 88340
(505) 464-7777
Website: www.innofthemountaingods.com
Map: **#4** (90 miles N.E. of Las Cruces)

Toll-Free Number: (800) 545-9011
Rooms: 250 Price Range: $199-$269
Suites: 23 Price Range: $299-$399
Restaurants: 4 Liquor: Yes
Buffets: Brunch-$15.50 (Sat/Sun) B-$9.50
 L-$12.00 D-$16.50/$24.00 (Wed)/$18.50 (Fri/Sat)
Hours: 8am-4am/24 Hours (Fri/Sat)
Casino Size: 38,000 Square Feet

Other Games: S21, MB, P, PGP, LIR, TCP, FCP, CW
Overnight RV Parking: Free/RV Dump: No
Senior Discount: 20% off buffet if 62+
Special Features: 18-hole golf course.

Isleta Casino Resort
11000 Broadway S.E.
Albuquerque, New Mexico 87105
(505) 724-3800
Website: www.isletacasinoresort.com
Map: **#3**

Toll-Free Number: (800) 843-5156
Restaurants: 3 Liquor: Yes
Buffets: B-$7.95 (Sat/Sun) L-$6.95/$7.95 (Fri/ Sat)/$8.95 (Sun) D-$8.95/$16.95 (Fri)/$14.95 (Sat)/$12.95 (Sun)
Hours: 8am-4am/24 Hours (Thu-Sun)
Casino Size: 30,000 Square Feet
Other Games: P, CSP, LIR, TCP, BG
Overnight RV Parking: Free/RV Dump: No
Special Features: Convenience store. Gas station. Three nine-hole golf courses. Alcohol is only served at sports bar in casino.

Ohkay Casino Resort
P.O. Box 1270
San Juan Pueblo, New Mexico 87566
(505) 747-1668
Map: **#5** (24 miles N. of Santa Fe)

Toll-Free Number: (800) PLAY-AT-OK
Room Reservation (877) 829-2865
Rooms: 101 Price Range: $79-$97
Suites: 24 Price Range: $109-$127
Restaurants: 2 Liquor: Yes
Buffets: B-$6.99 (Sat/Sun) L-$7.99
 D-$14.99 (Fri)/$10.99 (Sat)
Hours: 8am-4am/24 hrs (Fri-Sat)
Casino Size: 30,000 Square Feet
Overnight RV Parking: Free/RV Dump: No
Special Features: Hotel is Best Western. Sporting clays club.

Palace West Casino
State Road 45
Albuquerque, New Mexico 87105
(505) 869-4102
Web: www.isletacasinoresort.com/palace.html
Map: **#3** (at Coors & Isleta Road)

Hours: 8am-Midnight Daily
Other Games: Only gaming machines
Overnight RV Parking: Free/RV Dump: No
Special Features: Completely nonsmoking.

Route 66 Casino
14500 Central Avenue
Albuquerque, New Mexico 87121
(505) 352-7866
Website: www.rt66casino.com
Map: **#13** (20 miles W. of Albuquerque)

Toll-Free Number: (866) 352-7866
Restaurants: 2 Liquor: No
Buffets: L-$7.95 D-$11.95/$15.95 (Thu/Fri)
Hours: 8am-4am/24 Hours (Fri-Sun)
Other Games: P, PGP, LIR, TCP, BG
Overnight RV Parking: Free/RV Dump: No
Special Features: Johnny Rockets restaurant.
New 154-room hotel expected to open in
December 2007.

San Felipe Casino Hollywood
25 Hagan Road
Algodones, New Mexico 87001
(505) 867-6700
Website: www.sanfelipecasino.com
Map: **#6** (17 miles N. of Albuquerque)

Toll-Free Number: (877) 529-2946
Restaurants: 1 Liquor: No
Buffets: B-$4.25 L-$6.25 D-$7.50
Hours: 8am-4am/24 Hours (Fri-Sat)
Overnight RV Parking: Must use RV park
Special Features: 100-space RV park ($10 per
night). Adjacent to Hollywood Hills
Speedway.

Sandia Resort & Casino
30 Rainbow Road NE
Albuquerque, New Mexico 87113
(505) 796-7500
Website: www.sandiacasino.com
Map: **#9**

Toll-Free Number: (800) 526-9366
Rooms: 198 Price Range: $139-$189
Suites: 30 Price Range: $269-$339
Restaurants: 4 Liquor: Yes
Buffets: B-$6.95 L-$8.95/$12.95 (Sun)
        D-$10.95/$23.95 (Fri)/$14.95 (Sat)
Hours: 8am-4am/24 Hours (Fri-Sun)
Casino Size: 65,000 Square feet
Other Games: P, CSP, LIR, TCP, PGP, BG, K, MB
Overnight RV Parking: Free/RV Dump: No
Special Features: 4,200-seat theater. 18-hole
golf course. Smoke-free slot room.

Santa Ana Star Casino
54 Jemez Dam Canyon Road
Bernalillo, New Mexico 87004
(505) 867-0000
Website: www.santaanastar.com
Map: **#6** (17 miles N. of Albuquerque)

Restaurants: 5 Liquor: No
Buffets: B-$6.95 L-$8.95/$10.95 (Sun)
        D-$11.95/$12.95 (Sat)/$19.95 (Sun)
Hours: 8am-4am/24 Hours (Thurs-Sat)
Casino Size: 19,000 Square Feet
Other Games: P, LIR, TCP, FCP
Overnight RV Parking: Free/RV Dump: No
Senior Discount: Various Mondays if 50+
Special Features: 36-lane bowling alley. 18-
hole golf course. Spa. Smoke shop. 3,000-seat
event center.

Sky City Casino Hotel
P.O. Box 519
San Fidel, New Mexico 87049
(505) 552-6017
Website: www.skycitycasino.com
Map: **#1** (50 miles W. of Albuquerque)

Toll-Free Number: (888) 759-2489
Rooms: 132 Price Range: $69-$99
Suites: 15 Price Range: $110-$130
Restaurants: 1 Liquor: No
Buffets: B-$7.95 L-$8.95
        D-$10.95/$15.95 (Fri)
Hours: 8am-4am/24 Hours (Fri/Sat)
Casino Size: 30,000 Square Feet
Other Games: TCP, BG
Overnight RV Parking: Free/RV Dump: No

Taos Mountain Casino
P.O. Box 1477
Taos, New Mexico 87571
(505) 758-4460
Website: www.taosmountaincasino.com
Map: **#8** (50 miles N.E. of Santa Fe)

Toll-Free Number: (888) 946-8267
Restaurants: 1 Deli   Liquor: No
Hours: 8am-1am/2am (Thu-Sun)
Other Games: No Roulette, TCP
Overnight RV Parking: No
Special Features: Entire casino is nonsmoking.

Pari-Mutuels

The Downs Racetrack and Casino at Albuquerque
P.O. Box 8510
Albuquerque, New Mexico 87198
(505) 266-5555
Website: www.abqdowns.com
Map: **#9**

Restaurants: 1
Buffets: L-$7.95
Hours: 10am-1am/2am (Fri/Sat)
Other Games: Only gaming machines
Overnight RV Parking: No
Senior Discount: $2 off buffets if 55+
Special Features: Live horse racing April through early June and during New Mexico State Fair in September. Daily simulcasting of horse racing.

Ruidoso Downs & Billy The Kid Casino
1461 Highway 70 West
Ruidoso Downs, New Mexico 88346
(505) 378-4431
Website: www.ruidosodownsracing.com
Map: **#4** (90 miles N.E. of Las Cruces)

Restaurants: 2
Hours: 10am-Midnight/1am (Fri/Sat)
Other Games: Only gaming machines
Overnight RV Parking: No
Senior Discount: Various Wed 2pm-9pm if 55+
Special Features: Live horse racing (Thu-Sun) late May through early September. Daily simulcasting of horse racing.

Sunland Park Racetrack & Casino
1200 Futurity Drive
Sunland Park, New Mexico 88063
(505) 874-5200
Website: www.sunland-park.com
Map: **#10** (5 miles W. of El Paso, TX)

Restaurants: 5
Buffets: L-$8.95 D-$8.95/$15.95 (Fri)
Hours: 9:30am-12:30am/2am (Fri/Sat)
Other Games: Only gaming machines
Overnight RV Parking: Free/$5 w/hookups
Senior Discount: $1 off lunch buffet and special coupon book if 55+
Special Features: Live thoroughbred and quarter-horse racing November through April. Daily simulcasting of horse racing.

SunRay Park and Casino
#39 Road 5568
Farmington, New Mexico 87401
(505) 566-1200
Website: www.sunraygaming.com
Map: **#11** (150 miles N.W. of Santa Fe)

Restaurants: 1
Hours: 11am-2am/3am (Thu)/4am (Fri)
10-am-4am (Sat)/10am-2am (Sun)
Other Games: Only gaming machines
Overnight RV Parking: No
Special Features: Live horse racing (Thu-Sun) from mid-June through early September. Daily simulcasting of horse racing.

Zia Park Race Track & Black Gold Casino
3901 W. Millen Drive
Hobbs, New Mexico 88240
(505) 492-7000
Website: www.blackgoldcasino.net
Map: **#14** (70 miles N.E. of Carlsbad)

Toll-Free Number: 888-942-7275
Restaurants: 3
Buffets: Brunch-$11.95 (Sun) L-$9.95
D-$11.95/$16.95 (Fri)/$14.95 (Sat)
Hours: 9am-12:30am/2am (Fri)/ 2:30am (Sat)
Other Games: Only gaming machines
Overnight RV Parking: Free/RV Dump: No
Special Features: Live horse racing mid-September through early December. Daily simulcasting of horse racing.

NEW YORK

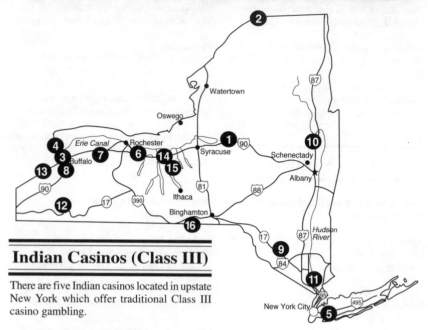

Indian Casinos (Class III)

There are five Indian casinos located in upstate New York which offer traditional Class III casino gambling.

The terms of the compact between the tribes and the state allow table games and slot machines, including video keno and video poker. These machines do not pay out in cash. Instead, they print out a receipt which must be exchanged for cash. All casinos also offer a cashless system whereby you have to go to a cashier cage, or a kiosk, get a "smart" card and deposit money to that card's account. The machines will then deduct losses from, or credit wins to, your account.

All of these casinos are open 24 hours and offer the following games: blackjack, craps, roulette and Caribbean stud poker. Some casinos also offer: Spanish 21 (S21), baccarat (B), mini-baccarat (MB), big six wheel (B6), keno (K), poker (P), pai gow poker (PGP), let it ride (LIR), three-card poker (TCP) and four-card poker (FCP).

The minimum gambling age is 21 at the three Seneca casinos and 18 at the other two casinos. For more information on visiting New York call the state's travel information center at (800) 225-5697 or go to: www.iloveny.com.

Akwesasne Mohawk Casino
Route 37, Box 670
Hogansburg, New York 13655
(518) 358-2222
Web Site: www.mohawkcasino.com
Map: **#2** (65 miles W. of Champlain)

Toll-Free Number: (888) 622-1155
Restaurants: 2   Liquor: Yes Valet Park: Free
Buffets: L-$7.99 D-$12.99
Casino Size: 40,000 Square Feet
Other Games: S21, P, LIR, TCP, B6
Overnight RV Parking: Free/RV Dump: No

Seneca Allegany Casino & Hotel

777 Seneca Allegany Boulevard
Salamanca, New York 14779
(716) 945-9300
Web Site: www.senecaalleganycasino.com
Map: **#12** (65 miles S. of Buffalo)

Toll-Free Number: (877) 553-9500
Rooms: 189 Price Range: $150-$270
Suites: 23 Price Range: $240-$290
Restaurants: 3 Liquor: Yes Valet Park: Free
Buffets: B-$9.99 L/D-$18.99
Casino Size: 48,000 Square Feet
Other Games: P, TCP, FCP, LIR, BG
Overnight RV Parking: No
Special Features: Buffet discount for slot club
members.

Seneca Buffalo Creek Casino

1 Fulton Street
Buffalo, New York 14204
(716) 853-7576
www.senecagamingcorporation.com/sbcc
Map: **#3**

Restaurants: 1 Snack Bar Liquor: Yes
Valet Park: Free
Hours: 10am-2am Daily
Casino Size: 5,000 Square Feet
Other Games: Only Gaming Machines
Overnight RV Parking: No

Seneca Niagara Casino

310 Fourth Street
Niagara Falls, New York 14303
(716) 299-1100
Web Site: www.senecaniagaracasino.com
Map: **#4**

Toll-Free Number: (877) 873-6322
Rooms: 574 Price Range: $139-$265
Suites: 30 Price Range: $239-$305
Restaurants: 4 Liquor: Yes Valet Park: Free
Buffets: B-$13.99 (Sat/Sun) L-$17.99
         D-$20.99
Other Games: S21, B, MB, P, PGP,
         TCP, LIR, B6, K
Overnight RV Parking: No
Special Features: Buffet discount for slot club
members.

Turning Stone Casino Resort

5218 Patrick Road
Verona, New York 13478
(315) 361-7711
Web Site: www.turning-stone.com
Map: **#1** (adjacent to NY State Thruway exit
33 at Verona, off Route 365, 30 miles E. of
Syracuse)

Toll-Free Number: (800) 771-7711
Rooms: 572 Price Range: $120-$229
Suites: 143 Price Range: $179-$395
Restaurants: 14 Liquor: No Valet Park: $5
Buffets: B-$12.95/$15.95 (Sun) L-$15.95
         D-$21.95
Casino Size: 122,000 Square Feet
Other Games: S21, B, MB, P, LIR, PGP, BG,
         TCP, K, B6, Casino War, Acey-Deucey
Overnight RV Parking: No
Special Features: Three golf courses. Gift shop.
Discount smoke shop. 800-seat showroom.
175-space RV park ($45 per night/$55
weekends).

Indian Casinos (Class II)

There are five Indian casinos that offer Class
II gambling which consist of electronic
gaming machines which look like slot
machines, but are actually games of bingo and
the spinning video reels are for "entertainment
purposes only." No public information is
available concerning the payback percentages
on the video gaming machines.

Some of these casinos also offer high-stakes
bingo and poker, as shown in the "Other
Games" listings.

Lakeside Gaming - Seneca Falls

2552 State Route 89
Seneca Falls, New York 13148
(315) 568-0994
Map: **#14** (50 miles W. of Syracuse)

CLOSED AT PRESS TIME - EXPECTED REOPENING
DATE IS UNKOWN - CALL BEFORE VISITING
Restaurants: None Liquor: No Valet Park: No
Hours: 10am-10pm/Midnight (Fri/Sat)
Overnight RV Parking: Free/RV Dump: No
Special Features: Non-smoking casino.

Lakeside Gaming - Union Springs
271 Cayuga Street
Union Springs, New York 13160
(315) 889-5416
Map: **#15** (55 miles S. W. of Syracuse)

CLOSED AT PRESS TIME - EXPECTED REOPENING
DATE IS UNKOWN - CALL BEFORE VISITING
Restaurants: None Liquor: No Valet Park: No
Hours: 10am-11pm/2am (Fri/Sat)
Overnight RV Parking: Free/RV Dump: No

Mohawk Bingo Palace
202 State Route 37
Hogansburg, New York 13655
(518) 358-2246
Web Site: www.mohawkpalace.com
Map: **#2** (65 miles W. of Champlain)

Toll-Free Number: (866) 452-5768
Restaurants: 1 Liquor: No Valet Park: No
Hours: 10am-8am Daily
Other Games: Bingo
Overnight RV Parking: Free/RV Dump: No

Seneca Gaming - Irving
11099 Route 5
Irving, New York 14081
(716) 549-6356
Web Site: www.senecagames.com
Map: **#13** (38 miles S.W. of Buffalo)

Toll-Free Number: (800) 421-BINGO
Restaurants: 1 Liquor: No Valet Park: No
Hours: 9:30am-2am/4:30am (Fri/Sat)
Other Games: Bingo, Poker
Overnight RV Parking: Free/RV Dump: No
Special Features: Discount smoke shop.

Seneca Gaming - Salamanca
768 Broad Street
Salamanca, New York 14779
(716) 945-4080
Web Site: www.senecagames.com
Map: **#12** (65 miles S. of Buffalo)

Toll-Free Number: (877) 860-5130
Restaurants: 1 Liquor: No Valet Park: No
Hours: 9:30am-1am/2am (Fri/Sat)
Other Games: Bingo
Overnight RV Parking: No

Pari-Mutuels

In October 2001, legislation was passed to allow for the introduction of slot machine-type video lottery machines at New York racetracks. Officially referred to as *Video Gaming Machines* (VGM's), they are regulated by the New York State Lottery Division.

All VGM's offer standard slot machine-type games, plus keno in denominations from five cents to $10. The machines all accept cash but do not pay out in cash. They print a receipt which must be taken to a cashier.

The VGM's do not operate like regular slot machines. Instead, they are similar to scratch-off-type lottery tickets with a pre-determined number of winners.

According to a spokesperson at the Lottery's headquarters, "no public information is available concerning the actual payback percentages on the machines." However, the legislation authorizing the VGM's states, "the specifications for video lottery gaming shall be designed in such a manner as to pay prizes that average no less than ninety percent of sales."

As of July 2007 all New York tracks offered VGM's, except for Aqueduct, which was expected to have them in operation by late 2008.

All Video Gaming Machine facilities are open from 10am to 2am daily and all are non-smoking. Admission is free to all facilities and the minimum gambling age is 18 for playing VGM's, as well as for betting on horse and harness racing.

Aqueduct
110-00 Rockaway Boulevard
Jamaica, New York 11417
(718) 641-4700
Website: www.nyra.com/aqueduct
Map: **#5** (15 miles E. of Manhattan)

Admission: $1   Clubhouse: $3
Valet: $5
Restaurants: 2
Special Features: Live thoroughbred racing
Wed-Sat. Daily simulcasting of thoroughbred
racing. Video Gaming Machines expected to
be in operation by late 2008. Call ahead to
check on the status of their VGM's.

Batavia Downs Gaming
8315 Park Road
Batavia, New York 14020
(585) 343-3750
Website: www.batavia-downs.com
Map: **#7** (35 miles E. of Buffalo)

Toll-Free: (800) 724-2000
Restaurants: 2   Valet Parking: No
Buffets: D-$8.95 (Wed)/$12.95 (Sat)
Overnight RV Parking: No
Special Features: Live harness racing Wed/Fri/
Sat from early August through early December.
Daily simulcasting of thoroughbred and
harness racing.

Empire City at Yonkers Raceway
8100 Central Avenue
Yonkers, New York 10704
(914) 968-4200
Website: www.yonkersraceway.com
Map: **#11** (20 miles N. of Manhattan)

Restaurants: 3
Valet: $10
Special Features: Year-round live harness
racing Mon-Sat evenings. Daily simulcasting
of thoroughbred and harness racing.

Fairgrounds Gaming & Raceway
5600 McKinley Parkway
Hamburg Fairgrounds
Hamburg, New York 14075
(716) 649-1280
Website: www.buffaloraceway.com
Map: **#8** (15 miles S. of Buffalo)

Toll-Free: (800) 237-1205
Restaurants: 2   Valet Parking: No
Casino Size: 27,000 Square Feet
Overnight RV Parking: No
Special Features: Live harness racing Wed/Fri-
Sun from February through July. Simulcasting
Wed-Sun of thoroughbred and harness racing.

Finger Lakes Gaming & Racetrack
5857 Route 96
Farmington, NY 14425
(585) 924-3232
Website: www.fingerlakesgaming.com
Map: **#6** (25 miles S. of Rochester)

Restaurants: 3   Valet Parking: $3
Buffets: L-$12.95 D-$16.95
Casino Size: 28,267 Square Feet
Overnight RV Parking: Call for permission
Senior Discount: Various Tue if 60 or older
Special Features: Live thoroughbred horse
racing (Fri-Tue) mid-April through late
November. Daily simulcasting of harness and
throroughbred racing.

Monticello Gaming & Raceway
204 Route 17B
Monticello, New York 12701
(845) 794-4100
Website: www.monticelloraceway.com
Map: **#9** (50 miles W. of Newburgh)

Toll-Free: (866) 777-4263
Admission: Free   Self-Parking: Free
Restaurants: 1   Valet Parking: $2
Buffets: B-$9.99 (Sat/Sun)/$6.95 (Fri)
    L-$11.95 D-$17.95/$22.95 (Fri/Sat)/
    $12.95 (Tue/Wed)
Overnight RV Parking: Free/RV Dump: No
Senior Discount: Breakfast discount if 55+
Special Features: Year-round live harness
racing Mon-Thu. Daily simulcast of
thoroughbred and harness racing.

Saratoga Gaming and Raceway
342 Jefferson Street
Saratoga Springs, New York 12866
(518) 584-2110
Website: www.saratogaraceway.com
Map: **#10** (25 miles N. of Schenectady)

Toll-Free: (800) 727-2990
Restaurants: 5   Valet Parking: $3
Buffets: L-$12.95 D-$14.95
Casino Size: 55,000 Square Feet
Overnight RV Parking: Free
Special Features: Live harness racing Wed-Sat evenings from February through mid-December. Daily simulcasting of thoroughbred and harness racing.

Tioga Downs
2384 West River Road
Nichols, New York 13812
Website: www.tiogadowns.com
Map: **#16** (30 miles W. of Binghamton)

Toll-Free: (888) 946-8464
Restaurants: 2   Valet Parking: $3
Buffets: B-$16.99 (Sun) L-$9.99/$7.99 (M/Tu)
    D-$16.99/$9.99 (M/Tue)/$13.99 (Wed)
Casino Size: 19,000 Square Feet
Overnight RV Parking: Free
Special Features: Live harness racing from May through mid-September. Daily simulcasting of thoroughbred and harness racing.

Vernon Downs
4229 Stuhlman Rd
Vernon, New York 13476
(315) 829-2201
Website: www.vernondowns.com
Map: **#1** (30 miles E. of Syracuse)

Toll-Free Number: (877) 888-3766
Room Reservations: (866) 829-3400
Suites: 175 Price Range: $79-$159
Restaurants: 1   Valet Parking: $2
Casino Size: 28,000 Square Feet
Overnight RV Parking: Free/RV Dump: No
Special Features: Live harness racing Thu-Sat evenings late April through mid-November. Daily simulcasting of thoroughbred and harness racing.

Canadian Casinos

If you are traveling to the Buffalo area there are two nearby Canadian casinos just across the border in Niagara Falls, Ontario.

All winnings are paid in Canadian currency and the minimum gambling age is 19. Both casinos are open 24 hours and offer the following games: blackjack, Spanish 21, craps, baccarat, mini-baccarat, pai-gow poker, Caribbean stud poker, three-card poker and let it ride.

Casino Niagara
5705 Falls Avenue
Niagara Falls, Ontario L2G 3K6
(905) 374-3589
Website: www.discoverniagara.com/casino
Map: **#4**

PRICES ARE IN CANADIAN DOLLARS
Toll-Free Number: (888) 946-3255
Restaurants: 6   Valet Parking: $5
Buffets: B-$6.95 L-$11.95 D-$16.95
Casino Size: 100,000 Square Feet
Overnight RV Parking: Free/RV Dump: No
Senior Discount: Various Tue if 55 or older
Special Features: Free shuttle to/from Niagara Fallsview Casino.

Niagara Fallsview Casino Resort
6380 Fallsview Boulevard
Niagara, Ontario L2G 7X5
(905) 358-3255
Web: www.discoverniagara.com/fallsviewcasino
Map: **#4**

PRICES ARE IN CANADIAN DOLLARS
Toll-Free Number: (888) 325-5788
Room Reservations: (888) 888-1089
Rooms: 340 Price Range: $239-$350
Suites: 28 Price Range: $359-$559
Restaurants: 10   Valet Parking: $20
Buffets: B-$10 L-$15 D-$20
Other Games: Pai Gow (tiles), Casino War, Big 6 Wheel, Sic Bo, Poker
Casino Size: 180,000 Square Feet
Overnight RV Parking: No
Special Features: Spa/fitness center. 1,500-seat theatre. Free shuttle to/from Casino Niagara. Additional Hilton hotel connected by walkway.

NORTH CAROLINA

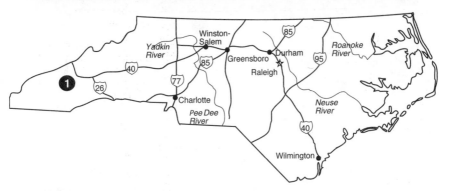

North Carolina has one Indian casino. In August, 1994 the state's Eastern Band of Cherokee Indians signed a compact with the governor to allow forms of video gambling. According to the terms of the compact, the video machines must be games of skill and they are required to return a minimum of 83% and a maximum of 98%.

No table games are offered at the Cherokee Casino, only video slots, video poker, and digital verisons of blackjack, craps and baccarat. The slots are different than slots you will find in other casinos because of the required "skill" factor. With these "skill" slots you have two opportunities to spin the reels. The "skill" factor comes into play because after seeing the results of your first spin you then have to decide whether to keep none, one, two, or all three of the symbols on each reel before you spin them again.

The casino is open 24 hours and the minimum gambling age is 21.

For more information on visiting North Carolina call the state's division of travel & tourism at (800) 847-4862 or go to: www.visitnc.com.

Harrah's Cherokee Casino
777 Casino Drive
Cherokee, North Carolina 28719
(828) 497-7777
Website: www.harrahs.com
Map: **#1** (55 miles S.W. of Asheville)

Toll-Free Number: (800) HARRAHS
Rooms 555 Price Range: $129-$199
Suites: 21 Price Range: Casino Use Only
Restaurants: 5   Liquor: No
Valet Parking: $8
Buffets: B-$9.00 (Sat/Sun)
           L-$11.00 D-$15.00/$22 (Wed/Fri)
Overnight RV Parking: No
Special Features: 1,500-seat entertainment pavilion.

NORTH DAKOTA

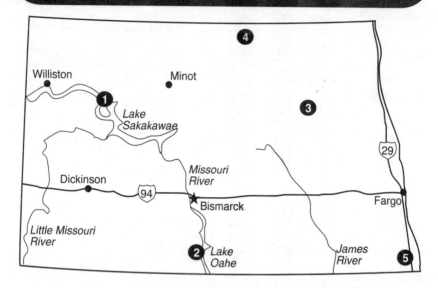

North Dakota has more than 800 sites throughout the state that offer blackjack, with betting limits of $1-$25, for the benefit of charities.

There are also six Indian casinos which are limited by law to the following maximum bet limits: blackjack-$100 (two tables in a casino may have limits up to $250), craps-$60, roulette-$50, slots/video poker-$25 and poker-$50 per bet, per round with a maximum of three rounds.

The terms of the state's compact with the tribes require gaming machines to return a minimum of 80% and a maximum of 100%. However, if a machine is affected by skill, such as video poker or video blackjack, the machines must return a minimum of 83%.

All casinos are open 24 hours and offer: blackjack, craps, roulette, slots, video poker and video keno. Optional games include: Spanish 21 (S21), Caribbean stud poker (CSP), let it ride (LIR), poker (P), three-card poker (TCP), keno (K), bingo (BG), big-6 wheel (B6) and off-track betting (OTB). The minimum age requirement is 21 for casino gambling and 18 for bingo.

For information on visiting North Dakota call the state's tourism office at (800) 435-5663 or go to: www.ndtourism.com.

Dakota Magic Casino
16849 102nd Street SE
Hankinson, North Dakota 58041
(701) 634-3000
Website: www.dakotamagic.com
Map: **#5** (50 miles S. of Fargo)

Toll-Free Number: (800) 325-6825
Rooms: 111 Price Range: $55-$110
Suites: 8 Price Range: $150-$250
Restaurants: 1 Liquor: Yes Valet Parking: No
Buffets: Brunch-$9.95 (Sat/Sun) L-$7.95
D-$9.95/$12.95(Fri-Sun)
Casino Size: 24,000 Square Feet
Other Games: P
Overnight RV Parking: Free/RV Dump: Fee
Senior Discount: Various on Mon if 55 or older
Special Features: 25-space RV park ($10 summer/$5 winter). 10% off rooms for seniors.

Four Bears Casino & Lodge
202 Frontage Rd
New Town, North Dakota 58763
(701) 627-4018
Website: www.4bearscasino.com
Map: **#1** (150 miles N.W. of Bismarck)

Toll-Free Number: (800) 294-5454
Rooms: 97 Price Range: $74
Suites: 3 Price Range: $105
Restaurants: 2 Liquor: Yes Valet Parking: No
Buffets: B-$6.95 L-$7.95
       D-$9.95/$18.95 (Wed)/$13.95 (Sun)
Other Games: P, TCP, LIR
Overnight RV Parking: Free/RV Dump: No
Senior Discount: Various Tue/Thu if 55+
Special Features: 85-space RV park ($12 per night). Nearby marina. 1,000-seat event center.

Prairie Knights Casino & Resort
7932 Highway 24
Fort Yates, North Dakota 58538
(701) 854-7777
Website: www.prairieknights.com
Map: **#2** (60 miles S. of Bismarck)

Toll-Free Number: (800) 425-8277
Rooms: 92 Price Range: $65-$75
Suites: 4 Price Range: $90-$135
Restaurants: 2 Liquor: Yes Valet Parking: No
Buffets: B-$6.50 L/D-$9.95/$19.95 (Sun)
Casino Size: 42,000 Square Feet
Other Games: TCP, LIR, No Roulette
Overnight RV Parking: Free/RV Dump: Free
Senior Discount: $6.95 buffet 11am -3pm
       (Mon-Fri) if 55 or older
Special Features: 12-space RV park ($5 per night) at casino. 32-space RV park ($10 per night) at marina. Free RV dump at marina. $45 rooms for slot club members. Convenience store.

Sky Dancer Hotel & Casino
Highway 5 West
Belcourt, North Dakota 58316
(701) 244-2400
Website: www.skydancercasino.com
Map: **#4** (120 miles N.E. of Minot)

Toll-Free Number: (866) 244-9467
Rooms: 70 Price Range: $60-$70
Suites: 27 Price Range: $60-$70
Restaurants: 2 Liquor: Yes Valet Parking: No
Buffets: L-$5.95 (Mon-Fri)
       D-$7.95/$9.95 (Mon)/$16.95 (Fri/Sat)
Casino Size: 25,000 Square Feet
Other Games: P, LIR, BG, OTB (Tue-Sun),
       No Craps
Overnight RV Parking: Free/RV Dump: Free
Special Features: Gift shop.

Spirit Lake Casino & Resort
Highway 57
Spirit Lake, North Dakota 58370
(701) 766-4747
Website: www.spiritlakecasino.com
Map: **#3** (6 miles S. of Devil's Lake)

Toll-Free Number: (800) WIN-U-BET
Rooms: 108 Price Range: $60-$95
Suites: 16 Price Range: $90-$150
Restaurants: 3 Liquor: No Valet Parking: Free
Buffets: B-$5.50/$9.95 (Sat) L-$6.50
       D-$9.95/$16.50 (Wed)/$11.95 (Sat)
Casino Size: 45,000 Square Feet
Other Games: P, BG, No roulette
Overnight RV Parking: Free/RV Dump: No
Senior Discount: Various on Monday if 55+
Special Features: 15-space RV park ($18 per night). Gift shop. Discount smoke shop. 32-slip marina. Slot club members get 10% off rooms.

Turtle Mountain Chippewa Mini-Casino
Highway 5 West
Belcourt, North Dakota 58316
(701) 477-6438
Map: **#4** (120 miles N.E. of Minot)

Restaurants: 1 Liquor: Yes Valet Parking: No
Other Games: Only Machines - No Table Games
Overnight RV Parking: Free/RV Dump: No
Special Features: Affiliated with and located four miles east of Sky Dancer Hotel and Casino.

OKLAHOMA

All Oklahoma Indian casinos are allowed to offer both Class II and Class III gaming machines.

Most casinos offer only Class II machines which look like slot machines, but are actually games of bingo and the spinning video reels are for "entertainment purposes only." Some casinos also offer traditional Class III slots.

In either case, the gaming machines are not allowed to accept or payout in coins. All payouts must be done by a printed receipt or via an electronic debit card. No public information is available concerning the payback percentages on gaming machines in Oklahoma.

All casinos offering card games such as blackjack, let it ride or three-card poker, etc., can only offer a player-banked version where players must pay a commission to the house on every hand they play. The amount of the commission charged varies, depending on the rules of each casino, but it's usually 50 cents to $1 per hand played. Roulette and dice games are not permitted in Oklahoma.

There are also three horse racing facilities in Oklahoma which feature Class II gaming machines.

All Oklahoma Indian casinos offer gaming machines. Other games include: blackjack (BJ), mini-baccarat (MB), poker (P), three-card poker (TCP), pai gow poker (PGP), let it ride (LIR), bingo (BG) and off-track betting (OTB).

Not all Oklahoma Indian casinos serve alcoholic beverages and the individual listings note which casinos do serve it. Unless otherwise noted, all casinos are open 24 hours. The minimum gambling age is 18 at some casinos and 21 at others.

For more information on visiting Oklahoma call the Oklahoma Tourism Department at (800) 652-6552 or go to: www.travelok.com

Ada Gaming Center
1500 North Country Club Road
Ada, Oklahoma 74820
Website: www.chickasaw.net
(580) 436-3740
Map: **#2** (85 miles S.E. of Oklahoma City)

Restaurants: 1   Liquor: No
Hours: 9:00am-7:00am Daily
Casino Size: 22,482 Square Feet
Other Games: BJ, P, OTB
Overnight RV Parking: No
Special Features: Located in travel plaza with gas station and convenience store.

Ada Travel Plaza
201 Latta Road
Ada, Oklahoma 74820
(580) 310-0900
Website: www.chickasaw.net
Map: **#2** (85 miles S.E. of Oklahoma City)

Restaurants: 1 Snack Bar   Liquor: No
Overnight RV Parking: No
Special Features: Located in travel plaza with gas station and convenience store.

Baby Grand Casino
4901 South Highway Drive
McLoud, Oklahoma 74851
(405) 964-7263
Map: **#23** (31 miles E. of Oklahoma City)

Restaurants: 1 Snack Bar   Liquor: No
Overnight RV Parking: Free/RV Dump: No

Black Gold Casino
288 Mulberry Lane (on Route 70)
Wilson, Oklahoma 73463
(580) 668-9248
Website: www.chickasaw.net
Map: **#39** (112 miles S. of Oklahoma City)

Hours: 9:00am-6:30am Daily
Casino Size: 3,744 Square Feet
Restaurants: 1 Snack Bar   Liquor: No
Overnight RV Parking: Free/RV Dump: No
Special Features: Located in travel plaza with gas station and convenience store.

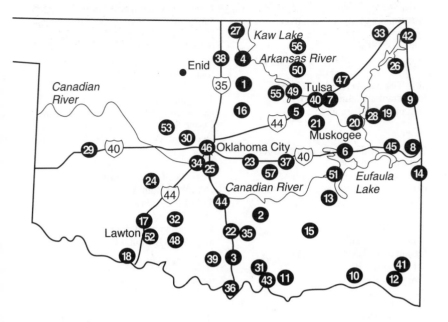

Blue Star Gaming and Casino
20 White Eagle Drive
Ponca City, Oklahoma 74601
(580) 765-0040
Map: **#4** (106 miles N. of Oklahoma City)

Restaurants: 1   Liquor: No
Hours: Noon-12am/2am (Thurs-Sat)
Other Games: BG (Wed-Sun)
Overnight RV Parking: Free/RV Dump: No

Bordertown Bingo and Casino
130 W. Oneida Street
Seneca, Missouri 64865
Website: www.bordertownbingo.com
(918) 666-1126
Map: **#42** (90 miles N.E. of Tulsa)

Toll-Free Number: (800) 957-2435
Restaurants: 1   Liquor: Yes
Other Games: BJ, TCP, LIR, BG, OTB
Overnight RV Parking: Must use RV park
Special Features: 30-space RV park ($9 night).
Casino is located directly on the Oklahoma/
Missouri border near Wyandotte.

Bristow Indian Bingo
121 West Lincoln
Bristow, Oklahoma 74010
(918) 367-9168
Map: **#5** (35 miles S.E. of Tulsa)

Restaurants: 1   Liquor: Yes
Hours: 2pm-12am/Closed Sunday
Other Games: BG (Mon)
Overnight RV Parking: Free/RV Dump: No

Buffalo Run Casino
1000 Buffalo Run Boulevard
Miami, Oklahoma 74354
(918) 542-7140
Website: www.buffalorun.com
Map: **#33** (89 miles N.E. of Tulsa)

Restaurants: 1   Liquor: Yes
Other Games: BJ, P, TCP, OTB
Overnight RV Parking: Free/RV Dump: No
Special Features: 2,000-seat showroom.

Cash Springs Gaming Center
West First and Muskogee Streets
Sulphur, Oklahoma 73086
(580) 622-2156
Map: **#35** (84 miles S. of Oklahoma City)

Toll-Free Number: (866) 622-2156
Restaurants: 1   Liquor: No
Overnight RV Parking: No

Checotah Indian Community Bingo
830 North Broadway
Checotah, Oklahoma 74426
(918) 473-5200
Map: **#6** (120 miles E. of Oklahoma City)

Restaurants: 1
Hours: 10am-1am/3am (Fri/Sat)
Casino Size: 8,000 Square Feet
Other Games: BG
Overnight RV Parking: No

Cherokee Casino and Resort
19105 East Timbercrest Circle
Catoosa, Oklahoma 74015
 (918) 384-7800
Website: www.cherokeecasino.com
Map: **#7** (a suburb of Tulsa)

Toll-Free Number: (800) 760-6700
Rooms: 130 Price Range: $56-$126
Suites: 20 Price Range: $157-$269
Restaurants: 4   Liquor: Yes
Buffets: B-$6.25 L-$8.50/$10.95 (Sun)
        D-$12.75/$18.95 (Fri)/$16.95 (Sat)
Casino Size: 80,000 Square Feet
Other Games: BJ, MB, PGP
Overnight RV Parking: Free/RV Dump: No
Senior Discount: Various Mon if 50 or older.

Cherokee Casino - Ft. Gibson
US Highway 62
Ft. Gibson, Oklahoma 74338
(918) 478-9526
Website: www.cherokeecasino.com
Map: **#20** (50 miles S.E. of Tulsa)

Restaurants: 1 Deli   Liquor: No
Overnight RV Parking: Free/RV Dump: No

Cherokee Casino - Roland
Interstate 40 and Highway 64
Roland, Oklahoma 74954
(918) 427-7491
Website: www.cherokeecasino.com
Map: **#8** (175 miles E. of Oklahoma City)

Toll-Free Number: (800) 256-2338
Restaurants: 1 Deli   Liquor: Beer Only
Casino Size: 28,000 Square Feet
Overnight RV Parking: Free/RV Dump: No

Cherokee Casino - Sallisaw
1621 West Ruth Avenue
Sallisaw, OK 74955
(918) 774-1600
Website: www.cherokeecasino.com
Map: **#45** (160 miles E. of Oklahoma City)

Toll-Free Number: (800) 256-2338
Restaurants: 1   Liquor: Yes
Casino Size: 22,000 Square Feet
Other Games: BJ, P
Overnight RV Parking: Free/RV Dump: No

Cherokee Casino - Siloam
7300 West US Highway 412
W. Siloam Springs, Oklahoma 74338
(918) 422-6301
Website: www.cherokeecasino.com
Map: **#9** (85 miles E. of Tulsa)

Toll-Free Number: (800) 754-4111
Restaurants: 1 Deli   Liquor: Yes
Othe Games: BJ, P
Overnight RV Parking: Free/RV Dump: No

Cherokee Casino - Tahlequah
16489 Highway 62
Tahlequah, Oklahoma 74464
(918) 207-3600
Website: www.cherokeecasino.com
Map: **#19** (83 miles S.E. of Tulsa)

Restaurants: 1 Snack Bar   Liquor: No
Other Games: BJ, P
Overnight RV Parking: Free/RV Dump: No

Chisholm Trail Casino
7807 N. Highway 81
Duncan, Oklahoma 73533
(580) 255-1668
Website: www.chickasaw.net
Map: **#48** (79 miles S. of Oklahoma City)

Hours: 8:00am-6:00am Daily
Casino Size: 22,000 Square Feet
Restaurants: 1   Liquor: No
Overnight RV Parking: Free/RV Dump: No
Other Games: BJ

Choctaw Casino - Broken Bow
1790 South Park Drive
Broken Bow, Oklahoma 74728
(580) 584-5450
Website: www.choctawcasinos.com
Map: **#41** (235 miles S.E. of Oklahoma City)

Restaurants: 1 Snack Bar   Liquor: No
Hours: 10am-1am/24hrs (Thur-Sat)
Other Games: Bj, P
Overnight RV Parking: Free/ RV Dump: No

Choctaw Casino - Durant
3735 Choctaw Road
Highway 69/75
Durant, Oklahoma 74701
(580) 920-0160
Website: www.choctawcasinos.com
Map: **#11** (150 miles S.E. of Oklahoma City)

Toll-Free Number: (800) 788-2464
Room Reservations: (580) 931-8340
Rooms: 40 Price Range: $79-$89
Suites: 4 Price Range: $99-$119
Restaurants: 2   Liquor: No
Buffets: L- $8.99 D-$9.99
Casino Size: 36,000 Square Feet
Other Games: BJ, BG, OTB, P
Overnight RV Parking: Free/RV Dump: No
Special Features: Free shuttle buses from
Dallas and Fort Worth.

Choctaw Casino - Grant
Route 1 Box 17-1
Grant, Oklahoma 74738
(580) 326-8397
Website: www.choctawcasinos.com
Map: **#10** (200 miles S. of Oklahoma City)

Restaurants: 1 Deli   Liquor: No
Other Games: BJ, P
Overnight RV Parking: No

Choctaw Casino - Idabel
1425 Southeast Washington
Idabel, Oklahoma 74745
(580) 286-5710
Website: www.choctawcasinos.com
Map: **#12** (240 miles S.E. of Oklahoma City)

Toll-Free Number: (800) 634-2582
Restaurants: 1   Liquor: No
Hours: 8am-4am/24 Hours (Fri-Sat)
Other Games: BJ, OTB
Casino Size: 11,000 Square Feet
Overnight RV Parking: Must check-in at
front desk/RV Dump: No

Choctaw Casino - McAlester
1638 South George Nigh Expressway
McAlester, Oklahoma 74501-7411
(918) 423-8161
Website: www.choctawcasinos.com
Map: **#13** (130 miles S.E. of Oklahoma City)

Toll-Free Number: (877) 904-8444
Restaurants: 1   Liquor: No
Hours: 9am-5am/24 Hours (Fri-Sat)
Other Games: OTB
Casino Size: 17,500 Square Feet
Overnight RV Parking: Free/RV Dump: No

Choctaw Casino - Pocola
3400 Service Road
Pocola, Oklahoma 74902
(918) 436-7761
Website: www.choctawcasinos.com
Map: **#14** (195 miles E. of Oklahoma City)

Toll-Free Number: (800) 590-5825
Restaurants: 2   Liquor: No
Buffets: L-$8.00 D-$10.00
Other Games: BJ, OTB, P
Overnight RV Parking: Free/RV Dump: No

Choctaw Casino - Stringtown
895 North Highway 69
Stringtown, Oklahoma 74569
(580) 346-7862
Website: www.choctawcasinos.com
Map: **#15** (163 miles S.E. of Oklahoma City)

Restaurants: 2   Liquor: No
Hours: 9am-1am (Sun)/10am-1am (Mon-
Wed)/10am-4am (Thurs-Fri)/9am-4am (Sat)
Overnight RV Parking: Free/RV Dump: No

Cimarron Casino
821 W. Freeman Avenue
Perkins, Oklahoma 74059
(405) 547-5352
Website: www.iowanation.org
Map: **#16** (60 miles N. of Oklahoma City)

Restaurants: 1 Snack Bar   Liquor: Yes
Other Games: P
Overnight RV Parking: No

Comanche Nation Casino
402 South East Interstate Drive
Lawton, Oklahoma 73502
(580) 354-2000
Website: www.comanchenationcasino.com
Map: **#17** (86 miles S.W. of Oklahoma City)

Toll-Free Number: (866) 354-2500
Restaurants: 1   Liquor: Yes
Other Games: BJ, BG (Wed-Sun), P, OTB
Overnight RV Parking: Free (With Hook
Ups)/RV Dump: No

Comanche Red River Casino
Highway 36 and Highway 70
Devol, Oklahoma 73531
(580) 299-3378
Website:
www.comancheredrivercasino.com
Map: **#18** (125 miles S.W. of Oklahoma City)

Toll-Free Number: (866) 280-3261
Restaurants: 1   Liquor: Yes
Casino Size: 52,500 Square Feet
Other Games: BJ, P, C
Overnight RV Parking: Free (With Hook
Ups)/RV Dump: No
Special Features: Drive-thru smoke shop.

Comanche Spur
9047 US Highway 62
Eldon, Oklahoma 73538
(580) 492-5502
Website: www.comanchespur.com
Map: **#19** (83 miles S.E. of Tulsa)

Restaurants: 1   Liquor: No
Hours: 7am-11pm/10am-10pm (Sun)
Overnight RV Parking: No
Special features: Smoke shop. Convenience
store.

Comanche Star Casino
Rt 3 and Hwy 53
Walters, Oklahoma 73572
(580) 875-2092
Website: comanchenation.com/starcasino.html
Map: **#52** (25 miles S.E. of Lawton)

Restaurants: 1   Liquor: No
Hours: 10am-12am/2am (Fri/Sat)
Casino Size: 7,000 Square Feet
Overnight RV Parking: No

Creek Nation Casino - Eufaula
806 Forest Avenue
Eufaula, Oklahoma 74432
(918) 689-9191
Map: **#51** (135 miles E. of Oklahoma City)

Restaurants: 1 Snack Bar   Liquor: No
Hours: 10am-3am/4am (Fri/Sat)
Overnight RV Parking: No

Creek Nation Casino - Muscogee
3420 West Peak Boulevard
Muskogee, Oklahoma 74403
(918) 683-1825
Website: www.muscogee-casino.com
Map: **#20** (50 miles S.E. of Tulsa)

Restaurants: 1   Liquor: No
Other Games: BJ, P, BG
Casino Size: 22,500 Square Feet
Overnight RV Parking: Free/RV Dump: No

Creek Nation Casino - Okemah
1100 S. Woodie Guthrie
Okemah, Oklahoma 74859
(918) 623-0051
Website: www.creeknationcasino.com
Map: **#37** (72 miles E. of Oklahoma City)

Hours: 8am-6am Daily
Restaurants: 1   Liquor: No
Other Games: BJ, P, BG
Overnight RV Parking: Free/RV Dump: No

Creek Nation Casino - Okmulgee
1901 North Wood Drive
Okmulgee, Oklahoma 74447
(918) 756-8400
Website: www.cncokmulgee.com
Map: **#21** (40 miles S. of Tulsa)

Restaurants: 1   Liquor: No
Casino Size: 10,000 Square Feet
Other Games: BJ, P
Overnight RV Parking: Free/RV Dump: No

Creek Nation Casino - Tulsa
1616 East 81st Street
Tulsa, Oklahoma 74137
(918) 299-8518
Website: www.creeknationcasino.com
Map: **#40**

Toll-Free Number: (800) 299-2738
Restaurants: 1   Liquor: No
Casino Size: 81,000 Square Feet
Other Games: BJ, P, TCP, BG
Overnight RV Parking: Free/RV Dump: No
Special Features: Separate nonsmoking
casino. Free shuttle to/from local hotels.

Creek Nation Travel Plaza
Highway 75 and 56 Loop
Okmulgee, Oklahoma 74447
(918) 752-0090
Map: **#21** (40 miles S. of Tulsa)

Restaurants: 1 Snack Bar   Liquor: No
Overnight RV Parking: Free/RV Dump: No
Special Features: Gas station and convenience
store. Burger King.

Davis Trading Post
Interstate 35 and Highway 7
Davis, Oklahoma 73030
(580) 369-5360
Website: www.chickasaw.net
Map: **#22** (75 miles S. of Oklahoma City)

Restaurants: 1   Liquor: No
Overnight RV Parking: Free/RV Dump: No

Duck Creek Casino
10085 Ferguson Road
Beggs, Oklahoma 74421
(918) 267-3468
Map: **#21** (35 miles S. of Tulsa)

Restaurants: 1 Snack Bar   Liquor: No
Hours: 9am-7am Daily
Casino Size: 5,000 Square Feet
Overnight RV Parking: Free/RV Dump: No

Feather Warrior Casino
1407 S. Clarence Nash Boulevard
Watonga, Oklahoma 73772
(580) 623-7333
Map: **#53** (70 miles N. W. of Okla. City)

Restaurants: 1 Snack Bar   Liquor: No
Hours: 11am-2am/10am-2am (Fri/Sat)
Casino Size: 2,200 Square Feet
Overnight RV Parking: Free/RV Dump: No

Fire Lake Entertainment Center
1601 S. Gordon Cooper Drive
Shawnee, Oklahoma 74801
(405) 273-2242
Website: www.potawatomi.org
Map: **#23** (38 miles E. of Oklahoma City)

Restaurants: 1   Liquor: Yes
Other Games: BJ, P, BG, OTB
Overnight RV Parking: Free/RV Dump: No

Fire Lake Grand Casino
777 Grand Casino Boulevard
Shawnee, Oklahoma 74851
Website: www.firelakegrand.com
(405) 964-7263
Map: **#23** (38 miles E. of Oklahoma City)

Restaurants: 3   Liquor: Yes
Buffets: B-$4.99 L-$4.99/$6.99(Fri) D-$8.99
Casino Size: 125,000 Square Feet
Other Games: BJ, P, C
Overnight RV Parking: Free/RV Dump: No
Special Features: 3,000-seat event center.

Fort Sill Apache Casino
2315 East Gore Boulevard
Lawton, Oklahoma 73502
(580) 248-5905
Map: **#17** (86 miles S.W. of Oklahoma City)

Restaurants: 1   Liquor: No
Casino Size: 7,700 Square Feet
Overnight RV Parking: Free/RV Dump: No

Gold Mountain Casino
1410 Sam Noble Parkway
Ardmore, Oklahoma 73401
(580) 223-3301
Website: www.chickasaw.net
Map: **#3** (100 miles S. of Oklahoma City)

Restaurants: 1   Liquor: No
Hours: 9am-7am Daily
Casino Size: 8,620 Square Feet
Overnight RV Parking: Free/RV Dump: No
Special Features: Tobacco shop.

Gold River Bingo and Casino
Highway 281
Anadarko, Oklahoma 73005
(405) 247-6979
Website: www.goldriverok.com
Map: **#24** (60 miles S.W. of Oklahoma City)

Toll-Free Number: (800) 280-1018
Restaurants: 1   Liquor: No
Hours: 9am-4am/24 hrs(Fri/Sat)
Casino Size: 12,000 Square Feet
Other Games: BJ
Overnight RV Parking: Free/RV Dump: No

Golden Pony Casino
Hwy. I-40, Exit 227 Clearview Rd.
Okemah, Oklahoma 74859
(918) 623-2620
Website: www.goldenponycasino.com
Map: **#37** (72 miles E. of Oklahoma City)

Restaurants: Snack Bar   Liquor: No
Overnight RV Parking: Free/RV Dump: No

Goldsby Gaming Center
1038 West Sycamore Road
Norman, Oklahoma 73072
(405) 329-5447
Website: www.chickasaw.net
Map: **#25** (21 miles S. of Oklahoma City)

Restaurants: 1   Liquor: No
Hours: 8am-6am Daily
Other Games: BJ, BG
Casino Size: 23,007 Square Feet
Overnight RV Parking: Free/RV Dump: No

Grand Lake Casino
24701 S. 655th Road
Grove, Oklahoma 74344
(918) 786-8528
Map: **#26** (90 miles N.E. of Tulsa)

Toll-Free Number: (800) 426-4640
Restaurants: 1   Liquor: Yes
Other Games: BJ, P, TCP
Overnight RV Parking: No

High Winds Casino
61475 E. 100 Road
Miami, Oklahoma 74354
(918) 541-9463
Map: **#33** (89 miles N.E. of Tulsa)

Restaurants: 1   Liquor: Yes
Other Games: BJ
Overnight RV Parking: Free/RV Dump: No

Kaw Southwind Casino
5640 North LaCann Drive
Newkirk, Oklahoma 74647
(580) 362-2578
Website: www.southwindcasino.com
Map: **#27** (106 miles N. of Oklahoma City)

Toll-Free Number: (866) KAW-BINGO
Hours: 9am-2am/24 Hours (Thu-Sat)
Restaurants: 1   Liquor: No
Other Games: BJ, BG, P
Overnight RV Parking: Free/RV Dump: No

Keetoowah Casino
2450 South Muskogee
Tahlequah, Oklahoma 74464
 (918) 456-6131
Map: **#28** (15 miles S.E. of Tulsa)

Restaurants: 1   Liquor: No
Hours: 8am-2am/24 hrs (Thurs-Sat)
Overnight RV Parking: No

Kickapoo Casino
25230 East Highway 62
McLoud, Oklahoma 74851
(405) 964-7322
Map: **#23** (31 miles E. of Oklahoma City)

Restaurants: 1   Liquor: No
Other Games: BJ, MB, TCP
Overnight RV Parking: Free/RV Dump: No

Kiowa Casino
County Road 1980
Devol, Oklahoma 73531
(580)299-3333
Website:www.kiowafuncasino.com
Map: **#18** (125 miles S.W. of Oklahoma City)

Toll-Free Number: (866)370-4077
Restaurants: 3   Liquor: Beer Only
Buffets: L-$8.99 D-$10.99/$14.99 (Fri)
Other Games: P, BJ
Overnight RV Parking: Free/RV Dump: No

Lucky Star Casino - Clinton
101 N. Indian Hospital Road
Clinton, Oklahoma 73601
(580) 323-6599
Website: www.luckystarcasino.org
Map: **#29** (85 miles W. of Oklahoma City)

Restaurants: 1   Liquor: No
Other Games: P, BJ
Overnight RV Parking: Free/RV Dump: No

Lucky Star Casino - Concho
7777 North Highway 81
Concho, Oklahoma 73022
(405) 262-7612
Website: www.luckystarcasino.org
Map: **#30** (35 miles N.W. of Oklahoma City)

Restaurants: 1   Liquor: Yes
Other Games: BJ, P
Casino Size: 40,000 Square Feet
Overnight RV Parking: Free/RV Dump: Free
Special features: Free RV hookups (must register first).

Lucky Turtle Casino
64499 East Highway 60
Wyandotte, Oklahoma 74370
(918) 678-3767
Map: **#42** (90 miles N.E. of Tulsa)

Restaurants: 1   Liquor: No
Casino Size: 4,000 Square Feet
Overnight RV Parking: No
Special Features: Convenience store.

Madill Gaming Center
902 South First Street
Madill, Oklahoma 73446
(580) 795-7301
Map: **#31** (122 miles S. of Oklahoma City)

Restaurants: 1   Liquor: No
Casino Size: 2,071 Square Feet
Overnight RV Parking: No

Marlow Gaming Center
Route 3
Marlow, Oklahoma 73055
(580) 255-1668
Website: www.chickasaw.net
Map: **#32** (79 miles S. of Oklahoma City)

Restaurants: 1   Liquor: No
Hours: 8am-6am Daily
Overnight RV Parking: Free/RV Dump: No

Miami Tribe Entertainment
202 South 8 Tribes Trail
Miami, Oklahoma 74354
(918) 542-8670
Map: **#33** (89 miles N.E. of Tulsa)

Restaurants: 1   Liquor: No
Overnight RV Parking: No

Million Dollar Elm Casino - Bartlesville
222 Allen Rd.
Bartlesville, Oklahoma 74003
(918) 335-7519
Website: www.milliondollarelm.com
Map: **#56** (50 miles N. of Tulsa)

Restaurants: 2   Liquor: No
Hours: 10am-12:00am(Mon-Wed)/10:00am-
2:00am (Thurs)/10:00am-3:00am (Fri/Sat)
Other Games: BJ, P
Overnight RV Parking: No

Million Dollar Elm Casino - Hominy
Highway 99
Hominy, Oklahoma 74035
(918) 885-2990
Website: www.milliondollarelm.com
Map: **#49** (44 miles N.W. of Tulsa)

Restaurants: 1   Liquor: No
Hours: 10am-12:20am(Mon-Wed)/10:00am-
2:00am (Thurs)/10:00am-3:00am (Fri/Sat)
Other Games: BJ, P
Overnight RV Parking: Free/RV Dump:No

Million Dollar Elm Casino - Pawhuska
201 N.W. 15th Street (at Highway 99)
Pawhuska, Oklahoma 74056
(918) 287-1072
Website: www.milliondollarelm.com
Map: **#50** (a suburb of Tulsa)

Restaurants: 1   Liquor: No
Hours: 10am-12:20am(Mon-Wed)/10:00am-
2:00am (Thurs)/10:00am-3:00am (Fri/Sat)
Overnight RV Parking: Free/RV Dump: No

Million Dollar Elm Casino - Sand Springs
301 Blackjack Drive (on Highway 97T)
Sand Springs, Oklahoma 74063
(918) 699-7727
Website: www.milliondollarelm.com
Map: **#40** (a suburb of Tulsa)

Toll-Free Number: (877) 246-8777
Restaurants: 2   Liquor: Yes
Other Games: BJ, P
Overnight RV Parking: No

Million Dollar Elm Casino - Tulsa
951 W. 36th Street North
Tulsa, Oklahoma 74127
(918) 699-7740
Website: www.milliondollarelm.com
Map: **#40**

Toll-Free Number: (877) 246-8777
Restaurants: 1   Liquor: Yes
Casino Size: 47,000 Square Feet
Other Games: BJ, P, BG
Overnight RV Parking: Free/RV Dump: No

Mystic Winds Casino
12052 Highway 99
Seminole, OK 74868
(405)382-3218
Map: **#57** (60 miles S.E of Oklahoma City)

Restaurants: 1 Snack Bar   Liquor:No
Other Games: BJ, P
Overnight RV Parking: Free/RV Dump: No

Native Lights Casino
12375 N. Highway 77
Newkirk, Oklahoma 74647
(580) 448-3100
Website: www.nativelightscasino.com
Map: **#27** (106 miles N. of Oklahoma City)

Toll-Free Number: (877)468-3100
Restaurants: 1   Liquor: Yes
Other Games: BJ, P
Overnight RV Parking: Free/RV Dump: No

Newcastle Gaming Center
2457 Highway 62 Service Road
Newcastle, Oklahoma 73065
(405) 387-6013
Website: www.chickasaw.net
Map: **#34** (19 miles S. of Oklahoma City)

Restaurants: 1   Liquor: Yes
Casino Size: 44,622 Sqaure Feet
Other Games: BJ, OTB, P
Overnight RV Parking: Free/RV Dump: No

Pawnee Trading Post Casino
291 Agency Road
Pawnee, Oklahoma 74058
(918) 762-4466
Website: www.tradingpostcasino.com
Map: **#55** (57 miles N.W. of Tulsa)

Restaurants: 1   Liquor: No
Hours: 6am-2am(Mon-Thurs)
        24hrs (Fri/Sat)/6am-11pm (Sun)
Casino Size: 3,600 Square Feet
Overnight RV Parking: No
Special Features: Convenience store/gas station.

Peoria Gaming Center
8520 S. Hwy 69A
Miami, Oklahoma 74354
(918) 540-0303
Map: **#33** (89 miles N.E. of Tulsa)

Restaurants: 1 Snack Bar Liquor: No
Hours: 10am-Midnight/2am (Fri/Sat)
Overnight RV Parking: No
Special features: Adjacent to Buffalo Run Casino which allows overnight RV parking.

Quapaw Casino
58100 E. 66th Road
Miami, Oklahoma 74355
(918) 540-9100
Website: www.quapawcasino.com
Map: **#33** (89 miles N.E. of Tulsa)

Restaurants: 1   Liquor: Yes
Other Games: BJ
Overnight RV Parking: Free/RV Dump: No

Riverwind Casino
1544 W. State Highway 9
Norman, Oklahoma 73072
(405) 364-7171
Website: www.riverwindcasino.com
Map: **#25** (21 miles S. of Oklahoma City)

Toll-Free Number: (888) 440-1880
Restaurants: 2   Liquor: No
Buffets: L-$10.95/$12.95 (Sun)
         D-$12.95/$14.95 (Sat)
Casino Size: 60,000 Square Feet
Other Games: BJ, P, OTB
Overnight RV Parking: Free/RV Dump: No
Special Features: 1,500-seat showroom.

Sac and Fox Casino
42008 Westech Road
Shawnee, Oklahoma 74804
(405)275-4700
Web Site: www.sandfcasino.com
Map: **#23** (40 Miles E. of Okalhoma City)

Restaurants: 1   Liquor: Yes
Casino Size: 8,600 Sqaure Feet
Other Games: P, BJ
Overnight RV Parking: Free/RV Dump: No

Seven Clans Paradise Casino
7500 Highway 177
Red Rock, Oklahoma 74651
(580) 723-4005
Map: **#1** (82 miles N. of Oklahoma City)

Toll-Free Number: (866) 723-4005
Restaurants: 1   Liquor: Yes
Casino Size: 23,000 Square Feet
Other Games: BJ
Overnight RV Parking: Must use RV park
Senior Discount: Various Tue/Thu if 55 or older
Special Features: 7-space RV park ($10 per night). Convenience store and gas station.

Silver Buffalo Casino
620 East Colorado Drive
Anadarko, Oaklahoma 73005
(405) 247-5471
Website: www.silverbuffalocasino.com
Map: **#24** (60 miles S.W. of Oklahoma City)

Restaurants: 1   Liquor: Beer Only
Hours: 10am-2am/4am (Fri/Sat)
Overnight RV Parking: Free/RV Dump: No

The Stables Casino
530 H Street Southeast
Miami, Oklahoma 74354
(918) 542-7884
Website: www.the-stables.com
Map: **#33** (89 miles N.E. of Tulsa)

Toll-Free Number: (877) 774-7884
Restaurants: 1   Liquor: Yes
Other Games: BJ, OTB
Overnight RV Parking: Free/RV Dump: No

Texoma Gaming Center
HC 68 Box 13
Kingston, OK 73439
(580) 564-6000
Website: www.chickasaw.net
Map: **#43** (130 miles S. of Oklahoma City)

Restaurants: 1   Liquor: No
Hours: 9am-6am Daily
Other Games: BJ, P
Overnight RV Parking: No
Special Features: Convenience store and KFC.

Thackerville Travel Plaza
Interstate 35, Exit 1
Thackerville, Oklahoma 73459
(580) 276-4706
Website: www.chickasaw.net
Map: **#36** (124 miles S. of Oklahoma City)

Restaurants: 1 Snack Bar   Liquor: No
Hours: 8am-6am Daily
Overnight RV Parking: Free/RV Dump: No

Thunderbird Casino
15700 East State Highway 9
Norman, Oklahoma 73026
(405) 360-9270
Map: **#25** (21 miles S. of Oklahoma City)

Toll-Free Number: (800) 259-5825
Restaurants: 1   Liquor: Yes
Other Games: BJ, P, TCP
Casino Size: 40,000 Square Feet
Overnight RV Parking: No

Tonkawa Casino
1000 Allen Drive
Tonkawa, Oklahoma 74653
(580) 628-2624
Website: www.tonkawacasino.com
Map: **#38** (91 miles N. of Oklahoma City)

Restaurants: 1 Snack Bar   Liquor: No
Hours: 9am-3am Daily
Overnight RV Parking: Free/RV Dump: No

Treasure Valley Gaming Center
I-35, Exit 55 (Highway 7)
Davis, Oklahoma 73030
(580) 369-2895
Website: www.chickasaw.net
Map: **#22** (75 miles S. of Oklahoma City)

Rooms: 59   Price Range: $73-$89
Suites: 2   Price Range: $99-$109
Restaurants: 2   Liquor: No
Buffets: L-$5.99
         D-$6.99/$7.99 (Sat)/$13.99 (Fri)
Casino Size: 19,666 Square Feet
Other Games: BJ, P
Overnight RV Parking: Free/RV Dump: No
Special Features: RV park ($15 per night).

Washita Gaming Center
P.O. Box 307
Paoli, Oklahoma 73074
(405) 484-7777
Website: www.chickasaw.net
Map: **#44** (52 miles S. of Oklahoma City)

Restaurants: 1   Liquor: No
Casino Size: 6,335 Square Feet
Overnight RV Parking: No
Special Features: Convenience store.

Wilson Travel Plaza
354 Route 1
Wilson, Oklahoma 73463
(580) 668-9248
Website: www.chickasaw.net
Map: **#39** (112 miles S. of Oklahoma City)

Restaurants: 1   Liquor: No
Overnight RV Parking: Free/RV Dump: No

WinStar Casino
Interstate 35, Exit 1
Thackerville, Oklahoma 73459
(580) 276-4229
Website: www.winstarcasinos.com
Map: **#36** (124 miles S. of Oklahoma City)

Toll-Free Number: (800) 622-6317
Restaurants: 5   Liquor: No
Buffets: L-$10.00 D-$11.00/$15.99 (Fri)
Other Games: BJ, P, BG, OTB
Casino Size: 169,824 Square Feet
Overnight RV Parking: Free/RV Dump: No
Senior Discount: $1 off buffets if 55 or older
Special Features: $3.99 buffet 3pm-5pm daily.

Wyandotte Nation Casino
100 Jackpot Place
Wyandotte, Oklahoma 74370
(918) 678-4946
Website: www.winstarcasinos.com
Map: **#33** (90 miles N.E. of Tulsa)

Toll-Free Number: (866) 447-4946
Restaurants: 2   Liquor: Yes
Other Games: BJ, P, TCP
Overnight RV Parking: Free/RV Dump: No

Pari-Mutuels

Oklahoma has three horse tracks which offer Class II electronic video gaming machines as well as pari-mutuel betting on horse races. Admission is free to all casinos, but there is an admission charge for horse racing. The minimum gambling age is 18.

Blue Ribbon Downs Racino
3700 W. Cherokee Street
Sallisaw, Oklahoma 74955
(918) 775-7771
Website: www.blueribbondowns.net
Map: **#45** (160 miles E. of Oklahoma City)

Hours: 10am-Midnight/4am (Fri/Sat)
Self-Parking: Free   Valet Parking: $6
Restaurants: 2
Overnight RV Parking: Free/RV Dump: No
Special Features: Live horse racing May-September. Daily simulcasting of horse racing.

Cherokee Casino Will Rogers Downs
20900 S. 4200 Road
Claremore, Oklahoma 74017
(918) 343-5900
Map: **#47** (30 miles N.E. of Tulsa)
Website: www.willrogersdowns.com

Hours: 10am-1am/1:30am (Fri/Sat)
Self-Parking: Free
Restaurants: 1
Overnight RV Parking: Must use RV park
Special Features: Live horse racing Feb-May. Daily simulcasting of horse racing. 400-space RV park ($18 per night).

Remington Park Racing • Casino
One Remington Place
Oklahoma City, Oklahoma 73111
(405) 424-1000
Map: **#46**
Website: www.remingtonpark.com

Toll-Free Number: (800) 456-4244
Hours: 10am-12am/2am (Thu)3am (Fri/Sat)
Self-Parking: Free   Valet Parking: Free
Restaurants: 2
Buffet: L-$11.99 Brunch-$14.99 (Sun)
        D-$14.99/$19.99 (Thurs)/$18.99 (Fri)
Overnight RV Parking: No
Special Features: Live horse racing Fri-Mon. Daily simulcasting of horse racing. Buffet dicount for slot club members.

OREGON

Oregon law permits bars and taverns to have up to six video lottery terminals that offer various versions of video poker. Racetracks are allowed to have no more than 10 machines. The maximum bet allowed is $2 and the maximum payout on any machine is capped at $600.

These machines are the same as regular video gaming devices but are called lottery terminals because they are regulated by the state's lottery commission which receives a share of each machine's revenue. The machines accept cash but do not pay out in cash; instead, they print out a receipt which must be taken to a cashier.

According to figures from the Oregon Lottery, during its fiscal year from July 1, 2006 through June 30, 2007, the VLT's had an approximate return of 93.29%.

There are nine Indian casinos in operation in Oregon. According to the governor's office which regulates the Tribe's compacts, "there is no minimum payback percentage required on the Tribe's machines. Each Tribe is free to set their own limits on their machines."

All casinos offer blackjack, slots and video poker. Some casinos also offer: craps (C), roulette (R), poker (P), Pai Gow Poker (PGP), let it ride (LIR), three card poker (TCP), four card poker (FCP), big 6 wheel (B6), bingo (BG), keno (K) and off track betting (OTB). Unless otherwise noted, all casinos are open 24 hours and the minimum gambling age is 21 (18 for bingo).

For Oregon tourism information call (800) 547-7842 or go to: www.traveloregon.com.

Chinook Winds Casino Resort
1777 N.W. 44th Street
Lincoln City, Oregon 97367
(541) 996-5825
Website: www.chinookwindscasino.com
Map: **#4** (45 miles W. of Salem)

Toll-Free Number: (888) CHINOOK
RV Reservations: (877) 564-2678
Room Reservations: (877) 423-2241
Rooms: 146 Price Range: $139-$184
Suites: 81 Price Range: $169-$244
Restaurants: 4 Liquor: Yes
Buffets: B-$6.95 L-$7.95
      D-$11.95/$14.95 (Fri/Sat)
Other Games: C, R, P, LIR, TCP, PGP, K, BG
Overnight RV Parking: Free/RV Dump: No
Senior Discount: Meal discounts if 55 or older
Special Features: 51-space RV Park ($28/$32 per night). Childcare center. Video arcade. 18-hole golf course.

Kah-Nee-Ta High Desert Resort & Casino
6823 Highway 8
Warm Springs, Oregon 97761
(541) 553-1112
Website: www.kahneeta.com
Map: **#5** (100 miles E. of Portland)

Toll-Free Number: (800) 554-4786
Rooms: 109 Price Range: $150-$206
Suites: 30 Price Range: $180-$265
Restaurants: 2 Liquor: Yes
Casino Size: 25,000 Square Feet
Spring/Summer Hours: 8:30am-2am Daily
Fall/Winter: 10am-2am/8:30am-2am (Fri/Sat)
Other Games: P
Overnight RV Parking: Free/RV Dump: No
Special Features: 51-space RV park ($39 per night). 18-hole golf course. Horseback riding. European spa.

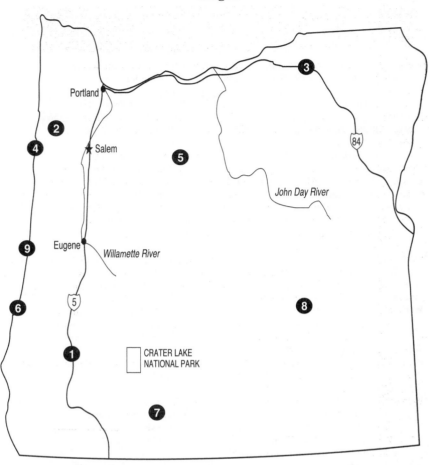

Kla-Mo-Ya Casino
34333 Hwy 97 North
Chiloquin, Oregon 97624
(541) 783-7529
Website: www.klamoyacasino.com
Map: **#7** (20 miles N. of Klamath Falls)

Toll-Free Number: (888) 552-6692
Restaurants: 2   Liquor: No
Buffets: B-$8.99 (Sun) L-$7.49
 D-$9.99/$15.99 (Fri)$10.99 (Sat)/$15.95 (Sun)
Overnight RV Parking: Free/RV Dump: No
Senior Discount: Various on Mondays if 55+
Special Features: Buffet discounts for slot club
members.

The Mill Casino Hotel
3201 Tremont Avenue
North Bend, Oregon 97459
(541) 756-8800
Website: www.themillcasino.com
Map: **#6** (75 miles S.W. of Eugene)

Toll-Free Number: (800) 953-4800
Rooms: 109 Price Range: $79-$145
Suites: 3 Price Range: $159-$239
Restaurants: 4 Liquor: Yes
Buffets: B-$14.95 (Sun) D-$15.95/$18.95 (Fri/Sat)
Other Games: C, R, P
Overnight RV Parking: Free/RV Dump: No
Senior Discount: 10% off food if 55 or older
Special Features: 65-space RV park ($32/$68
per night). Free local shuttle. Room and food
discounts for slot club members.

The Old Camp Casino
2205 W. Monroe Street
Burns, Oregon 97720
(541) 573-1500
Website: www.oldcampcasino.com
Map: **#8** (250 miles S. of Pendleton)

Toll-Free Number: (888) 343-7568
Restaurants: 1 Liquor: Yes
Summer Hours: 9am-Midnight/2am (Fri/Sat)
Winter Hours: 10am-10pm (Wed/Thu/Sun)
            10am-Midnight (Fri/Sat)
Other Games: P (Fri-Sun), BG (Sun/Wed)
Overnight RV Parking: Must use RV park
Special Features: Liquor sold in lounge and
restaurant only. 15-space RV park ($6 per
night/$15 w/hookups). BJ only played Fri-Sun.

Seven Feathers Hotel & Casino Resort
146 Chief Miwaleta Lane
Canyonville, Oregon 97417
(541) 839-1111
Website: www.sevenfeathers.com
Map: **#1** (80 miles S. of Eugene)

Toll-Free Number: (800) 548-8461
Room Reservations: (888) 677-7771
Rooms: 146 Price Range: $99-$129
Restaurants: 4 Liquor: Yes
Buffets: B-$20.50 (Sun) D-$14.25/$15.25 (Fri)
Casino Size: 27,300 Square Feet
Other Games: C, R, P, LIR, TCP, FCP, K, BG
Overnight RV Parking: Free/RV Dump: No
Special Features: 32-space RV park ($28/$35
per night). 18-hole golf course.

Spirit Mountain Casino
P.O. Box 39
Grand Ronde, Oregon 97347
(503) 879-2350
Website: www.spiritmountain.com
Map: **#2** (85 miles S.W. of Portland)

Toll-Free Number: (800) 760-7977
Reservation Number: (888) 668-7366
Rooms: 94 Price Range: $104-$164
Suites: 6 Price Range: $174-$234
Restaurants: 5 Liquor: Yes
Buffets: B-$6.95 L-$7.95 D-$11.95/$15.95 (Wed)
Other Games: C, R, P, PGP, LIR, TCP, K
Overnight RV Parking: Free/RV Dump: Free
Special Features: Childcare center. Video
arcade. Slot club members receive a $20 room
discount.

Three Rivers Casino
1845 US Highway 126
Florence, Oregon 97439
(541) 997-7529
Website: www.threeriverscasino.com
Map: **#3** (61 miles W. of Eugene)

Restaurants: 3 Liquor: Yes
Overnight RV Parking: Free/RV Dump: No

Wildhorse Resort & Casino
72777 Highway 331
Pendleton, Oregon 97801
(541) 278-2274
Website: www.wildhorseresort.com
Map: **#3** (211 miles E. of Portland)

Toll-Free Number: (800) 654-9453
Rooms: 100 Price Range: $70-$95
Suites: 5 Price Range: $99- $119
Restaurants: 4 Liquor: Yes
Buffets: B-$9.95 (Sun)
Casino Size: 80,000 Square Feet
Other Games: S21, C, R, P, TCP, K, BG
Overnight RV Parking: Free/RV Dump: No
Senior Discount: Various on Tuesdays if 55+
Special Features: 100-space RV park ($18/$20
per night). Cultural Institute. 18-hole golf
course. Health spa. Child care center.

PENNSYLVANIA

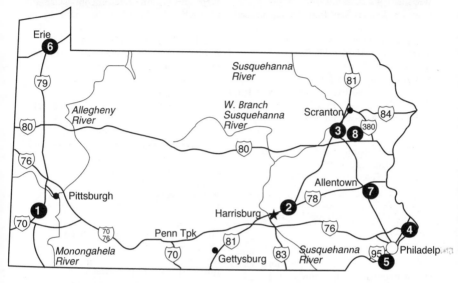

In July 2004 the Pennsylvania legislature authorized the legalization of slot machines at 14 locations throughout the state.

Licenses were awarded to the six racetracks shown below and slots are in place at all of them, except for Hollywood Casino at Penn National, which expects to have them in operation by early 2008. Additionally, one slot license is reserved for a future harness track which has not yet been built or named.

Two slot casinos will be built on the Philadelphia waterfront: Foxwoods Casino Philadelphia and SugarHouse Casino. The earliest that either casino is expected to open is late 2008. For more current information, visit their websites at sugarhousecasino.com or foxwoods.com

In Pittsburgh's North Shore area, the Majestic Star will be building a slot casino. Late 2008 is the earliest that casino is expected to open.

Bethlehem (map location #7) will be home to the Sands Bethworks Casino which is expected to open in mid-2008. For more current information, go to sandsbethworks.com

The state's 12th casino will open at the Mount Airy Lodge Resort in Mt. Pocono (map location #8). and it is expected to open by late 2007.

Finally, two slot parlors are allowed at two as-yet-to-be-determined hotels which each must have a minimum of 275 rooms. As of August 1, 2007 there were four applications for these casinos, but the decision to award the two licenses was not expected to be made until early 2008.

Pennsylvania gaming regulations require that gaming machines return a minimum of 85%. All casinos are open 24 hours and admission is free. The minimum gambling age is 18 for pari-mutuel betting and 21 for gaming machines.

For the period from January 1, 2007 through July 22, 2007 the average return on gaming machines was 92.03% at The Meadows; 91.12% at Philadelphia Park; 90.67% at Presque Isle; 90.66% at Mohegan Sun; and 90.59% at Harrah's Chester.

For more information on visiting Pennsylvania call their Office of Tourism at (800) 237-4363 or visit their website at www.visitpa.com.

Harrah's Chester Casino & Racetrack
35 E. 5th Street
Chester, Pennsylvania 19013
(484) 490-2207
Website: www.harrahs.com
Map: **#5** (8 miles S. of Philadelphia airport)

Toll-Free Number: (800) 480-8020
Valet Parking: $5/$10 (Fri-Sun)
Restaurants: 6
Buffets: L-$12.95 D-$16.95
Special Features: Live harness racing from early July through mid-December. Daily simulcast of harness and thoroughbred racing.

Hollywood Casino at Penn National
720 Bow Creek Road
Grantville, Pennsylvania 17028
(717) 469-2211
Website: www.pennnational.com
Map: **#2** (16 miles N.E. of Harrisburg)

Restaurants: 1
Special Features: Live thoroughbred horse racing Wed-Sat evenings all year long. Daily simulcast of harness and thoroughbred racing. Slots expected to open in early 2008.

The Meadows
PO Box 499
Meadow Lands, Pennsylvania 15347
(724) 225-9300
Website: www.meadowsgaming.com
Map: **#1** (25 miles S.W. of Pittsburgh)

Valet Parking: $3
Restaurants: 3
Special Features: Live harness racing various evenings all year long. Daily simulcast of harness and thoroughbred racing.

Mohegan Sun at Pocono Downs
1280 Highway 315
Wilkes-Barre, Pennsylvania 18702
(570) 831-2100
Website: www.poconodowns.com
Map: **#3** (20 miles S.W. of Scranton)

Valet Parking: Not Offered
Restaurants: 4
Special Features: Live harness racing various evenings early April through mid-November Daily simulcast of harness and thoroughbred racing. New expansion to open in mid-2008.

Mount Airy Resort & Casino
44 Woodland Road
Mount Pocono, Pennsylvania 18344
(570) 243-4800
Website: www.mtairyresort.com
Map: **#8** (30 miles S.E. of Scranton)

Toll-Free Number: (877) 682-4791
Rooms: 175 Price Range: Not Set at Press
Suites: 25 Price Range: $299-$449
Restaurants: 3
Casino Size: 68,000 Square Feet
Special Features: 18-hole golf course. Spa.

Philadelphia Park Casino and Racetrack
3001 Street Road
Bensalem, Pennsylvania 19020
(215) 639-9000
Website: www.philadelphiapark.com
Map: **#4** (18 miles N.E. of Philadelphia)

Toll-Free Number: (888) 442-6366
Valet Parking: $5
Restaurants: 3
Buffets: L-$12.99 D-$16.99
Special Features: Thoroughbred horse racing Sat-Tue afternoons all year long. Friday racing added January and February. Daily simulcast of harness and thoroughbred racing.

Presque Isle Downs & Casino
8199 Perry Highway
Erie, Pennsylvania 16509
Website: www.presqueisledowns.com
Map: **#6**

Toll-Free Number: (866) 374-3386
Valet Parking: $3
Restaurants: 4
Buffets: B-$4.95 L-$7.95 D-$10.95
Special Features: Live thoroughbred horse racing during September. Daily simulcast of harness and thoroughbred racing.

RHODE ISLAND

Rhode Island has two pari-mutuel facilities which both feature video lottery terminals (VLT's). These machines are the same as regular video gaming devices but are called lottery terminals because they are regulated by the state's lottery commission which receives a share of each machine's revenue. The machines accept cash but don't pay out in cash; instead, they print out a receipt which must be taken to a cashier.

All VLT's are programmed to play at least six different games: blackjack, keno, slots and three versions of poker (jacks or better, joker poker and deuces wild).

The Rhode Island Lottery does not provide figures to determine the actual paybacks on its VLT's. However, according to officials at the Rhode Island Lottery, the VLT's are programmed to pay back the following amounts over time:

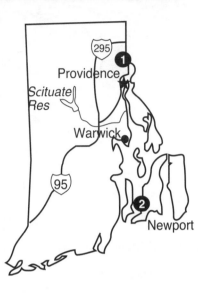

Blackjack - 99.1%
5¢, 10¢, 25¢ Video Poker - 95%
50¢ Video Poker - 96.5%
$1 Video Poker - 98%
5¢, 10¢, 25¢ Slots - 92%
50¢ Slots - 94%
$1 Slots - 96%
25¢ Keno - 92%
50¢ Keno - 94%
$1 Keno - 96%.

The minimum gambling age in Rhode Island is 18. For information on visiting Rhode Island call the state's tourism division at (800) 556-2484 or go to: www.visitrhodeisland.com.

Newport Grand
150 Admiral Kalbfus Road
Newport, Rhode Island 02840
(401) 849-5000
Web Site: www.newportgrand.com
Map: **#2**

Toll-Free Number: (800) 451-2500
Restaurants: 1   Valet Parking: $2.50
Hours: 10am-1am Daily

Admission: Free
Overnight RV Parking: No
Special Features: Daily simulcasting of horse racing, dog racing and jai-alai.

Twin River
1600 Louisquisset Pike
Lincoln, Rhode Island 02865
(401) 723-3200
Web Site: www.twinriver.com
Map: **#1** (10 miles N. of Providence)

Toll-Free Number: (877) 827-4837
Restaurants: 4   Valet Parking: Free
Buffets: L-$13.95 D-$16.95
Hours: 9am-2am Daily
Admission: Free
Overnight RV Parking: No
Special Features: Live dog racing (Mon/Wed/Fri/Sat) throughout the year. Daily (except Tuesday) simulcasting of horse and dog racing.

SOUTH CAROLINA

South Carolina has two casino boats which sail three miles out into international waters where casino gambling is permitted.

Both boats offer: blackjack, craps, roulette, three card poker, slots and video poker. Due to security restrictions, you must present a photo ID or you will not be allowed to board.

For more information on visiting South Carolina go to: www.discoversouthcarolina.com or call their tourism department at (800) 872-3505

Diamond Casino Cruises
4491 Waterfront Avenue
Little River, South Carolina 29566
(843) 249-9811
Website: www.diamondcasinocruises.com
Map Location: **#1** (35 miles N. of Myrtle Beach)

Reservation Number: (877) 250-5825
Ship's Registry: U.S.   Gambling Age: 18
Food: Pre-boarding buffet included
Schedule:
   11:00am - 4:00pm   (Mon-Fri)
    7:00pm - 12:00am (Sun-Thu)
    7:00pm - 1:00am   (Fri/Sat)
  12:00pm - 5:00pm   (Sat/Sun)
Price: $10
Port Charges: None   Parking: Free

Other Games: Poker, Three Card Poker
Special Features: 600-passenger *Diamond Girl II* sails from Little River waterfront. Free shuttle available from Myrtle Beach. Must be 18 or older to board.

SunCruz Casino - Myrtle Beach
99705 Mineola Avenue
Little River, South Carolina 29566
(843) 280-2933
Website: www.suncruzcasino.com
Map Location: **#1** (35 miles N. of Myrtle Beach)

Ship's Registry: U.S.   Gambling Age: 18
Buffets: L-$7 D-$10
Schedule:
   11:00am - 4:15pm (Mon-Fri)
     Noon - 5:15pm (Sat/Sun/Holidays)
    7:00pm - 12:15am (Sun-Thu)
    7:00pm - 1:15am (Fri/Sat)
Price: $10
Port Charges: Included   Parking: Free
Other Games: Let It Ride, Three Card Poker
Senior Discount: Free buffet Mon if 55+
Special Features: 600-passenger *SunCruz VIII* sails from Little River waterfront. Must be 18 or older to board.

SOUTH DAKOTA

South Dakota's bars and taverns are allowed to have up to 10 video lottery terminals (VLT's) that offer the following games: poker, keno, blackjack and bingo. These machines are the same as regular video gaming devices but are called lottery terminals because they are regulated by the state's lottery commission which receives a share of each machine's revenue. The machines accept cash but don't pay out in cash; instead, they print out a receipt which must be taken to a cashier. The maximum bet is $2 and the maximum payout allowed is $1,000.

Slot machines, as well as blackjack and poker are only permitted at Indian casinos and in Deadwood.

Deadwood was once most famous for being the home of Wild Bill Hickok who was shot to death while playing cards in the No. 10 Saloon. The hand he held was two pairs: black aces and black eights, which is now commonly referred to as a "dead man's hand." Wild Bill is buried in the local cemetery along with another local celebrity: Calamity Jane.

The first casinos in Deadwood opened on November 1, 1989. All of the buildings in the downtown area are required to conform with the city's authentic 1880's architecture. Many of the casinos are located in historic structures but there are also some new structures which were designed to be compatible with the historic theme of the town. The old No. 10 Saloon is still operating and you can actually gamble in the same spot where old Wild Bill bit the dust!

South Dakota law limits each casino licensee to 30 slot machines and no one person is allowed to hold more than three licenses. Some operators combine licenses with other operators to form a cooperative which may look like one casino but in reality it's actually several licensees operating under one name.

The state's gaming laws originally limited blackjack, poker, let it ride and three-card poker bets to a maximum of $5, however, in late 2000 the law was changed to allow maximum bets of $100.

In addition to the Deadwood casinos, there are also nine Indian casinos in South Dakota. These casinos are also subject to the $100 maximum bet restrictions.

Here are statistics from the South Dakota Commission on Gaming for the payback percentages on all of Deadwood's slot machines for the one-year period from July 1, 2006 through June 30, 2007:

Denomination	Payback %
1¢ Slots	90.79
5¢ Slots	90.96
25¢ Slots	90.76
50¢ Slots	91.51
$1 Slots	91.98
$5 Slots	93.59
$25 Slots	95.09
Average	91.29

Some of the larger casinos are open 24 hours but most of the smaller ones are open from 8 a.m. until midnight Sunday through Thursday and 8 a.m. until 2 a.m. on the weekends.

The Deadwood Trolly runs a scheduled shuttle service to all of the casinos that operates from 8 a.m. to midnight weekdays and 7 a.m. to 3 a.m. on weekends. During the summer months the weekday hours are extended until 1:30 a.m. The cost is $1 per ride.

Unless otherwise noted, all casinos offer slot machines and video poker. Some casinos also offer: blackjack (BJ), let it ride (LIR), three-card poker (TCP), Caribbean stud poker (CSP) and poker (P). Most of the Indian casinos also offer bingo (BG).

The minimum gambling age is 21 at all Deadwood and Indian casinos (18 for bingo at Indian casinos). South Dakota's casinos have very liberal rules about allowing minors in casinos and virtually all of the casinos will allow children to enter with their parents until about 8 p.m. Additionally, South Dakota is the only jurisdiction that will allow children to stand next to their parents while they are gambling.

For South Dakota tourism information call (800) 732-5682. For information on visiting Deadwood call the city's Chamber of Commerce at (800) 999-1876, or visit their website at www.deadwood.org.

Deadwood

Map: **#1** (in the Black Hills, 41 miles N.W. of Rapid City. Take I-90 W. Get off at the second Sturges exit and take Hwy. 14-A into Deadwood)

B. B. Cody's
681 Main Street
Deadwood, South Dakota 57732
(605) 578-3430

Restaurants: 1
Special Features: Video arcade.

Best Western Hickok House
137 Charles Street
Deadwood, South Dakota 57732
(605) 578-1611
Website: www.bestwestern.com

Best Western Reservations: 800-837-8174
Rooms: 38   Price Range: $69-$119
Restaurants: 1
Special Features: Hot tub and sauna.

Bourbon Street
667 Main Street
Deadwood, South Dakota 57732
(605) 578-1297

Special Features: Free mardi gras beads and dirty rice daily.

Buffalo-Bodega Gaming Complex
658 Main Street
Deadwood, South Dakota 57732
(605) 578-1162

Restaurants: 1
Other games: BJ
Special Features: Oldest bar in Deadwood. Steakhouse restaurant. Ice cream parlor.

Bullock Express
68 Main Street
Deadwood, South Dakota 57732
(605) 578-3476
Website: www.historicbullock.com/be.htm

Reservation Number: 800-526-8277
Rooms: 38   Price Range: $45-$75
Restaurants: 1

Bullock Hotel
633 Main Street
Deadwood, South Dakota 57732
(605) 578-1745
Website: www.historicbullock.com/bh.htm

Reservation Number: 800-336-1876
Rooms: 26   Price Range: $65-$99
Suites: 2 Price Range: $135-$159
Restaurants: 1
Hours: 24 Hours Daily
Special Features: Deadwood's oldest hotel.

Cadillac Jacks's Gaming Resort
360 Main Street
Deadwood, South Dakota 57732
(605) 578-1500
Website: www.cadillacjacksgaming.com

Toll Free Number: (866) 332-3966
Rooms: 92 Price Range: $79-$169
Suites: 11 Price Range: $229-$310
Restaurants: 1
Hours: 24 Hours Daily
Casino Size: 10,000 Square Feet
Other Games: BJ, P, TCP
Special Features: Hotel is AmericInn. 15% off rooms for slot club members. Free valet parking.

Celebrity Hotel & Casino
629 Main Street
Deadwood, South Dakota 57732
(605) 578-1909
Website: www.celebritycasinos.com

Toll-Free Number: (888) 399-1886
Rooms: 9 Price Range: $69-$129
Suites: 3 Price Range: $99-$159
Hours: 24 Hours Daily
Special Features: Car and motorcycle museum. Free to hotel guests, otherwise admission charge. Includes the **Mint Casino.**

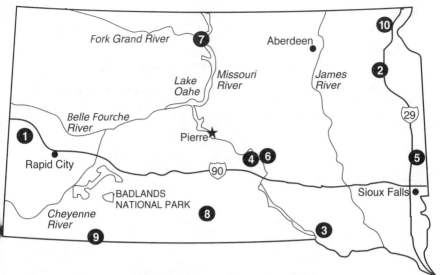

Deadwood Dick's Saloon and Gaming Hall
51 Sherman Street
Deadwood, South Dakota 57732
(605) 578-3224
Website: www.deadwooddicks.com

Toll Free Number: (877) 882-4990
Rooms: 5 Price Range: $50-$85
Suites: 6 Price Range: $110-$200
Restaurants: 1
Special Features: Antique mall with 30 dealers.

Deadwood Gulch Resort
304 Cliff Street
Deadwood, South Dakota 57732
(605) 578-1294
Website: www.deadwoodgulch.com

Reservation Number: (800) 695-1876
Rooms: 95 Price Range: $59-$119
Restaurants: 1
Hours: 24 Hours Daily
Casino Size: 7,500 Square Feet
Other Games: BJ
Special Features: Free breakfast for hotel guests.

Deadwood Gulch Saloon
560 Main Street
Deadwood, South Dakota 57732
(605) 578-1207

First Gold Hotel & Gaming
270 Main Street
Deadwood, South Dakota 57732
(605) 578-9777
Website: www.firstgold.com

Reservation Number: (800) 274-1876
Rooms: 101 Price Range: $39-$99
Suites: 1 Price Range: $89-$229
Restaurants: 2
Hours: 24 Hours Daily
Casino Size: 11,000 Square Feet
Other Games: BJ, TCP
Senior Discount: 10% off room if 55 or older
Special Features: 79¢ breakfast 6-11am. RV park located next door. Includes **Blackjack** and **Horseshoe** casinos.

Four Aces
531 Main Street
Deadwood, South Dakota 57732
(605) 578-2323
Website: www.fouracesdeadwood.com

Toll Free Number: (800) 834-4384
Rooms: 59 Price Range: $109-$179
Suites: 5 Price Range: $179-$264
Restaurants: 1
Buffets: B/L-$6.99 D-$12.99/$14.99 (Fri/Sat)
Hours: 24 Hours Daily
Casino Size: 24,000 Square Feet
Other Games: BJ, LIR, TCP
Senior Discount: room/food discounts if 55+
Special Features: Hotel is Hampton Inn.

Goldberg's
670 Main Street
Deadwood, South Dakota 57732
(605) 578-1515

Restaurants: 1
Hours: 9am-2am Daily
Casino Size: 2,500 Square Feet
Special Features: Ice cream parlor.

Gold Country Inn
801 Main Street
Deadwood, South Dakota 57732
(605) 578-2393

Reservation Number: (800) 287-1251
Rooms: 53   Price Range: $35-$79
Restaurants: 1

Gold Dust Gaming & Entertainment Complex
688 Main Street
Deadwood, South Dakota 57732
(605) 578-2100
Website: www.golddustgaming.com

Toll-Free Number: (800) 456-0533
Rooms: 56 Price Range: $39-$149
Suites: 22 Price Range: $139-$190
Restaurants: 1
Buffets: B-$5.99 L-$7.99
          D-$11.99/$13.99 (Fri/Sat)
Hours: 24 Hours Daily
Casino Size: 30,000 Square Feet
Other Games: BJ, P, TCP
Senior Discount: $1 off buffets if 55 or older
Special Features: Hotel is Holiday Inn Express.
Largest gaming complex in Deadwood with
nine casinos. Free continental breakfast for
hotel guests, indoor pool, gym, whirlpool,
arcade. Includes **French Quarter**, **Legends**
and **Silver Dollar** casinos.

Gulches of Fun
225 Cliff Street
Deadwood, South Dakota 57732
(605) 578-7550
Website: www.gulchesoffun.com

Reservation Number: (800) 961-3096
Rooms: 66 Price Range: $60-$130
Suites: 5 Price Range: $79-$149
Restaurants: 1
Hours: 24 Hours Daily
Special Features: Hotel is Comfort Inn. Family
amusement center with rides and mini-golf.

Hickok's Iron Horse
27 Deadwood Street
Deadwood, South Dakota 57732
(605) 578-7700

Toll Free Number: (877) 815-7974
Rooms: 19 Price Range: $59-$124
Suites: 4 Price Range: $99-$239
Casino Size: 1,000 Square Feet
Hours: 24 Hours Daily

Hickok's Saloon
685 Main Street
Deadwood, South Dakota 57732
(605) 578-2222
Website: www.hickoks.com

Other Games: BJ, TCP
Special Features: Video arcade.

Lucky 8 Gaming Hall/Super 8 Motel
196 Cliff Street
Deadwood, South Dakota 57732
(605) 578-2535
Website: www.deadwoodsuper8.com

Reservation Number: (800) 800-8000
Rooms: 47 Price Range: $40-$95
Suites: 4 Price Range: $85-$135
Restaurants: 1
Hours: 24 Hours Daily
Special Features: Video arcade. Free
continental breakfast for hotel guests.

Nestled in the Black Hills of South Dakota, the entire city of Deadwood has been designated a national historic landmark. Free historic walking tours are offered daily.

McKenna's Gold
470 Main Street
Deadwood, South Dakota 57732
(605) 578-3207

Midnight Star
677 Main Street
Deadwood, South Dakota 57732
(605) 578-1555
Website: www.themidnightstar.com

Toll-Free Number: (800) 999-6482
Restaurants: 2
Other Games: BJ, LIR, TCP
Special Features: Sports Bar & Grill.

Mineral Palace Hotel & Gaming Complex
601 Main Street
Deadwood, South Dakota 57732
(605) 578-2036
Website: www.mineralpalace.com

Reservation Number: (800) 84-PALACE
Rooms: 63 Price Range: $89-$159
Suites: 4 Price Range: $109-$329
Restaurants: 1
Hours: 24 Hours Daily
Other Games: BJ, TCP
Special Features: Cappuccino/espresso bar.
Liquor store.

Miss Kitty's Gaming Emporium
647 Main Street
Deadwood, South Dakota 57732
(605) 578-1811
Website: www.historicbullock.com/mk.htm

Restaurants: 2
Hours: 24 Hours Daily
Special Features: Chinese restaurant.

Mustang Sally's
634 Main Street
Deadwood, South Dakota 57732
(605) 578-2025

Old Style Saloon #10
657 Main Street
Deadwood, South Dakota 57732
(605) 578-3346
Website: www.saloon10.com

Toll-Free Number: (800) 952-9398
Restaurants: 1
Casino Size: 4,000 Square Feet
Other Games: BJ, P, TCP
Special Features: During summer there is a reenactment of the "Shooting of Wild Bill Hickok" at 1, 3, 5 and 7 p.m. Wild Bill's chair and other Old West artifacts on display. Italian restaurant.

Oyster Bay/Fairmont Hotel
628 Main Street
Deadwood, South Dakota 57732
(605) 578-2205

Restaurants: 1
Special Features: Historic restoration of 1895
brothel, spa and underground jail cell. Oyster
bar.

**Silverado - Franklin Historic Hotel &
Gaming Complex**
700-709 Main Street
Deadwood, South Dakota 57732
(605) 578-3670
Website: www.silveradocasino.com

Toll-Free Number: (800) 584-7005
Reservation Number: (800) 688-1876
Rooms: 80   Price Range: $49-$115
Suites: 15 Price Range: $79-$199
Restaurants: 1
Buffets: B/L-$6.95 D-$11.95/$13.95 (Fri/Sat)
Hours: 24 Hours Daily
Casino Size: 20,000 Square Feet
Other Games: BJ, P, LIR, TCP, CSP
Special Features: 50-cent breakfast special.

Tin Lizzie Gaming
555 Main Street
Deadwood, South Dakota 57732
(605) 578-1715
Web Sit: www.tinlizzie.com

Toll-Free Number: (800) 643-4490
Restaurants: 1
Buffets: B-$3.99
Hours: 24 Hours Daily
Casino Size: 8,300 Square Feet
Other Games: BJ
Senior Discount: Various if 50 or older

Veterans Of Foreign War
10 Pine Street
Deadwood, South Dakota 57732
(605) 722-9914

Hours: 9:30am-10pm Daily

Wild West Winners Casino
622 Main Street
Deadwood, South Dakota 57732
(605) 578-1100
Website: www.historicbullock.com/wwc.htm

Toll-Free Number: (800) 873-1876
Restaurants: 1
Special Features: Steakhouse restaurant. Ice
cream parlor. Includes **Jackpot Charlie's**
casino.

Wooden Nickel
9 Lee Street
Deadwood, South Dakota 57732
(605) 578-1856

Special Features: Includes **Martin Mason**
casinos.

Indian Casinos

Dakota Connection
RR 1, Box 177-B
Sisseton, South Dakota 57262
(605) 698-4273
Website: www.dakotanationgaming.com
Map: **#10** (165 miles N. of Sioux Falls)

Toll-Free Number: (800) 542-2876
Restaurants: 1   Liquor: No
Buffets: B-$6.50 (Sat/Sun) L-$7.50 (Sun)
Hours: 24 Hours Daily
Other Games: BG
Overnight RV Parking: Free/RV Dump: No

Dakota Sioux Casino
16415 Sioux Conifer Road
Watertown, South Dakota 57201
(605) 882-2051
Website: www.dakotanationgaming.com
Map: **#2** (104 miles N. of Sioux Falls)

Toll-Free Number: (800) 658-4717
Rooms: 88 Price Range: $59-$79
Suites: 12 Price Range: $99-$199
Restaurants: 1 Liquor: Yes
Buffets: B-$4.95 L-$7.95/$9.95 (Sat/Sun)
   D-$6.95 (Mon)/$18.95 (Tues)
   $10.95 (Wed/Fri)$14.95 (Thu)/$12.95
Hours: 24 Hours Daily
Other Games: BJ, P
Overnight RV Parking: Free/RV Dump: Free
Senior Discount: Specials on Mon if 55+
Special Features: 18-space RV park (Free,
including hookups).

Fort Randall Casino Hotel
East Highway 46
Pickstown, South Dakota 57367
(605) 487-7871
Website: www.fortrandall.com
Map: **#3** (100 miles S.W. of Sioux Falls)

Room Reservations: (800) 362-6333
Rooms: 57 Price Range: $59-$69
Suites: 2 Price Range: $79-$100
Restaurants: 1 Liquor: Yes
Buffets: B-$6.95 (Sat/Sun) L-$7.95
   D-$9.95/$10.95 (Fri)/$13.95 (Sat)
Hours: 24 Hours Daily
Other Games: BJ, P, BG (Wed-Sun)
Overnight RV Parking: Free/RV Dump: Free
Senior Discount: Specials on Wed if 50+
Special Features: 20-space RV park (Free,
including hookups).

Golden Buffalo Casino
321 Sitting Bull Street
Lower Brule, South Dakota 57548
(605) 473-5577
Website: www.lbst.org/casino.htm
Map: **#4** (45 miles S.E. of Pierre)

Room Reservations: (605) 473-5506
Rooms: 38 Price Range: $39-$54
Restaurants: 1 Liquor: Yes
Hours: 8am-1:30am/2am (Fri/Sat)
Casino Size: 9,000 Square Feet
Other Games: BG (Wed), No blackjack
Overnight RV Parking: Free/RV Dump: Free
Senior Discount: Specials on Mon if 50+

Grand River Casino and Lodge
P.O. Box 639
Mobridge, South Dakota 57601
(605) 845-7104
Website: www.grandrivercasino.com
Map: **#7** (240 miles N.E. of Rapid City)

Toll-Free Number: (800) 475-3321
Rooms: 38 Price Range: $60-$105
Suites: 2 Price Range: $85-$129
Restaurants: 1 Liquor: Yes
Buffets: B-$6.95 (Sat/Sun)
         D-$8.95/$11.95 (Sat)/$10.95 (Sun)
Hours: 24 Hours Daily
Other Games: BJ, P (Sat/Sun)
Overnight RV Parking: Free/RV Dump: No
Special Features: 10-space RV park ($10 per
night).

Lode Star Casino
P.O. Box 140
Fort Thompson, South Dakota 57339
(605) 245-6000
Website: www.lodestarcasino.com
Map: **#6** (150 miles N.W. of Sioux Falls)

Room Reservations: (888) 268-1360
Restaurants: 1 Liquor: Yes
Rooms: 50 Price Range: $39-$62
Hours: 7am-2am/4am (Fri/Sat)
Other Games: BJ, P (Mon/Wed/Thu)
Overnight RV Parking: Free/RV Dump: No

Prairie Wind Casino
HC 49, Box 10
Pine Ridge, South Dakota 57770
(605) 867-6300
Website: www.prairiewindcasino.com
Map: **#9** (85 miles S.E. of Rapid City)

Toll-Free Number: (800) 705-9463
Rooms: 78 Price Range: $56-$91
Suites: 6 Price Range: $126-$156
Restaurants: 1 Liquor: No
Buffets: B-$4.95 L-$6.95
   D-$7.95/$9.95 (Wed)/$$8.95 (Fri/Sun)
Hours: 24 Hours Daily
Other Games: BJ, TCP
Overnight RV Parking: Free/RV Dump: No
Special Features: Casino is located 12 miles
East of Oelrichs off Hwy. 385 and 8 miles West
of Oglala on Hwy. 18.

Rosebud Casino
Highway 83 (on SD/NE stateline)
Mission, South Dakota 57555
(605) 378-3800
Website: www.rosebudcasino.com
Map: **#8** (22 miles S. of Mission)

Toll-Free Number: (800) 786-7673
Room Reservations: (877) 521-9913
Rooms: 58 Price Range: $79-$99
Suites: 2 Price Range: $89-$109
Restaurants: 2 Liquor: Yes
Buffets: Brunch-$8.99 (Sun) D-$9.99
Hours: 24 Hours Daily
Other Games: BJ, P (Fri-Tue), BG
Overnight RV Parking: Free/RV Dump: No
Senior Discount: Various if 55 or older
Special Features: Hotel is Quality Inn.

Royal River Casino & Hotel
607 S. Veterans Street
Flandreau, South Dakota 57028
(605) 997-3746
Website: www.royalrivercasino.com
Map: **#5** (35 miles N. of Sioux Falls on I-29)

Toll-Free Number: (800) 833-8666
Rooms: 108 Price Range: $55-$60
Suites: 12 Price Range: $90-$95
Restaurants: 2 Liquor: Yes
Buffets: B-$7.45 L-$8.00
    D-$10.95/$15.95 (Mon)/$11.95 (Fri/Sat)
Hours: 24 Hours Daily
Casino Size: 17,000 Square Feet
Other Games: BJ, P (Thu-Sun), LIR, OTB
Overnight RV Parking: Free/RV Dump: No
Special Features: 21-space RV park ($10 per night).

TEXAS

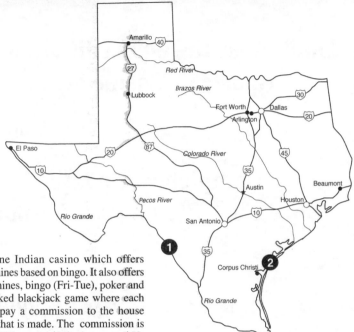

Texas has one Indian casino which offers gaming machines based on bingo. It also offers pull tab machines, bingo (Fri-Tue), poker and a player-banked blackjack game where each player must pay a commission to the house for each bet that is made. The commission is 50¢ for $3-$50 bets and $1 for bets over $50. The minimum gambling age is 21 and the casino is open 24 hours daily. For more information on visiting Texas call (800) 888-8TEX or go to: www.traveltex.com.

Kickapoo Lucky Eagle Casino
Lucky Eagle Drive
Eagle Pass, Texas 78852
(830) 758-1995
Website: www.kickapooluckyeaglecasino.com
Map: **#1** (140 miles S.W. of San Antonio)

Toll-Free Number: (888) 255-8259
Restaurants: 1 Liquor: Yes Valet Parking: No
Buffets: B/L-$8.00 D-$9.00
Casino Size: 16,000 Square Feet
Overnight RV Parking: Free/RV Dump: Free
Special Features: 20-space RV park (Free, including hookups).

Texas has one casino boat which sails nine miles out into the Gulf of Mexico where casino gambling is permitted. The boat offers: blackjack, craps, roulette, poker, Caribbean stud poker, let it ride, three card poker, slots and video poker. You must provide a photo ID or you won't be allowed to board.

Texas Treasure Casino Cruises
1401 W. Wheeler Avenue
Aransas Pass, Texas 78336
(361) 758-4444
Website: www.txtreasure.com
Map: **#2** (10 miles N.E. of Corpus Christi)

Reservation Number: (866) 468-5825
Gambling Age: 21 Ship's Registry: U.S.
Meal Service: Buffet Included
Schedule/Prices:
12:00pm - 6pm (Sun) $19.95
11:00 am - 5pm (Tue-Fri) $15/$10 (Tue)
11:00 am - 5pm (Sat) $19.95
7:00pm - 12:30am (Sun) $15
6:30pm - 12:30am (Tue-Thu) $15/$10 (Tue)
6:30pm - 1:30am (Fri/Sat) $19.95
Port Charges: Included Parking: Free
Senior Discount: $5 off $19.95 cruises if 55+
Special Features: 1,010-passenger *Texas Treasure* sails from Port Aransas at the ferry crossing. Must be 21 or older to board.

WASHINGTON

There are 26 Indian casinos operating in Washington. Twenty-four of the casinos are affiliated with tribes that have compacts with the state allowing them to offer table games, as well as electronic 'scratch' ticket games which use a finite number of tickets with a predetermined number of winners and losers.

These video gaming machines have a maximum bet of $5 and aren't allowed to accept cash. Instead, a cashless system is used whereby you have to go to a cashier cage, or a kiosk, get a "smart" card and deposit money to that card's account. The machines will then deducts losses from, or credit wins to, your account. Ticket-in ticket-out (TITO) receipts are also used in some casinos.

The remaining two casinos (Chewelah and Two Rivers) are affiliated with the Spokane Tribe which has an ongoing dispute with the state and their casinos are operating without a compact. These casinos offer regular spinning-reel slots which accept cash, plus an assortment of table games.

All of the state's Tribes are not required to release information on their slot machine percentage paybacks. However, according to the terms of the compact between the Tribes and the state, the minimum prize payout for electronic 'scratch' ticket games is 75%.

Most Washington casinos are not open on a 24-hour basis and the hours of operation are noted in each casino's listing.

All casinos offer blackjack, craps, roulette, slots, video poker and pull tabs. Optional games offered include: baccarat (B), mini-baccarat (MB), poker (P), pai gow poker (PGP), Caribbean stud poker (CSP), three-card poker (TCP), Spanish 21 (S21), big 6 wheel (B6), keno (K), Off-Track Betting (OTB) and bingo (BG). The minimum gambling age is 21 for casinos and 18 for bingo or pari-mutuel betting.

Although most of the casinos have toll-free numbers be aware that some of these numbers will only work for calls made within Washington.

For more information on visiting Washington call their tourism department at (800) 544-1800 or go to: www.experiencewashington.com.

Angel of the Winds Casino
3438 Stoluckquamish Lane
Arlington, Washington 98223
(360) 474-9740
Website: www.angelofthewinds.com
Map: **#22** (50 miles N. of Seattle)

Restaurants: 1 Liquor: Yes Valet Parking: Free
Hours: 8am-4am Daily
Other Games: P, TCP, FCP
Overnight RV Parking: Free/RV Dump: No
Special Features: Must be 21 or older to gamble.

Chewelah Casino
2555 Smith Road
Chewelah, Washington 99109
(509) 935-6167
Website: www.chewelahcasino.com
Map: **#13** (50 miles N. of Spokane)

Toll-Free Number: (800) 322-2788
Restaurants: 1 Liquor: No Valet Parking: No
Buffets: B- $10.95 (Sun)
          L-$6.95 (Sat)
          D-$9.95 (Thu)/$9.50 (Fri)
Hours: 9am-2am/4am (Fri/Sat)
Casino Size: 22,000 Square Feet
Overnight RV Parking: Free/RV Dump: No
Senior Discount: Various Wed if 55+
Special Features: Regular slots. One block from Double Eagle Casino. 20-space RV park ($10 per night). Gambling age is 18.

Coulee Dam Casino
515 Birch Street
Coulee Dam, Washington 99155
(509) 633-0766
Website: www.colvillecasinos.com
Map: **#11** (190 miles E. of Seattle)

Toll-Free Number: (800) 556-7492
Restaurants: 1 Deli Liquor: No
Hours: 9am-1am/24 Hours (Fri/Sat)
Other Games: Only gaming machines
Overnight RV Parking: Free/RV Dump: No
Special Features: Gambling age is 18.

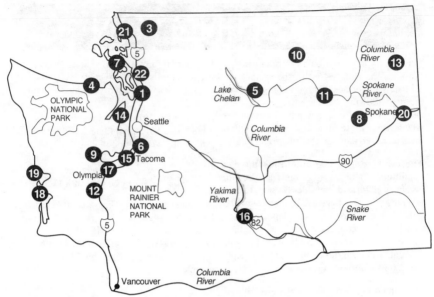

Emerald Queen Hotel & Casino - Fife
5700 Pacific Highway East
Fife, Washington 98424
(206) 594-7777
Website: www.emeraldqueen.com
Map: **#15** (a suburb of Tacoma)

Toll-Free Number: (888) 820-3555
Rooms: 130 Price Range: $89-$109
Suites: 10 Price Range: $189-$239
Restaurants: 1 Liquor: Yes Valet Parking: No
Hours: 10am-6am/24 Hours (Fri-Mon)
Other Games: Only gaming machines/keno
Overnight RV Parking: No
Special Features: Gambling age is 21.

Emerald Queen Casino at I-5
2024 East 29th Street
Tacoma, Washington 98404
(206) 383-1572
Website: www.emeraldqueen.com
Map: **#15** (a suburb of Tacoma)

Toll-Free Number: (888) 831-7655
Restaurants: 3 Liquor: Yes Valet Parking: Free
Buffets: B-$12.95 (Sat)/$14.95 (Sun) L-$9.95
        D-$15.95/$19.95 (Mon/Fri/Sat)
Hours: 10am-6am/24 Hours (Fri-Mon)
Other Games: S21, PGP, CSP, LIR
Overnight RV Parking: Free/RV Dump: No
Special Features: Sports bar. Gambling age is 21.

Little Creek Casino Resort
91 West Highway 108
Shelton, Washington 98584
(360) 427-7711
Website: www.little-creek.com
Map: **#9** (23 miles N. of Olympia off Hwy 101/108 interchange)

Toll-Free Number: (800) 667-7711
Rooms: 92 Price Range: $79-$109
Suites: 6 Price Range: $139-$209
Restaurants: 2 Liquor: Yes Valet Parking: Free
Buffets: B-$7.00/$13.00 (Sun) L-$9.00
        D-$14.00/$19.00 (Fri/Sat)/$17.95 (Sun)
Hours: 9am-4am/5am (Fri/Sat)
Casino Size: 30,000 Square Feet
Other Games: S21, P, PGP, TCP, K, BG
Overnight RV Parking: Free/RV Dump: No
Senior Discount: Various Mon-Wed if 50+
Special Features: Indoor pool. Gift shop. Gambling age is 21.

Lucky Dog Casino
19330 N. Highway 101
Shelton, Washington 98584
(360) 877-5656
Website: www.theluckydogcasino.com
Map: **#9** (23 miles N. of Olympia)

Toll-Free Number: (877) LUCKY-4-U
Restaurants: 1 Liquor: No Valet Parking: No
Hours: 10am-12:00am/2am (Wed-Sat)
Casino Size: 2,500 Square Feet
Other Games: TCP, PGP, P
Overnight RV Parking: Call Ahead/RV Dump: No
Senior Discount: Various Mon-Thu if 50+
Special Features: Will reimburse up to two days of RV parking fees at participating RV parks. Call for details. Gambling age is 21.

Lucky Eagle Casino
12888 188th Avenue SW
Rochester, Washington 98579
(360) 273-2000
Website: www.luckyeagle.com
Map: **#12** (26 miles S. of Olympia)

Toll-Free Number: (800) 720-1788
Rooms: 65 Price Range: $99-$129
Suites: 4 Price Range: $119-$259
Restaurants: 5 Liquor: Yes Valet Parking: No
Buffets: L-$8.25/$11.50 (Sun)
    D-$11.50/$14.95 (Sat)/$23.95 (Fri)
Hours: 9am-4am/6am (Fri/Sat)
Casino Size: 75,000 Square Feet
Other Games: S21, P, PGP, TCP, K, BG
Overnight RV Parking: Free/RV Dump: No
Senior Discount: Various specials Mon if 55+
Special Features: 20-space RV park ($14 per night). Gambling age is 21.

Mill Bay Casino
455 E. Wapato Lake Road
Manson, Washington 98831
(509) 687-2102
Website: www.colvillecasinos.com
Map: **#5** (200 miles N.E. of Seattle on the N. shore of Lake Chelan)

Toll-Free Number: (800) 648-2946
Restaurants: 1 Liquor: No Valet Parking: No
Buffets: B-$4.95 (Sat)/$7.77 (Sun)
    D-$19.99 (Fri)/$13.95 (Sat)
Other Games: S21, PGP
Overnight RV Parking: Free/RV Dump: No
Senior Discount: Various Tuesdays if 55+
Special Features: Gambling age is 18.

Muckleshoot Casino
2402 Auburn Way South
Auburn, Washington 98002
(253) 804-4444
Website: www.muckleshootcasino.com
Map: **#6** (20 miles S. of Seattle)

Toll-Free Number (800) 804-4944
Restaurants: 5 Liquor: Yes Valet Parking: Free
Buffets: L-$9.95 (Sat/Sun) D-$19.50
Other Games: S21, B, MB, P, PGP, CSP, TCP,
    Sic Bo, K, BG
Overnight RV Parking: Free/RV Dump: No
Senior Discount: $2 off Sat buffet if 55+
Special Features: Two casinos in separate buildings, one is non-smoking. Gambling age is 21.

Nooksack River Casino
5048 Mt. Baker Highway
Deming, Washington 98244
(360) 592-5472
Website: www.nooksackcasino.com
Map: **#3** (14 miles E. of Bellingham)

Toll-Free Number (877) 935-9300
Restaurants: 4 Liquor: Yes Valet Parking: Free
Buffets: B-$9.95 (Sat)/$16.95 (Sun) L-$9.95
    D-$18.95/$14.95 (Wed)/$27.95 (Fri)
Hours: 8am-3am/24 Hours(Fri/Sat)
Casino Size: 21,500 Square Feet
Other Games: S21, MB, P, PGP, K
Overnight RV Parking: Free/RV Dump: No
Senior Discount: Various on Wed if 55 or older
Special Features: 6-space RV park ($10 per night). $2 off buffets for slot club members. Gambling age is 21.

Northern Lights Casino
12885 Casino Drive
Anacortes, Washington 98221
(360) 293-2691
Website: www.swinomishcasino.com
Map: **#7** (70 miles N. of Seattle, between I-5 and Anacortes on Hwy. 20)

Toll-Free Number: (888) 288-8883
Restaurants: 2 Liquor: Yes Valet Parking: Free
Buffets: L-$8.49/$10.95 (Sat/Sun)
D-$11.99/$10.95 (Wed)/$19.99 (Fri/Sat)
Hours: 11am-4am/6am (Fri/Sat)
Casino Size: 23,000 Square Feet
Other Games: P, PGP, TCP, BG, K, OTB
Overnight RV Parking: Must use RV park
Senior Discount: Buffet discount if 55+
Special Features: 35-space RV park ($17/$20 per night). Gift shop. Gambling age is 21.

Northern Quest Casino
N. 100 Hayford Road
Airway Heights, Washington 99001
(509) 242-7000
Website: www.northernquest.com
Map: **#20** (10 miles W. of Spokane)

Toll-Free Number (888) 603-7051
Restaurants: 4 Liquor: Yes Valet Parking: Free
Buffets: B-$12.95 (Sun)
        D-$13.95 (Mon/Wed)/18.95 (Tues)
Hours: 9am-5am/24 Hours (Fri/Sat)
Casino Size: 21,500 Square Feet
Other Games: S21, PGP, TCP, K, OTB
Overnight RV Parking: Free/RV Dump: No
Senior Discount: $2 Buffet discounts if 55+
Special Features: Gambling age is 18.

Okanogan Bingo Casino
41 Appleway Road
Okanogan, Washington 98840
Website: www.colvillecasinos.com
(509) 422-4646
Map: **#10** (165 miles E. of Seattle)

Toll-Free Number: (800) 559-4643
Restaurants: 1 Snack Bar Liquor: No
Hours: 9am-2am/24 Hours (Fri/Sat)
Other Games: Only machines & bingo (Fri-Tue)
Overnight RV Parking: Free/RV Dump: No
Senior Discount: Various Wednesdays if 55+
Special Features: Gambling age is 18.

The Point Casino
7989 Salish Lane NE
Kingston, Washington 98346
(360) 297-0070
Website: www.pointnopointcasino.com
Map: **#14** (18 miles W. of Seattle via Bainbridge Ferry)

Toll-Free Number (866) 547-6468
Restaurants: 1 Liquor: Yes Valet Parking: No
Buffets: B-$10.95 (Sun) L-$10.95
        D-$12.95(Wed)/$19.95 (Thu)/
        $14.95 (Fri/Sat)/$10.95 (Sun)
Casino Size: 18,500 Square Feet
Hours: 8am-5am/24hrs (Fri/Sat)
Other Games: S21, PGP
Overnight RV Parking: Free/RV Dump: No
Senior Discount: Various on Sundays if 55+
Special Features: $15 of Seattle and Edmonds Ferry fees reimbursed after one hour of play. Gambling age is 21.

Quil Ceda Creek Nightclub & Casino
6410 33rd Avenue N.E.
Tulalip, Washington 98271
(360) 551-1111
Website: www.quilcedacreekcasino.com
Map: **#1** (30 miles N. of Seattle)

Toll-Free Number: (888) 272-1111
Restaurants: 1 Liquor: Yes Valet Parking: No
Hours: 10am-6am/24hrs (Wed-Sun)
Casino Size: 52,000 Square Feet
Other Games: S21, PGP, TCP, No craps
Overnight RV Parking: Free/RV Dump: No
Special Features: Gambling age is 21.
One mile from Tulalip Casino.

Quinault Beach Resort and Casino
78 Route 115
Ocean Shores, Washington 98569
(360) 289-9466
Website: www.quinaultbeachresort.com
Map: **#19** (90 miles W. of Tacoma)

Toll-Free Number: (888) 461-2214
Rooms: 159 Price Range: $109-$179
Suite: 9 Price Range: $300-$449
Restaurants: 2 Liquor: Yes Valet Parking: Free
Casino Size: 16,000 Square Feet
Hours: 9am-3am daily
Other Games: S21, P, PGP, LIR, TCP, K
Overnight RV Parking: Free (must register first at front desk)/RV Dump: No
Senior Discount: Various on Wed if 55+r
Special Features: Gambling age is 21.

Red Wind Casino
12819 Yelm Highway
Olympia, Washington 98513
(360) 412-5000
Website: www.redwindcasino.net
Map: **#17**

Toll-Free Number: (866) 946-2444
Restaurants: 1 Liquor: Yes
Buffets: B-$8.95 L-$10.95
　　　　Brunch-$12.95 (Sun)
　　　　D-$14.95/$21.95 (Fri/Sat)
Hours: 9am-5am/24 hrs (Fri/Sat)
Casino Size: 12,000 Square Feet
Other Games: S21, P, PGP, LIR, K
Overnight RV Parking: Free/RV Dump: No
Senior Discount: Various Mon-Fri if 55+
Special Features: Gambling age is 21.

7 Cedars Casino
270756 Highway 101
Sequim, Washington 98382
(360) 683-7777
Website: www.7cedarscasino.com
Map: **#4** (70 miles N.W. of Seattle via ferry)

Toll-Free Number: (800) 4-LUCKY-7
Restaurants: 2 Liquor: Yes
Buffets: B-$10.95 (Sun) L-$10.95 D-$9.95
(Mon)/$10.95 (Tues)/$12.95 (Wed/Thurs)
Hours: 10am-3am/4am (Fri/Sat)
Other Games: S21, P, PGP, LIR, TCP, K,
　　　　BG (Mon-Sat), OTB (Wed-Mon)
Overnight RV Parking: Free (Must check-in
　　　　first)/RV Dump: No
Special Features: Gambling age is 21.

Shoalwater Bay Casino
4112 Highway 105
Tokeland, Washington 98590
(360) 267-2048
Map: **#18** (75 miles S.W. of Olympia)

Toll-Free Number: (888) 332-2048
Restaurants: 1 Liquor: No Valet Parking: No
Hours: 10am-Midnight/2am (Thu-Sat)
Casino Size: 10,000 Square Feet
Other Games: S21, No Craps or Roulette
Overnight RV Parking: No
Senior Discount: Various on Tue if 55 or older
Special Features: 15-space RV park across the
street ($15 per night). Gambling age is 21.

Silver Reef Hotel • Casino • Spa
4876 Haxton Way
Ferndale, Washington 98248
(360) 383-0777
Website: www.silverreefcasino.com
Map: **#14** (7 miles N. of Bellingham)

Toll-Free Number: (866) 383-0777
Rooms: 105 Price Range: $119-$149
Suite: 4 Price Range: $269-$289
Restaurants: 4 Liquor: Yes Valet Parking: No
Casino Size: 48,000 Square Feet
Other Games: S21, PGP, TCP, LIR
Overnight RV Parking: Free/RV Dump: No
Special Features: Gambling age is 21.

Skagit Valley Casino Resort
5984 N. Darrk Lane
Bow, Washington 98232
(360) 724-7777
Website: www.theskagit.com
Map: **#7** (75 miles N. of Seattle)

Toll-Free Number: (877) 275-2448
Room Reservations: (800) 895-3423
Rooms: 74 Price Range: $105-$125
Rooms: 29 Price Range: $180-$225
Restaurants: 3 Liquor: Yes Valet Parking: No
Buffets: B-$7.25 (Sat) L-$9.95/$14.95 (Sun)
　　　　D-$15.95/$17.95 (Fri/Sat)/$18.95 (Wed)
Hours: 9am-3am/5am (Fri/Sat)
Casino Size: 26,075 Square Feet
Other Games: S21, PGP, LIR, TCP, K
Overnight RV Parking: No
Senior Discount: Various on Mon if 55 or older
Special Features: Gambling age is 21. Two 18-
hole golf courses. 2,700-seat outdoor events
center. Health spa.

Suquamish Clearwater Casino Resort
15347 Suquamish Way N.E
Suquamish, Washington 98392
(360) 598-8700
Website: www.clearwatercasino.com
Map: **#14** (15 miles W. of Seattle via
Bainbridge Ferry)

Toll-Free Number: (800) 375-6073
Room Reservations: (866) 609-8700
Restaurants: 4 Liquor: Yes Valet Parking: Free
Buffets: B-$11.95 (Sat/Sun) L-$8.95
　　　　D-$13.95/$21.95 (Fri/Sat)
Hours: 9am-5am/24 Hours (Fri/Sat)

Casino Size: 22,000 Square Feet
Other Games: S21, P, PGP, CSP, TCP, LIR, K
Overnight RV Parking: Free/RV Dump: No
Senior Discount: 50% off Sun buffets if 55+
Special features: Seattle and Edmonds Ferries fee reimbursed with qualified play. Gambling age is 18.

Tulalip Casino
10200 Quil Ceda Boulevard
Tulalip, Washington 98271
(360) 651-1111
Website: www.tulalipcasino.com
Map: **#1** (30 miles N. of Seattle)

Toll-Free Number: (888) 272-1111
Restaurants: 4 Liquor: Yes Valet Parking: Free
Buffets: L-$9.95/$13.95 (Sun)
         D-$16.95/$21.95 (Tues)
Hours: 10am-6pm/24 Hours (Thurs-Sat)
Casino Size: 45,000 Square Feet
Other Games: S21, B, MB, P, PGP, CSP,
         TCP, LIR, K, BG
Overnight RV Parking: Free/RV Dump: No
Senior Discount: Various on Tue if 50+
Special Features: 2,300-seat amphitheatre. One mile from Quil Ceda Creek Casino. Gambling age is 21.

Two Rivers Casino & Resort
6828-B Highway 25 South
Davenport, Washington 99122
(509) 722-4000
Website: www.tworiverscasinoandresort.com
Map: **#8** (60 miles W. of Spokane)

Toll-Free Number: (800) 722-4031
Restaurants: 1 Liquor: No Valet Parking: No
Buffets: B-$7.95 (Sun) L-$6.25 (Tue)
         D-$9.95 (Thu)/$8.95 (Sat)
Hours: 8am-1am/24 Hours (Fri/Sat)
Casino Size: 10,000 Square Feet
Overnight RV Parking: Must use RV park
Special Features: Regular slots. 100-space RV park ($25 to $30 per night). 260-slip marina and beach. Gambling age is 18.

Yakama Nation Legends Casino
580 Fort Road
Toppenish, Washington 98948
(509) 865-8800
Website: www.yakamalegends.com
Map: **#16** (20 miles S. of Yakima)

Toll-Free Number: (877) 7-COME-11
Restaurants: 2 Liquor: No Valet Parking: No
Buffets: L-$8.99/$12.99 (Thu/Sun)
         D-$12.99/$18.99 (Thu)
Hours: 9am-4am/5am (Fri/Sat)
Casino Size: 45,000 Square Feet
Other Games: S21, P, PGP, TCP, LIR, K
Overnight RV Parking: Free/RV Dump: No
Senior Discount: Various on Tue if 55 or older
Special Features: Childcare center. Indoor waterfall. Gambling age is 18.

Card Rooms

Card rooms have been legal in Washington since 1974. Initially limited to just five tables per location, the law was changed in 1996 to allow up to 15 tables. One year later, a provision was added to allow house-banked games. Permissible games include: blackjack, Caribbean stud poker, pai gow poker, let it ride, casino war and numerous other card games. Baccarat, craps, roulette and keno are not allowed.

The maximum bet at each card room is dependant on certain licensing requirements and is capped at either $25 or $100. Additionally, the rooms can be open no more than 20 hours per day. These card rooms are now commonly called "mini-casinos." The minimum gambling age in a card room is 18.

Each city and county has the option to ban the card rooms so they are not found in every major city (Seattle has none). Due to space limitations we don't list all of the Washington card rooms in this book.

For a list of card rooms, we suggest that you contact the Washington State Gambling Commission at (360) 486-3581, or visit their website at: www.wsgc.wa.gov

WEST VIRGINIA

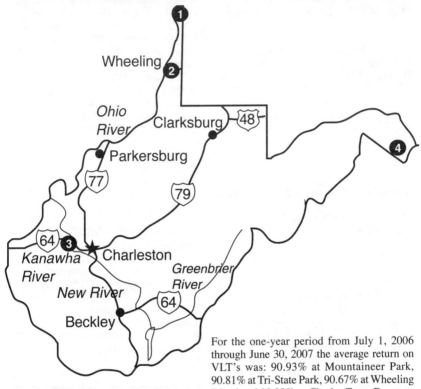

West Virginia has four pari-mutuel facilities that feature video lottery terminals. The VLT's are the same as regular video gaming devices but are called lottery terminals because they are regulated by the state's lottery commission which receives a share of each machine's revenue.

The maximum allowable bet on a machine is $2 and there is no limit on the prize payouts. Most of the gaming machines pay out coins or tokens, but there are also some machines which will only print out a receipt which must be taken to a cashier.

West Virginia law requires that VLT's return a minimum of 80% to a maximum of 95%. VLT games include: slots, blackjack, keno and numerous versions of poker. The minimum gambling age is 18 and admission is free to all casinos.

For the one-year period from July 1, 2006 through June 30, 2007 the average return on VLT's was: 90.93% at Mountaineer Park, 90.81% at Tri-State Park, 90.67% at Wheeling Island and 90.08% at Charles Town Races.

West Virginia law also allows bars, as well as restaurants that serve alcohol, to have up to five VLT's. Fraternal organizations are also allowed to have up to 10 VLT's. All of these machines are identical to the machines found at the racetracks, except they only print out tickets and do not pay out in cash.

In early 2007 the state legislature authorized a referendum in the home county of each of the four pari-mutuel facilities to allow table games at each track. The amendment passed in every county except for Jefferson County, home of Charles Town Races & Slots. The earliest that table games are expected to be in operation at the other three tracks is early 2008.

For West Virginia tourism information call (800) 225-5982 or go to: www.callwva.com.

Charles Town Races & Slots
P.O. Box 551
Charles Town, West Virginia 25414
(304) 725-7001
Website: www.ctownraces.com
Map: **#4** (320 miles N.E. of Charleston, on the Virginia border)

Toll-Free Number: (800) 795-7001
Restaurants: 4　Valet Parking: $4/$6 (Fri-Sun)
Buffets: L-$11.99/$13.99 (Sat)/ $16.99 (Sun)
　　　　D-$14.99/$21.99 (Fri)/$19.99 (Sat)
Hours: 7am-4am Daily
Overnight RV Parking: Free/RV Dump: No
Special Features: Live thoroughbred racing Wed-Sun. Daily simulcasting of horse and dog racing. Food court with five fast-food outlets.

Mountaineer Race Track & Gaming Resort
State Route #2
Chester, West Virginia 26034
(304) 387-2400
Website: www.mtrgaming.com
Map: **#1** (35 miles N. of Wheeling)

Toll-Free Number: (800) 804-0468
Room Reservations: (800) 489-8192
Rooms: 337　Price Range: $109-$169
Suites: 22　Price Range: $159-$219
Restaurants: 8　Valet Parking: $5
Hours: 7am-4am Daily
Overnight RV Parking: Free/RV Dump: No
Special Features: 18-hole golf course. Spa and fitness center. Live thoroughbred racing Sat-Tue. Daily simulcasting of horse/dog racing. Expected to have table games by early 2008.

Tri-State Racetrack & Gaming Center
1 Greyhound Drive
Cross Lanes, West Virginia 25313
(304) 776-1000
Website: www.tristateracetrack.com
Map: **#3** (10 miles N.W. of Charleston)

Toll-Free Number: (800) 224-9683
Restaurants: 5　Valet Parking: $3
Hours: 11am-3am Daily
Casino Size: 30,000 Square Feet
Overnight RV Parking: Free/RV Dump: No
Special Features: Live dog racing Wed-Mon. Daily simulcasting of horse and dog racing. Expected to have table games by early 2008.

Wheeling Island
Racetrack & Gaming Center
1 S. Stone Street
Wheeling, West Virginia 26003
(304) 232-5050
Website: www.wheelingisland.com
Map: **#2**

Toll-Free Number: (877) 946-4373
Room Reservations: (877) 943-3546
Rooms: 142　Price Range: $129-$165
Suites: 9　Price Range: $175-$250
Restaurants: 4　Valet Parking: $5
Buffets: L-$9.99　D-$12.49/$14.99 (Fri/Sat)
Hours: 7am-4am Daily
Casino Size: 50,000 Square Feet
Overnight RV Parking: Free/RV Dump: No
Senior Discount: Various on Wed if 55+
Special Features: Live dog racing daily except Tue/Thu. Daily simulcasting of horse and dog racing. Expected to have table games by early 2008.

WISCONSIN

All Wisconsin casinos are located on Indian reservations.

The Tribes are not required to release information on their slot machine percentage paybacks, but according to the terms of the compact between the state and the tribes "for games not affected by player skill, such as slot machines, the machine is required to return a minimum of 80% and a maximum of 100% of the amount wagered."

All casinos offer blackjack, slots and video poker. Some casinos also offer: craps (C), roulette (R), mini baccarat (MB), poker (P), Pai Gow Poker (PGP), let it ride (LIR), big 6 wheel (B6), bingo (BG), keno (K) and off-track betting (OTB). Unless otherwise noted, all casinos are open 24 hours and the minimum gambling age is 21 (18 for bingo).

For visitor information contact the state's department of tourism at (800) 432-8747 or their web site at: www.travelwisconsin.com..

Bad River Lodge Casino
U.S. Highway 2
Odanah, Wisconsin 54861
(715) 682-7121
Website: www.badriver.com
Map: **#1** (halfway between Ironwood, MI and Ashland, WI; 45 miles east of Duluth, MN on US 2)

Toll-Free Number: (800) 777-7449
Lodge Reservations: (800) 795-7121
Rooms: 42 Price Range: $40-$55
Suites: 8 Price Range: $65-$75
Restaurants: 2 Liquor: Yes
Casino Size: 19,200 Square Feet
Hours: 8am-2am Daily
Other Games: C, R, P, TCP, LIR
Overnight RV Parking: Free/RV Dump: Free
Senior Discount: Various dining specials throughout the week if 55+.
Special Features: 20-space RV park (Free). Gas station. Grocery store.

Dejope Gaming
4002 Evan Acres Rd.
Madison, WI 53718
(608)223-9576
Website: www.dejope.com
Map: **#17**

Toll-Free Number: (888)248-1777
Restaurants: 1 Liquor: No
Hours: 7am-4am Daily
Casino Size: 22,000 Square Feet
Other Games: Only Gaming Machines
Senior Discount: $5 free play on Wed if 55+

Ho Chunk Casino and Hotel
S3214 Highway 12
Baraboo, Wisconsin 53913
(608) 356-6210
Website: www.ho-chunk.com
Map: **#4** (40 miles N. of Madison. On Hwy. 12 just S. of Delton)

Toll-Free Number: (800) 746-2486
Room Reservations: (800) 446-5550
Rooms: 295 Price Range: $89-$150
Suites: 20 Price Range: $140-$275
Restaurants: 4 Liquor: Yes
Buffets: B-$6.99 (Sat-Sun) L-$8.99
       D-$11.99/$24.99 (Wed) $13.99 (Fri)/
       $14.99 (Sat)
Casino Size: 90,000 Square Feet
Other Games: BG (Tue-Sun)
Overnight RV Parking: Free/RV Dump: No
Special Features: Smoke shop. Free local shuttle. Kid's Quest childcare center.

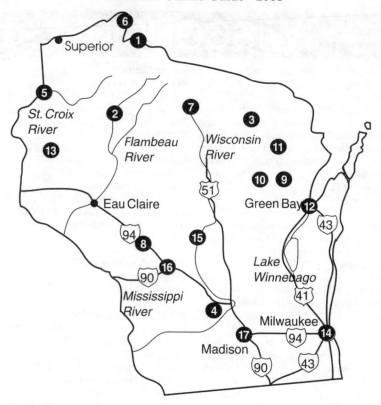

Hole In The Wall Casino & Hotel
P.O. Box 98, Highways 35 & 77
Danbury, Wisconsin 54830
(715) 656-3444
Website: www.holeinthewallcasino.com
Map: **#5** (26 miles E. of Hinckley, MN)

Toll-Free Number: (800) 238-8946
Rooms: 45 Price Range: $60-$65
Suites: 1 Price Range: $80
Restaurants: 1 Liquor: Yes
Hours: 8am-2am/4am (Fri/Sat)
Casino Size: 22,500 Square Feet
Other Games: C, R
Overnight RV Parking: Must use RV park
Special Features: Craps and Roulette only
offered on weekends. 35-space RV park ($15
per night). $10 off room for slot club members.

Isle Vista Casino
Highway 13 North, Box 1167
Bayfield, Wisconsin 54814
(715) 779-3712
Map: **#6** (70 miles E. of Duluth, MN on Hwy.
13, 3 miles N. of Bayfield)

Toll-Free Number: (800) 226-8478
RV Reservations: (715) 779-3743
Restaurants: 1 Liquor: Yes
Hours: 10am-12am/2am (Thu-Sat)
Other Games: Bingo (Thu/Sat/Sun)
Overnight RV Parking: Must use RV park
Special Features: Campground and 30-space
RV park ($30 per night). 34-slip marina.

Lake of the Torches Resort Casino
510 Old Abe Road
Lac du Flambeau, Wisconsin 54538
(715) 588-7070
Website: www.lakeofthetorches.com
Map: **#7** (160 miles N.W. of Green Bay.
Heading N. on Hwy. 51, go left on Hwy. 47,
12 miles to casino)

Toll-Free Number: (800) 25-TORCH
Room Reservations: (888) 599-9200
Rooms: 88 Price Range: $100-$145
Suites: 13 Price Range: $150-$185
Restaurants: 2 Liquor: Yes
Buffets: B-$5.95 L-$7.50/$10.95 (Sat/Sun)
       D-$12.95/$14.95 (Sat)/$21.95 (Fri)
Other Games: BG (Tue-Sun)
Overnight RV Parking: Free/RV Dump: No
Special Features: Slot club members get 20%
off room and other discounts.

LCO Casino, Lodge & Convention Center
13767 W County Road B
Hayward, Wisconsin 54843
(715) 634-5643
Website: www.lcocasino.com
Map: **#2** (55 miles S.E. of Duluth, MN. 3 miles
N.E. of Hayward on county trunk B)

Toll-Free Number: (800) 526-2274
Room Reservations: (800) LCO-LODGE
Rooms: 53 Price Range: $54-$89
Suites: 22 Price Range: $80-$130
Restaurants: 2 Liquor: Yes
Buffets:B-$5.95 L-$8.95/$10.95(Sun) D-$9.95
Casino Size: 35,000 Square Feet
Other Games: C, R, P, LIR, BG (Sun-Fri)
Overnight RV Parking: Free (must register first
at customer service)/RV Dump: No
Special Features: Nearby 8-space RV park
(Free). Sports lounge. Gift shop.

Majestic Pines Casino, Bingo & Hotel
W9010 Highway 54 East
Black River Falls, Wisconsin 54615
(715) 284-9098
Website: www.mpcwin.com
Map: **#8** (110 miles M.W. of Madison on Hwy.
54, 4 miles E. of I-94)

Toll-Free Number: (800) 657-4621
Rooms: 60 Price Range: $49-$78
Suites: 6 Price Range: $88-$115
Restaurants: 2 Liquor: Yes
Buffets: B-$6.50 L-$8.00/$9.00 (Sun) D-$11.00
Hours: 8am-2am/24 Hrs (Fri/Sat)
Open 24 hours daily Memorial to Labor Day
Size: 35,000 Square Feet
Other Games: BG, C, R, TCP, LIR
Overnight RV Parking: Free/RV Dump: No
Senior Discount: $5 off bingo Sundays if 55+
Special Features: 10% off food/hotel for slot
club members.

Menominee Casino Bingo & Hotel
P.O. Box 760, Highways 47 & 55
Keshena, Wisconsin 54135
(715) 799-3600
Website: www.menomineecasinoresort.com
Map: **#9** (40 miles N.W. of Green Bay on Hwy.
47, 7 miles N. of Shawano)

Toll-Free Number: (800) 343-7778
Rooms: 100 Price Range: $60-$80
Suites: 8 Price Range: $100-$135
Restaurants: 1 Liquor: Yes
Casino Size: 33,000 Square Feet
Other Games: C, R, P, LIR, TCP, BG
Overnight RV Parking: Free/RV Dump: No
Special Features: 60-space RV park ($10 per
night/$15 w/hookups). Gift shop. Smoke shop.

Mohican North Star Casino & Bingo
W12180A County Road A
Bowler, Wisconsin 54416
(715) 787-3110
Website: www.mohicannorthstar.com
Map: **#10** (50 miles N.W. of Green Bay)

Toll-Free Number: (800) 775-2274
Restaurants: 2 Liquor: Yes
Hours: 8am-2am/24 Hours (Fri-Sun)
Other Games: C, R, LIR, TCP,
              BG (Sun/Mon/Wed-Fri)
Overnight RV Parking: Free/RV Dump: Fee
Special Features: 57-space RV park ($15/$18
per night). Smoke shop.

Mole Lake Casino & Bingo
Highway 55
Mole Lake, Wisconsin 54520
(715) 478-5290
Website: www.molelake.com
Map: **#3** (100 miles N.W. of Green Bay on
Hwy. 55, 7 miles S. of Crandon)

Toll-Free Number: (800) 236-9466
Motel Reservations: (800) 457-4312
Rooms: 25 Price Range: $46-$74
Restaurants: 2 Liquor: Yes
Hours: 10am-2am/3am (Fri-Sat)
Other Games: BG (Fri-Tue)
Overnight RV Parking: Free/RV Dump: No
Special Features: Motel is two blocks from
casino.

Oneida Bingo & Casino
2020 Airport Drive
Green Bay, Wisconsin 54313
(920) 494-4500
Website: www.oneidabingoandcasino.net
Map: **#12** (across from Austin Straubel Airport,
take Interstate 43 to Highway 172)

Toll-Free Number: (800) 238-4263
Reservation Number: (800) 333-3333
Rooms: 408 Price Range: $109-$159
Suites: 40 Price Range: $169-$429
Restaurants: 3 Liquor: No
Buffets: L-$8.95 D-$12.95
Hours: 10am-4am (Tables)/24 Hours (Slots)
Other Games: C, R, P, LIR, TCP, BG, OTB
Overnight RV Parking: Free/RV Dump: No
Special Features: Two casinos. One is
connected to Radisson Inn where hotel rooms
are located. Free local shuttle. Smoke shop.

Potawatomi Bingo Casino
1721 W. Canal Street
Milwaukee, Wisconsin 53233
(414) 645-6888
Website: www.paysbig.com
Map: **#14**

Toll-Free Number: (800) PAYS-BIG
Restaurants: 4 Liquor: Yes
Buffets: B-$15.99 (Sun)
        L-$9.99 D-$14.99/$15.99 (Fri/Sun)/
        $19.99 (Wed/Sat)
Casino Size: 38,400 Square Feet
Other Games: C, R, P, LIR, BG
Overnight RV Parking: Free/RV Dump: No
Special Features: Alcohol served in sports bar,
not in casino. Smoke-free casino on 2nd floor.

Potawatomi Bingo-Northern Lights Casino
Highway 32
Wabeno, Wisconsin 54566
(715) 473-2021
Website: www.cartercasino.com
Map: **#11** (85 miles N. of Green Bay on Hwy.
32)

Toll-Free Number: (800) 487-9522
Lodge Reservations: (800) 777-1640
Rooms: 70 Price Range: $75-$95
Suites: 29 Price Range: $85-$125
Restaurants: 2 Liquor: Yes
Casino Size: 25,000 Square Feet
Other Games: C, R, LIR, TCP, BG (Wed-Sun)
Overnight RV Parking: Must use RVpark
Senior Discount: Specials on Thu if 50+
Special Features: 10-space RV park ($15 per
night). 10% off room for slot club members.
24-hour gas station and convenience store.

Rainbow Casino
949 County Road G
Nekoosa, Wisconsin 54457
(715) 886-4560
Website: www.rbcwin.com
Map: **#15** (50 miles S. of Wausau)

Toll-Free Number: (800) 782-4560
Restaurants: 2 Liquor: Yes
Buffets: B/L-$10.95 (Sun)
Hours: 8am-2am/24 hours (Fri/Sat)
Other Games: R, P, LIR, TCP
Overnight RV Parking: Free (must check-in
              first with security)/RV Dump: No
Senior Discount: Specials on Thu if 55+
Special Features: Smoke and gift shop.
Convenience store.

St. Croix Casino & Hotel
777 US Highway 8
Turtle Lake, Wisconsin 54889
(715) 986-4777
Website: www.stcroixcasino.com
Map: **#13** (105 miles S. of Duluth, MN on Hwy. 8)

Toll-Free Number: (800) 846-8946
Room Reservations: (800) 782-9987
Rooms: 145 Price Range: $61-$73
Suites: 8 Price Range: $110-$135
Restaurants: 2   Liquor: Yes
Buffets: B-$3.95 L-$7.95
          D-$10.95/$21.95 (Thu)
Casino Size: 95,000 Square Feet
Other Games: MB, C, R, P
Overnight RV Parking: Must use RV park
Special Features: 20% off rooms for slot club member. 18-space RV park ($20 per night).

Whitetail Crossing Casino
27867 Highway 21
Tomah, Wisconsin 54660
(608) 372-3721
Map: **#16** (3 miles E. of Tomah on Hwy 21)

Restaurants: 1 Snack Bar Liquor: No
Hours: 8am-Midnight Daily
Casino Size: 2,000 Square Feet
Other Games: Only Gaming Machines
Special Features: Convenience store. Open 24 hours Fri-Sat during the summer.

WYOMING

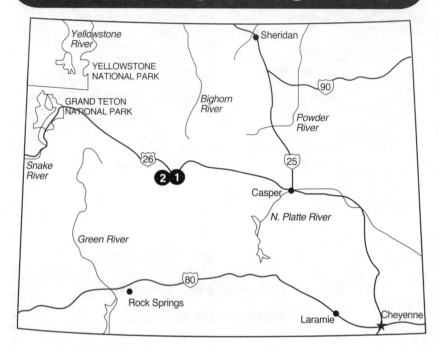

Wyoming has two Indian casinos that offer Class II bingo-type gaming machines, plus traditional Class III slot machines.

The machines don't pay out in cash. Instead they print out a receipt which must be cashed by a floor attendant or taken to the cashier's cage. You can also make bets via a cashless system whereby you get a "smart" card and deposit money to that card's account. The machines will then deducts losses from, or credit wins to, your account.

No public information is available regarding the payback percentages on Wyoming's gaming machines. Both casinos are open 24 hours daily and the minimum gambling age is 18.

For Wyoming tourism information call (800) 225-5996 or visit their web site at: www.wyomingtourism.org

Little Wind Casino
690 Blue Sky Highway
Ethete, Wyoming 82520
(307) 335-8703
Map: **#2** (140 miles W. of Casper)

Restaurants: 1 Liquor: No Valet Parking: No
Casino Size: 1,920 Square Feet
Overnight RV Parking: Free/RV Dump: No
Special Features: Convenience store and deli.

Wind River Casino
10369 Highway 789
Riverton, Wyoming 82501
(307) 856-3964
Website: www.windrivercasino.com
Map: **#1** (125 miles W. of Casper)

Toll-Free Number: (866) 657-1604
Restaurants: 1 Liquor: No Valet Parking: No
Casino Size: 8,000 Square Feet
Overnight RV Parking: Free/RV Dump: No

Casino Index

Reference Map of U.S.

2008 American Casino Guide
America's Favorite Casino Awards

We want to know your favorites! Please take a moment to fill out this form and mail it back to us, or enter your votes on our web site at www.americancasinoguide.com/favorites.shtml All entries we receive by April 30, 2008 will be entered into a drawing to receive a FREE autographed copy of the 2009 edition of the American Casino Guide.
10 winners will be chosen. Good luck!

Las Vegas

Favorite Strip Casino_____

Favorite Off-Strip Casino_____

Favorite Downtown Casino_____

Favorite "Locals" Casino_____

Reno

Favorite Casino_____

Lake Tahoe

Favorite Casino_____

Laughlin

Favorite Casino_____

Atlantic City

Favorite Casino_____

Mississippi Gulf Coast

Favorite Casino_____

Tunica

Favorite Casino_____

Chicago-Area

Favorite Casino_____

Connecticut

Favorite Casino_____

South Florida

Favorite Casino_____

Kansas City

Favorite Casino_____

St. Louis

Favorite Casino_____

_____
Name

_____
Address

_____
City, State, Zip

Limit: one ballot per person. Ballot must be received by April 30, 2008.
Mail to: Favorite Casino Awards, PO Box 703, Dania, FL 33004
Vote on our website at www.americancasinoguide.com/favorites.shtml

COUPON CHANGES

Coupon offers can change without notice.

To see a list of any coupon changes, go to:

americancasinoguide.com/changes.shtml

We will list any coupon changes on that page.

Coupon Directory

Notice

**Listen to FREE monthly Podcasts
hosted by American Casino Guide author
Steve Bourie.**

**During each show Steve features
an interview with a special guest
from the world of casino gambling!**

**Listen on our website at:
www.americancasinoguide.com**

**Receive our FREE monthly
newsletter by e-mail!**

**Get informative stories from some of
America's best gaming writers, plus
details on special money-saving offers.**

**Sign up on our website at:
www.americancasinoguide.com**

COUPON CHANGES

Coupon offers can change without notice.

To see a list of any coupon changes, go to:

americancasinoguide.com/changes.shtml

We will list any coupon changes on that page.

AMERICAN CASINO GUIDE

$20 Off!

- Reserve a compact through fullsize car, minivan, or SUV in the United States, Latin America, Caribbean or Asia Pacific.
- Valid for a rental of at least 4 days
- Valid through 12/31/08
- For best rates book online at **alamo.com** or call 1-800-462-5266 or your travel agent. Be sure to request I.D. Number 641394 and Coupon Code AD3694KFR at time of reservation.

See terms and conditions on reverse side of this coupon.

CASINO COUPON   AD3694KFR

AMERICAN CASINO GUIDE

One FREE Day!

- Reserve a compact through fullsize car in the U.S., Canada, Latin America, Caribbean or Asia Pacific.
- Valid for a rental of at least 5 days.
- Valid through 12/31/08.
- For best rates book online at alamo.com or call 1-800-462-5266 or your travel agent. Be sure to request I.D. Number 641394 and Coupon Code AF2525JDR at time of reservation.

See terms and conditions on reverse side of this coupon.

CASINO COUPON   AF2525JDR

AMERICAN CASINO GUIDE

Save Up to 20% with Alamo®

See the world one stop at a time with special rates from Alamo. As an American Casino Guide reader, you'll receive up to 20% off great retail rates year-round and unlimited mileage. Alamo always goes that extra mile to make your car rental experience a fun part of your trip. Call Alamo at 1-800-462-5266 or book online at *alamo.com.* Be sure to request ID #641394. This is not a coupon.

See terms and conditions on reverse side.

CASINO COUPON

Terms and Conditions

- One coupon per Alamo rental and void once redeemed.
- Original coupon must be presented at counter upon arrival.
- Discount applies to base rate, which does not include taxes (including VAT), other overnmentally-authorized or imposed surcharges, license recoupment/air tax recovery and concession recoupment fees, airport and airport facility fees, fuel, additional driver fee, one-way rental charge, or optional items.
- Offer is subject to standard rental conditions.
- Blackout dates may apply.
- Not valid with any other discount or promotional rate, except your member discount.
- Subject to availability and valid only at participating Alamo locations.
- Some countries may convert coupon value into local currency.
- 24-Hour advance reservations required.
- Offer not valid in San Jose, CA.
- Coupon VOID if bought, bartered or sold for cash.

Terms and Conditions

- One coupon per Alamo rental and void once redeemed.
- Original coupon must be presented at counter upon arrival.
- Free day is prorated against base rate for entire rental period, which does not include taxes (including VAT/GST), other governmentally-authorized or imposed surcharges, license recoupment/air tax recovery and concession recoupment fees, airport and airport facility fees, fuel, additional driver fee, one-way rental charge, or optional items.
- Offer is subject to standard rental conditions.
- Subject to availability and valid only at participating Alamo locations.
- Not valid with any other discount or promotional rate, except your member discount.
- Blackout dates may apply.
- 24-Hour advance reservations required.
- Offer not valid in Manhattan, N.Y. or San Jose, CA.
- Coupon VOID if bought, bartered or sold for cash.

Terms and Conditions

Discount applies to base rate only. Taxes (including GST/VAT), other governmentally-authorized or imposed surcharges, license recoupment/air tax recovery and concession recoupment fees, airport facility fees, fuel, additional driver fees, one-way rental charge and optional items are extra. Renter must meet standard age, driver and credit requirements (may vary by country). 24-Hour advance reservation required. May not be combined with other discounts. Availability is limited and valid only at participating locations. Subject to change without notice. Blackout dates may apply.

Save $20 Off a Weekly Rental! - Terms and Conditions

One coupon per National rental and void once redeemed. Original coupon must be presented at counter upon arrival. Discount applies to base rate only, which does not include taxes (including VAT), governmentally-authorized or imposed surcharges, license recoupment/air tax recovery and concession recoupment fees, airport and airport facility fees, fuel, additional driver fee, one-way rental charge or optional items. Some countries may convert coupon value into local currency. Renter must meet standard age, driver and credit requirements. Blackout dates may apply. May not be combined with other discounts or promotions, except your member discount. Availability is limited. Valid only at participating National locations. Offer not valid in San Jose, CA. Coupon VOID if bought, bartered or sold for cash.

nationalcar.com

One Car Class Upgrade! - Terms and Conditions

One coupon per National rental and void once redeemed. Original coupon must be presented at counter upon arrival. Renter must meet standard age, driver and credit requirements. Blackout dates may apply. May not be combined with other discounts or promotions, except your member discount. Valid only at participating National locations. Offer not valid in San Jose, CA. Valid for a one car class upgrade from the car class reserved. Coupon VOID if bought, bartered or sold for cash.

nationalcar.com

Up to 20% Discount - Terms and Conditions

Discount applies to base rate only, which does not include taxes (including GST/VAT), governmentally-authorized or imposed surcharges, license recoupment/air tax recovery, concession recoupment fees, airport and airport facility fees, fuel, additional driver fees, one-way rental charge or optional items. Renter must meet standard age, driver and credit requirements (may vary by country). 24-Hour advance reservation required. May not be combined with other discounts. Availability is limited. Subject to change without notice. Blackout dates may apply. This is not a coupon. Percentage discount is reflected in the reserved rate.

nationalcar.com

AMERICAN CASINO GUIDE

FREE CATALOG **FREE CATALOG**

BOOK GBC **SHOP**

EST. 1964

Gambler's Book Shop

10% Off Your Purchase!

Save 10% on your order from the world's oldest and largest bookstore specializing in books, software and videos for casino, sports and racing fans!

CASINO COUPON

AMERICAN CASINO GUIDE

FREE Copy of *The Crapshooter* Newsletter! A $7 Value!

This coupon entitles you to receive one FREE copy of *The Crapshooter* newsletter. The only publication devoted exclusively to the game of casino craps! You'll also receive a FREE catalog and a special FREE offer! See reverse for details.

CASINO COUPON

AMERICAN CASINO GUIDE

FREE $19.95 Value
Selection of 5 Gambling eBooks

Follow instructions on the reverse and we will send you FREE this great collection of Gambling eBooks via email download.

We will also include in the package or Collection of Gambling Systems that people use to try and beat the Casino Games.

For more information visit:

www.wedoitallvegas.com

CASINO COUPON

300 E. Bennett Ave.
Cripple Creek, CO 80813
(719) 689-3517
(877) 244-9469
www.coloradogrande.com

The Cornerstone of Cripple Creek™ CO
209 East Bennett Avenue
Cripple Creek, CO 80813
(719) 689-2646
www.grushcasino.com

AMERICAN CASINO GUIDE

**\$5 CASH for New Members
After Earning 50 points on
Your Gold Exchange Club Card**

The Cornerstone of Cripple Creek™ CO

Bring this coupon to the Gold Exchange Club desk, sign up
as a new member, and get \$5 CASH after earning 50 points.
See reverse for more details.

A current American Casino Guide Discount Card must be
presented when redeeming this coupon, or offer is void

AMERICAN CASINO GUIDE

**50% Off
Appetizers**

Present this coupon to your server at Stadium Sports Bar &
Grill before ordering to receive 50% off any appetizer
order. Valid any day. See reverse for more details.

A current American Casino Guide Discount Card must be
presented when redeeming this coupon, or offer is void

AMERICAN CASINO GUIDE

HARD ROCK CAFE

**BUY ONE BURGER, SALAD, SANDWICH
GET ONE BURGER, SALAD, SANDWICH FREE**

HOLLYWOOD, FL

954.327.ROCK
1 Seminole Way I Hollywood, FL 33314
www.seminolehardrock.com

Expires: December 31, 2008

A current American Casino Guide Discount Card must be
presented when redeeming this coupon, or offer is void

AMERICAN CASINO GUIDE

HOLLYWOOD, FL

954.327.ROCK
1 Seminole Way I Hollywood, FL 33314
www.seminolehardrockhollywood.com

$10 FREE PLAY

TO NEW MEMBERS ONLY
PRESENT THIS COUPON AT PLAYERS CLUB

Expires: December 31, 2008

A current American Casino Guide Discount Card must be presented when redeeming this coupon, or offer is void

---

AMERICAN CASINO GUIDE

GRAND VICTORIA CASINO®

E L G I N

Buy One Buffet, Get One Free

Present this coupon at Club Victoria with your Club Victoria card to receive
one complimentary meal when a second meal of equal or greater value
is purchased at **Grand Victoria Buffet**. Some restrictions apply.

T99995

Coupon Code: 746

A current American Casino Guide Discount Card must be presented when redeeming this coupon, or offer is void

Expires on Dec 30, 2008

AMERICAN CASINO GUIDE

GRAND VICTORIA CASINO®

E L G I N

Buy One Entrée, Get One Free

Present this coupon at Club Victoria with your Club Victoria card to receive
one complimentary entrée when a second entrée of equal or greater value
is purchased at **Buckinghams**. Some restrictions apply.

T99995

Coupon Code: 747

A current American Casino Guide Discount Card must be presented when redeeming this coupon, or offer is void

Expires on Dec 30, 2008

HOLLYWOOD, FL

954.327.ROCK
1 Seminole Way I Hollywood, FL 33314
www.seminolehardrockhollywood.com

Must be 18 to play the games and redeem the ticket. Ticket is void if illegible, altered, counterfeit, incomplete, produced in error or fails any validation testing. The player is responsible for checking this ticket for accuracy, including the date and amount shown and must immediately notify attendant of any error. Cannot be combined with any other offer. For New Members Only.

Present with current and valid government issued photo ID and Club Victoria card at any Club Victoria booth prior to dining. Some restrictions apply. Club Victoria membership required. To sign up for a free Club Victoria membership, stop by a Club Victoria booth. After Club Victoria redemption, present this coupon at Grand Victoria Buffet to receive offer. Dine-in only. Valid Monday – Thursday only. Not valid on weekends or holidays. Alcohol and gratuities not included. May not be combined with other discounts, offers, or comp dollar purchases. Non-negotiable. No cash value. Subject to availability. Void if copied or altered. One coupon per person. Grand Victoria is not responsible for any typographical errors or misprints or for lost, stolen or expired offers, and reserves the right to modify or cancel this program at any time without prior notice. Redeemable only at Grand Victoria Casino, Elgin, Illinois. Must be 21. If you or someone you know has a gambling problem, call 1.800.GAMBLER.

Grand Victoria Casino Elgin • 250 S. Grove Avenue, Elgin, IL 60120 (847) 468-7000

Present with current and valid government issued photo ID and Club Victoria card at any Club Victoria booth prior to dining. Some restrictions apply. Complimentary entrée must be of equal or lesser value than purchased entrée. Club Victoria membership required. To sign up for a free Club Victoria membership, stop by a Club Victoria booth. After Club Victoria redemption, present this coupon at Buckinghams to receive offer. Reservations required. Call 847.468.7000. Dine-in only. Valid Monday – Thursday only. Not valid on weekends or holidays. Alcohol and gratuities not included. May not be combined with other discounts, offers or comp dollar purchases. Non-negotiable. No cash value. Subject to availability. Void if copied or altered. One coupon per person. Grand Victoria is not responsible for any typographical errors or misprints or for lost, stolen or expired offers, and reserves the right to modify or cancel this program at any time without prior notice. Redeemable only at Grand Victoria Casino, Elgin, Illinois. Must be 21. If you or someone you know has a gambling problem, call 1.800.GAMBLER.

Grand Victoria Casino Elgin • 250 S. Grove Avenue, Elgin, IL 60120 (847) 468-7000

AMERICAN CASINO GUIDE

GRAND VICTORIA CASINO®

E L G I N

Buy One Entrée, Get One Free

Present this coupon at Club Victoria with your Club Victoria card to receive
one complimentary entrée when a second entrée of equal or greater value
is purchased at **Fox & Hounds**. Some restrictions apply.

T99995

Coupon Code: 748   Expires on Dec 30, 2008

AMERICAN CASINO GUIDE

BUY ONE GET ONE FREE!

Buy one lunch or dinner buffet and get a second one FREE
(or 50% off when dining alone). See reverse for details.

AMERICAN CASINO GUIDE

$5 OFF YOUR NEXT ROUND

CHARIOT RUN
THE GOLF COURSE OF CAESARS

Behold the spectacular Chariot Run Golf Course! 18 uniquely
challenging holes spread out over 7,000 yards of beautiful Southern
Indiana landscape, featuring bent grass greens and upgraded bunkers.
Present this coupon and receive $5 off your next round for up to 8 players.

Present with current and valid government issued photo ID and Club Victoria card at any Club Victoria booth prior to dining. Some restrictions apply. Complimentary entrée must be of equal or lesser value than purchased entrée. Club Victoria membership required. To sign up for a free Club Victoria membership, stop by a Club Victoria booth. After Club Victoria redemption, present this coupon at Fox & Hounds to receive offer. Dine-in only. Alcohol and gratuities not included. May not be combined with other discounts, offers or comp dollar purchases. Non-negotiable. No cash value. Subject to availability. May exclude some holidays. Void if copied or altered. One coupon per person. Grand Victoria is not responsible for any typographical errors or misprints or for lost, stolen or expired offers, and reserves the right to modify or cancel this program at any time without prior notice. Redeemable only at Grand Victoria Casino, Elgin, Illinois. Must be 21. If you or someone you know has a gambling problem, call 1.800.GAMBLER.

Grand Victoria Casino Elgin • 250 S. Grove Avenue, Elgin, IL 60120 (847) 468-7000

SEIZE THE DAY
11999 Avenue of the Emperors
Elizabeth, IN 47117
1-877-237-6626
caesarsindiana.com

Present this coupon to the cashier at time of purchase. Offer valid Sunday-Thursday, excludes Sunday brunch and Tuesday dinner. When using as 2-for-1 coupon both buffets must be redeemed on same visit. Must be 21 or older to redeem. Tax and gratuiy not included. Coupon not redeemable for cash. Original coupon (no photocopies) must be presented to the cashier. One coupon per customer. Not valid with any other coupon or offer. Management reserves all rights. Valid through 12/31/08.

SEIZE THE DAY
11999 Avenue of the Emperors
Elizabeth, IN 47117
1-877-237-6626
caesarsindiana.com

Senior Tuesday rate, $37. Twighlight Weekday rate, $35 after 3 p.m. Twilight Weekend rate, $45 after 4 p.m. For a tee time, call 1-877-316-7336 or visit caesarsindiana.com for more information. Not valid with any other offer. Valid through 12/31/08. Rates show valid through 10/01/07. Must be 21 years or older to gamble. Know When To Stop Before You Start.® Gambling Problem? Call 1-800-522-4700. ©2007, Harrah's License Company, LLC.

AMERICAN CASINO GUIDE

$10

SLOT DOLLARS

FRENCH LICK
RESORT · CASINO

Present this coupon to the Resort Rewards at French Lick players' club desk along with a valid photo I.D. to receive your $10 Slot Dollars.

A current American Casino Guide Discount Card must be presented when redeeming this coupon, or offer is void

---

AMERICAN CASINO GUIDE

BUY ONE MEAL, GET ONE FREE AT PASSPORTS BUFFET

PASSPORTS A WORLD CLASS BUFFET

Present this coupon to the cashier at Passports Buffet to receive your buy one meal, get one free. Excludes alcohol and gratuity. No cash value. Valid through December 31, 2008. See back for complete details. CASINOG

Player Account Number _____

Majestic Star
CASINOS & HOTEL

A current American Casino Guide Discount Card must be presented when redeeming this coupon, or offer is void

---

AMERICAN CASINO GUIDE

FREE REGULAR CUP OF COFFEE AT JACKPOT JAVA

Present this coupon to the cashier at Jackpot Java for a free regular cup of coffee. Excludes alcohol and gratuity. No cash value. Valid through December 31, 2008. See back for complete details. CASINOG

Player Account Number _____

Majestic Star
CASINOS & HOTEL

A current American Casino Guide Discount Card must be presented when redeeming this coupon, or offer is void

---

AMERICAN CASINO GUIDE

EARN 25 POINTS, GET $10

After playing with your Club Majestic® card and earning
25 points, please present your coupon at Club Majestic®
and you will receive $10 in cash. Club Majestic® members
get exciting offers and rewards, fabulous benefits and
SAME DAY CASH BACK! Valid through December 31,
2008. See back for complete details. CASINOG

Majestic Star
CASINOS & HOTEL

Player Account Number _____

A current American Casino Guide Discount Card must be
presented when redeeming this coupon, or offer is void

AMERICAN CASINO GUIDE

$5 off any Buffet!

Present this coupon, along with your Terrible's Players Club Card,
to the cashier at the Bougainvillea Buffet to receive $5 off any
breakfast, lunch or dinner buffet. See reverse for more details.

A current American Casino Guide Discount Card must be
presented when redeeming this coupon, or offer is void

AMERICAN CASINO GUIDE

$5 Gas Discount!
(with gas purchase of $25 or more!)

Present this coupon, along with your Terrible's Players Club Card, to
the cashier at Terrible's convenience store and gas station to receive
a $5 discount on any gas purchase of $25 or more. See reverse for details.

A current American Casino Guide Discount Card must be
presented when redeeming this coupon, or offer is void

AMERICAN CASINO GUIDE

FREE Slot Play, Hat or T-shirt and deck of cards for new Slot Club members!

Sign up for a Terrible's Lakeside Casino Players Club Card and receive $5 in FREE Slot Play, a FREE t-shirt or hat and a FREE deck of cards. Only valid for new members. See reverse for details.

A current American Casino Guide Discount Card must be presented when redeeming this coupon, or offer is void

---

AMERICAN CASINO GUIDE

GREEKTOWN
CASINO
a Kewadin Casino™

Receive $5 in Bonu$ Play When You Earn 150 Points!

Use your CLUB Greektown Card and when you earn 150 points, you'll receive $5 in Bonu$ Play! See reverse for full details.

A current American Casino Guide Discount Card must be presented when redeeming this coupon, or offer is void

---

AMERICAN CASINO GUIDE

$79 ROOM OFFER

Plus $20 resort credits*
to be used at:

- Banana Cabana Gift Shop
- Restaurants
- The Spa at the Isle

Call **1-800-THE-ISLE** for reservations.
Mention Code: VENPCK

151 Beach Blvd.
Biloxi, MS, 39530
www.isleofcapricasino.com

A current American Casino Guide Discount Card must be presented when redeeming this coupon, or offer is void

2-For-1 Buffet

Present this coupon to the cashier at the *Clemens Café* to purchase one breakfast or lunch buffet at regular price and receive a second buffet for FREE (or 50% off when dining alone). See reverse for details.

A current American Casino Guide Discount Card must be presented when redeeming this coupon, or offer is void

Buy one entrée and get a second entrée at 50% off!

Buy one entrée at the *Clemens Café* and enjoy a second entrée of equal or lesser value at 50% off! See reverse for details.

A current American Casino Guide Discount Card must be presented when redeeming this coupon, or offer is void

50% Discount on any logo'd item in our Gift Shop!

Present this coupon to the cashier at Terrible's St. Jo Frontier Casino gift shop to receive 50% off the purchase price of any one logo'd item. See reverse for more details.

A current American Casino Guide Discount Card must be presented when redeeming this coupon, or offer is void

104 Pierce Street
LaGrange, MO 63448
(573) 655-4770
(866)454-5825
www.terribleherbst.com

Must be 21 years of age or older. Not valid on holidays. Not valid with any other offer. Limit one coupon per person. Discount is 50% off when dining alone. Resale prohibited. Original coupon must be presented (no photocopies). Gratuity and alcoholic beverages not included.

Management reserves the right to cancel or alter this coupon without prior notice. Offer expires 12/30/08.

Bet with your head, not over it.
Gambling Problem? Call 888-BETSOFF.

104 Pierce Street
LaGrange, MO 63448
(573) 655-4770
(866)454-5825
www.terribleherbst.com

- Offer valid for adults 21 years of age or older.
- Present original coupon (no photocopies) to server prior to ordering.
- Limit one coupon per person.
- Management reserves the right to cancel or alter this coupon without prior notice.
- Gratuity and alcoholic beverages not included.
- Offer expires 12/30/08.

Bet with your head, not over it.
Gambling Problem? Call 888-BETSOFF.

777 Winner's Circle
St Joseph, MO 64505
(816) 279-5514
(800) 888-2946
www.terribleherbst.com

Must be 21 years of age or older. Not valid with any other offer. Limit one coupon per person. Limited to a 50% discount on one item. Resale prohibited. Original coupon must be presented (no photocopies).

Management reserves the right to cancel or alter this coupon without prior notice. Offer expires 12/30/08.

Bet with your head, not over it.
Gambling Problem? Call 888-BETSOFF.

AMERICAN CASINO GUIDE

2-For-1 Bougainvillea Buffet

Present this coupon at the *Bougainvillea Buffet* to purchase one breakfast, lunch or dinner buffet at regular price and receive a second buffet for FREE (or 50% off when dining alone). See reverse for details.

A current American Casino Guide Discount Card must be presented when redeeming this coupon, or offer is void

AMERICAN CASINO GUIDE

Buy one entrée and get a second entrée FREE!

Buy one entrée at the *Bougainvillea Cafe* and enjoy a second entrée of equal or lesser value FREE! See reverse for details.

A current American Casino Guide Discount Card must be presented when redeeming this coupon, or offer is void

AMERICAN CASINO GUIDE

2-FOR-1 BUFFET

Please Present This Coupon To Your Server Before Ordering. Receive One (1) Free Buffet With The Purchase Of One (1) Buffet At Regular Price. One Coupon Per Party Of Two.

US Hwy 93 Boulder City, NV. 89005
(702) 293-5000 Toll free(800) 245-6380
www.haciendaonline.com

A current American Casino Guide Discount Card must be presented when redeeming this coupon, or offer is void

US Hwy 93
Boulder City, NV. 89005
(702) 293-5000
(800) 245-6380
www.haciendaonline.com

Overlooking Beautiful Lake Mead, Near Hoover Dam

One coupon per customer per day. May be used with: Blackjack-any bet, Craps-pass line or field only, Roulette-red/black or odd/even only. Must be 21 or older. Offer may be cancelled at any time. No cash value. No photocopies accepted. Not valid with any other offer. Expires 12/31/08.

1 Main Street
Jean, NV 89019
(800) 634-1359
www.stopatjean.com

To Redeem: 1) Present this coupon with club card (or join club) at the Gold Strike club booth to receive a validation slip. 2) Present this coupon and your validation slip to server before ordering entree or to cashier as you enter buffet.

Must be at least 21 years of age and a member of, or join, Jean's Cash & Comp Club. Offer may not be combined with any other offers or programs. Limit one redemption per club account. Offer not valid to employees of Gold Strike. Management reserves all rights. Offer expires 12/30/08.

Jean is located at Exit 12 off I-15
Just 20 minutes south of the world famous Las Vegas Strip.

111 Country Club Drive
Incline Village, NV 89451
(775) 832-1234
(800) 327-3910

Must be 21 years of age, or older. New accounts only. One offer per account. Management reserves the right to alter or change promotion at any time. Expires 12/31/08.

AMERICAN CASINO GUIDE

2-For-1 Breakfast or Lunch Buffet

Present this coupon to the buffet cashier at either Arizona Charlie's
Decatur or Arizona Charlie's Boulder to receive one FREE breakfast
or lunch buffet when you purchase one buffet at the regular price.
Not valid on holidays or specialty nights. See reverse for more details.

A current American Casino Guide Discount Card must be
presented when redeeming this coupon, or offer is void

AMERICAN CASINO GUIDE

2-For-1 Medium Size Pizza

Bring this coupon directly to the Brickhouse Pizza Kitchen between the
hours of 2pm – 9pm. Show your Wild Card, pay for one medium single
topping pizza and get the second for free. Extra toppings available at
additional charge. See reverse for complete details.

A current American Casino Guide Discount Card must be
presented when redeeming this coupon, or offer is void

AMERICAN CASINO GUIDE

2-For-1 Micro-Brewed Beer

Purchase one micro-brew at the bar at Barley's and receive a second brew
of equal or lesser value FREE! Must present this coupon to your server
at the bar **before** ordering. See reverse for complete details.

A current American Casino Guide Discount Card must be
presented when redeeming this coupon, or offer is void

4575 Boulder Highway
Las Vegas, NV 89121
(702) 951-9000 • (800) 362-4040
www.arizonacharlies.com

740 S. Decatur Boulevard
Las Vegas, NV 89107
(702) 258-5200 • (800) 342-2695
www.arizonacharlies.com

Must be 21 years of age or older. Must present your A.C.E. Rewards card and surrender this original coupon (no photocopies) to the cashier before being seated. Limit one coupon per person. Resale prohibited. Management reserves all rights. Not valid on holidays or specialty nights. Non-negotiable. Valid through December 30, 2008.

ACBUFF07D/ACBUFF07B

4500 E. Sunset Road #30
Henderson, NV 89014
(702) 458-2739
www.stationcasinos.com

Must be 21 or older. Must be a Wild Card member. Offer expires December 31, 2008.

Offer valid daily during normal pizza kitchen hours. Tax & Gratuity not included. Offer has no cash value. Non-transferable. Not responsible for lost or stolen coupon. Management reserves all rights. Not valid with any other offer or promotion. Offer void if sold.

Offer may be changed or discontinued at anytime at the discretion of management. Settle to #151-140

4500 E. Sunset Road #30
Henderson, NV 89014
(702) 458-2739
www.stationcasinos.com

Must be 21 or older. Valid 24 hours per day. Purchase one micro brew and receive a second brew of equal or lesser value for free. Tax and gratuity not included. Offer void if sold. Expires December 26, 2008.

Not responsible for lost or stolen coupon. Management reserves all rights. Offer may be changed or discontinued at anytime at the discretion of management. Settle to #151-140

Bella Panini
2-For-1 Menu Item

Present this coupon at Bella Panini in the Venetian Hotel Grand Canal Shops, purchase your choice of any menu item and receive your choice of a second menu item of equal or lesser value FREE!

A current American Casino Guide Discount Card must be presented when redeeming this coupon, or offer is void

Grand Canyon South Rim Bus Tour
$85.99 (Regular $149.99)

Book a Grand Canyon South Rim Bus Tour for only $85.99 Present this coupon at check-in to receive discount. Coupon only valid by calling Best Tours directly at (702) 851-8436. Not valid with any other offer or promotion. Offer expires 12/31/08.

mention code: ACG

A current American Casino Guide Discount Card must be presented when redeeming this coupon, or offer is void

2,500 Slot Club Points For New Members

Present this coupon at the Bigshot Players Club booth to receive 2,500 FREE slot club points when you join as a new member.
See reverse for more details.

A current American Casino Guide Discount Card must be presented when redeeming this coupon, or offer is void

Bella Panini
Venetian Hotel Grand Canal Shops

Must present coupon to cashier prior to ordering. Offer has no cash value. Not valid with any other offer. One coupon per person. Subject to change or cancellation without prior notice. Offer valid through December 31, 2008.

- Guided tour thru Boulder City, Lake Mead and a 15 minute stop at Hoover Dam for photos.

- Three major stops at the Grand Canyon

- Lunch included

- Duration: Approx. 14 hours

- Reservations: 702-851-8436

Best Tours
Grand Canyon • Hoover Dam
Airplane • Helicopter • Bus • Hummer

Terms and Conditions: Not valid with any other offers, must call direct and mention code ACG

BIGHORN Casino
RESTAURANT & LOUNGE

3016 E. Lake Mead Blvd.
N. Las Vegas, NV 89030
(702) 642-1940

Valid for new accounts only. Must be 21 or older. Cannot be combined with any other offer or promotion. Non-transferable. Offer void if sold. Please allow up to 48 hours for points to reflect on account balance.

Must present original coupon (no photocopies). Not responsible for lost or stolen coupon. Management reserves all rights. Offer may be changed or discontinued at anytime at the discretion of management. Offer expires December 30, 2008.

AMERICAN CASINO GUIDE

$10 Blackjack Matchplay

Present this coupon at any blackjack table, along with your
Bigshot Players Club card, prior to the start of a hand and
we'll match your bet of $10 if you win. See reverse for details.

A current American Casino Guide Discount Card must be
presented when redeeming this coupon, or offer is void

AMERICAN CASINO GUIDE

2-for-1 Lunch or Dinner Entrée

Buy one lunch or dinner entrée in our restaurant and
get one entrée of equal or lesser value FREE! Present to
server before ordering. See reverse for more details.

A current American Casino Guide Discount Card must be
presented when redeeming this coupon, or offer is void

AMERICAN CASINO GUIDE

One FREE Cocktail at any Casino Bar

Present this coupon to the server at any casino bar
at Bill's Gamblin' Hall & Saloon to receive
one FREE cocktail. See reverse for details.

A current American Casino Guide Discount Card must be
presented when redeeming this coupon, or offer is void

3016 E. Lake Mead Blvd.
N. Las Vegas, NV 89030
(702) 642-1940

Limit: one coupon per person, per month. Cannot be redeemed for cash. Must be 21 or older. Cannot be combined with any other offer or promotion. Non-transferable. Offer void if sold.

Must present original coupon (no photocopies). Not responsible for lost or stolen coupon. Management reserves all rights. Offer may be changed or discontinued at anytime at the discretion of management. Offer expires December 30, 2008.

3016 E. Lake Mead Blvd.
N. Las Vegas, NV 89030
(702) 642-1940

Limit one coupon per person. Must be 21 years or older. Purchase one lunch or dinner entrée to receive the second one of equal or lesser value free. Coupon is void if altered or duplicated. Must present original coupon (no photocopies).

Tax, beverages and gratuity are not included. Not valid with any other offers or discounts. Management reserves the right to cancel or modify offer at any time. Coupon has no cash value. Offer expires December 30, 2008.

3595 Las Vegas Blvd. S.
Las Vegas, NV 89109
(702) 737-2100
(866) 245-5745
www.billslasvegas.com

Must be 21 years of age or older. Excludes specialty drinks in souvenir glasses. Excludes restaurant bars. Gratuity not included. Please present before ordering. Original coupon must be presented (no photocopies accepted). Resale prohibited.

Management reserves the right to cancel or alter this coupon without prior notice. Offer expires 12-30-08.

AMERICAN CASINO GUIDE

FREE Hot Dog and a Beer!

Present this coupon at the hot dog cart located in the Sports Lounge and receive one free hot dog and a beer. See reverse for complete details.

A current American Casino Guide Discount Card must be presented when redeeming this coupon, or offer is void

---

AMERICAN CASINO GUIDE

Downtown Las Vegas Since 1951

Gambling Hall & Hotel

Buy One $11.99 Steak & Lobster Dinner and get a second one FREE

Valid 11 a.m. to 11 p.m. Sunday thru Thursday (holidays and special events excluded.) in Binions Coffee Shop. Subject to availability. Must mention ACG.

A current American Casino Guide Discount Card must be presented when redeeming this coupon, or offer is void

ACG 004-2008

AMERICAN CASINO GUIDE

Downtown Las Vegas Since 1951

Gambling Hall & Hotel

Buy one Deli Sandwich get one FREE

Pay for the first deli sandwich and receive the second deli sandwich free. Valid Sunday thru Thursday (holidays and special events excluded.) Sandwiches subject to availability. Must mention ACG.

A current American Casino Guide Discount Card must be presented when redeeming this coupon, or offer is void

ACG 001-2008

3595 Las Vegas Blvd. S.
Las Vegas, NV 89109
(702) 737-2100
(866) 245-5745
www.billslasvegas.com

Must be 21 years of age or older. Not valid with any other offer. Resale prohibited. Limit one coupon per person. Gratuity not included. Original coupon must be presented (no photocopies).

Management reserves the right to cancel or alter this coupon without prior notice. Offer expires 12-30-08.

Downtown Las Vegas Since 1951

Gambling Hall & Hotel

128 East Fremont St.
Las Vegas, NV 89101
800.937.6537 • 702.382.1600
www.binions.com

This coupon entitles the bearer to one free Steak & Lobster entrée in at Binion's Coffee Shop with the purchase of $11.99 Steak and Lobster entree. Must present and surrender this coupon upon ordering. No exceptions. Not available in conjunction with any other offer or discounts. Management reserves the right to change or cancel this offer without prior notice. Must be 21 or older. Limit one free entrée per party. Gratuity and tax not included. Coupon has no cash value. Offer Expires Dec. 27, 2008

Downtown Las Vegas Since 1951

Gambling Hall & Hotel

128 East Fremont St.
Las Vegas, NV 89101
800.937.6537 • 702.382.1600
www.binions.com

This coupon entitles the bearer to one free deli sandwich at Binion's Gambling Hall & Hotel's first Floor Deli with the purchase of a sandwich. Free sandwich must be of equal or lesser value than sandwich purchased at full price. Must present and surrender this coupon upon ordering. No exceptions. Not available in conjunction with any other offer or discounts. Management reserves the right to change or cancel this offer without prior notice. Must be 21 or older. Limit one free sandwich per person. Gratuity and tax not included. Coupon has no cash value. Offer Expires Dec. 30, 2008

AMERICAN CASINO GUIDE

Downtown Las Vegas Since 1951

Gambling Hall & Hotel

Second Room Night FREE

Pay for one room night at the prevailing rate and receive a second consecutive room night FREE at Binion's Gambling Hall & Hotel.

ACG 002-2008

A current American Casino Guide Discount Card must be presented when redeeming this coupon, or offer is void

AMERICAN CASINO GUIDE

Downtown Las Vegas Since 1951

Gambling Hall & Hotel

Buy 1 Entrée get one FREE at Binion's Ranch Steakhouse

ACG 003-2008

A current American Casino Guide Discount Card must be presented when redeeming this coupon, or offer is void

AMERICAN CASINO GUIDE

BOULDER STATION
HOTEL · CASINO

2-For-1 Room

Pay for one night and get the second night FREE! Good Sunday through Thursday. Holidays and convention periods excluded. Black out dates may apply. Subject to availability. Offer expires December 26, 2008. For reservations call: 1-800-683-7777 and ask for Operator #M38.

A current American Casino Guide Discount Card must be presented when redeeming this coupon, or offer is void

$10 Match Play on any Table Game

Make a minimum $10 bet with this coupon at any table game and you'll receive an extra $10 if you win! Coupon must be surrendered after bet wins or loses. See reverse for more details.

2-For-1 Lunch or Dinner Buffet
(or 50% off when dining alone)

Buy one lunch or dinner buffet and get a second one FREE (or 50% off when dining alone). Offer valid Sunday-Thursday, excludes Sunday brunch and Thursday dinner. When using as 2-for-1 coupon both buffets must be redeemed on same visit. See reverse for more details.

FREE Hat or T-shirt, plus a deck of cards for new Slot Club members!

New members only, present this coupon at the All American Can Club booth, sign up for a card and receive a FREE hat or T-shirt, plus a FREE deck of cards! See reverse for details.

2121 E. Craig Road
N. Las Vegas, NV 89030
(702) 507-5700
(866) 999-4899
www.cannerycasinos.com

Make a $10 minimum bet at any table game, along with this coupon, and receive an extra $10 if your bet wins. Even-money bets only. Coupon must be surrendered after bet wins or loses. Cannot be redeemed for cash. Not valid with any other offer. Must be 21or older to redeem. Limit: one coupon per person, per year. No photocopies accepted. Management reserves all rights. Offer expires12/31/08.

2121 E. Craig Road
N. Las Vegas, NV 89030
(702) 507-5700
(866) 999-4899
www.cannerycasinos.com

Present this coupon to the cashier at time of purchase. Must be 21 or older to redeem. Tax and gratuity not included. Coupon not redeeemable for cash. Original coupon (no photocopies) must be presented to the cashier. One coupon per customer. Not valid with any other coupon or offer. Management reserves all rights. Offer void if sold. Valid through 12/31/08.

2121 E. Craig Road
N. Las Vegas, NV 89030
(702) 507-5700
(866) 999-4899
www.cannerycasinos.com

Present this coupon at the Cannery's All American Can Club booth. Sign up for a Player's Club card and receive a FREE hat or t-shirt, plus a FREE deck of cards. Only valid for new members. Must be 21 years of age or older. Not valid in conjunction with any other offer. No photocopies accepted. Offer void if sold. Management reserves all rights. Offer expires12/31/08.

AMERICAN CASINO GUIDE

FREE FUN BOOK!

Present this coupon at either the Market Express across from THE Steak House, or Headliners located on the Promenade Level. Must be at least 21 years of age.

Be Adventurous.

A current American Casino Guide Discount Card must be presented when redeeming this coupon, or offer is void

AMERICAN CASINO GUIDE

 **Hotel & Casino**

$10 Free Slot Play!

$10 free slot play for new or current members of Jackie's Club Cortez. See reverse for details.

A current American Casino Guide Discount Card must be presented when redeeming this coupon, or offer is void

AMERICAN CASINO GUIDE

 **Hotel & Casino**

50% off at Roberta's Steakhouse

Redeem this coupon for a 50% discount on your total bill, up to a maximum of $25 at Roberta's Steakhouse. Coupon valid Sunday-Thursday only. Reservations recommended.

A current American Casino Guide Discount Card must be presented when redeeming this coupon, or offer is void

AMERICAN CASINO GUIDE

2-For-1
Room Offer!

Redeem this coupon for one night free room. Book one night
at the special rate of $30 and get your second night free. Rate
is for Vintage or Pavilion rooms. You may stay additional
nights at casino rate. Blackout dates apply.

A current American Casino Guide Discount Card must be
presented when redeeming this coupon, or offer is void

AMERICAN CASINO GUIDE

2-For-1
Menu Item

Present this coupon, along with your Passport Players Club Card, at the Restaurant
or BBQ in Ellis Island Casino & Brewery to receive one FREE menu item when
you purchase one item at the regular price. See reverse for more details.

A current American Casino Guide Discount Card must be
presented when redeeming this coupon, or offer is void

AMERICAN CASINO GUIDE

4 FREE Cocktails
at the Casino Bar!

Present this coupon, along with your Passport Players Club Card,
at the Casino Bar inside Ellis Island Casino & Brewery to receive
four FREE cocktails of your choice. See reverse for more details.

A current American Casino Guide Discount Card must be
presented when redeeming this coupon, or offer is void

600 E. Fremont Street
Las Vegas, NV 89101
(702) 385-5200
(800) 634-6703
www.elcortezhotelcasino.com

Please tell reservation agent you are booking for the American Casino Guide coupon book. First night of stay must be Sunday-Wednesday. Offer is subject to availability. You must present and surrender coupon upon check-in and be at least 21 years of age. Customer is responsible for tax, telephone, room service, and all other additional charges. This offer is not available in conjunction with any other offer or coupon.

Offer Expires 12/28/08.

4178 Koval Lane
Las Vegas, NV 89169
(702) 733-8901
www.ellisislandscasino.com

Present this original coupon (no photocopies) to the hostess in the restaurant or the BBQ, along with your Passport Players Club Card, to receive one FREE menu item from the regular menu with the purchase of another menu item at the regular price. The FREE item must be of equal or lesser value. Limit: one coupon per customer. No cash value. Must be 21 years of age or older. Tax and gratuity not included. Management reserves all rights. Offer expires 12/30/08.

4178 Koval Lane
Las Vegas, NV 89169
(702) 733-8901
www.ellisislandscasino.com

Must be 21 years of age or older. No restrictions on brands. Gratuity not included.

Please present before ordering. Original coupon must be presented (no photocopies) along with your Passport Players Club Card. Resale prohibited. Management reserves the right to cancel or alter this coupon without prior notice. Offer expires 12/30/08.

AMERICAN CASINO GUIDE

$10 Match Play for Any Even-Money Table Game Bet

(with your Passport Players Club Card)

Make a $10 even-money bet at blackjack, craps or roulette with this coupon and your Passport Players Club Card and receive a FREE $10 Match Bet!

A current American Casino Guide Discount Card must be presented when redeeming this coupon, or offer is void

AMERICAN CASINO GUIDE

Buy One Entrée Get One FREE!

Come in and enjoy the luck of the Irish. Buy one entrée at our Emerald Island Grille and get the second entrée of equal or lesser value FREE! See reverse for more details.

A current American Casino Guide Discount Card must be presented when redeeming this coupon, or offer is void

AMERICAN CASINO GUIDE

 2-For-1 Feast Buffet

Valid once at Sunset Station, Boulder Station, Texas Station, Santa Fe Station, Green Valley Ranch, or Red Rock. Present this coupon to the cashier. Pay for one Feast Buffet and get the second Feast Buffet free! Valid Sunday through Thursday only. Offer expires December 26, 2008. Settle to comp BS 82-965, GVR 00694, SS 13-279, TS 82-295, SF 41328, RR 33069.

A current American Casino Guide Discount Card must be presented when redeeming this coupon, or offer is void

4178 Koval Lane
Las Vegas, NV 89169
(702) 733-8901
www.ellisislandscasino.com

Must be 21 years of age or older and a Passport Players Club member. Make a $10 minimum even-money bet at any Ellis Island Casino blackjack, craps or roulette game, along with this original coupon (no photocopies), and receive a $10 Match Bet. Valid for one bet only and coupon must be surrendered after play. No Cash Value. Limit: one coupon per customer. Not valid with any other offer. Management reserves all rights. Offer expires 12/30/08.

120 Market Street
Henderson, NV 89015
(702) 567-9160

The *Jewel* of Henderson

"Where Every Day is Promotion Day!"

Redeem this coupon at Club Jewel Rewards Center prior to dining. Must be at least 21 years of age and a Club Jewel Rewards Member. Limit one coupon per member. Gratuities not included. Coupon has no cash value. Copies are not accepted. Offer expires December 31, 2008.

www.emeraldislandcasino.com

Sunset Station • Boulder Station • Texas Station
Santa Fe Station • Green Valley Ranch • Red Rock

Offer valid one time at any of the above Station Casinos Properties

This ticket entitles bearer to one free breakfast, lunch, or dinner in The Feast Buffet when accompanied by a paying guest. Tax and gratuity not included. One coupon per person. Coupon must be presented to cashier. Coupons are not transferable and are not redeemable for cash. Must be 21 years of age or older. Not a line pass. Valid Sunday through Thursday only. Not valid on holidays. Not valid with any other offer. Offer may be changed or discontinued at any time at the discretion of management. This offer is void if sold.

AMERICAN CASINO GUIDE

2-For-1 Room!

Pay for one night and get the second night FREE! Valid for Sunday-Wednesday
check in. Convention periods excluded. Subject to availability. Black out
dates may apply. Offer expires December 26, 2008. For Reservations call:
1-800-388-8334 and ask for Fiesta Operator #M38.

A current American Casino Guide Discount Card must be
presented when redeeming this coupon, or offer is void

AMERICAN CASINO GUIDE

2-For-1 Festival Buffet!

Present this coupon to the cashier at the Festival Buffet at either
Fiesta Rancho or Fiesta Henderson. Pay for one buffet and get
the second buffet FREE! Valid Monday through Friday only.
Offer expires 12/30/08. Settle to FH 41-353/FR 28-305

A current American Casino Guide Discount Card must be
presented when redeeming this coupon, or offer is void

AMERICAN CASINO GUIDE

Sign up for an Amigo Card and receive 1,500 bonus points!
Present this coupon to the Amigo Club when you sign up for
an Amigo Card and receive 1,500 bonus points! Valid at either
Fiesta Rancho or Fiesta Henderson. See reverse for details.

A current American Casino Guide Discount Card must be
presented when redeeming this coupon, or offer is void

777 W. Lake Mead Drive
Henderson, NV 89015
(702) 558-7000 • (866) 469-7666
www.stationcasinos.com

2400 N. Rancho Drive
Las Vegas, NV 89130
(702) 631-7000 • (800) 731-7333
www.stationcasinos.com

This voucher entitles the bearer to one free room night at Fiesta Henderson or Fiesta Rancho, with the purchase of one night at the prevailing rate. Must have advance reservations. Must present original voucher (no photocopies) upon check-in. Not valid in conjunction with any other offer. Management reserves the right to cancel this promotion at any time. Credit card or cash deposit required. Guest is responsible for tax, telephone, room service and all other additional charges. Must be 21 or older. Limit one free room per person. Offer expires December 26, 2008. Settle to #41386

777 W. Lake Mead Drive
Henderson, NV 89015
(702) 558-7000 • (866) 469-7666
www.stationcasinos.com

2400 N. Rancho Drive
Las Vegas, NV 89130
(702) 631-7000 • (800) 731-7333
www.stationcasinos.com

Must be 21 or older. Management reserves all rights. Not a line pass. Tax and gratuity not included. Coupons are not transferable and are not redeemable for cash. Original coupon (no photocopies) must be presented to the cashier. Not valid on holidays. Not valid with any other offer. Valid through December 30, 2008. Offer void if sold. Settle to: FH 41-353 / FR 28-305

777 W. Lake Mead Drive
Henderson, NV 89015
(702) 558-7000 • (866) 469-7666
www.stationcasinos.com

2400 N. Rancho Drive
Las Vegas, NV 89130
(702) 631-7000 • (800) 731-7333
www.stationcasinos.com

Offer only valid for first time sign up for the Amigo Card. Original coupon (no photocopies) must be presented at Amigo Club. Must be 21 or older. Management reserves all rights. One coupon per person. Valid through December 30, 2008.

AMERICAN CASINO GUIDE

**One Complimentary Appetizer
or Dessert With the purchase of
two entrees at Don B's Steakhouse**

Present this coupon to your server before ordering to
receive one complimentary appetizer or dessert with the
purchase of two entrees at Don B's Steakhouse
See reverse for more details.

A current American Casino Guide Discount Card must be
presented when redeeming this coupon, or offer is void

AMERICAN CASINO GUIDE

**Earn 50 Base
Reward Credits and
get $5.00 in COMPS!**

Base Reward Credits must be earned within 72 hours. Present coupon
to the Total Rewards Center at the Flamingo after Base Reward Credits
have been earned. See the Total Rewards Center for more details.

A current American Casino Guide Discount Card must be
presented when redeeming this coupon, or offer is void

AMERICAN CASINO GUIDE

**Join Total Rewards at
Flamingo Las Vegas
and get a FREE Gift!**

Present this coupon at the Flamingo Las Vegas when you first
sign up for a Total Rewards Card and receive a FREE gift!
See the Total Rewards Center for more details.

A current American Casino Guide Discount Card must be
presented when redeeming this coupon, or offer is void

301 Fremont St.
Las Vegas, NV 89101
(702) 388-2400
1-800-274-LUCK
fitzgeraldslasvegas.com

Must be 21 years of age or older. Tax and gratuity not included. Reservations recommended. Please call (702) 388-2460. Coupon has no cash value and may be revoked/cancelled at anytime. Employees of Fitzgeralds are not eligible. Not valid with any other offer. Offer valid through 12/28/08.

LAS VEGAS

3555 Las Vegas Blvd. S.
Las Vegas, NV 89109
(800) 732-2111
www.flamingolasvegas.com

Valid only at Flamingo Las Vegas. Must be 21 or older to participate. One coupon redemption per account, per month. Base Reward Credits must be earned within 72 hours. Cannot be used in conjunction with any other offer or promotion. Original coupon must be presented (no photocopies). Management reserves the right to cancel or alter this offer without prior notice. Offer Code: AC06. Offer valid through 12/30/08.

Must be 21 or older to gamble. Know When To Stop Before You Start.® Gambling Problem? Call 1-800-522-4700.
©2007, Harrah's License Company, LLC.

LAS VEGAS

3555 Las Vegas Blvd. S.
Las Vegas, NV 89109
(702) 733-3111
(800) 732-2111
www.flamingolasvegas.com

Valid only at Flamingo Las Vegas and only valid for new members. Must be 21 or older to participate. Cannot be used in conjunction with any other offer or promotion. Original coupon must be presented (no photocopies). Management reserves the right to cancel or alter this offer without prior notice. Offer Code: ACM06. Valid through 12/30/08.

Must be 21 or older to gamble. Know When To Stop Before You Start.® Gambling Problem? Call 1-800-522-4700.
©2007, Harrah's License Company, LLC.

AMERICAN CASINO GUIDE

Double Points (Up to 100) for members of the Royal Players Club™

Double your Royal Players Club™ points (up to 100) with this coupon! See reverse for more details.

A current American Casino Guide Discount Card must be presented when redeeming this coupon, or offer is void

AMERICAN CASINO GUIDE

2-for-1 Lunch or Dinner Entrée in Magnolia's

Buy one lunch or dinner entrée in Magnolia's and get one entrée FREE! See reverse for more details.

A current American Casino Guide Discount Card must be presented when redeeming this coupon, or offer is void

AMERICAN CASINO GUIDE

$10 in FREE Slot Play!

New members only, present this coupon at the Royal Players Club™ booth, sign up for the Royal Players Club™ card and receive $10 in FREE slot play. See reverse for more details.

A current American Casino Guide Discount Card must be presented when redeeming this coupon, or offer is void

202 Fremont Street
Las Vegas, NV 89101
(702) 385-4011
(800) 634-6045
www.fourqueens.com

Limit one coupon per person. Coupon has no cash value. Must be 21 years or older. Points must be earned on day of redemption. Offer valid for Royal Players Club™ members only. Double points will be added to account within 48 hours. Management reserves the right to cancel or modify offer at any time without notice. Coupon is void if altered or duplicated. Offer expires December 30, 2008.

202 Fremont Street
Las Vegas, NV 89101
(702) 385-4011
(800) 634-6045
www.fourqueens.com

Limit one coupon per person. Must be 21 years or older. Purchase one lunch or dinner entrée (equal or greater value) to receive the second one free. Offer valid only in Magnolia's. Coupon is void if altered or duplicated. Tax, alcoholic beverages and gratuity are not included. Not valid with any other offers or discounts. Management reserves the right to cancel or modify offer at any time. Coupon has no cash value. Offer expires December 30, 2008.

202 Fremont Street
Las Vegas, NV 89101
(702) 385-4011
(800) 634-6045
www.fourqueens.com

Must be 21 years or older. Not valid with any other offers or discounts. Management reserves the right to cancel or modify offer at any time. Limit one coupon and $10 in Free Slot Play per account. Must show valid I.D. and RPC card to receive your $10 in Free Slot Play. Coupon has no cash value. $10 must be played on a slot machine and cannot be cashed out. Free Slot Play rules apply. Coupon is void if altered or duplicated. Non-transferable. $10 in Free Slot Play is valid through December 30, 2008.

AMERICAN CASINO GUIDE

$5 Match Play

Present this coupon to casino dealer with equal wager of real chips or cash. See reverse for full details.

A current American Casino Guide Discount Card must be presented when redeeming this coupon, or offer is void

AMERICAN CASINO GUIDE

2-For-1 Food Special

Bring this coupon to Digger Dan's at the Gold Rush Casino to receive 2-for-1 on any menu item! See reverse for more details.

A current American Casino Guide Discount Card must be presented when redeeming this coupon, or offer is void

AMERICAN CASINO GUIDE

Established 1906
GOLDEN GATE
HOTEL & CASINO • ONE FREMONT STREET • LAS VEGAS

Second Room Night FREE

Pay for one room night Sunday through Thursday at the prevailing rate and receive a second consecutive room night FREE. See reverse side for full details.

A current American Casino Guide Discount Card must be presented when redeeming this coupon, or offer is void

AMERICAN CASINO GUIDE

Established 1906

2-for-1 Menu Item at Bay City Diner or Shrimp Bar & Deli

Present this coupon to your server at the Bay City Diner or the Shrimp Bar & Deli. Purchase any menu item and receive a second menu item of equal or lesser value FREE! Shrimp cocktail not included. See reverse for more details.

A current American Casino Guide Discount Card must be presented when redeeming this coupon, or offer is void

AMERICAN CASINO GUIDE

LAS VEGAS

Receive $60 in Poker Chips for $50

Receive $60 in chips for a $50 buy-in in our non-smoking Poker Room. See reverse for more details.

A current American Casino Guide Discount Card must be presented when redeeming this coupon, or offer is void

AMERICAN CASINO GUIDE

LAS VEGAS

2-For-1 Show Tickets

Receive One Complimentary Ticket to Defending the Caveman with the purchase of a second ticket. See reverse for more details.

A current American Casino Guide Discount Card must be presented when redeeming this coupon, or offer is void

AMERICAN CASINO GUIDE

2-For-1 Menu Item

Present this coupon at any Haagen Dazs shop listed on the back, purchase your choice of any menu item and receive your choice of a second menu item of equal or lesser value FREE!

A current American Casino Guide Discount Card must be presented when redeeming this coupon, or offer is void

---

AMERICAN CASINO GUIDE

LAS VEGAS CASINO & HOTEL

Earn 50 Base Reward Credits and get $5.00 in COMPS!

Base Reward Credits must be earned within 72 hours. Present coupon to the Total Rewards Center at Harrah's after Base Reward Credits have been earned. See the Total Rewards Center for more details.

A current American Casino Guide Discount Card must be presented when redeeming this coupon, or offer is void

---

AMERICAN CASINO GUIDE

LAS VEGAS CASINO & HOTEL

Join Total Rewards at Harrah's Las Vegas and get a FREE Gift!

Present this coupon at Harrah's Las Vegas when you first sign up for a Total Rewards Card and receive a FREE gift! See the Total Rewards Center for more details.

A current American Casino Guide Discount Card must be presented when redeeming this coupon, or offer is void

MGM Grand Hotel - Star Lane Mall
MGM Grand Hotel - Food Court
New York New York Hotel • Bally's Hotel
The Venetian Hotel • Fashion Show Mall
Monte Carlo Hotel

Must present coupon to cashier prior to ordering. Offer has no cash value. Not valid with any other offer. One coupon per person. Subject to change or cancellation without prior notice. Offer valid through December 31, 2008.

LAS VEGAS CASINO & HOTEL
3475 Las Vegas Blvd. S.
Las Vegas, NV 89109
(800) HARRAHS
www.harrahs.com

Valid only at Harrah's Las Vegas. Must be 21 or older to participate. One coupon redemption per account, per month. Base Reward Credits must be earned within 72 hours. Cannot be used in conjunction with any other offer or promotion. Original coupon must be presented (no photocopies). Management reserves the right to cancel or alter this offer without prior notice. Offer Code: ACM07. Offer valid through 12/30/08.

Must be 21 or older to gamble. Know When To Stop Before You Start.® Gambling Problem? Call 1-800-522-4700.
©2007, Harrah's License Company, LLC.

LAS VEGAS CASINO & HOTEL
3475 Las Vegas Blvd. S.
Las Vegas, NV 89109
(702) 369-5000
(800) HARRAHS
www.harrahs.com

Valid only at Harrah's Las Vegas and only valid for new members. Must be 21 or older to participate. Cannot be used in conjunction with any other offer or promotion. Original coupon must be presented (no photocopies). Management reserves the right to cancel or alter this offer without prior notice. Offer Code: ACM06. Valid through 12/30/08.

Must be 21 or older to gamble. Know When To Stop Before You Start.® Gambling Problem? Call 1-800-522-4700.
©2007, Harrah's License Company, LLC.

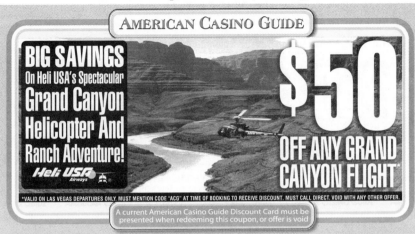

HOTEL & CASINO • CENTER - "STRIP" • LAS VEGAS
3535 LAS VEGAS BLVD. S. • LAS VEGAS, NV 89109
www.imperialpalace.com

Management reserves all rights. Other restrictions may apply.
Must be 21 years of age or older. Cannot be combined with any
other offer. Excludes holidays. Original coupon must be presented
at the Show and Tour Desk at least two hours before performance.
Limit one coupon per customer. Offer expires 12/30/08.

1821 Las Vegas Boulevard North
N. Las Vegas, NV 89030
(702) 399-3000 • www.jerrysnugget.com

Limit one coupon per customer. Must be a More Club Plus member. More Club
membership is free. Present this coupon with your More Club card to cashier in Uncle
Angelo's Pizza Joint upon paying and receive a free 12" pizza with one topping when
purchasing a 16" or larger pizza. Maximum value on 12" pizza is $6.00. Cannot be
used with any other offer. No split checks. Not valid on holidays. No take-out order.
Tax and gratuity not included. No cash value. Must be 21 years of age or older to
redeem. Management reserves all rights. Offer expires December 31, 2008.

1821 Las Vegas Boulevard North
N. Las Vegas, NV 89030
(702) 399-3000 • www.jerrysnugget.com

Limit one coupon per customer. Applies to New More Club members only. Present
this coupon at the More Club Center, sign up for More Club Plus and receive your free
gift and 300 More Club points. No cash value. Points may be adjusted up to 5 working
days from date of redemption. Must be 21 years of age or older to redeem.
Management reserves all rights. Offer expires December 31, 2008.

$5 Blackjack Match Play with your More Club Plus Card

Make a $5 bet at a "21" table and receive a $5 Match Bet ($5 minimum bet required). See reverse for more details.

A current American Casino Guide Discount Card must be presented when redeeming this coupon, or offer is void

CASA
NiCOLA
RISTORANTE

$20 Towards the Purchase of Two Entrées in Casa Nicola!

Serving modern Italian cuisine prepared from authentic recipes in an open exhibition kitchen. Open daily 5:30 p.m. to 10:30 p.m. See reverse for more details.

A current American Casino Guide Discount Card must be presented when redeeming this coupon, or offer is void

$20 Towards the Purchase of Two Entrées at TJ's Steakhouse!

Serving prime steaks broiled over mesquite charcoal, succulent chops and fresh fish in a cozy atmosphere. Open daily 5:30 p.m. to 10:30 p.m. See reverse for more details.

A current American Casino Guide Discount Card must be presented when redeeming this coupon, or offer is void

AMERICAN CASINO GUIDE

Las Vegas

Hilton

A RESORTS INTERNATIONAL DESTINATION

$10 Match Play for the Table Game of Your Choice!

Present this coupon and your Resorts Destination Casino Club card to the dealer at the table game of your choice for a $10 match play. See reverse for more details.

A current American Casino Guide Discount Card must be presented when redeeming this coupon, or offer is void

---

AMERICAN CASINO GUIDE

 澳門酒廊

100 Coin Bonus on Four-of-a-Kind

Present this coupon to the floorperson when you win a four-of-a-kind (no wild cards) on any denomination video poker machine at the Little Macau Casino and receive a 100-coin bonus. You must present a valid ID and you must be playing maximim coins in order to receive this bonus. See reverse for more details.

A current American Casino Guide Discount Card must be presented when redeeming this coupon, or offer is void

---

AMERICAN CASINO GUIDE

2,500 Slot Club Points For New Members

Present this coupon at the Bigshot Players Club booth to receive 2,500 FREE slot club points when you join as a new member. See reverse for more details.

A current American Casino Guide Discount Card must be presented when redeeming this coupon, or offer is void

Las Vegas

Hilton

A RESORTS INTERNATIONAL DESTINATION

3000 Paradise Road
Las Vegas, NV 89109
(702) 732-5111
(800) 732-7117
www.lvhilton.com

Present this coupon and your Resorts Destination Casino Club card to the dealer at the table game of your choice to redeem. $10 match play coupon must be accompanied by a minimum $10 bet. If you do not have a player's club card, sign up at our Resorts Destination Casino Club Center to begin earning player rewards. Cash value: 1/10 of $.01. Your wager may exceed the stated value of the coupon. Limit one coupon per customer and one coupon per week. To be used only at designated locations. Even money bets only. Coupon valid for one decision only. Nontransferable. Not redeemable for cash. Not valid in conjunction with any other offer. Management reserves all rights. Must be 21 or older to gamble or consume alcohol. Expires 12/28/08.

little **MACAU** 澳門酒廊
ULTRA TAVERN

3939 Spring Mountain Road
Las Vegas, NV 89102
(702) 222-3196

Must be 21 or older to redeem. Natural four-of-a-kind only. Maximum coins bet. Must present valid ID. Floor person must verify. Management reserves the right to cancel, alter or discontinue promotion at any time. Original coupon (no photocopies) must be presented. Limit one coupon per person per year. Valid through 12/31/08.

Date_____

Name_____

Signature_____

5288 Boulder Highway
Las Vegas, Nevada 89122
(702) 435-9170
(800) 825-0880

Valid for new accounts only. Must be 21 or older. Cannot be combined with any other offer or promotion. Non-transferable. Offer void if sold. Please allow up to 48 hours for points to reflect on account balance.

Must present original coupon (no photocopies). Not responsible for lost or stolen coupon. Management reserves all rights. Offer may be changed or discontinued at anytime at the discretion of management. Offer expires December 30, 2008.

AMERICAN CASINO GUIDE

$10 Blackjack Matchplay

Present this coupon at any blackjack table, along with your Bigshot Players Club card, prior to the start of a hand and we'll match your bet of $10 if you win. See reverse for details.

A current American Casino Guide Discount Card must be presented when redeeming this coupon, or offer is void

AMERICAN CASINO GUIDE

2-for-1 Lunch or Dinner Entrée

Buy one lunch or dinner entrée in our restaurant and get one entrée of equal or lesser value FREE! Present to server before ordering. See reverse for more details.

A current American Casino Guide Discount Card must be presented when redeeming this coupon, or offer is void

AMERICAN CASINO GUIDE

Madame Tussauds
LAS VEGAS

2-For-1 General Admission
Sunday through Thursday

Receive one FREE ticket with the purchase of a full-price adult general admission ticket at Madame Tussauds Interactive Wax Attraction located in front of the Venetian Resort on Las Vegas Boulevard. Only valid Sunday through Thursday.

A current American Casino Guide Discount Card must be presented when redeeming this coupon, or offer is void

AMERICAN CASINO GUIDE

2-For-1
Food Special

Bring this coupon to Star of the Valley at the Magic Star Casino
to receive 2-for-1 on any menu item! See reverse for more details.

A current American Casino Guide Discount Card must be
presented when redeeming this coupon, or offer is void

AMERICAN CASINO GUIDE

2-For-1
Menu Item

Present this coupon at any Natahn's listed on the back,
purchase your choice of any menu item and receive your
choice of a second menu item of equal or lesser value FREE!

A current American Casino Guide Discount Card must be
presented when redeeming this coupon, or offer is void

AMERICAN CASINO GUIDE

2-For-1
Dinner Buffet
(or 50% off when dining alone)

Buy one dinner buffet and get a second one FREE (or 50% off when
dining alone). Valid Sunday-Thursday. When using as 2-for-1 coupon
both buffets must be redeemed on same visit. See reverse for more details.

Note: Casino name will change to Cannery Eastside in late 2008.
Coupon will still be honored after the name changes to Cannery Eastside.

A current American Casino Guide Discount Card must be
presented when redeeming this coupon, or offer is void

AMERICAN CASINO GUIDE

40 Coin Bonus on Four-of-a-Kind

Present this coupon to the floorperson when you win a four-of-a-kind (no wild cards) on any denomination video poker machine at the Nevada Palace Hotel and Casino. Your Players Circle Card must be properly inserted while playing and you must be playing maximim coins in order to receive this bonus. See reverse for more details.

Note: Casino name will change to Cannery Eastside in late 2008.
Coupon will still be honored after the name changes to Cannery Eastside.

A current American Casino Guide Discount Card must be presented when redeeming this coupon, or offer is void

AMERICAN CASINO GUIDE

$10 Match Play on any Table Game

Make a minimum $10 bet with this coupon at any table game and you'll receive an extra $10 if you win! Coupon must be surrendered after bet wins or loses. See reverse for more details.

Note: Casino name will change to Cannery Eastside in late 2008.
Coupon will still be honored after the name changes to Cannery Eastside.

A current American Casino Guide Discount Card must be presented when redeeming this coupon, or offer is void

AMERICAN CASINO GUIDE

2-For-1 Menu Item

Present this coupon at any New York Pretzel listed on the back, purchase your choice of any menu item and receive your choice of a second menu item of equal or lesser value FREE!

A current American Casino Guide Discount Card must be presented when redeeming this coupon, or offer is void

5255 Boulder Highway
Las Vegas, NV 89122
(702) 458-8810
(800) 634-6283
www.nvpalace.com

5255 Boulder Highway
Las Vegas, NV 89122
(702) 458-8810
(800) 634-6283
www.nvpalace.com

$20 FREE Play in Blackjack

Present this coupon, along with your Silver Rewards card, at any blackjack table to receive an additional $20 in promotional chips when you buy-in for $20 or more. See reverse for details.

A current American Casino Guide Discount Card must be presented when redeeming this coupon, or offer is void

Buy One Entrée Get One Free

Purchase one entrée in Cadillac Joe's Restaurant and get a second entrée for FREE. See reverse for details.

A current American Casino Guide Discount Card must be presented when redeeming this coupon, or offer is void

2-For-1 Fajita Dinner

Present this coupon to your server at *Don Miguel's* to purchase one beef or chicken fajita dinner at regular price and receive a second beef or chicken fajita dinner of equal or lesser value for FREE (or 50% off when dining alone). See reverse for complete details.

A current American Casino Guide Discount Card must be presented when redeeming this coupon, or offer is void

**2542 Las Vegas Blvd. N.
N. Las Vegas, Nevada 89030
(702) 649-8801**

Limit one offer per person, per day. Must enroll in Silver Rewards Club, or be a current member. Promotional chips must be bet and cannot be redeemed for cash. Winning bets made with promotional chips will be paid with regular negotiable chips. Must be 21 years of age or older. No cash value. Management reserves the right to modify, change or cancel this offer at any time without prior notice. Offer expires 12/30/08.

**2542 Las Vegas Blvd. N.
N. Las Vegas, Nevada 89030
(702) 649-8801**

Present this original coupon to your server in the restaurant, along with your Silver Rewards Club card, to receive one FREE entree with the purchase of another entree at the regular price. The FREE entree must be of equal or lesser value. Limit: one coupon per customer, per day. No cash value. Must be 21 years of age or older. Tax and gratuity not included. Management reserves all rights. Offer expires 12/30/08.

**4500 W. Tropicana Ave.
Las Vegas, NV 89103
(702) 365-7111
(800) ORLEANS
www.orleanscasino.com**

Must be 21 years of age or older. Not valid on holidays. Not valid with any other offer. Limit one coupon per person. Resale prohibited. Original coupon must be presented (no photocopies). Discount is 50% off when dining alone. Gratuity not included. Management reserves the right to cancel or alter this coupon without prior notice. Offer expires 12-30-08.

4500 W. Tropicana Ave.
Las Vegas, NV 89103
(702) 365-7111
(800) ORLEANS
www.orleanscasino.com

Must be 21 years of age or older. Not valid on holidays. Not valid with any other offer. Limit one coupon per person. Resale prohibited. Original coupon must be presented (no photocopies). Discount is 50% off when dining alone. Gratuity not included. Management reserves the right to cancel or alter this coupon without prior notice. Offer expires 12-30-08.

4500 W. Tropicana Ave.
Las Vegas, NV 89103
(702) 365-7111
(800) ORLEANS
www.orleanscasino.com

Must be 21 years of age or older. Excludes specialty drinks in souvenir glasses. Excludes Showroom and restaurant bars. Gratuity not included.

Please present before ordering. Original coupon must be presented (no photocopies). Resale prohibited. Management reserves the right to cancel or alter this coupon without prior notice. Offer expires 12-30-08.

3555 Las Vegas Blvd. S.
Las Vegas, NV 89109
(702) 697-2767

Present this original coupon to the Flamingo or O'Shea's Box Office. Not valid with any other coupon, offer or discount. No cash value. Subject to availability. Must be 21 or older. Management reserves all rights. Coupon valid through 12/30/08.

Must be 21 or older to gamble. Know When To Stop Before You Start.® Gambling Problem? Call 1-800-522-4700. ©2007, Harrah's License Company, LLC.

AMERICAN CASINO GUIDE

2-For-1 Room

Pay for one night and get the second night FREE! Good Sunday through Thursday. For reservations call 1-800-683-7777 and ask for Operator #M38. Holidays and convention periods excluded. Black out dates may apply. Subject to availability. Offer expires December 26, 2008.

AMERICAN CASINO GUIDE

FREE Mystery Gift!

Get a FREE mystery gift when you earn 500 points in one day. Must present Boarding Pass with this coupon. See reverse for more details

AMERICAN CASINO GUIDE

Free Glass of House Wine with the Purchase of any Entrée at Pasta Palace!

Pay for one Entrée in Pasta Palace and receive a FREE Glass of Wine! See reverse for more details.

2411 W. Sahara Avenue
Las Vegas, NV 89102
(702) 367-2411
(800) 634-3101
www.stationcasinos.com

This voucher entitles the bearer to one free room night at Palace Station Hotel & Casino, with the purchase of one night at the rack rate. Must have advance reservations. Must present voucher upon check-in. Not valid in conjunction with any other offer. Management reserves the right to cancel this promotion at any time. Credit card or cash deposit required. Guest is responsible for all incidental charges and hotel service fee of $4.95 per day. Must be 21 or older. Limit one free room night per visit. No more than one coupon may be redeemed per room. Offer expires December 26, 2008.

2411 W. Sahara Avenue
Las Vegas, NV 89102
(702) 367-2411
(800) 634-3101
www.stationcasinos.com

Present this coupon to the Rewards Center to redeem after you have earned 500 points in one day. Coupon has no cash value. Management reserves all rights. Valid only at Palace Station. Offer expires December 30, 2008.

BP#_____

Date: _____

2411 W. Sahara Avenue
Las Vegas, NV 89102
(702) 367-2411
(800) 634-3101
www.stationcasinos.com

Redeem this original coupon (no photocopies) at the Palace Station Pasta Palace.

Offer not valid with specials of the day. Must be 21 years or older to redeem. Valid Seven Days a Week. May not be combined with any other offers. Management reserves all rights. No cash value. Offer expires December 30, 2008. Settle to 47073.

AMERICAN CASINO GUIDE

$10 in FREE Slot Play!

New members only, present this coupon at the Club Palms booth, sign up for the Club Palms card and receive $10 in FREE slot play. See reverse for complete details.

A current American Casino Guide Discount Card must be presented when redeeming this coupon, or offer is void

AMERICAN CASINO GUIDE

3X Points!

Present this coupon at the Club Palms booth and receive 3X points for one day's play from 12:01am to 11:59pm. See reverse for more details.

A current American Casino Guide Discount Card must be presented when redeeming this coupon, or offer is void

AMERICAN CASINO GUIDE

HOTEL AND CASINO

Buy 1 Domestic Draft Beer and Get 1 FREE!

Present this coupon at ANY Casino Bar to purchase one Domestic Draft beer at regular price and get a second Domestic Draft beer FREE! See reverse for details.

C9221

A current American Casino Guide Discount Card must be presented when redeeming this coupon, or offer is void

Buy 1 Buffet Get 1 FREE!

HOTEL AND CASINO

Present this Coupon to the Cashier at the Plaza Buffet to purchase one buffet at regular price and get a second buffet FREE! See reverse for details.

C9220

Receive 500 Bonus Points When You Earn 500 Points!

HOTEL AND CASINO

Enroll in the Play Club and use your Play Club Card. Earn 500 points your first day and we'll give you 500 bonus points! See reverse for full details.

FREE Bingo Red Pack A $6 Value!

Make any bingo buy-in of $3 or more and receive a FREE Red Pack! A $6 value. See reverse for complete details.

HOTEL AND CASINO
1 Main Street
Las Vegas, NV 89101
(702) 386-2110
(800) 634-6575
www.plazahotelcasino.com

Subject to Availability. Not valid with any other offers. Alcoholic Beverages, tax and gratuity not included.

Must be 21 years of age or older. Subject to change or cancellation. Management reserves all Rights. Valid through December 26, 2008.

HOTEL AND CASINO
1 Main Street
Las Vegas, NV 89101
(702) 386-2110
(800) 634-6575
www.plazahotelcasino.com

One coupon per person. New Club Enrollments Only. Must be 21 years of age or older. Management reserves all rights.

Play Club Membership required and rules apply. No Cash Value. No Reproductions. Not valid with any other offer. Management reserves the right to modify or cancel this promotion at any time. Offer valid through December 26, 2008.

The Poker Palace
2757 Las Vegas Blvd. N.
N. Las Vegas, NV 89030
(702) 649-3799

Limited to one coupon per customer per week. Must join or be a member of the Gold Club. Not valid in conjunction with any other offer or coupon. Must be 21 years of age or older and present picture ID. Coupon is non-transferable and cannot be redeemed for cash. Offer void if sold. Coupon expires December 30, 2008.

Gold Club Member #_____

AMERICAN CASINO GUIDE

$10 Blackjack Matchplay

Present this coupon and your Poker Palace Gold Club Card at any blackjack table prior to the start of a game and **we'll match your bet of $10** if you win. See reverse for complete details.

A current American Casino Guide Discount Card must be presented when redeeming this coupon, or offer is void

AMERICAN CASINO GUIDE

2-FOR-1 Menu Item at Maddy's Paddys Café

Buy one menu item and get one menu item of equal or lesser value free at Maddy's Paddys Café. Must present this coupon along with your Gold Club card. See reverse for complete details.

A current American Casino Guide Discount Card must be presented when redeeming this coupon, or offer is void

AMERICAN CASINO GUIDE

RAMPART CASINO
AT THE RESORT AT SUMMERLIN

FREE Hat or T-shirt, plus a deck of cards for new Slot Club members!

New members only, present this coupon at the Rampart Rewards Desk, sign up for a card and receive a FREE hat or T-shirt, plus a FREE deck of cards! See reverse for details.

A current American Casino Guide Discount Card must be presented when redeeming this coupon, or offer is void

The Poker Palace
2757 Las Vegas Blvd. N.
N. Las Vegas, NV 89030
(702) 649-3799

Limit: one coupon per person, per day. Cannot be redeemed for cash. Must be 21 or older and present picture ID. Non-transferable. Cannot be combined with any other offer or promotion. Offer void if sold.

Must join or be a Poker Palace Gold Club member and must present original coupon (no photocopies). Not responsible for lost or stolen coupon. Management reserves all rights. Offer may be changed or discontinued at anytime at the discretion of management. Offer expires December 30, 2008.

Gold Club Member #_____

The Poker Palace
2757 Las Vegas Blvd. N.
N. Las Vegas, NV 89030
(702) 649-3799

Limited to one coupon per customer per week. Must join or be a member of the Gold Club. Not valid in conjunction with any other offer or coupon. Must be 21 years of age or older and present picture ID. Does not include tax and gratuity. Coupon is non-transferable and cannot be redeemed for cash. Offer void if sold. Coupon expires December 30, 2008.

Gold Club Member #_____

RAMPART CASINO
AT THE RESORT AT SUMMERLIN

221 N. Rampart Boulevard
Las Vegas, NV 89128
(702) 507-5900
(877) 869-8777

Present this coupon at the Rampart Rewards Desk. Sign up for a Player's Club card and receive a FREE hat or t-shirt, plus a FREE deck of cards. Only valid for new members. Must be 21 years of age or older. Not valid in conjunction with any other offer. No photocopies accepted. Offer void if sold. Management reserves all rights. Offer expires 12/31/08.

AMERICAN CASINO GUIDE

$20 Match Play
on any Table Game

Make a minimum $20 bet with this coupon at any table game and you'll receive an extra $20 if you win! Coupon must be surrendered after bet wins or loses. See reverse for more details.

AMERICAN CASINO GUIDE

2-For-1 Lunch
or Dinner Buffet
(or 50% off when dining alone)

Buy one lunch or dinner buffet and get a second one FREE (or 50% off when dining alone). Offer valid Sunday-Thursday, excludes Sunday brunch and Thursday dinner. When using as 2-for-1 coupon both buffets must be redeemed on same visit. See reverse for more details.

AMERICAN CASINO GUIDE

2 for 1
Show
Tickets!

Voted best Comedy Club in Las Vegas. Shows perform nightly. Please call the Riviera Box Office at 702-794-9433 for performance schedule. See reverse for more details.

221 N. Rampart Boulevard
Las Vegas, NV 89128
(702) 507-5900
(877) 869-8777

Make a $20 minimum bet at any table game, along with this coupon, and receive an extra $20 if your bet wins. Even-money bets only. Coupon must be surrendered after bet wins or loses. Cannot be redeemed for cash. Not valid with any other offer. Must be 21or older to redeem. Limit one coupon per person, per year. No photocopies accepted. Management reserves all rights. Offer expires 12/31/08.

221 N. Rampart Boulevard
Las Vegas, NV 89128
(702) 507-5900
(877) 869-8777

Present this coupon to the cashier at time of purchase. Must be 21 or older to reeem. Tax and gratuity not included. Coupon not redeeemable for cash. Original coupon (no photocopies) must be presented to the cashier. One coupon per customer. Not valid with any other coupon or offer. Management reserves all rights. Valid through 12/31/08.

2901 Las Vegas Blvd. So.
Las Vegas, NV 89109
(702) 734-5110
(800) 634 3420

Original coupon must be presented to Riviera Box Office (no photocopies) to buy one ticket at regular price and get another FREE! Must be 21 or older. Not valid Saturdays or Saturday & Sundays of a holiday weekend or with any other offer. One coupon per person. Offer may be cancelled at any time without notice. No cash value. Offer expires 12/30/08.

AMERICAN CASINO GUIDE

2 for 1 Show Tickets!

Las Vegas' Sexiest Topless Revue
Voted #1 Showgirls

Voted Sexiest Topless Revue in Las Vegas. Shows perform nightly. Please call the Riviera Box Office at 702-794-9433 for performance schedule.
See reverse for more details.

A current American Casino Guide Discount Card must be presented when redeeming this coupon, or offer is void

AMERICAN CASINO GUIDE

2 for 1 Show Tickets!

Norbert Aleman's

Starring
FRANK MARINO
as Joan Rivers
and an All-Star cast of Female Impersonators

Voted best show in Las Vegas. Shows perform nightly. Please call the Riviera Box Office at 702-794-9433 for performance schedule.
See reverse for more details.

A current American Casino Guide Discount Card must be presented when redeeming this coupon, or offer is void

AMERICAN CASINO GUIDE

$5 Off Thrill Pass

Unlimited Rides, All Day Long!

Quicken your pulse with unlimited rides on these great attractions!
Regular price $19.95

One coupon per person. Coupon may not be duplicated and has no cash value. Coupon cannot be combined with any other offer. Management reserves the right to modify or cancel this promotion at any time. Each member of party must be 21. Offer expires December 23, 2008. Comp #842

A current American Casino Guide Discount Card must be presented when redeeming this coupon, or offer is void

AMERICAN CASINO GUIDE

2 for 1 BUFFET

Breakfast-Monday thru Friday. 7a.m. to 10:30a.m.
Lunch-Monday thru Friday. 10:30a.m. to 4p.m.
Not valid for weekend or holiday brunch.
Dinner-Good seven days a week, 4p.m. to 10p.m.

One coupon per person. Coupon may not be duplicated and has no cash value. Coupon cannot be combined with any other offer. Management reserves the right to modify or cancel this promotion at any time. Each member of party must be 21. Offer expires December 23, 2008. Comp #183

HOTEL · CASINO · LAS VEGAS

A current American Casino Guide Discount Card must be presented when redeeming this coupon, or offer is void

---

AMERICAN CASINO GUIDE

$5 Blackjack Matchplay

Present this coupon and your Club Sahara Card
at any blackjack table prior to the start of a game
and we'll match your bet of $5 if you win.
Even money bets only. See reverse for details.

SAHARA
HOTEL · CASINO · LAS VEGAS

A current American Casino Guide Discount Card must be presented when redeeming this coupon, or offer is void

---

AMERICAN CASINO GUIDE

San Gennaro Grill
2-For-1 Menu Item

Present this coupon at the San Gennaro Grill in the Venetian Hotel
Grand Canal Shops, purchase your choice of any menu item and receive
your choice of a second menu item of equal or lesser value FREE!

A current American Casino Guide Discount Card must be presented when redeeming this coupon, or offer is void

Sahara Hotel and Casino

2535 Las Vegas Blvd. South
Las Vegas, NV 89109

1-888-696-2122

saharavegas.com

2535 Las Vegas Blvd. South
Las Vegas, NV 89109
(702) 737-2111
(800) 634-6645

Limit: One coupon per person, per day. Cannot be redeemd for cash. Must be 21 or older. Cannot be combined with any other offer or promotion.

Must be a Sahara Club member and must present original coupon (no photocopies). Not responsible for lost or stolen coupon. Management reserves all rights. Offer may be changed or discontinued at any time at the discretion of management.

Offer expires December 23, 2008.

San Gennaro Grill
Venetian Hotel Grand Canal Shops

Must present coupon to cashier prior to ordering. Offer has no cash value. Not valid with any other offer. One coupon per person. Subject to change or cancellation without prior notice. Offer valid through December 31, 2008.

4949 N. Rancho Drive
N. Las Vegas, NV 89130
(702) 658-4900
(866) 767-7770
www.stationcasinos.com

This voucher entitles the bearer to one free room night at Santa Fe Station, with the purchase of one night at the prevailing rate. Maximum three nights. Must have advance reservations. Must present voucher upon check-in. Not valid in conjunction with any other offer. Management reserves all rights to cancel this promotion at any time. Credit card or cash deposit required. Guest is responsible for tax, telephone, room service and all other additional charges. Must be 21 years or older. Limit one free room per person. Offer Expires December 26, 2008.

4949 N. Rancho Drive
N. Las Vegas, NV 89130
(702) 658-4900
(866) 767-7770
www.stationcasinos.com

The bearer of this coupon is entitled to 1 (one) free Game of Bowling anytime!

One coupon per person, per day. Must present original coupon (no photocopies). Management reserves all rights. Offer expires December 30, 2008.

Settle #41331

2140 Las Vegas Blvd. N.
N. Las Vegas, Nevada 89030
(702) 399-1111

Present this original coupon to your server in the restaurant, along with your Silver Rewards Club card, to receive one FREE entree with the purchase of another entree at the regular price. The FREE entree must be of equal or lesser value. Limit: one coupon per customer, per day. No cash value. Must be 21 years of age or older. Tax and gratuity not included. Management reserves all rights. Offer expires 12/30/08.

$20 FREE Play in Blackjack

Present this coupon, along with your Silver Rewards card, at any blackjack table to receive an additional $20 in promotional chips when you buy-in for $20 or more. See reverse for details.

$25 in FREE Bingo

$25 in FREE bingo when you earn 200 slot points or when you purchase $10 in bingo cards.
See reverse for details.

SILVERTON
Casino • Lodge • Las Vegas

Join the Player's Club and receive $10 in FREE Slot Play!

New Player's Club members only. Must redeem at Silverton's Player's Club and sign up as a new Club member. Good for one time use only. Expires December 30, 2008. See reverse for more details.

2140 Las Vegas Blvd. N.
N. Las Vegas, Nevada 89030
(702) 399-1111

Limit one offer per person, per day. Must enroll in Silver Rewards Club, or be a current member. Promotional chips must be bet and cannot be redeemed for cash. Winning bets made with promotional chips will be paid with regular negotiable chips. Must be 21 years of age or older. Management reserves the right to modify, change or cancel this offer at any time without prior notice. No cash value. Offer expires 12/30/08.

2140 Las Vegas Blvd. N.
N. Las Vegas, Nevada 89030
(702) 399-1111

Limit one offer per person, per day. Must enroll in Silver Rewards Club, or be a current member. No cash value. Must be 21 years of age or older. Management reserves the right to modify, change or cancel this offer at any time without prior notice. Offer expires 12/30/08.

Silverton Hotel and Casino
3333 Blue Diamond Road
Las Vegas, NV 89139
www.silvertoncasino.com
702-263-7777 • 866-946-4373

Present this original coupon to the Silverton's Player's Club. Must sign up as a new club member to receive the offer. Player's Club membership is free. Offer is non-transferable, may not be used in conjunction with any other offer or promotion and has no cash value. Management reserves all rights. Must be 21 years of age or older, with a valid form of ID. Offer void if sold. Expires 12/30/08.

AMERICAN CASINO GUIDE

2-For-1
Seasons Buffet
(or 50% off when dining alone)

Must redeem at Silverton's Player's Club to receive actual voucher.
Must purchase one Seasons buffet at regular price, to receive a second
buffet, of equal or lesser value, for free. Good for one time use only.
Expires December 30, 2008.

A current American Casino Guide Discount Card must be
presented when redeeming this coupon, or offer is void

AMERICAN CASINO GUIDE

20% Off
Hotel Stay

Please mention "American Casino Guide" at time of reservation
and present coupon at check-in to receive discount.
See reverse for more details.

A current American Casino Guide Discount Card must be
presented when redeeming this coupon, or offer is void

AMERICAN CASINO GUIDE

Free Deck of Cards
<u>and</u> Fun Book

Present this coupon at the Slots-A-Fun Gift
Shop to receive a FREE deck of cards. FREE
Fun Book is available at the Free Pull Booth and
"Players Club" Booth. See reverse for more
details.

A current American Casino Guide Discount Card must be
presented when redeeming this coupon, or offer is void

Silverton Hotel and Casino
3333 Blue Diamond Road
Las Vegas, NV 89139
www.silvertoncasino.com
702-263-7777 • 866-946-4373

Present this original coupon to the Silverton's Player's Club. Must be a Player's Club member, or sign up as a new club member to receive the offer. Player's Club membership is free. Limit one per customer. Offer is non-transferable, may not be used in conjunction with any other offer or promotion and has no cash value. Management reserves all rights. Must be 21 years of age or older, with a valid form of ID. Offer does not include gratuity. Offer void if sold. Expires 12/30/08.

Silverton Hotel and Casino
3333 Blue Diamond Road
Las Vegas, NV 89139
www.silvertoncasino.com
702-263-7777 • 866-946-4373

This voucher entitles bearer to 20% off rack room rate at Silverton Casino Lodge. Must have advance reservations. Must present voucher upon check-in. Not valid in conjunction with any other offer. Management reserves all rights to cancel this promotion at any time. Credit card or cash deposit required. Guest is responsible for tax, telephone, room service and all other additional charges. Must be 21 years or older. Limit one discounted room per person. Offer expires December 30, 2008. Settle to Marketing #148.

LOCATED NEXT TO CIRCUS CIRCUS

Must be 21 years or older to receive this promotion. Offer void if sold. Limited to one free offer per person. Management may revoke this offer at any time without notice. Must present original coupon (no photocopies accepted). Offer valid through December 31, 2008.

Present this coupon at the Players Club Booth from 9am until 9pm to receive your complimentary card good for a giant 1/2-pound hot dog and a 21-oz Pepsi, or an ice cold bottle of beer, or an ice cold bottle of water FREE!

Must be 21 years or older. Gratuity not included. Offer void if sold. Limit one coupon per person per trip. Management reserves all rights. Must present original coupon (no photocopies accepted). No cash value. Non-transferable. Offer expires December 29, 2008.

LAS VEGAS
LOCATED NEXT TO CIRCUS CIRCUS

9777 Las Vegas Blvd. South,
Las Vegas, NV 89123
(702) 796-7111 • (866) 796-71111
www.southpointtcasino.com

Valid only at Don Vito's, Silverado Steakhouse, Coronado Café and Big Sur Oyster Bar. Must be 21 years of age or older. Gratuity not included. Please present before ordering. Original coupon must be presented (no photocopies). Resale prohibited. Management reserves the right to cancel or alter this coupon without prior notice. Offer expires 12-31-08.

9777 Las Vegas Blvd. South,
Las Vegas, NV 89123
(702) 796-7111 • (866) 796-71111
www.southpointtcasino.com

Must be 21 years of age or older. Excludes specialty drinks in souvenir glasses. Also excludes Showroom, Night Club, restaurants and High Roller Bar. Gratuity not included. Please present before ordering. Original coupon must be presented (no photocopies). Resale prohibited. Management reserves the right to cancel or alter this coupon without prior notice. Offer expires 12-31-08.

AMERICAN CASINO GUIDE

NORTH LAS VEGAS

FREE T-SHIRT
When You
Join Player's Club
See reverse for details

AMERICAN CASINO GUIDE

NORTH LAS VEGAS

FREE DRINK
at any
CASINO BAR
See reverse for details

AMERICAN CASINO GUIDE

NORTH LAS VEGAS
See reverse for details

Two for One Entree
at Rookies Bar and Grill

3227 Civic Center Drive
N. Las Vegas, NV 89030
1-8SPEEDWAY-1 • 702.399.3297
www.speedwaycasino.com

Restrictions apply. See Players Club for complete rules. Limit one shirt per customer. This offer is non-transferrable, non-refundable and has no cash value. MUST mention ACG. Must present and surrender this coupon upon use. No exceptions. Not available in conjunction with any offer, Management reserves all rights. Must be 21 or older. Offer subject to change or cancellation at any time without notice. Offer expires December 30, 2008.

3227 Civic Center Drive
N. Las Vegas, NV 89030
1-8SPEEDWAY-1 • 702.399.3297
www.speedwaycasino.com

Restrictions apply. Limit one per customer. This offer is non-transferrable, non-refundable, and has no cash value. MUST mention ACG. Must present and surrender this coupon upon use. No exceptions. Not available in conjunction with any offer, Management reserves all rights. Must be 21 or older. Offer subject to change or cancellation at any time without notice. Gratuity not included. Offer expires December 30, 2008.

3227 Civic Center Drive
N. Las Vegas, NV 89030
1-8SPEEDWAY-1 • 702.399.3297
www.speedwaycasino.com

Present this coupon to your server at Rookies at time of purchase to receive one free entree when another entree of equal or greater value is purchased. Gratuity not included. Must be 21 years of age. Not valid with any other offer or promotion. No cash value. Limit one coupon per person per year. Void if altered or copied in any way. Management reserves the rights to change or cancel this offer at any time without prior notice. Offer expires December 30, 2008.

American Superstars Two-For-One Show Tickets

Voted Las Vegas' Best Entertainment Value!

Get one FREE "American Superstars" Show with the purchase of one American Superstars Show ticket. Coupon must be presented at the Stratosphere Ticket Center. See back for full details.

*by Las Vegas Advisor

Two-For-One Show Tickets

Get one FREE "Bite" ticket with the purchase of one "Bite"ticket at full price. Coupon must be presented at the Stratosphere Ticket Center. See back for full details.

A MOLYNEUX CREATION ®

2-For-1 Room

SUNSET STATION HOTEL · CASINO

Pay for one night and get the second night FREE! Good Sunday through Thursday. Holidays and convention periods excluded. Subject to availability. Black out dates may apply. Offer expires December 26, 2008. For Reservations call: 1-888-786-7389 and ask for Operator #M38. See reverse for complete details.

2000 Las Vegas Blvd. S. • Las Vegas, NV 89104
(800) 99-TOWER • (702) 380-7777

Must be at least 18 years of age to attend show without being accompanied by an adult. Some material may be inappropriate for children; parental discretion recommended. Must be at least 5 years of age to attend the show. Subject to availability. Show times subject to change. Offers cannot be combined. Management reserves all rights. Not for resale. Valid through December 27, 2008. **(Coupon must be presented at the Stratosphere Ticket Center.)**

2000 Las Vegas Blvd. S. • Las Vegas, NV 89104
(800) 99-TOWER • (702) 380-7777

Must be at least 18 years of age to attend the show. Subject to availability. Show times subject to change. Offers cannot be combined. Management reserves all rights. Not for resale. Valid through December 27, 2008. **(Coupon must be presented at the Stratosphere Ticket Center.)**

1301 W. Sunset Road
Henderson, NV 89014
(702) 547-7777
(888) 786-7389
www.stationcasinos.com

This voucher entitles the bearer to one free room night at the Sunset Station Hotel & Casino, with the purchase of one night at the prevailing rate. Must have advance reservations. Must present original voucher (no photocopies) upon check-in. Not valid in conjunction with any other offer. Management reserves the right to cancel this promotion at any time. Credit card or cash deposit required. Guest is responsible for tax, telephone, room service and all other additional charges. Must be 21 or older. Limit one free room per person. Offer expires December 26, 2008.

$5 FREE
Slot Play
when you join
Player's Club!

Receive $5 in FREE slot play when you sign up for Terrible's
Player's Club. Must be a new sign up. See reverse for more details.

A current American Casino Guide Discount Card must be
presented when redeeming this coupon, or offer is void

2-For-1
Bowling

Present this coupon to get one FREE game of bowling with the
purchase of one game of bowling at the regular price.
See reverse for more details.

A current American Casino Guide Discount Card must be
presented when redeeming this coupon, or offer is void

One FREE Game
of Bowling Anytime!
(including Cosmic Bowling)

The bearer of this coupon is entitled to one FREE Game of Bowling
anytime (including Cosmic Bowling). One coupon per person,
per day. Management Reserves All Rights. Offer expires
December 26, 2008. See reverse for complete details.

A current American Casino Guide Discount Card must be
presented when redeeming this coupon, or offer is void

Terrible's Town Henderson
642 S. Boulder Hwy.
Henderson, NV 89015
(702) 564-7118
www.terribleherbst.com

Must be 21 years of age or older. No cash value. Not valid with any other offer.

Subject to cancellation without prior notice. One coupon per person. May not be reproduced. Management reserves all rights. Expires 12/30/08.

Terrible's Town Henderson
642 S. Boulder Hwy.
Henderson, NV 89015
(702) 564-7118
www.terribleherbst.com

Must be 21 years of age or older. No cash value. Not valid with any other offer. Must present original coupon (no photocopies).

Subject to cancellation without prior notice. One coupon per person. Management reserves all rights. Expires 12/30/08.

2101 Texas Star Lane
N. Las Vegas, NV 89032
(702) 631-1000
(800) 654-8888
www.stationcasinos.com

This coupon entitles the bearer to one FREE game of bowling during regular business hours when open play is available at the Texas Station Hotel & Casino Bowling Center. Does not include shoe rental. Must present original voucher (no photocopies). Not valid in conjunction with any other offer. Management reserves the right to cancel this promotion at any time. Limit one free game per person, per day. Offer expires 12/26/08.

2-For-1 Room

Pay for one night and get the second FREE! Good Sunday-Thursday. Holidays and convention periods excluded. Subject to availability. For reservations call 1-800-654-8888 and ask for operator #M38. Offer expires December 26, 2008.
See reverse for more details.

HOTEL AND CASINO

Buy 1 Domestic Draft Beer and Get 1 FREE!

Present this coupon at ANY Casino Bar to purchase one Domestic Draft beer at regular price and get a second Domestic Draft beer FREE! See reverse for details.

HOTEL AND CASINO

Receive 500 Bonus Points When You Earn 500 Points!

Enroll in the Play Club and use your Play Club Card. Earn 500 points your first day and we'll give you 500 bonus points! See reverse for full details.

2101 Texas Star Lane
N. Las Vegas, NV 89032
(702) 631-1000
(800) 654-8888
www.stationcasinos.com

This voucher entitles the bearer to one free room night at the Texas Station Hotel & Casino, with the purchase of one night at the prevailing rate. Must have advance reservations. Must present original voucher (no photocopies) upon check-in. Not valid in conjunction with any other offer. Management reserves the right to cancel this promotion at any time. Credit card or cash deposit required. Guest is responsible for tax, telephone, room service and all other additional charges. Must be 21 or older. Limit one offer per guest. Subject to availability and blackout dates apply. Offer expires 12/26/08.

HOTEL AND CASINO
18 E. Fremont Street
Las Vegas, NV 89101
(702) 385-1664
(800) 634-6532
www.vegasclubcasino.net

Subject to Availability. Not valid with any other offers. Must be 21 years of age or older.

Excludes specialty drinks. Excludes restaurant bars. Gratuity not included. Subject to change or cancellation. Management reserves all rights. Valid through December 26, 2008.

HOTEL AND CASINO
18 E. Fremont Street
Las Vegas, NV 89101
(702) 385-1664
(800) 634-6532
www.vegasclubcasino.net

One coupon per person. New Club Enrollments Only. Must be 21 years of age or older. Management reserves all rights.

Play Club Membership required and rules apply. No Cash Value. No Reproductions. Not valid with any other offer. Management reserves the right to modify or cancel this promotion at any time. Offer valid through December 26, 2008.

AMERICAN CASINO GUIDE

FREE
1/4 lb. Burger & Fries
with purchase of a beverage

Bring this coupon to Dante's Restaurant, show your
Wild Card, and receive a FREE 1/4 lb. burger with fries
when you purchase a beverage! See reverse for more details.

A current American Casino Guide Discount Card must be
presented when redeeming this coupon, or offer is void

AMERICAN CASINO GUIDE

2-For-1
Food Special

Bring this coupon to Dante's Restaurant, show your
Wild Card and receive 2-for-1 on any menu item!
See reverse for more details.

A current American Casino Guide Discount Card must be
presented when redeeming this coupon, or offer is void

AMERICAN CASINO GUIDE

FREE
Draft Beer!

Present this coupon to any bartender to receive a
complimentary draft beer at the Loose Trax Lounge.
See reverse for more details.

A current American Casino Guide Discount Card must be
presented when redeeming this coupon, or offer is void

1901 N. Rancho Drive
Las Vegas, NV 89106
(702) 648-3801

www.stationcasinos.com

Must be 21 or older. Must be a member of the Wildfire Player's Club. Valid one time. Not valid with any other offer or promotion.

Valid Sunday through Thursday only. Tax and gratuity not included. Must purchase a beverage. Non-transferable. Must present original coupon (no photocopies). Offer has no cash value. Management reserves all rights. Coupon expires December 26, 2008. Settle to comp #00430.

1901 N. Rancho Drive
Las Vegas, NV 89106
(702) 648-3801

www.stationcasinos.com

Must present coupon and Wild Card to server prior to ordering. Tax and gratuity not included. Excludes prime rib and porterhouse steak special. Must be 21 or older. Non-transferable.

Offer has no cash value. Management reserves all rights. One coupon per person. Offer may be changed or discontinued at anytime at the discretion of management. Offer expires December 31, 2008. Settle to comp #70144.

3330 W. Tropicana Ave.
Las Vegas, NV 89103
(702) 740-0000
(800) 634-3488
www.stationcasinos.com

- Must be 21 or older

- Present original coupon (no photocopies) to bartender prior to ordering.

- Limit one coupon per person.

- Management reserves all rights.

- No Cash Value.

- Offer expires December 31, 2008.

- Settle to comp #41397

AMERICAN CASINO GUIDE

2-For-1 Room
Don't forget to pick up your FREE gift just for staying with us!

Present this coupon when you check in at the front desk Monday-Thursday. Pay for one night at the prevailing rate and get the second night FREE. For reservations call (702) 367-2441 and ask for Operator #M38. See reverse for more details.

A current American Casino Guide Discount Card must be presented when redeeming this coupon, or offer is void

AMERICAN CASINO GUIDE

Buy one Breakfast, Lunch or Dinner entrée, get the second entrée FREE!

Buy one entrée at the Gambler's Grill and enjoy a second entrée of equal or lesser value FREE!
See reverse for more details.

A current American Casino Guide Discount Card must be presented when redeeming this coupon, or offer is void

AMERICAN CASINO GUIDE

AQUARIUS
CASINO RESORT
Laughlin, NV

2-For-1 Lunch Buffet

Present this coupon to the cashier at the Windows on the River Buffet to receive one FREE lunch buffet when you purchase one lunch buffet at the regular price. Not valid on holidays.
See reverse for more details.

A current American Casino Guide Discount Card must be presented when redeeming this coupon, or offer is void

Buy one, get one FREE
Turn A $20 Into More entry
($20 value)

Present this coupon at the *Turn A $20 Into More* promotions desk and get one FREE *Turn A $20 Into More* entry when you buy one entry at the regular price. See reverse for more details.

Buy One Appetizer - Get One FREE!

Present this coupon at the Range Steakhouse at Harrah's Laughlin at time of seating. Buy one appetizer at the Range and receive one appetizer of equal or lesser value FREE. Valid only at Harrah's Laughlin. Offer code: 176

Buy One Pizza - Get One FREE!

Present this coupon at the Beach Cafe at Harrah's Laughlin at time of seating. Buy one pizza at the Beach Cafe and receive one pizza of equal or lesser value FREE! Valid at Harrah's Laughlin only. Offer code: 176

1900 S. Casino Drive
Laughlin, Nevada 89029
(702) 298-5111
www.theaquarius.com

Must be 21 years of age or older. No Cash Value. Limit: one coupon per customer, per day. May not be used in conjunction with any other offer, discount or promotion. Management reserves all rights. Offer expires 12/31/08.   #00080

2900 South Casino Drive
Laughlin, Nevada 89029
(702) 298-4600 • (800) HARRAHS
www.harrahs.com

Management reserves the right to modify this offer at any time without prior notice. Original coupon must be presented (no photocopies). Not valid on weekends (Friday/Saturday) or holidays. Cannot be combined with any other offer, advertisement or mailing. Must be 21 years of age or older. Limit one coupon per person per visit. Subject to availability. Gratuity not included. Offer valid through 12/15/08.

2900 South Casino Drive
Laughlin, Nevada 89029
(702) 298-4600 • (800) HARRAHS
www.harrahs.com

Management reserves the right to modify this offer at any time without prior notice. Original coupon must be presented (no photocopies). Not valid on weekends (Friday/Saturday) or holidays. Cannot be combined with any other offer, advertisement or mailing. Must be 21 years of age or older. Limit one coupon per person per visit. Subject to availability. Gratuity not included. Offer valid through 12/15/08.

2900 South Casino Drive
Laughlin, Nevada 89029
(702) 298-4600 • (800) HARRAHS
www.harrahs.com

LAUGHLIN CASINO & HOTEL

5870 Homestead Rd
Pahrump, NV 89048
775-751-7770 • 888-558-5253
www.terribleherbst.com

5870 Homestead Rd
Pahrump, NV 89048
775-751-7770 • 888-558-5253
www.terribleherbst.com

AMERICAN CASINO GUIDE

$10 Blackajck Match Play!

Make a $10 bet at blackjack with this coupon and your Terrible's Players Card and receive a FREE $10 Matching Bet! See reverse for more details.

A current American Casino Guide Discount Card must be presented when redeeming this coupon, or offer is void

---

AMERICAN CASINO GUIDE

PRIMM VALLEY CASINO RESORTS
BUFFALO BILL'S • PRIMM VALLEY • WHISKEY PETE'S

Buy One Ride on the Desperado Roller Coaster Get one FREE!

Present this coupon to the attraction's cashier and receive one FREE Desperado roller coaster ride when you purchase one ride at the regular price. See reverse for more details.

A current American Casino Guide Discount Card must be presented when redeeming this coupon, or offer is void

---

AMERICAN CASINO GUIDE

PRIMM VALLEY CASINO RESORTS
BUFFALO BILL'S • PRIMM VALLEY • WHISKEY PETE'S

Buy One Carolee's Movie Theatre Ticket - Get one FREE! Plus, a FREE small popcorn!

Present this coupon to the Carolee Theatre cashier to receive one FREE movie ticket when you purchase one ticket at the regular price, plus one FREE small popcorn. See reverse for more details.

A current American Casino Guide Discount Card must be presented when redeeming this coupon, or offer is void

FREE T-Shirt when you join Player's Club!

Receive a FREE T-shirt when you sign up for the Primm Rewards Club. Must be a new sign up. See reverse for more details.

A current American Casino Guide Discount Card must be presented when redeeming this coupon, or offer is void

$5 in FREE Food at Sierra Café

Present this coupon at the Ranch Rewards Club for $5 in FREE food at the Sierra Café. See reverse for more details.

A current American Casino Guide Discount Card must be presented when redeeming this coupon, or offer is void

FREE Drink at Kantina Bar

Present this coupon to your server at the Kantina Bar for one FREE domestic beer or well drink. See reverse for more details.

A current American Casino Guide Discount Card must be presented when redeeming this coupon, or offer is void

PRIMM VALLEY CASINO RESORTS

BUFFALO BILL'S • PRIMM VALLEY • WHISKEY PETE'S

31900 Las Vegas Boulevard South
Primm, NV 89019
1-800-FUN-STOP
www.primadonna.com

35 miles south of Las Vegas on I-15
at the California/Nevada state line

Must be 21 or older. No cash value. Not valid with any other offer. Limit one t-shirt per person.

Subject to cancellation without prior notice. One coupon per person. May not be reproduced. Expires 12/15/08.

TERRIBLE'S GOLD RANCH

CASINO & RV RESORT

320 Gold Ranch Road
Verdi, NV 89439
(775) 345-6789
(877) 927-6789
www.goldranchrvcasino.com

- Offer valid for adults 21 years of age or older.
- Present original coupon (no photocopies) to Ranch Rewards Center.
- Limit one coupon per person.
- Management reserves the right to cancel or alter this coupon without prior notice.
- Dine-in only.
- Gratuity not included.
- Offer expires 12/30/08.

TERRIBLE'S GOLD RANCH

CASINO & RV RESORT

320 Gold Ranch Road
Verdi, NV 89439
(775) 345-6789
(877) 927-6789
www.goldranchrvcasino.com

- Offer valid for adults 21 years of age or older.
- Present original coupon (no photocopies) to server prior to ordering.
- Limit one coupon per person.
- Management reserves the right to cancel or alter this coupon without prior notice.
- Gratuity not included.
- Offer expires 12/30/08.

320 Gold Ranch Road
Verdi, NV 89439
(775) 345-6789
(877) 927-6789
www.goldranchrvcasino.com

- Offer valid for adults 21 years of age or older.
- Present original coupon (no photocopies).
- Limit one coupon per account.
- Management reserves the right to cancel or alter this coupon without prior notice.
- Not valid with any other offer.
- Offer expires 12/30/08.

GRAND SIERRA RESORT
AND CASINO

2500 E. Second St.
Reno, NV 89595
(775) 789-2000
(800) 648-5080
www.grandsierraresort.com

Present this coupon to the cashier at time of purchase. Must be 21 or older to redeem. Tax and gratuity not included. Coupon not redeemable for cash.

Original coupon (no photocopies) must be presented to the cashier. One coupon per customer. Not valid with any other coupon or offer. Offer may be changed or discontinued at anytime at the discretion of management. Offer void if sold. Offer valid through December 30, 2008.

GRAND SIERRA RESORT
AND CASINO

2500 E. Second St.
Reno, NV 89595
(775) 789-2000
(800) 648-5080
www.grandsierraresort.com

Valid for new accounts only. Must be 21 or older. Must have valid photo ID. Cannot be combined with any other offer or promotion. Non-transferable. Offer void if sold.

Must present original coupon (no photocopies). Not responsible for lost or stolen coupon. Management reserves all rights. Offer may be changed or discontinued at anytime at the discretion of management. Offer valid through December 30, 2008.

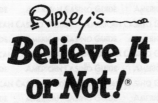

AMERICAN CASINO GUIDE

TRUMP
P L A Z A

25% Room Discount

Experience the excitement first hand and rediscover all that Trump Plaza has to offer with a 25% discount on one-night accommodations Monday through Thursday. For Reservations, call 1-800-677-7378. Must present this coupon at check-in to receive discount. See reverse for more details.

A current American Casino Guide Discount Card must be presented when redeeming this coupon, or offer is void

---

AMERICAN CASINO GUIDE

TRUMP
TAJ MAHAL

Buy One Sultan's Feast Buffet Get One FREE!

Present this coupon to the cashier at the Sultan's Feast Buffet to purchase one buffet at regular price and get a second buffet FREE. Not valid on holidays. See reverse for more details.

185

A current American Casino Guide Discount Card must be presented when redeeming this coupon, or offer is void

---

AMERICAN CASINO GUIDE

FREE GIFT
— FROM THE —
STAR REWARDS CLUB

SANTA ANA STAR
CASINO

This is YOUR Casino!™

See reverse side for details.

A current American Casino Guide Discount Card must be presented when redeeming this coupon, or offer is void